THE WORD

OF THE LORD

FROM JERUSALEM

366 MEDITATIONS
FROM THE BIBLE

(IN CONSECUTIVE ORDER, IN CONTEXT)

BY
NEWTON H. FRITCHLEY

© Copyright by Newton H. Fritchley
All rights reserved. Published 2013

Printed in the United States of America

ISBN-10: 0615788432

No portion of this publication may be
Reproduced in any manner without the
written permission of the author.

Book designed and edited by
Charge the Cannons Publishing

CHARGE THE CANNONS
PUBLISHING
MECHANICSBURG, PA

Now it shall come to pass in the latter days
That the mountain of the home of the LORD
Shall be established as the highest of the mountains,
And shall be raised above the hills;
And all nations shall flow to it.
And many people shall come and say,
"Come, and let us go up to the mountain of the LORD,
To the house of the God of Jacob;
That He may teach us His ways,
And we shall walk in His paths."
For out of Zion shall go forth the law,
And the word of the LORD from Jerusalem.

Isaiah 2:2-3

Dedication

Hovering over the writing of this volume has been the spirit of my cherished wife, Delores. To her this work is dedicated, since we walked the world together in love — especially in the city which the Lord has always loved, Jerusalem.

Acknowledgements

Would that there was a more inclusive word than "gratitude" to express my full feelings about those who have given valuable guidance in this study: The Rev. Dr. Lewis Parks; The Rev. Dr. Paul Herring; Dr. Dale Condit, colonel and professor at the U.S. Air Force Academy; and Mrs. Sandy Kornish.

The editor, Kimberly Largent-Christopher, knowing the intricacies of an increasingly nuanced profession has smoothed the entire highway.

Once again, Mrs. William (Donna) Sherman has untangled my hieroglyphic handwritten manuscript.

Much gratitude to Mrs. Kari Werner for tackling innumerable jobs quickly, quietly, and with no quibbling.

Thank yous are more adequately expressed in newly minted definition as: **T**he **H**eartfelt **A**ttitude **N**ever **K**nows **S**ufficiency.

Cheers!

WHO IS THIS MAN NEWTON FRITCHLEY?

Reflections of an Enduring Friendship with the Consummate Pulpit Preacher

Now also when I am old and grayheaded, O God, do not forsake me, until I declare Your strength to this generation, your power to everyone who is to come.   Psalm 71:18 (NKJV)

Who is this man Newton Fritchley? On the surface this is an easy question to answer: the minister at my home church, Maple Grove United Methodist Church in Columbus, Ohio. Oh but much more than this.

I remember back in 1973, when I was a young Air Force Captain stationed at Wright-Patterson AFB in Dayton, just 75 miles from my home in Columbus, my mother called and said, quite enthusiastically, "You must come listen to the new minister we have at Maple Grove, Dale."

Now, my mother never expressed much excitement about anybody—except perhaps for my father who had died some sixteen years earlier—so this *was* different. Perhaps needless to say, that call got my attention. I do not recall that I made a special trip to Columbus on the basis of my mother's telephone call, but I was there not long afterward and attended church with her. I remember it as if it were yesterday.

When the time arrived for the sermon, this diminutive, unprepossessing man in his mid-fifties ascended into the pulpit. He was almost ghostlike in his black robe and with his nearly all-gray hair combed straight back over his head. And he just stood there gazing out over our heads for several seconds, taking our measure perhaps and waiting for absolute quiet to descend upon the sanctuary.

Then he intoned—and that is exactly what it was: *intoned*—"Our subject for this morning is...." I do not now recall the subject of that first sermon I heard, but I remember thinking to myself, "Oh, brother, what am I in for here?"

But that did not last long. He then began his sermon, standing ramrod straight, hands at his sides, looking now around at the congregation, and sharing his message without ever looking down—without ever referring to a note and yet offering as carefully crafted a message as I had ever heard. I was astonished—more so, I was captivated, captured by this man who was the son of Methodist missionaries, grew up and was educated in India, emigrated to the United States, and completed graduate work at Boston University before entering the ministry.

Wow! I spent a lot of Sundays back in Columbus after that. I was fascinated by Dr. Fritchley's sermons—and can only smile when, in my mind's ear, I can still hear, "Our subject for this morning is..." But this was only the beginning. The quality of his sermons was masterful. Why? Because of his incisive use of the English language, his turn of a phrase, such as "epistle-packing apostle," his pacing and voice control from slow whispers to drumbeat cadences. And, of course, there was always "the hook." Almost every sermon drew you in with some kind of story or argument, only to "hook" you and draw you inevitably toward the message that he was driving home. He "reeled me in" every time!

Of course, as a public speaker myself, I was always impressed by the fact that he *never* used a note. I asked him about this once. He told me that, during the week, he did prepare a complete written text of his sermon, then went over and over it until he had it down nearly word for word. Clearly reminiscent Manchester's recounting of General MacArthur's last, presumably extemporaneous speech at West Point in 1961—the "duty, honor, country" speech to the Cadets.

As you might suspect, among the many great sermons I have heard in my lifetime, the best sermon I ever heard was Dr. Fritchley's Easter sermon "Man

Alive!" It contained all the elements that made his sermons a joy to the ear and a fascination to the mind—and, lest I not forget, a clear, unequivocal message to the Christian soul.

I remember begging him many times to give it again, and he did so on the last Easter he preached at Maple Grove in 1987. As he offered then, it was being delivered by "special request," and I do regret to this day that I did not return to Columbus for that Easter. This was his *tour de force*, and I am lucky enough to have it on tape. I listen to it occasionally, and it never fails to send shivers up my spine, especially with that crescendo at the end when he says, "Man alive, what a Savior!" then turns toward the altar and repeats, "What a Savior," so that it echoed back into the sanctuary. Man alive, *what a preacher!*

Over the time that I was close to Columbus early in my Air Force career, Dr. Fritchley and I developed a close relationship that has endured to this day. We occasionally had quite interesting discussions.

When I was a Captain, I was visiting with him in his office after a church service one Sunday, and he quite casually asked me, "What is it that you want in your life, Dale?"

Now, at this age, I had not read the Bible cover to cover nor had I been a Sunday school teacher as I now have been, so my answer was more innocent than it might have sounded at the time. I answered, "Wisdom."

After all these years, this is still true, even though I now know I was only reiterating Solomon's response to God's similar query. Dr. Fritchley's response to me was characteristic, though: "Be sure you do not spend your whole life acquiring it and none in dispensing it." I have tried to heed that counsel to the best of my God-given ability.

Once I moved to the faculty at the Air Force Academy, I became involved in the chaplains' programs there. As they often invited guest ministers to come to the Academy, I could think of none better than Dr. Fritchley and recommended him.

The command chaplain invited him; and, as suspected, Dr. Fritchley thoroughly impressed chaplains and Cadets alike with his style and message.

Then, too, Dr. Fritchley and I had our toe-to-toe once—about my seeing Martin Scorsese's movie The Last Temptation of Christ—when I was a Colonel. He was astonished that I would see a movie that was so antithetical to the truth about Christ. My view was that, had I not seen it, I would have been unable to counsel any of my younger brethren who asked about it, as I perceived many others were doing in ignorance.

As always, he had the incisive Biblically based response, speaking to Paul's admonition in Corinthians that we should guard our own behavior lest we tempt our weaker brothers to sin. A salient point—
but, being the Abraham-type who would contend even with God, I still believe in my own point as well.

I am not sure to this day why the Methodist Church was "hiding" this man. I have heard a lot of well-known preachers in my life, both in person and on television—Billy Graham, Norman Vincent Peale, Robert Schuller, James Kennedy, Charles Stanley—but Newton Fritchley is the best of all of them in my view. Why is this?

He is clearly a man of God, who walks in the path of Christ, and is imbued with the Spirit. And that Spirit has made him the master of his craft; the consummate pulpit preacher.

He retired those many years ago to Carlisle, Pa. But he and his beloved wife, Dee, never really retired, as they continued to be involved with two or three small churches in that area—and who would not want to hear Newton Fritchley on a regular basis?

And now, at age 94, he has published his second book, a wonderful devotional titled *The Word of Our Lord from Jerusalem*. [His first book is titled *The Personal Touch of God's Word*.]

He is a man who is teaching us all how to live our winter years when they are upon us—live them actively in service to others, with humility, grace, and good humor — marvelous virtues all.

And who loves him? God, most certainly — but I also know that Dale Condit loves him and prays that God shall continue to bless him — this day *and always*.

Colonel Dale O. Condit
United States Air Force (Retired)

Foreword

World travelers who have an acceptable scale of comparison would agree with Lowell Thomas, this planet's plenipotentiary if there ever was one, that, "Jerusalem is the most dramatic of the cities of this earth, even more so than Athens, Rome, or Paris."

"Dramatic" could neither mean a sort of Times Square ever-throbbing with superficial excitement, for Jerusalem is light-years removed from that. Nor is it dramatic in a publicity-hungry sense, as is Hollywood; nor a bustling marketplace such as London's Oxford Street. Rather, Jerusalem's drama puts each individual on the world's stage. There, unheard voices speak to one's innermost being. "The place whereon thou standest is holy ground." There, the heartbeats of 5,000 years of history are audible. The clouds of witnesses are dense. Even the stones cry out their experiences under Abraham's feet, Jesus' blood, and Stephen's stoning. The valley re-echoes the Savior's sobs. "O Jerusalem, how often would I have gathered your children together...but you would not." Even the sparrows seem to know their ancestors, two of which were sold for a penny. And the wildflowers in sprightly dance on Zion's slopes, rejoice that even Solomon, a fellow city dweller, was not arrayed like one of them. Indeed, Jerusalem's holy ground pulsates with meaning from the past, the present, and in the future.

Since this Holy City is unarguably the world's central city, the home of the soul, little wonder that the psalmist vowed, "If I forget you, Jerusalem, may my right hand wither away; let my tongue cleave to the roof of my mouth if I do not remember you, if I do not set Jerusalem above my chief joy." (Ps. 137:5-6)

To remember Jerusalem, many ways may be taken: historically, archaeologically, militarily, geographically, culturally. But, as the Bible deals with Jerusalem in almost two-thirds of its sixty-six books, to meditate 366 times on what the Prophetic Chroniclers have garnered from centuries of study of this city extraordinaire—is to become better acquainted, now, with our eternal home, the New Jerusalem. For isn't this what the Bible is all about? **B**asic **I**nstruction **B**efore **L**eaving **E**arth...

Contents

Genesis
The Sermon on the Mount: Moriah 33
Gen. 22:2 God said, "Take your son, your one and only son Isaac whom you love, and go to the land of Moriah. There you shall offer him as a sacrifice on one of the heights which I shall show you."

Joshua
Fear Begone 34
Jsh. 10:1-2 When King Adonizedek of Jerusalem heard that Joshua had captured and destroyed Ai, dealing with Ai and its King as he had dealt with Jericho and its King, and also that the inhabitants of Gibeon had come to terms with Israel and were living among them, he was greatly alarmed.

To Gather Together 36
Jsh. 15:63 At Jerusalem, the men of Judah failed to drive out the Jebusites living there, and to this day Jebusites and men of Judah live together in Jerusalem.

Judges
Thataway to Truth 38
Judg. 1:7 Adoni-bezek said, "I once had seventy kings with their thumbs and big toes cut off who were picking up scraps under my table. What I have done, God has done to me." He was brought to Jerusalem, and he died there.

Awake, My Soul 40
Judg. 19:12 His master replied, "No, not into a strange town (Jerusalem) where the people are not Israelites, let us go on to Gibeah."

1 Samuel
When the Ideal Becomes Real 42
1 Sam. 17:54 David took Goliath's head and carried it to Jerusalem, but he put Goliath's weapons in his own tent.

2 Samuel
Can't Stop Now 44
2 Sam. 5:7 Nonetheless, David did capture the stronghold of Zion, and it is now known as the City of David.

Peace Capital of the World 46
2 Sam. 5:9 David took up his residence in the stronghold and called it the City of David. He built up the city around it, starting at the Millo and working inward.

THE BEAUTY OF HOLINESS 48
2 Sam. 6:9 David was afraid of the Lord that day and said, "How can I harbour the Ark of the Lord after this?"

ON THIS ROCK I WILL BUILD 50
2 Sam. 6:12 When David was informed that the Lord had blessed Obed-edoms' family and all that he possessed because of the Ark of God, he went and brought the Ark of God from the house of Obed-edom up to the city of David (another name for Jerusalem) amid rejoicing.

LOVE FINDS A WAY 52
2 Sam. 14:28 Absalom lived in Jerusalem for two whole years without entering the King's presence.

HIS WAY EVERY DAY...54
2 Sam. 15:16 The King set out (from Jerusalem), and all his household followed him except ten concubines whom he left in charge of the palace.

LIVE IT, GIVE IT 56
2 Sam. 15:27 The King went on to say to Zadok the priest, "Are you not a seer?" Or the alternative expression, "Can you make good use of your eyes?"

LIFE'S UPPER SLOPES 58
2 Sam. 15:30 David wept as he went up the slope of the Mount of Olives.

TRUTH BEGINS AND ENDS WITH A T (A CROSS)...... 61
2 Sam. 16:1 When David had moved on a little from the top of the ridge, he was met by Ziba the servant of Mephibosheth.

I WILL FOLLOW JESUS, ANYWHERE 63
2 Sam. 20:2 All the men of Israel deserted David to follow Sheba, son of Bichri, but the men of Judah stood by their King and followed him from the Jordan to Jerusalem.

FROM THRASHING TO THRESHING 64
2 Sam. 24:16 The angel stretched out his arm toward Jerusalem to destroy it; but the Lord repented of the evil and said to the angel who was destroying the people, "Enough! Stay your hand." At that moment the angel of the Lord was at the threshing floor of Araunah the Jebusite.

THE SHAPER OF LIFE 66
2 Sam. 24:21 Araunah the Jebusite said, "Why has your majesty come to visit his servant?" David answered, "To buy the threshing floor from you so that I may build an altar to the Lord, and the plague which has attacked the people may be stopped."

1 KINGS

THE SOURCE OF SIN 68
1 Kings 1:5 Now Adonijah...was boasting that he was to be King.

FROM THE FIRST DEEP BREATH 70
1 Kings 2:1 When the time of David's death drew near, he gave his last charge to his son Solomon.

ONE GREATER THAN DAVID IS HERE 72
1 Kings 2:10-11 So David rested with his forefathers and was burned in the City of David, having reigned over Israel for 40 years, 7 in Hebron and 33 in Jerusalem.

THE VALUE OF CABINETS 74
1 Kings 4:1 King Solomon reigned over Israel.

THE SOUL'S ABIDING PLACE 76
1 Kings 6:1 Four hundred and eighty years after the people of Israel came out of the land of Egypt, in the fourth year of Solomon's reign over Israel, in the month of Ziv, which is the second month, he began to build the house of the Lord.

ON ANSWERING LOADED QUESTIONS 78
1 Kings 10:1 The queen of Sheba heard of Solomon's fame and came to test him with hard questions.

THE COMPLETION OF WISDOM 80
1 Kings 10:26 And Solomon got together many chariots and horses, he had 1,400 chariots and 12,000 horses, and he stabled some in the chariot-towns and kept others at hand in Jerusalem.

AN ODE OWED TO SOLOMON 82
1 Kings 11:3-4 He (Solomon) had 700 wives, all princesses, and 300 concubines, and they influenced him, for as he grew old, his wives turned his heart to follow other gods, and he did not remain wholly loyal to the Lord his God as his father David had been.

TO LOVE LIKE CHRIST 84
1 Kings 12:4-5 Your father laid a cruel yoke upon us; but if you lighten the cruel slavery he imposed on us and the heavy yoke he laid on us we will serve You.

2 KINGS

KEEPING THE MARRIAGE CONTRACT ON TRACK 86
2 Kings 8:18 He (Joram) had married Ahab's daughter; and he did what was wrong in the eyes of the Lord.

HIGH HOPES—ON THE ROPES 88
2 Kings 10:1-2 The Queen of Sheba heard of Solomon's fame and came to test him with enigmatic questions. She arrived in Jerusalem

with a very large retinue, camels laden with spices, gold in vast quantity, and precious stones...

A GARBLED FACTS MACHINE 90
2 Kings 18:22 And if you tell me that you are relying on the Lord your God, is he not the god whose shrines and altars Hezekiah has suppressed, telling Judah and Jerusalem they must worship at his altar in Jerusalem?

HIS WINNING WAY 92
2 Kings 19:10 How can you be deluded by your God on whom you rely when He promises that Jerusalem shall not fall into the hands of the King of Assyria?

ON BEING DISHED 94
2 Kings 21:13 I shall use against Jerusalem the measuring line used against Samaria and the plummet used against the house of Ahab. I shall wipe Jerusalem as one wipes a plate and turns it upside down.

1 CHRONICLES
VICTORIOUS LIVING 96
1 Chron. 18:13 The Lord gave victory to David wherever he went.

FROM DAVID'S CITY TO OURS 98
1 Chron. 28:8 Now therefore, in the sight of all Israel, the assembly of the Lord, and in the hearing of our God, I say to you: Study carefully all the commandments of the Lord your God, in order that you may possess this good land and hand it down as an inheritance for all time...

2 CHRONICLES
A LITURGY FOR THE AGES 100
2 Chron. 2:4 Now I am about to build a house for the name of the Lord my God and to consecrate it to him, so that I may burn fragrant incense in it before him, and present the rows of the Bread of the Presence regularly...

OUR CHRIST-LIKE GOD 102
2 Chron. 6:6 I chose Jerusalem for my Name to be there.

TEMPLED SOULS 104
2 Chron. 8:6 And Baalath, as well as all his store-cities, and all the towns where he quartered his chariots and horses. He carried out all his cherished plans for building in Jerusalem, in the Lebanon, and throughout his whole dominion.

ALL, OR NONE AT ALL 106
2 Chron. 12:8 The (God's) people will know the difference between serving me (God) and serving the rulers of other countries.

OH, HOW HE GIVES **107**
2 Chron. 16:9 The eyes of the Lord range through the whole earth, to bring aid and comfort to those whose hearts are loyal to him.

O JOY **109**
2 Chron. 30:26 There was great rejoicing in Jerusalem, the like of which had not been known there since the days of Solomon, son of King David of Israel.

HE SEES WHAT WE CANNOT **111**
2 Chron. 36:23 This is the Word of Cyrus King of Persia: The Lord the God of heaven has given me all the Kingdoms of the earth, and he himself has charged me to build him a house at Jerusalem.

EZRA

DIVINELY REVVED UP **113**
Ezra 1:1 So that the word of the Lord spoken through Jeremiah (Jer. 29:10; 31:38) might be fulfilled, the Lord stirred up the heart of Cyrus King of Persia.

THE POWER OF ONE **115**
Ezra 3:1 The Israelites now settled in their towns, the people assembled as one man in Jerusalem. Then Jeshua...

VICTORY IN THE SHADOWED VALLEY **117**
Ezra 4:4-5 Then the people of the land caused the Jews to lose heart...

PROFITABLE PROPHETS **119**
Ezra 5:2 Then Zerubbabel, son of Shealtil and Jeshua, son of Jozadak, with the prophets of God at their side to help them, began at once to rebuild the house of God.

UP FROM THE PITS **121**
Ezra 10:1 While Ezra was praying and making confession, prostrate in tears before the house of God, there gathered round him a vast throng of Israelites, men, women, and children, and there was widespread lamentation among the crowd.

MOMENTUM FROM IN FRONT **123**
Ezra 10:2 In spite of this, there is still hope.

NEHEMIAH

A WALL IN YOUR WILL **125**
Neh. 6:9 They were all trying to intimidate us in the hope that we should then relax our efforts and that the work would never be completed...

WALLED IN HIS EVERLASTING ARMS **127**
Neh. 6:12 Then it dawned on me: God had not sent him. His prophecy aimed at harming me and Tobiah and Sanballat had bribed him to utter it.

HOW GOD SPEAKS TO US 129
Neh. 8:8 They read from the book of the law of God clearly, made its sense plain, and gave instruction in what was read.

FOR INSURED SUCCESS 131
Neh. 11:1 The leaders of the people settled in Jerusalem; and the rest of the people cast lots to bring one in every ten to live in Jerusalem, the Holy City.

REJOICE, THE LORD IS KING...133
Neh. 12:43 The rejoicing in Jerusalem was heard a long way off.

HOLY SABBATH 135
Neh. 13:19 When the entrances to Jerusalem had been cleared in preparation for the Sabbath, I gave orders that the gates should be shut and not opened until after the Sabbath...

ESTHER
AS THE TWIG IS BENT..137
Esther 2:6 [Mordecai] had been taken into exile from Jerusalem among those whom King Nebuchadnezzar of Babylon had carried away with King Jeconiah.

PSALMS
THE KING IS COMING..139
Ps. 2:6 I have enthroned my King on Zion my holy mountain.

PO$$E$$ED 141
Ps. 5:2 Heed my cry for help, my King and my God.

A DIVINE RESCUE OPERATION.....................................143
Ps. 9:13 Thou who hast lifted me up and caught me back from the gates of death.

OUR CARING COMPANION 145
Ps. 11:1 Why do you say to me, "Flee to the mountains like a bird"?

GOD HELP US..147
Ps. 14:7 If only Israel's deliverance might come out of Zion.

HIS EVER-ENLIVENING WORD.......................................149
Ps. 15:1 O Lord, who may lodge in Thy tabernacle? Who may dwell on Thy holy mountain?

SEEK HIS FACE AND GRACE...151
Ps. 27:4 One thing I ask of the Lord.

GOD'S WORLD ON HIS SHOULDERS............................153
Ps. 29:1 Ascribe to the Lord glory and might.

TAKE THE REFRESHING COURSE 155
Ps. 42:1 As a hind (deer, hart) longs for the running streams, so do I long for Thee, O God.

MY FATHER'S WORLD 157
Ps. 48:14 Such is God.

THE RIDDANCE OF SIN 159
Ps. 51:1 Be gracious to me, O God, in Thy true love; in the fullness of Thy mercy blot out my misdeeds.

THANKSGIVING DAILY 161
Ps. 65:1 We owe thee praise, O god, in Zion; thou hearest prayer, vows shall be paid to thee.

HOW TO HANDLE THIS STRESS 164
Ps. 69:17 I am thy servant, do not hide thy face from me. Make haste to answer me, for I am in distress.

GOD'S GOLDEN OLDIES 166
Ps. 71:18 Now also when I am old and gray-headed, O God, do not forsake me, until I declare Your strength to this generation, Your power to everyone who is to come.

EYES RIGHT! 168
Ps. 73:3 The boasts of sinners roused my envy when I saw how they prosper.

THIS WAY OUT 170
Ps. 79:1 The heathen have invaded your domain, God; they have defiled your holy temple and laid Jerusalem in ruins.

DON'T GRUDGE THE TRUDGE 172
Ps. 84:5 Happy the men whose refuge is in thee, whose hearts are set on the pilgrim ways!

OUR WORLD'S CAPITAL 174
Ps. 87:7 Singers and dancers alike say, "All my springs are in you."

THE ONE AND ONLY GOD 176
Ps. 99:1 The Lord is King.

HOW TO RENEW A NATION 178
Ps. 101:1 I will sing of loyalty and of justice; to thee, O Lord, I will sing.

OUR FOUNDATION LAYER (V. 25) 180
Ps. 102:17 He turns to hear the prayer of the destitute and does not scorn them when they pray.

VIRTUOUS UNBELIEVERS? 182
Ps. 119:25 My soul cleaves to the dust...

THE CHURCH EXEMPLAR 184
Ps. 122:3 Jerusalem that is built to be a city where people come together in entity.

A PILGRIM'S PEACE PRAYER.................................. 186
Ps. 122:6 Pray for the peace of Jerusalem: May those who love you prosper.

MOUNTAINOUS SECURITY....................................... 188
Ps. 125:2 As the mountains surround Jerusalem, the Lord surrounds His people.

MIRACLES IN MOMENTS.. 190
Ps. 126:4 Turn once again our fortune, Lord.

REST IN HIM 192
Ps. 132:14 This is my resting place forever; here will I make my home for such is my desire.

WHEN WE HANG UP OUR LYRES 194
Ps. 137:4 How could we sing the Lord's song in a foreign land?

THE MUSIC OF THE SPHERES 196
Ps. 150:1 O praise God in his holy place.

ECCLESIASTES
JOY IN THE LORD 198
Eccles. 2:7 I acquired male and female slaves and had my home-born slaves...I owned possessions, more flocks and herds than any of my predecessors in Jerusalem.

SONG OF SONGS
O LOVE, THAT WILL NOT LET ME GO 200
The Song of Songs 2:7 I charge you, maidens of Jerusalem, by the spirits and the goddesses of the field: Do not rouse or awaken love until it is ready.

ISAIAH
LONGSIGHT 201
Isa. 1:1 The vision which Isaiah son of Amoz had about Judah and Jerusalem during the reigns of Uzziah, Jotham, Ahaz, and Hezekiah, Kings of Judah.

LIFE-SAVIORS 203
Isa. 1:9 If the Lord of hosts had not left us a few survivors, we should have been like Sodom.

THE WORD FROM THE MOUNT 205
Isa. 2:1 This is the message which Isaiah, son of Amoz, received in a vision about Judah and Jerusalem.

THE SIGNATURE MEDITATION IN ISAIAH.............. 207
Isa. 2:3 Out of Jerusalem comes the Word of the Lord.

NO FIGS FROM THISTLES 209
Isa. 3:8 Jerusalem is brought low, Judah has come to grief, for in word and deed they defied the Lord, in open rebellion against his glory.

EVEN SO, COME LORD 277
Isa. 4:3 Then those who are left in Zion, who remain in Jerusalem, every one whose survival in Jerusalem was decreed will be called holy.

REVIVAL MODE 212
Isa. 4:4-5 When the Lord washes away the filth...he will create.

GLIMPSE OF GLORY 215
Isa. 6:1 In the year that King Uzziah died I saw the Lord seated on a throne, high and exalted.

O COME, IMMANUEL 217
Isa. 7:4 Say to him (King Ahaz): Remain calm and unafraid; do not let your nerve fail because of the blazing anger of (your enemies).

WALKING IN THE LIGHT 219
Isa. 8:11,20 The Lord spoke thus to me with his strong hand upon me and warned me not to walk (and talk) in the way of this people, saying "Surely for this word which they speak there is no dawn."

WHEN GLOOM GOES BOOM 221
Chapter 8 closed with dreary verse 33: They shall look to the earth, but behold, distress and darkness, the gloom of anguish; and they will be thrust into thick darkness.

GOD'S HIDDEN PURPOSES 223
Isa. 10:12 When the Lord has finished all that he means to do against Mt. Zion and Jerusalem, he will punish the King of Assyria for the words which spring from his arrogance and for his high and mighty men.

THE IMP IN IMPERIOUS 225
Isa. 10:17 So the Light of Israel will be for a fire, and his Holy One for a flame.

WHEN THY KINGDOM COMES 227
Isa. 11:9 There will be neither hurt nor harm in all my holy mountain (another term for Jerusalem).

RIGHT FROM THE START 230
Isa. 22:1 Tell me, what is amiss that you have all climbed on to the roofs.

KEEPER OF THE KEYS 232
Isa. 22:21 I shall invest him with your robe, equip him with your sash

of office, and invest him with your authority; he will be a father to the inhabitants of Jerusalem and to the people of Judah.

ON BEING IN A UNITED STATE 234
Isa. 27:13 On that day a great trumpet will be sounded, and those who are lost in Assyria and those dispersed in Egypt will come to worship the Lord in Jerusalem's holy mountain.

GOD'S PROMISED PROSPERITY 235
Isa. 29:1 Woe betide Ariel! Ariel the city where David encamped. When another year has passed, with its full round of pilgrim feasts.

REFRESHING GRACE 238
Isa. 30:19 People of Zion, dwellers in Jerusalem, you will weep no more.

OUR SHIELD AND DEFENDER 240
Isa. 31:4 So the Lord of Hosts will come down to do battle on the heights of Mt. Zion.

FIXED ARITHMETIC 242
Isa. 32:5 The scoundrel will no longer be thought noble, nor the villain considered honorable.

THE ETERNAL CITY 244
Isa. 33:20 Look to Zion, city of our sacred feasts, let your eyes rest on Jerusalem, a secure abode, a tent that will never be moved, whose pegs will never be pulled up, whose ropes will none of them be snapped.

REDEEMED—HOW I LOVE TO PROCLAIM IT! 246
Isa. 35:10 The ransomed of the Lord shall return and come to Zion with singing.

ALL THE NEWS THAT'S FIT TO MINT 248
Isa. 40:9 Climb to a mountaintop, you that bring good news to Zion; raise your voice and shout aloud, you that carry good news to Jerusalem, raise it fearlessly; say to the cities of Judah, "Your God is here!"

TO WHOM ELSE SHALL WE GO? 250
Isa. 40:25 To whom will you liken me, whom set up as my equal? asks the Holy One.

FRIEND, COME UP HIGHER 252
Isa. 42:1 Behold my servant, whom I uphold, my chosen, in whom my soul delights.

HALLELUJAH, WHAT A SAVIOR 255
Isa. 43:11 I, I am the Lord, and besides me there is no savior.

TRES-PASSES 257
Isa. 43:25 I alone, I am He, who for his own sake wipes out your transgressions, who will remember your sins no more.

JERUSALEM HOW FIRM A FOUNDATION 259
Isa. 44:8 Is there a God besides Me? Indeed there is no other Rock; I know not one.

IN THE BLEAK MIDWINTER CHEERS 262
Isa. 45:3 I will give you the treasures of darkness, And hidden riches of secret places.

HOW SILENTLY THE WONDROUS GIFT IS GIVEN ... 264
Isa. 46:3-4 Hearken to me, O house of Jacob, all the remnant of the house of Israel, who have been borne by me from your birth, carried from the womb; even to your old age I am He, and to grey hairs I will carry you. I have made, and I will bear; I will carry and will save.

GET THE L OUT OF GOLD 266
Isa. 46:5-6 To whom will you liken me and make me equal, and compare me, that we may be alike...

HOW TO GAIN—AGAIN AND AGAIN 268
Isa. 48:18 If only you had listened to my commands.

SERVANT OF GOD, WELL DONE 271
Isa. 49:1 The Lord called me before I was born.

AS ONCE HE SPOKE IN ZION 273
Isa. 51:1 Listen to me, all who follow after the right, who seek the Lord.

ON RISING TO THE OCCASION 275
Isa. 51:17 Arouse yourself; rise up, Jerusalem.

A PORTRAIT OF THE GREAT HEALER 277
Isa. 53:5 But he was wounded for our transgression, he was bruised for our iniquities; upon him was the chastisement that made us whole, and with his stripes we are healed.

THE LORD'S LEGACY FOR YOU 280
Isa. 54:17 This is the heritage of the servants of the Lord.

HIS LIFE-SUSTAINING WORD 282
Isa. 55:10-11 As the rain and snow come down from heaven...

ON BEING ONE IN HIM 284
Isa. 56:8 Thus says the Lord God, who gathers the outcasts of Israel.

THE SYMPATHIZING SAVIOR 287
Isa. 57:4 Are you not the children of transgression, the offspring of deceit?

DARE TO DECLARE 289
Isa. 58:1 Declare to my people their transgressions.

OUR ALL-SUFFICIENT SAVIOR 291
Isa. 59:1 Behold, the Lord's hand is not shortened, that it cannot save, or his ear dull, that it cannot hear.

HOME AT LAST 294
Isa. 60:2 Darkness shall cover the earth, and thick darkness the peoples; but the Lord shall arise upon you.

EARNED STARS 296
Isa. 60:15 I will make you majestic forever, a joy from age to age.

WIDENING HORIZONS 298
Isa. 61:1 The Spirit of the Lord God is upon me, because the Lord has anointed me...

HIS NAME SHALL BE CALLED 301
Isa. 62:2 You will be called by a new name which the Lord Himself will announce.

THE GROUNDBREAKING QUALITY OF LOVE 303
Isa. 63:1 Who is this coming from Edom, from Bozrah with his garments stained red?

THE VITALITY OF PRAYER 305
Isa. 63:7 I will recount the steadfast love of the Lord.

CONTENTED COWORKERS 307
Isa. 63:15 Look down from heaven and see, from thy holy and glorious habitation. Where are thy zeal and thy might?

LISTEN TO THE LESSON 309
Isa. 65:1 I was ready to be sought by those who did not ask for me.

BEHOLD, WHAT IS CREATED 311
Isa. 65:17 For behold, I create.

CUSTOM MADE FOR HIM 314
Isa. 66:2 The one for whom I have regard.

AND NOW, A BENEDICTION BY ISAIAH 316
Isa. 66:10 Rejoice with Jerusalem, and be glad for her.

JEREMIAH
IS IT I? 318
Jer. 2:2-3 Go, make this proclamation in the hearing of Jerusalem: These are the words of the Lord: I remember in your favor the loyalty of your youth, your love during your bridal days, when you followed me through the wilderness, through a land unsown...

ANANIAS CLUB 319
Jer. 7:4 This catchword of yours is a lie; put no trust in it.

MY GOD 321
Jer. 10:6 Where can one be found like thee, O Lord?

FREE AT LAST 324
Jer. 10:17 Living as you are under siege.

THE DIVINE LETTER WRITER 326
Jer. 11:4 If you obey me and do all that I tell you, you shall become my people and I will become your God.

THIS IS THE DAY OF SALVATION 328
Jer. 18:11 Go now and tell the people of Judah and the citizens of Jerusalem that these are the words of the Lord: I am framing disaster for you and perfecting my designs against you. Turn back, every one of you, from his evil conduct, mend your way...

FROM SIN TO THE SON 329
Jer. 23:14 Among the prophets of Jerusalem I see a thing most horrible: adulterers and hypocrites. They encourage evildoers, so that no one turns back from sin; to me all her inhabitants are like those of Sodom and Gomorrah.

BE NOT AFRAID 331
Jer. 26:7-9 The priests, the prophets, and all the people heard Jeremiah say this in the Lord's house and, when he came to the end of what the Lord had commanded him to say to them, priests, prophets and people seized him and threatened him with death.

A FAITH THAT'S FIT 333
Jer. 27:4-5 These are the words of the Lord of Hosts the God of Israel: Say to your masters: I made the earth with my great strength and with outstretched arm, I made man and beast on the face of the earth and I give it to whom I see fit.

OPEN THE GATES OF THE TEMPLE 335
Jer. 29:4-7 These are the words of the Lord of Hosts the God of Israel: To all the exiles whom I have carried from Jerusalem to Babylon...Build...plant...marry (that)...you may increase there and not dwindle away.

OUT OF THE DEPTHS 337
Jer. 32:2 At that time the forces of the Babylonian King were besieging Jerusalem, and the prophet Jeremiah was imprisoned in the court of the guard house attached to the palace.

THE ONLY COMPLETE CURER 339
Jer. 33:6 I will heal and cure.

NEW—THROUGH AND THROUGH 341
Jer. 33:10-11 These are the words of the Lord: You say of this place, "It lies in ruins, without people or animals throughout the towns of Judah and the streets of Jerusalem. It is all a waste, inhabited by neither man nor beast." Yet in this place will be heard once more the sounds of joy and gladness...

A ROSE BETWEEN TWO THORNS 343
Jer. 34:1 The word which came to Jeremiah from the Lord when King Nebuchadnezzar of Babylon and his whole army, along with all his vassal Kingdoms and nations, were attacking Jerusalem and all her towns.

"WILT THOU BE MADE WHOLE?" 344
Jer. 35:13 These are the words of the Lord of Hosts the God of Israel: Go and say to the Judeans and the citizens of Jerusalem: "Will you never accept correction and obey my word?" Says the Lord.

HIS WORD IN OUR WORLD 346
Jer. 36:10 Then Baruch (the scribe) read Jeremiah's words (from God) in the house of the Lord out of the book in the hearing of all the people.

UP THE DOWN STAIRCASE 348
Jer. 43:2 (A group) had the effrontery to say to Jeremiah "You are lying; the Lord our God has not sent you to forbid us to go and make our home in Egypt."

LAMENTATIONS
SINGING IN THE REIGN OF TERROR 350
Lam. 1:7 In the days of Jerusalem's misery and restlessness she called to mind all the treasures which were hers from days of old, when her people fell into the power of adversaries and she had no one to help her...

CLEANSE ME 352
Lam. 1:8 Jerusalem had sinned greatly, and so she was treated like a filthy rag.

TASTE AND SEE 354
Lam. 2:13 How can I cheer you? Whose plight is like yours, daughter of Jerusalem? To what can I compare you for your comfort, virgin daughter of Zion? For your wound gapes as wide as the ocean—who can heal you?

FINALLY SONSHINE 356
Lam. 4:11, 12 The Lord glutted his rage and poured forth his anger; he kindled a fire in Zion, and it consumed her foundations. This no one believed.

EZEKIEL

THE SOURCE OF PURITY 358
Ezek. 4:14 O Lord God, I have never been made unclean, never in my life.

DEM BONES 360
Ezek. 4:16 He then said, "O man, I am cutting short their daily bread in Jerusalem; people will weigh out anxiously the bread they eat, and measure with dismay the water they drink."

THE "I" IN IDOL 361
Ezek. 8:17 He said to me, "Man, do you see that? Is it because they think these abominations a trifle, that the Jews have filled the country with violence?"

FINDING FAVOR IN HIS SIGHT 363
Ezek. 9:11 The man clothed in linen...brought back word, saying, "I have done as thou didst command me."

ABIDE WITH HIM 365
Ezek. 11:16 For a while I became their sanctuary.

TO SUIT THE CASE 367
Ezek. 12:4 Bring out your belongings, packed as if for exile.

GOD'S WHISTLEBLOWERS 369
Ezek. 13:1-2 The word of the Lord came to me: Son of man. Prophesy against the prophets of Israel.

ON MAKING HIS THREE 371
Ezek. 14:14 Even if those three men were living there, Noah, Daniel and Job, they would save none but themselves by their righteousness.

TOO BAD TO BE TRUE 373
Ezek. 14:21 The Lord God says: How much less hope is there for Jerusalem when I inflict on her these four terrible punishments of mine, sword, famine, wild beasts, and pestilence, to destroy both people and cattle!

GRAFTED TO THE CHRISTLY VINE 375
Ezek. 15:6 The Lord God says: As the wood of the vine among all kinds of wood from the forest is useful only for burning, even so I treat the inhabitants of Jerusalem.

THE LIFE-SAVING POTENTIAL OF POISON 376
Ezek. 16:60 I will remember.

ALL MY NATURE REFINE 379
Ezek. 22:19 Therefore, these are the words of the Lord God: Because you are all alloyed, I shall gather you into Jerusalem.

THE LORD'S LAST CALL 380
Ezek. 23:2-4 There were two women...they played the harlot in Egypt...As for their names, Oholah is Samaria, and Oholibah is Jerusalem.

PRIDE'S LAST RIDE 382
Ezek. 26:1-2 The word of the Lord came to me: "Son of man, because Tyre said concerning Jerusalem, aha, the gate of the peoples is broken, it has swung open to me; I shall be replenished, now that she is laid waste."

A CARING MINISTRY 384
Ezek. 34:8 My shepherds have not asked after the sheep but have cared only for themselves.

ON BEING SINGLED OUT 386
Ezek. 34:17 As for you, my flock, these are the words of the Lord God: I will judge between one sheep and another.

FLOCK TO HIM 388
Ezek. 36:38 As Jerusalem is filled with sheep offered as holy gifts at times of festivals, so will their ruined cities be filled with flocks of people. Then they will know that I am the Lord.

ARISE, YE SAINTS 390
Ezek. 37:3 Can these bones live again?

DANIEL
BRIDGED TO HIM 392
Dan. 1:3,4 The King ordered to take certain of the Israelite exiles...and fit (them) for service in the royal court.

NO FOOLING 393
Dan. 5:2 Under the influence of the wine, Belshazzar gave orders for the vessels of gold and silver which his father Nebuchadnezzar had taken from the temple at Jerusalem to be fetched, so that he and his nobles, along with his concubines and courtesans might drink from them.

WINE, WOMEN, AND WRONG 395
Dan. 5:2 Under the influence of the wine, Belshazzar gave orders for the vessels of gold and silver which his father Nebuchadnezzar had taken from the Temple at Jerusalem to be fetched, so that he and his nobles, along with his concubines and courtesans might drink from them.

ON SHUTTING LIONS' MOUTHS 397
Dan. 6:10 When Daniel learned that this decree had been issued, he went into his house. It had in the roof-chamber windows open toward Jerusalem; and there he knelt down three times a day and offered

prayers and praises to his God as was his custom.

DIVINE INSTRUCTION **399**
Dan. 9:2 I, Daniel, was reading the scriptures.

THE BOOKS OF DANIEL **401**
Dan. 9:2 I, Daniel, was reading the scriptures and reflecting on the 70 years which, according to the Word of the Lord to the prophet Jeremiah, were to pass while Jerusalem lay in ruins.

THE INNER BRACES OF PRAYER **402**
Dan. 9:7 Lord, the right is on your side; the shame, now as ever, belongs to us, the people of Judah and the citizens of Jerusalem, and to all the Israelites near and far in every land to which you have banished them for their disloyal behavior toward you.

UP THE DOWN STAIRCASE **404**
Dan. 9:16 Lord, by all your saving deeds we beg that your wrath and anger may depart from Jerusalem, your own city, your holy hill; on account of our sins and our father's crimes, Jerusalem, and your people have become a byword among all our neighbors.

ON LIVING AGAIN—AND AGAIN **406**
Dan. 12:2 An angel says to Daniel: "Many of those who sleep in the dust of the earth will wake, some to everlasting life..."

JOEL
THE EVERLIVING WORD **408**
Joel 2:28 And it shall come to pass afterward, that I will pour out my spirit on all flesh.

JOEL'S FIRST NOEL **410**
Joel 2:32 Then everyone who invokes the Lord's name will be saved; on Mt. Zion and in Jerusalem there will be a remnant as the Lord has promised, survivors whom the Lord calls.

A WONDERFUL SAVIOR IS JESUS **411**
Joel 2:32 Everyone who invokes the Lord by name shall be saved.

JUDGMENT AHEAD **413**
Joel 3:1 When I reverse the fortunes of Judah and Jerusalem...

WHY BE HOLY? **415**
Joel 3:17 Thus you will know that I am the Lord your God, dwelling in Zion, my holy mountain; Jerusalem will be holy, and foreigners will never again set foot in it.

AMOS
A CALL FROM CENTRAL INTELLIGENCE **417**
Amos 1:2 He (Amos) said, the Lord roars from Zion and thunders

from Jerusalem; the shepherds' pastures are dried up and the choicest farmland is parched.

FROM THE STRONG COMES SWEETNESS 418
Amos 1:2 The Lord roars from Zion.

BREATHE ZION'S ENLIVENING ATMOSPHERE 421
Amos 6:1 Shame on you who live at ease in Zion.

OBADIAH
SELF REFLECTIONS? 423
Obad. 11 On that day when you stood aloof, while strangers carried off his wealth, while foreigners passed through the gates and shared out Jerusalem by lot, you were at one with them.

MICAH
FULLY ANSWERED QUESTIONS 425
Mic. 1:5 All this for Jacob's crime and Israel's sin. What is the crime of Jacob? Is it not Samaria? What is the sin of Judah? Is it not Jerusalem?

RECLAIMING RUINS 426
Mic. 3:12 Therefore, because of you Zion will become a ploughed field, Jerusalem as heap of ruins, and the temple mount rough moorland.

CAPSULED CHURCHMANSHIP 428
Mic. 4:2 "Let us go up to the mountain of the Lord, to the house of Jacob's God, that he may teach us his ways and we may walk in his paths."

A WHOLE AND HOLY PEACE 430
Mic. 4:3 They shall beat their swords into mattocks (plowshares) and their spears into pruning knives.

WAR BEGONE 432
Mic. 4:3 Neither shall they learn war any more.

LISTEN UP 434
Mic. 6:1-2 Up, state your case...Hear the Lord's case.

ZEPHANIAH
LIVING GOD—LIVE IN US 436
Zeph. 1:4 I shall stretch my hand over Judah, over all who live in Jerusalem. I shall wipe out from that place the last remnant of Baal, every memory of the heathen priests.

THE MIGHT OF LIGHT 438
Zeph. 1:12 At that time I will search Jerusalem by lantern-light and punish all who are ruined by complacency like wine left on its lees, who say to themselves "the Lord will do nothing, neither good nor bad."

JOY WITHOUT ALLOY **439**
Zeph. 3:14 Zion, cry out for joy; raise the shout of triumph, Israel; be glad, rejoice with all your heart, daughter of Jerusalem!

ZECHARIAH
BACK TO A BRIGHT FUTURE **441**
Zech. 1:17 Proclaim once more: These are the words of the Lord of Hosts; My cities will again brim with prosperity; once again the Lord will comfort Zion, once again he will make Jerusalem the city of His choice.

OUR ALL EMBRACING GOD **442**
Zech. 2:5 "I myself shall be a wall of fire all round it (Jerusalem)," says the Lord, "and a glorious presence within it."

THE WRECK OF THE SATANIC **444**
Zech. 3:2 The angel said to Satan, "The Lord silence you, Satan! May the Lord, who has chosen Jerusalem, silence you..."

THE KING IS COMING **446**
Zech. 9:9 Daughter of Zion, rejoice with all your heart; shout in triumph, daughter of Jerusalem! See your King is coming to you, his cause won, his victory gained, humble and mounted on a donkey, on a colt, the foal of a donkey.

ARMS AND THE MAN **447**
Zech. 9:10 He will banish the chariot from Ephraim, the warhorse from Jerusalem; the warrior's bow will be banished, and he will proclaim peace to the nations...

THE SECRET OF SUCCESS **448**
Zech. 12:5 Then the families of Judah will say in their hearts, "The inhabitants of Jerusalem find their strength in the Lord of Hosts, their God."

HE LEADETH ME, O BLESSED THOUGHT **450**
Zech. 12:8 On that day the Lord will shield the inhabitants of Jerusalem; on that day the weakest of them will be like David, and the line of David godlike, like the angel of the Lord going before them.

WHOLE HOLINESS **451**
Zech. 14:21 Every pot in Jerusalem and Judah will be holy to the Lord of Hosts, and all who come to sacrifice will use them for boiling the flesh of the sacrifice. When that time comes, no longer will any trader be seen in the house of the Lord of Hosts.

MALACHI
A TREASURED ENDING—OR BEGINNING **453**
Mal. 3:1 Look, I am sending my messenger.

Matthew

BORN TO SET US FREE **455**
Matt. 2:1 Jesus was born in Bethlehem in Judaea during the reign of Herod. After his birth astrologers from the east arrived in Jerusalem.

BLESSINGS IN UNEXPECTED PLACES **456**
Matt. 4:5 The devil then took Him to the Holy City and set Him on the parapet...

LORD OF ALL **458**
Matt. 4:25 Large crowds followed him, from Galilee, and the Decapolis, from Jerusalem and Judaea, and from Transjordan.

WHERE ACTIONS NEED TO SPEAK LOUDER **459**
Matt. 5:35 Nor by the earth, for it is his footstool, nor by Jerusalem, for it is the city of the great King.

HOLD THE GARNISH **461**
Matt. 15:1 Then Jesus was approached by a group of Pharisees and scribes from Jerusalem, with the question...

EVEN BEYOND FOREVER **462**
Matt. 16:21 From that time Jesus began to make it clear to his disciples that he had to go to Jerusalem and endure great suffering at the hands of the elders, chief priests, and scribes, to be put to death, and to be raised again on the third day.

GETTING TO KNOW HIM **464**
Matt. 21:10 When he entered Jerusalem the whole city went wild with excitement. 'Who is this?' people asked.

THIS IS MY FATHER'S HOUSE... .... **465**
Matt. 21:13 My house shall be called a house of prayer, but you are making it a bandits' cave!

THE WONDERS OF HIS LOVE **466**
Matt. 21:15 When the chief priests and scribes saw the wonderful things he did, and heard the boys in the temple shouting, "Hosanna to the Son of David!" they were indignant.

THE AUTHOR IN OUR AUTHORITY **468**
Matt. 21:23 So they answered, "We do not know," and Jesus said: "Then I will not tell you either by what authority I act."

THE RIGHT OF WAY **469**
Matt. 21:32 For when John came to show you the right way to live, you did not believe him but the tax-collectors and prostitutes did; and even when you had seen that, you did not change your minds and believe him.

LET'S GET GROWING 471
Matt. 21:33 There was a landowner who planted a vineyard: he put a wall round it, hewed out a wine-press, and built a watchtower; then he let it out to vine-growers and went abroad.

THE REWARDED REMNANT 472
Matt. 22:14 Many are invited, but few are chosen.

TRYING TO FOOL JESUS 474
Matt. 22:18 Jesus was aware of their malicious intention and said, "You hypocrites! Why are you trying to catch me out?"

ON BEING BIBLE BASED 475
Matt. 22:29 Jesus answered: "How far you are from the truth! You know neither the scriptures nor the power of God..."

WHEN TWO BECOME FLESH 477
Matt. 22:36 "Teacher, which is the greatest commandment in the law?"

THE GODFORSAKEN CHURCH 478
Matt. 23:38 Look! There is your temple, forsaken by God and laid waste.

HIS WORD FOR OUR CHURCH 480
Matt. 24:1-2 Jesus left the temple and was walking away when his disciples came and pointed to the temple buildings. He answered, "Yes, look at it all. Truly I tell you: not one stone will be left upon another; they will all be thrown down."

THE BIRTH OF THE BEST 482
Matt. 24:8 All these things are the first birth pangs of the new age.

PRUDENTIAL LIVING 483
Matt. 25:8 The foolish said to the prudent, "Our lamps are going out; give us some of your oil."

ONLY TRUST HIM 484
Matt. 26:2 "You know that in two days' time it will be Passover, when the Son of Man will be handed over to be crucified."

JESUS, I COME 486
Matt. 26:22 Greatly distressed at this they asked him one by one, "Surely you do not mean me, Lord?"

FROM HERE TO FRATERNITY 487
Matt. 26:29 I tell you, never again shall I drink from this fruit of the vine until that day when I drink it new with you in the Kingdom of my Father.

OUR GO AHEAD SAVIOR 489
Matt. 26:32 But after I am raised, I shall go ahead of you into Galilee.

STAY WITH HIM AND PRAY WITH HIM 490
Matt. 26:36 Jesus then came with his disciples to a place called Gethsemane.

HIS CENTRAL CALM 491
Matt. 26:51 At that moment one of those with Jesus reached for his sword and drew it, and struck the high priest's servant, cutting off his ear.

ARMED WITH HIS WORD 493
Matt. 26:55 Jesus spoke to the crowd: "Do you take me for a bandit, that you have come armed with swords and cudgels to arrest me? Day after day I sat teaching in the temple, and you did not lay hands on me."

WOUNDED FOR ME 494
Matt. 27:42 Let him come down now from the cross, and then we shall believe him.

DEATH, BEGONE 496
Matt. 27:53 And coming out of their graves after his resurrection entered the Holy City, where many saw them.

THE LORD'S NEED OF US 497
Matt. 27:55 A number of women were also present, watching from a distance; they had followed Jesus from Galilee and looked after him.

A TOMB FULL OF JOY 499
Matt. 28:8 They hurried away from the tomb in awe and great joy, and ran to bring the news to the disciples.

MARK

THE FORERUNNER'S BATON 500
Mark 1:5 And everyone flocked to [John the Baptist] from the countryside of Judaea and the city of Jerusalem and they were baptized by him in the River Jordan, confessing their sins.

WHAT'S A CHURCH FOR? 502
Mark 11:16 And he would not allow anyone to carry goods through the temple court.

TAKE THAT! 504
Mark 12:9 He will...give the vineyard to others.

A TALE OF TWO CITIES 505
Mark 12:15 He saw through their duplicity.

THE EVER-LIVING WORD 507
Mark 12:24 Jesus said to them, "How far you are from the truth! You know neither the scriptures nor the power of God."

ONCE UPON A SCRIBE 509
Mark 12:34 When Jesus saw how thoughtfully he answered, he said to him, "You are not far from the Kingdom of God."

I SURRENDER ALL 511
Mark 12:41 He watched the people dropping their money into the chest.

THE HANDS OF HIS TIME 513
Mark, Chapter 13

UNITE THE UNTIED 515
Mark 14:15 Make the preparations for us there.

DO YOU KNOW HIM? 516
Mark 14:71 I do not know this man you are talking about.

A MOCKUMENTARY OF JESUS 518
Mark 15:20 When they had finished their mockery they stripped off the purple robe and dressed him in his own clothes.

WHEN THE CASUAL BECOMES CAUSAL 520
Mark 15:21 A man called Simon, from Cyrene, the father of Alexander and Rufus, was passing by on his way in from the country, and they pressed him into service to carry his cross.

HOW TO SAVE A WORLD 522
Mark 16:8c Afterwards Jesus himself sent out by them, from east to west, the sacred and imperishable message of eternal salvation.

LUKE
THE LOOK OF REVELATION 524
Luke 2:38 Coming up at that very moment [Anna] gave thanks to God; and she talked about [Jesus] to all who were looking for the liberation of Jerusalem.

TO FIND AND BE FOUND 526
Luke 2:40 Why did you search for me? he asked. Did you not know that I was bound to be in my Father's house?

THE SHUN IN TEMPTATION 528
Luke 4:9 The devil took him to Jerusalem and set him on the parapet of the temple. "If you are the son of God," he said, "throw yourself down from here."

NO OTHER GOD 530
Luke 19:44 You did not recognize the time of God's visitation.

STANDING ON THE PROMISES 531
Luke 21:19 By standing firm you will win yourselves life.

A VERY PRESENT HELP 533
Luke 22:4 *And he (Judas) went to the chief priests and temple guards to discuss ways of betraying Jesus to them.*

HOW COME UNION? 535
Luke 22:24 *Then a dispute began as to which of them should be considered the greatest.*

SEE HERE 537
Luke 22:64 *They blindfolded him, and kept asking him, "If you are a prophet, tell us who hit you?"*

THE DIFFERENCE FAITH MAKES 538
Luke 22:71 *At that they said, "What further evidence do we need? We have heard this ourselves from his own lips."*

KNOW THE REST OF THE STORY 540
Luke 23:5 *His teaching is causing unrest among the people.*

HIGH COMMUNION FIND 541
Luke 23:12 *That same day Herod and Pilate became friends; till then there had been a feud between them.*

RING THE DECIBELS FOR HIM 543
Luke 23:23 *But they persisted with their demand, shouting that Jesus should be crucified. Their shouts prevailed.*

THE FUTURE IS NOW 545
Luke 23:31 *For if these things are done when the wood is green what will happen when it is dry?*

FROM NOTHING RIGHT TO NOTHING WRONG 546
Luke 23:41 *In our case it is plain justice; we are paying the price for our misdeeds. But this man has done nothing wrong.*

GOOD GRIEF 548
Luke 23:56 *Then they ("the women who had accompanied Jesus from Galilee," v. 55) went home and prepared spices and perfumes; and on the Sabbath they rested in obedience to the commandment.*

ON SAVING APOSTLES! 550
Luke 24:7 *The Son of Man must be given into the power of sinful men and be crucified, and must rise again on the third day.*

STAND BY ME 552
Luke 24:36 *As they were talking about all this, there he was standing...*

JOHN

UPSET TO SET UP 554
John 2:15 *He made a whip of cords and drove them out of the temple,*

sheep, cattle, and all. He upset the tables of the money-changers, scattering their coins.

THE CHURCH ETERNAL 555
John 2:21 But the temple he was speaking of was his body.

ON REMOVING THE RUST FROM TRUST 557
John 2:23-24 While he was in Jerusalem for Passover many put their trust in him when they saw signs that he performed. But Jesus for his part would not trust himself to them. He knew them all.

GROWN BY HIM AND FOR HIM 559
John 3:3 Jesus answered, "In very truth I tell you, no one can see the Kingdom of God unless he has been born again."

THE YOU IN TRUTH 561
John 3:21 Those who live by the truth come to the light so that it may be clearly seen that God is in all they do.

THE WILL TO BE WELL 563
John 5:6 Jesus saw him lying there, and knowing that he had been ill a long time he asked him, "Do you want to get well?"

OUR TIRELESS PROTECTOR 565
John 5:17 He defended himself by saying, "My Father continues to work, and I must work too."

THE LORD'S BEST KEPT SECRET 567
John 5:24 In very truth I tell you, whoever heeds what I say and puts his trust in Him who sent me has eternal life; he does not come to judgment, but has already passed from death to life.

HIS SHUT-OUT WORD 569
John 5:38 His word has found no home in you, because you do not believe the one whom he sent.

THE FELLOWSHIP OF THE UNASHAMED 571
John 7:13 No one talked freely about him, however, for fear of the Jews.

GRAND CANYONS 573
John 7:43 Thus he was the cause of a division among the people.

UNLOOSE HIM 574
John 7:45 The temple police went back to the chief priests and Pharisees, who asked them, "Why have you not brought him?"

TOUGH LOVE 576
John 8:11 Go; do not sin again.

RIGHT SIGHT BY HIS LIGHT 578
John 8:12 Once again Jesus addressed the people: "I am the light of

the world. No follower of mine shall walk in darkness; he shall have the light of life."

THE HE(ART) OF SOUL-WINNING 580
John 8:30 As he said this, many put their faith in him.

O COME, ALL YE FAITHFUL 582
John 10:22 It was winter.

TO BE CONTINUED—NATURALLY............................584
John 12:2 They gave a supper in [Jesus'] honor at which Martha served, and Lazarus was among the guests with Jesus.

A STIR AT EASTER 586
John 12:16 At the time his disciples did not understand this, but after Jesus had been glorified, they remembered that this had been written about him and that this had happened to him.

THE COST OF DISCIPLESHIP 588
John 12:21 [Some Greeks, Gentiles] approached Philip, who was from Bethsaida in Galilee, and said to him, 'Sir, we should like to see Jesus.'"

ON BEING SAVED 590
John 12:42 For all that, even among those in authority many beloved in him, but...

HIS NIGHT LIGHT..592
John 13:30 It was night.

SHOW ME THE WAY TO GO HOME............................594
John 13:33 Where I am going you cannot come.

START AT THE HEART 596
John 15:25 "They hated me without reason."

FROM GRIEF TO BLISSFUL BELIEF............................598
John 16:20 You will weep and mourn, but the world will be glad, but though you will be plunged in grief, your grief will be turned to joy.

THE UNVEILING OF TRUTH...600
John 16:25 Till now I have been using figures of speech; a time is coming when I shall no longer use figures, but tell you of the Father in plain words.

ONE WITH THE FATHER 602
John 17:8 I have taught them (the men whom in you gave me out of the world [v. 6]) what I learned from you, and they have received it: they know with certainty that I came from you, and they have believed that...

ON KNOWING JESUS 605
John 18:2 The place was known to Judas.

THE LORD'S TURN (LUKE 22:61) 607
John 18:27 A cock crowed.

HEART AND HAND JOINTS... 609
John 18:20 The Jews themselves stayed outside the headquarters to avoid defilement, so that they could eat the Passover meal.

THE HOLY ARMOR OF GOD 611
John 19:23 When the soldiers had crucified Jesus they took his clothes and, leaving aside the tunic, divided them into four parts, one for each soldier...

THE CENTERPIECE OF OUR FAITH 613
John 19:41 Near the place where he had been crucified there was a garden, and in the garden a new tomb...

FIRST CLASS...615
John 20:4 They ran together, but the other disciple ran faster than Peter and reached the tomb first.

OH SAY CAN YOU SEE? 617
John 20:18 Mary of Magdala went to tell the disciples, "I have seen the Lord!"

HIS BREATHING BUSINESS 619
John 20:22 Then he breathed on them, saying, "Receive the Holy Spirit!"

AN OPEN SECRET 621
John 20:29 Happy are they who find faith without seeing me.

ACTS

THEY ALSO SERVE 623
Acts 1:4 He (Jesus) directed them not to leave Jerusalem: "You must wait," He said.

FROM WHENCE OUR SIGNALS COME....................... 626
Acts 1:26 They drew lots, and the lot fell to Matthias; so he was elected to be an apostle with the other eleven.

PURPOSE DRIVEN SCRIPTURE 628
Acts 2:14 But Peter stood up with the eleven, and in a loud voice addressed the crowd: "Fellow Jews, and all who live in Jerusalem, listen and take note of what I say."

I SURRENDER ALL 630
Acts 3:2 Now a man who had been a cripple from birth used to be

carried there and laid every day by the temple gate called Beautiful to beg from people as they went in.

THE PRIZE IN SURPRISE **632**
Acts 3:12 Peter saw them coming and met them with these words: "Men of Israel, why be surprised at this?"

I SERVE A RISEN SAVIOR **634**
Acts 4:2 Annoyed because they were proclaiming the resurrection from the dead.

UP THE DOWN STAIRCASE **637**
Acts 4:4 But many of those who had heard the message became believers, bringing the number of men to about five thousand.

DRAW ME NEARER **639**
Acts 4:13 ...took note that they (Peter and John) had been companions of Jesus.

TELL IT OUT **641**
Acts 4:18 They then called them in and ordered them to refrain from all public speaking and teaching in the name of Jesus.

PROCEED WITH HIS PROCEDURE **643**
Acts 4:24 When they (the Christian fellowship) heard it (the mandate placed upon the apostles by the court), they raised their voices with one accord and called upon God.

CONSECRATED, LORD, TO THEE **646**
Acts 4:36-37 For instance...Barnabas...sold an estate which he owned; he brought the money and laid it at the apostles' feet.

ALL OR NOT AT ALL **648**
Acts 5:9 Why did the two of you conspire...?

WHAT PRISON? **650**
Acts 5:23 "We found the jail securely locked at every point, with the warders at their posts by the doors, but on opening them we found no one inside."

THE DNA OF OUR FAITH **653**
Acts 5:31, 32 God exalted him at his right hand as leader and savior, to grant Israel repentance and forgiveness of sins. And we are witnesses to all this, as is the Holy Spirit who is given by God to those obedient to him.

WHEN ACTIONS SPEAK LOUDEST **656**
Acts 5:33 But a member of the council rose to his feet, a Pharisee called Gamaliel, a teacher of the law held in high regard by all the people.

DIVIDE AND CONQUER **657**
Acts 6:2,4 It would not be fitting for us to neglect the word of God in order to assist in the distribution...then we can devote ourselves to prayer and to the ministry of the word.

COME AWAY **660**
Acts 7:2-3 The God of glory appeared to Abraham...while he was in Mesopotamia, before he had settled in Harran and said: "Leave your country and your kinsfolk, and come away to a land that I will show you."

FAITH, IN SPITE OF **662**
Acts 7:4-5 God led him (Abraham) to migrate to this land (the Holy Land) where you now live. He gave him no foothold in it...

GIVE OF YOUR BEST TO THE MASTER **665**
Acts 7:22 So Moses was trained in all the wisdom of the Egyptians, a powerful speaker, and a man of action.

CLOSER DRAWN TO HIM **667**
Acts 7:31 Moses was amazed at the sight, and as he approached to look more closely, the voice of the Lord came to him.

AFTER HIS PATTERN (V. 44) **670**
Acts 7:44 Our forefathers had the Tent of the Testimony in the Desert.

TURN EVIL TO LIVE **672**
Acts 7:58 The witnesses laid their coats at the feet of a young man named Saul.

THE CONVERT AND THE REVERT **674**
Acts 8:14 When the apostles in Jerusalem heard that Samaria had accepted the Word of God, they sent off Peter and John.

ON BEING A RECYCLED DISCIPLE **676**
Acts 9:26 On reaching Jerusalem [Saul] tried to join the disciples, but they were all afraid of him because they did not believe that he really was a disciple.

THE CHURCH TRIUMPHANT **679**
Acts 9:31 Meanwhile the church, throughout Judaea, Galilee, and Samaria, was left in peace to build up its strength, and to live in the fear of the Lord...

STICK TO THE FACTS **681**
Acts 11:4 Peter began laying before them facts as they had happened.

PETER AT HEAVEN'S GATE **683**
Acts 12:9 Peter followed him out, with no idea that the angel's intervention was real.

THE TEMPLED HOME 685
Acts 12:12 Once he had realized this, he made for the house of Mary, the mother of John Mark, where a large company was at prayer.

NOT TO WORRY 687
Acts 12:18 When morning came, there was consternation among the soldiers: what could have become of Peter?

WHEN GOD CALLS 689
Acts 12:28 Barnabas and Saul, their task fulfilled, returned from Jerusalem, taking John Mark with them.

THE BEAUTY OF THE CANYON 691
Acts 15:6 The apostles and elders met to look into this matter.

A MNASONIC BOOM 693
Acts 21:16 Some of the disciples from Caesarea came along with us, to direct us to a Cypriot named Mnason, a Christian from the early days...

AT GOD'S DISPOSAL 695
Acts 21:23 Our proposal is this...

OUR UNFAILING FRIEND 697
Acts 21:30 The whole city was in turmoil, and people came running from all directions.

BORN AGAIN 699
Acts 22:6 What happened to me on my journey was this

POSSIBILITIES BEYOND CLOSED DOORS 701
Acts 22:22 Up to this point the crowd had given him a hearing; but now they began to shout, "down with the scoundrel He is not fit to be alive!"

RUBBING OUT THE RUBBISH 704
Acts: 22:27 The Commandant came to Paul and asked, "Tell me, are you a Roman citizen?"

GOD'S SECRET SERVICE OPERATIVES 706
Acts: 23:16 The son of Paul's sister, however, learned of the plot and, going to the barracks, obtained entry, and reported it to Paul.

A SERMON ON THE MOUNTS 708
Acts 23:24 And provide mounts for Paul so that he may be conducted under safe escort to Felix the governor.

ROMANS
ROCK OF AGES 710
Romans 9:33 Here I lay in Zion a stumbling stone and a rock to trip them up; but he who has faith in him will not be put to shame.

CENTRAL COMMAND 712
Romans 15:19 I have completed the preaching of the gospel of Christ from Jerusalem as far round as Illyricum

GIFTED GIVING 715
Romans 15:25 I am on my way to Jerusalem on an errand to God's people...

1 CORINTHIANS
A BUDGET BLUEPRINT 717
1 Cor. 16:3 Carry your gift to Jerusalem.

GALATIANS
THE BEDROCK OF FAITH 719
Gal. 1:18 Three years later I did go up to Jerusalem to get to know Cephas, and I stayed two weeks with him.

OUR RACE AT HIS PACE 721
Gal. 2:1-2 Fourteen years later, I went up again to Jerusalem with Barnabas and we took Titus with us...to make sure that the race...should not be in vain.

GOD'S ALL-SUFFICIENT WORD 723
Gal. 4:24-26 This is an allegory; the two women stand for two covenants. The one covenant comes from Mt. Sinai; that is Hagar, and her children are born into slavery. Sinai is a mountain in Arabia and represents the Jerusalem of today, for she and her children are born in slavery. But the heavenly Jerusalem is the free woman (Sarah); she is our mother.

HEBREWS
THE CROWN AWAITS THE CONQUEST 725
Heb. 12:22 You have come to Mount Zion, the city of the living God, the heavenly Jerusalem.

REVELATION
KINGDOM GIFTS 728
Rev. 3:12 I shall write on them the name of my God, and the name of the city of my God, that new Jerusalem.

JERUSALEM 728
THE GREATER CITY OF GOD 730
Rev. 11:26 (The outer court of the temple) has been given over to the Gentiles, and for forty-two months they will trample the Holy City underfoot.

TOWARD THE BRIGHTER DAY 732
Rev. 14:1 Then I looked, and on mount Zion stood the Lamb.

THE HOME OF GOD'S ELECT 733
Rev. 21:2 I saw the Holy City, new Jerusalem, coming down out of heaven from God.

THE LAND OF BEGINNING AGAIN 736
Rev. 21:10 So in the spirit he (an angel) carried me away to a great and lofty mountain, and showed me Jerusalem, the Holy City, coming down out of heaven from God.

THE SOUL'S SUNSHINE 738
Rev. 21:23 The city did not need the sun.

HIS NOURISHING WORD 739
Rev. 22:10 Do not seal up the words of the prophecy that are in this book.

THY PERFECT LIGHT 741
Rev. 22:16 I, Jesus...am...the bright star of dawn.

NO TINKERING WITH THE WORD 743
Rev. 22:19 If anyone takes away from the words in this book of prophecy, God will take away from him his share in the tree of life and in the Holy City which are described in this book.

THE SERMON ON THE MOUNT: MORIAH

Gen. 22:2 *God said, "Take your son, your one and only son Isaac whom you love, and go to the land of Moriah. There you shall offer him as a sacrifice on one of the heights which I shall show you."*

Much had happened to Abraham since he first went to Jerusalem (the land of Moriah) and was blessed by the Priest—King Melchizedek. Now history was to repeat itself. As Abraham was born when his father was 130 years old, so Isaac was born when his father Abraham was 100. And this time Abraham was commanded by God to go up to Jerusalem to receive another blessing, which, at the moment, Abraham was unaware of.

Though dramatic, this episode is an unnerving one to read in the Bible, that is, until the moment of relief comes, and the execution is stayed. Then the divine blessing descends as a benediction upon father and son—and later upon the waiting, hoping mother. The blessing did not stop there.

For one thing, Abraham's unconditional faith has been the bedrock for the world's three great faiths: Judaism, Islam, Christianity.

Because of the coronation of faith on Mt. Moriah, David set up a Tabernacle there, and on that site his son Solomon built a second-to-none Temple. Four hundred years later when it was destroyed by the Babylonians, the Temple was rebuilt by Nehemiah, Ezra, and Zerubbabel. After 500 years, that place of worship was replaced by Herod's Temple.

From that very site, in the seventh century A.D., Mohammed is believed to have ascended to heaven on his winged steed, El Burak. There now stands the Mosque of Omar.

In that Temple area Jesus was presented as a babe, schooled and taught and condemned to die.

Moreover, there is a close parallel between the sacrifice of Isaac and that of Jesus Christ.

First, scripture allows only Abraham to be a type of God the Father—who also sacrificed His son Jesus on the hill of Calvary ("one of the heights"). Second, on the third day "Abraham looked up." (v. 4) At Easter, a "third day," there was a looking up because there had been a rising up from the grave. Third, Abraham said to his helpers, "Stay here...while I...go on ahead." (v. 5) In Gethsemane, Jesus said to His helpers, "Sit here while I go over there..." (Matt. 26:36) Fourth, Isaac says, "Father." (v. 7) On the cross, Jesus says, "Father." (Luke 23:34,46) Fifth, Isaac is laid on the wood, (v. 9) as Jesus was on the cross. Sixth, there's the ram caught in a thicket, (v. 13) as Jesus, the Lamb of God, was caught in the thick of it. Seventh, Abraham received an "abundant" blessing, (v. 17) as the world has through our Lord Jesus Christ.

PRAYER: *Thank You, Lord, for the extended blessing—that all nations on earth will be blessed as Abraham's descendents are blessed, because Abraham was obedient to You. (Gen. 22:18) Amen.*

FEAR BEGONE

Jsh. 10:1-2 *When King Adonizedek of Jerusalem heard that Joshua had captured and destroyed Ai, dealing with Ai and its King as he had dealt with Jericho and its King, and also that the inhabitants of Gibeon had come to terms with Israel and were living among them, he was greatly alarmed...*

This is the first time in the Bible that Jerusalem is specifically mentioned by the name we call it today. Then Joshua, author of this book, is off to the races. He mentions Jerusalem four times in this one chapter. Each time the city is named with its King, who started a tragic chain reaction.

Learning, as the whole country had, of Joshua's military strategies and victories, Jerusalem's King suddenly felt vulnerable. Perhaps he would be next on Joshua's hit list, and he wasn't taking any chances. He would launch a pre-emptive strike on his not-to-be-trusted neighboring city—state of Gibeon.

Enlisting the help of four neighboring Kings, the ruler of Jerusalem declared war on Gibeon. Gibeon, in turn, called on ally Joshua, who arrived after an overnight march, and was still supremely triumphant. Finding the five enemy Kings hiding in a cave, Joshua had them brought out—and the rest is history. (Jsh. 10:23) Even their lands were appropriated by Joshua, all except Jerusalem.

What havoc fear works upon us. It is often self-fulfilling. We fear something so much, for so long, that we actually draw the imaginary out of hiding, and subconsciously construct it into reality. Joshua could have been of the same cowering mind as Jerusalem's leader. After all, he was a newcomer in that land. His army was untried. Most of his men had been born out in the Sinai desert during Israel's forty-year trek. Oh, there had been Jericho. But there had been no battle—just walking around the walls, trumpeting, shouting. The people of Jericho collapsed through thinking of what might happen—but didn't! Now facing five armies, Joshua could have been the one to collapse, if God had not reassured him, "Do not be afraid; I have delivered these Kings into your hands, and not one of them will be able to withstand you." (Jsh. 10:8) And they didn't. Nor do they ever, as God continues to send that message through His Son, Jesus Christ.

In his book *Crossing the Threshold of Hope*, Pope John Paul II wrote, "I state right from the outset: 'Be not afraid'...Christ addressed this invitation many times to those He met. The angel said to Mary: 'Be not afraid!' (Luke 1:30) The same was said to Joseph, 'Be not afraid!' (Matt. 1:20) Christ said the same to the apostles, to Peter, in various circumstances, and especially after His Resurrection. He kept telling them, 'Be not afraid!'" Our Lord goes even further—not just giving us advice and then backing away to let us fend for ourselves. There comes to us the personal touch: "Lo, I am with you always, even unto the end of the world." With Him by our side, we are assured of victory.

PRAYER: *Thank You, Lord, for Your Presence always. Amen.*

To Gather Together

Jsh. 15:63 *At Jerusalem, the men of Judah failed to drive out the Jebusites living there, and to this day Jebusites and men of Judah live together in Jerusalem.*

Though traditionally, the first-born son inherited the birthright (twice as much of the father's belongings as anyone else in the family), Jacob's first three sons were passed up. The fourth, Judah, and the eleventh, Joseph, were co-contenders for the favored position. Perhaps this is why Judah was anxious to sell Joseph into slavery. Judah's bloodline then became the chosen one from which the Messiah was to come.

Five hundred years later, the descendents of

Judah, aware of their major role among the new occupiers of the Promised Land, tried but "failed to drive out the Jebusites living" in the highly desirable city of Jerusalem.

The Jebusites were among the cursed descendents of Ham, Noah's second son. The evil spell had been pronounced because Ham had been disrespectful toward his father. Such an accused race should have been easy to dislodge by the premier Judean men of war. But it didn't happen.

What to do—carry on an endless vendetta? Withdraw? Find excuses?

The words "live together" offer a clue. They show how former antagonists can have a peaceful co-existence. And the phrase "to this day" can be equated with "lived happily ever after." Or, at least, for the next 400 years, after which David captured Jerusalem. (2 Sam. 5:7)

Daily life is full of things that are not as we want them. The specter of death stalks through our homes and down our streets. War, disease, lawlessness, physical handicaps, poverty, wrongdoing—there doesn't seem to be much that can be done to outlaw them. Well might we declare with William Orpen: "I am a joke, thou art a joke, he is a joke, we are jokes, you are jokes, they are jokes."

What did the Judahites and the Jebusites do when things were not as they wanted? First, they accepted the disagreeable as a part of life—thinking in terms of future fertility instead of immediate utility, praying possibly after the manner of Reinhold Niebuhr: "God, give me the serenity to accept the things I cannot change, courage to change the things I can, and wisdom to know the difference."

Second, as people who had a knowledge of God, isn't it likely that they put themselves in His hands? Who else can give victory over life's undesirables? Maude Royden had it right: "If anybody asks me to explain suffering, I say I can't, I say I have a power that can surmount it."

PRAYER: *Lord, lift us up to higher ground, where the playing field is flat. Amen.*

THATAWAY TO TRUTH

Judg. 1:7 *Adoni-bezek said, "I once had seventy kings with their thumbs and big toes cut off who were picking up scraps under my table. What I have done, God has done to me." He was brought to Jerusalem, and he died there.*

The city-state of Bezek, not many miles north of Jerusalem, was captured by the men of Judah and their allies. Adoni (the king) of Bezek fled. Nabbed, he was subjected to punishment common for that time (when there were no war crimes trials)—chopping off thumbs and big toes. Such dismemberment was not only a stinging humiliation for a king, but it also rendered him unfit to bear arms or to lead his foot soldiers in a rout with an enemy.

But this King refused to be subdued. Arrogantly he responded to his conquerors that he had in like manner mutilated seventy Kings (a number no doubt exaggerated by revenge, pain, blood). Then, unable to thumb his nose at the enemy, he made light of such amputations, adding that the severed seventy, though humiliated, were still handily dexterous enough to pick up tiny objects from dark places under tables. Bah! Who needs an opposable thumb?

But what about those big toes? Did Adoni-bezek know that we humans walk some 65,000 miles in a lifetime, or two and a half times around the world? Was he sure that the loss of his toes was no big deal; that when a bone breaks, osteoblasts—or the pothole fillers of the bone—get to work, and in two or three months usable repairs are complete? Through the bombast, one can hear the note of confidence.

Then the King's conscience kicked in. At a time when ethical principles were almost non- existent, this man exhibited, for all of history to see, a clean confession of his misdeeds. He admitted to enough sensitive hearers around him, so that it was recorded for posterity, that he was reaping what he had sown. And God has seen to that, not his conquerors.

Why the man was transported to Jerusalem, when the punished enemy was usually left to die on the field of battle, is a question left unanswered.

Could it be that he had touched the sensitivities of those who stood over him, gloating? Did they feel that here, after all, was a life worth saving? Yet, it was not to be.

But the principle he raised to the top of the mast still flies. Many thanks, your Majesty. At least your fingers keep pointing us in the right direction. Jesus, in the millennial relay, carried the message forward. As did St. Paul, who finished the course saying, "Make no mistake about this: God is not to be fooled; everyone reaps what he sows. If he sows in the field of his unspiritual nature, he will reap from it a harvest of corruption; but if he sows in the field of the spirit, he will reap from it a harvest of eternal life." (Gal. 6:7-8)

PRAYER: *Lord, make us, in word and deed, to be pointers of the way to eternal life. Amen.*

Awake, My Soul

Judg. 19:12 *His master replied, "No, not into a strange town (Jerusalem) where the people are not Israelites, let us go on to Gibeah."*

Chapter 19 starts by informing us that Israel was still in those days without a King. And, although this is called the Book of Judges, there were no judges in the sense of their being legal functionaries. Leaderless, people did what was right in their own eyes, which amounted to doing as they pleased. It is easy to follow this story that keeps extending itself into three full chapters. It is unbelievably horrifying even for our day with its daily news menu of murder and mayhem. Were it on television, there would be a list of precautionary advisements.

An unnamed man makes a long journey to retrieve his secondhand runaway wife. On the return journey, it was late and stormy, and, being near Jerusalem, the servant suggested that they turn in for the night. But the master put his foot down. This was still some 400 years before David occupied the city of Jerusalem and took the Ark there—the Ark where God resided. For this reason it was deemed a place unfit to spend even one night, Gibeah would be safer, the master decided, if it was Israelite; Jerusalem was not.

But surprise! The town of Gibeah may have been Israelite and apparently safe, but it was inhumanely inhospitable. "Nobody took them into his house for the night." (v. 15) Later that evening an old man, returning from work, took the travelers into his home because they were from the same home country as he was.

Then came the fireworks. "Some of the most depraved scoundrels surrounded the house, beating the door violently and shouting to the old man, whose home it was, 'Bring out the man who has come to your house, for us to have intercourse with him.'" (v. 22) When those outsiders couldn't be argued out of their passionate desire, and since women in those days were considered nothing but the expendable goods of men, the traveler pushed his "wife" through the door for the predators to fall upon. Which they did, all night, raping her to death.

When the word spread, Israelites everywhere were in shock. Nothing like this had happened among them since Moses brought the Israelites out of Egypt 200 years ago.

A cleansing movement was started to rid the land of such gross wickedness. Bloodshed was seen up and down the Land of Promise. And all this in spite of the people promising Moses, and his successor, Joshua, that they would be obedient children of God.

Yet, slowly becoming leaderless, rudderless, they drifted. They saw no evil, heard no evil, spoke no evil, did no evil while they sat on their hands. The trouble was that they couldn't even distinguish evil from good—even when evil was hidden in plain sight. The love for the golden calf had never really been purged from their lives. More than a thousand years later, Jesus faced the same problem, and told people the parable of the Two Sons. (Matt. 21:28-32) "Truly," Jesus said, "I tell you tax-collectors and prostitutes are entering the Kingdom of God ahead of you" (you who profess to be religious). In Christian America we are still genuflecting before Fort Knox and Dow Jones, pornography, and prevailing fads. Let us move on to a new life in Christ.

PRAYER: *Gracious God, forgive us for promising to do better, and not keeping our promise. "Revive us again; fill each heart with Thy love; may each soul be rekindled with fire from above."*[1] *Amen.*

WHEN THE IDEAL BECOMES REAL

1 Sam. 17:54 *David took Goliath's head and carried it to Jerusalem, but he put Goliath's weapons in his own tent.*

Another dreadful verse! If David was on the Lord's side, why did he stoop to such a ghastly deed as decapitating the giant? Wasn't David's slingshot enough? It felled the foe, even if Goliath was unconscious for a while. Why finish the man off with unholy homicide—beheading?

Although David was severely punished for later plotting the death of Uriah (one of his very own fine military commanders), not a hair of David was touched by either God or man, regarding the butchering of the gargantuan Philistine.

From Stone Age times and even before, it was believed that the soul of a human being resided in one's head. In that section of the human anatomy there was said to be a vaporous substance which bursts, fertilizing the earth. Plants are thereby nurtured, and in time reenter human bodies to propagate the species. Headhunting, for this and cannibalistic purposes, has been recorded all over the world—until the early twentieth century. The practice was known in Ireland, Scotland, across Europe, Borneo, Australia, New Zealand, and North and South America. If heads were not shrunken to the size of a small monkey, they were tattooed

---

[1]William P. Mackay

and sold as curios, or scalped with the thought that the soul-strength was in the hair—as with Samson. Even Jesus' cousin, John the Baptist, had his head presented on a platter. Vestigial remains of this gruesome operation are still around. Any day, anywhere the macabre expression can be heard, that if a certain person comes this way "heads will roll." In certain secret societies the members continue to drink out of skulls. Since the law now forbids such skullduggery, plastic is shaped in skull form. Yet the ancient perception very obviously persists. Up to the minute: In Boston, Mass. a man decapitated a prostitute and several other persons.

David, then, was clearly following a deeply ingrained custom. His understanding of God's Ten Commandments from Sinai was immature. His religious faith was more in word than in deed. Unfortunately, before his experience could catch up with his words, he committed a sin that disqualified him from what he wanted most of all to do—build a Temple to the Lord of Hosts. That honor was left to his son Solomon.

It takes time for words and deeds to come together. The process is seen more clearly in the great fisherman Simon Peter.

First, there has to be exposure. And Peter's brother exposed him to the Way, the Truth, the Light of the World, saying, "We have found the Messiah." (John 1:41) Second, there must be repeated exposures to the good, to God. And Peter had those as he watched and heard his Master teaching, healing, and raising the dead. Third, there must be understanding, as Jenny Lind (the Swedish nightingale) sang, "I *know* that my Redeemer liveth." Fourth, there must be conviction. When Jesus asked His disciples "Who do people say the Son of Man is?" they replied, "Some say John the Baptist, others Elijah, others Jeremiah, or one of the prophets." "And you," He pressed His listeners, "who do you say I am?" Simon Peter answered, "You are the Messiah, the Son of the living God." (Matt. 16:13-16) Ah, conviction at last! Fifth, there must be application. David said: "I shall teach transgressors your ways, and sinners will return to you." (Ps. 51:13)

PRAYER: *Heavenly Father, "Let us not love in word, neither in tongue (theory); but in deed and in truth." (1 John 3:18) Amen.*

CAN'T STOP NOW

2 Sam. 5:7 *Nonetheless, David did capture the stronghold of Zion, and it is now known as the City of David.*

Here comes the man whose name is at the top of the list in Hebrew history: David. And he comes to the city that has borne his name ever since.

For 1,000 years Jerusalem had been the habitat of the Jebusites. It had their name—Jebu to Jeru, with "salem" added to identify the area as the City of Peace.

But now David had his eye on it. It was in just the right strategic position to pull together the southern and northern sections of Israel and become the nation's capital. But the Jebusites had their own ideas. Nobody was going to take their prized possession from them—least of all David. Others, many others, had tried this dispossessing trick on them and failed. So, with a centuries-old confidence, with noses in the air, they flicked David off their sleeves with scorn, "You will never come in here..." (2 Sam. 5:6) Those words had turned back others, but not David. The word "never" was the wrong one to use with David. Others had used it with him—and the rest is history.

When he was a young shepherd, David had heard the "never" word from Goliath. That nine-foot giant was heavily armored. Who was this kid coming to challenge him with a sling and stones? Goliath prepared to make short work of this youngster, and give his flesh to the vultures and the carnivores of the field.

Lions and bears had also thought that of David. But the young man had some ideas too. With a sling made of goat hair (still used to commemorate David), he practiced until he was proficient, able to bull's-eye every target. The swaggering giant was no different—he got it between the eyes with a pebble from a stream.

And that's how the "nevers" were forevermore treated, Jerusalem included.

Winston Churchill learned that lesson. During World War II when Britain was hard-pressed and alone, Churchill challenged his countrymen to never give up. Even if their little country was invaded they were to fight in the streets, from house to house, with whatever weapons that were handy—shovels, rakes, drainpipes. Later, with that same spirit, invited to speak at a well-known school, Churchill cleared his throat and said "never, never, never, never, give up." Then he sat down.

A cartoon portrays it graphically. A stork has swallowed a frog. But the frog thinks quickly and gets its legs around the storks neck so that it can't complete the swallow. The stork has to cough up the frog—or die. The frog turns the odds around to become his enemy's odds.

> Courage is not just to bare one's bosom
> to the saber thrust alone in daring.
> Courage is to grieve, to have the hurt and
> make the world believe you are not caring.
> Courage does not lie alone in dying for
> a cause, to die is only giving.
> Courage is to feel the daily daggers of
> relentless steel and go on living.

PRAYER: *Lord Jesus, our own "nevers" become squishy without the assurance of Your "I will never leave you nor forsake you." Thank You. Amen.*

PEACE CAPITAL OF THE WORLD

2 Sam. 5:9 *David took up his residence in the stronghold and called it the City of David. He built up the city around it, starting at the Millo and working inward.*

David had been living in Hebron. It was there he ruled as King over Judah for seven and a half years. But when he was crowned King of all Israel, Hebron was nothing but a birdcage for his soaring ambitions. He needed space and a lofty fortress. And what better fitted his needs than that natural stronghold—Jerusalem, with its mountains and valley, just nineteen miles northeast of Hebron?

The great-grandson of Ruth and Boaz, David had been born and brought up in Bethlehem, just five miles south of Jerusalem. He knew the impregnability of Jerusalem. Men of Judah, who had co-existed with the Jebusites for years in Jerusalem, provided David with helpful intelligence about the city. Yet the current residents, the Jebusites, were not about to give up their city without a fight. That's what they thought. With comparative ease, "David took up his residence in the stronghold and called it the City of David." There he reigned as King for thirty-three years.

What a reign. And what a city. David made it so attractive, and gathered in all the plans and materials for a Temple that all his son Solomon had to do was construct it. Then nobody could keep their hands off the place. Through the centuries came the Babylonians, Persians, Greeks, Romans, Byzantines, Arabs, Crusaders, Turks, and British. All have seen in Jerusalem a possible world capital of Peace.

On 13 May 1995, Feisel Husseini, the PLO representative in Jerusalem, made a speech during a demonstration protesting against the confiscation of Arab land. Standing beneath the walls of the old city in what had once been No Man's Land, Husseini said, "I dream of the day when a Palestinian will say 'Our Jerusalem' and will mean Palestinians and Israelis, and an Israeli will say 'Our Jerusalem' and will mean Israelis and Palestinians." In response, 700 prominent Israelis, including writers, critics, artists, and former Knesset members, signed this joint statement:

Jerusalem is ours, Israelis and Palestinians—Muslims, Christians, and Jews. Our Jerusalem is a mosaic of all cultures, all the religions, and all the periods that enriched the city from the earliest antiquity to this very day—Canaanites and Jebusites and Israelites, Jews and Hellenes, Romans and Byzantines, Christians and Muslims, Arabs and Mamelukes, Ottomans and Britons, Palestinians and Israelis. They and all the others who make their contribution to the city have a place in the spiritual and physical landscape of Jerusalem.

Our Jerusalem must be united, open to all and belonging to all its inhabitants, without borders and barbed wire in its midst.

Our Jerusalem must be the capital of the two states that will live side by side in this country— West Jerusalem the capital of the State of Israel and East Jerusalem the capital of the State of Palestine.

Our Jerusalem must be the Capital of Peace.[1]

Indeed, that is what is promised us by David's greater Son, the King of Kings, our Lord Jesus Christ, in the New Jerusalem. (Rev. 22:1-5)

PRAYER: *Even so, come, Lord Jesus. Amen.*

THE BEAUTY OF HOLINESS

2 Sam. 6:9 *David was afraid of the Lord that day and said, "How can I harbour the Ark of the Lord after this?"*

After what? Israel was having a happy time accompanying the Ark for its first entry into Jerusalem. The Ark of the Covenant, a portable throne for the invisible presence of God, and mentioned more than 200 times in the Old Testament with twenty-two different names, was Israel's most prized possession. Now God was coming home— to the City of God, Jerusalem. Suddenly everything went askew. The Ark was in an ox-drawn cart. Coming to a sacred spot, of which the oxen were aware but the humans were not, the animals missed their footing. One man, nearest the oxen, reached out in an attempt to help the beasts (thereby revealing more of a concern for the oxen

---

[1] Karen Armstrong, *Jerusalem*, p. 419

than for the place made holy by God), was struck dead, sending a shock wave through the enormous procession, and triggering David's fear of handling the Ark.

It was just that David and the others were slow to recall from their memory bank how the Ark came into being, and the precautions surrounding it. It had been 400 years since God ordered Moses to build the Ark in the Sinai Wilderness. The acacia wood box was to contain the Ten Commandments, a pot of Manna, and the Pentateuch—the first five books of the Bible written by Moses. On top was God's throne! But the no-nonsense security measures guarding the Ark were not to be trifled with. One misstep, as in the above procession, and death was the result. It is seen in the case of Ananias and Sapphira who fraudulently "kept back part of the price." (Acts 5:1-12)

When God came to Mt. Sinai in the combination of a volcano and a thunderstorm, it was to impress upon His people for the last time His divine authority and His laws, the prime importance of God's presence, and that each worshipper must be physically and spiritually prepared before approaching God's holiness. And these reminders abide despite Jesus' "user friendly" promise to be with us always. For example, at worship, personal bodily gratifications (drinking, smoking, idle chatter and other trendy [cell phone] contemporary jingoisms) are unacceptable.

In earlier times a Saturday night on the town was considered an inappropriate introduction to Sunday morning worship, especially when Holy Communion was to be served. In time, though some of the restrictions were loosened, the respect factor was maintained. Clothes were referred to as "Sunday best." "Blue Laws" were still in effect; that is, weekday labor came to a standstill on the Sabbath. All stores were closed, as were movie houses and stadiums. Following World War II there came a slow but widespread disappearance of the Commandment to keep the Sabbath Day holy; in fact, to keep anything holy. All of which has caused western society to become materialistic. Pluralistic, with an unrecognizably mushy Christianity. May David's experience "revive in our collective memory the poetry and power of ancient stories and past visual art, both of which are threatened with extinction by the sterile images and jejune (not amounting to much) stories offered daily by contemporary culture."[1]

PRAYER: *"Jesus, where'er Thy people meet, There they behold, Thy mercy seat; Where'er they seek Thee, Thou art found, And every place is hallowed ground."*[2] Amen.

ON THIS ROCK I WILL BUILD

2 Sam. 6:12 *When David was informed that the Lord had blessed Obed-edoms' family and all that he possessed because of the Ark of God, he went and brought the Ark of God from the house of Obed-edom up to the city of David (another name for Jerusalem) amid rejoicing.*

Today on Mt. Moriah, the Muslims have a mosque called the Dome of the Rock. That great slab of rock was once a threshing floor. It was purchased by David, and on it he placed the pre-

---

[1]Regis DeBray, *The Old Testament Through 100 Masterpieces of Art*, p. 17
[2]William Cowper

cious Ark of the Covenant. For David the place was special. It was also the spot where Abraham was about to sacrifice his son Isaac. And, as the area became increasingly honored and sacred, because of the Ark's meaning that here God dwelt on earth, Solomon's once-in-a-millennium temple was built on that site. In fact, for the next 1,000 years three Jewish Temples dominated the heights of Mt. Moriah (Solomon, Zerubbabel, and Herod) right into the era of Jesus Christ. That is, the Hebrew-Christian act of worship was built on two rock-solid convictions—threshing and sacrifice.

Threshing, or thrashing, separating grain from chaff or plant seeds from husks or pods, was done from earliest times until the tenth century A.D., with flails. The flail is still used for this purpose in parts of the world. By 1833 there were some 700 variants of threshing machines. So crucial was threshing—getting to the core, to the vitalizing center—that the term entered the sacred precincts. "Holy" means separated. The pure, the righteous is set apart from the sinful. The word "holy" is found under every letter of the alphabet, which indicates that all through everyday life there is a job to be done on separating good from evil, the wheat from the weed, "the breakfast of champions" from the worthless.

Sacrifice, as Abraham showed on the threshing floor of Mt. Moriah, is giving our best to the Lord. At first they were material offerings which cost, and hurt the pocketbook—oxen, sheep, vegetables, and money. But when the Temple was destroyed or the Hebrews were exiled, and had no worship center to do their sacrificing—other ways were found, or no ways.

David determined the direction in which both

these worship experiences could go—Temple or not. We see them in his great penitential, Ps. 51.

"Sprinkle me with hyssop, so that I may be cleaned." (v. 7) Hyssop was used for the cleansing of lepers, and here David courageously and rightly identifies himself as a moral leper. "Wash me, and I shall be whiter than snow." (v. 7) There were two kinds of washing: soap, with warm water poured over the hands, dishes, or the body as in a shower and, the other, as they still wash clothes (in some countries) down by the river, thrashing the clothes on the rocks. This latter is the kind of washing that David is asking the Lord to do on him. "Thrash me on the rocks, get all the filth out of me."

As for the sacrifice, David says to the Lord, "You have no delight in sacrifice; if I were to bring a whole-offering you would not accept it. God, my sacrifice is a broken spirit; you, God, will not despise a chastened heart." (v. 16-17) And the writer to the Hebrews updates it: "If sprinkling the blood of goats and bulls...consecrates those who have been defiled and restores their ritual purity, how much greater is the power of the blood of Christ; through the eternal spirit he offered himself without blemish to God." (Heb. 9:13-14)

PRAYER: *"I praise Thee, Lord, for cleansing me from sin; Fulfill Thy Word, and make me pure within; Fill me with fire, where once I burned with shame; Grant my desire to magnify Thy name."*[1] *Amen.*

LOVE FINDS A WAY

2 Sam. 14:28 *Absalom lived in Jerusalem for two whole years without entering the King's presence.*

---
[1] Edwin Orr

King David's name means "beloved"; his son Absalom's (Ab-shalom) name means "peace." But there was no love lost, and little peace between the two.

The estrangement, strangely, was started by neither. James Naylor reminded us that "King David and King Solomon led merry, merry lives, with many, many lady friends, and many, many wives..." Thus, David had many, many children. His son and heir, Amnon, fell in love with his half-sister Tamar, then seduced and raped her. Tamar's full brother, Absalom, second in line for the throne, was enraged, and arranged for Amnon's assassination. Then, fearing reprisals, Absalom took refuge among his mother's relatives. And it gets even more complicated. "Oh, what a tangled web we weave, when first we practice to deceive."

Over the next three years, David slowly became reconciled to the death of his firstborn son, and conceded to inviting Absalom to come home to Jerusalem—but with the understanding that he should keep his distance from his dad.

What a different Prodigal Son story this is—compared with the one in Jesus' parable. There the father comes running out (with a different shoe on each foot, he's so excited), flings his welcoming arms around his son, kisses him, stops him in mid-confession, orders: "Quick! Fetch a robe, the best we have (denoting the son's restoration to the family), put a ring on his finger (one of two mentions of a finger-ring in the New Testament, a signet, making the occasion official), and sandals on his feet (only slaves went barefooted, not family members), bring the fatted calf...and let us celebrate with a feast." (Luke 15:22-23) It was a red-carpet day, with fireworks.

How clearly the lines are drawn here between the Old and New Testaments, and the need for having both in our Bible. The Old gives a rawbones description of how and why humans behave as they do. And, throughout, there are correctives given as to how humans can surmount their savagery. The New, stepping up, shows by God incarnate, how to live and love and die nobly; God's people are put back on the road of righteousness, of which they began to wander away from in the Garden of Eden.

Certainly in David's present case, the matter of polygamy (his many wives and concubines) made family relations stickier than normal. Jesus emphasized the one-man, one-woman marriage bond as being the most enduring. In David's day they were like a buck and a herd of doe; a group of sex-induced and produced dissimilars who could never quite coalesce. Essentially they were strangers to one another. And, as long as family life follows pre-Christian patterns, just so long will the world remain stone-aged, overrun with alley cats. Jesus showed the upper road to the glory land.

PRAYER: *David's greater Son, have mercy on us for knowing better and doing worse. We will arise and depart from the "far country"—and look forward to Your welcome home. Amen.*

HIS WAY EVERY DAY

2 Sam. 15:16 *The King set out (from Jerusalem), and all his household followed him except ten concubines whom he left in charge of the palace.*

Such women were in charge of palaces and other places. Such were the times. And not first at a time when the King was fleeing for his life. Sex was in charge. Then why were they being left behind?

Learning that his son was leading a revolt against him, King David, being an old hand at such contingencies, knew the consequences. He would be on the move, using dodging tactics, running low on food, living out of tents, often not knowing where he was going, or if he would survive the day. Of what use were concubines amid such perils? They would be an added burden. Leave the unnecessary baggage behind?

Yet it was for none of these reasons that those ten women were "not wanted on the voyage" as the old ship luggage labels used to say.

There was a custom that when a King died his harem went to his successor. In fact, to claim the palace harem was as good as claiming the throne. Now the new ruler had acquired all the rights of the former head of state. That is why, when David's son asked his counselor for advice as to what to do next, he was told: "Have intercourse with your father's concubines whom he left in charge of the palace." (v. 16:21) This was not done in secret. Rather, the whole event had the overlay of religion, and was made to look like a marriage ceremony. The counselor had given David's son to believe that when David was put to death, "I will bring all the people (of Israel) over to you as a bride is brought to her husband." (v. 17:3) Accordingly, a bridal tent (still used in Jewish practice) was set up on the roof, so that all who wished to view this public display of sexuality (and the claiming of the Kingdom by the new ruler) might do so.

Through this historical event, God was fulfilling

His intent to punish David for his sinful act with Bathsheba. Said He: "I will bring trouble upon you from within your own family; I will take your wives and give them to another man before your eyes, and he will lie with them in broad daylight. What you did was done in secret; but I will do this in the light of day for all Israel to see." (v. 12:11-12)

Nothing we say or do escapes the Heavenly Watchman. "God alone understands the way to it, He alone knows its source; for He can see to the ends of the earth and observe every place under heaven." (Job 28:23-24) More explicitly there is Jesus: "I tell you this; every thoughtless word you speak you will have to account for it on the day of judgment. For out of your own mouth you will be acquitted, and out of your own mouth you will be condemned." (Matt. 12:36-37)

The Lord is watching the concubines, numbering them and the hairs on their heads that minutely. Somewhere His recording is being set down to be settled, in His own good time with rewards or punishments. He is never off duty. What a comfort to know that He is always with us—to help and heal and make us ready to be claimants of His Kingdom, now and ever.

PRAYER: *Although it is sometimes unnerving, Lord, to have You looking over our shoulder, it is comforting to know that You are always doing it for our good. We praise You for Your creative companionship. Amen.*

LIVE IT, GIVE IT

2 Sam. 15:27 *The King went on to say to Zadok the priest, "Are you not a seer?" Or the alternative expression, "Can you make good use of your eyes?"*

Knowing that his son was leading a revolt against him, King David was exiting Jerusalem in fast-forward mode. But known as a hardened warrior and one who could be "savage as a bear in the wilds robbed of her young," (v. 17:8) David made sure that, first, his intelligence service was in operation. It was nothing new. Two thousand years before David, the Egyptians had a well-organized secret service, which could be defined as "the attempt to obtain clandestinely or under false pretenses information concerning one government for transmission to another government." And David, as an old campaigner in the field, was aware that success, in large measure, depended upon the accuracy of information about the enemy. Accordingly, David set up his espionage system: two loyal priests, their sons, and another trusted official, working from inside Jerusalem where the occupation troops were about to enter, the informers were to pass along significant happenings to David.

The next two chapters, 16 and 17, read like a detective story, with information, misinformation, intelligence, and counterintelligence. Always the spies had to make use of their eyes, and all their faculties. And David was victorious.

Though the bush telegraph and grapevine have become highly complex and sophisticated, as in Britain's Scotland Yard, Russia's KGB, USA's CIA, and Interpol—the International Police network, to say nothing about Israel's topflight system, the basic act of gathering and spreading vital information is the same as in David's day: Can you make good use of your eyes? That is why the essential elements are used in almost all aspects of daily life.

In courtship there are the coded "come" or "stay away" signs: a wink, a nod, a dropped hanky as if by accident, a frown. No words are spoken, but volumes of messages and life-changing decisions are exchanged. And it is common knowledge that in politics, industry, agriculture, labor, and most other human activities, their cherished successes are artfully concealed until they are safely secured. With the World Wide Web, and other such earth links, sensitive messaging has gone underground, with ever-newer defensive encoding.

In such a dog-eat-dog era, our faith dare not desert the privilege of telling it out among the nations that the Lord is King. Refined, put to work for the Kingdom's cause, the good old person-to-person approach, which was good enough for King David, and David's Greater Son, should be good enough for us. Especially in the present day, when enemies of the faith are determined to silence the Good News, to misinterpret it, spin it into something unrecognizable to Bible believers. When St. Paul was converted, he converted the communication system he had learned as an unbeliever. He used it to our advantage, in obedience to Jesus Commission "go therefore to all nations and make them my disciples...and teach them all that I have commanded you. I will be with you always, to the end of time." (Matt. 28:19-20)

PRAYER: *Remind us often, gracious Lord, "the best of all the preachers are the ones who live their creeds. For to see good put into action is what everybody needs." Amen.*

LIFE'S UPPER SLOPES

2 Sam. 15:30 *David wept as he went up the slope of the Mount of Olives.*

A thousand years later Jesus wept on Olivet. Today there is a Church on the Mount to commemorate the occasion. It is called the Tear Drop Church. It is tiny, but worshipfully and exquisitely designed in the shape of a teardrop.

At that early time, the host of people leaving Jerusalem were all crying. "The whole countryside resounded with their weeping." (v. 15:23) Nobody knew if they would ever return home to their capital city. Yet, though the future was uncertain, bleak, David's order of the day—tear or not, blurred journey ahead or not—was "March On!" As people passed their courageous King, they took heart. With a leader like that they couldn't and wouldn't lose.

Centuries later, in England, the army won a great victory in the face of impossible odds. Asked how they did it, they replied: "We had a touch of Harry in the night." During the night before the battle, King Henry had moved through the encampment inspiring his men, cheering them, sharing with them his indomitable will to win.

In Jerusalem there was a touch of David, in broad daylight, as he publicly and trustfully left everything in God's hands to "do what he pleases." (v. 15:26) That, too, was Gen. Dwight D. Eisenhower's approach as he watched the launching of the D-Day invasion in World War II. By which history confirms the fact that anything is safest when put in the hands of the "Man who stilled the waters" of Galilee.

Having supervised the crossing of his people across the Kidron Valley, it was David's turn to climb Mount Olivet. From there one gets the most emotionally moving panoramic view of the Holy

City, north to south—from Mt. Zion and Mt. Moriah to Bethlehem and on to Sinai, and east to west and the Mediterranean Sea. And here was David having to say goodbye, perhaps for the last time, to his own "City of David." No wonder he wept, especially as he thought of all this misery being caused by his own beloved son Absalom. "Salom," shalom, Peace on the Mount of Olives with its olive branches of Peace. It was too much. The tears couldn't be restrained.

Then there was the priest close to David, who had become a turncoat. Christ, too, had His Judas, who went and hanged himself. (v. 17:23)

Still, David had friends to whom he said, "You can help me." (v. 15:34) And they did, the Lord being their helpers.

It all sounds so familiar, a synopsis of life's journey with its unceasing farewells and crying spells, the uphill slogging, the self-recriminations, the tiptoeing through minefields, the hurt and bleeding feelings caused by traitorous friends—not all at once, thank heaven, but still they come.

Not to be outdone, however, is the encouraging order to march on. 'Tis God's will. Knowing our every move, He sends His angelic helpers flying in to aid us when they are most needed. Besides, Jesus, "though He was a Son...He learned obedience by the things which He suffered. And having been perfected, He became the author of eternal salvation to all who obey Him." (Heb. 5:8-9)

PRAYER: *Lord, we sing: "It is glory just to walk with Him...He will guide my steps aright, Thro' the vale and o'er the height; It is glory just to walk with Him."*[1] *Amen.*

---

[1] Avis M. Burgeson

TRUTH BEGINS AND ENDS WITH A T
(A CROSS)

2 Sam. 16:1 *When David had moved on a little from the top of the ridge, he was met by Ziba the servant of Mephibosheth.*
    This story goes from A to Z. As Absalom entered one end of Jerusalem, Ziba was awaiting David at the other end. Surprised, David asked two questions: "What are you doing with these?" (lots of food, loaded on donkeys) and "Where is your master's grandson?" The food and pack animals were for King David's journey. But it was Mephibosheth whom David was more concerned about. He was the son of David's best friend, Jonathon, and the grandson of King Saul whose troubled spirit David had once calmed while playing on his lyre. Both those elders were now gone, and as it was the custom to execute all family members of the former King, David, instead, had taken the young man under his wing. Especially because Mephibosheth was a cripple. When he was five years old, in an emergency situation his nurse had dropped him, breaking both his legs. Since then, Ziba, with his fifteen sons and twenty slaves, was appointed to look after the disabled prince. Now Ziba replied to David's question that Mephibosheth was staying on in Jerusalem, "for he thought that the (invaders) might now restore to him his grandfather's throne." (v. 16:3) Annoyed at such arrogant ingratitude, David, on the spot, gave all the young man's belongings to this servant.
    Later, when David returned to Jerusalem in triumph, one who went out to welcome him was Mephibosheth. And "Why did you not go with

me?" asked the King. The reply was, "My servant deceived me...his stories set your majesty against me." (v. 19:25-27) Unable to make out who was fibbing, David divided the estate between the two of them. Both men had David in their crosshairs as they hungered for more possessions and power. As a result both were poorer.

Did Solomon, David's son, learn this bit of administrative justice from his dad? As in the case of the two women who claimed the same baby as her own? Both women were persuasive. Both had good arguments. Was it then that Solomon's "Wisdom" reminded him of what dad had once done in a case: cut it in two? "Fetch me a sword," ordered Solomon, "cut the living child in two and give half to one woman and half to the other." (1 Kings 3:24-25) That revealed the true mother—the one who was unwilling to have her child sliced in half.

Mephibosheth's response to King David was, "Let him (Ziba) have it all." (v. 19:30) Truth has a way of coming to the surface, as the cream always does.

David, himself, had learned that painful lesson in the Bathsheba incident. He thought he had all bases covered, all doors locked, covered all peepholes. But there were people who changed the bed linen and swept the floors, and who whispered. And the prophet Nathan's grapevine got the message! As John Wolcot put it:

> The sages say Dame Truth delights to dwell
> (Strange Mansion) in the bottom of a well:
> Questions are then the Windlass and the Rope
> That pull the grave old gentlewoman up.

"Putting away lying, speak every man truth with his neighbor." (Eph. 4:25)

PRAYER: *"Send down thy truth, O God: Too long*

the shadows frown; Too long the darkened way we've trod,
Thy truth, O Lord, send down."[1]

I WILL FOLLOW JESUS, ANYWHERE...

2 Sam. 20:2 *All the men of Israel deserted David to follow Sheba, son of Bichri, but the men of Judah stood by their King and followed him from the Jordan to Jerusalem.*

Sheba (no relation of or any connection to the Queen), is called a "scoundrel" in verse one. It is the same word that is used of David in 2 Sam. 16:7. Here, David's accuser elaborates on what he means by "scoundrel." David, he yelled, as he showered stones right and left, was a man of blood, one on whom the Lord had taken vengeance for stealing Saul's throne; a murderer whose crimes had overtaken him.

Opposite to that partisan opinion of David, the description of "scoundrel" fitted Sheba snugly. Sensing dissent in the ranks and sniffing the sweet smell of possible kingship for himself, Sheba blew a ram's horn to get public attention. To his listeners he proclaimed a pithy message, which promptly split the ranks. The army of Israel chose to follow the scoundrel, where the men of Judah stood stolidly with King David.

How that following of the worst by deserting the best has reverberated through the corridors of time. And you would think that by now we would have learned enough to once and for all have a turn around.

But no, David's greater son, Jesus, knew the grief of being deserted. And for the same reason it happened to David: dissent in the ranks. When

---
[1] Edward R. Sill

"Jesus spoke to the crowd: 'Do you take me for a bandit that you have come out with swords and cudgels to arrest me?'" (Matt. 26:55) His disciples viewed Him from the public's standpoint. Why else would the crowd have come armed—except to subdue a marauder, a scoundrel? And Jesus' threat: "Do you suppose that I cannot appeal for help to my Father, and at once be sent more than twelve legions of angels?" (Matt. 26:53) sounded like empty bragging. Then, as with David, "the disciples all deserted [Jesus] and ran away." (Matt. 26:56)

An X-ray of desertion reveals a fatal fascination with the opposition. David saw it; so did Jesus; so do we. Hearing that in a pluralistic society everyone must be given equal opportunity to witness to the finality of Christ is to be considered a kook, a boat-rocker, a disturber of the peace. In like manner, "when Jesus said these things in the synagogue as he taught in Capernaum...many of his disciples exclaimed, 'This is more than we can stand! How can anyone listen to such talk?'...From that moment many of his disciples drew back and no longer went about with him." (John 6:59,60,66)

How the Lord still needs those who will stand by their King. The reward and grandeur of future history is theirs.

PRAYER: *Lord, stand with me, as I stand with Thee. Amen.*

FROM THRASHING TO THRESHING

2 Sam. 24:16 *The angel stretched out his arm toward Jerusalem to destroy it; but the Lord repented of the evil and said to the angel who was destroying the people, 'Enough! Stay your hand.' At that moment the angel of the Lord*

was at the threshing floor of Araunah the Jebusite.

Repeated for its importance in 1 Chron. 21, this incident also repeats history, and supplies hinges on which future imperatives depend.

Something went wrong in a natural census taking, and David took the blame for it. Given a choice of three punishments, David chose three days of pestilence upon the land. As a result 70,000 people died. Then, just as Jerusalem was to be destroyed, as Isaac was, and in the same place, the hand of the slayer was again held back. Then there is introduced a line which at first appears irrelevant, namely, that the sparing of Jerusalem took place at a threshing floor. So what?

To David, however, the spot was of supreme importance. It appealed to the historian in him to learn from the locals that this was none other than the noted area on which Abraham almost slew his son on a sacrificial altar. And David was convinced that he should become the owner of it.

It was nothing but a threshing floor. There was a board, studded on the underside, which a horse or bull dragged around and around to separate the grain from the chaff. Sure the owner consented King David could have it—cattle, boards, yokes, the whole operation—for nothing. Yet David's modus operandi was that he would never make an offering to God that cost him nothing.

That, then, became the site of David's altar, which later was included in Solomon's magnificent Temple. And the rest is history, epicentral history.

How deftly God turns disappointments into His appointments, and a lemon into Le Monde. In the imminent destruction of Jerusalem He saw emerging glory.

On a mountainside, far from food and water,

with 5,000 people in need of victualing, Jesus converted an unsettling condition into a settlement of citizens sustained in body, mind, spirit. God continues to find blessings in unexpected places.

At Greyfriars Churchyard in Edinburgh, Scotland, homes are built along the churchyard wall. One home has a window that looks out between two high headstones. Many people live with a grave outlook on life. But that is precisely the kind of outlook that the Lord can turn into an uplook.

When millions were dying from malaria, there seemed to be no hope for a cure. But today, in Calcutta, India, they show you where Ronald Ross wrote: "This day relenting God hath placed within my hand a wondrous thing." He had found a cure.

PRAYER: *We are grateful, Lord, that with Edna St. Vincent Millay we can push the grass apart and lay a finger on Thy heart. Amen.*

THE SHAPER OF LIFE

2 Sam. 24:21 *Araunah the Jebusite said, "Why has your majesty come to visit his servant?" David answered, "To buy the threshing floor from you so that I may build an altar to the Lord, and the plague which has attacked the people may be stopped."*

Still on the heights of Mt. Moriah, and at the end of the two books on Samuel, one gets a rearview of where David has come from and a forward view of where he is headed.

Whether King David rightly understood God's orders, he commanded a national census to be taken. After ten months of labor it was reported that the country had more than a million "able-bodied men, capable of bearing arms." (v. 9) Aha! Was David bursting with pride at the potential power of his armed forces? What sinister motives were festering in his fertile mind in fetid hours? For the next thing we learn is that "David's conscience smote him." (v. 10) The Lord didn't have to be told. He knew, and the punishment was quick in coming. A pestilence came upon the land, and the Lord was also ready to destroy Jerusalem. (v. 16) But He desisted.

When David pleaded for mercy, he was instructed through the Lord's prophet to set up an altar on the threshing floor of Araunah on Mt. Moriah. And, large-hearted Araunah was ready to give his King the whole estate—for free. He even provided oxen and fuel for an on-the-spot sacrificial offering. But David was not one who would take something for nothing. He paid handsomely. And the pestilence stopped.

As we noted in yesterday's Meditation, that area on Moriah has borne three Temples and a Mosque for almost 3,000 years.

What a process—from painful conscience to punishment to penitence to purchase to the pinnacle of the Temple. It looks so zig-zaggy, so unnecessarily out of joint, but so familiar. That is the way the course of life proceeds, almost every day. Why? Having reached a summit of successful endeavor, isn't it possible to remain there—as Jesus' disciples wanted to do on the Mount of Transfiguration? That, they felt in their innermost being, was what life was all about. They didn't want to break the spell. Let's settle here. But, as always, it was meant to be. At the bottom of the mountain, heartache awaited them, and the whole process repeated itself.

Yet, a backward look takes the mist out of the mystery. God is not the author of confusion, but of order—logical and methodical. What at the moment seems screwed up is caused more by our inability to get the long view, where the most satisfactory results await us. And there the score is always "Advantage God." His overview is consistently more dependable than our partial view, or even our full view—through a glass, darkly.

It is not that we must sit with crossed legs and fingers, hoping for the magical arrival of manna and quails. Increasingly attuned to the Lord's words and movements, thinking His thoughts after Him (as we do with those around us who we know best), we must pursue our earthly course to the best of our limited and flawed abilities. And, as with David, God's angel (helpers in myriad forms), will be standing at the next crossroads—pointing us in His desired direction. "Be still my soul, the Lord is on Thy side...in every change He faithful will remain...leads to a joyful end."

PRAYER: *Eternal Pathfinder: We follow You closely, confidently. Amen.*

THE SOURCE OF SIN

1 Kings 1:5 *Now Adonijah...was boasting that he was to be King.*

This history book of Kings, which can be as dry as Sinai, flies off the starting block like a novel.

King David, 70 years old, is cold. Nothing warms him. But the palace servants—especially those responsible for his bedclothes—know the King better than he knows himself. They know that his problem is not with the temperature of the air, but that he was in "heat," and that a pretty girl would provide the warmth that their highly sexed monarch needed. But even that left the old man cold. So much for sex.

Yet, that news was not lost on Adonijah, David's oldest surviving son. The gorgeous girl may have left Dad still freezing, but she fanned Adonijah's passion into white heat. And since verse 6 says that he was "very handsome," his uncontrolled imagination took off at rocket speed. He could see himself on his father's throne, with Miss Palestine as his Queen. So he boasted "that he was to be King."

Before anyone knew what was happening, with the help of good friends in high places, Adonijah began celebrating his accession to the throne. A done deal! How easy could it get?

It was Nathan the prophet who blew this secret behind-the-scenes maneuver into the open.

Nathan had a knack for doing this. Years before, through his well-ordered grapevine network of information, he had heard about David's sexual encounter with Bathsheba, and had blown David's cover with the paralyzing accusation: "You are the man."

Now Nathan did the same thing to David's son. Cold or not, Father David must be told and reminded that he had promised son Solomon that he was next in line as King of Israel, and not Adonijah. And that is the way it turned but with David's blessing.

The moment Adonijah bragged that he was King, the poison of pride was running through the intravenous lines into the center of his soul. And, as always, it led to a pratfall. "That pride is the source of our failure" is the verdict not only of religious thinkers but also of many psychiatrists. Alfred Adler points out rather frequently how all the ills of the human personality are related to this desire of the self to receive adulation, pleasure, recognition. Henry C. Link in *Return to Religion* makes the great paradox of Jesus (Mark 8:35) the center of his diagnosis of the ills of man. And in his book *Psychiatry and Mental Health*, John Rathbone Oliver writes: "...of so many, many patients, I have felt that I could diagnose their entire complex cases in those few words of our Lord's 'He loved his life; and so he lost it.'"[1]

Jesus came right to the point when he noticed how the guests were trying to secure the place of honor, He spoke to them in a parable. "When you receive an invitation, go and sit in the lowest place, so that when your host comes he will say, 'Come up higher, my friend.'" (Luke 14:7,10)

PRAYER: *Everlasting Father of David, Solomon, Adonijah and us—You know the worst of the seven deadly sins to which we still fall prey. While we still have the opportunity to learn from our forebears, make us like the lowly Jesus. In His name we pray. Amen.*

FROM THE FIRST DEEP BREATH

1 Kings 2:1 *When the time of David's death drew near, he gave his last charge to his son Solomon.*

With death stalking him, King David gave his son Solomon instructions on how to be the kind of person God cherishes.

This advice takes three verses (2:2-4), nine lines, in one breath. Pretty good for a dying elder.

But how was twenty-four-year-old Solomon supposed to remember the ten different critically

---

[1] Lance Webb, *The Seven Deadly Sins,* p. 41

important demandments for upright living, especially when his dad's voluptuous nurse was hugging the old man to keep him warm? Perhaps the most lasting effect of this deathbed exhortation showed up in Solomon's biography—where he is reported by historians to have had 700 wives and 300 concubines!

Dying breath is not strong enough to impress upon a young buck the seriousness of godly living. It has to begin with the child's first breath.

Look at the expectations that David lists for his son. They cannot be attained at a single bound. They must be grown into from day one. Be strong. (v. 3) You cannot get up some spring morning and be strong. We have to build the ladder of power by which we rise from the lowly earth to the vaulted skies. We mount to its summit round by round—eating healthily; exercising; resting in body, mind, and spirit. And consistently, not just on weekends—golfing and/or churching.

Be a man. (v. 3) In 1 Kings 3:3 it says that Solomon loved the Lord and kept all his father's precepts. But he "also" served two masters sacrificing to and worshiping at the pagan shrines which he had built for his foreign, pagan, non-Hebrew wives, most of whom were accumulated through political expediencies and exchanges. No surprise then that upon Solomon's death his Kingdom collapsed.

Surely there's a better way to place one's mantle on a successor's shoulders.

Look at how it happened with Jesus—which shows again the necessity of a New Testament in the Bible which testifies to improvements in text and in truth.

Jesus' parents, of simple peasant stock, learned from their stumbling forebears how to do better with David's Greater Son.

At Jesus' birth, the Shepherds and Wise Men of the East proclaimed His Saviorhood. When He was presented at the Temple in Jerusalem, Simeon and Anna (the prophetess) echoed the proclamation. The parents caught on, and guided the boy's growth in wisdom, stature, and in favor with God and man. Quite at home among the doctors of the law in the Temple, Jesus asked them questions and answered theirs. So that when it came time for Jesus to graduate into public ministry, the heavenly Father, laying the mantle of Redeemer of the world on Jesus' shoulder saying: "Here is my servant whom I have chosen, my beloved, in whom I take delight." (Matt. 12:18) Even Solomon in one of his most quoted proverbs noted (wistfully): "Train up a child in the way he should go, and when he is old he will not depart from it." (Prov. 22:6)

PRAYER: *Father, be Thou our guide while life shall last. Amen.*

ONE GREATER THAN DAVID IS HERE

1 Kings 2:10-11 *So David rested with his forefathers and was burned in the City of David, having reigned over Israel for forty years, seven in Hebron and thirty-three in Jerusalem.*

Reader's Digest has always done well in condensing its subject matter. In its publication *Who's Who in the Bible*, it neatly packs David's life into capsule form, thus: "Shepherd, builder, sinner, saint, failed father, ideal King! Who in the Bible but David appears in so many roles? His name occurs more than 1,000 times in the Old and New Testaments, more than any other. He has a prominent place not only in the political and military history of his people but also in their theology and poetry and even in their hopes for the future." (p. 72)

Born in Bethlehem in 1040 B.C., he is best remembered in his youth for doing the impossible: killing the towering giant, Goliath, with a single slingshot. Moving up the ladder of success, David was popularly proclaimed King of all Israel in 1003 B.C. Capturing Jerusalem, he made it a religious capital by giving the Ark of the Covenant a central position. But most important for Christians is the fact that David started the bloodline which gave us Jesus—"David's Greater Son," who was also born in Bethlehem. (Matt. 1:1; 22:41-46)

Adding to David's charisma is how the site of the first Temple in Jerusalem (built by David's son Solomon) was selected. It is still, after 3,000 years, the city's epicenter. 2 Sam. 24:16-24 tells of how Jerusalem was about to be destroyed by the angel of the Lord. But the Lord said, "Stay your hand." At that moment the angel was standing on Araunah's threshing floor.

One thousand years before, Abraham's hand (holding a knife) was stayed from offering his son Isaac as a sacrifice, at that very same place, which eventually became the area on which Solomon's Temple was constructed! For the very same day that the angel was stopped from destroying Jerusalem, God came to David and said to him, "Go and set up an altar to the Lord on the threshing floor of Araunah." (2 Sam. 24:18)

Taking the long view of God's mysterious workings, there are at least two messages. One is that the Lord, in his mercy, stops destruction at the last moment and brings new life. This is what God in Christ did for the penitent thief on Calvary. "Today, shalt thou be with me in paradise." Two, is that the Temple, the Church, is also in the threshing business. (Matt. 3:12; Luke 3:17; 1 Cor. 9:10) There must be a separation of wheat from chaff, right from wrong, good from the not-so-good. That is not as easy to do among church members as it is on a threshing floor. But it must be done, or we get to looking like one and the same thing. And anything goes.

Returning to David's tomb, since archaeologists and "scholars" have been unable to make up their minds about exactly where David was buried, they have left it to the locals, who know better, to put David's final resting place on Mt. Zion. There, too, the messaging is full of hope. For, adjacent to the Tomb, in an Upper Room, is where Jesus had His Last Supper, saying, "Do this as often as you can in remembrance of Me." In this same room, Jesus appeared to His disciples after Easter. Here, too, the new church was born on the Day of Pentecost: David's star, on the Israeli flag still flies over Jerusalem.

PRAYER: *David's Lord, and ours, though we cannot rise to the heights that David did, through Christ we can be more than conquerors. Amen.*

THE VALUE OF CABINETS—
PRESIDENTIAL AND KITCHEN

1 Kings 4:1 *King Solomon reigned over Israel.*

By now, 400 years after the Exodus, the rulers of Israel had learned the lesson of leadership initiated by Moses at the suggestion of his father-in-law, Jethro. Seeing Moses' handling the whole expedition by himself, Jethro said, "This is not the best way to do it. You will wear yourself out ...search for capable, God-fearing men...and appoint them over the people as officers...In this way your burden will be lightened, as they will be sharing it with you." (Exod. 18:17-18, 21-22) Solomon, seeing the wisdom of such governmental strategy, chose nine officers as his "Cabinet."

One officer was in charge of the Calendar. A daily schedule is compulsory to keep everyone on track and from bumping into each other—year round, every year. Time reckoning was left to the priests who coordinated the special festivities and religious observances with the calendar, as it still is in the present day. Always Easter must be first located under three conditions. Fixing the day of Easter must be done without any possibility of mistake. Many systems of time reckoning have been used: Chinese, Egyptian, Babylonian, Assyrian, Jewish, Hindu, Greek, Roman, Mayan, Mexican, and Muslim.

It was no easy task for Solomon's Keeper of the Calendar, either.

Another cabinet officer was a priest, responsible for overseeing the operation of the state-run religion, leading national observances, in touch with the masses, and keeping the king up to date on all critical issues. In short, the priest was in charge of the spiritual life of the nation although Solomon himself played a priestly role, as seen in chapter 8, where he offers the opening prayer (one of the longest in the Bible) at the dedication of the first Temple in Jerusalem.

Another officer was titled "King's Friend." Who doesn't need a friend? Even Kings do. Even the Pope has his close companion and a Father Confessor. In fact, to keep the all-powerful Pope aware of his mortality, every so often he is required to climb into a casket and lie there. Human as we all are, we need someone in whose presence we can be at our best. Solomon did.

In addition to the regular Commander of the Army and Secretary of State, and such, there was the Comptroller of the household who got down to the nitty-gritty—overseeing the upkeep of the palace and grounds, horses and chariots, curtains, bed linen, food, and furniture...If a woman's work is never done, think of this Comptroller!

As dear old Jethro tells us across the ages—both Kings and commoners—we can't do it all by ourselves. We need the Lord, and our fellow humans.

PRAYER: *Controller of our business and private lives, guide us into the company of persons who will help to make us well pleasing in Your sight. Through Jesus Christ our divine Friend. Amen.*

THE SOUL'S ABIDING PLACE

1 Kings 6:1 *Four hundred and eighty years after the people of Israel came out of the land of Egypt, in the fourth year of Solomon's reign over Israel, in the month of Ziv, which is the second month, he began to build the house of the Lord.*

For Jews the most important historical event is the Exodus. It came after 400 years of residence, much of it with enforced labor, in Egypt. Surely it is not without the utmost significance that the Exodus, here, is on a par with the building of Solomon's Temple (with his father David's blueprint) in Jerusalem.

The question that follows this surprising comparison is—Why? Is a building, no matter how expensive and architecturally exquisite deserving of an honored place beside the liberation of millions of God's chosen people? After all, those people had been without a building for worship for almost five centuries. Then, for another forty years in the Sinai their worship center was portable. They took it all the way into the Promised Land. The Ark of the Covenant (in a tent) was their spiritual dynamo. Wasn't that sufficient? Why "build the house of the Lord?"

To be sure, God felt left out when He saw people building their homes and structures, many, as it turned out, more elaborate than the Temple. So the building was started in which the Lord could abide forever.

But why a building, particularly when we remember that after a while the Ark of the Covenant disappeared, and has never been found. And Solomon's Temple, though destroyed and rebuilt several times, was finally demolished in A.D. 70, and has never been rebuilt or replaced except by the Moslem Mosque of Omar. By all this has God been trying to impress on His people that a Temple (church) building is unnecessary?

That is how Hebrew-Christians started out. Persecuted for worshipping in public, they hid and worshipped in catacombs and homes. In many countries the faithful have taken their practice of worship underground, because worship buildings continue to evoke problems. And not just from public dissent, worshippers are forever drawing fire and ire from members of their own congregations.

Cost of the building's upkeep calls perennially upon members to dig deeper into their billfolds. Furnishings, food, more room, less room, obeying community laws and by-laws and in-laws are hidden explosives with the potential for imploding at any time. At the site of many restaurants, apartment buildings, museums, senior citizen centers, one can say, "Once upon a time there was a church here." If it is not necessary to have a church building, what are the true options? Or must we live with worship centers that become institutionalized with a bland churchianity? "As the Lord is patient with many another such disconcerting paradox, He does so with this one. Ours is not to scrap the continuance of the temple, but to align it with His will as much as is humanly possible—until His coming again. Then, as John saw, there will be no temple in the Holy City new Jerusalem, 'for its temple was the Sovereign Lord God and the Lamb.' (Rev. 21:22) With God the focus of all temple activities now dwelling with mankind. (Rev. 21:3) He will be all the church we need."[1]

PRAYER: *Our Father who art in heaven, You are all the God and Church we need, now and ever. Amen.*

ON ANSWERING LOADED QUESTIONS

1 Kings 10:1 *The queen of Sheba heard of Solomon's fame and came to test him with hard questions.*

The Queen of Sheba had no King. The King of Israel (Solomon) had no Queen—although he

---

[1]*The Personal Touch of God's Word*, Newton H. Fritchley, p. 522

had 700 wives. On an official visit, Sheba makes a huffy statement about Solomon's "happy wives" in the same breath as she chortles about his "happy courtiers." Her tone of voice is the same as if she was talking about contented cows, and by contrast extolling the only Queen present—herself. Happy wives and courtiers could be corralled, as Solomon seemed to have done, at a dime a dozen. But not a Queen!

How subtly she orchestrated the pairing of herself and Solomon, cunningly calculating that in his wisdom he would recognize in a flash the rightness of this King-Queen bond. Little surprise, then, that he gave her whatever she asked for. (1 Kings 10:13) Since by her intonation she had asked for one, Sheba went home carrying Solomon's baby. Tradition has it that their child started the royal line of Abyssinia. And without a formal wedding!

One of the hard questions for us in the present day is: Are people in the twenty-first century reverting to solomonic practices? No marriage—just have a baby? For if Solomon's 1,000 women didn't make up an enormous flourishing assembly line for babies, what does?

Polygamy in the Bible, which for too long has slipped under the radar without much comment or criticism, appears to be making a comeback. If multiple wives and harems were acceptable among biblical notables, why not now?

Actually it is now widely practiced under all kinds of convoluted laws and excuses. It could burst out of its confines someday soon, as has marriage of same-sex couples. The cry for freedom could be "Let's be Davidic, Solomonic, Abrahamic."

A cartoon shows the world in ruins, while one chimp says to another: "Oh no, not again."

The world of Solomon's time, be it remembered, was before Christ came to redeem and transform the world. One Adam and one Eve for their unity to be a holy estate "instituted by God and signifying unto us the mystical union which exists between Christ and His Church. It is therefore not to be entered into unadvisedly, but reverently, discreetly, and in the fear of God."

Harems did Bible characters no good. But in using these persons for His own purposes, God showed His patience, beneficence, and love.

No doubt that humans have a lot more cocoons to grow out of—but only in the direction that David's Greater Son orders. He's not for retreat. He is for those fundamental tenets that have stood the test of time. For this is not the first time this monstrous problem has lifted its ugly head. But God's people have survived, and still can.

PRAYER: *Understanding Lord, who knows how easily the human sex drive goes into overdrive without the moral foot power to slam on the brakes, save us from our weaknesses. In Thy holy name we implore Thee. Amen.*

THE COMPLETION OF WISDOM

1 Kings 10:26 *And Solomon got together many chariots and horses, he had 1,400 chariots and 12,000 horses, and he stabled some in the chariot-towns and kept others at hand in Jerusalem.*

Nor was this all the horseflesh that Solomon owned. In 1 Kings 4:26 we learn that "Solomon had 40,000 chariot horses in his stables and 12,000 cavalry horses." And these took money to buy and transport from the lands where they were born and bred, required feed and harness, and needed pay keepers to look after them. And money was made through trading. As Nelson Glueck explains, "In addition to being a famous sage and a strong-handed, wise ruler, Solomon may also be called a copper King. He was a renowned trader and in the literal sense of the word a horse dealer on an international scale. (1 Kings 10:28-29) His Tarshish ships built and manned with the help of the Phoenicians, sailed from Ezion-Geber (modern Eilat) laden with, among other things, copper ingots or copper disks, fish hooks, pins, nails, and utensils of various kinds and brought back in exchange for gold and other valuable goods, either obtainable in Arabia or transshipped there from Africa and India."[1] These ships went on three-year-long voyages.

As for horses, 4,000 years ago in Central Asia, an ugly, shaggy type of horse was domesticated. From there the horse migration spread into the world. Each country bred and adapted the animals for the local area's particular needs—farm work, riding, or for battle. And Solomon, desiring to be the nuclear power of his time, built an enormous equine war machine. Strategist that he was, Solomon spread his chariot horses and charioteers up and down the land so that they could deal with troubling situations in their own localities or assemble more quickly for a national call to arms. Especially in the north, at Megiddo, where the remains of a heavy concentration of stables has been unearthed. The danger to guard up there near the valley of Jezreel (Armageddon—of the Book of Revelation) was a narrow defile through

---

[1] Nelson Glueck, *The Other Side of the Jordan*, p. 100

which all foreign invaders had to enter. Further, in our text for today, it mentions stables in Jerusalem. There, today, near the Mosque of Omar (where Solomon's Temple stood with his palace nearby), one is pointed to where the stables were. Had the king's life been in danger, he could have escaped on horseback from the secret underground stables.

All of which showed that Solomon, with all his wisdom, was not just a theorist. Yes, he wrote 3,000 proverbs, 1,005 songs, the books of Proverbs, Ecclesiastes, Song of Solomon, and the Wisdom of Solomon in the Apocrypha. No, not only a theorist, but also a pragmatist. Both are necessary in religion. The balance must be maintained. The bookwork is akin to schooling. There one learns ABCs, lays foundations, becomes acquainted with one's own talents and weaknesses. On the other hand, to skip school, and to try to make a go of it in the workaday world has been done, but only by a tiny handful of people. The Bible is emphatic about "and works."

PRAYER: *Heavenly Father, instead of following Solomon's example of horsing around, we can see wisdom in his theory and practice. Help us to do our best with each to Thy honor and glory. Amen.*

AN ODE OWED TO SOLOMON

1 Kings 11:3-4 *He (Solomon) had 700 wives, all princesses, and 300 concubines, and they influenced him, for as he grew old, his wives turned his heart to follow other gods, and he did not remain wholly loyal to the Lord his God as his father David had been.*

As James B. Naylor saw it, "old age crept over them, with many, many qualms, King Solomon wrote the Proverbs and King David wrote the Psalms."

Here however, Solomon was writing "Finis" to his forty-year reign—an anticlimax, a dropping out on the last lap, a disgracefully written last act.

It was not so much that he had gathered these 1,000 women into his fleshly treasure house. It was the thing to do among his kingly contemporaries. That was the way Rulers fulfilled their dynastic ambitions and made political alliances—by marrying each other's daughters, and exchanging sexual playmates. Even Solomon's spiritual mentors did not appear to frown on that part of his life. The glowering came with the kind of women in his fold, and his folding under their evil influence.

The majority of Solomon's wives were pagans. To stroke their religious requests and requirements the right way, Solomon built shrines for them, mostly on the southern tip of the Mount of Olives, which, for that reason, is today called the Mount of Offence; or Mount of Corruption, or Scandal. And why not? The first two commandments of the Decalogue are "Thou shalt have no other God besides me" and "Thou shalt not worship any graven image."

Even if Solomon was not 100 percent in agreement with his most aggressive wives, neither, notes the text, was he "wholly loyal to the Lord his God." He was trying to serve two masters, a trapeze act that ends in a fatal free fall.

Then there was the incessant clamor for his coital companionship. So much so that at the age of sixty Solomon was worn out, giving the appearance of an old man. To say nothing of the shameful example he set for those who came after him. He brought the Golden Age to a potty end, and, in a few years, his unflattering image was seen reflected in the life of King Ahab, "wickedest of all the Kings of Israel," whose pagan queen Jezebel, the devil incarnate, introduced Baal worship into Israel.

Saint Paul's admonition bears the test of time. "If you think you are standing firm, take care, or you may fall." (1 Cor. 10:12) You may be standing on shaky premises—wealth, fame, a super intellect, a timepiece that says any or every moment is just sex o'clock. Apparently these were the premises on which Solomon took his stand—and fell.

Oh that our daily chant may be, "On Christ the solid rock I stand, All other ground is sinking sand."

PRAYER: *God of our forefathers, help us to learn from their seismic faults, lest we are doomed to repeat them. Amen.*

TO LOVE LIKE CHRIST

1 Kings 12:4-5 *Your father laid a cruel yoke upon us; but if you will now lighten the cruel slavery he imposed on us and the heavy yoke he laid on us, we will serve You.*

When King Solomon was in his extensive building program—the Temple, palace, shrines for his foreign-born wives, he needed laborers. At first he used men who were not Israelites. As the need for more workmen increased, even native born Israelites were drafted into the forced labor contingents.

Noting the capabilities of Jeroboam, King Solomon appointed him head of Labor. (1 Kings 11:28)

One day, on a lonely road north of Jerusalem, Jeroboam met a prophet named Ahijah. Apparently it was one of those accidentally-on-purpose happenstances, blueprinted by God. The prophet tore his cloak into twelve strips, giving Jeroboam ten, denoting that ten tribes of Israel would belong to him and only one tribe would go to Solomon because he had been a disappointment to the Lord. (1 Kings 11:33)

When Solomon heard of this, he attempted to kill Jeroboam. But Solomon's onetime fair-haired boy was ready to leave Solomon's employ—not only because he couldn't enforce the slavish work conditions that Solomon insisted upon, but also because this brutality was creating conflict between the tribes of Israel. So he fled to Egypt and sought the protection of Pharaoh.

When Solomon died, Jeroboam returned to Palestine, and as the new leader of the northern section of the country, kindly sought unity with the southern section whose leader was Solomon's son Rehoboam.

After three days, Rehoboam replied, "My father made your yoke heavy; I will make it heavier. My father used the whip on you; but I will use the lash" (or "Scorpions" as some versions put it). (1 Kings 12:14-15)

Jeroboam's request was very much in the spirit of Jesus; gentle Jesus. Both had witnessed the results of harsh, dominating behavior—Jeroboam at the heartless treatment of laborers employed in the building of God's Temple(!), and Jesus shocked at the merciless Roman storm troopers. We've seen the same in our time—the humiliation of African-Americans; the death camps and holocaust of the Nazi era; the Islamic terrorist beheadings; the wreckage of lives and property; and globally the purposeful enslavement of humans by sex, drugs, money, and political intrigue. None of it works for good. But kindness does, and love and serving one another (as Jeroboam was pleading for). That is why "Independence" day (July 4) lacks character. It allows for bossy Solomons and Rehoboams to rule the roost. Better to have "Interdependence" days and lives where you do unto others as you would have them do unto you. Instead of having a tyrannical ruler you have a Golden Ruler. Shortly after the Soviet Union broke up, a visitor from America to one of those former communist countries was passing a church. Its bulletin board caught his eye. In large letters it proclaimed: THE LAMB WINS. Indeed The history books show that the Caesars, Genghis Khans, Napoleons, Hitlers...all come to naught. Who wins but Christ—swordless, riding on an ass. We can, too, with Him.

PRAYER: *Monitor of the ages: You have seen it all. Help us who have seen so little to be on the side of the everlastings—like LOVE. Amen.*

KEEPING THE MARRIAGE CONTRACT ON TRACK

2 Kings 8:18 *He (Joram) had married Ahab's daughter; and he did what was wrong in the eyes of the Lord.*

Here is a young man who would lead anyone to believe that he had everything going for him. His very name was tied in with Jehovah. Joram and his father are mentioned in Jesus' lineage (Matt. 1:8)—no small distinction.

At age thirty-two, palace-born and -bred Joram ascended a throne that was the envy of the kings of the earth, since it was in the line of David and Solomon.

Having married Ahab's daughter, Joram was attracted to her side of the family. Why? Was she the stronger one of the two? More influential? Know her husband's emotional life better than he did? Was more desirous for him to be like her family than his own? Whoever or whatever the stronger tide was, Joram was drawn into his in-laws way of living. (2 Chron. 22:3; 24:7) The results are found in the history book. The Jewish historian Josephus tells of Joram's miserable death, which came from "a disease of the intestines after a long period of torment, when from excessive corruption of his inward parts, his bowels [fell] out, so that he [could] look on his own misery." The Bible reports that because of Joram's evil doings, "his people made no fire in his honor...and he departed with no one's regret." (2 Chron. 21:19-20) And all because of his marital connection. He was too much of a funky weakling to resist. And instead of going up the ladder to crowning achievements, he skidded on that banana skin of a marriage—right into obscurity.

But see what he missed, and by a hair's breadth. Edom, to the east, stood like a sentry blocking the southern entrance to the Gulf of Aqaba. Both David and Solomon had seen the marketing value of Ezion-Geber (modern Eilat) at Aqaba. From there Solomon's merchant ships and navy put in at Arabian ports, East Africa and India. They took Solomon's merchandise far beyond their shores and returned with treasures after two-year voyages. The same treasure troves were open to Joram. So he took his mighty force of charioteers to flatten Edom.

But something went wrong in a campaign launched at night. Did the commander-in-chief, accustomed to doing wrong things in the eyes of the Lord, do wrong things in the eyes of his fellow warriors? Instead of the mighty military machine from Jerusalem taking charge, it was "surrounded"—indicating poor strategy on Joram's part, and he was "defeated."

Yet, God in His mercy held to His promise to keep David's name aflame through his progeny. Joram's flame was reduced to a flicker, but by the grace of God it did not go out. As Jesus helpfully reminded us, "a bruised reed He shall not break, and the smoldering wick He will not quench." (Matt. 12:20) The Lord raises His own witnesses in His good time. They fan the flames of faith. They are the reformers, the revivalists who bring rebirths "for all time" (v. 19), the Lord being their Restorer.

So the Joram's of the world come and go with their large professions and their paltry deeds. But still standing tall is the divine One who points to a Land of Promise, and it is up to His faithful followers to press toward that mark.

PRAYER: *Eternal Watcher of our daily lives, help us make the right marital decisions, knowing the crucial part they play in all of life. Amen.*

HIGH HOPES—ON THE ROPES

2 Kings 10:1-2 *The Queen of Sheba heard of Solomon's fame and came to test him with enigmatic questions. She arrived in Jerusalem with a very large retinue, camels laden with spices, gold in vast quantity, and precious stones. When she came to Solomon, she talked to him about everything she had on her mind.*

One can only imagine the pomp and circumstance that accompanied the arrival of Sheba's

Queen. And she was just one of many dignitaries who made the long journey to Jerusalem, to rub themselves against the world class reputation of King Solomon. (1 Kings 10:23-25) Even the arrival of the Three Wise Men, centuries later, in that same city, pales in contrast with not only their three camels, but also who knows how many camels burdened with...and the detailed treasures are listed.

Besides gifting Solomon sumptuously, this Queen had come to pick her host's renowned brain. Whereas other gift-givers and favor-seekers go unrecognized, unnamed, Her Eminence was pedestalled by the historians. Why?

For one thing, this royal visit exposes, albeit in capsule form, the glittering splendor of the capital city of Israel's empire. There was the Temple, the most expensive and eye-catching building of its time. There was the King's Palace with an ivory throne overlaid with gold, and with every vessel made of gold. There was a constant inflow of priceless commodities from "the ends of the earth." That was no problem. Solomon had a navy headquartered at the head of the Red Sea. The ships would make two-year journeys to lands afar, collecting whatever the King's heart desired. The whole operation was as sophisticated as the times could boast of.

Then there was Solomon's almost divine wisdom. He was a student, a naturalist, an author. He wrote 1,005 songs, 3,000 proverbs, the Book of Ecclesiastes. "The wisdom of Solomon" is still cited as the acme of all knowingness. This was given exposure in panoramic dimensions, by the Queen of Sheba. Yet what did this do for her? And for Solomon? Little. Why?

Jesus saw through the hypnotic effect of externals—to the defining need of the human soul. "What doth it profit a man if he gains the whole world but loses his soul, or what shall a man give in exchange for his soul?" (Matt. 16:26) And that was concisely what happened to Solomon. Having gained the whole world and enriched his soul, he would have been of all men most joyously fulfilled. Instead, revealing his spiritual lostness he wrote: "The words of the Speaker, the son of David, King in Jerusalem.

"Futility, utter futility, says the speaker everything is futile. I have seen everything that has been done here under the sun; it is all futility and a chasing of the wind...I applied my mind to understanding wisdom and knowledge, madness and folly, and I came to see that this too is a chasing of the wind." (Eccles. 1:1,2,14,17)

Jesus had it right, not Solomon. "Store up treasure in heaven." (Matt. 6:20) "Seek first the Kingdom of God and His righteousness, and all these other things will be added unto you." (Matt. 6:33)

PRAYER: *Lord, help us to fill our spiritual treasury with Your unsearchable riches. In You we find that a greater-than-Solomon is here. (Matt. 12:42) Amen.*

A GARBLED FACTS MACHINE

2 Kings 18:22 *And if you tell me that you are relying on the Lord your God, is he not the god whose shrines and altars Hezekiah has suppressed, telling Judah and Jerusalem they must worship at his altar in Jerusalem?*

Jerusalem was under siege by the Assyrian army. Inside the city were King Hezekiah and his Hebrew people. It was another Goliath and David confrontation—with gigantic forces on the outside.

Three representatives from each side met to negotiate. The Assyrians took the approach of intimidation, as swaggering powerhouses do. They urged the besieged to capitulate. Then, in the text for today, undermine the Hebrew's confidence in God. The Assyrians very well knew that Hezekiah had been ruthless with the pagan shrines and altars that his wayward predecessors had built and idolized. Sacred poles and pillars, phallic symbols, used by fertility cults, had been ordered smashed by Hezekiah. Even the bronze serpent, which Moses made in the wilderness that had come to be wrongfully used by the Hebrews as an object of worship, was destroyed. Knowing all this, the Assyrians still tried to confuse the Hebrew people into believing that their God of these evil icons was not worth much; therefore, His and their demolition had been ordered by Hezekiah, who nevertheless insisted on worship at such an altar!

But there was no confusing and fooling the Hebrews. They had confidence in their King, who had prepared them for this hour. To the Assyrian spokesman's question they made no reply. Not that their tongues were tied with fear. Rather, "the heart has its reasons, which reason does not know."

In their hearts they knew that they had worked hard to strengthen the walls of Jerusalem. Then there was that remarkable engineering feat of quarrying and removing 850 cubic yards of rock to make the 1,749-foot tunnel which brought the Gihon Spring into the city, cutting off the enemy's water supply. The work had been completed in an estimated 200 days—with picks and shovels. Meanwhile, King Hezekiah "did what was right in the eyes of the Lord, as his ancestor David had done," (v. 3) in facing another Goliath. Hezekiah turned to the prophet Isaiah, through whom marching orders were coming down from the Supreme Commander—the living God. And Hezekiah prayed. And he went into the Temple of the Lord, and talked the whole situation out with God; how the Assyrians had laid low every other country that came in their way; how at the walls of Jerusalem they were taunting the living God. Then Hezekiah prayed: "Now, Lord our God, save us." And He did, that very night. The entire Assyrian army was struck down.

There are steps to victory—without aggression.

PRAYER: *Release Your power, Lord "that all the Kingdoms of the earth may know that you alone, Lord, are God." (2 Kings 19:19) Amen.*

HIS WINNING WAY

2 Kings 19:10 *How can you be deluded by your God on whom you rely when He promises that Jerusalem shall not fall into the hands of the King of Assyria?*

The speaker, Sennacherib, King of Assyria, was the greatest conqueror of his time. In one campaign after another he had mowed down his opponents, taking hundreds of thousands of prisoners and wealth incalculable. Now it was famed Jerusalem's time to be hit. And here Sennacherib begins by attempting to shake loose the morale of Jerusalem's leader, King Hezekiah. After all, wasn't the God of the Jews just another handcrafted idol? What assistance could he give? What Sennacherib, in his pagan unbelief couldn't discern was that this God had created the universe; this God had dealt with swaggering imperialists, outmaneuvering them by using them to perform His desires. (Isa. 44:28) Which is the way it turned out in favor of Jerusalem. As 2 Kings 19:35 reports: "That night the angel of the Lord went out and struck down 185,000 men in the Assyrian camp; when morning dawned, they all lay dead." Verse 36 describes the whipped Sennacherib with his tail between his legs, breaking camp, and slinking home—where he stayed. And though he had kept voluminous records of all his other campaigns, there is not a word about how this one ended. Other historians have joined the dots and found that on the night the Assyrian army was no more, it had been accomplished by an overnight infestation of field mice that gnawed the soldier's bowstrings—making the warriors militarily ineffective—and infecting those fighters with bubonic plague. It was not very long after this that a thoroughly humiliated Sennacherib was assassinated by two of his sons.

Learning from God that the worst can be used to fulfill His desired outcomes, His pupils have followed His example. Walking across the campus of the Vellore hospital in South India, we saw a young woman being wheel-chaired from one building to the next. It was Dr. Mary Verghese, who as a new medical school graduate had been on an outing with friends when she was involved in an automobile accident. After a long, painful recovery, the stark fact emerged that Mary would never walk again. Might as well give up her burning ambition to be a surgeon. But no, dedicating her ten fingers to God, Mary learned how to operate while sitting, and became an inspiration for disabled persons the world over. So that others, with the loss of hands, have taken to writing or painting by holding pen or brush between their teeth or with their toes. Nothing stops their dauntless thrust-through spirit. They are not physically perfect, but they are perfectly wonderful in their accomplishments. They never rest until they have topped their Everest. They are world Olympians without medals.

Snarling Sennacheribs come in many forms. They are menacing, intimidating, and appear to be hands-down winners. But there is always Isaiah's admonition (2 King 19:20-21) to lean more heavily on the Lord's promises and powers. He is the One who takes the worst and swings it around to be a thing of beauty and a joy forever. Surprise!

PRAYER: *Wise and Holy Father of mankind, forgive us for our feverish, childish ways of combating enemies. You know how to do it all right. Show us how we can be of help with Your planned surprises. Amen.*

ON BEING DISHED

2 Kings 21:13 *I shall use against Jerusalem the measuring line used against Samaria and the plummet used against the house of Ahab. I shall wipe Jerusalem as one wipes a plate and turns it upside down.*

Just when we thought that Jerusalem had it made since God's residence was in the Temple, in His chosen city, in His Promised Land, here comes King Manasseh to make a beginning for the end of Jerusalem.

Manasseh, son of esteemed Hezekiah, had the longest and worst reign of any Hebrew ruler. He was the complete opposite of his father. He turned his dad's Reformation into a Deformation of the holy city and country. The stringencies demanded by father were deemed unnecessary by son. The prophet Isaiah, the spokesman of God, and the conscience of the Kingdom, was silenced. He was sawn in two. Manasseh's son was incinerated as a burnt offering to some pagan god. The idolatrous shrines were rebuilt. Unopposed, king, priests and people did whatever they desired.

But the Divine Judge was watching. He made known that He intended to take four steps to put a stop to this frenzied shedding of standards.

First, He was going to use a measuring line that He had used in a similar situation with which the deformers were familiar. He would measure how far from the commandments they had drifted. That is always a good indication of a person's ability to get back to his moorings, or to prove that he has passed beyond the point of no return. Also, numbers can be measured. Exactly who, and how many are drifters? What is the extent of their wrongdoing? And values can be measured. Whose values are being used, and why, and where and how? And the Lord, alone, knows how many other ways there are to measure misdemeanored lives.

Second, God was going to use a plummet, which was an earlier term for a plumb line. As Amos (7:8) later saw in a vision, God's plumb line detects how much out of the straight we are. Well known is the fact that even when tiny inaccuracies are built-in, in an earthquake they can cause massive collapses in buildings and lives.

Third, having put Jerusalem in the balance and found it woefully wanting, God turns to the figure of a plate—using easily understood language so that His message could be understood on the run.

Fourth, the plate is wiped! Nothing is left on it. Even if a meal was about to be eaten, or was half eaten! There were no more chances. That was it. And the upside-down plate symbolized not only what Manasseh had done to his father's legacy, but it also symbolized a readiness for a new beginning. No more banquets of consequences.

Golden ages don't last forever—on automatic pilot. Each must work out its own salvation, under God's direction. Individuals that have ears, let them hear what the Spirit says to the ages.

PRAYER: *Evaluate us, Lord—up, down, sideways. When we meet Your expectations, fill our plate that we may taste and see that the Lord is good. Amen.*

VICTORIOUS LIVING

1 Chron. 18:13 *The Lord gave victory to David wherever he went.*

The Chronicler has first listed some of David's victories—over the Philistines, Moabites, Edemites, Ammonites, Amalekites. Other conquests had been over the Syrians, and enemy nations from Egypt to the Euphrates. But were the victories *wherever* David went? Knowing God's love for David, and well aware that battles are not all fought on foreign fields, it is more likely that God gave David victories, yes—*wherever* he went: in the family, in the workplace, in personal life. Who dares to say nay to the fact that daily life has its intensive infighting? David's did. Look at a few such incidents within his family: His wife, Michal, laughed David to scorn for having danced in the streets like any nightclub entertainer while escorting the sacred Ark of the

Covenant to its final resting place in Jerusalem. Or follow David's son Absalom as he stalks his father with intent to kill him. Or there was David's overnighter with Bathsheba. One can only imagine the bedlam in the harem the next morning, with dozens of wives and concubines and their children, David had more warlike conditions within the confines of his palace than he had abroad. Were all these women to be re-ranked as to which one would get the higher ranking in the King's bed? In such an emotional tangle we can almost hear David pleading, "Give me a world war, or give me death."

Then there were David's inner conflicts. In making Bathsheba pregnant, and then putting her husband to death, David broke at least five of the Ten Commandments. He had promoted murder, engaged in treachery, lust, intrigue, adultery. To confess to any one of these would have been agony. To own up to all of them must have been torture. But he bore it, asking God to make him a new person. And God did—giving victory to David *wherever* he went. "So David steadily grew stronger, for the Lord of Hosts was with him." (1 Chron. 11:9)

Strength comes slowly, since there are setbacks by illness, or a bad habit, or an ineffective diet. But rectifying errors, and persisting with the healthful regimens, strength builds and rebuilds. "Heaven is not reached at a single bound, but we build the ladder by which we rise from the lowly earth to the vaulted skies and we mount to its summit round by round"—by painful round. Besides, the good results of physical exercise last only about forty-eight hours. Much depends upon the continuity of the course. Nor is the spiritual fitness program different, or there wouldn't be the emphasis on daily devotions, prayer, church attendance. Our Muslim friends knew the danger of forgetfulness and carelessness and counterbalanced them by praying five times a day.

Look at what faithfulness attendance to the Lord brought to David—victory *wherever* he went. Who could ask for or expect any more in a life, which has face-offs and post-deployment trauma almost daily? Only the Lord can grant victory for all seasons, for all reasons.

PRAYER: *No Davids, Lord, are we, but we are Yours. Knowing that faith (in You) is the victory that overcomes the world, we will strive to grow steadily stronger in faith. Amen.*

FROM DAVID'S CITY TO OURS

1 Chron. 28:8 *Now therefore, in the sight of all Israel, the assembly of the Lord, and in the hearing of our God, I say to you: Study carefully all the commandments of the Lord your God, in order that you may possess this good land and hand it down as an inheritance for all time to your children after you.*

At the close of his life, Moses gave final instructions to his people. (Deut. 31:3-8) That tearful occasion was recounted often in the 400 years that followed. "Now therefore," David, approaching his own final curtain, reprises his famed ancestor, also "in the sight of all Israel." But this time it was a sight and sound affair—"in the hearing of our God."

And what was this expansive public event all about? The Ten Commandments. So vital were they, and so neglected, that David minted and measured minutely every word of his farewell message. Then, as he had learned to his personal satisfaction, the top priority concerning the Decalogue is to study them carefully, for they are tightly packed with wisdom. Any lengthier, and people would have an added reason to discard them. Nor must these Laws given by God be picked over in order to find only those that are untroubling to one's conscience. *All* must be carefully studied. It is possible that already people were thinking in terms of not Ten, but Two Commandments as Jesus did later: love God and your neighbor. (Matt. 22:37-40) But whereas Jesus realized that it was only in fully understanding the Ten that you would know where the Two should be applied, people of David's time chose the Two as a shortcut to salvation. It's a Decalogue, not a Monologue. These are not ten choices in a true or false test. These are Ten Demandments, with no plea-bargaining. Not ten suggestions, but ten uncompromising, unequivocal statutes, the keeping of which guarantees "an inheritance for all time."

And who are the beneficiaries? All Israel. And Jesus, in that line of fortunates, passed the blessings on to all who believe in Him. Those blessings, in turn, are not just for our immediate family members, but also for those who keep on coming after us—our spiritual offspring too.

What an epochal accomplishment it is to carefully study God's commands from Sinai. It involves more than a series of lessons in Sunday School, or Sunday sermons. It takes a lifetime to understand what was on the two stone tablets, to say nothing about their application to myriad aspects of daily living, the world over. And what endless rewards! William Barclay writes about the Ten Commandments that they are "the universal foundation, not only of Jewish ethics, but of all ethics...the necessary laws of nationhood, the charter of democracy."

PRAYER: *Father God, for Your guidelines to glory we are grateful. Grant that Your Holy Spirit may interpret the written Word for our edification. In Jesus name. Amen.*

A LITURGY FOR THE AGES

2 Chron. 2:4 *Now I am about to build a house for the name of the Lord my God and to consecrate it to him, so that I may burn fragrant incense in it before him, and present the rows of the Bread of the Presence regularly, and whole-offerings morning and evening, on the Sabbaths and at the new moons and appointed festivals of the Lord our God; for this is a duty laid on Israel for ever.*

The books of Kings and Chronicles are twins. What is seen in one is noticeable in the other. As with today's text. Solomon's intention to build the Temple is by now a familiar theme. God had laid out the general plan, David had worked out the details and collected the materials, and all that Solomon had to do was to put the building blocks together. It took 180,000 workers seven and a half years to do that. The Temple might have lasted longer than 400 years if it had not been destroyed by the Babylonians.

In a letter to King Huram (or Hiram) of Tyre, the supplier of building materials, Solomon here gives a rough outline of what he proposes for the Temple in Jerusalem. Temples were a dime a dozen at the time. But Solomon's was unique in that it was dedicated to the God of Israel. If a church is purpose-driven, unless the sole purpose is total commitment to the Lord our God, forget about any other so-called purpose, it's inconsequential.

Next on the Temple's agenda was the burning of incense. Not only did that spread a pleasing odor, but also it symbolized the fragrant prayers of worshippers, prayers that ascended to God, and were sweet and acceptable to Him.

The Bread of the Presence, consisting of twelve loaves, laid out in two rows of six each, pertained to the sustenance that God supplied His people by His presence in the Holy of Holies. The Bread was also offered as a token of gratitude to God for His prodigal generosity toward His chosen people. That Bread was eaten by the priests, and only in the sanctuary, on the Sabbath. The replacement of loaves came immediately with freshly baked loaves. This has been seen as a long shadow of our Lord's supper: "This is my body."

Then there were to be times and a place for offerings, not just collections. As indicated in the text, offerings can be presented in varying forms and cannot be confined to one day and time. As worshippers move through their myriad yearlong experiences, they are prodded by changing conditions to confer with the Lord. There are penitentiary offerings for self, family, nation. And adoration offerings, when one glories in exclaiming, "O for a thousand tongues to sing my great Redeemer's praise." And there are the offerings of confession, "exteriorizing our rottenness," and asking forgiveness.

Nor is this entire list of worship items a past enjoinder. It is a "forever" "duty."

PRAYER: *Lord, save us from making these tested and tried worship experiences just items in the Sunday bulletin. Embolden us to make them come alive in our Christian discipleship. Amen.*

Our Christ-like God

2 Chron. 6:6 *I chose Jerusalem for my Name to be there.*

The Word of the Lord from Jerusalem has spread into all the world, and will continue to permeate the entire plant until the endtime. That word had been written, spoken, sung, inwardly intoned. Prophets have relayed that Word, as well as saints and sinners. It has echoed down the centuries through fair weather and floods, in war and in peace. But why has it persisted, in spite of being thrown into bonfires, criticized, mocked out of context, officially banned by the politically correct, and caricatured?

The answer comes from wise old Solomon's reminder during his ceremony of dedicating the Temple in Jerusalem. Solomon recalled God's own words, "I chose Jerusalem for my Name to be there."

What is so penetratingly meaningful about that?

Early on, a name carried enormous weight, which it doesn't in the present day (except in the marketplace, where all-important iconic money is the central concern).

Names were indicators of character, ability, actions. And although the name "God" is defined nowhere in the Bible, His character and activities cannot be missed on any page. Fortunately there is a definition of God that is more widely accepted than any other, and found in the *Westminster Shorter Catechism*: "God is a Spirit, infinite, eternal, and unchangeable, in his being, wisdom, power holiness, justice, goodness and truth." In the Hebrew Old Testament all of God's attributes, it was believed, were brought together in the one word "Yahweh." That word was used more than any other in their Bible—6,800 times. But by the third century B.C. the consensus of opinion was that to use the word "Yahweh" was too revealing of God's reality; too holy to be on sinful man's tongue. Accordingly, the substitute word "Adonai" (Lord) was activated. In very fact, none of these special words and definitions are necessary since the Bible overflows with descriptions of God's multifaceted Person and creative activities.

He is our light and our salvation. (Ps. 27:1) He is Spirit and truth. (John 4:23-24) He is alpha and omega. (Rev. 22:13) He is our Father in heaven. (Matt. 6:9) He is our refuge and strength. (Ps. 46:1) He is our shepherd. (Ps. 23:1) He is the Word. (John 1:1) He is the God of glory, (Acts 7:2) of peace, (Rom. 15:33) of love, (2 Cor. 13:1) of patience and comfort. (Rom. 15:5) "God has spoken in His Son." (Heb. 1:1) "The fool says in his heart 'there is no god.'" (Ps. 14:1) "The heavens declare the glory of God and the firmament shows His handiwork." (Ps. 19:1)

It is the word of this omnipotent, omnipresent, omniscient God who speaks from His personally chosen and established central command—Jerusalem.

Yet, with due respect to the *Shorter Catechism*, there is no clearer, more definitive understanding of God than to turn one's eyes upon Jesus. As He said to Phillip who requested, "Show us the Father, we ask no more." (John 14:8) "Do you not believe that I am in the Father and the Father in me? (v. 10) Anyone who has seen me has seen the Father." (v. 9)

SEE LISTEN LIVE FOREVER

PRAYER: *Lord Jesus, all the God we need; You, too, spoke from ground zero in Jerusalem. We are listening and translating it into service for You. Amen.*

TEMPLED SOULS

2 Chron. 8:6 *And Baalath, as well as all his store-cities, and all the towns where he quartered his chariots and horses. He carried out all his cherished plans for building in Jerusalem, in the Lebanon, and throughout his whole dominion.*

It should have been enough for Solomon to build his ever-remembered Temple in the nation's capital. But no, he put even more time and attention and fortune into building "throughout his whole dominion." Much of this chapter is devoted to that phase of frenzied construction. And the economy, then as now, depending heavily on the building trades, boomed. It was not enough for Solomon to put as many of his own countrymen to work as possible, it became necessary, with the enormity of the undertaking, to supplement the workforce with foreign laborers. These, in turn, needed their own quarters, and food, clothes, entertainment in off-hours. The country buzzed with activity—all directed from the hub, Solomon's palace in Jerusalem.

Being no warrior like his father, David, Solomon never waged a large-scale war against anyone. But he did erect fortifications up and down the land as a safeguard against power-hungry intruders. Baalath, along with upper and lower Beth Horan, were such walled and bar-gated bastions together with store-cities, which were not only armories but also centers of storage for food and related necessities in times of war. The 12,000 horsemen and 1,400 charioteers, and all the equipment such a striking force called for, were located in strategic places known to be entry points for invaders.

What a brag sheet for builders this must have been. And Solomon soaked up all the credit. He luxuriated in it—and it finally did him in. For, instead of building for eternity a character that was well-pleasing in the sight of the Lord, Solomon built for transient time, which, before long, crumbled his buildings and his character. He had not learned that "The Lord does not see as a mortal sees; mortals see only appearances but the Lord sees into the heart." (1 Sam. 16:7) There is fame and fortune in building architectural wonders—skyscrapers, bridges, dams, a Great Wall of China, a Fort Knox, towers, tunnels, canals. To be sure, such products of human genius can be erected to God's glory, as was Solomon's Temple. Unfortunately the masterpiece too quickly can become the object of worship. The better approach is the building of one's character. "Build thee more stately mansions, O my soul, As the swift seasons roll! Leave thy low-vaulted past! Let each new temple, nobler than the last, Shut thee from heaven with a dome more vast, Till thou at length art free, Leaving thine outgrown shell by life's unresting sea."[1] Making sacred faith the foundation of our lives, we can build one another up. (Jude 1:20 and 1 Thess. 5:11) "Do you not know that your body is a temple of the indwelling Holy Spirit?" (1 Cor. 6:19) That's where the essential building must be done.

PRAYER: *Carpenter of Nazareth, help us to be Your coworker's in putting together our personal lives in a manner fit for Your service. Amen.*

---

[1] O. W. Holmes, *The Chambered Nautilus*

ALL, OR NONE AT ALL

2 Chron. 12:8 *The (God's) people will know the difference between serving me (God) and serving the rulers of other countries.*

In 1 and 2 Sams., 1 and 2 Kings, and 1 and 2 Chrons., we find many incidents repeated. But just when there appears to be a vast sameness, variants show up. And this episode, about Rehoboam, is one of the thirty-nine Kings mentioned. Only seven were good. The rest were bad, extra bad, mostly bad, and devilish. Rehoboam was half-and-half.

When his kingdom was on a firm footing, Rehoboam became stubborn.

There are leaders like that when they are in a winning position, they immediately take the credit. They claim that nobody but themselves had the vision, the qualities, the admiring supporters, the financial backing to pull off such an unheard-of triumph. They then feel qualified to go it alone. God? What can He do that they cannot? And that's when Rehoboam met his nemesis.

Noting his haughtiness, God allowed Rehoboam to be attacked by an Egyptian Pharaoh whom nobody could stop. Rehoboam, realizing his error, bowed to the Lord's might, and was allowed to barely escape annihilation. Instead, God ordered it so that Rehoboam and his people became servants of the Pharaoh, so that God's stubborn people would know the difference between serving the Lord and serving the rulers of other nations.

That's where the crunch and the ouch come for all who turn their backs on the heavenly Father. Convinced that He is the Super spoilsport, the Frown Prince of the Universe, people flee from the Lover of their souls right into the arms of the destroyer of souls, the demon of despair.

One sees it in Judas Iscariot turning from the Savior Christ to Silver coins. Or there's Peter taking refuge in denial. One went out and hanged himself, the other went out and wept bitterly, tear-washing away the stain of sin. Judas saw too late that he had turned away to serve the wrong master. Peter realized in time that he had been serving the right Master.

Rehoboam was an in-betweener. He was not utterly destroyed (v. 12), neither was he wholly for God. He was like the lukewarm church of Laodicea to which the Lord said uncompromisingly: "because you are neither cold nor hot, I will spew you out of my mouth." (Rev. 3:16) John 3:16 and Rev. 3:16 show the results of serving the Lord or serving somebody or something else. The first can claim "everlasting life," the other gets the door shut in his face, "Depart from Me, I never knew you," or the spew. Phew.

"Who is on the Lord's side, who will serve the King, who will be His helpers, other lives to bring?" "Lovest thou Me more than these?" (John 21:14) That's the ever returning, burning question. The Lord is not appreciative of the split-tongued submission: "Lord, I am all Yours, maybe." Rather His directive is: "You follow Me." (John 21:22)

PRAYER: *Heavenly Father we want to be soldiers of the cross, and not useless Humpty Dumptys sitting on some walled-off Astoria. Amen.*

OH, HOW HE GIVES

2 Chron. 16:9 *The eyes of the Lord range through the whole earth, to bring aid and comfort to those whose hearts are loyal to him.*

King Asa, briefly treated in 1 Kings 15, is here portrayed in full length, giving us an adequate picture of persons who are "good and right in the eyes of the Lord." (2 Chron. 14:12) This is helpful, for it is easy for anybody to do whatever they please, and thereby do wrong, as most of those kings did.

Asa was different. Learning the central truth that "the Lord is with you when you are with Him, if you look for Him, He will let Himself be found," (2 Chron. 15:2) Asa proceeded accordingly. It is not to have faith that the Lord will work all things together for our good. He will, if He sees that we are interested enough to do two things: Seek until we find Him and add works to faith.

So for Asa it became habitual to be God's man. In seeking the Lord and finding much in the way that were barriers, Asa hacked down all forms of worship of foreign gods. Then not dwelling on the negative, he issued a national edict for all people to keep the law and commandments. Now they would have long-tested rules to live by and not their own little pleasantries. And, right away, the Lord was true to His promises. There was peace and security on every side. Elsewhere by contrast "the inhabitants of every land had their fill of trouble; there was ruin on every side." (2 Chron. 15:5)

Not for Asa and his nation, for he had even made the supreme sacrifice of depriving his beloved grandmother of her rank as Queen Mother. Perhaps in a moment of vanity, when she felt that as the king's grandma she could do no wrong, she had set up for worship the image of a lewd goddess. Disregarding disrespect for granny, Asa had the obscenity ground to powder and burned. The old Lady's tears did not stop the King, nor did his fond memories of all the nice things the Queen Mother had done for him and others. Justice, as they say, is blind—especially to loved ones.

Jesus, too, was of this opinion. How He loved His Mother. She had been precious to Him all through life. Thoughtfully, despite the agony of the cross, He made arrangements for her final care, "Behold thy Son; behold thy Mother." Yet, when He said, "Seek first the Kingdom of God," He meant it, in spite of what his Mother may have thought when He said: "If anyone comes to Me and does not hate his father and mother, wife and children, brothers and sisters, even his own life, he cannot be a disciple of mine. No one who does not carry his cross and come with me can be a disciple of mine." (Luke 14:26-27) Those are granitic, sacrificial requirements. But to do any less would be to retract to being a teetering tottering Rehoboam, who gets just what he deserves. Jesus wants full consecration from those who serve Him, as King Asa and his countrymen required of themselves to be God's people.

Indeed, "the eyes of the Lord range through the whole earth." He doesn't miss a thing as He sorts out just who are unequivocally for Him, those who are not, and those who are in the grey area on some beautiful isle of somewhere.

PRAYER: *Watchful Redeemer: We would be watchful, too, hearing Your call for our all. Now. Amen.*

O JOY

2 Chron. 30:26 *There was great rejoicing in Jerusalem, the like of which had not been known there since the days*

of Solomon, son of King David of Israel.

What a grim city Jerusalem had become. A humorless hub for three centuries. Perhaps there was some giggling around the edges, but nothing to equal the ecstatic outburst that radiated throughout the land, and came to rest in the history books.

Could such jubilation be cloned? Is the mood of a rock concert or a Mardi Gras festival what is desired? If so, the rest is a cinch. A parade with floats? A fireworks display? A chariot race of Ben Hur proportions in the coliseum? An air show by the Blue Angels? Yet, while such adrenalin-boosters would thrill and chill, they could hardly be expected to reach the soul's depths. But this is what claimed the lives of Jerusalem's citizens in the time of King Hezekiah. They were wholly soul-satisfied. And, if this is what brings "great rejoicing," what is the spark (or sparks) that set the nation alight?

For any kind of light to appear, the obstacles must be removed. Perhaps the people here were dim and grim because they still had pagan altars and questionable worship practices. Having found these to be unrewarding, they were flung into the garbage dump. And, as the priests had led the way from God, now they took the initiative in turning back to Him. They acknowledged their transgressions, purified themselves, and made the offerings to God that had been neglected, or observed irregularly. Even his majesty the King interceded in prayer for his people—and healing came to them.

Apparently the observance of the Passover festival had not meant much to the people. But now, with new religious fervor, they had such an uplifting seven days, that, in total agreement, they extended the observance for another seven days. That would be the equivalent of Christians having such a glorious Easter, that by national consent they extended Easter to the next Sunday, and the next, and...—as successful Revival services have been. Little wonder that rejoicing appears four times in this chapter—the magic three, and then some! There hadn't been anything like such euphoria in 300 years—longer than the United States of America has been in existence. Now that's something worth looking into, and emulating. It has been likened to the joy of those who made the Exodus out of Egypt, and the freedom from the Babylonian Exile. And such triumph can be ours in the present day. "Happy days are here again" can be our theme song—not because of winning a Powerball lottery, or because of status, genes, good looks...but by coming to the Lord. Said Jesus: "If you dwell in me, and my words dwell in you, ask whatever you want, and you shall have it...I have spoken thus to you, so that my joy may be in you, and your joy complete." (John 15:7,11) This, mark you, was also said in Jerusalem at Passover time. Great rejoicing can indubitably be ours.

PRAYER: *Shine in and through us, Lord, that we may know true joy, Your joy, now and forever. Amen.*

HE SEES WHAT WE CANNOT

2 Chron. 36:23 *This is the Word of Cyrus King of Persia: The Lord the God of heaven has given me all the Kingdoms of the earth, and he himself has charged me to build him a house at Jerusalem.*

How did this fellow Cyrus, a non-Jew, an unbeliever, ever become one of God's fair-haired boys? Cyrus was right, nobody was greater than he was at the time. Nebuchadnezzar had been in that top position for forty-three years. When God's people, the Jews, had turned against God, and their King had cut God's Laws into pieces and burned them, the Lord had used Nebuchadnezzar as His instrument to punish the Jews. They were taken under escort to Babylon where they remained in exile for seventy years. But when they came to their senses and were reformed, and when God saw that they were deserving of release and that the Holy Land was ready to receive them, there was no one to release them from their Babylonian bondage. Enter Cyrus.

A wily strategist, Cyrus noted the weakness of Nebuchadnezzar's successor and laid siege to the capital city of Babylon, and captured it. Watching, God, the Supreme Strategist, having used Nebuchadnezzar to punish the sinful Jews, now uses Cyrus to release the repentant Jews. As Cyrus, filling out our text for today, says: "To every man, of his (God's) people now among you I say, the Lord his God be with him, and let him go up (back to Jerusalem)."

Instead of rejoicing at their release, and the permission to return to their homeland, the Jews showed how far they had drifted from their understanding of God's ways and means. How could God send them such contorted signals? Why use unbelievers to punish then heal believers? Doesn't make sense.

While in no way obligated to explain His dealing with idol worshipping foreigners, God, who so loves the world of humans, takes the time to explain.

Too often we are like the clay cross-questioning the Potter: "Mr. Potter, what in heaven's name do you think you are doing? Just look at this oddball jug. It doesn't have handles. A housewife will have to hold it by the neck. How preposterous the whole thing is, how jammed down the neck is, what an ignorant wreck it is."

The Lord replies, "Woe to him who strives with his Maker." (Isa. 45:9) Remember, He made the earth, and humans, and the heavens, and all that is found in the heavens. Besides, God's "woe" is a warning that such backtalk (as distinguished from a conversation with Him) is sacrilege. In 1632, Sir Henry Spelman wrote in his book *The History and Fate of Sacrilege*: "Our Saviour, Christ, cometh into the world; and though reproving it of all kinds of sins, he punisheth not one, save only sacrilege." (p. 25) Then comes the definition: "Sacrilege is the robbing of God by alienating, detaining, purloining, or perverting that which is God's own by Divine Right." (p. 266) Father, in heaven, knows best.

PRAYER: *Lord, we would be humble for we know (and often don't know) our weaknesses. We look to Thee from whence comes our help for all conditions. Amen.*

DIVINELY REVVED UP

Ezra 1:1 *So that the word of the Lord spoken through Jeremiah (Jer. 29:10; 31:38) might be fulfilled, the Lord stirred up the heart of Cyrus King of Persia.*

Most strongly does the word of the Lord come from Jerusalem through the books of Chronicles, Ezra, Nehemiah—all written by Ezra, who is known in the apocrypha as Esdras.

Though exiled for decades in Babylon (now

Iraq), Ezra was a Jerusalemite to the core, with a life-absorbing interest in that city's Temple. It is that house of worship around which Ezra's documentation revolves. But the narrative begins 900 miles east in Babylon, at the time under the rule of Persian King Cyrus.

Though "God works in a mysterious way His wonders to perform," more bewildering is the way this Book of Ezra opens, with God stirring up the heart of Cyrus.

Mind you, this was the God of the Jews who had allowed His chosen people to be ignominiously defeated and taken as exiles to Babylon. And this Cyrus was no man of God. On the "Cyrus Cylinder," now in the British Museum in London, one can read how Cyrus gave credit for his wartime victories to the pagan god Marduk!

So, our God gets together with a pagan king and stirs up the unbeliever's heart to do something nice for the once-believing, but now unbelieving Jews!

Wait a minute. In which direction are we going? Why does God have to be incomprehensible, even if He is about to perform wonders?

Whether we understand God's strange strategies, here He urges Cyrus to guide the distraught Jews on how to go home to Jerusalem. And responding, Cyrus proclaims: "Go up to Jerusalem." (v. 3) But that was easier said than done. It was a four-month journey, and the Jews confined in exile for seventy years, and now free, may wander off into new, exciting lands along the way. It would be a wearying jaunt, with all their goods and thousands of pack animals—horses, mules, camels, donkeys—having their own needs. Besides, many of these returnees had been born and raised in Babylon. They had taken Babylonian names, had intermarried; Palestine was the foreign land for them. Next, he proclaims: "Rebuild the house of the Lord." (v. 3) That had been the Temple Solomon built—the grandest building in the world of its time. To construct it had taken the labor of 30,000 Jews, 153,000 Canaanites more than seven and a half years to complete. Were these newcomers equal to such a task? It is more likely that they yearned for the fleshpots of Babylon. Next, every Jew could claim from his neighbor gold, silver, goods, cattle. (v. 4) Eight hundred years before, in exiting Egypt the Jews made similar claims upon their Egyptian neighbors. (Exod. 11:2; 12:35) Now the Babylonians get squeezed. Finally, probably as a penalty for destroying the Jerusalem Temple, the Babylonians are now asked to dig deeper into their pockets "for voluntary offerings for the house of God in Jerusalem." (v. 4) And they responded, even volunteering to help in the rebuilding project in Jerusalem. As Ezra wrote later (9:9), God "has made the Kings of Persia so well pleased towards us as to give us the means of renewal." Let us allow Him to perform such wonders in our lives.

PRAYER: *With Robert Browning we will trust You, Lord, see all, nor be afraid, for the best is yet to be. Amen.*

THE POWER OF ONE

Ezra 3:1 *The Israelites now settled in their towns, the people assembled as one man in Jerusalem. Then Jeshua...*

If we have never been quite sure of the answer to the ancient question: "What kind of a church would my church be if every member were just like me?"

Newly returned to their homeland from decades of servitude in strangely different surroundings, the Jews were like scattered sheep. They had lost their identity. Many had been born abroad, so that their so-called "homeland" was the real puzzler. Nor did they know each other, having intermarried with foreigners. How to become one flock, one nation, under God, ("with liberty and justice for all") as their forefathers had been?

Sheep do not know how to unite. They are good followers, and in following they draw together. Likewise with sheep-like humans. Ten percent of them think. Ten percent think that they think. And the rest would rather die than think. So they follow. And how fortunate for these Diaspora Jews, out of the meadow's haze stepped just the kind of flock master they needed—Jeshua.

How, behind the scenes the Lord intervenes. Watching His aimless, wandering-in-all-directions flock, He prepares a Shepherd-like leader for them.

The prophet Zechariah recorded it like this: "Then he showed me Joshua (Jeshua) the high priest standing before the angel of the Lord, with Satan standing at his right hand to accuse him. The angel said to Satan, 'the Lord silence you, Satan! May the Lord who has chosen Jerusalem, silence you! Is not this man a brand snatched from the fire?' Joshua was wearing filthy clothes as he stood before the angel, who now said to those in attendance on him, 'Take off his filthy clothes.' Then to Joshua he said, 'See how I have taken away your guilt from you; and I shall clothe you in fine vestments.'" (Zech. 3:1-4)

Set apart, and invested with authority to do the Lord's work, the very first thing Jeshua and his helpers did was to "put the altar in place." (Ezra 3:3) It was more than twenty years since the exiles had returned to Jerusalem. Their job had been to rebuild the city and the Temple. But it had been such an immense undertaking that the very thought unnerved them to a standstill. The whole area was a blackened, discouraging sight. Where to begin—if at all? Then Jeshua, with a jaw set that had made up its mind, drew the populace into a similar commitment—and, instead of beginning with the upbuilding of walls and gates and other peripherals, they got to the command center of life itself: worship. They felt assured that when they were healed of heart, they would be equal to any endeavor. And that is the way it worked out. It always does.

John Wesley, the founder of Methodism, was rescued as a boy from his father's burning vicarage. Thereafter John referred to himself as perhaps Jeshua did, as "A brand plucked from the burning." (Zech. 3:2) All Wesley's finest endeavors were also as filthy rags, until he came to know Christ as his Savior, in a worship setting. Sheepherding God's people in a time when, after every few homes there was a gin-shop or a brothel. But the Wesleyan revival moved from one man whose heart was strangely warmed—to people across Europe and around the world.

PRAYER: *Lord, we sing our prayer today with Samuel O'Maley Cluff: "When Jesus has found you, tell others the story, that my loving Savior is your Savior too; Then pray that your Savior will bring them to glory. And prayer will be answered—'twas answered for you!" Amen.*

VICTORY IN THE SHADOWED VALLEY

Ezra 4:4-5 *Then the people of the land caused the Jews to lose heart and made them afraid to continue building.*

Sooner or later one learns that you cannot do anything worthwhile without drawing the fire from the enemy's ire. It was no different with the well-meaning, committed Jews who had returned to the Holy Land from a distant imprisonment.

They were well on their way to rebuilding the shattered city of their dreams—Jerusalem. But they were too successful for the jealous opposition, and a reign of terror erupted. As predatory animals do, the rebels went first for the obvious weaknesses—all those reasons why the city had been laid waste (4:16) by a marauding nation from afar.

Instead of making a whip (as Jesus later did) and with it driving out the dens of iniquity in one clean sweep, God added humiliation and a long period of exile to His efforts to cleanse the Holy City and Land, by using the power of a pagan Empire (Babylon) to teach His own people a lesson of historic proportions. It has, in fact, been placed beside the 400-year exile of the Jews in Egypt.

God had His reasons for allowing the dissolution of the City of His presence. From king to commoner the nation had turned its back on the Lord. More attracted by the undisciplined, fleshly behavior of the idol worshippers around them, the Jews had no time for God's 10 Demandments. Flouting those laws for sane, sanitary, serene living, God's chosen people became positively poisonous.

But this was all now in the past. God's chastised people had learned their lesson, confessed their faults, and returned to their promised land with a new determination to rebuild their personal lives, their country and its once famed capital city. And they were doing well at it. Why, then, were they being hassled by local officials? Orders came down from the top that the rebuilding of Jerusalem was to be forcibly brought to a full stop. (4:23)

But why? Why was the Lord allowing this unnecessary and unlawful extension of affliction upon His now penitent people? And if He could do that with impunity, isn't it possible for Him to do the same to us—latter day sinners?

Ezra is showing us here, that God is most interested in reinstating backsliders in His affection. But He wants to see if we are really in earnest. Will we be loyal to Him this time around? Does our loyalty now have the tensile strength it had been lacking? New occasions teach new duties. Are we ready to submissively learn to adjust to His guidance? The testing will continue in perpetuity, for our own good. This wise though rough requirement is supported by God's word, and human experience.

Said the Psalmist: "Before I was afflicted I went astray, but now I have kept thy word." (Ps. 119:67) In a further word, Thomas Guthrie adds: "As in nature and in the arts, so in grace it is rough treatment that gives souls, as well as stones, their luster. The more the diamond is cut, the brighter it sparkles, and in what seems hard dealings God has no end in view but to perfect our graces. He sends tribulations, but tells us their purpose that 'tribulation worketh patience, and patience experience, and experience hope.'"

PRAYER: *Thank You, Lord, for allowing us to stumble into situations that we do not understand at the moment, but which, in time, can produce miracles. Amen.*

PROFITABLE PROPHETS

Ezra 5:2 *Then Zerubbabel, son of Shealtil and Jeshua, son of Jozadak, with the prophets of God at their side to help them, began at once to rebuild the house of God in Jerusalem.*

Born in Babylon during the Exile of the Jews in that country, Zerubbabel had grown up hearing about the recent history of his people. Thousands of them had been taken as prisoners after the conquest of their land.

But a new day came, with new rulers, allowing the Jews to return to their homeland. And Zerubbabel, who had earned the right, led the first wave of returnees—who numbered 42,360 Jews, 7,337 servants, 200 singers, together with hundreds of horses, donkeys, mules, camels. It was a responsible undertaking, especially in "safeguarding the 5,400 gold and silver vessels which had been filched from Solomon's fabulous Temple in Jerusalem." So adroit was Zerubbabel's leadership that he was not only appointed as Governor of the Hebrew nation, but also the new Temple that was built was done so under his watchful eye, on the site of Solomon's destroyed structure. It lasted longer than did the Temples of Solomon and Herod the Great combined. To crown his fame, Zerubbabel's name is included in Jesus' genealogy. (Matt. 1:12-13)

However, after the long, perilous foot-journey from Babylon, together with the opposition that awaited him in Jerusalem, Zerubbabel was stopped in his weary tracks. He could have rested back in ease and solitude and never taken up the challenge of rebuilding God's house—if it hadn't been for the prophets of God.

Fortunately these were not just prophets. Many had disgraced themselves, as clergy still do, leading people astray. "False prophets" they were rightly designated by prophetic voices who had exceptional insight and integrity. (See Mic. 3:5 and Jer. 28; 29:8) On hand (how God raises up His witnesses in the places and at the times they are most needed) were dependable, proved prophets, not named in the above text, but now known to have been Haggai and Zechariah. They were two of the Twelve Minor prophets—minor only in the length of their writings, not the quality. Through their preaching, these two, and other prophets, fired up the emotions and energies of Zerubbabel and his associates. And the work of rebuilding began, in spite of continued harassment and opposition. Nor did the prophets just pile on the words; they piled on bricks, stones, and whatever else the building called for. They sweated side by side with the carpenters and stonecutters, the plasterers and hewers of wood. Nor was there any more slacking. "At once" was the order of each day—until the job was completed.

How prophetic preachers are always needed to get the populace growing. Otherwise, how can they hear of the Lord, or have faith in Him, and call on Him without those very welcome messengers of good news? (Rom. 10:13-15) "I the Preacher was King." (Eccles. 1:12) Now there's humbling, enthusing entitlement!

PRAYER: *Give us the prophets, Lord, even if they are to be unnamed. The times demand their kindling ministry. Amen.*

UP FROM THE PITS

Ezra 10:1 *While Ezra was praying and making confession, prostrate in tears before the house of God, there gathered round him a vast throng of Israelites, men, women, and children, and there was widespread lamentation among the crowd.*

Seventy-nine years after Zerubbabel's trek to

Jerusalem, Ezra did the same journey accompanied by a much smaller assemblage than his predecessor did. It was now fifty-nine years since the completion of the Temple. All fronts should have been in the pink of condition for Ezra's arrival. Instead, we find him praying, confessing, crying, lamenting. What had gone wrong?

The distressing news that Ezra swerved into was that fellow returnees from the Babylonian exile had settled down in Israel and had married persons of other races and cultures—leftovers from earlier foreign invasions.

With insight, hindsight, and foresight nurtured by his study of the scripture, Ezra noted the inherent danger in such a mish mash setting. It was not so much the foreignness of spouses, as their paganism that rocked Ezra. He, under whose guidance the Jewish canon of scripture was completed, could hear the Word of god condemning such a practice. The Decalogue was against it. Solomon's pitiful example proved its eventual self-destruction. And this was the reason why God permitted the Exile of His people. It couldn't go on, on Ezra's watch. But how to incise the corruption and remove it entirely? After all, love was involved in these marital couplings, children too. What was to happen to the rejected spouses and children, if it was imperative that there had to be divorce to re-establish the purity of the Jewish race and faith? Who would harbor these castaways, refugees from "God's fierce anger"? (10:14) The situation was desperate. Still, one of the elders silver-lined the storm clouds: "We have broken faith with our god in taking foreign wives from the peoples of the land. But in spite of this, there is still hope for Israel." (10:2)

And how was that hope realized? It wasn't easy, it never is, but it can be done, and was. First, through prayer, because "God warms His hands at man's heart when he prays." (John Masefield) Second, through confession. The reformation can't take place until the wrong conformations are acknowledged as such. Third, strong action must be taken. (10:4)

Therein lies the recipe for solving the immoralities of each age. To debate them until doomsday, without ever coming to a knowledge of the truth, is to remain alienated from God. St. Paul was hewing to Scripture's line when he said, "Do not team up with unbelievers. What partnership can righteousness have with wickedness? Can light associate with darkness? Can Christ agree with Belial...?" (2 Cor. 6:14-15)

Israel was saved from disaster. And so can we be.

PRAYER: *Lord, the foreign alliances come to us as persons, possessions, positions...Take us and make us Your own. Amen.*

MOMENTUM FROM IN FRONT

Ezra 10:2 *In spite of this, there is still hope.*

What a life raft of a text this is in a tempestuous time: money market meltdown, wars, tsunamis, earthquakes. Isn't that enough? We know all the rest too well. Rowing our way through wavelengths of untimely upsets. There is the ever-present and ever-haunting question: Is there still hope of survival?

In a typically hopeless situation, the prophet sees a break in the storm clouds, and the sun shines through. He dared to believe that hope springs eternal.

The turbulence had come about slowly. Jews born abroad, not just exiles, had grown up alongside neighbors of a different color, class, creed. Neither knew that they were any different from each other. They played together, studied, and labored together, and attracted by certain traits in each other fell in love, married, had families.

Then the axe fell. When the prophets saw how widespread this had become, and how it was causing imbalance in faith issues, they went into action. Especially Ezra. Seeing that the roiling intermarriage storm had reached tornado-sized proportions, Ezra went straight to his knees in prayer and confession. (10:1)

How, to our tragic loss in this post-religious age, have we forgotten the old but sustaining stand-by, "More things are wrought by prayer than this would dreams of." (Tennyson) Even Jesus' disciples, though raised in a culture of prayer, and had heard and seen Jesus at prayer, made a beggarly request of Him: "Lord, teach us to pray." And He did—in the same praying tradition that Ezra had known.

First, "Our Father, who art in heaven." One turns first and always to the Giver of every good and perfect gift. Do you notice how at funerals, people, regardless of their beliefs, are ready to fall on their knees before the Lord in order that He might reverse the death process? The fact is that He can do anything at anytime, if it is for our good. "Thy will be done."

Second, "Forgive us our trespasses." Ezra acknowledged his failures in being a part of the problem. "Prostrate in tears before the house of God." (10:1) Ezra showed as Jesus did, that one's tears and sweat, in such intensity of purpose, can be the equivalent of drops of blood. Nor is the Lord a disinterested bystander. He never is. Ezra's pleading and bleeding found favor in the Lord's sight. For people came in "a very great crowd" to follow the example of the Prophet and more. Recognizing that there was still hope, they pledged themselves to God that they would be the answer to this tangled problem of intermarriage. Coleridge believed that "He is the best physician who is the most ingenious inspirer of hope." Jeremiah (17:7) does better.

PRAYER: *Lord, help us to be like Mahatma Gandhi who, in his Christianized Hinduism, prayed that "You must be the change you want to see in the world." Amen.*

A WALL IN YOUR WILL

Neh. 6:9 *They were all trying to intimidate us in the hope that we should then relax our efforts and that the work would never be completed. Strengthen me for the work, was my prayer.*

Who would dare to intimidate Nehemiah? He had come to Jerusalem thirteen years after Ezra, protected by a contingent from the Persian army now occupying Babylon. Appointed by the King of Persia as Governor of Judah, Nehemiah was assigned the task of rebuilding the wall around Jerusalem. That wall, which had been the protective shield around the city, had been flattened by marauders 142 years before. It was a daunting enough undertaking, under ideal conditions. But old-time enemies of the Jews, who had their own plans for occupying Jerusalem some day, were determined to hurry and worry and flurry and bury the work of the rebuilders. This,

Nehemiah saw as aggressive intimidation.

But why was it so venomous? What wrongs had he committed? The paradox is that such hatred and ridicule and guile are most often not aimed at evil doers, but at those who are doing well, are super-achievers as was Nehemiah. Under his catch-fire leadership the wall was completed in fifty-two days. Even his enemies, getting the word about the remarkably sprint-like finish, with every I dotted and every T crossed, approved crowingly: "a very wonderful achievement." (6:16)

The lessons learned here speak more loudly and disseminate more widely and rocket ahead more swiftly than these words.

Certainly Nehemiah would want all his readers to know that, for one thing, a wall makes a statement. Think of the better-known ones—the Berlin Wall, the Great Wall of China. All have eyes, ears, tongues. And, mainly, as Robert Frost keenly observed, "Something there is that doesn't love a wall, that wants it down." Every ruse will be tried to tear down such a barrier, whether it be made of stone, or whether it pertains to the prohibition of immorality, or a blockage of any pernicious social issue. Expect it to be attacked as Nehemiah found, with anger, ridicule, sarcasm, phony forensics, lies, physical threats, harassment, two-faced "friends."

Note that the value of prayer moves steadily onward through the pages and stages of history. And here it is again assuring victory. Therefore, it ought to be taken more seriously, since it is a weapon of mass destruction, getting rid of every sin that can so easily beset us. Of course the vaporizing power of prayer belongs to the One who presses the hot button—the God who is implored.

It is His defensive action, safeguarding His people. It is His offensive action that is directed at those satanic opponents in a way that will be most effective. "I will repay," says the Lord. His commander-in-chief strategies strengthen His warriors in their daily combat, enabling them to be more than conquerors.

PRAYER: *Called to be wall-builders, separating good from evil, sheep from goats, purity from filth, we beseech Thee to be our guide while life shall last, O Lord, our God. Amen.*

WALLED IN HIS EVERLASTING ARMS

Neh. 6:12 *Then it dawned on me: God had not sent him. His prophecy aimed at harming me and Tobiah and Sanballat had bribed him to utter it.*

Nehemiah had come to prominence as the trusted cupbearer of the King of Persia. A Jew, and learning that his beloved Jerusalem was an unsafe habitat for humanity, since its city walls lay in ruins, Nehemiah, was granted permission to return to the land of his birth and provide leadership in the reconstruction of Jerusalem.

Always, in any sizable city, the main concern was the enfolding wall that protected the citizens from marauders. So very important was this wall, that a religious significance was attached to it: "I myself shall be a wall of fire all around it (Jerusalem), says the Lord, and a glorious presence in it." (Zech. 2:5) Also, such a wall was a symbol of truth and strength: "To withstand them I shall make you strong, an unscaled wall of bronze. Though they attack you, they will not prevail, for I am with you to save and deliver you, says the Lord." (Jer. 15:20) Also salvation: "We have a strong city with walls and ramparts built for our safety. Open the gates! Let a righteous nation enter, a nation that keeps faith." (Isa. 26:1-2) Little wonder that Jerusalem still treasures its wailing (or western) wall, which is a 1,560-foot portion, of the two and a half mile wall that encircles the old city.

Nehemiah, and thousands of his fellow Jews coming back from exile, set to work with a tenacious will to rebuild their beloved central city. But local enemies raised buffered reasons to dishearten the laborers and bring their earnest endeavors to a standstill. Worst of the opposition were prophets who spread whatever falsities their wealthy donors ordered them to say. Nastiest was the rancid rumor that Nehemiah and his minions were so ruggedly intent on their reconstruction project because of the alleged conspiracy to make Nehemiah the King of Jerusalem, and then start a rebellion against the Persian overlords who at the time owned Jerusalem and surrounding areas.

That raised Nehemiah's hackles. "Should a man like me run away?" (Neh. 6:11) was his defiant retort. "Strengthen me for the work, is my prayer." (Neh. 6:9) "So I applied myself to it with greater energy." (Neh. 6:9) And his teammates inspired by his intrepid leadership, set to with a will and finished the job in 52 days. (Neh. 6:15)

When surrounding nations saw the results, "they thought it a very wonderful achievement, and they recognized that this work had been accomplished by the help of our God." (Neh. 6:16)

Unprofitable prophets are still in the Church but outside the Kingdom they doublespeak—uttering brilliance for whichever side offers them the most money and fame. They are wolves in lamb's wool. The Judas's of every age. Double agents.

But Nehemiah shows us that such persons don't have to have the last word. Through prayer and hard work, even naysayers can see the unarguably acceptable finished product. And the Judases have a way of hanging themselves.

PRAYER: *"And tho' this world with devils filled, Should threaten to undo us; We will not fear, for God hath willed, His truth to triumph through us. The prince of darkness grim—We tremble not for him; His rage we can endure, For lo! His doom is sure, One little word shall fell him."*[1] *That one word is Jesus, in whose Name we pray. Amen.*

How God Speaks to Us

Neh. 8:8 *They read from the book of the law of God clearly, made its sense plain, and gave instruction in what was read.*

That, in essence, was what the national day of worship was designed to do. None of this fast-food stuff for the soul's sustenance. As Moses had outlined centuries before, in Deut. 31:9-13, the day was carefully planned to allow plenty of time for a balanced intake to give maximum spiritual vitality.

With the Temple and the city wall finished to everyone's satisfaction, the more pressing type of building beckoned, the inner temples and fortifications of believer's lives. Without sturdy foundations and granite wills, impregnable walls are quickly breached.

So Ezra the priest comes back on stage, literally—"a wooden platform made for the purpose," (v. 4) something he had learned in Babylon. Taking

---

[1] Martin Luther

the first five books of Moses, Ezra made the opening of the scroll a distinctive act. So moving was the baring of God's word to the assembled multitude, that they instinctively rose to their feet. As Ezra read the Word, "from early morning till noon," (v. 3) people responded with "Amens," and by bowing their heads and prostrating themselves in actions of jubilation and humility. Then, following Ezra's example, a dozen or more teachers either broke the large congregation into a dozen manageable groups, or else they took turns at addressing the entire gathering. But all took four steps.

First, they read from the holy Word of God. There must have been a temptation, as there still is, to read something less forbidding. Or, at least, to read some novel, comedic, watered-down version of the said scripture. For example, a recent newspaper headline read: "New Bible is tailored to teens' lifestyles." The first paragraph went like this: "For teenagers bored by the Bible, an evangelical publisher has given the good book a radical turboboost of features geared to make Scripture more accessible for the skateboard-and-shopping-mall set." Although teens were among Ezra's listeners ("...and all who were capable of understanding what they heard..." [v. 2]), no tailoring of the scripture was done, no amendments to make it politically correct. After all, who is there to tell God what He ought to have said?

Second, the reading was done clearly. To the best of the Teacher's ability the text was read in a language, with understandable pronunciation, and with an audible tone that would include everyone present.

Third, "made its sense plain." As Jesus did in His

parables. They were earthly stories with heavenly meanings. Sure the scripture is often difficult and contradictory. But further study under the Holy Spirit's guidance can provide answers to which one can add Q. E. D.

Finally, instruction was given as to how the Word could become deed, flesh, action. For this is the focus of the divine Word.

PRAYER: *Lord, make us to be sensible, sensitive, instructors of Your Word. Amen.*

FOR INSURED SUCCESS

Neh. 11:1 *The leaders of the people settled in Jerusalem; and the rest of the people cast lots to bring one in every ten to live in Jerusalem, the Holy City.*

Back in Jerusalem after a long exile in Babylon, Nehemiah superintended the reconstruction of the Temple and the city. Careful about details, he did not overlook the rebuilding of the city's infrastructure.

In exile, the Jews had not been permitted to practice many of their religious traditions. Without a temple there had been no worship center to which they could take their many annual offerings. Without property of their own there was no land to cultivate, therefore no "first fruits" to offer God, no farm animals for ritual sacrifices.

Now in their homeland again, the Hebrew people were putting together a whole new way of life, many of them for the first time since they had been born abroad. Commitment was needed for the daily grinding work. Yet see how smoothly the author makes his thought flow from chapter 10 to chapter 11, connecting tithes and offerings to the now more-needed tithing and offering of human life itself. For in today's text the author introduces the resurging idea of tithed humans, one in ten—an enormous output of energy. No wonder that the work on city temple, homes, and farmland was completed in record time. That's what tithed lives can do, anywhere. It was not just the offering of bulls, sheep, goats, doves as sacrifices. It was not the mere giving of fruit, veggies, money, clothing, shelter. These, while necessary, though hard on the pocketbook, still leave the energy and talents of the contributor untouched.

Untouched also are one's *prayers*. If "more things are wrought by prayer than this world dreams of," what power is turned off without private and public prayer? Starting any endeavor with God at the center is empowering. Look at the resources of heaven and earth that He puts at our disposal, to say nothing of the fire of enthusiasm He stokes in our hearts.

Untouched by material giving is one's *presence*. You don't even have to "be there" to make an offering. These days it can be done through the Internet while you're on vacation in Hawaii. To give of one's Presence personalizes the gift. Under certain conditions a stand-in, a proxy is permissible. Otherwise it can be an insult to the Giver of every good and perfect gift. To be present, in person, can be sacrificial. Therefore acceptable *talents* are untouched by a $100 bill on the collection plate. Ones' talents, reserved strictly for the making of a living, amount to selfishness, greed—weapons of mass personal destruction. To give is to live. To deny is to die. What enrichment of life comes to those who share some expertise? Nor does one have to be exceptional. Whatever one's talents—they are blessed in the very sharing.

Then there is *service*. What a giant divide there can be between servicing and donating. One can be done from afar, whereas service requires hands-on giving of all that is required in the changing moments.

To this list has been recently added *"witness."* But if we're not witnessing by our prayers, presence, talents, service, what's the use of adding one unnecessary word? Tithed living gathers all the requirements together.

PRAYER: *Inspired by Thy people in the Holy City, we would be as giving of ourselves even in the unholy situations to which we have been appointed by Thee, O Lord. Amen.*

REJOICE, THE LORD IS KING

Neh. 12:43 *The rejoicing in Jerusalem was heard a long way off.*

Talk about a Wailing Wall, this one that went up under Nehemiah's supervision was assuredly another. What blood, sweat, and tears were mixed into its mortar. But when at last it stood in all its resplendent completion, the very stones and bricks cried out for a national celebration. And the population responded with an unforgettable dedication of all out "rejoicing, with thanksgiving and song, to the accompaniment of cymbals, lutes and harps," (Neh. 12:27) which was heard far and wide.

The lesson brought out for today, and every day, is that our religion is one of joy. That theme is threaded through both Testaments. In the forty-third verse Nehemiah uses the blissful word four or five times. It is characteristic of God. (Ps. 105:31) It is part of the nine-fold harvest of the Spirit. (Gal.

5:24) St Paul echoes it in Phil. 4:4: "Rejoice in the Lord always; again I will say, Rejoice." And whereas happiness is dependent on happenings—a Thanksgiving dinner, a Santa-filled stocking, a clear day for a picnic—joy holds hands with sorrow and makes of it a helpful companion. Jesus showed how it was done: "For the joy that was set before Him, endured the cross, despising the shame, and is set down at the right hand of the throne of God." (Heb. 12:2) George Matheson, the blind preacher-poet, sang triumphantly: "O Joy that seekest me through pain, I cannot close my heart to thee; I trace the rainbow through the rain, and feel the promise is not vain, that morn shall tearless be." Why, then, don't we exude such joy?

National magazines don't have all the answers, but every once in awhile they give us dots, which, when joined, outline a mirror in which we can see ourselves. In *Newsweek* issue Dec. 28, 2009-Jan. 4, 2010, p. 98, editors wanted to find out what the bestsellers of 2009 had to say about us. Combing through top books, movies, music, TV shows, they found that 70 percent of Americans bought into violence; 60 percent, money; 45 percent, sex; 40 percent, youth; 20 percent, vampires; and 10 percent each for politics and God. His presence was felt in just two books! Join the dots and we get *violence*; though needed sometimes for defense, it will turn to mush apart from God's guidance. When David approached Goliath "in the name of the Lord of hosts," his slingshot found its mark.

Money, lacking divinely guided stewardship, soon feels the ominous judgment: "You fool, this very night you must surrender your life, and the money you have made, who will get it now?" (Luke 12:20)

Sex, permitted by the Creator for procreation, is a coveted builder of families. Apart from Him sex is a vice in a vise.

To give the strength of *Youth* to the Master is to move toward a promising maturity.

Vampires and *politics* are all that one is left with when God is left out. Yet the Lord can mould politics into statesmen of stature. Without Him, politicians can be bought and sold for a vote. All things betray us when we betray Him. But there is joy in heaven if one sinner repents.

PRAYER: *Now we know, Lord, why we are bulging and our souls' starving. So we pray: "Here I give my all to Thee—Friends, and time and earthly store; Soul and body Thine to be, wholly Thine for evermore."*[1] *Amen.*

HOLY SABBATH

Neh. 13:19 *When the entrances to Jerusalem had been cleared in preparation for the Sabbath, I gave orders that the gates should be shut and not opened until after the Sabbath; and I posted some of my men at the gates to ensure that no load came in on the Sabbath.*

The state of Nehemiah's countrymen was reverting to the time of their forefathers. So immoral had that earlier generation become, that the Lord didn't prevent their being conquered and led away to years of exile. Now Nehemiah could detect similar danger signs. Mosaic laws were being neglected, which led to a slippage in all forms of daily behavior. This, the prophet deduced, was stemming from a breakdown in Sabbath observance. The desecration of the Sabbath was flagrant. Winepresses worked

---

[1] William McDonald

full tilt; produce of all kinds was trundled in the city; buying and selling was no different on the day of rest than on any other day of the week. It had to be stopped. And Nehemiah, as governor, took the initiative. As Rabbi Hayim Donin explains: "Scripture defines what work on the Sabbath means. It does not leave it up to each person to define for himself what should or should not constitute [work]. If it did, there might as well be no Sabbath at all. Any law in any legal system, that is vague and obscure and which can be interpreted in any way one sees fit, is a useless law and serves no purpose."[1]

Incoming workers, then, were stopped at their entryways. Today Jerusalem's walls have eight gates. Whatever gates they had in Nehemiah's day were closed to traffic. That brought to a halt the trafficking of goods and services within the city walls—until sundown on the Sabbath.

The bolted gates, shut out the Thou-shalt-nots, and shut in the Thou-shalts of Sabbath requirements. The line was drawn, and once again the fourth commandment was taken seriously. And again the results were recognized as a kin to the Exodus from Egypt. People who had felt restricted by Sabbath prohibitions, and kicked off the traces to enjoy their freedom, now found true liberty. They enjoyed the changes of pace, even for a day. There was more time for togetherness, as families, as worshipping fellowships. Most of all, there was soul refreshment, and a physical rejuvenation that sent people into the new workweek afire. Indeed, it was an Exodus to a Promising tomorrow. How sad, that "In our Western culture the day of rest has now be-

---

[1] H. H. Donin, *To Be A Jew*, pp. 89-90

come another day of busy work, filled with amusements and restless diversions not essentially different from the routine of the workweek, particularly in America. From the Sunday morning scramble through the metropolitan newspapers to the distracting tedium of the motor car excursion, we continually activate leisure time instead of letting all work and routine duties come serenely to a halt."[2]

PRAYER: *Lord Jesus, who said, "I am the door," (John 10:7) help us to shut out all Sabbath distractions. Shut us in with Yourself that we may have a week of content. Amen.*

AS THE TWIG IS BENT

Esther 2:6 *[Mordecai] had been taken into exile from Jerusalem among those whom King Nebuchadnezzar of Babylon had carried away with King Jeconiah of Judah.*

Although this is the only mention of Jerusalem in the Book of Esther, what a germinal part the city played in the preparations for the Savior's arrival 400 years later. For it was in Jerusalem that Mordecai received his basic training in spiritual matters. It was to that home city and land that he was ever devoted. For their ultimate upbuilding, he used his wisdom and court connections. Little wonder that he takes top honors in the book named for his cousin (and adopted daughter), and why, for centuries, this book was placed right after the precious Pentateuch—the first five books of the Old Testament, once the only scriptures the Jews possessed.

In spite of being mentioned as being in the company of a King, Jeconiah, Mordecai was a no-

---

[2]Lewis Mumford

body in captivity in Babylon, even when his adopted daughter Esther won a beauty contest and married the King of Babylon. In fact, Mordecai came under suspicion and was in danger of losing his life, and causing the extermination (holocaust-like) of all fellow Jews. He had angered the Prime Minister by not bowing in the presence of his Eminence. Even a seventy-five-foot-high gallows was erected to hang Mordecai in public. His end was near. And he was fully informed about it, knowing also that Esther, who was a key player in the drama, was waffling about helping him.

Then it was that Mordecai sent a wake-up message to Esther (the sort that Admiral Nelson conveyed to his navy: "England expects every man to do his duty.") Said Mordecai: "If you remain silent at such a time as this, relief and deliverance for the Jews will appear from another quarter (God); but you and your father's family will perish. And who knows whether it is not for a time like this that you have become queen." (v. 14)

That night the King couldn't sleep. Instead of taking a sleeping potion, he did the next best—call for the Journal in which Scribes recorded noteworthy matters of state. One item, which caught the monarch's attention, concerned the time when Mordecai saved the King from being assassinated by two thugs. And there was no record of Mordecai being rewarded?! That shame had to be reversed. In the skillfully worded documentary, the tables were turned on the Prime Minister, who was hanged on the gallows he had set up for Mordecai's strangling.

From then on the King couldn't do enough for the Jews. Mordecai was made Prime Minister, and

Nehemiah was granted permission to fortify Jerusalem—at government expense, mind you. Jerusalem's bread, cast upon the water, came back to sustain it after many years.

PRAYER: *O Thou who seest the end for which the first was made, build us aright in all our beginnings, that Thy goals for us will be met. Amen.*

THE KING IS COMING

Ps. 2:6 *I have enthroned my King on Zion my holy mountain.*

We come now to "the height of God-given literature," the longest book in the Bible with its 150 chapters, the most cherished book in the Old Testament—the Book of Psalms. Across all religious lines it has been found to be the most comforting and uplifting in its messages. More than any other book, it bridges the Old and New Testaments, pointing accurately to the coming Messiah in prophecies which were fulfilled. Of the 283 New Testament quotations from the Old Testament, 116 are from the Psalms. This is immediately brought to our attention in Ps. 2:7, which is used at the most important of junctures in the life of Messiah Jesus: His baptism, (Matt. 3:17) His transfiguration, (Matt. 17:5) and His resurrection. (Acts 13:33)

And with reference to our current purpose, the Book of Psalms has more references to Jerusalem than any other Bible book. That was to be expected, since David wrote seventy-three of these psalms, plus many of the fifty "anonymous" psalms, and Solomon wrote two, both gentlemen lifelong residents of the city set on God's "holy mountain."

This Royal psalm was used for generations by

those who followed David and Solomon to their throne. On the day of their coronation, each King would intone this monumental text in the presence of his subjects. In time, however, this psalm has become the possession of us commoners.

The opening question, "Why are the nations in turmoil?" never appears to be out-of-date. Peoples of the world are always up in arms against God, His followers, neighbors, themselves. Most of life's unhappiness originates in this central enmity. Running through all human thoughts and activities is the fire of destructiveness and malice. Were their feelings put on a sound track, there would be worldwide bedlam.

Then there is God. Though He is poetically pictured as sitting in heaven, enthroned, He is never unmindful of anything happening on earth. As proof, He laughs at those who work against Him. It is not a happy, approving laugh. It is scornful, rebuking. It indicates that the evildoers will, in time, be broken as shatteringly as a clay pot when hit with an iron rod.

As for the faithful, the Lord makes a generous offer: "Ask of me what you will: I will give you nations as your inheritance." (v. 8) And who echoed that promise but David's greater Son, Jesus?

Not to worry about world turbulence. Jesus, too, reassures us, "I have overcome the world." Our concern is to be mindful to "worship the Lord with reverence." (v. 10) Learning there from what to ask the Lord for, then enjoying the happiness of finding our refuge in Him." (v. 6:12)

In Rio de Janeiro, Brazil, the statue of Christ stands atop the highest promontory in the area, and can be seen from anywhere. We're beginning to see the Master way back in the

Book of Psalms. Rejoice.

PRAYER: *Through the mists of actuality we see You appearing, Lord Jesus. O Happy Day, that fixed my choice on Thee my Savior and my God. Amen.*

PO$$E$$ED

Ps. 5:2 *Heed my cry for help, my King and my God.*

These Psalms or songs that were twanged out on various musical instruments, come in seven categories: hymns, national psalms, thanksgiving psalms, those giving instructions on various themes, Messianic psalms for times of need, or psalms in special groupings such as Acrostics and Songs of Ascent. Psalm 5 is for individuals in need, and has been found to be most comforting in the night—when the day's errors and terrors are magnified to scary proportions. It is also believed that this psalm was written by one, who, the next morning, was to answer a false accusation against him.

Whatever its origin, it continues to perform its healing ministry across the world.

Appealing to the Divine Shepherd in a three-fold call for help "listen," "consider," "heed," the psalmist tries to figure out what kind of person would get a response from God, certainly not a wicked arrogant, lying traitor, slick talker. And he was not one of those. He had prayed and sacrificed and worshipped in the Temple. After all, he insisted this is "my King my God."

Two ministers were doing a summer hike in the Welsh mountains. During one of their rest stops, they chatted with a shepherd boy who was tending his flocks. The ministers noted that the young man didn't know much about the scriptures so they told him about what they thought would be of interest to him—the Shepherd's Psalm. They suggested that when he was in trouble he should look at his left hand, starting with the thumb, and say five words: "The Lord is my Shepherd."

The next summer the pastors were in the same mountainous area when they stopped at a cottage to ask for directions. The lady of the house invited them in for refreshments. Looking at a picture on the mantel one minister said to the hostess, "That's a familiar face, who would that be?" The motherly woman replied, "Oh, you wouldn't know him. That's my son. Last winter, while rounding up the sheep in a storm, he fell down the hillside and was killed. The ministers then recounted their time with the lad the previous summer. With a strange look, the mother said, "Then maybe you can explain what has been puzzling us. When the rescuers found the boy, he was dead. But they said that with his right hand he was tightly grasping the third finger of his left hand." "Why, of course we can explain it," replied one of the clergymen. And he told about the Shepherd's Psalm. In his dying moments the young shepherd had remembered from where help came, and hung on to that—"The Lord is MY Shepherd."[1]

It is that same third finger of the left hand that is a symbol of possession. "He is mine." "She is mine." On no other finger is that gold wedding ring slipped, that ring that has no beginning and no end. The commitment to each other that it symbolizes is endless. And as the ancients be-

---

[1] L. D. Weatherhead, *A Shepherd Remembers*, pp. 25-27

lieved, there is a nerve in that third finger of the left hand that goes directly to the heart—the centerpiece of love.

Clinging to MY King and MY God, the psalmist, too, was assured that he was safe in the arms of the divine shepherd, the Great Lover of the World, and that he would dwell in the house of the Lord forever. MY, MY, What a Savior is ours.

PRAYER: *Lord, we hold on to Your promise to never leave us—in good times or sullen. Amen.*

A DIVINE RESCUE OPERATION

Ps. 9:13 *Thou who hast lifted me up and caught me back from the gates of death.*

Psalms 9 and 10 started out as one acrostic poem. An acrostic is when each line starts with consecutive letters of the alphabet, ABC...In the Hebrew alphabet there are 22 letters.

Poets have used acrostics in numerous ways. You see them in the eight psalms that appear in the Book of Psalm (9-10,34,37,111,112,119,145).

Being in alphabetical order, these acrostic psalms were easier to memorize. In later editing and re-editing Ps. 9-10 were separated, and the alphabetizing was rendered incomplete. But the message is a single thread weaving its way through Ps. 9:1-20 to Ps. 10:1-18.

When it was decided that the 149 Psalms for this Bible book needed an introduction that would give the gist of all the others, Psalm 1 was written, and the last was put first. In substance it tells of the two forces that are constantly at war in this world: good and evil, "the way of the righteous," and "the way of the wicked." (1:6)

In Ps. 9-10, the pith of the message is found in

9:13-14, "the gates of death" and "the gates of Zion" (Jerusalem), the city in which God chose to dwell.

Psalm 9 opens with the poet praising God. While singing about all the wondrous things the Lord has done, the psalmist finds that he is actually talking to the Lord.

And there's a point to ponder, namely that when we sincerely and step-by-step recall the blessings we have received, quite normally, and quite without being aware of it, we find ourselves talking directly to the g/Giver of every good and perfect gift. Welcome to a face-to-face relationship with the Best Friend we could ever have. No more long distance communication. Just put down the cell phone and pick up the soul phone. It's far more effective, with unlimited range.

For example, there was a seemingly impossible task. But we asked the Lord for help, and He gave it. In thanking Him for the intricate zigzags through which He maneuvered us, we suddenly find ourselves saying (perhaps) aloud, "Lord, when I was about to give up, Tom appeared with just the word of assurance and the helping hand that changed the whole picture. That was no accident, Lord, You and only You could have produced Tom in that split second. Your timely intervention from behind the scenes saved the day and my life."

Moreover, talking confidently and confidentially to our Divine Companion, strengthens the bonds between us, and gives us the desire to lean more earnestly on the everlasting arms—the next time, and the next. Especially when "the gates of death" swing open like the consuming jaws of some monster ready to devour the unwatchful and unattended. How prone we humans are to have the gates of evil close behind us, when we could just as readily give ourselves to the wide-open gates of Zion, the place where God dwells. He knows the dangers, the addictions to which we are chained, and He is a past Master in the rescue business.

PRAYER: *Savior of the world: As times revert to chaotic unbelief, guide us to Your open-gated city of safety. Amen.*

OUR CARING COMPANION

Ps. 11:1 *Why do you say to me, "Flee to the mountains like a bird"?*

Having asked the disquieting question: "When foundations are undermined, what can the good man do?" (v. 3) the psalmist waits for answers. It doesn't seem to be an earthquake that has shaken his nerves. It's worse. Evildoers are at it again. The wicked "shoot down honest men out of the darkness." (v. 2) Lovers of violence (v. 3) brandishing their power and superiority see no need for rules, decency, God. What to do with the devil in control?

One would-be helper suggests that the mountains would be a safe retreat. Have we not been exhorted to lift up our eyes unto the hills from where our help comes? The birds know better than to wait for the shaking of the earth's foundations before taking off for the craggy mountains in which to hide. And there are caves where animals hibernate, and crevices into which snakes slither for shelter, or hideaways in which ascetics and monastics get away from it all. Are these elevations the places to seek out for the solace of the soul?

The mountain goats and eagles think so. But you can't be too sure. A sportsman tells of looking through his field glasses and learning a lesson for life. He watched as an eagle swooped down and grabbed a tasty looking lizard. Rising to the upper air, the bird, no doubt, was headed for his mountain roost there in leisure to have his feast. But as the sportsman watched the drama unfold, he saw the bird lose altitude and drop to the ground, while the lizard scurried away into the bushes. Upon examining the eagle, the sportsman found that the lizard had bitten into the bird's neck and sucked away its life.

Why flee to the mountains like a bird? You can't be sure of refuge there.

In a Burmese forest, everything was pristine. The trees were untouched by woodcutters hungry for valuable teak wood. No wildlife was on the "extinct" list. Yet, right in the middle of this no-man's land was a Buddhist training center for priests. They believe that the only way you can escape from the evils of human society is to withdraw to the isolation of the wilderness.

Our psalmist has heard all these suggestions and arguments for preserving his life from unbelievers who fire their fatal arrows from out of dark corners. And after carefully considering the pros and cons of the best shielded spots, he joyfully announces: "In the Lord I have found my refuge." (v. 1) Not subterfuge or centrifuge, but Refuge. And where was his refuge to be found? Not the mountains, underground tunnels, or Fort Knox-like imperviousness. It was on the holy hills of Jerusalem, the center of the world at that time: the Temple of the Lord.

That would be accessible for citizens of Jerusalem, but what about the rest of the world?

Not to worry, the Lord has made arrangements about that too. For the next line assures us that "the Lord's throne is in heaven [and] His eye is upon mankind, he takes their measure at a glance." (v. 4) How's that for total security? How unlike earthbound watchmen who can't take things in at a glance, who, in fact, are often known to go to sleep on the job. Our ever-watchful heavenly Father doesn't miss a thing—even when Jerusalem is ransacked and the Temple destroyed. "His eye is upon mankind." Relax. Rejoice.

PRAYER: *In Thy embrace, dear Lord, we are SAFE, now and forever. We cling to Thy merciful affection. Amen.*

GOD HELP US

Ps. 14:7 *If only Israel's deliverance might come out of Zion.*

Once Psalms 14 and 53 were considered identical. They still have much in common, but they have been separated because Ps. 53 has been found to have the answer to and the cause of the atheism in Ps. 14:1, "The impious fool says in his heart, 'There is no God.'"

In both psalms the deliverance from godlessness should have come from Zion, the City of God. And why wasn't it coming? Because the root of the trouble lay with the corruption of the priesthood in the Temple—the hub of the Jewish faith.

If we find it incomprehensible to believe that the priests could be "rotten to the core," (v. 3) a look at Mal. 1:6-2:9 gives a disgusting and disillusioning list of priestly indecencies: priests who despise God's name. (Mal. 1:6) These priests defiled the offerings laid on the altar, and thereby despised the name of the Lord. Although the priests had Kosher animals to sacrifice, they used defective animals, brazenly showing how little esteem they had for the Lord. For such disrespect the Lord said that He would turn their blessings into a curse (Mal. 2:2), and banish them from His presence. (Mal. 2:3) And the Lord gave further reasons for His stern action since people "hang on the words of the priest and seek knowledge and instruction from him, because he is the messenger of the Lord of Hosts. But you have turned aside from that course; you have caused many to stumble with your instruction...So I in my turn shall make you despicable and degraded in the eyes of all the people, inasmuch as you disregard my way and show partiality in your interpretation of the law." (Mal. 2:7-9)

With good reason, then, what the psalmist is saying is that foolish priests say in their heads, "There is no God." (Ps. 14:1)

As this psalm has been one of those eternally contemporary psalms, it means that the rot in the priesthood can be repeated in any age.

Is it, in ours?

When Jane Healy, in *Failure to Connect*, p. 18, observes that we are grasping at a techno centric quick fix for a multitude of problems we have failed to address—the unraveling of present-day society is laid bare. The mix-up in moral values can be traced to the mixed signals being sent out by the moral leadership (also known as the clergy of our time). Lacking unity in the understanding of substantive values, and therefore unable to translate them into workaday activities, techno centric quick fixes (which sound scientific and attractive) are tried and found wanting. The result is a throwback to the babbling cacophony of the Tower of Babel. There's no coherence about or commitment to God in Christ. Bedlam at the center resonates to the outer reaches in villages and huts.

Charles Colson, a shrewd analyst of our time, writes of "today's Biblically illiterate Church with its rampant doctrinal ignorance."

PRAYER: *Strict but loving Lord, Keep a tight rein on all persons in positions of moral leadership in the Church, the home and places of work. To whom more has been given and more shall be required for Thy Kingdom's growing glory. Amen.*

HIS EVER-ENLIVENING WORD

Ps. 15:1 *O Lord, who may lodge in Thy tabernacle? Who may dwell on Thy holy mountain?*

The children of Israel have been pilgrims since 1400 B.C. if not before. Exiting Egypt through the Sinai wilderness, wherever they tented, it was a move closer to the Promised Land. Even when they arrived there, and settled down, and built a Temple some 500 years later, their pilgrimage continued in the belief that "here we have no lasting city (or Temple), but we are seekers after the city which is to come." (Heb. 13:14)

In pilgrim mode they would remind themselves of their ongoing journey by periodically coming to the Temple gates in Jerusalem and intoning our text for today. Inside the Temple entrance the answer was said or sung by priests. This answer was in the form of the Commandments given by God to Moses on Mt. Sinai. These 10 words (not commands or demands) were to be learned by heart and lived out in daily life, readying the pilgrims for entry, not only into the Temple precincts, but also into God's eternal dwelling.

These ten Words in Ps. 15, reconstructed to sound like the Decalogue from Sinai, look like this:

1. Thou shalt walk uprightly and do what is right. (v. 2)
2. Thou shalt speak in truthfulness of heart. (v. 2)
3. Thou shalt refrain from slanderous gossip. (v. 3)
4. Thou shalt do no evil to thy neighbor. (v. 3)
5. Thou shalt not insult thy nearest kin. (v. 3)
6. Thou shalt honor those who fear the Lord. (v. 4)
7. Thou shalt reject those whom the Lord despises. (v. 4)
8. Thou shalt not change what thou hast sworn for something worse. (v. 4)
9. Thou shalt not lend out thy money at interest. (v. 5)
10. Thou shalt not accept a bribe against the innocent man.[1] (v. 5)

Through the Bible, other such "Words" have been proposed. Isaiah offers six (Isa. 33:15-16); Micah has three (Mic. 6:8); Isa. 56:1 mentions another two; Amos puts all his eggs in *one* basket. (Amos 5:4) Jesus has eight Beatitudes (Matt. 5:8-12), or else He boils down the ten words from Sinai to two—Love God and love your neighbor. (Matt. 22:36-40)

The ten from Ps. 15, conforming with the ten

---

[1] Elmer A. Leslie, *The Psalms*, p. 188

from Sinai, have been given more than ordinary attention because of their association with pilgrims, and with those later Pilgrims to America in 1620.

With that in mind, President Franklin Roosevelt, at a Thanksgiving service, quoted the last line of Ps. 15: "He who does these things shall never be brought low." (v. 5) Then the president added a closing comment: "The old ship of state is still on the same course, because the nation has leased its life on [these] moral principles." Amen and Amen.

PRAYER: *Father of mankind: in whichever age Your word is spoken, in ten words or one, it is a life giver. Speak, Lord, Your servants are listening. Amen.*

SEEK HIS FACE AND GRACE

Ps. 27:4 *One thing I ask of the Lord.*

When it comes to asking the Lord for anything, laundry and grocery lists shrink in comparison. Hearing that "thou art coming to a King, large petitions with thee bring, for His strength and power are such, thou canst never ask too much"—this psalmist starts modestly. There's only one request on his list. Then, sensing that the meek shall inherit the earth, his gimme list lengthens to at least thirteen items. Not to worry, we can never ask too much.

The one prayer request here is that the psalmist may "gaze upon the beauty of the Lord in His temple." (v. 4) Not expecting the Lord to do everything, this person is prepared to do his part and seek until he finds—using the word "seek" four times to show his earnestness.

Then, to enable him in his search and research, he first makes himself *teachable*, praying: "Teach me Thy way, O Lord." (v. 11) The seeker isn't going to get very far in his quest if he's not willing to be a student—especially of the Lord. And that entails not only God's holy word as it is found in the Bible, but also as Maltbie Babcock found "in the rustling grass I hear Him pass, He speaks to me everywhere." Indeed, He does, even in the silence, and in the buzz of the confounding city's razzle-dazzle.

Next, the psalmist makes himself *Guide-able:* "Lead me." (v. 12) Did you ever try to get a horse to go where you wanted when he was close to his stable? How we all want stable conditions. "Here am I, Lord, send John Jones." How unguideable Jonah was. The Lord wanted him to head for Nineveh, but Jonah stubbornly took a ship going in the opposite direction—Tarshish. Wanting that "one thing," the appropriate plea is, "guide me, O thou great Jehovah." Then, as our Shepherding Lord leads us beside still waters and in the paths of righteousness, can we follow?

Finally, the psalmist was *Convince-able.* "Well I know that I shall see the goodness (beauty) of the Lord in the land of the living." (v. 13) If he sought his heart's desire under the teaching and guidance, the psalmist was convinced that he would find that "one thing," and Jesus put His stamp of approval on that. "Set your mind on God's Kingdom and his justice before everything else, and all the rest will come to you as well." (Matt. 6:33) That's the starting place for being the recipient of manifold blessings which we never thought about or asked for. It calls for songs of praise to the Lord. (v. 6)

In India there were people called Untouchables. They belonged to the lowest caste, outcasts.

Today the untouchables are everywhere. They are the unteachable, the unreachables. You can tell that they are university educated, but you can't tell them much. They know it all. A recent college graduate asked Professor Einstein (without knowing who he was) what his main interest was. "Mathematics," replied Einstein briefly. "Mathematics" echoed the horrified recent graduate. "Why I finished with mathematics in my freshman year."

Teach me, guide me, convince me, O Lord, now and ever.

PRAYER: *Heavenly Father: Let the beauty of Jesus be seen in me, All His wondrous compassion and purity, O thou Spirit divine, all my nature refine, Let the beauty of Jesus be seen in me. Amen.*

GOD'S WORLD ON HIS SHOULDERS

Ps. 29:1 *Ascribe to the Lord glory and might.*

While the forces of nature do their thing through the centuries, we humans take the rain, thunder, oceanic turbulence, and the rest in our stride. Or try to. Sorting out the mechanics of these weather patterns—what causes them where they occur, what destruction they can cause—we build defenses against them: lightning conductors, umbrellas, sea-worthy procedures, fire protection, snow shelters, or even seeding clouds to induce rainfall. Often, nothing that we do will suffice. Massive tsunami-like results crumple lives and property.

Though we carry on the most heroic peaceful co-existence with nature's more terrifying elements, there comes a time (which can be anytime) when we have to admit that nature is the ultimate winner. Which is to say that there is a power which is seen and felt that is overwhelmingly greater than anything we humans possess, especially when we factor in volcanoes, tornadoes, floods, and being bombarded by meteorites. And when one considers an ordered universe emerging from a formless void (Gen. 1:2) (however the big-bang scientists explain it), there's a super-power "ascribe to the Lord glory and might." (v. 1,9) In verse 4 it states that "the voice of the Lord is power." So powerful is His voice that it reverberates seven times. In the lower level of the Taj Mahal, a priest cups his hands to his mouth and, with a loud voice, calls out the one word: "Allah" (God). Then you hear "God" echoing and re-echoing seven times through the marble chambers and halls.

Listen now as the voice of the Lord echoes seven times through Ps. 29.

1. "The voice of the Lord echoes over the waters," (v. 3) denoting how God silences the power of disorder. His is the ultimate word of authority.
2. "The voice of the Lord is power." (v. 4) Within nature's power is the power of God that created it.
3. "The voice of the Lord is majesty." (v. 4) He wields His power for constructive, admirable, regal purposes.
4. "The voice of the Lord breaks the cedars (of Lebanon)." (v. 5) Those trees are still much sought after, serving as a good description of pride. That the Lord has His stellar way of subduing.
5. "The voice of the Lord makes flames of fire burst forth." (v. 7) This is not only a reminder of God speaking to Moses through the fearful thunder and lightning on Mt. Sinai, but also of the tongues of fire that appeared on the heads of

those who were assembled in the Upper Room at Pentecost. Which is why, in later years, Ps. 29 became the chosen reading on the Day of Pentecost.

6. "The voice of the Lord makes the wilderness writhe in travail." (v. 8) Much the same as Five.
7. "The voice of the Lord makes the hinds calve and brings kids early to birth." (v. 9) As thunder caused early birth in animals, the Lord is anxious for new life on earth. Then, after all the turmoil, the last and most powerful word is "Peace."

PRAYER: *"God of grace and God of glory, On Thy people pour Thy power, Crown Thine ancient Church's story, Bring her bud to glorious flower."*[1] Amen.

TAKE THE REFRESHING COURSE

Ps. 42:1 *As a hind (deer, hart) longs for the running streams, so do I long for Thee, O God.*

This famous verse introduces a two-poem song. Originally Ps. 42-43 were one, and still should be since the same theme runs through both, in the same style with the same chorus.

The Psalmist is in misery, feeling far removed from and forgotten by God, especially when people ask him all day, "Where is your God?" (v. 3,11)

Then he must have seen this deer, frantic for a drink of water. He knows how the animal feels because that's the way he felt—crazy for the water of life that only God could supply. Neither he nor the deer could have their raging thirst quenched. The pain of unfulfillment must have been worse for the Psalmist since, at the moment, he was in the very watershed of the Holy Land. (v. 6) At

---

[1] H. E. Fosdick

Mizar (Banias) four sources of the River Jordan come together with the chilling water from 10,000-foot snowcapped Mt. Hermon. The psalmist needed living water, and the deer looking for "still waters" (Ps. 23) at which it could drink, and finding nothing but cataracts and a full-blown rushing river, was frightened into a maddening thirst. Although in Leslie Weatherhead's *A Shepherd Remembers* (pp. 51-53), there is another point of view even more distressing.

The difficulty arises in why should the hart pant if he is already standing over the water brooks? James Neil, from his intimate knowledge of the Holy Land, argues that the word translated "water brooks" (or "running streams") should be translated "aqueducts." Everyone who has visited Palestine has been impressed by the way in which water is carried from one place to another along stone channels that are closed in at the top to protect them from being fouled.

Aqueducts are, and always must have been, very common and familiar objects in the Holy Land, where the entire absence of rain for seven months and the universal and extensive practice of horticulture render them so necessary. Ruined remains of such aqueducts are to be found throughout the country, some of a most costly and elaborate kind. It is, therefore, almost certain that the inspired writers must have alluded to these precious water channels; and that in the primitive, rich, precise Hebrew of the Old Testament there must be a special technical term for them. This term is translated "water brooks," but should be translated "aqueducts."

If a closed-in aqueduct is what is meant, the famous opening of Ps. 42 carries a much more significant meaning. The hart can hear the running water, and even scent the precious, refreshing current. She/he might even see it through one of the infrequent air holes; but she cannot reach it, and lifts up her head in a wail of frustrated desire. A literal translation would be, "As the hart wails over the aqueduct, so cries my soul for Thee, O God."

Believing that the Lord will lead him to the Temple's altar, where he will find God, his heart's desire, the Psalmist, who is a harpist, looks forward to expressing his joy in the Lord—across his vibrant strings. (Ps. 43:3-4) That's God's way of ending our misery—through delight in Him.

PRAYER: *Lord, we sing with Louis Spohr: "As pants the hart for cooling streams, When heated in the chase, So longs my soul, O God, for Thee, And Thy refreshing grace." Amen.*

MY FATHER'S WORLD

Ps. 48:14 *Such is God.*

When Martin Luther drew from Ps. 46 for his well-known Battle Hymn of the Reformation "A Mighty Fortress is our God," there is little doubt that he also drew upon Ps. 47-48, since these three are considered a trilogy. They use the same language, themes, and had the same author, King David. Originally they were used together during the celebration of God's sovereignty in His holy city of Jerusalem.

Of course, Ps. 46 stands out because of the recognition brought to it by Luther. James Moffatt (the famed Bible translator), called Ein Feste Burg, for which Luther also composed the music, "the greatest hymn of the greatest man in the greatest period of German history." It was sung by the whole army before the Battle of Leipzig in 1631. Eminent composers have used it in cantatas and symphonies, as in Mendelssohn's Reformation Symphony. Such widespread publicity over several centuries has caused many people to believe that Luther wrote Ps. 46! However, James Naylor reminds us that "King David and King Solomon led merry, merry lives, with many, many lady friends, And many, many wives; But when old age crept over them, with many, many qualms, King Solomon wrote the Proverbs and King David wrote the Psalms."

Though the Protestant Reformation was built on three principles: 1. reestablishment of the scriptures, 2. clarification of the means of salvation, and 3. restoration of congregational singing, Luther's trilogy was based, first, on the Supremacy of God. It is summed up at the end of Ps. 48:14 in three words: "Such is God."

Such as? For instance, there is one nation under gods and goddess—of all kinds. There are persons who believe they are the only God there is. There are the Hindu gods—Brahma, Vishnu, Shiva; Jupiter and his fellow gods on Mt. Olympus; the Medicine man; the belief that all the forces of nature are manifestations of god. "A picket frozen on duty, A mother starved for her brood, Socrates drinking the hemlock, And Jesus on the rood; And millions, who, humble and nameless, The Straight, hard pathway trod—some call it Consecration, And others call it God." (W. H. Carruth)

David, however, was a monotheist who believed that God was a shelter (Ps. 46:1) as Jesus later offered to be. David saw God as the "great sovereign over all the earth!" (Ps. 47:2) and "our guide eternally." (Ps. 48:14)

We learn that God is like a river that gives life to Jerusalem. Although there is no river in or near the city, (Ps. 46:4) it conveys the idea that God, through His distributaries—witnesses "for me in Jerusalem, Judea, Samaria, and in the farthest corners of the earth." (Acts 1:8) Such a gospel (good news) will gladden people everywhere.

Finally, Jerusalem "the city of our God, upon his holy hill, Fair and lofty, the joy of the whole earth" (Ps. 48:1-2) is given full-blown praise. The city, by several designations, is mentioned seven times. In its Temple God's love is reenacted, and His judgments gratefully accepted. (Ps. 48:11)

PRAYER: *"O Triune God, with heart and voice adoring, Praise we the goodness that doth crown our days; Pray we that now Thou wilt hear us still imploring, Thy love and favor kept to us always."*[1]

THE RIDDANCE OF SIN

Ps. 51:1 *Be gracious to me, O God, in Thy true love; in the fullness of Thy mercy blot out my misdeeds.*

Of this greatest of the seven penitential psalms in the Psalter, one commentator asserts that "Almost every word in this tremendous psalm will ask for our attention. What it has to say is timeless; it is also universal."

David had sinned. It happened one night when he was unable to sleep. Walking out on the palace terrace, David looked over the sleeping city of Jerusalem. Suddenly he became aware of a graceful

---

[1]William C. Doane

young woman on a nearby housetop. Blissfully unaware that she was being watched, the woman filled a basin with water and washed herself. David stood transfixed at her beauty. His passion became uncontrollable, and he sent for Bathsheba. (2 Sam. 11ff)

Later, when David learned that this woman was to bear him a child, he had her husband put to death—just accidentally on purpose!

Then Nathan, the prophet, hearing about all this from secret sources, confronted David with it, and David knew the jig was up. Going into a deep period of mourning and contrition, King David came out with this psalm of penitence.

His first step to newness of life was confession of his sin. He cries, "I acknowledge my transgressions: and my sin is ever before me." (v. 3) Confessing must have been doubly difficult for David, since he had received so many added blessings from God. Then he went and broke at least five of the Ten Commandments. The second step to spiritual renewal was cleansing. David cries, "Purge me with hyssop and I shall be clean; wash me, and I shall be whiter than snow." (v. 7) Hyssop was an aromatic oil which was sprayed on lepers and others with loathsome diseases. And, in using the word *hyssop*, David identifies himself as a moral leper who needs the most potent cleanser available. In the Hebrew there are two meanings for the word *wash*. The first meaning is to wash one's hands. The other meaning, in a modern idiom would be, "soak me in Clorox, and put me through the Laundromat."

The third step David took was to plead for deep-down cleansing. He cries, "Create in me a clean heart, O God, and renew a right spirit within me." (v. 10)

When David did his part, God stepped in to do His part, and complete the job of renewing David's life.

The city of Venice, in Italy, is built on dozens of tiny islands. It is the only city in that world where you see no wheels. All transportation takes place by water. There are waterbuses, water taxis, even funeral barges. Those waterways, like the busy streets of a city, get their share of rubbish. And you are sure that Venice must be the most dangerously polluted city on earth. But one forgets the tide. Twice a day the tide comes in with all the mighty force of the Adriatic Sea behind it, and washes Venice spotlessly clean.

So it was with David's life. God's mighty cleansing power rolled in over David's life, washing away the sins, and freeing David for a new start.

This is what renewal can mean in your life and mine. The promise is to us, "they that wait upon the Lord *shall* renew their strength." (Isa. 40:31)

PRAYER: *"Lord Jesus, I long to be perfectly whole; I want Thee forever to live in my soul, Break down ev'ry idol, cast out ev'ry foe; Now wash me, and I shall be whiter than snow."*[1]

THANKSGIVING DAILY

Ps. 65:1 *We owe thee praise, O god, in Zion; thou hearest prayer, vows shall be paid to thee.*

At first this psalm sounds so prosaic. It is

---

[1] James Nicholson

about two humdrum subjects: gratitude and nature. Nature confronts us everywhere, so what? There are countless reasons for being grateful—ho-hum. But this is precisely why special consideration needs to be given to these matters which are intertwined with our lives, yet taken for granted, with our minds in neutral. As the poet pointedly remarks, when it comes to praising and thanking God, a service He deserves with unbroken frequency, we are always up to our necks in debt. With attention affixed to the material aspects of getting through each day, the unseen spiritual imperatives are put on hold. Hence the pile up of indebtedness—"We owe thee."

Or look at our misdeeds, which "are too heavy for us." (v. 3) Try as we may to get rid of them by ceaseless labor, counseling, cultivating a slick forgettery, or taking long journeys to immerse ourselves in entirely different situations, we are never free from the terrifying knock-knock of a troubled conscience.

The psalmist is right, only God can lift the burden of sin and cast it aside, so that, as they say in the Eskimo language for the word "forgiveness," you can't think about it anymore. (v. 3) Whew! Is that a relief—and another reason to give thanks to the Lifter of heartloads.

Then there's gratitude to be expressed for enjoying the house of the Lord. (v. 4) For it isn't always an enjoyable place. Divisive gossip marks many a congregation, or cockamamie ideas about Jesus, where spiritually diminutive critics climb their sycamore trees from which to view the Master.

To be able to rejoice in the Lord as a fellowship (and again I say rejoice), is a prime reason to give thanks to the Lord. Oh, how indebted we are to Him in the area of Thank-yous.

Come now to Nature, which, disproportionately, is left in the hands of botanists, conservationists, Earth Day devotees, and the John Muirs of the world. When, as Wordsworth keenly observed "one impulse from the vernal wood may teach you more of man, of moral evil and of good than all the sages can."

This psalmist was of the Wordsworth school, or vice versa, for in verse 12 one can almost see and hear Julie Andrews skipping happily in an Alpine setting singing "The hills are alive with the sound of music," a picture beloved the world over for decades. And with what added gratitude, Julie would sing now were her loss of voice restored!

In his land of skimpy rainfall, a dousing shower was something to skip and be thankful about, aware that "back of the loaf is the snowy flour, and back of the flour the mill, and back of the mill is the wheat and the shower and the sun, and the Father's will." Everyone realizes that the year is going to be crowned with God's good gifts (v. 11)—from the family's back yard, to the mass producer of fruits and veggies. Even "the meadows are clothed with sheep" (v. 13) whose tails are so huge with fat that a little trailer was attached to the animal to carry the tail! Then, for a bottom-liner, the psalmist could only conclude by reporting that "they (all the people) shout, they break into song." (v. 13) Let's follow suit.

PRAYER: *For what we are about to receive, Lord, we would be truly thankful, and debt-free. Amen.*

How to Handle This Stress

Ps. 69:17 *I am thy servant, do not hide thy face from me. Make haste to answer me, for I am in distress.*

On learning that Ps. 69 has been traditionally used in Good Friday worship services, and that it has been quoted more often (except for Ps. 22) than any other in the New Testament, we are assured of its affinity with Jesus' cross-laden, tortured trudge to Calvary, and the Savior's closing experiences in Lent.

The psalm gives a vivid description of one who is drowning, and cries "save me." (v. 1) Weighted with a spirit broken by false accusations, the down drag is too much for him. No lifeguards no hope, no family members to the rescue. He hears the bawdy laughter of drunks, and the scoffing of city gossips. "Help!" But, no one does.

Angry and sinking, the abandoned one curses his enemies: May they and their families be made to suffer, may their torments be multiplied, and may they be blotted out of the book of life. There! Take that, and that!

Oh, how this world needed Jesus to show us a better way. Although suffering all the pangs, and more, of this psalmist, see the road to victory that our Lord took—in seven steps:

1. "Father forgive them. (Luke 23:34) During World War II when Belgium was suffering under Nazi dictatorship, a group of Belgian school children knelt at a wayside shrine to say the Lord's Prayer. But when they came to "forgive us our trespasses as we..." they choked up. Their teacher tried to lead them in finishing the prayer, but failed. Suddenly, from behind them came a strong voice concluding the prayer. Looking around, teacher and

children saw that it was their own Emperor, King Albert of Belgium, who had taken upon himself the responsibility of forgiving the enemy. Indeed, that is what Jesus, the King of Kings, did for us on Calvary.

2. "Today shalt thou be with me in Paradise." (Luke 23:43) This fellow to whom Jesus addressed this lovely promise was a fellow sufferer with the Master at Galgotha. In Persian the word "paradise" means a walled garden. And if the Persian King was to bestow a special favor on someone, he would invite this person to walk with him in the palace garden-paradise. What a glowing favor Jesus did for this penitent thief—to walk in the beauties of heaven—that very day! "What wondrous love is this, O my soul...that caused the Lord of bliss to bear the dreadful curse for my soul."

3. "Woman, beloved, thy son!...Behold, thy mother." (John 19:26-27) Disregarding His own agony, Jesus makes provision for His widowed Mother, and for the "beloved disciple" John. What a loving triangle.

4. "My God, my God, why hast Thou forsaken me?" (Matt. 27:46; Mark 15:34) "But His God had not forsaken: He was still beside the Son, Closer He than John or Mary, Arms of love about His own."

5. "I thirst." (John 19:28) "But more than pains which racked Him then, was the deep longing thirst divine that thirsted for the souls of men: Dear Lord! And one was mine"[1]

6. "It is finished." (John 19:30) "Are we still waiting for the end, Expecting Jesus' power to wane? Oh, Master, ages, spread the news that they who wait

---

[1]Cecil Frances Alexander.

shall wait in vain!"[1]

7. "Father, into Thy hands I commend my Spirit." (Luke 23:46) "Everyone who hears these words of mine and does them will be like a wise man who built his house upon the rock." (Matt. 7:24)

PRAYER: *These are beautiful words, wonderful words of life, dear Lord. Help us to live them out, for Thy Names' sake. Amen.*

GOD'S GOLDEN OLDIES

Ps. 71:18 *Now also when I am old and gray-headed, O God, do not forsake me, until I declare Your strength to this generation, Your power to everyone who is to come.*

This is a much-discussed subject in America at the moment—in the health care system. In these financially strapped days the government is looking for ways to save money. And where has their attention finally come to a focused rest than upon care for the elderly. You can't take it out on the younger generation: they are too healthy, go for the old! They are a sure bet. They have had more years on earth than most. Why throw good money at a dying cause, an empty mine? Why pour out non-existent money on expensive pacemakers, amputations, postsurgical care, when the patient's expiration date is just around the corner?

Much depends on which side of the health care dateline you are. Those on the far side have their needs and feelings too. Still in fair health, with creative projects in the works they hope for more time, even if it is borrowed. Those without hands have been known to do drawings with their toes. Lacking feet, they have used their teeth.

---

[1] George Wiseman

There's no way to obstruct a keen motivator on the basis of age. As Noah showed, when you are 600 years old you may be called upon to build a cruise ship! Before "Two By Two" was staged on Broadway, lead actor Danny Kaye had an accident. But he went ahead and played the part of Noah in a wheelchair. And how can one forget Danny singing out, "Oh, to be 90 again!"

Those days lie ahead, accompanied, for many, by the shivers. Who is going to care—give? So help me God, especially, as Tennyson wrote, "Some work of noble note may yet be done."

It is not that our psalmist was unmindful of what we face at the present time. They had their infirmities in Old Testament times too. Listen to the writer of the Book of Ecclesiastes. 12:3-5,7. "The keepers of the house tremble" (shaking legs) "the strong men are bent" (arthritic back and knees). "The grinders are few" (no teeth). "Those who look through the windows are dimmed" (failing eyesight). "The doors on the street are shut" (poor hearing). "All the daughters of song are brought low" (feeble voice). "The almond tree blossoms" (white hair) "and the dust returns to the earth as it was, and the spirit returns to God who gave it."

Ah! There we have it—the Prime Care-Giver, the "God who gave"—is the One who still gives, and will forever give every good gift. In his own way the psalmist was singing the message which Katharina von Schlegel later put into words, to which Sibelius added the music of "Finlandia": "Be still my soul the Lord is on thy side; Bear patiently the cross of grief and pain; Leave to thy God to order and provide; In every change He faithful will remain. Be still my soul: thy best thy heavenly Friend thro' thorny ways leads to a joyful end." Nor does the psalmist wait for God to do all the providing. He himself continues, with rugged determination to declare the power of the heavenly Father to everyone.

PRAYER: *Dear Lord, everyone suffers from that terminal ailment, LIFE. When we are wrinkled with service stripes, we will still look to Thee. Where else shall we go—our Strength and our Redeemer. Amen.*

EYES RIGHT!

Ps. 73:3 *The boasts of sinners roused my envy when I saw how they prosper.*

What a problem, and ever has been according to the number of psalms (17) and treatises devoted to its solution. Logic demands that the practice of uprightness and purity of heart are to be rewarded with prosperity. Sin is to be punished—isn't it! Yet, in the daily grind, the opposite pushes ahead to sour the situation.

This psalmist had the typical experience. Where evildoers should have been going around with their heads bowed with shame and remorse—surprise! They were sleek and sound in limb, suffering no pangs of conscience, "not plunged in trouble as other (righteous) men are," (v. 4-5) and rogues amass great wealth, (v. 12) so, as many have argued, "It ain't no use to do right."

See it in a real-life situation. A young man and woman saw, at first, that transgression in its every form was attractive. Who really wants to be good and clean, anyway? It's against ones grain—isn't it? It's tough going, and it's boring. So these youngsters, fed up with the banality of home life, departed to live as they pleased. They didn't care for conventional clothes or hair-dos or diets. They dressed as wildly as they chose, and ate what they pleased, when they pleased. Refusing to be bored, as they claimed others were, they sailed off into the fantasy world of drugs. The girl started with marijuana, saying "My first high was beautiful, because for a while it made everything seem so simple. Then I had my first acid trip. I was sold on acid real fast. Then I went to speed." Revolting against sexual decency, these young people, still unmarred, indulged.

To the person who is trying to live honestly, whose home life has its arid spots, whose church life is at times prosaic—to such a person, the devil-may-care existence of these young people may be enticing, as it was for our psalmist who confesses that his feet almost slipped, his "foot hold had all but given way." (v. 2) Yet, all that glitters is not gold. Or as another put it: "I wanted the gold and I got it; came out with a fortune last fall. But somehow life's not what I thought it would be, and somehow the gold isn't all."

This young man and woman found, not much later, that the ungodly are like the chaff that the wind driveth away. Detached from home, they placed themselves beyond the reach of provably helpful community agencies. Sloppy about dress, they lowered their standards on other personal matters—like hygiene, and thus proved Napoleon right when he said, "One becomes the man of one's uniform." Eating improperly those young people picked up infections more easily. On drugs—they craved increasing doses, which, by the way, you don't get for nothing. The procurement of these drugs, though starting as incidental, becomes a full-time job very quickly. And who in the wide world can afford that kind of money, every day of the year, year in and year out—who, but those who rob and murder to get the money to buy these drugs?

Our psalmist, believing that his chief good was to be near God (v. 28), was led "into God's sacred courts," and there, he concludes triumphantly, "I saw clearly what their (sinners) end would be." (v. 17)

PRAYER: *Thank You, Lord, for those helps from the sanctuary, and just in time. They give us mini-resurrections along the way. Amen.*

THIS WAY OUT

Ps. 79:1 *The heathen have invaded your domain, God; they have defiled your holy temple and laid Jerusalem in ruins.*

Scholars are unsure of the horrific incident referred to here. Which was it? The invasion by King Nebuchadnezzar of Babylon in 586 B.C., or the earlier invasion by the Pharaoh, King Shishak of Egypt who "carried away the treasures of the house of the Lord and of the King's palace, and seized everything, including the gold shields made for Solomon." (2 Chron. 12:9)

The exact historical event is immaterial, considering the fact that Jerusalem remains as the most invaded and disrupted city in human history. What this psalmist nationally laments is the same cry of humanity in life's calamities. That grabs everyone's attention.

First, there's the psalmist's cry of total despair. Whatever could go wrong, did. Ungodly nasties had laid waste the Holy Land, the Holy Temple, the Holy City. The sky had fallen in. Nothing worse could follow. Yet that was only the physical blown apart.

Second, was the emotional agony. "We suffer the taunts of our neighbors, the gibes and mockery of those about us." (v. 4) And because the Jews believed that they were exempt from suffering, since they were God's chosen, their collapse was met with a gleeful derision by unbelievers. And that was wounding.

Third, was the explosion of pent-up resentments. "Pour out your wrath on nations that do not acknowledge you." (v. 6) Why should we get dumped on? We are the Lord's people. Who does He have to call His own but us? We pray to Him, offering Him our tithes and gifts. Yet it is those who disown Him who are untouched by misfortune. "It ain't fair, I tell you. Level the playing field. Do unto others what has been done to us. Let them have it, sevenfold." (v. 12) Oh how the split-tongued venom spurts out.

Fourth, spent with physical, emotional, spiritual exhaustion there is a remorseful cry for help. Human resources are inadequate. "Let your compassion come swiftly to meet us...Help us, God our Savior." (v. 8-9) Because...

Finally, the Lord is our Shepherd (v. 13), we shall not want. To whom else shall we go? He has the words of eternal life. He leads us all the way, sustaining us in the midst of enemies—until we reign with Him forever. Amen.

Whose personal crackup is not outlined by this psalmist? And does he not provide for our torn-apartness—a balm in Gilead?

PRAYER: *Good Shepherd, with Your leadership we can get through the deepest shadowed valleys. Amen.*

Don't Grudge the Trudge

Ps. 84:5 *Happy the men whose refuge is in thee, whose hearts are set on the pilgrim ways!*

Here is another Bible Beatitude. Those who walk in pilgrim ways are the happy ones.

But how can that be? Trudging the pilgrim way, or motoring, sailing, flying is no picnic. It takes planning, money, time, hardships, patience, commitment, discipline, an ordered devotional life. Any one of these can be a grim pill for the pilgrim to swallow.

Look at the major religions and note the solemnity in their history of pilgrimage.

The Hindus probably have the longest experience with their ever-present River Ganges (Mother Gunga). To reach her sacred waters the faithful first go flat on their faces. Then, length by body length, they inch along for miles. Reaching the holy water they bathe in it, drink it, take lotas (brass containers) of it to purify their homes.

The Jews made Jerusalem their goal. Hadn't it been chosen for them by God? It became especially desirous when the Temple was built there as God's dwelling place. And having been scattered because of wars and persecutions, Hebrews were drawn to the center of worship from the ends of the earth.

After Christ's coming, the Christians entered the pilgrimage routes, not only to Jerusalem, but also to the many places touched by the Lord's blessed presence.

Then came Islam with its chief sanctuary in Mecca, birthplace of Muhammad. With every Muslim on earth hoping to make one hajj or pilgrimage to the

Black Stone (which is believed to have been given by Gabriel to Abraham, and which is placed at a convenient height where it is kissed) in a lifetime. They center on Mecca in the largest and best-organized pilgrim program in the world.

It is serious business in all religions, and gives us pause, as Lou Werner has ably put it to "question our own absolute assumptions about the fault-lines of religious conflict."[1]

But our textual Beatitude is right about the happy results of a pilgrimage. For the way of the pilgrim is not just taking a trip to the Holy Land, which may never materialize. There is built into the human make-up a migratory urge granted also to the animal kingdom. It takes us to different climes at different times for varying purposes. So the goal must be set, and the homing instinct tuned in. For, after all, life is pilgrimage. The daily drudge in the home, school, office, church, is a part of it, which, as in every pilgrimage brings the promised happiness. There's the joy of coming to Jesus in Spirit and in truth, and not just to walk where Jesus walked 2,000 years ago—getting sidetracked by donkeys, camels, and the tantalizingly delightful whiffs of shish kebob. Rather, the daily round, the common task is guided and energized by our traveling companion, Jesus, who said, "Lo, I am with you always."

In a poem, William Blake talks of building "Jerusalem in England's green and pleasant land." Indeed, our pilgrimage is right where we are pressing toward the mark of the high calling of God in

---

[1] *Saudi Aramco World* Sept.-Oct. 2009, p. 42

Christ Jesus." Happy day!

PRAYER: *Lord, with Isaac Watts we sing: "Come, we that love the Lord, and let our joys be known, join in a song with sweet accord, and thus surround the throne. We're marching to Zion...the beautiful City of God." Amen.*

OUR WORLD'S CAPITAL

Ps. 87:7 *Singers and dancers alike say, "All my springs are in you."*

Yesterday in Ps. 84 we saw that Jerusalem is the focal point of life's journey, here and hereafter (in the New Jerusalem). Psalm 87 makes the conclusive statement that the Holy City is also the world's central city, the axis on which a peaceful world turns. It affirms that all people, even the wicked ones, and former enemies and conquerors of God's people will all be considered citizens of God's specially chosen city (v. 4-6), in the Creator's eyes all were born there. And for another valid reason, all our springs are in Jerusalem. (v. 7) What could that mean?

Well, what are springs? Do they not start as a gift of ground water that is pure? As with a newborn child. Which is why Jesus saw that unless we become as pure as innocent infants we cannot enter the Kingdom of heaven. Pure spring water is a life-rejuvenator, as purity of heart makes for righteousness, which must be sought first if we are to get anything else of worth in life. (Matt. 6:33)

But a spring has other purposes, so it trickles along looking for its own water-level. Other springs doing likewise find each other along the way and become a stream. Those "still waters" are soul restorers. (Ps. 23:2-3) In continuing action, streams, like springs, are tributaries to other running waters that change their names to rivers. Now whole cities have all their water needs fulfilled. Unembraced by land, which would otherwise form a lake, rivers empty their contents into the sea, the ocean, enabling the global community to have a ready food supply and a way to be in touch.

Nor does the sea world remain static. Unwilling to be a Dead Sea, it submits to the uplifting power of temperature, which moves the moisture back over the land to descend in showers of blessing—starting the circular process over again and again. In other words, it keeps the world going. That is how our psalmist saw Jerusalem in operation. The whole life-system begins at its core—in Jerusalem.

And again, why? Because the Lord of life is the Divine operator. Seeing that the world population could not fit into Jerusalem, the Lord made His favorite city into the prototype for making the place where we live well in God's sight. The place doesn't have to be green and pleasant. The Lord makes the pleasantry, not the land, or anyone else.

Knowing also the inability of the United Nations organization to keep the sparring peoples of the world together, God, who so loves the world, sent His only begotten Son to show how it can be done. If Mahatma Gandhi, a Hindu (who lived by Christian principles), could, through a civil disobedience campaign and nonviolent noncooperation, bring the powerful British Empire to its knees, are we to suppose that Jesus cannot do better? Said He: "Peace is my parting gift to you, my own peace, such as the world (the U.N.'s and the Gandhi's) cannot give. Set your troubled hearts at rest, and banish your fears." (John 14:27)

PRAYER: *Gracious heavenly Father, we "see the*

streams of living waters, springing from eternal Love, Well supply thy sons and daughters And all fear of want remove; Who can faint while such a river ever flows their thirst to assuage? Grace which like the Lord, the giver, Never fails from age to age."[1]

THE ONE AND ONLY GOD

Ps. 99:1 *The Lord is King.*

But this kind of King, introduced by an enthronement hallelujah, is different. Seated on the ark, his throne, He takes His exclusively exalted position in the Holy of holies. He is the King of Kings and Lord of Lords.

Which is unnerving and disturbing for humans. (v. 1) They cannot cope with such overall greatness. Earth quivers at this incomprehensible power (v. 1), when we learn that God has the ability to do with power all that power can do, especially when this superhuman power is a combination of justice, equity, righteousness, answers to calls for help, and forgiveness of sins. (v. 4-8)

Instead of giving three cheers, at this point the Psalmist's raise in praise ascends to a threefold gloria, Holy (v. 4), Holy (v. 5), Holy (v. 9). And since Zion (Jerusalem is the greatest of cities—see Ps. 87), here is One who is even greater than Zion. Also as the Temple made Zion great, Jesus was acknowledged to be greater than the Temple. (Matt. 12:6) Here, then, is the triple holy Trinity which stands above and beyond all else—the ultimate ultimacy of our God.

What a necessary belief this has to be, finally. Otherwise we get distracted and distraught by the al-

---

[1] John Newton

leged power of man's intellectualism, or the frighteningly massive powers in the operations of the universe, or the awesomeness of the gods of other people.

To know and believe in an all-powerful God is the only resting place anyone can have.

Without such a Standard of reference, earth's humanity, though patting itself on the back for all its civilized advancements, is not the duck it might have been. It refuses to admit that it's still dabbling around in the barnyard muck of a despoiled Eden, beguiled by the split-tongued "serpents" that put us in two minds about the Creator-God who placed us in this world for purposes closer to His will than we could ever think or hope for.

It is when we "exalt the Lord our God" (v. 9) that we can enjoy the Edenic bounties. He has long stored up for us.

To be sure, we earthlings still strive to define God in terms of our own liking, questioning His Omnipotence, Omniscience, Omnipresence. Others do better as Luther with his: "A Mighty fortress is our God." Or Charles Wesley's "O for a thousand tongues to sing my great Redeemer's praise." Or Matthew Bridges' "Crown him with many crowns...and hail him as thy matchless King through all eternity." Or Walter Smith's "Immortal, invisible God only wise in light inaccessible hid from our eyes, Most blessed, most glorious, the Ancient of Days, Almighty, victorious, Thy great Name we praise."

Let us therefore rejoice and believe in our trice Holy Triune God. And, since Jesus is all the God we need, why worry. We know who He is.

PRAYER: *Heavenly Father, we, too, have found, with*

this prophetic psalmist, that there is no one superior to You. There we rest our faith both now and ever. Amen.

HOW TO RENEW A NATION

Ps. 101:1 *I will sing of loyalty and of justice; to thee, O Lord, I will sing.*

And why shouldn't he sing? This is David speaking; the Sweet Singer of Israel, harpist, composer, vocalist.

King David doesn't expect his subjects to do what he fails to do. Rather, he hopes that they will follow his example so he sets high standards for himself, using the personal "I" thirteen times in the eight verses that make up this psalm.

At appropriate festivals both King and countrymen would sing this song, knowing that regular repetition of their pledge to live ordered, Godly lives was necessary in a world where Kaleidoscopic changes take place every day.

Nor was David's moral agenda for governmental use only. This one-size-fits-all plan was for all community life—from city to village to home to the individual.

Accordingly, the psalm leaves one feeling like that deer that was panting for water. (Ps. 42:1-2) We cry: "How long, O Lord, must we wait for this kind of Davidic moral leadership in the residence of the nation's appointed head person, in the halls of Justice, in the fractured and abused ethical principles of the country's infrastructure, the bastardizing of marriage vows, and the citizen's unfamiliarity with God's will for their lives?" Oh, that his psalm might be a Sinaitic Proclamation for this and every age.

It is not because David had a treasure chest of

high ideals left him by the prophets and we have none. There is evidence that David opened that safety deposit box of morality to learn of mercy from Hosea; justice from Amos; truth from Isaiah; help from Proverbs, Noah, Enoch, Micah.

The fact is that we have those same riches and a lot more in our Holy Bible. The trouble with us, from the top down, is that we had good schools, but disinterested students; good homes, but prodigal children who prefer life among the hog pens; a Savior who offers help to persons who shun Him. Thanks, but no thanks.

David couldn't help but see this kind of dissension among his own people and how untamed human nature slinks in the bushes until it hears the Voice of Authority calling, "Adam, where are you?" (Gen. 3:9)

Wisely, then, David started to get his own life in order, pledging his personal allegiance to a life acceptable in God's sight, the One who is Perfect and against whose perfection all goodness must be gauged. Any other standard is an inadequate rubberized measuring tape, and a joke.

Having set his own life and house in order, this noble monarch of a psalmist now moves with confidence to ensure his nation that their joining him in building morally sturdy lives, the capital city of Jerusalem will be cleansed (v. 8), and will spread its holiness countrywide and beyond. Here, come to think of it, is a heaven-approved blueprint for the reformation of any nation.

PRAYER: *Forerunner of the Universe: We would not wait for others to set the pace for bringing about a reformed nation. Begin with us, Lord, as we take our cues from You. Amen.*

OUR FOUNDATION LAYER (V. 25)

Ps. 102:17 *He turns to hear the prayer of the destitute and does not scorn them when they pray.*

The author of this cry for help is in exile in Babylon. Far from home (Jerusalem), he feels equally far from God whose residence is in the Holy of Holies in the Holy City. Adding to his aloneness, the author is disquieted by his intestinal ailment, which is terminal. Equally depressing, if not worse, was the emotional battering from enemies and, unbelievably, from God, who this accuser feels has thrown him under a bus.

Having learned from brave souls before him, this psalmist believes that as God was about to reconstruct a destroyed Jerusalem, so He could do with the writer's emaciated life. After all, this caller upon God was still young, still desiring to be of service in God's Kingdom on earth, as Jesus was at that age in His early thirties. Why a cross just when you are beginning to hit your stride? It's a god-forsaking experience, as Jesus found.

Why, then, a cross, not just for this psalmist and the crucified Christ, but also for every person born on this planet to have an earthly life that is cross-shaped?

See how slowly the light of understanding dawns upon this seeming mystery, where the mist is lifted from the mystery.

First, there is the stark, general announcement of our creation: "God created human beings in his own image...God blessed them and said to them: 'Be fruitful and increase, fill the earth and subdue it...'" (Gen. 1:27-28)

Later, in Ps. 139, an insightful person probes the birth process how we are "fearfully and wonderfully made." "Knitted together" in mother's womb. (v. 13-14)

Then the Apostle John, in introducing Jesus to the world, slips in the astounding fact that the Lord was present at and part of the Creative procedure. "He was with God at the beginning, and through Him all things came to be; without Him no created thing came into being." (John 1:2-3)

With increasing light being thrown on this subject, St. Paul, in his letter to the Colossians, included words, which at the time had nothing to do with medical research (unless Luke, the physician, suggested this idea to Paul somewhere in their missionary journeyings): Christ "exists before all things, and all things are held together (adhere, cohere) in Him." (Col. 1:17)

Now, with all the minute medical research that has been done, we find that we humans are held together by laminin—cell adhesion molecules, which, as their definition says "are a family of proteins that are an integral part of the structural scaffolding of basement membranes in almost every animal tissue."

Then came the shocker. Photographed, these basic cohesive cells that literally keep our bodies together are in the form of a +. Which is to say that at the creation of the world, the cross was, by divine wisdom, inserted at the core of our physical being. The cross purpose of life is to help us fulfill what we were made for: held together and thus enabled to overcome the intense hardships of human existence. It is conceivable that this psalmist did recover. His intestinal fault was replaced with intestinal fortitude allowing him to write this therapeutic song and prayer.

Sensing such connectives, Sir John Frederic Herschel wrote (before the discovery and photographing of laminin): "All human discoveries seem to be made only for the purpose of confirming more and more strongly the truths that come from on high and are contained in the sacred writings."

PRAYER: *"For the love which from our birth over and around us lies; Lord of all, to thee we raise this our hymn of grateful praise."*[1] *Amen.*

VIRTUOUS UNBELIEVERS?

Ps. 119:25 *My soul cleaves to the dust; revive me according to thy word.*

At one time this psalm was supposed to bring the Psalter to a close, even as Psalm One was designed to be just the right opener for this longest chapter in the longest book in the Bible. It would have been a spectacular finish with Ps. 119 in the form of an acrostic, beginning each paragraph with a letter of the twenty-two-letter Hebrew alphabet. Each paragraph, with eight lines, has given this psalm "a well crafted balance of 176 verses, mostly summarizing all the previous psalms which tell of God's love and law."

The author of this unusual psalm was a young man, well-educated in Jerusalem, moving in high-end financial and political circles who had found that the playboy mentality leaves one moaning: "I wanted the gold and I got it, came out with a fortune last fall. But somehow life's not what I thought it, and somehow the gold isn't all."

So this author-scholar outlines for himself a course of study and devotion that will develop his

---

[1] F. S. Pierpoint

life blamelessly, for this is the only kind of life that is well-pleasing to the Lord. Accordingly, this student of God's Word repeats the Lord's commandments, statutes, decrees—seven times a day.

With all this emphasis on the psalmist's love of the Lord, it is quickly noticeable that every time the psalmist thrills and chills and fills with emotion about his divine Instructor, he looks over his shoulder at what the evildoers are up to, and maligns them mercilessly.

This would not have drawn any attention had it been done occasionally. But the constant comparison between the psalmist's excitement about God and His word and the stink of malicious men, is attention-getting, and raises the question: On which side are his affections, really? Is he secretly wishing to do the things for which he is condemning others? Repeated several times it makes the psalmist look as if he is cheering, not for the dull saints but for the exciting sinners!

Perhaps this is why thirty-one more psalms were added on after this moral balancing act of Ps. 119. How wonderful to close with that jubilant Ps. 150!

The lesson of Ps. 119, then, is to watch the soul that cleaves to the dust. We cannot serve two masters. We must despise one and love the other. Leave the dust, and cleave to the Lord and His word. We have to be harder on ourselves than this psalmist seems to have been in slamming shut his personal preference for passionate pleasures.

In the very last verse the picture becomes clear, as the truth of the matter emerges. The psalmist admits that he has forgotten the commandments. Why should he—saying them seven times a day. But they hadn't reached his heart, for "I have strayed like a lost sheep; come, search for thy servant."

We can be more than conquerors through Him who loves us and gave Himself for us.

PRAYER: *Merciful Lord, save us from being two-faced fence-sitters, "definite" and "maybe" never coming to a knowledge of the truth. We would be Thine, and thine alone, now and ever. Amen.*

THE CHURCH EXEMPLAR

Ps. 122:3 *Jerusalem that is built to be a city where people come together in entity.*

Following the ancient liturgical use of this Psalm, the General Assembly of the Church of Scotland, in its closing session, sings this psalm. Then the members return to their local churches across the United Kingdom. What makes this Psalm so fitting for the early (before Christ) worshippers of God, and the modern?

First, because the house of the Lord, the worship center, the church, is a place for rejoicing.

To many persons the church means just the opposite of being upbeat. For them it's downbeat, grim, boring. Real happiness, it is maintained, is to be found in a dance hall, a bar room, a nudist colony. There the rulebook is thrown into the fireplace, and you do as you please. The aftermath of such orgiastic hooplas, the uneasy conscience, the soiled relationships with others, go unmendable. To say nothing of the financial strain.

To be sure, the church's joy lies not in gossip or a garage sale, but in the bliss in knowing the good news of God, the giver of every good and perfect gift. Among such church-bred believers, one finds the most dependable persons in the land. They have been through the valley of the shadow, and can testify to the victory gained from their divine traveling companion.

Second, because of the unity of the worshipping fellowship with thousands of splintered groups calling themselves Old or New Testament followers of the Lord, where is the unity, one may ask. Yet it is remarkable how the Hebrew-Christian union, unlikely partners at times, complement each other and stand together in stormy times, since, basically, we are one in the Spirit and one in the Lord—an amiable co-existence.

Third, justice is enthroned. Outside the religious community courtroom, proceedings are sadly influenced by politics and high finance. For example, there are "celebrity lawyers," who take cases where much publicity and remuneration are involved, whether they win or lose. The very circumstances determine that the kind of justice meted out will be unfair, unbalanced, untruthful, with twisting of facts to suit the wealthier of the clients. The Lords' people, on the other hand, strive to be just for truth's sake—knowing that God is watching, and is the ultimate Judge.

Fourth, Peace plays a central role among God's people. The word "Peace" is mentioned three times in this psalm, and peace is further buttressed by the use of the word "Jerusalem" three times—where the "salem" or shalom, has a fourfold meaning:

i. This "peace" is more than just a greeting.

Throughout the Bible it means tranquility, which comes from a right relationship with God, through our Lord Jesus Christ. (Rom. 5:1)

ii. Security. Verse 7 says there will be peace in towers, ramparts, battlements, and all those places made for war. To have those shut down and used for peaceful purposes gives a city another protective coat of security.

iii. Prosperity is conventionally thought of in terms of all that money can buy. But this psalmist suggests a more achievable prosperity, for more people forever—even in palaces peace, which moth and rust do not corrupt, and for which thieves do not break in and steal.

iv. Verse 8 says, "Peace be within you." That peace, which the world cannot give nor take away, is a gift from the Lord of life. "My peace I give unto you." (John 14:27)

PRAYER: *Thank You, Lord, for Your church: its joy, and unity, justice and peace, which passes all understanding and misunderstanding. Amen.*

A PILGRIM'S PEACE PRAYER

Ps. 122:6 *Pray for the peace of Jerusalem: May those who love you prosper.*

Since pilgrims had to slog up the 2,300-foot ascent to Jerusalem, this is called a song of the ascents. It was also an ascending spiritual experience, as worshippers lifted their hands, hearts, voices, songs, prayers, aspirations to God in worship.

This particular pilgrim was happy to be invited to make this ascending journey. (v. 1) And in the next verse, he can hardly believe that he has arrived at the desired haven, because, as one historical reporter states, such pilgrimages "required far more than booking a flight through a travel agent. It was an extraordinarily long and difficult marathon across often-unforgiving terrain, and an individual's travel could take years or even decades if he had to stop en route to work and save before setting out again. The land routes were often littered with the remains of caravans ravaged by raiding tribes, stricken by disease, short of water or just plain lost, and every seafaring pilgrim knew that the sea had swallowed many a boat. The risks often taxed pilgrims to their limits, but this did little to inhibit the remarkably steady flow [of pilgrims]. It outlasted empires and persisted through war, famines, and plagues."[1]

Looking around at the city about which he had heard so much while traveling, our pilgrim's first impression is that Jerusalem is compact—no wasted space, and it is solid, giving the feeling of all being well and secure. Now, relaxed and confident, the pilgrim can get on with the whole purpose for his coming.

The festival lasted seven days, and the city was organized and prepared to serve every need of a tidal wave of visitors. There were markets for buying (and selling), entertainment centers, courtrooms for settling legal matters, and, mainly, the Temple. That's where the various kinds of sacrifices were offered, and where worship services were held. It was at public worship and private that the pilgrim prayed along with brothers and friends (v. 8), for the peace and prosperity of this dear city that had come to mean so much to so many. Here, it pleased the Lord to bless His peo-

---

[1] *Saudi Aramco World*, Jan./Feb. 2004, p. 4

ple, His Temple, His city, this Promising Land, making it a pattern to be reproduced wherever His committed followers have the will, and a pilgrim's determination. And we can. At a Christmas Eve service in Bethlehem's Church of the Nativity, we heard the bishop of Jerusalem say: "Here is where the Prince of Peace and the principle of peace was born." He can be born in us today.

PRAYER: *Lord of all being, help us to actualize our prayers for peace, that our town, too, may be called Shalom (Salem) a place of peace. Amen.*

MOUNTAINOUS SECURITY

Ps. 125:2 *As the mountains surround Jerusalem, so the Lord surrounds His people.*

In this another song of the ascents, the pilgrim is in awe of Mt. Zion, where most of the festival activities are taking place. The mountain's dimensions, its pleasing configuration, its eternal quality, well describe the person who trusts in the Lord. (v. 1)

Then, letting his eyes rove across the landscape, the pilgrim notes that the city is enveloped by mountains, in the same way that the Lord throws His loving arms about His chosen people, keeping them close to His heart.

There was Mt. Moriah, where Abraham was about to sacrifice his son; where Araunah had his threshing floor, and where Solomon built his Temple. Moriah, then, was a reminder of superlative human faith, and a faith honoring a god to be worshipped.

To the east, the pilgrim would see the Mt. of Olives, with its northern most peak, Mt. Scopus, towering over the entire area at 2,900 feet. The word Scopus, in fact, means range of outlook. It also gives us words like microscope, telescope, periscope, and all those other scopes which help one to view the whole range of earth.

Another peak along the two and a half mile ridge of Olivet, is the Mount of Ointment, as the Talmud calls it, or the Healing Mountain. The reference is to the healing ointment which was made out of olive oil—from the abundant olive groves which gave the mountain its name.

The southernmost peak on the Olivet range was the Mount of Offence. In Hebrew, the words for "destroyer" and "oil," that is, olive oil, are much the same. And in the Old Testament, when the writer mentions the Mount of Olives, instead of using the meaning of the Mount of healing olive oil, the writer uses the other meaning. He calls it the Mount of the Destroyer. Why? Because, as we have already learned in 1 Kings 11:1-13, many of King Solomon's wives were pagan. For them he built pagan shrines on the southern tip of the Mount of Olives. Later, when King Josiah tore down those impious shrines, that peak was given the shameful name of the Mount of Offence, the Mount of Corruption, the Mount of Evil Counsel, the Mount of Scandal. Take your pick. Each is as smelly as the other.

Indeed, the Lord surrounds His people as the mountains surround Jerusalem. He makes His beloved as awe—inspiring as Mt. Zion. He honors their faith while granting them worshipping privileges as at Mt. Moriah. He gives them healing and wholeness as from the Mount of Ointment. He shields them from the Destroyer of their souls. "So the Lord surrounds his people both now and evermore." (v. 2)

PRAYER: *What more could we ask for, Lord, than to be encircled by, and held closely within Your arms? Amen.*

Miracles in Moments

Ps. 126:4 *Turn once again our fortune, Lord.*

Exiled Hebrews in Babylon were remembering how they were freed, overnight, without a fight.

Such a triumph seemed impossible considering Babylon's titanic world power. Yet, like another Titanic about which it was unthinkable to be sinkable, Babylon crashed.

There was no way to get in over the walls. But Cyrus sharply noticed that the River Euphrates flowed under the walls and through the city. Directing his engineers (helped by two Babylonian deserters) to divert the river, a dry riverbed provided a way for troop entry under the walls.

Meanwhile, on the inside, King Belshazzar of Babylon, cocksure that his "Queen of Cities" was impenetrable, threw a banquet for his government officials—with plenty of flirting with females and booze.

Cyrus, (the Persian invader) with information from undercover agents, saw his window of opportunity and invaded. King Belshazzar was slain, and the mighty Babylonian empire was toppled.

The new Persian overlords were generous with their Hebrew exiles, granting them freedom to return to Jerusalem.

What a dream come true. What a turn of events. The exiles were beside themselves with rapture. Their cup overflowed with excited laughter. They did crazy things as we witnessed after World War II. There had been hopeful songs about four-leafed clover on the white Cliffs of Dover, and how the lights would come on again all over the world. Then, suddenly, it happened. O Joy!

Remembering, but now needing another such turn of events, the Hebrews pleaded with the Lord.

Commentators have also called this a New Year's supplication rather than a list of resolutions that evaporate with the dawn, and a yawn, in another year that is about to duplicate the previous one. Instead, give the Lord His turn to make all things new, as only He can do. (Rev. 21:5) As He did for St. Paul on the Damascus road. Paul's virulent violence (Acts 9:1-2), in three short days, was turned into visible virtues.

When Jonah took ship for distant Tarshish, trying to escape from the Lord's assignment for him in Nineveh, God turned Jonah around. He was swallowed by a whale, which saved him from being run through by a swordfish or whipped by a stingray. Politely the whale disgorged Jonah on the beach from which he had sought to flee from the Lord.

And how the Lord can resurrect. The Prodigal son's father learned that. With tears of joy he blubbered: "This my son was dead, and is alive again." Tears not only clear the eyes, but through divine alchemy can also make us deliriously happy. Or as Henry Ward Beecher explained, "God washes the eyes by tears until they can behold the invisible land where tears shall come no more."

In St. Paul's Cathedral, London, John Wesley heard the choirboys sing Ps. 130, "Out of the depths have I cried unto Thee, O Lord." It echoed the cry for help in Wesley's own soul. That night at a meeting on Aldersgate Street, Wesley's heart was strangely warmed, and an international date line was drawn through his life.

PRAYER: *More than anything, Lord, turn us in Your direction, for it is to You we belong. Amen.*

REST IN HIM

Ps. 132:14 *This is my resting place for ever; here will I make my home, for such is my desire.*

Two points are made in these 18 verses: a Person and a Place. When God whispered His desire to dwell among His people on earth (2 Sam. 7:5-6), those who had learned how to turn up the volume heard God's request loud and clear. And the one who was in the best position to make the choice of a Place that received God's amen, was King David. (Ps. 132:1-5) No paragon of perfection endued with all the weaknesses of mortal man, he nevertheless struggled his way into the affectionate embrace of his Lord—which is why he was chosen as a progenitor of "David's Greater Son"—Jesus. Having found a Person whose future was assured all the way to eternity, the second point could be attained, namely, where should the Lord be headquartered?

What an assignment in a world 25,000 miles in circumference and from pole to pole, and in a time of limited travel facilities. With a better vantage point than the first moon walkers had of earth, God pinpointed His first and only choice: Jerusalem.

Prior to the building of the Lord's first dwelling place on earth (Solomon's Temple), the Lord had been His people's traveling companion, the Ark of the Covenant was His dwelling. A small box made of acacia wood (the only lumber to be found in the Sinai wilderness) held the original tablets of the ten Commandments, a pot of manna, and the first five books of the Bible—the Pentateuch—written by Moses. On top was a diminutive throne between two Cherubim. The Ark held the Presence of God until it was taken by Israel's enemies. Won back after twenty-one years it was taken with pomp and ceremony to become the Holy City's Centerpiece. When Solomon built the Temple, the Ark was placed in the Holy of holies. Yet the Temple was not to last. Destroyed by enemy action it was rebuilt by Zerubbabel. Torn apart again, it was rebuilt by Herod the Great. Flattened by the Romans, it has never been rebuilt and may never be again.

What then has this Psalm to say about the Person therein, and the Place?

Jesus, David's greater Son, remains as God's Presence. "I am with you always." Also, fully confident that His Great Commission to take the good news into all the world would be obeyed, the Place of God's abode would be adapted to changing conditions. Referring to His body, Jesus said, "Destroy this temple and in three days I will raise it up again." (John 2:19) Paul took the temple adaptation even further. "Do you not know that your body is a temple of the indwelling Holy Spirit?" (1 Cor. 6:19) With templed lives and homes we can do without a Temple building if we have to, as people have had to when they were exiled, dispersed (diaspora) or when enemy activists have demolished houses of worship, replacing them with housing developments, schools, restaurants, or brothels.

No, the promise of the continuing Presence

and Place is unending, regardless of wild world changes. The ingenious human mind, aided by the unsleeping efforts of the Creator of the Universe, finds ever-new strategies of spiritual survival. The writer of Ps. 132 anticipated and outlined operational Procedures for God's people, until times end. Rejoice!

PRAYER: *All-knowing Creator: In times of puzzling change we rest back confidently on Your trustworthiness. Now and ever. Amen.*

WHEN WE HANG UP OUR LYRES

Ps. 137:4 *How could we sing the Lord's song in a foreign land?*

The Babylonian super-power had captured Jerusalem, taking many of the Hebrew people captive back to Babylon. Then these prisoners were asked, they felt insultingly, to sing and play some of the songs of Zion for which they were well-known. How could these brokenhearted, defeated people oblige? Instead they chose to hang up their musical instruments on the weeping willows and weep and curse their captors, making this psalm the only example of its kind in the entire Book of Psalms. But why couldn't they have obliged? They had much for which to be grateful. Should they sing only when conditions were perfect? Did they realize how much blessing they could bring to their conquerors by returning good for evil, and how much damage they could do to themselves, to others, to their cause (their religion), by pouting and withholding goodwill?

They had a chance to spread their musical message far beyond the limited confines of Jerusalem and its Temple. What an opportunity those

Hebrew musicians had to captivate and convert their captors. Bishop Berggrav did that when he was imprisoned by the Nazis. The military authorities couldn't change the Bishop's guard quickly enough to keep up with the rapidity with which the Bishop converted those guards to Christ.

But it was not so with those Hebrew Exiles. Muting their good works, they hurt themselves and their potential converts. They didn't give an attractive account of their own religious faith. How different it was with that Man who hung on a cross, asking forgiveness for those who did Him in. You would want to embrace that man's faith. Or Ada Lee's faith. After losing six of her children in the Darjeeling landslide disaster, Mrs. Lee inscribed these words on their gravestone: "Thanks be to God who giveth us the victory through our Lord Jesus Christ." Who is not magnetized by a faith like that which sings despite disaster?

Listen to Rupert Brooke, upbeat in the midst of a World War: "Now God be thanked who matched us with this hour." Or Albert Schweitzer in Africa: "What do all the disagreeable features (the meagerness of food, the exilic living conditions, the unhygienic setting for hospital) count for—compared with the joy of being here, working and helping."

When Martin Luther and Philipp Melanchthon were depressed, Luther said, "Come now, Philipp, let us sing the forty-sixth psalm. 'God is our refuge and strength, a very present help in trouble.'" These pilgrims, caught in numberless strange situations, have expected their faith to sing—and it has from the depths of their hearts. Their hallelujahs have helped them to become stronger, have encouraged others, and have made disciples for their Lord and Master.

In spite of the most compelling arguments to the contrary, there stands Saint Paul's authoritative communication, Brethren "Rejoice always...give thanks in all circumstances, for this is the will of God in Christ Jesus for you." (1 Thess. 5:16-18)

In more than one language "think" and "thank" are closely related. And if, as Cicero remarked, gratitude "is not only the greatest of all virtues but also the parent of all others," we can make what otherwise might have been life's Via Dolorosa into a Via Gloriosa.

PRAYER: *Merciful, Lord: We know how easy it is to slap the hands of our ancient brethren. Forgive us, and help us to be at our best in the worst of times. Amen.*

THE MUSIC OF THE SPHERES

Ps. 150:1 *O praise God in his holy place.*

We come at length to the bookend that holds the one and a half hundred psalms together. They make up the best-loved book in the Old Testament. Out of the 283 quotes from the Old Testament to be found in the New Testament, 116 are from Psalms. How right on target the one is who wrote: "To open the Book of Psalms is to open the door into the worship of all believers in all countries of the world in all centuries from 1000 B.C. till the present time."

The last editor of the Psalter, Ezra, made a wise choice in using Ps. 150, a musical extravaganza as the finale. It is in keeping with the interests and creations of the major contributor to the Book of Psalms—David.

Worship, accompanied by music, both vocal

and instrumental, was initiated by David, which continued (1,000 years) in essentially the same form until the time of Christ.

David wrote the words of seventy-three songs (psalms), and composed the music. He invented musical instruments, formed choirs and orchestras, and made Temple choir singing a paid profession. For the entry of the Ark into Jerusalem, David pulled out all the stops—orchestrating the entire occasion with soldiery, flower girls, dancers, singers, and instrumentalists. He, himself, danced in the streets, leaping and whirling with abandon—to the embarrassment of his wife (King Saul's daughter) Michal. (2 Sam. 6:16)

Psalms 146-150 are called Hallelujah psalms, since they begin and end with "Hallelujah," which means "Praise the Lord." Psalm 150 has twelve hallelujahs, well numbered to fit in with the twelve tribes of Israel and later with Christ's twelve apostles. The total message is for worshippers to Praise the Lord for the whole Word of God, the Bible, both Old and New Testaments. This enhancement of the Book of Psalms added to its original importance when the several separate collections of psalms were put together in the third century B.C., in five books: Ps. 1-41, 42-72, 73-89, 90-106, 107-150. These five were set beside the first five books of the Bible (the Pentateuch), which had been written by Moses. The five books of the Psalms became a sort of second Pentateuch, and in time, have come to be better known and more quoted than Moses' five books.

In Ps. 150, the Psalmist answers our questions.

1. Where is God to be praised? (v. 1)
2. Why is God to be praised? (v. 2)
3. How is God to be praised? (v. 3-5) Musical instruments mentioned in the Bible are lyre, flute, tambourine, bell, shofar (ram's horn), trumpet, harp, psaltery, oboe, rattle, cymbals. Of these, Ps. 150:3-5 name trumpet, harps, lyres, drum, stringed instruments, flute, clanging cymbals, clear cymbals.
4. Who are to praise the Lord? (v. 6)
The final half line, "Praise ye the Lord," is a doxology ("Praise God from whom all blessings flow"), which was inserted by the last editor.

What a rich assortment of songs we have here, covering most of our human needs for any era in history. There are National psalms, prayers for individuals in times of need, thanksgiving psalms. You name the need. The remedy is here. Praise God.

PRAYER: *Gracious conductor of universal harmony, we praise You for giving these psalmists messages to keep Your people going through all of life's emotional discords. Enable us to pass on the good news, through Christ our Lord. Amen.*

JOY IN THE LORD

Eccles. 2:7 *I acquired male and female slaves, and I had my home-born slaves as well; I owned possessions, more flocks and herds than any of my predecessors in Jerusalem.*

Those who disclaim the traditional view that Solomon wrote the Book of Ecclesiastes are hard put to then explain who uttered such a statement that only Solomon could rightfully make. Now was he bragging, though this was but one item in a catalog of claims?

In truth, he was conducting a test to see if

pleasure was really what made his, and everyone else's, world go round. Isn't this what all humans commonly believe?

So the experimenter lists every sort of pleasure for which human passion yearns and burns. Laughter was engaged in, and wine—although he didn't become a slobbering drunk. He kept a tight rein on his indulgence. "My mind was guided by wisdom, not blinded by folly." (v. 3) Then he tried great works, building houses, planting vineyards, gardens, parks, fruit-trees, irrigation systems. Then, as above, he had slaves, possessions (palaces—not mentioned here, but elsewhere). Consulting the history books he found that he had set a record in the number of livestock that he owned. He amassed silver and gold, singers of both sexes, "and all that man delights in." (v. 8) Nothing that titillated the senses was overlooked. "Whatever my eyes coveted, I refused them nothing." (v. 10) And, oh, yes, there was sex—with 700 wives and 300 concubines. What other alleged bringers of satisfaction could there possibly be under the sun? This man had drained the ocean dry.

And what was his verdict? Had he proved to himself, and for all others, for all time, that this is what life is all about? And nobody else has been in quite the same position to try such a full-scale experiment. The flesh appeasers of our time are chump change compared with this sensual seeker of Solomonic proportions.

His conclusion—almost foregone—was, "I saw that everything was emptiness and chasing the wind, of no profit under the sun." (v. 11)

But that's too negative. Nobody can live with that, and neither could Solomon. He keeps the best for the last: "Fear God and obey His commandments; this sums up the duty of mankind." (12:13)

Patiently the Lord has been watching our wanderings in the far country, waiting for our return home to Him. In Him we live and move and have our being, now and ever.

PRAYER: *To whom else shall we go, Lord, You have all we need for a lifetime of joy. Amen.*

O LOVE, THAT WILL NOT LET ME GO

The Song of Songs 2:7 *I charge you, maidens of Jerusalem, by the spirits and the goddesses of the field: Do not rouse or awaken love until it is ready.*

Having composed more than a thousand songs and proverbs, Solomon puts this Song on the summit of his performances. It is a love song believed to have been written to celebrate his marriage to the fairest maiden of them all. That is itself was a command performance—that Solomon had that much passion left after gathering 700 wives and 300 concubines into his cuddly corral. But here, in a charge made three times (also in 3:5 and 8:4), for special emphasis, Solomon addresses the ladies of Jerusalem "by the spirits and goddesses of the field." Here the naturalist in Solomon comes to the fore as he refers (in other translations, to the "gazelles" and "hinds" of the forest). Those, everyone of the time knew, were symbols of sexual virility. Then comes the specific request to leave the lover for as long as she wishes to be in the intimate presence of the one whose banner over her is LOVE. (v. 4)

This is such a tender, above-board, delightful picture of how unquenchable and indissoluble marital life was meant to be, that Jews have seen fit to read from this Song at Passover. For it was at the time of the first Passover, in Egypt, that God and Israel came into what cannot better be described than a wedded relationship. (Jer. 3:1; Ezek. 16:23) Christians likewise have seen here the kind of union there is between Christ and His bride, the Church. (Matt. 9:15, 25:1; John 3:29; 2 Cor. 11:2; Ephesians 5:23; Rev. 19:7; 21:2; 22:17) All of which set a standard for true love and marital bliss.

God knows how far off the sex track humans have deviated. And since the home, the family, is the cornerstone of the commonwealth, the deviates' effects reach out into all segments of society. Even religious faith is contaminated by it. And that is why and where, in the past, God has stepped in with harsh measures. Love His creation though He does and ever will, His right must prevail.

Unfortunately, as often happens, Solomon failed to live up to his own standards and the walls of his empire were reduced to dust.

The standards remain. It's the staying power that is in short supply. Where can we find more married couples, celebrating their golden anniversaries, still saying: "When I hear his/her voice, my heart beats faster with excitement"?

PRAYER: *O God of love, teach us the exacting meaning of love, and how to live it. For "love is the perfect of the verb 'to live.'" Amen.*

LONGSIGHT

Isa. 1:1 *The vision which Isaiah son of Amoz had about Judah and Jerusalem during the reigns of Uzziah, Jotham, Ahaz, and Hezekiah, Kings of Judah.*

The School of the Prophets, started by Samuel, was by now bearing fruit abundantly. As with Isaiah, the first of the Major Prophets, who wrote the longest book with sixty-six chapters—a small Bible (which has 66 books).

Learning at School that visions of future events come when one's faculties are coordinated, and as we say, running on all cylinders, and that vision must be written down plainly, so that even he who runs may read it—Isaiah, at age twenty, began to inscribe what he had envisioned. Having lived in Jerusalem and in the larger area of Judah, Isaiah was well versed in what made the demography of the province tick. And pre-dating the futurists who through polls, censuses, and the like, forecast trends, Isaiah's predictive skills were sharpened. Through the governance of four Judean Kings, Isaiah was able to see the end from the beginning.

First, there was King Uzziah. Ascending the throne when he was just sixteen, Uzziah was tutored "in the fear of God" (2 Chron. 26:5) and "as long as he sought the Lord, God made him to prosper." Military defenses were strengthened and a port for foreign traders was built on the Gulf of Aqaba. Uzziah's reign of fifty-two years could have been unquestioned. Sadly, when in his pride he assumed a priestly function in the Temple and was scolded for it; he responded with such anger at the insult that he became an instant leper, ending his days in quarantine.

Jotham, Uzziah's son, continued with the building for which his father had a reputation. But after a short, unimpressive record, Jotham died in his early forties.

Jotham's son, Ahaz, was next on the throne.

Afraid of Assyria's power, Ahaz kowtowed in spite of Isaiah's cautioning. The King was so awed by Assyria that he embraced that faith confused and vacillating; Jotham sacrificed his son in the belief that it would appease the wrath of the gods.

Then came the best of Kings, Hezekiah. Just the opposite of his father Ahaz, Hezekiah had the Hebrew faith, with his friend Isaiah's guidance. And when the Assyrian army was about to flatten Jerusalem, God's word of assurance came through Isaiah that the City of God would be saved. It was. Overnight the enemy was completely wiped out.

More than this, Isaiah foresaw the coming of the Messiah, Jesus' life perfectly matched the seer's prophecies, from birth to death.

PRAYER: *Lord, lift the fog from the mountaintops that we may see, and foresee, beyond the far horizon. Amen.*

LIFE-SAVIORS

Isa. 1:9 *If the Lord of hosts had not left us a few survivors, we should have been like Sodom.*

Even "a few survivors" were cause for hope. The rest of the population (in Jerusalem) and their country of Israel were a disaster—unclean throughout. Animals knew their owners and masters (1:2) but humans did not. They despised God their heavenly Father, steeped as they were in evil doing. (1:4) "Unclean lips" (6:5) were not their only fault. You name a misdeed and these people were up to their necks in it. Even their once lovely city of Jerusalem was sorely tainted. The prophet here portrays the city not just with one crumbling word picture—but three. Once this "daughter of

Zion" was as inviting as a sumptuous vineyard, but now it was nothing more than a hastily thrown-together shelter; once a mouth-watering cucumber field, now Jerusalem resembled a mere hiding place for a watchman on the lookout for thieves at harvest time. Once an attractive city, it now appeared as one under siege by aliens. Jerusalem's destiny clearly belonged in the era of Sodom and Gomorrah, destroyed 1,300 years before—cities that are now under the southern waters of the Dead Sea. But the Lord had mercy on His favorite city and permitted "a few survivors." How precious a handful of the faithful are. Without them the smelly masses would be extinct. As Michelangelo put it, "Trifles make perfection, and perfection is no trifle."

Gideon learned that. (Judg. 7) At first he was sure that it would take a colossal army to be victorious. Then he found that just 300 committed, maneuverable troops could do better. And they did. There's an endless line of splendor through the ages to prove the workability of a dozen dedicated disciples. Jesus' apostolic fellowship was exponentially adequate for the fulfillment of His world mission. Or there was Martin Luther declaring, "Here I stand I can do no other, so help me God."

Those of us who couldn't get lost in Calcutta, India, remember the Squalor and how visitors from abroad dubbed it as "the city of statues and stinks." Along the streets were open garbage dumps off which wandering ownerless cattle and packs of stray, mangy dogs fed. Mental cases, men and women, stark naked, talking to themselves while walking in the middle of the street; lepers galore, heartbreakingly disfigured blind children begging for handouts; and everywhere the abhorrent odors. Then into this vale of tears came a nun. In her pure white habit, she moved across the city quietly doing what she could, where she could, when she could. And the rest is history. Later she was acclaimed worldwide as the sainted Mother Teresa. Indeed, Isaiah was more prophetic than perhaps he realized. "If the Lord of hosts had not left us a few survivors," God's own, the world could be Sodomized tomorrow. So the need for such surviving saviors still cries out for enlistees. Said Thomas Guthrie: "The greatest things ever done on earth have been done by little and little—little agents, little persons, little things—by everyone doing his own work, filling his own sphere, holding his own post and saying, 'Lord, what wilt thou have me to do?'"

As the Lord has done for and with others who were unable to do the big things, He helped them to do the small and few things in a big way. He can do the same for us.

PRAYER: *Gracious Lord, we see how in Heb. 11:33-40, unnamed, unnumbered persons are listed in Faith's Hall of Fame. But "only with us can they reach perfection." Make us worthy of the task. Amen.*

THE WORD FROM THE MOUNT

Isa. 2:1 *This is the message which Isaiah, son of Amoz, received in a vision about Judah and Jerusalem.*

Isaiah's vision, extending through four Kingships and beyond, has been outlined in general terms. Now the meaning of the vision begins to be stated in local and detailed terms.

Mt. Moriah, the mountain on which the Temple stood, could not be elevated above the surrounding peaks, but the prophet, with his telescopic insight, sees the worldwide importance of Moriah dwarfing all neighboring elevations. As in Rio de Janeiro the elevated statue of Christ can be seen from anywhere in the city, the loftiness of Jerusalem's templed mount would draw the attention and the attendance of "all the nations." (v. 2) And it has; and they do "stream toward it" (v. 2) by the millions every year. Though touring briefly, none leaves without an inner resolve to be instructed by God's words and to "walk in his paths." (v. 3)

Such transformed souls, then, go back home, and, under the leadership of the Holy Spirit work to bring God's family into a loving relationship. Swords are turned into plowshares, and spears into pruning hooks (v. 4) in a multitude of ways.

After every war, munitions and many of the countless other articles it takes to keep the war engine fired up, are left behind on the battlefield. They are too costly to cart home. Locals have seized such leftovers and have survived on their conversion into helps in the home, the garden, the factory, the impoverished mission outpost, and more.

Then, learning from such conversion experiences, God's people have attempted to forestall war by transforming explosive emotions into propellant endeavors in high-tech research and for peace conferences. The urge to fight other humans has been directed toward combating disease, hunger, homelessness, mental disabilities, and race discrimination. Adoration of military might seen for its utter failure to bring warring factions together has been better served by presenting it to God our Creator.

Yet, as Isaiah learned from his divinely delivered message, humans insist on bowing "down to their own handiwork, to objects their fingers have fashioned" (v. 8) so that mankind is brought low (v. 9) and a general reversal takes place. Plowshares are turned into swords, and pruning hooks into spears. (Joel 3:10)

The vision of a warless world remains, however, albeit among a remnant of the Lord's faithful. That is the hope in the vision—that momentum from in front, pulling us toward the actualization of the possible. And where people have no such vision, they perish. (Prov. 29:18)

PRAYER: *We hear Your message from the soul's Central City, Lord. Help us to enflesh it. Amen.*

THE SIGNATURE MEDITATION IN ISAIAH

Isa. 2:3 *Out of Jerusalem comes the Word of the Lord.*

Who in the wide world would dare to make such a bold claim? Who, knowing Jerusalem with all that it lacks to make even a decent village, should choose the site for its divinely appointed premier position in the world—forever? Why not Damascus or Thebes, Babylon, Athens? They were on commercially prosperous trade routes. Their water supply was attractive to a growing population. Natural resources promised rich yields. Why then settle in isolated, sparsely spring-fed Jerusalem, which stands on ninety-foot deep-rock solid mountains?

Mt. Sinai was as unpromising to be made into the City of God. There, too, God spoke in thunderous accents. There He taught the ten basics for a sound society with Saint Catherine's Monastery, and other communities, and the steady inflow of pilgrims. Sinai looks as if it would have made a burgeoning Holy City. Or Mount Tabor, the location of Jesus' transfiguration. Certainly the "inner circle" apostles made a strong case for settling there. But Tabor, too, was bypassed. God saw in Jerusalem—despite its negatives and all the destruction of city and people that awaited them in the thousands of years to come—a city of Salem (Peace). That had the "ace" in it. Which means that it was not to be what human frailties and falsities want as priorities in their capitals. God sees not as man.

Instead, God prepared a place where His only begotten Son could show the world how a Godlike life ought to be lived on planet Earth, in readiness for eternal life. And Jerusalem was the best possible classroom in which such divine instruction could be given in word and deed. This is what Isaiah saw with his prophetic distance vision, and here puts it into his written record—to be verified by us latter-day believers: First, "that He may teach us His ways." (v. 3) After three years of teaching the apostles (which accounts for three years in seminary), Jesus assumed that the Twelve were ready to graduate as Christian Leaders, so He said: "You know the way I am taking." (John 14:4) That's when Jesus realized that His instructions were not enough, or that they were not fully understood, for Thomas broke in, asking, "Lord, we do not know where you are going, so how can we know the way?" (v. 5) Jesus replied, "I am the Way, the Truth, and the Life; no one comes to the Father except by Me." (John 14:6) Just as a married person approaches everything with new thought-patterns of "our," "us," and "we," instead of "I," "me," "mine," so is the *way* we take when we become one in Christ Jesus. Always the inner silent commitment to Him determines the direction in which we move on any issue. Likewise with *Truth*. The Pilates of the world still flounder at this point. "What is truth?" they ask, and in the very asking reveal their ignorance. Christ is truth, and all that is true is that which conforms to His standards. *Life* for Jesus meant living in Him and He in us, now and ever. Second, "that we may walk in his paths" (Isa. 2:7) not just "walking today where Jesus walked," pausing at the stations of the Cross and other holy places—though these have their value. It is, rather, entering the straight gate and walking the narrow, disciplined road that leads to life eternal—as Jesus did.

PRAYER: *There had to be an entranceway for Your Word, Lord. Thank You for making Jerusalem Your carefully chosen way, which will also be the entrance to heaven—the new Jerusalem. Amen.*

NO FIGS FROM THISTLES

Isa. 3:8 *Jerusalem is brought low, Judah has come to grief, for in word and deed they defied the Lord, in open rebellion against his glory.*

When a country was conquered, to keep it subdued its props and stays were removed. Persons who had been the mainstays of that society were rendered silent and immobile. Security forces were stripped of weapons and responsibilities. Judges were defrocked. Captains of industry "and men of good standing" (v. 3) were muzzled. And that was the sad situation of the nation of Judah, in general, and the sunken level of Jerusalem in particular, as God wanted it. For His people had defied Him.

They were conversant with God's commands. Ever since their proclamation at Sinai, God's ten standards for upright living had been read at worship centers, taught at home and school, driven deep into the Hebrew culture. Yet this generation, like those before and after, thumbed their noses at the word of the Lord. They were to honor their parents and elders, were they? Well, they just jolly well wouldn't. (v. 5) Who said that they couldn't have as many gods as they wanted? God? Too bad. Indeed, there was "open rebellion against his glory." Not only in the blasphemous words they spat in His direction, but also in deeds. "Like Sodom they proclaim their sins, parading them openly." (v. 9) And what was Sodom destroyed for—but Sodomy? The condemnation is upon all who go and do likewise, in every age.

The defiant word is heard when, with cunning casuistry, doubts are cast upon God's word as to what He really meant. Doesn't the meaning of this translation disprove that one? Shouldn't we listen to this great scholar or that movie producer rather than to the prophetically relayed word from the Lord? Then, having set up straw men and defeated them with rapier-like word play, the defiant deed is enacted. Abandoning biblically based beliefs, anything goes. I'm okay. You're okay. Everyone's okay. Any god is okay. Aren't we all headed for the same place? And then, just as the hip-hop, flip-flop, eat, drink, and be merry happy hour begins, there is a shuddering silence as a hand writes on the wall, and that unmistakable voice says, "Thou fool, this night thy soul shall be required." What then? "Woe betides the wicked! All goes ill with them; they reap the reward they have earned." (v. 11)

PRAYER: *Forgive us, Lord for those times of barefaced rebellion against You. Redeem our lives from destruction. Amen.*

EVEN SO, COME LORD

Isa. 4:3 *Then those who are left in Zion, who remain in Jerusalem, every one whose survival in Jerusalem was decreed will be called holy.*

The "then" with which this text begins, indicates that something pivotal has occurred to cause a complete turnaround of God's people. They were pretty low at the end of Chapter 3. And at the beginning of this chapter, they were sub-zero. What made the difference between verses 1 and 3? What cleansed the people and made them holy?

In verse two Isaiah tells for the first time not *what* is going to be a lifesaver, a cleanser of hearts, a purger of iniquity, but *who*—the Messiah. From now on the message is repeated in clearer and louder tones in Isa. 11:1, 53:2; Jer. 23:5, 33:15; Zech. 3:8, 6:12. Here the forecasters were thrilled to announce that a Branch would sprout from David's fallen family tree. This person, for whom the ages had been yearning, would purify His people, and through them set the world right side up. And this holiness movement would start in Jerusalem.

Who, then, is this Messiah, and what is this holiness that He initiates? The record shows that the books of the Old Testament would be like a lot of beads of unequal sizes and unrelated to one theme. That gives cohesion and meaning to the Old Testament, for every book except Proverbs and Ecclesiastes has a wide-screen prevision of the one Majestic Person who was to come with Salvific effects. The bottom line is that this Person turned out to be none other than Jesus Christ.

The word "holy" is used in a bewildering number of ways. In one library I found this word "Holy" under every letter of the alphabet—all the way from Holy Alliance, and Bible, and City—to Holy Year of Jubilee, and the Holy Mt. Zion. And there are probably scores of other combinations in which the term is used. An elderly Roman Catholic worshipper, complaining about the new order of worship, said: "With all this yakking, I don't feel holy anymore."

Since the people of Jerusalem and Judah had incurred God's wrath by being like Sodom (3:9), they were sin-sick. Impurity, in the final analysis, is a despisal of God. Purity and impurity cannot peacefully co-exist. Only the Purifier of sins, the Messiah, could cure such a sickness. Which is to say, that to be healed and to be holy are the same thing. As St. Paul appealed to the brethren: "Present your bodies as a living sacrifice, holy and acceptable to God." (Rom. 12:1)

Accordingly, "every one whose survival in Jerusalem was decreed will be called holy," having been cleansed, healed, made whole, by the Messianic Physician.

PRAYER: *Lord, make us wholly Thine. Amen.*

REVIVAL MODE

Isa. 4:4-5 *When the Lord washes away the filth...he will create.*

First there must be cleansing before there is creation. "In the beginning God created." (Gen. 1:1) No cleaning had to be done. The earth was vast and formless. But when sin brought filth and malformations, the flood gates were opened that the malcontents might be flushed away, and the world re-created. And that is the order that is still followed weekly, if not daily in worship. First the confession of misdeeds, the exteriorizing of rottenness, then the regenerating.

This was what the Lord was teaching early on through Isaiah. And although this washing away of filth was aimed at the "women of Zion" and their monthly bloodstains, it was actually referring to the messy situation in which the citizens of the Holy City wallowed. The faithful city had become a harlot. (1:21)

It happened, as it always does, in myriad ways and Isaiah painstakingly sorts out the main culprits and labels each.

The root of all evil, wealth, gets the first hit. "There is no end to their treasures." (2:7) Thinking that this is what gives them the joys of life, people bow in adoration before the items which their bank accounts provide, and then wonderingly ask, "who needs God?" Then, having no God, persons put their trust in anything that comes down the pike, become vulnerable, and the playthings of sharpies.

God saw this happening to His people, in His city, while the people were retardedly unaware of their condition. Mercifully, the Lord retrieved His chosen people, and, first, by cleansing. "By a spirit of judgment burning like fire." The dress had to be consumed, by whatever means it took—even decades of exile; and the gold in human character to be refined.

Then came the new creation, as with Moses

and the Exodus. Those who had been exiled in Babylon, exited that land of bondage, heading for home—the Holy Land, and the Holy City, and the Holy Temple, with one addition—the promise of the coming of the Holy One of God, Jesus Christ.

Out of some fifty Old Testament passages quoted in the gospels, twenty-one are from Isaiah. The prophet looks ahead to the One who will come from David's family (David's Greater Son), be born of a virgin, live in Galilee at Nazareth, with a mission to the Gentiles, dealing with healing, teaching in parables, despised and rejected, entering triumphantly into Jerusalem. Other prophets filled out other details in the life of the coming Messiah.

What a gemstone of a reason for which to return to Jerusalem, One had to prepare for the coming of the King of Kings. There had to be cleaning of country and city and personal lives. The infrastructure had to be re-aligned. Plenty to be done and, in fact, it took 700 years to actualize Isaiah's blueprint for preparation. "Clear a road through the wilderness for the Lord, prepare a highway across the desert for our God. Let every valley be raised, every mountain and hill brought low, uneven ground be made smooth, and steep places become level. Then will the Glory of the Lord be revealed." (Isa. 40:3-5)

PRAYER: *"Have Thine own way, Lord! Have Thine own way! Search me and try me, Master, today! Whiter than snow, Lord, Wash me just now, As in Thy presence, Humbly I bow."*[1] Amen.

---

[1] Adelaide Pollard

GLIMPSE OF GLORY

Isa. 6:1 *In the year that King Uzziah died I saw the Lord seated on a throne, high and exalted.*

The young man Isaiah was noticeably disturbed. After a reign of forty-one years, his cousin, King Uzziah died—a leper. The King had accomplished much for the improvement of his country. The military and defenses were strengthened, valuable caravan routes secured, and the port of Elat (still important to Jordan and Israel) on the Gulf of Aquba was built. At the same time, King Uzziah neglected religion. The breaking point happened in the Temple when the King, puffed up about his successes, disobeyed the priests, flew into a rage, and was struck, on the spot, with leprosy.

In addition to this emotionally searing memory, Isaiah learned that the King's weakness and withdrawal from palace duties had emboldened enemies who were ready to pounce. And this shoe, ready to fall, hung there, terrifyingly, for seventy years.

That jangled the nerves of God's people, who were already in a dilapidated state spiritually. This Isaiah knew. The populace would have to be upbraided, and Isaiah felt himself being drawn into the center of the storm as the one who would have to do the upbraiding. That, recent clinical studies have shown, is the most stressful condition for the human body: to stand up and speak out in public. This, with the other additives, raised Isaiah's stress threshold too high to step over. So he went to church (the Temple in Jerusalem) and came face-to-face with the only One who could help him—the Lord, the King of Kings.

Unlike that which was around him, on a low, depressed, leprous level, Isaiah's soul was stirred by this uplook to One who was high and exalted. Then, as it were, the curtains were pulled back to reveal a fuller view of what, obviously, was heaven. Six-winged angels, more maneuverable than birds or humans, did their Lord's bidding, and witnessed to His holiness. Even Rudolf Otto, the eminent German theologian, failed to adequately describe this absoluteness of God in his landmark volume on "The Idea of the Holy"—the mysterium tremendium, that luminous numinous, that strangely felt Presence which is beyond understanding. But Isaiah got the picture, which immediately made him aware of his own unworthiness. It was akin to Moses experience on Mt. Sinai in receiving the Ten Commandments from the hand of God Himself. And not with Charlton Heston and sound effects on a movie set.

Isaiah confessed his double uncleanliness—personal and social and was instantly purified, and, at last, was God's man, the one whom the Lord was waiting for. Breaking into a heavenly conversation where the Lord was asking, "Whom shall I send? Who will go for us?" Isaiah, now confident of his own ability and availability, replied. "Here am I, send me," not caring whether he might dislike what he asked for. His was an unconditional commitment, providing a Bible—centered critical mass for the ages to ponder and strive to duplicate. For here is the outline for personal and congregational worship: *Adoration* of the "Holy, holy, holy Lord of Hosts" (6:3); *Confession* of sin: "I, a man of unclean lips" (6:5); *Cleansing*: "your sin is wiped out" (6:7); *Offertory*: "Send me" (6:8); *Commission*: "Go, tell." (6:9)

PRAYER: *Thank You Lord, for the Book of Isaiah, the most Jerusalem-centered book in the Bible, and for life-*

commitment as its central theme. Take us, make us, and the world what You will. Amen.

O COME, IMMANUEL

Isa. 7:4 *Say to him (King Ahaz): Remain calm and unafraid; do not let your nerve fail because of the blazing anger of (your enemies).*

Now we learn of the Lord's concern. (Isa. 6:8) He could see enemies making alliances to come, en masses, against Jerusalem. Worse yet, He saw that Jerusalem's King Ahaz was off track and inviting defeat. He needed to be shown road signs to lead him back to regaining control. So Isaiah, God's newest prophet, now loaded for bear, was given the assignment.

Finding the King's hidden nervousness in full display (he was examining the city's water supply), Isaiah tried to induce his majesty to be calm. Fluster was a buster. "Be calm in thy soul, each thought and each motive beneath His control." "He leadeth me beside the still waters" for a very good reason. Unruffled, I can get my act together, faster. Then, seeing fear written all over the King, Isaiah supportively suggested that there was nothing to fear. If the Lord is on your side, who can overcome you? Even if the enemy is ganging up against you and promises doom, and your knees are knocking, "Be still, my soul, the Lord is on thy side...He faithful will remain...Thy best, thy heavenly friend, through thorny ways, leads to a joyful end."

Even if this advice, this word of the Lord, went unheeded, there was Isaiah's son's name, which meant "a remnant will return." That, too, was a signpost for the King. There was hope and help and healing in all the Lord's provisions.

Still King Ahaz would not listen—determined to take his own bridge to nowhere.

Enter Isaiah's second son, Immanuel, to impress upon the King that "God is with us." That, too, was spurned. Fortunately the promise of God's presence had larger dimensions than the capped condition in which it first appeared. Seven hundred years later, Matthew reported that Jesus' birth "happened in order to fulfill what the Lord declared through the prophet (Isaiah)." "A virgin will conceive and bear a son, and he shall be called Emmanuel, a name which means 'God is with us.'" (Matt. 1:22-23) That gift, too, has been largely spurned.

Determined to be of help to a needy King and his people, God tries to speak through Isaiah's third son, whose name is the longest in the Bible (Isa. 8:1), and tells of coming judgment upon those who disobey the Lord's guidance.

The powers of darkness still threaten and oppress God's people in many forms. If not war, the godzillas and mastodons of the financial world invade the homeland's security. Or nature takes its turn at testing human survivability through tsunamis, floods, earthquakes, fires, volcanic action. Or the pests of the world have an uprising and for a joining of forces to wreak their vengeance upon mankind, mosquitoes, locusts, snakes, rodents, hornets, stink bugs. One can never tell what combinations of disaster will strike next. But the Lord is watching, sending help through His prophets, sons, signs, and a Savior. God is with us. "Have firm faith, or you will not stand firm." (Isa. 7:9)

PRAYER: *Because You first loved us, Lord, You are there to help even before the storm strikes. Forgive our slowness to realize and believe it. Amen.*

WALKING IN THE LIGHT

Isa. 8:11,20 *The Lord spoke thus to me with his strong hand upon me and warned me not to walk (and talk) in the way of this people, saying "Surely for this word which they speak there is no dawn."*

In spite of all God's proffered help, His people would not listen. There was no dawn in their behavior; no tomorrow, no hope. Why not? Instead of turning to God for help, they consulted "mediums and the wizards who chirp and mutter," (v. 10) and they consulted "the dead on behalf of the living," (v. 19) through séances and spiritualism and necromancy. The people dabbled in the weird, making that, for all practical purposes, their god. Little wonder that without the fixed arithmetic of God's tested and trustworthy guidance, the people were stumbling and falling and breaking and snared and captured. (v. 15)

By way of the contrast to these five ways in which the godless were falling apart, Isaiah is shown five ways, more accurately—five definitions, of God.

First, He is a sanctuary. (v. 14) Solomon in his wisdom recognized that "the name of the Lord is a tower of strength, where the righteous may run for refuge." (Prov. 18:10) More than that, as one new convert happily reported: "I came looking for shelter, I found a shell. And then, in that shell, I found a pearl" of great price! That, in itself, is worth the price of admission into the Lord's safe keeping. Nor is the Lord's sanctuary just a physical refuge. He is where one worships. There we go to find ourselves; it is so easy to get lost in the world.

There renewal of Spirit is generated. There dawn breaks upon the soul. Light does the opposite of its disappearing act at nightfall—and increases its intensity, enabling us to turn off our flickering little candle lights and let the sun of our universe take charge for bringing our planet to life. And that is exactly what God's Son does for us in His sanctuary, in worship. With Him, the Light of the World, we are better able to see those stones, those rocks, those obstacles that get between Him and ourselves, that shut off our access to Him, and which, as a result, could cause us to stumble. Yet, for the unenlightened, God is, *Second,* a stone of offense, and *Third,* a Rock of Stumbling. How and why does this happen at the hand of a good and loving God? D. T. Niles put the words together rightly: "Men are under necessity to find faith in God at the place and in the person where God humbled Himself," that is, in the Person of Jesus Christ. For the Hindu, however, that is offensive. He stumbles over that proposition, since for him Christ is just one in a galaxy of gods. Take your pick! Likewise the Muslim. The claim that Christ is God is offensive to the Islamic belief that there is only one God—Allah, and Muhammad is his apostle. Muslims stumble over the idea of incarnation. How can God come in the flesh? He is God, not sinful man! Buddhism too, is offended by, and trips over the idea of an unseen God. For the Buddhist it is as difficult to believe in such a God as it is to believe that day will not follow night. No dawn!

A *Fourth* and *Fifth* definition of God revealed to Isaiah, were a trap and a snare. Unbelievers are trapped like birds flying blind; entrapped like predatory animals. Where is the dawn in such dead-end living? Don't take that way of walking and talking.

PRAYER: *"Light of the world, illumine, This darkened earth of Thine, Till everything that's human, Be filled with the divine; Till every tongue and nation, From sin's dominion free, Rise in the new creation, Which springs from love and thee."*[1]

WHEN GLOOM GOES BOOM

Chapter 8 closed with dreary verse 33: *"They shall look to the earth, but behold, distress and darkness, the gloom of anguish; and they will be thrust into thick darkness."*

Chapter 9 opens with a "But," and we are left holding our breath in the deafening, questioning silence. But what? Something worse than the downward steps to the hellish blackout aforementioned? Surely not possible. But, yes, surprise, the past is epilogue, finis. For, as 9:1 reads: "But there will be no gloom for her that was in anguish." And why not? Saint Matthew, quoting the text for the day, Isa. 9:2, answers—because "those who sat in the region and shadow of death Light has dawned." (Matt. 4:16, NKJV) And with the coming of dawn Isaiah goes into spasms of joy. He says it's like the rejoicing over an abundant harvest, over winning a war—such as Gideon did when, with 300 men, he conquered 120,000 Mideanites. (Judg. 6-8) Indeed, Isa. 9:1-5 is full of the rocket's red glare, with bombs bursting in air. His cup is running over. It's a new day, in fact, a new world. The reason is found in Isa. 9:6, which

---

[1] John Monsell

Bible reference has appeared on countless e-mails and cables to families, announcing the birth of a new family member: "For unto us a child is born, to us a Son is given."

It is part of a Psalm, possibly composed by Isaiah for the coronation of a King in Jerusalem. Isaiah was experienced at this. He had witnessed the crowning of four Kings. (Isa. 1:1) The new emperor was considered a son of God. But his passage of scripture (v. 6-7) was not confined to Jerusalem's Kings. Dimensionally open on all sides, especially to seven centuries ahead, it came to rest, as did the natal star, over the place where the Baby Jesus lay, lightening everyone coming into the world. (John 1:9) And as in those coronations the new King was given five new names—Throne names. Those names fitted Jesus even better than they had fitted the kings of Jerusalem. For Jesus was finally revealed as the King of Kings and Lord of Lords. Little wonder that Handel made these Throne-names central in his Christmas Cantata, "Messiah."

The government will be upon His shoulder. How could anyone take on such a broad-shouldered responsibility of being the Savior of the world, except by being tempted in all points, like us earth dwellers, and dying for our sins? No royalty before or since Jesus has ever done that.

Wonderful Counselor. Not all Counselors, however well-qualified and university-degreed, are of value. They come in grades. Jesus earned a special, super standing, since "never man spoke like" Him. He "knew what was in man" and knew how to get the best out of people, and work all things together for their good. His counseling had wondrous outcomes.

Mighty God—and not just one of a multitude of deities made of clay, wood, or precious metals on an assembly line. Nor was He a Jupiter, head honcho of an Olympian dream team. He was all powerful—saving the strong from their stupidities, and empowering the weak.

Everlasting Father. No other father is everlasting. Each is subject to his own human frailties and limitations. Not Jesus. Said He: "I and the Father are One." The Eternal Father.

The Prince of Peace, and the Principle of Peace. He has it all, and we can have all of Him, and have a life full of Hallelujah choruses.

PRAYER: *We rejoice in Your Throne names, Lord. Reign in us, now and forever. Amen.*

GOD'S HIDDEN PURPOSES

Isa. 10:12 *When the Lord has finished all that he means to do against Mt. Zion and Jerusalem, he will punish the King of Assyria for the words which spring from his arrogance and for his high and mighty men.*

Why was the Lord intent on punishing His chosen people and city? Because, as the pagan King of Assyria noted (v. 10-11), there should have been a difference between godless cities and the City of God, Jerusalem. But there wasn't. Jerusalem was rife with idolatry. That made it not only an abysmal moral failure in the Lord's sight, but also a good reason to be conquered by those whom the living God used as His instrument of chastisement. What happened next, then, was that God used a heathen king to punish the Lord's people.

Those Hebrews were fascinated by idols. During their 430-year residence in Egypt they had a long time exposure to the whole spectrum of idol worship.

That worship had been in the making since 3000 B.C., and it was 1,000 years old by the time the Hebrews arrived. So imbued were they with the veneration of nature—sun, moon, birds, animals, that the worship of the golden calf during the Exodus is quite understandable. Moreover, it is not without significance that the first two of the Ten Commandments from Sinai relate to idolatry. There were to be no other Gods nor any graven images. God recognized the danger, and early sought to nip it in the bud. Yet, here were the Hebrews, in Isaiah's time, 1,000 years after the Exodus, still hypnotized by idolatry, still breaking the first two commandments, and probably several of the others. Knock down the prime standards, and the domino effect goes into operation. And again, as at Sinai, punishment came to the offenders.

The Assyrians, however, were not going to get away scot-free. Though used by God for His own purposes, they, too, were offensive, arrogant, swaggering. They had to be cut down to size. And they were. God rains on the just and the unjust. There is a goodness and severity in God's dealings. (Rom. 11:22) With His people He was severe that they might be purged of their idolatry. He was good to them by keeping them, despite their backslidings, in the fold of His loving embrace. With those who had no time for Him, God was good in granting them victory over God's people (for a while). But those arrogant, Godless conquerors tasted God's severity when they were finally laid low before Him.

The Lord's goodness is never wishy-washy neutrality. Nor is His severity heartless. His goodness is robust—drained of its saccharin insincerities. His severity is redemptive, with the poison and barbs removed. Though chastised with scorpions, we are reminded that it is better for us to enter into life maimed, than to have all our limbs—and go to perdition.

PRAYER: *We trust Your judgment, Lord. Help us to understand, and accept with grace Your goodness and severity. Amen.*

THE IMP IN IMPERIOUS

Isa. 10:17 *So the Light of Israel will be for a fire, and his Holy One for a flame.*

One often forgets that Light, though beneficial, can be savagely destructive. And here, the Light of Israel, the Lord Himself, turns from illumination to eradication, but with every good reason. He has used the super power of Assyria to punish His own chosen people for their wrongdoing. Now, in His justice, Assyria itself gets its turn in the hot seat.

As in a doctor's consulting room there is usually a wall chart of those parts of the human body in which the doctor specializes, so Isaiah gives us a run-down on how the Assyrian rulers blew their own horns and patted themselves on the back. It is a composite picture of how those Kings unashamedly boasted of their conquests in many lands and in various venues. It is "I" "I" "I" all down the page. "By the strength of my hand I have done it." (v. 13) They weren't even Pentagonists with Joint Chiefs of Staff. They hogged all the credit for themselves. One bragged that he had "removed the boundaries of peoples." (v. 13) That is, in their world empire they re-created new peoples and countries. Old borderlines were scrapped, and land and population were reorganized under Assyrian rules. So thoroughly shuffled was everything, that few people knew where they belonged. Thus confused and intimidated, they were easier to handle.

Another Assyrian dictator tooted that he had plundered treasures. In fact, all of them did; that was their main and voracious desire. They became adept at it—taking from palaces, temples, and wherever else treasures were stored. One described it as easy as taking (stealing) eggs from an unguarded nest. Talk about nest eggs! Even when the parent birds are not around in such a nest-snatching, other birds emit the danger signals, and the forest is astir with alarm. But not with these Assyrians. The reporter says "There was none that moved a wing, or opened the mouth or chirped." (v. 14) People who were aware of the blatant robbery, smothered their distress calls. They knew too well the consequences.

Another aggressor, flip as they come, blithely announced: "like a bull I have brought down those who sat on thrones." (v. 13) Just like that! Bulldoze your way through life, butting into throne-rooms, acting like the proverbial bull in a china shop. And there was more . But by now the Lord had seen enough on Assyria's wall chart to know that much fixing had to be done—not alone for Assyria's good, but for the realignment of all such persons who are brazenly in love with their self-importance, and are pretty cocky about being able to get away with it. That's when the Lord lights His flaming torch, as He did in the Garden of Eden, to stop sin. (Gen. 3:24)

So that the Hebrew people (for whom this was written) would better understand how the Lord lowered the boom on the haughty Assyrians, the action moves to northern Israel—known for the dryness of the forests in summer, and their flammability. The destruction of Assyria would be as rapid as a wildfire stoked by thorns and briers, which were literally matchsticks, and scorching the fruited plain, into nothingness. The people of Assyria would likewise waste away in soul and body. (v. 18)

Assyria, be it remembered, was a prototype of what can happen and has happened, not just among nations, but within nations, cities, villages, homes. Solomon was right again: "Pride goes before destruction, and a haughty spirit before a fall. Better to be of a humble spirit with the lowly." (Prov. 16:18) Otherwise, "of all the lunacies earth can boast, the one that must please the devil the most is pride reduced to the whimsical terms, of causing slugs to despise the worms."[1]

PRAYER: *"Lead, kindly Light, I loved the garish day, and, spite of fears, Pride ruled my will: remember not past years."*[2] *Amen.*

WHEN THY KINGDOM COMES

Isa. 11:9 *There will be neither hurt nor harm in all* my holy mountain *(another term for Jerusalem).*

Just when there was nothing but hurt and harm, a vesuvian change occurs. We move from the depths of despair to the summits of serenity. The merciful Lord is always ahead of the curve, always preferring for His people to have what He originally planned for them to enjoy permanently.

---

[1] Robert Brough
[2] John Henry Newman

For this reason, Eusebius, in his fourth century book *Onomasticon*, describes the Garden of Eden with one word "Delight," and it is this pure delight which is about to become worldwide beginning at Jerusalem.

It will start in a small way with Someone coming out of the lineage of David, Someone in whom the fruits of the Spirit will be noticeable: Wisdom, understanding, counsel, power; "and in the fear (love) of the Lord will be his delight." (v. 3) Delight! He has the fragrance of Eden now upon him but within him, and immediately the connection is made with Jesus and two of His Beatitudes—on the poor and the meek—noticeable in verse 4. Jesus the Delightfully blessed One—the One who has everything that anybody needs, the One who can and will transform human behavior as unbelievably as having a wolf live with a lamb.

What we have come to expect is that the wolf slips into sheep's clothing in order to pull the wool over everyone's eyes, then snatch up the lamb and Little Red Riding Hood, and grandma, and carry them to the den where the wolf-pack can dine on them at leisure. Which behavior has been commonplace in the marketplace, at the home-base, even in the worship place. Wolves aplenty, seeking whom they may devour. In like manner, the narrative continues, the leopard will lie down with the kid. Really? Since when? Wasn't the leopard designed to lie down after his tummy was filled with goat meal? And what nonsense is this about a calf and a young lion feeding fraternally together? The lion is happy only when the fraternity is swallowed.

Then it goes on to be utterly senseless—about the infant playing over the cobra's hole and the young child dancing over the viper's nest. (v. 8) Who would allow such unconscionable unwatchfulness and dereliction of parental duty? Yet, it's going to happen. It says it at the top of this page: "There will be neither hurt nor harm." A new ball game!

Now we know who can bring about these stupendous changes. And we know that these changes are not particularly for nature conservancy or animal rights. Already some people are worried about the meat situation. If the animals all become docile and hippity-hoppity around together, and there are no more predators—animal or human—what are we going to do for meat on our tables and at our steak cookouts? All become vegetarians? The Lord provides where He guides. He will, as always, do more than His share to provide the Delightful Blessedness. But there is a part that we have to play—that is to "be filled with the knowledge of the Lord." (v. 9) How else can He communicate with us? How could we ever know what He wants us to do?

If we have been exhorted to know ourselves, it is imperative that we come to know the Lord, our Creator. How to know Him but through His Word—sometimes directly, and personally spoken by Him, sometimes through prophets and others who know Him well. Then we also come to know the Lord through prayer—talking to Him as a friend, pouring out our hearts to Him and taking time to hear and feel what He wants us to do. It is also valuable to learn from other persons about Him, others who are old, dependable friends of His. He is good, very good to know.

PRAYER: *Lord, "Teach us to utter living words of truth that all may hear, The language all men understand when love speaks loud and clear; Till every age and race and clime, Shall blend their creeds in one. And earth shall form one brotherhood, By whom thy will is done."*[1] *Amen.*

RIGHT FROM THE START

Isa. 22:1 *Tell me, what is amiss that you have all climbed on to the roofs.*

What was amiss in Jerusalem with people climbing to their rooftops en masse? Strictly speaking, this has never been much of a concern in Middle Eastern countries where most socializing is done on flat roofs. But here it was different. Fear stalked the land—fear of disease and of their army commanders and special forces deserting their posts in wartime. (v. 3) Terrified, the populace cried out for help, cries that echoed among the mountains. (v. 5)

Thinking that he knew what was amiss, namely that the Assyrian army was about to besiege Jerusalem, King Hezekiah had his stock of weaponry checked at the armory. This "House of the Forest" (v. 8) had been built 200 years before, during Solomon's fourteen-year building spree. It had "four rows of cedar columns, on top of which were laid lengths of rows of cedar. It had a cedar roof extending over the beams, which rested on the columns, fifteen in each row, and the number of the beams was forty-five." (1 Kings 7:2-3) Hez-

---
[1] Henry Tweedy

ekiah depended on this sturdy structure, as others had before him. But there was also the problem of water, which has always plagued the Holy Land. In a time of siege from where would Jerusalem get its water? That was when Hezekiah built his famous tunnel. (2 Chron. 32:3-4; 2 Kings 20:20) It still brings water into the city from the Gihon Spring. The tunnel was cut through solid rock for 1,700 feet—to the Pool of Siloam. At the entrance is an inscription which says, "while the stone cutters were lifting up the pick, each toward his neighbor (from opposite sides), there was heard a voice of one calling to another; and after that pick struck against pick; and the waters flowed from the spring to the Pool." Having provided for the water supply to the inner city, King Hezekiah saw to it that the invading army was deprived of water. All springs surrounding the city were blocked, or they were diverted into the new tunnel.

During the Second World War when Britain expected an invasion by the Germans, in British Coastal towns street names were changed to confuse the invaders. What Hezekiah did was to find the weakest spots in the wall around the city that could be breached. There, homes were torn down to create blockages and confusion for penetrating troops. And, no doubt, these were just a few of the many wartime strategies and trickeries that were thrown in the path of the advancing invaders. Still, with all these diversionary tactics, the question at the top of the page remained unanswered: What is amiss? What was glaringly missing was that God their Maker was not consulted for an answer. (v. 11) Trapped like a bird in a cage, Hezekiah was forced to pay an enormous amount of money to be released. This came from gold that was stripped off the temple doors and doorposts. When, at last, Hezekiah held steady under God's guidance, with the prophet Isaiah as intermediary, the enemy was wiped out in one night by an angel of the Lord.

How right Jesus is: "Set your mind on God's Kingdom and his justice before everything else, and all the rest will come to you as well." (Matt. 6:33) What we still miss in our problem solving, is going for help to the Lord, *first*.

PRAYER: *Immanuel, God with us, we would seek first Your Kingdom and righteousness, before being caged. That's for the birds. Amen.*

KEEPER OF THE KEYS

Isa. 22:21 *I shall invest him with your robe, equip him with your sash of office, and invest him with your authority; he will be a father to the inhabitants of Jerusalem and to the people of Judah.*

The verses that sandwich verse 21 fill out the picture. The Lord is telling the former high priest of Israel that his important position is passing to one named Eliakim. This man was to be invested with a robe that was a symbol of high office and authority. Also, at Eliakim's investiture he was to be fitted with a sash (girdle). As C. W. Slemming explains in *These Are the Garments* (pp. 46-47), "The ephod, curious girdle, and breastplate, were united to each other so that they became inseparably one. Inside the breastplate were deposited Urim and Thunim"—sort of dice, which were used to ascertain the will of God. Yet Eliakim would hardly have any use for such dicey decision-makers, when, in the next verse, the Lord places the Key of David's palace on Eliakim's shoulder, granting him the special power to open doors (to the throne room, the treasury, the armory...?) which no one dare shut, and to shut doors that nobody was allowed to open. Here was supreme authority, indeed.

Little did Eliakim know how he was to be taken as a pattern throughout coming ages.

Jesus was the first one to lift it out of His close reading of the Book of Isaiah—and apply it to the apostle Peter. (Matt. 16:19) Whatever Peter forbade on earth would be forbidden in heaven, and whatever he allowed on earth would be allowed in heaven. It gave Peter unusual authority to make decisions while establishing the fellowship of believers in Christ. And as the church grew in numbers, and spread to the uttermost parts, and as new leaders from differing backgrounds multiplied the problems, decision-making would have been well-nigh impossible but for Peter's God-given keys.

Then, in the Book of Revelation, John, with divine approval, sees Jesus as the final owner of the Key that opens doors no one can close, and shuts doors no one can open. (Rev. 3:7) And since Jesus is our Savior, Eliakim's gift finds an eventual application in us, personally. Praise the Lord for opening doors for us out of a sickness, out of alcohol and drug problems, out of depressing moods. Thanks be to God, who through Christ shuts doors no one can open—for our own good; grateful for what we might have been and done but were effectively kept from.

PRAYER: *Lord Jesus, we are thankful that You have the Keys, and not Eliakim or Peter, You are the Director of our lives, not the church. Amen.*

ON BEING IN A UNITED STATE

Isa. 27:13 *On that day a great trumpet will be sounded, and those who are lost in Assyria and those dispersed in Egypt will come to worship the Lord in Jerusalem's holy mountain.*

This "Isaiah apocalypse" comes to an end with great trumpeting. That is how the giving of the Decalogue ended on Mt. Sinai. Trumpeting denoted that there were to be only Ten Commandments. In like manner, Isaiah is here foretelling the end of the Jewish period of Exile. The trumpet in each case was the shofar, made from the horn of the wild goat, and in remembrance of Abraham's finding a ram in a thicket on the occasion of the intended sacrifice of Abraham's son. The ram, the substitutionary sacrifice, foreshadowed the substitutionary sacrifice of the Lamb of God (Jesus) for the sins of the world.

Yet, the trumpeting was not only an ending, but a beginning. It summoned the return of God's chosen people from the lands to which they had been dispersed by conquest and by commerce. There came to be more Jews outside Palestine than inside. Outside, they had become a vital part of the societies in which they had settled, maintaining their cultural connection with the homeland, and with one another—through their local synagogues and their scriptures. At best, however, these were all long-distance contacts. They were better than no linkages, but they were not the ideal. In every Jew's heart there was always the unexpressed yearning to return to the soul's capital—Jerusalem. And now the opportunity was being provided, not alone to return to Jerusalem's holy mountain, but there to enjoy the real family re-union of oneness in the Father

God, by the mass worship of Him.

Nor did Isaiah envision such a coming together as a onetime incident. Joel (2:15ff) caught that vision and passed it on. John in his apocalyptic Book of the Revelation, chapter 19, saw it as pertaining to the final homecoming of God's faithful followers in the New Jerusalem. Which would indicate that now and ever, and anywhere in the world, people of faith can find coherence in the Lord through private and public worship. Worship is the tie that binds.

David wrote Ps. 24 especially for the triumphal entry of the Ark into Jerusalem. There the choirs sang: "Who may go up the mountain of the Lord? Who may stand in his holy place? One who has clean hands and a pure heart." (v. 3-4) Thus, the eligible ones, coming into the Lord's presence, no matter from where, find themselves in a congregation of kindred spirits.

Trumpeter, do your stuff. This is the finale.

PRAYER: *Our Father who art in heaven, Thy thankful people come to worship and adore Thee—to the end of time. Amen.*

GOD'S PROMISED PROSPERITY

Isa. 29:1 *Woe betide Ariel! Ariel the city where David encamped. When another year has passed, with its full round of pilgrim feasts...*

Isaiah, the Prophet Laureate of Jerusalem and the most quoted of the Old Testament prophets in the New Testament (more than all the other writing-prophets put together), knew better than anyone else the sixty different names given to his hometown. Each name fills out the many facets of the city's character. As here in Ariel, with its yearly round of pilgrim feasts, chief of which were the Passover—a remembrance of the Exodus from Egypt; Pentecost, fifty days after Passover and the end of the wheat harvest; and Tabernacles, to mark the entrance into the Promised Land after forty years in the wilderness.

Then, since all feasts were celebrated in the Temple, and since the Temple was the centerpiece of Jerusalem that was the capital of the only Kingdom God has on earth, it was to that worship center that devout Jews flocked from all over the world at feast times. Tri-annually these multitudes of pilgrims required thousands of sacrificial animals for their burnt offering on the alter—bulls, calves, sheep, goats, and doves. With such a colossal use of the altar and of fire (talk about air pollution!), the city was referred to as the altar-hearth, as in Ezek. 43:15: "The altar-hearth was four cubits high and was surmounted by four horns a cubit high." But why use two words, altar-hearth, when you could describe it with one word—Ariel?

Being multipurposeful, Ari-el, as in El-ohim, means "of God." You notice "el" in names like Michael, Gabriel, Daniel, Joel, Ariel, then meaning Lion of God, "denoting Jerusalem's firm stance in facing up to and defeating overwhelming foes."

Ariel, with its altar-hearth perpetually soaked in blood, with the foul smell of burning flesh was often interpreted to mean this was the way the city was destined to be—reeking and bloodied and smelly and defeated, as indeed the city has been at times through the centuries. On the other hand the gory scene has been viewed as another Mt. Sinai out of the middle of whose cataclysmic thunder and fire and smoke came the healing, helping voice of God. As the Psalmist described it: "Those who trust in the Lord abides forever." (Ps. 125:11) Or looking through the viewfinder of "the multitudes of all nations that fight against Ariel." (Isa. 29:7) Jerusalem has seemed to be a pushover. One good puff and the old girl will fall down flat. Yet such blowhards have found and will continue to find that theirs was "like a dream, a vision of the night." (v. 7) Call it a pipe dream? Ariel, the lion of God, still stood strong—the King of the forest.

In a city centered on God, through worship of Him and offerings to Him, able therefore to face down insurmountable odds for centuries, could it have been the reason why such structural tenacity (built into it by people of sound character) resulted in physical blessings too? Reliable sources inform us that "myriads of private fortunes were deposited in the Temple." For Temple activities nothing but the best would do—in wood, wine, oil, grain, incense, "From as far as India came the material for the high priests vestment...and the twelve precious stones on his ephod were chosen from the most valuable jewels in the whole world...By means of the Temple treasury, to which every Jew had to pay his annual dues, the whole worldwide Jewry contributed to the commerce of Jerusalem." (Joachim Jeremias)

In times of global economic downturns, the character and fortunes of Ariel are worth reconsidering our pilgrim heritage, prior to Plymouth.

PRAYER: *Heavenly Father, "Gladness breaks like morning where'er Thy face appears; Thy cross is lifted o'er; We* *journey in its light, The cross awaits the conquest, Lead on, O God of might."*[1] *Amen.*

REFRESHING GRACE

Isa. 30:19 *People of Zion, dwellers in Jerusalem, you will weep no more.*

There had been good reasons for people to weep. They had sinned. Grant them the benefit of the doubt, though. In those undemocratic days when government was not by the people and for them, the reverting to inferior morals had seeped down from the top leadership who had made alliances with pagan nations, embracing policies, both domestic and foreign, that were contrary to God's will. Drifting from God, they drifted backward to the worship of handmade gods—"silver plated images and gold-covered idols." (v. 22) As punishment, therefore, the Lord fed these moral slackers with the "bread of adversity and the water of affliction" (v. 20) causing them to weep copiously.

Never less than gracious and merciful, the Lord now looks with favor upon these crybabies who plead for help. It is this pattern in three parts, that we now see recurring throughout the Book of Isaiah, a recurrence that should not be regretted or looked upon as boringly repetitive. In fact, we cannot be reminded of it often enough, since our frail humanity is attracted by the pigpen in which we prefer to squat, as did the Prodigal son; or else we spend much time on the judgment thereof—which gets us so depleted with weeping, feeding on the bread of adversity and the water of afflic-

---

[1] Ernest Shuertleff

tion, that we cannot find any way out of the imprisoning punishments.

Nor should we see in this tri-partite pattern of sin, judgment (punishment), and hope that because there is always a hopeful way out provided by God, we can sin to our heart's content. St. Paul addressed this slimy maneuver: "But where sin was multiplied, grace immeasurably exceeded it, in order that, as sin established its reign by way of death, so God's grace might establish its reign in righteousness, and result in eternal life through Jesus Christ our Lord. What are we to say, then? Shall we persist in sin, so that there may be all the more grace? Certainly not!" (Rom. 5:20-6:2)

A case in point is the financial tumble that the United States took in September and October of 2008, when the Dow took its greatest freefall ever.

The sin was greed basically, and a hip-joining with those who couldn't or wouldn't see beyond their deep investment in self interests. When the axe of judgment fell, there was a wild and general blaming of one another while all the time it was acknowledged that there was a way out of the tangle that had tempted the key players to take unnecessary risks anyway. The culprits (and who would put the finger of accusation on them?) with guile, and a prostitution of hope, crashed the world's economy.

Isaiah's drumbeat reminder of sin, judgment, and hope is rather to emphasize that though sin occurs and must be punished, we are not to take advantage of God's eventual mercy. Beginning by working with a gracious heavenly Father, we can move from strength to strength and victory to victory. The weeping over sin and chastisement can be left to the Prodigals to get their jollies from.

PRAYER: *O Thou, in whose presence our souls take delight; "Our hope is built on nothing less than Jesus' blood and righteousness." Amen.*

OUR SHIELD AND DEFENDER

Isa. 31:4 *So the Lord of Hosts will come down to do battle on the heights of Mt. Zion.*

Here come Israel's enemies once again, closing in on Jerusalem, determined to get their claws into this prize that sooner or later every country salivated to own. They forgot, however, who really owned the area. Piercing the tense situation, God, through His spokesman Isaiah, pictorially describes two action shots illustrating His tenacious love, and love that will not let go of His beloved city.

The first picture, filling up the rest of verse 4, introduces the King of the forest, the Lion King.

Since there are no lions in the Holy Land today, there is a temptation to believe that Isaiah went mythical at this point. History jerks us back to reality with the reminder that early on lions were found throughout Europe, Africa, Mesopotamia, and Western India. Since those lands come together at the Holy Land, it is hardly possible that the lion would have missed making its presence felt in that small central area. If it had, Samson wouldn't have had a lion to kill. Or David. Daniel wouldn't have had any in the den with him. These animals, with their admirable traits of phenomenal strength, royal bearing, family orientation, protectiveness, have been used in connection with the highest and best. "The Lion of Judah" (David). "The Lion of God" (Ariel).

Any day in Africa's game parks, from the safety of a Land Rover one can see Isa. 31:4 come alive. A pride of lions bring down a wildebeest. The pride settles down around the feast. Each is happy with his (her) lot, woe betide those who try a quick steal—whether it be jackals, hyenas, vultures, or other scavengers, or shepherds, or Masai tribesmen trying to frighten away the feeding animals. To be sure, it's a raw, bloody affair and in a way, it is unfortunate that it is used in the Bible to vivify the scene. Yet keeping central the exclusivism of the Commandment, "I, the Lord thy God am a jealous God," (Exod. 2:5) we can feel, each one of us, that we are wholly His. With such a Lover, Possessor, Protector, how dare we express any fear, mistrust, anxiety. He holds us fast, beyond dislodgment from His grasp. All of this is behind the first word in today's text—"So." Because of His great love for Jerusalem (and for all of us His loved ones), He comes down to do battle on our behalf.

Still, He is not finished. Abruptly the second action shot is presented "like a hovering bird." (v. 5) The Lord watches from on high—to get a fuller view of the situation. The lions were limited to their tall grass. With all its senses working full time, the bird's boundaries are almost limitless. Far-off enemies can be identified, and diversionary tactics used. The hovering, higher or lower or in wider circles like a "shield," overlaying those who are being protected with a covering above could draw the attention of other predators, in greater numbers! Delivery is the core. Get them out of harm's way. Take them piggy-back, if need be, to safe quarters.

The next step in the lifesaving operation is to "spare" the captives from any further fear and harm. Help from land-based allies can be called in. Aid could be dropped parachute-like into needy areas. Then comes the final "rescue," the Lord Protector thinks of everything. He holds on to His loved ones tenaciously, on land, sea, and air, doing what He can to defeat our adversaries (as He wiped out the Assyrian hordes overnight) and rescued Jerusalem from mortal danger. His rescue operation is not over. Wherever there is need, He is there like a lion, like a hovering bird, like a Savior.

PRAYER: *"Love that will not let me go, I rest my weary soul in Thee; I give Thee back the life I owe, That in Thine ocean depths its flow, May richer, fuller be"*[1]

FIXED ARITHMETIC

Isa. 32:5 *The scoundrel will no longer be thought noble, nor the villain considered honorable.*

As a matter of course screws get loose, and no less so than in our thinking and morality. When the screws are where they were designed to be for the best results, all systems and connections perform acceptably. With time and use and variable factors bearing down on weaknesses therein, the squeaks and rattles signal the approach of a meltdown—and no less so in morality.

The owner of a cannery told me that he could drive past his business and tell by the atmosphere, the smoke, and the smell how well or how ill things were going inside.

So it was with Isaiah. When a scoundrel was

---

[1] George Matheson

treated as nobility, and a villain as a right-honorable gentleman, watch out—something has gone screwy. And Isaiah called attention to these indicators. If they were not fixed, all of society, beginning in the Holy City, could be shaken to pieces. What to do but tighten the screws, get things back to where they ought to be, as they were made to be, not for some cockamamie, politically correct, lock-stepped, lock-jawed reason. There is danger in lying. Mark Twain aptly said the difference between a cat and a lie is that the cat has only nine lives.

The prophet catalogs the many life forms that lying took in the society around him. There were persons who hatched evil in their hearts, so that it came out, understandably, in their behaviors. They even lied to God—the habit had become so ingrained in them. The rising tide of evil finally spilled over into all of society's infrastructure: covenants were broken, treaties flouted, the land was parched and wilting. Once fertile areas became deserts and were stripped bare. The best of human efforts amounted to nothing but chaff and stubble. Countrysides had the appearance of thorn bushes crackling quickly into flame and being reduced to white ash.

"O what a tangled web we weave when first we practise to deceive," cried Sir Walter Scott.

Deception works subtly, convolutedly, with artful quibbles, and usually with the tongue—which is the strongest muscle in the human body. Peter O'Toole, superstar on stage and screen, says, for example, that he doesn't mind being a bad person because "you are only as good as you have the courage to be bad." It gets even more tangled by those who have a talent for bending things out of shape, especially when they are alcoholized and religiously disoriented. Their conscience is in pain, telling them that something basic is crying to be fixed. But the cry is smothered with tranquilizers in the belief that pain is a gift they can do without, and unaware that total painlessness denotes the presence of leprosy, either physical and/or spiritual.

The combinations of satanic thinking emanate in the most boa-constrictive contortions that make for the squirmiest explanations for law-breaking that police hear sound like a Sunday School Bible story. Halloween, even, doesn't parade anything so weird. Vanity of vanities, all is vanity declared the wisdom writer Addison found that "falsehood and fraud shoot up in every soil, the product of all climes."

Isaiah's recipe for overcoming all the nuanced evil of daily life, all the hairpin bends and off color words and deeds can be corrected when we make the Lord our mainstay. Calling on Him for assistance, we are granted wisdom and knowledge, which are the assurance of salvation. Our treasure is found in loving the Lord. He shows us how to snap our fingers at a bribe, to close eyes and ears to evil. Our yes will be yes, and our no not yet, a spade a spade, and the scoundrel the blackguard that he is.

PRAYER: *O Eternal Standard, You know how easily we sidetrack and do what is right in our own eyes. Straighten us out, now and forever. Amen.*

THE ETERNAL CITY

Isa. 33:20 *Look to Zion, city of our sacred feasts, let your eyes rest on Jerusalem, a secure abode, a tent that will never be moved, whose pegs will never be pulled up, whose ropes will none of them be snapped.*

Almost in the middle of the central chapter

in the Book of Isaiah, there is a clarion proclamation of hope. Oh how it was needed. On the outside, there were never-ceasing threats of enemy attacks. On the inside, moral decay seemed almost incurbable. All of which created a gloomy, soaking atmosphere of insecurity, of doomsday dread.

Suddenly, through the dark night of fright, the note of hope sounds forth to set people back on their feet with heads held high—looking upwards to Zion, the beautiful City of God.

Whoever is speaking, turns his hearer's attention first to the city's sacred feasts. That spells out its own message of prosperity and peace. No need for doom and gloom when food can be bought and prepared and enjoyed in homes and places of worship. Happy Passovers were still being commemorated, as was the Feast of Tabernacles (Booths), and other historical remembrance. Cheer up!

Then people's attention was turned to the City's reputation as a secure abode. That should stiffen their nerve and raise their sights.

At first it seems to be a silly idea—describing Jerusalem as secure as a tent. A Tent? Isn't that the first article to be blown away in a high wind? Yet, if this airborne shelter could be made immovable even in cyclonic conditions, if the weak could be made strong, why, anything was possible.

So the text goes on to affirm the stability of this tent. After all, the Israelites, during their forty-year sojourn in the wilderness, perfected the art of tent-making. For them it was not camping equipment but regular housing—for about two million people. The tents had to withstand wind, sandstorms, rain—and snow (at Mt. Sinai). These goat- and badger-skin tents sturdily bore the burden and heat of the trek. One, because the pegs were so skillfully designed that they never pulled up unless maneuvered out by the tent-dweller. The ropes, likewise, were unsnappable. The Israelites had learned rope-making in Egypt—rolling papyrus with the palm of the hand on a bare thigh. That rope had to be dependable, as it was used to tie knife handles to blades, and used on their ships. Isaiah knew what he was writing about. He never would have compared the rock-solid security of Jerusalem to a tent if he was not sure of tent-making and rigging. No, the tent was unarguably dependent. As the city was. As the city's God was. Let your troubled eyes REST on Jerusalem, God's city.

PRAYER: *In our weakness is Thy strength, O Lord. Thy tent shall be our home. Amen.*

"REDEEMED—HOW I LOVE TO PROCLAIM IT!"[1]

Isa. 35:10 *The ransomed of the Lord shall return and come to Zion with singing. (RSV)*

Where in a previous meditation (32:5) the scoundrel is considered noble, that is, the truth is falsified—and, thereafter, everything goes downhill, now the situation is reversed. The mirage (35:7), that is, the lie to the eye, is here for real. The mirage becomes a pool, a bubbling spring, and not just a tantalizingly imaginative oasis. In fact, all that follows is for real, especially our text for the day. It is so precious, so much of a national treasure, that it is duplicated word for word in Isa. 51:11. We can never have enough of the Good News—of the three R's: redemption, return, rejoicing.

---

[1] Fanny Crosby

Our text helpfully interconnects several outstanding historical events, life-changing experiences, and happy endings, allowing for their wider application, from the individual to the international to church, family, community.

"The ransomed of the Lord," or "The Lord's redeemed" (NEB) is a picture of a re-created person or persons we have seen too often. They have been in all kinds of scraps and scrapes personally and collectively. They have been naughty children of God—knowing better, but doing worse; knowing that God loved them, had given them all the best they had ever possessed, but still they mocked Him, turned their backs on Him, and sat down to a banquet of bitter consequences. They had been in the dumps, defeated, exiled repeatedly, pitiful, and pitied. Enter our redeeming God to re-create His sin-sick people.

The word "redemption" was originally borrowed from the marketplace. A redeemer was one who purchased a person out of slavery, and then set that person free. It also meant buying a rare opportunity (as in taking the tide at its flood). In the faith community God was looked to as the only worthy Redeemer, who, at the last trumpet call, would buy us all back from bondage, even the fallen angel—Satan. This not only resonated with Isaiah, whose name means "God is salvation," but it also reverberates through the New Testament in our purchase by the Blood of the Lamb of God.

"Shall return" is made possible by Redemption. You see it in the Exodus. There the Land was ready for the people. It was bursting with promise of every kind. The bunches of grapes were only a small portion of what limitless profits awaited the exiled returnees. Indeed, the Land was ready for them. The question was: Were they ready for the Land? Were the people promising? When redeemed, they were welcome.

However, homecoming is not a bed of roses for many persons. For them home is where the hurt is. You were taken to the woodshed, more than once, and you have the scars and stripes to prove it. One has outgrown the cocoon, why reenter its confinements? How are you going to keep 'em down on the farm after they've seen Paree?

Yet, our text has a different ending—with singing, rejoicing. It's the return of a prodigal soul. The lost is found, the dead—alive again. You hear the overtones of the Shepherd's Psalm (23). The return journey is through green pastures and beside still waters, with no scariness in the valley of the shadow. For just as goodness and mercy follow us all the days of our lives, here God is both vanguard and rearguard—till we dwell in the house of the Lord (where else?) forever.

PRAYER: *Thank You, Lord, for a happy ending that is no mirage. Amen.*

ALL THE NEWS THAT'S FIT TO MINT

Isa. 40:9 *Climb to a mountaintop, you that bring good news to Zion; raise your voice and shout aloud, you that carry good news to Jerusalem, raise it fearlessly; say to the cities of Judah, "Your God is here!"*

As returnees stream back from their exile in Babylon, they are invited to become part of a good news movement. Suggestions are then made as to how best to spread that breathtaking news.

Lacking mass media of communication, simple, natural means had to be used to their maximum. What, for one thing, would provide a loftier soap box from which to proclaim the urgent word—than a mountain-top? The proclaimer would have to possess a stentorian voice. And that voice, loud as it might be around the house, for this occasion would have to be revved up to mega-capacity. Running out of adequate vocabulary, Isaiah uses the word "raise" twice. Jack it up, more, more, he is appealing. Do it "fearlessly," he adds, since there is always the fear of not being heard, or being misunderstood—and causing untold problems.

Then comes the quintessential reason for all this full-throated broadcasting—the message, in four words, "Your God is here!" Previously, because of myriad misfortunes that had befallen Israel, the commonly held hopeless belief was that God had deserted His people, that God was nowhere to be found. Now comes the invigorating word that "nowhere" has been sliced in two, and, instead of God being nowhere, God is now here, and near.

He is here to bring comfort. (v. 1) And tenderness, since city names, in Hebrew, denote the feminine. (v. 2) Further tenderness is pictured in verse 11, where the shepherd carries "the lambs in his bosom and lead(s) the ewes to water."

Verses 3-5 have been reproduced by all four gospels (Matt. 3:3, Mark 1:3, Luke 3:4-6, John 1:23) to prove that God is, indeed, now here, in the advent of Jesus Christ, the Word of God made flesh—to be seen and heard and touched, and to be touched by. Immanuel, God with us.

More than providing comfort and tenderness

to Isaiah's countrymen, and to those of Jesus' time, the ever-present Lord extends further good news to us, in the closing verse of this chapter: "Those who look to the Lord will win new strength, they will soar as an eagles' wings; they will run and not feel faint, march on and not grow weary."

No wonder that many lecterns are shaped like eagle's wings. From there this good news must be spread—to the ends of the earth, through all time.

PRAYER: *Heavenly Father, source of this good news, make us to be recipients, examples, and conduits of this enlivening message, now and forever. Amen.*

TO WHOM ELSE SHALL WE GO?

Isa. 40:25 *To whom, then, will you liken me, whom set up as my equal? asks the Holy One.*

The good news to Jerusalem (v. 9) continues, this time emerging from a specific incident: the capture of God's people by the Babylonians.

In the land of exile far from home, the Hebrews were a defeated people—physically, emotionally, spiritually. Physically they had been overpowered by the world power of their time. Emotionally, as citizens of a conquered and imprisoned country, all their high hopes for the future had now turned to mush. Spiritually, in those days the conquest of your country was taken to mean that the conqueror's god was greater than your god, and their places of worship were more alive and effective than yours were. So turn your face to the wall. Forget your God. He's too small.

How up-to-the-minute that sounds. And how necessary it is to hear the Lord's rejoinder. Often. For in presenting His credentials, our Lord is granting us another needed dose of great good news. Or, perhaps we haven't quite understood our Father who is in heaven—whom He is and what He can do. Rushing into the future, with remarkable discoveries and inventions popping up all over the place, many people feel, as people always have, that God is still back there in antiquity. We're ahead of Him.

No, God asserts, He's ahead of us. He can hold the oceans in the palm of His hand, and all the earth's soil as well. Who but the Lord can weigh the mountains on a pair of scales? Nobody has taught Him discernment, justice, wisdom. God can do in a jiffy what we humans could not do in millenniums.

Nations, during their time in the sun, strut and talk as if their eminence will last forever. But Isaiah sharply returns us to reality, to God: "nations are but drops from a bucket, no more than moisture on the scales." (v. 15) History has proven that to be correct.

Others are persuaded that idols can very practically take God's place. These gods, though, are made by crafty hands. A goldsmith does his part with an overlay of gold to make the idol more attractive, adding studs of silver. (v. 19) Then this manufactured entity is expected to take care of us, answer our cries, and run the universe? Let's not smirk and say, "Give me a break until we uncover our own present-day idols—those antique cars, luxury-appointed private jets, baronial estates of those who are listed in the Fortune 500.

Rulers and princelings have also had their time in the sun as sons of righteousness, and God's equals. Or so they thought. But the Lord of heaven still cuts them down to size—grasshoppers. (v. 22) They are "as nothing." (v. 23) They are unstable, with no deep rootage. The first puff of wind and they are blown away. (v. 24) Even when they liken themselves to the famed Cedars of Lebanon—stately, aromatic, useful for building, fragrant as firewood. Yet, like those favorites of the forest, rulers have their inadequacies and insufficiencies.

In Babylon they believed that the stars ruled human destiny. Therefore, weren't those sparklers in the firmament—gods? Are the stars, then, the equals of the Holy One, or the nations, or idols or Rulers? Look up, He invites us. Consider who created the heavens (and all else) "through His great might, His strength and power." (v. 26) He has no equal.

PRAYER: *Divine Companion: We sing with Maltbie Babcock, "This is my Father's world: why should my heart be sad? The Lord is King; let the heavens ring! God reigns; let the earth be glad!" Amen.*

FRIEND, COME UP HIGHER

Isa. 42:1 *Behold my servant, whom I uphold, my chosen, in whom my soul delights. (RSV)*

In this first of four Servant Songs, God directs His workers toward a high-priority duty in their daily ministry. Apparently, He had noted their drift toward what they thought was important—but in His sight was not. The message was so strong, so clear, that Jesus couldn't mistake its primacy, and wisely injected it into the arteries of His own ministry—800 years later. (Luke 4:16-19)

Some thirty years later, when Saint Paul was at Troas (Troy) wondering in which direction he should turn in his missionary journeyings, he turned to Isaiah to see what help he might give. Sure enough, the Spirit directed Paul's attention to this section. Then, determined to be this kind of servant of the Lord, Paul crossed over to Europe to implement the divine agenda in and for the rest of his life.[1] (Acts 16:9)

At this point in the Hebrew-Christian tradition, the pivotal God-chosen word is, "Servant." Knowing all the dimensions of the value of such a person, God immediately puts His stamp of authority upon such a person with four personal attachments—"my servant," "I uphold," "my chosen," "my soul." And the bookends of this thirteen-word two-line text are "Behold" and "delights." Oh to be such a person who is so near to the heart of God.

Even with the privilege of being enwrapped by God's affection, not everyone jumps at the chance—especially when one learns what servanthood entails. For one thing, a servant "will bring forth justice to the nations." Placed first in the line of duty for a servant, justice is mentioned three times (v. 1,3,4) for added emphasis. Easy to be bent out of shape in the ongoing war of words, the thousands of languages and dialects, in myriad variant circumstances—justice could be anyone's guess. Yet, unless there's a gold standard for justice, the world will be retrograded to dancing mindlessly and confusedly around a golden calf in the town of Babel. Being a taker of justice unto the uttermost parts will identify us, when, as our Servant-Savior invited us to seek first His Kingdom and His right-

---

[1] Jerome Murphy-O'Connor, O.P., *Paul on Preaching*, pp. 112-113

eousness (justice), that all the other necessities may be credited to us. (Matt. 6:33)

Justice, to be specific, begins with championing the helpless, the vulnerable, like the blind and imprisoned (v. 7)—since it's a dog-eat-dog society out there, where, for the most part, people look out for number one!

When the parents died, the oldest child in the family took on the responsibility of looking after her younger siblings. She did all the housework and had an outside job as well. She literally worked herself to death. When she was dying of TB, one of those well-meaning visitors asked the girl if she had ever been baptized. "No." Was she ever in Catechism Class? "No." Did she ever join a church? "No." "Then, my dear," cried the visitor, "whatever are you going to tell God?" The dying girl brought out her work stained and said softly, "I'll show Him my hands." We only have to see Jesus' nail-pierced hands and feet, and His thorn-crowned brow to know what He's done to redeem our lives from destruction. And a servant is not greater than his Lord.

PRAYER: *"Lord Jesus, bless all who serve us, who have dedicated their lives to the ministry of others—all the teachers of our schools who labor so patiently with so little appreciation; all who wait upon the public, the clerks in the stores who have to accept criticism, complaints, bad manners, selfishness at the hands of a thoughtless public. Bless the mailmen, the drivers of buses who must listen to people who lose their tempers. Bless every humble soul who, in these days of stress and strain, preaches sermons without words."*[1] Amen.

---

[1] Peter Marshall, *Mr. Jones, Meet the Master*, p. 61

HALLELUJAH, WHAT A SAVIOR

Isa. 43:11 *I, I am the Lord, and besides me there is no savior. (RSV)*

From Central Command comes this no-holds-barred forthright statement from God.

In our uncourtly street language this would translate into: "Forget about any other Savior but God. There ain't any." And this, to others, is condemned as "The Scandal of Particularity." How dare anyone declare that there is no savior but the one who is lifted high in this Bible?!

Yet, everyone acknowledges the need of a Savior. As the opening of many a worship service intones: "We come here to find ourselves, it is so easy to get lost in the world." Indeed, there is so much lostness everywhere, wandering in the wilderness of Sinai for forty years is only a fractional account of mankind's meanderings. Sometimes it looks as if the Bible is nothing but the history of the Lost and Found department of the human race. Anything, anybody can be lost, and, sooner or later, is. If it's not a lost soul, it's a lost coin, or a prodigal son, or sheep. Or if the salt can lose its savor, can we be surprised about lost time, or hope, or a business deal, or losing loved ones, or our minds? Why go on—nibbling our unnerving earthly existence where we want to cry out for deliverance. Is there anyone, anything out there that can help us find ourselves and what else we seek?

It is understandable that God, aware of this persistent worldwide problem, addresses it as nobody else could.

To be sure, others have tried—and discovered that the moment they found the best coin, the whole world economy was in a meltdown in spite of the best efforts and wizardry of the high-octane economists. Or after the red-carpeted banquet for the returning prodigal son, we find his elder brother in the dumps and ready to fly the coop. And so it goes. Who, really, is an honest-to-goodness Savior?

Only the One who voices our text. And, lest a listener has hearing loss or is a slow learner, the Lord patiently repeats Himself, "I, I am the Lord, and besides me there is no Savior."

"What?" We may ask (as most people do), "What are His qualifications for the job?"

His subsequent support of His people gives the answer in the Old Testament. But in the New Testament, through His only begotten Son Jesus Christ, God shows, in words and deeds, the full answer. Jesus' concern for the last, the least, and the lost—throughout His life, defined His Saviorhood. It showed in all He did. Look at His teachings, the CBS parables (Luke 15:4-32) so called for easier recall: Coin, Boy, Sheep—all lost, and all found—the inanimate, the human, and the animal. Lostness in any form touched Him to the quick. As in Matt. 25:40, "Truly I tell you: anything you did for one of my brothers here, however insignificant (hungry, thirsty, a stranger, naked, ill, in prison), you did it for me." Or "Are not five sparrows sold for two pence? (You could get two sparrows for a penny. The fifth one was thrown in at no extra cost.) Yet not one of them is overlooked by God." (Luke 12:6) "I have not lost one of those you gave me." (John 18:9)

Look at His deeds. After feeding the 5,000, Jesus said to His disciples, "Gather up the pieces left over, so that nothing is wasted." (John 6:12)

Or the woman beyond medical help, who with a mere touch of Jesus' clothes, was healed by faith. (Mark 5:25-34) And it continued to the end with the penitent thief at Calvary being assured by the Savior that he would be in paradise with Jesus that very day. (Luke 23:43) As a climax Jesus will descend into hell to win Satan and his satellites back to God's fold, "That they all may be saved."

PRAYER: *Lord, we sing with John Newton: "Amazing grace! How sweet the sound, that saved a wretch like me! I once was lost, but now am found, was blind, but now I see." Amen.*

TRES-PASSES

Isa. 43:25 *I alone, I am He, who for his own sake wipes out your transgressions, who will remember your sins no more.*

Jerusalem was in ruins, and, as always, God's people couldn't or wouldn't identify the underlying reason for the downfall. So God gives them a lesson in salvation history.

Reviewing such histories is a spiritual restorative. The review mirror recalls where we were in imprisoning circumstances. Then came the day of rejoicing, and goodbyes to a past that belongs in a Dumpster. The road to the wide-open spaces with new faces—Ah! That's what we had lived for.

Yet, wretchedness persists in making the journey of life a three-legged race, with all the out-of-sync dangers that it entails. What options did we have for doing better the next time?

The Moses-led Exodus was a good jump starter, since all Exoduses have the same general outline. First there's the time away from home. For Moses' people it had been forty years. Other exilic experiences had been for decades longer. In the present day, in sin and not at home in the Lord—it depends! As with the Prodigal Son.

Then the heart strings twang us to the realization that there's no place like home—and preparations are made to go there.

What follows is the journey. There are outer pressures as with Pharaoh's charioteers who were determined to drag the Israelites back to Egypt and slavery. Or there are inner pressures—hunger and thirst, and the burning desire to return to the fleshpots of Egypt (they were tastier than what the Sinai desert offered). Or there was that inner magnet of wanting to worship the gods of Egypt. Hence the Golden Calf!

In fact, most of those Israelites never did make it to the Homeland because of persistent moral drawbacks. Those who took God as their guide made it to Home-sweet-Home. Sin is the destroyer of lives. This is what God is trying, yet again, to impress on His people—*US*, or is it *USA*?

Graciously the Lord makes His promises:

First, He will blot out our transgressions. That's a burden-lifter. Otherwise that backpack of personal wrongdoing saps our strength. Without it we can be the persons we were made to be.

Second, God promises not to remember our sins. And neither will we. When missionaries first went to Labrador, they couldn't find a word in the Eskimo language for "forgiveness," so they had to invent one. Literally it means, "not able to think about it anymore." That's pure joy. Now we have it on God's Word that He has not only blotted out the stain of sin, He who remembers the number of hairs on our heads is completely blank about our sins. And if He can't remember why should we? Herewith begins the New Exodus. The timely reminder here is that of Jesus forgiving the woman caught in the act of adultery. In dismissing her without condemnation, Jesus said, "Go: do not sin again." (John 8:11) Those final and critically meaningful five words are for us too. Therein lies the rub—where the rubber meets the road.

In December 2008, Charles Colson noted that "This financial crisis is in reality a crisis in character." Indeed. Analyze any critical situation honestly and it reveals Character, as the makeup of the word suggests is charred, blackened beyond recognition because it has been putting on an act, playing at being better than it is. This is exactly what God found His people to be. And their Temple (Church) and city (Jerusalem) had suffered accordingly. A New Exodus is necessary, a cleansing of sin by the Lord, and an entry into an at-homeness with Him. Lord, heal me at the heart, and let the world come in.

PRAYER: *"Once my heart was black but now, what joy. My sins are blotted out, I know! I have peace that nothing can destroy, My sins are blotted out, I know!"*[1] *Thank You, Lord. Amen.*

How Firm a Foundation

Isa. 44:8 *Is there a God besides Me? Indeed there is no other Rock; I know not one. (NKJV)*

God has proclaimed His uniqueness as a Savior, as a Forgiver of iniquities, and now as a Rock. We can understand the first two. But a Rock?

---

[1]Merrill Dunlop

The Psalms use the term plentifully. "The Lord is my rock and my fortress." (Ps. 18:2) "Who is a rock except our God?" (Ps. 18:31) "The Lord lives! Blessed be my Rock." (Ps. 18:46) "To You I will cry, O Lord my Rock!" (Ps. 28:1) "Their rock is not like our Rock." (Deut. 32:31)

The ancients knew and accepted the aptness of God as a Rock. And we should know better from the advancing study of Petrology—which has nothing to do with petrol, or oil, but with rocks. Jesus knew that. Remembering the Greek word for Rock was "Petros," Jesus answered, "I say to you: You are Peter, the Rock; and on this rock I will build my church, and the powers of death shall never conquer it." (Matt. 16:18)

Petrology has shown that in large measure the earth is made of rocks—even in the seas and oceans that cover the larger areas of earth. Submarine topography reveals that there are mountains below sea level that are almost a mile taller than Mt. Everest is above sea level, and that the strongest rocks are to be found on the ocean floor.

The earth is buttressed by rocks—from the Rock of Gibraltar to the Rocky Mountains (which are the backbone of the U.S.A., and a major topographical feature of the entire globe), to the Andes, Alps, Himalayas...Though there are some 1,500 minerals, only twelve come together to form the toughest of the rocks—granite, which covers enormous distances and remains solid on land and in sea for eons. And when, through all this act of creation the character of the Creator is revealed, that character is best described by the word that He Himself chose—Rock. From birthstones to tombstones we learn the character of this unspeakably fascinating backbone of planet earth—God.

The best definition of the word "God" is said to be found in the *Westminster Shorter Catechism*. But that was put together by theologians. Non-clergy persons have defined God in ways that have appealed to them personally. To Jesus, God was a "Father." But how did God think of Himself?

Jesus thought of Himself in many ways. "I am the door," or the "Good Shepherd" or "the Resurrection and the Life." Jesus saw that these were prior human needs and then strove to become the embodied fulfillment of those needs. As Dr. John Hunter wrote for us bunglers—dreams and deeds go their separate ways. In Jesus, however, dreams and deeds were fused, galvanized, since in Him all things cohere. And from whom did Jesus learn that but from His heavenly Father. In creating the world, God opened the secret regarding His own person. In response to seeing the mental sloth in humanity, and the moral rot and legal squishiness and under-the-counter dealings, God saw the need for stability, standardization, dependability, rock-like granitic character. And who or what could fulfill those qualifications but our Creator God? Is there anything to disqualify Him? Speak up, centuries. Let's hear from the wise. There's not a sound. What can they say? He had the last word: "I know not one."

But why the Rock? Isn't a diamond tougher, radiantly multifaceted? To be sure. Yet, consider its finitude (which means "limited to a small scale"). He is universal, now and forever, and has been, always.

PRAYER: *"While I draw this fleeting breath, When my eyes shall close in death, When I rise to worlds unknown, And* *behold Thee on Thy throne: Rock of Ages, cleft for me, Let me hide myself in thee."Amen.*[1]

IN THE BLEAK MIDWINTER CHEERS

Isa. 45:3 *I will give you the treasures of darkness, And hidden riches of secret places. (NKJV)*

What an astonishing promise! It is made by God to Cyrus who is an enemy of God's people. Cyrus, the head of the Medes and Persians, doesn't even know God. But God knows him, as God knows everyone since He has made us all, according to His own plans. He can use anyone to fulfill His purposes as He is about to do with Cyrus. "Reaching across the aisle" as the term is used on Capitol Hill, God extends a friendly "Right hand" (v. 1) across usually deeply traced exclusionary lines, to non-believer, alien Cyrus—and offers Cyrus a priceless gift that cannot be wrapped: "treasures of darkness." In fact, the promise is made a second time, in case it was unheard or misunderstood the first time: "hidden riches of secret places."

Few people receive such a gift. They don't even believe that there is anything of value in the pitch blackness out there. Unless it is hidden out in public in the glare of noon, its reality is questioned. But look at the fortunes that would have been missed if the dense fog had been taken for impenetrable nothingness.

Those who went after King Tut's tomb in the Valley of the Kings at Luxor, Egypt, labored in vain for years. Enormous amounts of money were spent on several expeditions. Tons of earth were

---

[1] Augustus M. Toplady

removed from the site and hopes sagged. Was it a case of a black cat in an unlighted room at midnight? But just when the explorers were about to quit, someone broke through a hole in the wall—and there it was, the most memorable archaeological discovery of the twentieth century. So massive was the find that at the Cairo Museum they had to build a special extension to accommodate the contents of the tomb. Millions of tourists have been enthralled by the thousands of showpieces, many of which have graciously been allowed to be exhibited all over the world, Treasures that had lain in darkness for thousands of years!

But God wasn't particularly thinking of gold and jewels in our text's promise. He Himself was up against a seemingly hopeless situation in the second verse of the Bible: "The earth was without form, and void; and darkness was on the face of the deep." How's that for a vast, formless waste, all blacked out? Where do you begin? Why even begin? Why not try somewhere else, that has even a single sunbeam of hope? Nope.

Well, there's the promise, do with it what you will. After all, it's on God's Word.

On Christmas Eve we are reminded of how on this day in 1818 in a little church in the Austrian mountains, mice had chewed the wires of the organ. What to do? Night coming on, a church service in peril. Worshippers to be turned away? Nope. Priest and organist sensed treasures in the darkness, hidden riches in secret places. Quickly they wrote the simple carol "Silent night," and at the midnight mass it was sung with guitar accompaniment, little realizing that every Christmas thousands would visit "The Silent Night Chapel" to sing "Stille Nacht." Now the world's favorite carol, it has been translated into more than 200 languages.

When Sir Ernest Shackleton needed recruits for one of his expeditions to the South Pole, he put this advertisement in *The Times of London*: "Men Wanted: For hazardous journey, small wages, bitter cold, long months of complete darkness, constant danger, safe return doubtful. Honour and recognition in case of success." They responded. And the world has benefitted geographically and morally.

PRAYER: *Lord, we remember how in the valley of the shadow You promise to be with us. You are our Treasure, now and ever. Amen.*

HOW SILENTLY THE WONDROUS GIFT IS GIVEN

Isa. 46:3-4 *Hearken to me, O house of Jacob, all the remnant of the house of Israel, who have been borne by me from your birth, carried from the womb; even to your old age I am He, and to grey hairs I will carry you. I have made, and I will bear; I will carry and will save. (RSV)*

It may come as a shocker to hear God claim that He has borne us, His people, from our birth, and carried us "from the womb." (v. 3) And here we've been thinking that we were getting along pretty well on our own, with the help of some people around us. The troubler has been that unthinkingly we have assumed that nobody but our parents did that for us—at least at life's beginning. We have veered sharply into the tangle between "born" and "borne."

Yes, we were born to our parents, and because of them. But the moment the umbilical cord was cut, we began to be distanced from our parents. We don't realize how we've been like a baton in life's relay race, and how we have been handed from one bearer to another—persons who have borne the responsibility of sharing in our ultimate winning or losing. How little aware we are of our dependence on one another.

Yes, Mother delivered us at the Maternity Center, or at home, but not without the assistance of a midwife, or nurse, or doctor, or the Emergency Service ambulance personnel, or an alert policeman in his squad car. Whoever they were, they handed the precious baby into the next pair of caring arms, and vanished into the fog of forgotten history. From there a new life may know a loving embrace or a hasty, loveless transfer to family members, friends, Orphan's Homes, Children's Welfare Societies—or a combination thereof.

The next handover is to School and Sunday School teachers of all kinds, with the subtle teaching that also goes on through each teacher's character and personality—good and bad.

By now the person is ready to commit his/her life to a job. Here again are teachers—fellow workers, managers, superintendents, bosses either officially or self-appointed.

Somewhere in this milieu, ones affections are handed to a lover, who becomes a spouse.

Then come the children who hand us around with the introductory, "This is my mom," "This is my dad," or grandmother or great-grandfather—until we hear even God saying, "to grey hairs I will carry you." (v. 4) And that's what He has been doing all along. Parents have been long since gone. The doctors, nurses, teachers work-bosses and associates, perhaps even the spouse, have all had similar experiences, and have preceded us to glory. Even if they were asked if they had known us, or what they had done for us—they would be at a loss for words. Yet, through the long, long trail a-winding, we were being slipped from one person's grasp to another's (and then forgotten?), while the one Divine Lover of our souls has been the only consistent never-failing connector. No one else has borne, carried us from womb to tomb, as He has. He says so in today's text. Since we didn't even know that He was looking out for us, without our asking for His protection. Now that we do, let us thank Him, and drop any fears we may have regarding the afterlife. He's "been there, done that."

"I am going to prepare a place for you. And if I go and prepare a place for you, I shall come again and take you to myself, so that where I am you may be also." (John 4: 2-3) (NEB)

PRAYER: *How grateful we are, Lord, for Your silently effective companionship, from here to eternity. Amen.*

GET THE L OUT OF GOLD

Isa. 46:5-6 *To whom will you liken me and make me equal, and compare me, that we may be alike? Those who lavish gold from the purse, and weigh out silver in the scales, hire a goldsmith, and he makes it into a God, then they fall down and worship! (RSV)*

On Sinai, God made it clear and imperative that "You must have no other God besides me...You must not make a carved image for yourself...You must not bow down to them in worship; for I the Lord, Your God, am a jealous God." (Exod. 20:3-5, NEB) Yet, as we have often noted, rebellious humans have never been able to keep these and the other commandments from being kicked around and bloodied. Their absoluteness, is a defiant challenge that is willingly accepted and battled by humans.

Knowing this, nobody has been more open to questions about the issue—even suggesting tricky twisters that partisan persons have hidden from their own view—than God Himself. He wants His loved ones to fully understand and obey His commands, which are fundamental to our faith.

From His vantage point He sees three dangers facing His people at the moment (that could apply to any era).

First, the Hebrew homeland was surrounded by idolatrous nations, some of whom had attractive features—certain customs, worship practices, military and economic strength, cities and buildings and monuments, which made outsiders salivate.

Second, there was gold, known from Genesis to Revelation, which had become the prime passion of all people. As Thomas Hood explains:

> Gold! Gold! Gold! Gold!
> Bright and yellow, hard and cold,
> Molten, graven, hammer'd, and roll'd;
> Heavy to get, and light to hold;
> Hoarded, barter'd, bought and sold,
> Stolen, borrow'd, squander'd, doled:
> Spurn'd by the young, but hugg'd by the old
> To the very verge of the churchyard mould;
> Price of many a crime untold:
> Gold! Gold! Gold! Gold!
> Good or bad a thousand-fold!
> How widely its agencies vary:
> To save—to ruin—to curse—to bless—

> As even its minted coins express,
> Now stamp'd with the image of
> Good Queen Bess,
> And now of a bloody Mary.

Then, when they found each other, that is, when idolatrous nations could find nothing more glittering than gold out of which to make their gods—those gods exerted a powerful influence over peoples (like the Hebrews) who didn't have such dazzling beauties to worship. For God's people it became a stumbling block to their faith.

Third, God had no defenders of His demandments, since the prophets of the time were all false and fakey. Even today one can see statues and engravings of such profitless prophets—drunks, staggering down the street, carrying their wine jugs. And those "prophets" were usually stark naked. Such dropouts couldn't be counted on to hear the word of God correctly, much less to interpret it aright to God's chosen people, even if it meant assassination for speaking forthrightly.

It was at times like this that God cried: "Whom shall I send? Who will go for us?" That is when Isaiah answered the call, saying, "Here am I! Send me." (Isa. 6:8) Not only did Isaiah speak out for the Lord, he wrote this Book of Isaiah with sixty-six chapters, a miniature Bible with its sixty-six books. No wonder Isaiah's end came when he was placed inside a hollow log and sawn in half.

PRAYER: *Lord, help us to be your person of the hour. Speak to and through us, now and ever. Amen.*

HOW TO GAIN—AGAIN AND AGAIN

Isa. 48:18 *If only you had listened to my commands…*

"If only" is the worst of forlorn cries. In a tiny

compass it contains a lifetime of lost opportunities, of what might have been. Eden at last. As with those who claimed that they had never seen Jesus hungry, thirsty, a stranger, naked, ill, in prison, and did nothing for Him. (Matt. 25:44) As with those who had been invited to take refuge under Jesus' protecting wings "as a hen gathers her brood under her wings" (Matt. 23:37), but they shoved away that "hen." As with those in today's text who refused to listen, even though the Lord had "from the beginning" not spoken in secret. (Isa. 48:16)

Well, what did the losers lose; what could they have immeasurably gained?

First, "your peace would have been like a river." (Isa. 48:18) Really? Isn't peace more like war in masquerade? Isn't it as Thomas Hardy found "that war makes rattling good history: but Peace is poor reading"? Peace? You mean that stupid improbability where "the wolf shall dwell with the lamb and the leopard shall lie down with the kid"? (Isa. 11:6) "No," replies the Lord, peace "like a river." That gives you an idea of the expansiveness and effectiveness of peace. One Christmas Eve in the Church of the Nativity in Bethlehem, I heard the Bishop of Jerusalem say, "Jesus is the Prince of Peace and the principle of peace." Indeed, princes practice throne-sitting in preparation for their accession to the throne. But the principle of peace works its way through the infrastructural life of the prince's Kingdom. Old Testament Isaiah came at it in another way. Had the people listened to God, Isaiah said, their peace would have been like a river, not the drip, drip, dripping of a leaky faucet. Some rivers depend on rain. When the monsoons pass, those rivers dry up. That is how peace is for most people—something the law courts try to do for a warring marriage—arrange an armistice. But that's usually a two-minute silence. A river that is fed by melting snows and abundant springs is ceaseless, and flows from age to age. Peace is more than an absence of conflict. It is a oneness with God.

Second, had people listened to God, their righteousness would have been like the waves of the sea. (v. 18) That seabird, the halcyon, is born, lives, dies on the sea waves. It makes its nest on seaweed and driftwood, and knows the right time to lay her young and care for the hatchlings. Righteousness is that kind of clean, open, expansive living, as long as oceans last.

Third, had people listened to God, their children would have been numberless as grains of sand (a reference to the promise made by God to Abraham in Gen. 22:17). Not everyone leaves a legacy like that. It is an unbroken bloodline for centuries where the family name is never cut off. (v. 19) Rather, honorably it continues to emblazon the family pedigree in an endless line of splendor.

In addition to these three promises regarding peace, righteousness and our ever-multiplying family—which are still possible of fulfillment if we listen to God's commands—He urges us to break out of our bondage (v. 20), for, like the Israelites who fled the coop after 400 years of being caged, we will be helped all along the journey to freedom in a very promising land. (v. 21) Hear ye the word of the Lord and thrive in peace, righteousness, and family fruitfulness. No more "if I had only."

PRAYER: *We hear, O Lord, Thy summons, And answer: Here are we! Send us upon Thine errand, Let us*

Thy servants be. Our strength is dust and ashes, Our years a passing hour, But Thou canst use our weaknesses, To magnify Thy power. Amen.[1]

SERVANT OF GOD, WELL DONE

Isa. 49:1 *The Lord called me before I was born.*

The "call" here refers to the servant ministry, in this first of three poems (49:1-6; 50:4-9; 52:3-5) devoted to the subject most dear to Isaiah's heart: servanthood.

Although originally the servant was understood to be the people of Israel, devout readers of these poems have rightly put themselves in the position of being the servant called by God.

Why so eager to join the ranks of the servers? When we see in the following ways how meticulously God prepares His workers for labor in His Kingdom, what precautions He plans, what compensation He offers, one hears the call in one's very bones, and responds wordlessly—"Here am I, send me."

First, "He made my tongue a sharp sword," (v. 2) not necessarily to speak cutting words, but like a sword to be a defender and protector of life.

How intuitively wise of the Lord to bring tongue and sword together as His servant's first requirement. As Jesus' brother James wrote, "The tongue is a fire...it sets the whole course of our existence alight." (James 3:6) And the sword seen first as guarding the garden of Eden, (Gen. 3:24) on to Heb. 4:12 where the word of God "cuts more keenly than any two-edged sword, piercing so deeply that it divides soul and spirit," on to Rev.

---

[1] John Haynes Holmes

19:21 where the sword comes "out of the rider's mouth," we see the connection and the awesome power of both tongue and sword. Knowing the dangers involved at this point, the Lord reassures His workers of the safety measure He provides—"in the shadow of His hand," (v. 2) which for emphasis is repeated in 49:16: "I have graven you in the palms of my hands." The olive-wood artisans of the Holy Land, picking on this lovely idea in Isaiah, have fashioned thousands of souvenirs of God's chosen person safe in God's hand. In fact, as the song chants, "He's got the whole world in His hands"—both of them nail-scarred.

Second, "he made me into a polished arrow." (v. 2) From earliest days the bow and arrow were man's constant companions for subsistence (shooting for food animals, birds, fish), and existence in warfare. A stiff polished arrow was necessary to withstand buckling under the enormous build-up of speed, from rest to 200 feet a second. And so must the Lord's servant be strong enough not to become bent out of shape when pressure and velocity are revved up. When the going gets tough, the tough are counted on to keep going.

Third, "in his quiver he hid me away." (v. 2) If hiding in His hand is not enough protection, there's always His handy quiver as a backup. Along with the other arrows (servants), one rests in Him, ready at His bidding to attend to the things that make for peace in an accurate feathery flight to the target's center.

So far the Lord has been doing all the giving: weaponizing His servants with a sword-like tongue. With the rigidity and dependability of an arrow; with reinforcements of the Lord's guiding hand and His quiver. He has even bestowed honor and strength upon His troopers. (v. 5) But since to whom much is given of them shall much be required, the Lord now makes His assignment known: "I will give you as a light to the nations, that my salvation may reach to the end of the earth." (v. 6) The Lord expects the best of His servants to help Him give the world the best He has in store for it: LIGHT. That is how it all started out, with His very first creative act: Light. It drove back the darkness had brought form out of chaos. And God wants that to happen again, with our help.

PRAYER: *We see Your plan, Lord, and our task. So we sing with William Pierson Merrill, "Rise up. O men of God, Have done with lesser things; Give heart and mind and soul and strength to serve the King of Kings." Amen.*

AS ONCE HE SPOKE IN ZION

Isa. 51:1 *Listen to me, all who follow after the right, who seek the Lord.*

The prophet, writing from Jerusalem-central, asks us to listen up to three short prophecies: First, (v. 1-2) "consider the rock from which you were hewn." That is a backward look, which deserves attention since too many persons turn their backs to it, considering history a great dust-heap. Yet, as Thomas Jefferson found that "history, by apprising (men) of the past will enable them to judge of the future"—a chart and compass for national endeavor. Pre-dating our recent history, there's Cicero's insightful comment that, "To be ignorant of what happened before you were born is to be ever a child. For what is man's lifetime unless the memory of past events is woven with those of earlier times?"

Listening then is communication, even when there's hearing loss, or loss of sight, or complete paralysis of the body. One such patient could only blink his eyes. Family members wrote the alphabet on a chalkboard. They would point to each of the letters on the board. When it was the right letter the patient would blink. So words were put together and he wrote a book.

Love, too, has its own language—independent of age, sex, creed, nationality. Eyes speak to eyes, and heart to heart. So here Isaiah is asking us to listen to the past. It has much to tell us about God—the Rock from whom we were chiseled, and Whom we can still hear. "In the rustling grass, I hear Him pass, He speaks to me everywhere." (Maltbie Babcock) Are we listening?

Before taking our eyes off the past with all its deserted ruinations, there is a little hymn of salvation (v. 3), in which we hear thanksgiving and joyous singing for the rebuilding and replanting and rejuvenation that is taking place. The past is not wasteland. It is ground for hope.

Second, Isaiah invites us to listen to the present: Look up to the heavens for they "tell you the glory of God, heaven's vault makes known his handiwork. One day speaks to another...and this without speech or language, or sound of any voice." (Ps. 19:1-3) Now look down for "This is my Father's world, And to my listening ears, All nature sings, and round me rings the music of the sphere." (Babcock)

Having listened to past and present, how about the unknown future? The unknown can give us the jimmies. Not so, says the Lord, who not only ask us to listen to Him but who also listens to us. He wants us to know that when we have His Law in our hearts (v. 7), and not some Church building or denominational or political system or some personally constructed philosophical razz-matazz, we will not be shaken by the crackling changes around us. We will, instead, remain as unmoved by seismic shock as the Rock from whence we were hewn. His promised last word, a refrain, is "my saving power will last forever, and my deliverance to all generations." (v. 8)

And all of this comes to us per kind favor of the Lord, from Jerusalem (v. 4), in deed and in truth and in time-sensitive opportunities which He observes will be for our good. He that has ears to hear, listen up to the past for the betterment of the present and the yet-unknown future. Blest Town, mouthpiece of the Lord.

PRAYER: *To Your incoming word, Lord, unblock our blurry sense. We want to hear the whole story, no less. Amen.*

ON RISING TO THE OCCASION

Isa. 51:17 *Arouse yourself; rise up, Jerusalem.*

The Lord's people were in hot water, which, in a way, was good. They got steamed up. Otherwise they were flat out—asleep. The prophet clears his bullhorn voice and gives a wake-up call. And, as the instruction goes: When you wake up, get up or you might go back to slumberland and miss even the alarm clock's extended snooze period. Besides, it had been too long a time of slouching, for "ages long past." (v. 9)

Meanwhile, the people had become a timid lot, bowing subserviently before their oppressors; going to the pits, unsure of daily bread. (v. 14) They had forgotten the Rock from whence they were hewn, and how He had sliced the dreaded sea monster in half when He parted the Red Sea, allowing the Exiles to make a safe crossing. (v. 10) And He could do it again, for them. Yet here they were, having produced out of all the sons they had borne—no leader to guide them or take their hands and comfortingly deliver them to a safe haven. (v. 18) Slouching spiritually, they blearily discover that the land is devastated, and the state of the populace is that of famine and sword. (v. 19) The picture was despairing, especially since those who were destined for future leadership had become "like antelopes caught in a net." (v. 20)

In passing, one wonders why Isaiah introduces antelopes. Couldn't another animal or bird have done as well? Hardly. A shrewd observer who micromanaged his words, the prophet was struck by the similarity between humans and antelopes. They come in different shapes, sizes, colors, abilities—from the Eland at five feet at the shoulders, to the dik-dik at thirteen inches. Beautiful animals, swift of foot free-spirits (where the deer and the antelope play), ready to outpace their predators, made to lead the herd to green pastures and beside still waters. Then, suddenly, horrors, the animal is trapped in a wary hunter's net! There's a desperate struggle for freedom, but it's too late.

So the wake-up call is repeated, this time not just to come awake and stand up, but also to put on strength. (52:1) And that takes time, if you have ever been in a physical (or soul) fitness program.

Now, exuding strength, there is a need for publishing the good news of what the Lord has done, for onlookers, usually time-bound and depending on immediate sensory perceptions, are persuaded that the miracle of transformation has come from some climate change, or medical break-through, or political finagling, or some world religion's dead scrolls—ignoring the fact that "Your God reigns (52:7), "Your God who leads the cause of His people." (51:22) Those tidings deserve publishing since, too often they are swept under the rug, stamped on, laughed at, zippered shut. Nobody seems to want to hear the "good tidings of good." (52:7)

To those with renewed strength finally comes the directive not just to stand there, strong, but also to "deport, go out" (52:11) get going, but "touch no unclean thing." How that echoes in Jesus' final word to the woman taken in adultery. So you're back on your feet: good—but watch it, or you can be back in a slouch as a couch potato. Mashed! Sin no more. Knowing that possibility, too, Isaiah gives a flashback to the shepherd's Psalm (23), that the Lord "will go before you" ("He leadeth me"). And He will be your rearguard ("Surely goodness and mercy shall follow me").

PRAYER: *Dear God: How You mercifully shepherd us slackers. Awaken, strengthen us to publish the glad tidings to those who are missing out on so much. Amen.*

A PORTRAIT OF THE GREAT HEALER

Isa. 53:5 *But he was wounded for our transgression, he was bruised for our iniquities; upon him was the chastisement that made us whole, and with his stripes we are healed.*

This text, part of the famous section of Isa.

52:13-53:12, which is known as the most original prophecy in the whole Book of Isaiah, is a "critical mass" for Christians. The question has been, does it or doesn't it apply to the life of Christ?

Theologians, we are aware, come in assortments. Some shamefully play the part of a chameleon and take on the protective coloration of the prevailing popular blend. Others, stubbornly independent, have maintained that this passage in Isaiah refers to King Cyrus, or Zerubbabel, or Jeremiah or Moses or even the author himself, or to Israel, or the community in Jerusalem. In close-ups, however, none of these fill the picture. Only One does—Jesus! Dr. Leslie Weatherhead, famed pastor of the City Temple, London, used to tell of going to the Royal Albert Hall to hear Handel's Messiah. Once, Weatherhead took his father-in-law. After standing up for the singing of the Hallelujah Chorus, the audience was seated and Weatherhead turned to his father-in-law and found the old gentleman in tears. What was the matter? The dear soul wept proudly, saying: "That's my Savior they were singing about."

That's the enraptured feeling one gets on reading this passage of Scripture: "That's my Savior, Jesus Christ, described in exquisite detail by Isaiah." That, too, is why Isaiah is called the Evangelist of the Old Testament. The spiritually sensitive prophet could feel the radiating presence of the coming Redeemer of the world. If radio transmitters and Internet devices can send and receive messages from the moon and planets, is it not conceivable for the world's Creator to do that on a mightier scale? Besides, forty-seven passages from throughout the Old Testament, seventeen Old Testament quotes in the New Testament, have done pinpointingly accurate accounting of Jesus' birth, ministry, death, and resurrection. To force someone other than Jesus to put on such a semblance of Messiahship is to see David, a shepherd boy in King Saul's armor. As David laid the armor aside, he mumbled disgustedly, "I cannot use these for I have not proved them." It was a misfit. (1 Sam. 17:39) And this passage from Isaiah is a disconnect unless it is understood as referring to Jesus of Nazareth. "Christ is the need of the world, and for Him it cries. Though it babble of gold and fame, it lies, it lies. Though it would not have us know, its secret it cannot keep. The Lord is the need of the world, and it tells it awake or asleep."

The significance of Jesus' connection with Isaiah was initiated by Jesus Himself at the beginning of His public ministry in His hometown synagogue in Nazareth. Handed the Isaiah scroll to read in public, Jesus found, without difficulty, the verses He wanted from Chapter 61. This was not as easy as it looks. Remember, chapters and verses had not yet been invented. In those days the lines just ran on and on. For the Master to have put His finger on the verses of His choice (recounted in Luke 4:18-19) was no small task. It showed in a flash His familiarity with the beloved text. Not stopping there, "He began to address them: 'Today' he said, 'in your hearing this text has come true.'" (Luke 4:21)

Isaiah is quoted 21 times in the New Testament, more than all the other writing prophets put together.

PRAYER: *Thank You, Lord, for granting Isaiah the insight to recognize Jesus coming down the Glory Road, 700 years before our Redeemer appeared. Hail to the only Messiah the world will ever have. Amen.*

THE LORD'S LEGACY FOR YOU

Isa. 54:17 *This is the heritage of the servants of the Lord.*

Addressing Jerusalem, the Lord calls them into a new era. They had been like high-spirited juveniles, taking the law into their own hands and rampaging around.

For their own good they were stopped in their tracks and were hurt by their own lunacies.

Now, judging them to be ready for a mature morality, the Lord envisions for them an expansion into all the world. Putting it in terms that would be understood by the tent-dwelling population that they were, He tells them to lengthen their cords, strengthen their stakes (v. 2), that is, cover increasing territory. Could this have been the place in Isaiah from which Jesus drew His great Commission to go into all the world and make disciples? (Matt. 28:19) Certainly John, in his Book of Revelation, plucked his construction of the New Jerusalem out of this chapter of Isaiah, verses 11 and 12.

With a bit of history, the Lord refers to Noah's Flood and how He had dealt with that wicked situation, likening it to how He had just washed Jerusalem clean. Further, as He had promised (with a rainbow) never again to flood the world, so He would never again be harsh with Jerusalem. "My covenant of peace shall not depart from you." (v. 10)

Then comes the legacy to the reformed people of Jerusalem. Not only will the city be beautified, but also the people will be.

1. They will be taught by the Lord. (v. 13) That's just what Jesus came to do. "Never man spoke like this

Man." Even as a twelve-year-old He had much to teach the wise men in the Temple. (Luke 2:46-47) Since the Lord fulfills Himself in many ways, He teaches through all those persons whom we meet daily, in person, by phone, correspondence, shopping...As for being one-on-one with the Lord, spirit with spirit do meet, closer is He then breathing, nearer than hands and feet. Then there are His angels of mercy, who by their soundless sacrifices and prayerful support teach us more about the goodness of the Lord in the land of the living than a stack of pseudo-pions pap books.
2. Prosperity will be part of the divine legacy. (v. 13) Across the world prosperity has indeed been one of the benchmarks of Jewish life deservedly. Delightfully this promissory note may be claimed by any of God's faithful—and has been.
3. Membership in the Righteousness Establishment—freedom to walk in the steps of the Savior. You can't get any closer to divinity for eternity than that.
4. The elimination of fear. He has scratched out the last two words of the much-quoted Presidential pronouncement, that "There is nothing to fear, but fear." (v. 14)
5. How the Lord rewards! In His will and Testament He has given us all the above blessings. But what about that Grim Reaper named War? It swoops down like a pack of wolves on the sheepfold. No one is spared. As is still done early in a war, each side aims at crippling the armament manufacturing plants of the opponent. And that's where the Lord intervenes. He goes beyond the arsenal to the designers and creators of weaponry, regardless of which side they are on—controlling their rapacity

(note the word "rape" tucked in there), and sending the blacksmith to smithereens. (v. 16)

6. Finally, there's that tongue again, which is mightier than the pen and the sword. Some people have the gift of the gab, using the tongue like a rapier to run you through or slash you into short cuts of meat. Yet, in the Lord's will for His people, it reads like this: "You shall confute every tongue that rises against you in judgment." (v. 17)

PRAYER: *Father, we are going to keep Your will in our bank vault. Often we will read it and rejoice, and praise Your Holy Name. Amen.*

HIS LIFE-SUSTAINING WORD

Isa. 55:10-11 *As the rain and snow come down from heaven...so it is with my word issuing from my mouth.*

Why so many words, Lord? We can't keep up with them. They come like rainfall upon the mown grass or as a snowstorm. At the moment I am watching such a snowfall, the flakes, no two alike, keep coming, each for its appointed purpose, regardless of what I think or say. The earth asks for subsistence, and the call is answered. In due season there is new growth and subsistence for humans and animals and plants. The silent miracle cycles and recycles itself, with no instructions from us. But someone is giving orders. It is He who prompted His prophet to write our text for today. I see that the snow comes down and stays. Snowplows and shovels push it aside and curse its unnecessary volume. But nobody attempts to shoot it back up to where it came. It has its own trajectory and purpose, and the rest is up to those who receive it. Some people use it as a plaything: skating, skiing, sledding—Olympic or otherwise. There are snowballs, snowmen, ice castles. Others take it seriously, studying temperatures, snowbirds and animals, avalanches, crevasses, wind chill and myriad factors associated with the Abominable Snowman—all for the purpose of enabling humans to negotiate climbing, navigating, flying in snowy climes.

This was the Lord's explanation regarding His unreturnable Word. It comes to us with a purpose. Some people shovel the Word aside, and there it lies. Others play games with God's word, pitching it at one another's heads—"God damn you," "Geez," "Hell with you," "For God's sake." Others put an old straw hat on his head, a pipe in his mouth, black buttons and a carrot for eyes and nose, a broom at his side. Very funny. But, oh, how the Lord yearns to be taken seriously. He has so much wrapped up for us in His gifted Words. To shovel that into the bushes is to risk a joyless earthly life. One commentator believes that "This is a chapter where God's love for all people and the dependability of His Word are celebrated as nowhere else in the Old Testament." (J. F. A. Sawyer)

Moreover, Isaiah did not use the Word "snow" as a poetic accident. Yes, it does snow in Jerusalem, with its 3,000-foot elevation. Since ancient times people have been interested in snow. And whether Isaiah knew what we now know about snow, the fact remains that there are similarities between snow crystals that are the most beautiful and have the greatest variation in form of all minerals—and the Word of God. For one thing, snowflakes crystallize with geometric symmetry, and give an accurate account of the air in which they originated and grew—some cottony flakes to several inches in diameter. In this light, the Word of God ought not to be doubted. Though it comes through earthly processes, it was put together in heavenly places by the Creator Himself. Though tine crystals, called "diamond dust" may take several hours to fall 1,000 feet, the average flake can drop that same distance in eight to ten minutes. Can we say that the Showers of Blessing come sometimes slowly, sometimes quickly? Nor is it only at certain times. Climatologists have found that in the summer, too, snow crystals can be seen in Cirrus clouds four to seven miles above the earth. Those clouds are made up almost entirely of ice crystals.

Then the Word became flesh and dwelt (and still does) among so that overhead and underfoot we are enveloped by His love.

PRAYER: *O Word of God, Incarnate, May I have a word with You, often? Amen.*

ON BEING ONE IN HIM

Isa. 56:8 *Thus says the Lord God, who gathers the outcasts of Israel.*

Just when the Book of Isaiah seems to have covered the whole waterfront of values necessary for being true children of God—a new door opens. It reveals a problem which Israel has swept under the rug. The chosen few assured themselves of divine protection. But what about the outcasts, were they to be forever shut-outs, even if they eagerly desired inclusion?

Foreigners wailed: "The Lord will surely separate me from his people. (v. 3) Unhappy Eunuchs cried in distress, "Behold, I am a dry tree." (v. 3)

Foreigners were not just those of other countries, but also like the Samaritans of the Holy Land who were of mixed blood. When Jews had been hauled off into a lengthy exile in Babylon, many Jews were left behind to keep the infrastructure intact. In time, as has eternally happened with foreign troops occupying the land, there was intermarriage and/or cohabitation with the native population. So that when Jews of pure descent returned from exile, there was an immediate divide between the true-bloods and the mixed. As for the Eunuchs, they were men who were either born that way—unable to procreate—or men who had convinced themselves that procreation was the root of all evil and had themselves castrated. These (also women, lepers, etc.), too, were shunned by the bluebloods. Foreigners and Eunuchs, many of whom in themselves had done nothing wrong, were already faithfully practicing the attractive Jewish faith. And although the heated animosities of the factions kept them apart, God saw that such infantile behavior was not in accord with His will. Not that He gave the outcasts a blank check to write in whatever they desired. Rather, He demanded a toeing of the line—righteousness and justice (v. 1), keeping the Sabbath (v. 4), loving and serving the Lord. (v. 6) Then they would be most welcome to the Holy City. (v. 7) We understand that the Prophet never lived to see that day. But the seed was sown, and though it took five centuries to come above ground, we see it beginning to flower through the teaching of Jesus: "Come unto me all who labor and are heavy laden." (God so loved the world...that whosoever...) In the Parable of the Good Samaritan, where the despised Samaritan did more commendably than the Jewish

Priests: "Go into all the world and make disciples of all nations." (The Samaritan woman at the well.) Then Peter, on the housetop at Joppa learns that "What god has cleansed call not thou common." Philip finds the Ethiopian Eunuch reading from Isaiah and preaches to him about Jesus. Then there was Paul, the apostle to the Gentiles. This growing world, inclusiveness is modestly illustrated on the Aleutian islands that stretch 1,200 miles between Sitka, Alaska, and the peninsula of Kamchatka, Russia. The Aleuts are of Eskimo stock, but of hybrid blood and customs. When the Russians occupied the area in 1741, they brutalized the natives. In 1867 Russia transferred the Aleutian archipelago and its possessions in northwestern America to the United States. Still the Aleuts were a separated people, not only from the rest of the U.S., but also because the International Date Line cut the island chain in half. That caused people living side by side to be worlds apart. According to the clock, one household is just starting the day, while the next door neighbor's clock is at midnight the day before.

Today the Aleuts are a happy people, with their rich international Christian faith. They intermingle, going back and forth on their stepping-stone islands. In the summer they share each others' cultures (American and Russian) with fairs, games, dances, and other hilarities. Any appearance of discriminating against each other is purely an optical Aleutian. The Lord is still gathering the outcasts everywhere.

PRAYER: *For one reason or another, Lord, we are all outcasts. But You, the God of love, have drawn a circle to take us all in. We thank You fervently. Amen.*

The Sympathizing Savior

Isa. 57:4 *Are you not the children of transgression, the offspring of deceit?*

We can better understand why God prefers the outcasts of society (see previous Meditation), especially when He sees the supposedly righteous in places of responsibility behaving like disgusting ingrates. That is what happens when we take more freedom than we can handle morally. Unrestricted freedom leads to a free-fall into free-doom.

Look at these Jerusalemites whom the Lord has picked out for a verbal flogging. They were in positions of leadership because they had once been considered worthy. Now look at them—guard dogs of society? They couldn't bark at the approach of danger (56:10), much less sense what was disastrous for their constituents and what was desirous; what should be booted and what coveted. The Lord does not hesitate to call them "dumb dogs" that are prone to curl up and drift off to dreamland.

These leaders were also supposed to shepherd the population. But, not good shepherds, they did their own thing—drink, drank, drunk (56:12)—when they were supposed to lead their flock beside still waters for the restoration of their souls. The castigation of these lousy leaders continues down their list of depravities. The Lord doesn't mince words. He next mentions the childish and vulgar habit of sticking out their tongues at persons who are decent and quite unlike their sordid selves. (v. 4) Then come the sex orgies in which these leaders indulged—whenever and wherever they got a chance. They did it indoors and out, even on the mountains and under the trees. They invited others to their bed, and frequented the beds of others. They wore brashly "hooked on nakedness" (v. 8) with all the burning lust of which the human body is capable. The settings, too, were purposefully orchestrated with perfumes and pleasantries to cause maximum arousals of emotion. (v. 9) Even hell was canvassed for its titillating input. (v. 9)

One learns, by now, that such lecherous, treacherous, lifestyles could only belong to those who had far removed themselves from God, which he now makes clear to these evildoers. The "smooth stones" mentioned in verse 6 refer to idol worship to which the Lord returns at the end of His tirade: "When you cry out (as such people eventually do in their desperation) let your collection of idols deliver you! The wind will carry them off, a breath will take them away." (v. 13) With no moral compass, no captain of their salvation, no divine pilot to steer them to the harbor of holiness, such persons are at the merciless breaker's smashing power. The elements overwhelm them with liquor, sex, rudeness, laziness, godlessness, a craving for money, and hell's worst. Yet the dumb dogs are also deaf: they will not listen. The ultimate danger was that with such leaders—the *people* could go to the dogs. How much worse could these bogus leaders have been? They had zeroed out on their main responsibilities. They wallowed in vices, turning their backs on the God who had done so much for them. He was right, they were "the children of transgression, the offspring of deceit."

Surely they deserved all the terrors by night that befell them. Still, God sees not as man sees.

In His finale (v. 13) God tells these slackers what they can still re-possess if they return to Him: "But he who takes refuge in me shall possess the land, and shall inherit my holy mountain (Jerusalem)." "What wondrous love is this, O my soul."

Nor is that the end. He who is the same yesterday, today, and forever can work the same miracle of renewal on any reader of this page, if we take refuge in Him. "Under His wings...Who from His love can sever?...Safely abide forever."[1]

PRAYER: *"When all Thy mercies, O my God, My rising soul surveys, Transported with the view I'm lost in wonder, love, and praise."*[2] *Amen.*

DARE TO DECLARE

Isa. 58:1 *Declare to my people their transgressions.*

This was the right day to make such a declaration: the Day of Atonement, the most important of the Jewish festivals. It was the only day in the year when the High Priest entered the Holy of Holies in the Temple. There he was in touch with God, in God's dwelling place on earth. There the High Priest interceded on behalf of the people, asking forgiveness for the people's sins.

Since absolutely nobody but the High Priest was permitted into the most holy place, a chain was put around his ankle, in case he fainted there, or died, he could be pulled out without anyone else having to enter and desecrate God's sacred confines.

When the High Priest had completed his duties in the most holy place, two goats were brought, one was sacrificed as a sin-offering; the

---

[1] William O. Cushing
[2] Joseph Addison

second had the sins of the people put upon it and it was driven out into the wilderness to be purposely lost, signifying the final disappearance and death of the sins of the people. It was this scapegoat that purified the people.

So far, everything was done for the people. Their part was twofold: one, fasting, and two, observing the Day of Atonement as another Sabbath—when there was to be no labor for man or animal; worship; and works of charity for those in need. Then God stepped in to declare the transgression of the people. They convinced themselves that they had observed this Holy Day correctly, "as if they were a nation which had acted rightly," (v. 2) when, in fact, they had not. Instead, they had ingeniously turned fasting to serve their own interests. (v. 3) Putting workmen to hard labor on that Day had led to quarrels and fisticuffs. "Is that what you call a fast?" asks the Lord. "A day acceptable to the Lord?" (v. 5)

When the burning desires of the flesh demanded a continued feeding of the fire (with dire consequences), one way to douse flaming human passions was on a bed of spikes. Islam chose to sit on beds of spikes. Islam chose fasting for a month at Ramadan. Christianity, born in the Jewish tradition, continued with fasting—but adapted to Jesus' weeks of suffering (forty days of Lent). And, as God found in early Judaism—the desecration of the Day of Atonement (both fasting and the Sabbath), so did Jesus, and so do we. The Lord told of two men who went up to the temple to pray. "The Pharisee stood up and prayed...'I thank you, God, that I am not like the rest of mankind—greedy, dishonest, adulterous—or, for that matter, like this tax collector. I fast twice a week, I pay tithes on all that I get.'" (Luke 18:10-12) In bragging, he was no better than those whom he condemned.

Our own observances of these sacred customs are hardly better. Certainly we Protestants have a shoddy record in the matter of fasting. If it's done at all in Lent, it is accompanied by some such snide remark as, "He gave up a fender for Lent." Or the fast is comfortably worked into the required dieting in a physical fitness program, or for diabetes, or for weight loss. Or, if fasting is honestly done as a spiritual discipline, with prayer, it can still turn into what Jesus saw, and said: "Do not look gloomy like the hypocrites: they make their faces unsightly so that everybody may see that they are fasting." (Matt. 6:16) Another form of bragging!

As for the Sabbath Day, it has become a Sabbath Hour, which doesn't have much influence on the ensuing week. But Thanksgiving has its fling, as do Presidential inaugurals and Super Bowl Sundays! Declare to my people their transgressions.

PRAYER: *"My faith looks up to Thee, Thou Lamb of Calvary, Savior divine! Now hear me while I pray, Take all my guilt away, O let me from this day, Be wholly Thine!"*[1]

OUR ALL-SUFFICIENT SAVIOR

Isa. 59:1 *Behold, the Lord's hand is not shortened, that it cannot save, or his ear dull, that it cannot hear.*

It sounds as if Isaiah had been hearing harsh criticisms concerning God, and why He was falling short in His divine duties. God must be deformed, the critics claimed, with arms so stunted he can't

---

[1] Ray Palmer

reach people's needs. He can't take anybody in His loving arms; can't defend them from attackers. What sort of everlasting arms are these, when they are unable to be the uplifters we need? And stumpy fingers would no doubt be part of the deformity, causing His loved ones to slip out of His hands. Arms, hands, are what we live by, work with. How can a God lacking such irreplaceable limbs do much if anything for mankind?

Worse yet, if He's hard of hearing, what's the use of prayers, or worship, or Temples and churches, or religion? If God is hearing a word here and there, now and again, we might as well be talking to ourselves (which many people believe we are doing, anyway, when praying). Not unlikely, other people probably think of God as suffering from other human insufficiencies such as poor eyesight, cloddering, mumbling, and other actions that squeak louder than words.

Yet, before going any further in cooking up the hilariously imaginative infirmities of God, Isaiah turns the spotlight away from God and onto the excuse-making people who claim that they can't be better persons because their God doesn't have what it takes to be what He's supposed to be—the Creator of the world. Isaiah swings the searchlight of truth on to the people's iniquities, revealing the real cause of the problem.

Some boys played a mean trick on Grandpa. When he was asleep on the porch, they smeared some evil-smelling cheese on his beard. When he awoke and went into the house, he complained that there was a nasty odor in the room. Moving through the house, Grandpa bellowed: "This whole place stinks." Going out into the yard and sniffing around, he exploded: "The whole world reeks."

Likewise, the people who complained about God's inabilities, were themselves the cause of the evil atmosphere in the Holy City. The words "you" and "yours" which appear nine times in verses 2-3, put the blame where it rightly belongs—on the iniquitous people. Then Isaiah proceeds, item by item to call the roll of the people's misdeeds: injustice, dishonesty, lying, and doing things which were as perilous and ugh as eating the eggs of poisonous snakes. (v. 5) Then there were still other stupidities attempted which Isaiah quaintly describes as being as unattainable as trying to make clothing out of spider webs, then frustrated because they couldn't wear those garments. (v. 6) And these were the mentally and spiritually deficient persons who had the nerve to question God!

But the finale is always in the Lord's hands. Verse 20 reads, "And he will come to Zion (Jerusalem) as Redeemer." He is the answer to the world's wrongs. Not quick fixes by the United Nations, or an intellectual elite, or a call for the creative geniuses of the globe to unite. Essentially they are all still eating viper's eggs. It is the soul of man that first and always needs redemption, and humans do their renewing (or try to) from the outside in. The Redeemer does His correcting beginning from the core of our being. When the inner man is in tune with the Man of God, the rest of the puzzle is solvable. Not the other way around.

PRAYER: *Lord, "Thou hast bought me with Thy blood, Opened wide the gate to God: Peace I ask, but peace must be, Lord, in being one with Thee."*[1]

---

[1] Mary A. S. Barber

HOME AT LAST

Isa. 60:2 *Darkness shall cover the earth, and thick darkness the peoples; but the Lord shall arise upon you.*

The history of Jerusalem is rollercoaster-designed. Just when you think it's going, going, gone—an upward climb begins. And when this summit is peaked, it seems like Everest—that's it. Then down she goes.

In today's section (Isa. 60:1-14) it's a hoist all the way, with the foretelling that no matter what upside turns may occur, the final indication is that the dawn of a bright new day is near. As in thermostatic control, what happens on the outside is similarly calibrated on the inside. So, what happens to Jerusalem will happen to the dwelling place of the Lord in your life and mine.

The scene opens some 200 years after Solomon had built Jerusalem into a city that was the envy of the world. Then came dismemberment of different parts of the country, the whole nation, and the famed capital city.

Now comes the command for Jerusalem to "Arise, shine," (v. 1) that is, to stand up to its full spiritual stature under Gods' sky, and show its potential for greatness. On seeing Jerusalem arise to action, the Lord shows how He does more than His share in the recovery process.

First come the exiles and the dispersed (diaspora) from many lands. They are all on a long journey home. Along the way they help each other. Like relatives they recall the past, and plan grand futures.

Since Solomon had organized maritime merchandising, the flow of goods was again turned toward Jerusalem. Ships came with their white sails flapping like homing pigeons. By land, too, came the riches on endless camel caravans from Africa, Arabia, India.

In the story of Jonah, that runaway couldn't think of a farther place away from God than Tarshish (Spain). For Jonah it was the world's jumping off place. But now came "ships from Tarshish," (v. 9) boatloads of Hebrew families to replenish the dwindling population of the Holy Land (as in more recent times). These returnees to the homeland also brought fortunes they had made in the burgeoning west. That would restore the Land of Solomonic proportions. As, indeed, it did. For when Jerusalem was destroyed by the Romans in A. D. 70, and the massive amount of gold in the Temple was released into the world market of the Roman Empire (which extended from Britain, Europe, to the middle east), the price of gold did a freefall.

Isaiah then prophesies (v. 10) that the return of greatness to Jerusalem would be so attractive, that even foreigners would count it a privilege to rebuild the shattered Capital. Even Kings would be honored to offer their services, as they had during the upscale reign of Solomon. A return to the glory days! It was customary, in all cities, for the city gates to be closed at night. Security was tight. But in verse 11 there is a dramatic change. The city gates in Jerusalem were to be left open—reflecting the absence of fear and insecurity, and the benediction of peace that now calmly rested upon the city of Peace.

Finally the centerpiece, the Temple, is made glorious (v. 8), not only with the prized lumber from the north—the famed cedars of Lebanon, the plane (Chestnut), and pine for the beautification and pleasant around of the sanctuary—but also God gives the place His personal attention. What a heaven on earth there is ahead of us. And more. Read on.

PRAYER: *"O Sweet and blessed country, the home of God's elect! O Sweet and blessed country That eager hearts expect! Jesus, in mercy bring us To that dear land of rest; Who art with God the Father, and Spirit, ever blest."*[1] Amen.

EARNED STARS

Isa. 60:15 *I will make you majestic forever, a joy from age to age.*

In the previous meditation, which covered the first half of chapter 60, all the pieces of Jerusalem are put together with satisfying orderliness. This is how we hope all of life could be all the time.

But no, here comes the slicing machine to cut chapter 60 in half, leaving the top part beautifully unfinished, and starting another upward climb from ground zero.

At halftime there was a toppling. Jerusalem again was forsaken, hated, lonely, (v. 15) entering another period of mourning. (v. 20) Why does such disheartening disaster repeat itself, not first in the life of a city, but in our personal lives?

It was helpful of Isaiah to return our attention (perhaps with boring repetition to this important aspect of daily life). As Christina Rossetti wrote: "Does the road wind uphill all the way? Yes, to the very end. Will the day's journey take the whole long day? From morn to night, my friend."

---

[1] Bernard of Cluny, 12th Century

Fed up with the seemingly impossible job of being on the up and up the livelong day, people lose heart, quit trying to be overcomers, and terminate life prematurely. Then why try the upward plod? It's at the point of personal discipline that we fail or succeed. Unable to handle failure, we see no need to soldier on. But it is Jesus' challenge: "What do you do more than others" that fires us onward and upward—in the doing of which we earn our stripes. And the Lord adds the stars, a heaven full of them.

1. One star is when we persevere, we take on a *majestic quality*. (v. 15) Part of this refined quality comes from the King of the universe, (v. 15) and some from persons who have cultivated a regal dignity with or without a crown. (v. 16)
2. Another star is that the paltry in us will be upgraded. No more rotting wood and rusting iron. Nothing but good, better, best—bronze, silver, gold. (v. 17)
3. Where other city walls were vulnerable to being tunneled under or scaled over, Jerusalem's walls were called "salvation." They saved from invasion and destruction. (v. 18) For us city-dwellers that's another star. We are saved, not by our own strenuous efforts but by God's grace.
4. To add another star to our record is that "the Lord will be your everlasting light." (v. 19) That is reassuring, since no other light is everlasting. The sun goes to bed each evening, the moon eclipses, power plants have their outages, candles snuff out, batteries have their expiration dates. Not so the Lord. He outshines and outlives all light givers. And He's ours, now and forever. "The Lord is my light and my salvation. Whom shall I fear? The Lord is the strength of my life of whom shall I be afraid?"

5. Then there is the star of promise: "Your people shall *all* be righteous." (v. 21) A veritable starry firmament. Usually the righteous laborers are few. The struggle in every church is for a multiplication of the righteous. What else is a church for? Yet hankering for even one more committed soul and not finding any. Churches shift the goal posts, accept lower standards, adapt to cheaper morals, and go with the flow and the undertow of those who don't have a clue as to the meaning of righteousness. In verse 21, however, all apprehensions disappear as the Lord brings in an unbelievable but universal state of righteousness—a peek into heaven.

In case we think that all these, like falling stars, will land in our laps right away, the Lord has His foot on the brake. Not so fast: The bottom line of verse 21 is: "in its time I will hasten it." His time is not ours. "A thousand years are but as yesterday in His sight." The last word, the end time are His to determine—with a brake, if it's still not the right time; with the accelerator if it is. Leave it to Him. He is in the driver's seat.

PRAYER: *"My times are in Thy hand. Whatever they may be; Pleasing or painful, dark or bright, As best may seem to Thee."* Amen.

Widening Horizons

Isa. 61:1 *The Spirit of the Lord God is upon me, because the Lord has anointed me to bring good tidings.*

This portion of scripture (Isa. 61:1-11) is the critical mass in our Hebrew-Christian faith. God preached the original sermon through Moses to

---

[1] William F. Lloyd

the Israelites. The site was on Mt. Sinai. Then Isaiah repeated the message (Isa. 61:1-11) for the Israelites of his time, more than 600 years after Moses. And Jesus repeated the sermon adapting it to His era, some 700 years after Isaiah.

What could be more God-in-Christ-centered than this portion of God's Word?

Let us consider this three-layered beauty for our spirited consumption: first, in Leviticus chapter 25, the Lord instructs His people as to how the Land of Promise is to be treated in order to keep it fruitful. Just as the people were to obey the fourth Commandment (Exod. 20:8) and keep the Sabbath Day holy by not working, and by prayer and worship, so with the Land. Every seventh year the Land must be given a sabbatical rest. Then, after seven of those sabbaticals (forty-nine years), on the fiftieth year would be the year of Jubilee—an extra sabbatical! Liberty would be proclaimed and captives of all kinds would be set free. And God meant what He ordered. When the people didn't take God seriously, and overworked the soil for 500 years (seventy Sabbath years), God allowed His people to be taken captive in Babylon. That was from 606 B.C. to 534 B.C., seventy-two years to make up for the years that the land was cheated out of its rest by the disobedience of God's people.

Second, Isaiah, knowing the cardinal weakness of people to quickly forget God's instructions, now introduces a Person who will incorporate the various ministries and their observances which God had outlined in His Leviticus sermon set apart by God for this task. The Person would be a conveyor of good tidings to people in straitened circumstances: the poor; the mourners; those who were imprisoned in body, mind, spirit. Wherever there was ruination, He would be there to rebuild. Nothing short of a worldwide conversion was His mission. And this, Jesus saw as His calling. Reading Isaiah's prophesy "The Spirit of the Lord God is upon me because the Lord has anointed me," and taking His baptism in the Jordan as His anointing, Jesus identified with this Isaianic Person.

The first such identification came when Jesus "armed with the power of the Spirit (Luke 4:14) went to worship in His hometown synagogue of Nazareth and was invited to read the scripture and preach. Without hesitation He read Isaiah chapter 61. Moving into His address, He said: "Today in your hearing this text has come true." (Luke 4:21) And Luke adds, "There was general approval." (v. 22)

Not only did Jesus identify Himself as the One chosen for this particular ministry, but also Jesus proceeded to implement God's desires at His very first opportunity—the Sermon on the Mount. He copied His heavenly Father's sermon on Mt. Sinai. The Sermon on the Mount has been conclusively acclaimed as the essence of Jesus' teachings. And the Beatitudes, with which He began this Sermon, are without a doubt the essence of this Sermon. Which is to say that the Beatitudes constitute the essence of the essence of Jesus' teachings. And note, each Beatitude begins with the word "Blessed," meaning blissful. "Good tidings" to the poor, sorrowful, meek, hungry, merciful, pure, peacemakers, and the persecuted. (Matt. 5:3-12) There's a full-orbed pastorate—with what a Pastor! Ours, now and ever.

PRAYER: *Lord of Heaven, as Isaiah took Your Words as Jesus took Isaiah's; so help us to take Jesus' Words, and with the support of the Holy Spirit translate them into an enriching earthly ministry. Amen.*

HIS NAME SHALL BE CALLED

Isa. 62:2 *You will be called by a new name which the Lord Himself will announce.*

The Lord was anxious for Jerusalem to be seen in a new attractive form, since for too long she had been termed "Forsaken" and "Desolate," (v. 4) a disastrous state brought about by Manasseh, the worst king Judah ever had. Son of Hezekiah, one of the finest kings Judah had, Manasseh "did what was evil in the sight of the Lord." (2 Kings 21:2) Whatever good his father had done, Manasseh did just the opposite. He reintroduced pagan worship, rebuilt shrines to Baal and altars for the worship of sun, moon, stars. He even sacrificed his sons, burning them to death. No surprise, then, that Jerusalem, the nation's capital, was God-forsaken. She was, indeed, in need of a total transformation—with a new name or several new names to remove the awful odor of its former rotting condition.

First of all, God sees Jerusalem as a "crown of beauty" (v. 3)—a beauty queen, a Miss World. Certainly Jerusalem is a world-class location. At an elevation of 3,000 feet, not far from the Mediterranean Sea breezes, it is the lock point at which Europe, Africa, and Asia find common ground. World unity is no more visibly possible than here. In fact, it has been just the opposite. More blood has been shed here, for a longer time than anywhere else. So precious is the place—everyone would love to own it.

Second, God calls Jerusalem "My delight is in her." (v. 4) How divinely clever of the Lord to give this description of the only woman in the Bible who fits it—"Hephzibah." (2 Kings 21:1) She was the wife of the great King Hezekiah, and mother of the worst King Manasseh. Undistracted, God rescues her beauty out of a mucky situation, and uses her attractiveness for His own glorious purpose—that of having Jerusalem take on her delightful character.

Third, God called Jerusalem "Married." "To him your land will be linked in wedlock." (v. 4) The Lord sees the sons of the City so infatuated with her that they marry her as it were. God uses the concept of marriage because to Him it means a promise of indissolubility. No tie is more bonding. Through marriage a new social unit emerges, so that marriage is not just for the growing together of husband and wife, but also for their stronger combined influence and the influence of their children and the enlarging family. There is a ministry to be performed in the sacramental conjoining of husband and wife. It ripples out into the uttermost parts. And this is what God foresaw in the new Jerusalem.

Fourth, Jerusalem was named "Sought out." (v. 12) God didn't make a random choice. He looked around, not for perfection but for those persons though sinners, who say penitently, "I will arise and go to my father..." (Luke 15:11-24) God seeks out prodigals returning to a Father who waits to reclaim them.

Throughout this exposition of scripture we

learn that Jerusalem is more than its geographical or historical importance, or any other aspects. It's the people. They earned these insignias: crown of beauty, my delight is in her, marriage, sought out, holy, redeemed. Such persons would make any place an attractive Jerusalem. The place whereon thou standest can be holy ground. Not that the ground itself is sacred, but that God-like people make it so. Do we?

PRAYER: *"Jesus, the name to sinners given, it scatters all their guilty fear, it turns their hell to heaven."[1] Amen.*

THE GROUNDBREAKING QUALITY OF LOVE

Isa. 63:1 *Who is this coming from Edom, from Bozrah with his garments stained red?*

Where the Old Testament closes with a curse, the New Testament ends on a happy note of gratitude. Such a contrast is not seen more strikingly than in the first six verses of Isaiah, Chapter 63, where the Prophet begins to terminate his own longest book in the Bible. This chapter opens with God returning from Bozrah, the chief city in the country of Edom. It was a 100-mile-long country located in a depression that extended from south of the Dead (Salt) Sea to the Gulf of Aqaba.

Edom also went by the name of Seir, named for Mt. Seir, the 3,300-foot range. It was originally settled by Esau, brother of Jacob. Because he had despised his birthright and was in a strained relationship with his family, Esau wanted to be as far removed from his relatives as possible. So he moved to Edom—actually on Mt. Seir.

Fade out on Esau, and fade in on God. Some-

---

[1]Charles Wesley

one asks Him why his clothes are red, as if he had been treading grapes in a vat.

"Red" immediately takes us back to Edom, which means red. That, again, takes us back to the time when Jacob had been hunting and bagged a mealy animal and was cooking it. Along came brother Esau, famished. He would give anything for some of Jacob's red stew. (Gen. 25:30) That is why Esau, upon exchanging his birthright for red stew, was thereafter called "Edom," "Red."

Old Red's descendents didn't do so well. They ended up being the only country that deserved no mercy in the sight of God. Hence their being crushed by an angry God (v. 3), as if He had trampled them in a winepress. Or as Julia Ward Howe put it: "Mine eyes have seen the glory of the coming of the Lord, he is trampling out the vintage where the grapes of wrath are stored; he hath loosed the fateful lightning of his terrible swift sword..." And here Isaiah sees God coming home to Jerusalem all bloodied, but triumphant. He had looked for someone else to do the dirty work of roundly punishing the Red rough rulers of Edom. He was appalled that no one saw the need for stamping out the evil doings down south so He did it all by Himself, pouring the blood of those miscreants upon the soil of their soiled land. (v. 3-6)

All typically Old Testament. There is *wrath* and *humans* trampled upon, and *wine*—turning us to the New Testament, but with different emphases, the difference Christ makes. Oh Christ exhibited wrath, too, whipping (or, at least cracking the whip) to get the secularists out of the Temple. Yet His first words from the cross were, "Father, forgive them. (Luke 23:34) Even suffering that all-aloneness of feeling forsaken: "My God, my God, why have you forsaken me?" (Mark 15:34) while the blood ran down His face and His slashed back, His riven hands and feet. He had trodden the wine-press alone. As for the wine, He had drunk it in the Upper Room with His close friends, saying, "This is my blood of the new covenant, which is poured out for many. Truly, I say to you, I shall not drink again of the fruit of the vine, until that day when I drink it new in the Kingdom of God." (Mark 14:24-25)

Anger was not the way to salvation. God tried that, and it didn't work. But love found a way—through His only begotten Son. Now can anyone resist such a Christ?

PRAYER: *Heavenly Father, You were bloodied for our sake. Yet You love us. We would strive to be worthy of Your redeeming grace. Amen.*

THE VITALITY OF PRAYER

Isa. 63:7 *I will recount the steadfast love of the Lord.*

This is the beginning of a long prayer. And what a fruitful way to pray, especially when we are at a loss about what to say to the King of Kings. At a leprosarium worship service the Leader asked the congregation to suggest an opening hymn. A hand went up. It had no fingers. Neither had the man a nose nor ears. Just holes. The suggested hymn: "Count your blessings." "Recount the steadfast love of the Lord." That removes the fog we're in, and misty and mystic doubts about God who sits in His heaven frittering the time away. Recounting what He has done jump-starts our stalled engine of opportunity, and we're on our way.

Look at the lovely things which the Lord did for the one in today's text. It gives us ideas about divine gifts that we have received but never thought worth counting, gifts which we now see are surmountably countable.

For one, "all that the Lord has granted us." (v. 7) Heavens! Where to begin on that one. He granted us life, and not abortion. And we have all our limbs, senses, faculties. Think of the millions who are aborted each year, when they could have been shining examples of humankind. Or consider the deformed and disabled many of whom, bless them, have gallantly forged ahead of us who had no defections. Have we done any better for our perfections? Then, Lord, you put us into a good family, with a rich upbringing—when others have had a wretched one. They haven't known who their parents were. They've been handed around to individuals and institutions. Then there was food, clothing, schooling, marriage...Now we get the picture.

Moreover, "in all their affliction he was afflicted." (v. 9) Really? You mean, when I got shingles He suffered along with me? And here I thought I was treading the wine-press alone. Not only the bodily tortures. There were the mental and spiritual times of our being bent out of shape. The Lord went through the valley of the shadow with us, and we didn't even realize that the "angel of His presence saved us." (v. 9) Now we recall who those angels were: those who, at the time of our affliction, came for a comforting visit, prayed with us over the phone; sent food, supportive letters, or silently wept with us. They were angels who could only have known what to do and when to do it by the still small voice of Him who promised (and never forgets, even if we do, that He promised). "Lo, I am with you always. I will never leave you nor forsake you." Behind the scenes He intervenes—through His divinely guided intercessors.

Furthermore, the Lord has a reputation "from days of old" for "lifting up and carrying." (v. 9) His children, as a concerned parent does when we can't make it on our own, as the Israelites couldn't at the Red Sea and at certain junctures in the Sinai, the Lord did the heavy lifting, carrying them across the suddenly dry sea bed. (v. 11-14) He makes us as surefooted as horses that are at home on the range (v. 13), and as rested as cattle beside the still waters. (v. 14) How amply the Lord cares for our every need: carrying us when our own abilities are impotent, granting steadiness on gravelly, rutted footpaths—and peace at the last. To "recount the steadfast love of the Lord," we find, becomes nothing less than the composition of a bracing symphony.

PRAYER: *"Every time I feel the Spirit moving in my heart, I will pray." Thank You, Lord, for listening, and answering. Amen.*

CONTENTED COWORKERS

Isa. 63:15 *Look down from heaven and see, from thy holy and glorious habitation. Where are thy zeal and thy might?*

Such direct conversation with God is more evident in the Old Testament than in the New. The Oldies never hesitated to tell God to His face what they thought of Him—as in today's text. "Where's Your zeal and Your much-talked-of might?" To our more domesticated decency that sounds crude, cocky. Yet, to feel free to give and take with

God has more of a parental feel which is natural, and unaffected, and unfettered; and easier to turn to at any time of day or night. Nowadays, unfortunately we feel that we have to wait for special times, places, postures, when God, in His majesty can be approached on bended knee, in a sacred setting. Or else we go to the other extreme and get too chummy with Him.

In the scripture before us, the one who is offering this prayer is having it out with God—asking Him to take a little time away from His cozy heavenly abode, and see where He is shortchanging His faithful followers. "Where are Your vaunted virtues of zeal, and might and compassion?" (v. 15) "After all, Lord, we have no Father to look after us but You." In the White Mountains of New Hampshire little Mary Moore was lost. She had strayed away into the woods from a family picnic. Hundreds of people joined the search—professional mountaineers, boy scouts, police, firemen, friends, and dogs. After hours of nerve-wracking disappointments, there was Mary. Put in touch with her father by radio, the first thing she said was, "Daddy, Daddy, where have you been?" She felt that she was not lost, her dad was.

That is the implication about our Father God when anything goes screwy. Where are You, and what did You do to prevent it, and what are You going to do about the consequences?

The accusations, though sharp, with jagged edges, would be acceptable if we are doing our part. That induced Jesus' insistence that we should Ask, Seek, Knock. We have a part to play. "We are not here to play, to dream, to drift. We have hard work to do and loads to lift. Shun not the struggle, face it: 'Tis God's gift." It is a gift in that it enables us to be coworkers with the Lord. We won't be looking for handouts from divinity as perpetual spiritual welfare recipients. For it never stops there. Convinced that we're not getting what is owed us, we automatically turn upon the giver of every good and perfect gift, and let Him have a barrage of invectives. Rather, if we want a level playing field, and a frequent walk and talk with Lord, which allows us to tap into His storehouse of riches, there is a part which He is looking for us to play. St. Paul got the point. Said he: "I have learned, in whatsoever state I am, therewith to be content." (Phil. 4:11) That didn't mean he could get along with God. It did mean that he was doing his part and when he couldn't, that the Lord would do the heavy lifting, carrying Paul safely over the minefields. You can't beat that kind of teamwork. Let's test its workability.

PRAYER: *Master, help us to talk and work life out with You on a daily basis. Equally yoked with You we are at our best. Amen.*

LISTEN TO THE LESSON

Isa. 65:1 *I was ready to be sought by those who did not ask for me.*

What an astonishing picture this is of our God of love. It deserves to be framed, and a copy hung in every room in the house. We can't be reminded enough of the readiness of God to help us. It is too soon forgotten, leaving us estranged as "those who did not ask for (Him)."

Just visualize the Lord sitting on the edge of His throne waiting to do anything for anyone who asked, sought, knocked. But no one did. Eager to hear any supplicants voice, He broke the silence, saying, "'Here am I, here am I,' to a nation that did not call on my name." (v. 1) But silence prevailed.

That should haunt us—or inspire us to know that we have a God who is ever ready at our service, putting all His resources at our disposal. No wonder that through the ages God's people lived in triumph through the worst of times. They had a Helper in constant readiness for every occasion. Greater love has no one than this. How much Jesus mirrored His heavenly Father. "How often would I have gathered you (Jerusalem) under my protective custody, as a hen does her brood—but you would have none of it." That restive cry led to the erection of the Tear Drop Church (in the form of a tear drop) on the Mount of Olives. At the spot where He stood you can still get a panoramic view of Zion, City of our God. There, too, we can weep to be forgiven for our disinterest in Him, turning to Him a deaf ear and a blind eye. But more, we can duck under His overall shield of defense, and abide there forever.

Making Himself available, but not being taken up on the offer, "following their own devices" (v. 2), it is not surprising that God sees the necessity for separating the responsive souls from the "no thank-yous." Actually such people make a division through their own glaringly divisive daily living. This has been called the separation of the sheep and goats. Poor goats. They did nothing to deserve such denigration. It probably came from a preference for sheep when a sacrifice was needed at the Temple. Then, of course David immortalized sheep in his universally cherished "The Lord is my Shepherd"—not my Goatherder. No, it's not the animals that deserve the discriminating ear tags. We human are the culprits, turning deaf ears and insolent backsides to Him. So the fault lines appear. The Lord has no choice but to concede: "Let the evildoers persist in doing evil and the filthy-minded continue in their filth, but let the good persevere in their goodness and the holy continue in holiness." (Rev. 22:11) That's the way they want it. But God remains the same, as always, readily available.

Taking to heart the lesson "Do not destroy it, for there is a blessing in it," (v. 8) the great Physician heals Himself, moving through eternity with love for all, while the canyon widens between the persistently evil and the perseveringly holy. The godly get to eat, drink, sing with gladness of heart, while those on the far side are deprived of these blessings. (v. 13-16) Well, they asked for it and not for the One whose hands stretched out for them on a cross.

The gentle Hindu poet laureate of India crafted our lesson for today into a single glowing sentence: "God loves to see in me not His servant, but Himself, who serves all."[1]

PRAYER: *"O Master, let me walk with thee in lowly paths of service free; tell me thy secret; help me bear the strain of toil, the fret of care."* [2] *Amen.*

BEHOLD, WHAT IS CREATED

Isa. 65:17 *For behold, I create.*

"In the beginning God created." (Gen. 1:1) "On the sixth day God brought to an end all the

---

[1]Rabindranath Tagore
[2]Washington Gladden

work he had been doing." (Gen. 2:2) That sounds as if the Creator's building of planet earth was completed. (Gen. 2:3) Now He could take the weekend off. Since "Finis" was written across the whole project, God could take a sabbatical, or retire. For further creative acts one could henceforth turn to the Darwinians. Yet, in today's scripture God is at it again. Creating three different times in Isa. 65:17-18, just as He did in Gen. 1:27. No part-time Creator, we find God still in the creation business at the promontory of this most prominent book in the Old Testament, Isa. 66:23-24, as well as at the end of the Bible, Rev. 21-22. The open-endedness of divine creativity is seen ever more clearly as the curtain begins to come down on this spirit-filled drama of Isaiah.

Earlier in the Isaiah narrative the Exodus is referred to repeatedly as if what was ahead was a new Exodus to a greater Land of Promise. Now the prospects change. The secret is out that though an Exodus is taking place, there will be a total displacement where "the former things shall not be remembered." (Isa. 65:17) The destination this time will not be a pre-owned land of Canaan, but an entirely new habitation.

Jerusalem's remaking will be the first visible transformation in the new era. As if the blessed Creator has found what will work and what won't, Jerusalem is re-created to make it joyful, and His people a joy to Him. (v. 19) Paradise regained. Now that the people have heavenly residence, they must be remade to fit the improved external conditions. Human life expectancy will be extended, otherwise what's the use of having new everythings with nobody to enjoy them to the fullest?

Accordingly, the human life span here is put in terms of tree-life, (v. 22) where an oak for instance, can live to the age of 800 or the Sequoia to 3,000 years. Other correctives will be made in all the disjointedness of the infrastructure of daily life. The Lord's chosen "shall long enjoy the work of their hands. They shall not labor in vain." (v. 22)

Certainly there had to be a new Jerusalem since the Temple in the Old City had been plundered eight times in 300 years. Following that destruction, and Jesus' major statements made with remorse about the city of His affection, Jerusalem has been without a Temple for a longer time than with one. It was time to turn over to a new page, a new Jerusalem. There, even prayer will be updated. Still unspoken, prayer will be heard in the whisper of our hearts. Our prayer requests will be anticipated and fulfilled. In all of this newness, both inside and out, physical and spiritual, even the lowly animals are not forgotten. Even the predatory nature of meat-eating creatures will experience an unheard-of conversion. Imagine the wolf feeding with, not upon, a lamb, and the King of beasts instead of stalking the wildebeest goes to pasture with it! Incredible. No, the Lord sternly affirms, "they shall not hurt or destroy in all my holy mountain (Jerusalem)." (v. 25) There's the closing portrait: one of tranquility in the City of Shalom, Salem.

Looking in the rearview mirror we see all the roughness, blood and thunder and blunder receding speedily into a background that can't be remembered anymore. Ahead must be heaven.

PRAYER: *Thank You, Lord, for these glimpses of what it is worth struggling for. With Your assist we'll make it. Amen.*

Custom Made for Him

Isa. 66:2 *The one for whom I have regard.*

Many another has put together the qualities of a person for whom they have regard. William Dillen wanted a girl "Just like the girl that married dear old Dad." Henry Van Dyke went further, believing that "Four things a man must learn to do if he would make his record true: to think without confusion clearly; to love his fellowman sincerely; to act from honest motive purely; to trust in God and heaven securely." Long before these the prophet Micah tried his hand at it: "do justice, love, kindness, and walk humbly with your God." (Mic. 6:8)

Our Lord's brother urged "let every man be swift to hear, slow to speak, slow to wrath." (James 1:19) Better than all, God in today's text, looks for persons with three virtues: Humility, contrite in Spirit, those who reverence His Word.

Why humility first and most urgently? Isn't our pride hammered enough into ground zero? Are we not just specks in an expanding universe, blips on a panoramic screen? On the contrary. Every commercial on the airwaves inflates our self-esteem. We are sweet-talked into believing that we can be super rich in no time, that our good looks can be enhanced a thousand-fold, that we can have the finest clothes for 75 percent off. How can one be humble under such a barrage of such persuasive compliments? In better moments we know that these are lies, but then we've also had it drilled into our heads and hearts that anyone can become the President of the United States.

Jesus quickly caught on to His heavenly Father's priority requirement: *Humility*—and also put it at the head of His "Be(happy)attitudes": "Blessed are the poor in Spirit, for theirs is the Kingdom of heaven." (Matt. 5:3) As William Barclay explains: "When we bring together the Greek and the Hebrew background of this word *poor*, we see that it describes the man who has fully realized his own inadequacy, his own worthlessness and his own destitution, and who has put his whole trust in God." Which leads straight into the second characteristic of a person who is well-pleasing in God's sight: *Contrition*. As Dr. Barclay further elucidates this basic truth about life, "that the way to goodness lies through the confession and the acknowledgment of sin."

One woman told me that she resented having to confess her sins in church every Sunday. She had asked forgiveness once and hadn't sinned since. What's to confess? That's an insult. She didn't realize that we dirty hands and wash them many times a day. We likewise dirty souls. The evils come in through our senses and if not washed away with confession, abide and infect the inner life.

And how does one learn the graces of humility and the acts of contrition except from God's *Word*, even apart from the church (especially these days when there is teaching in the Church that is heretical). Studying God's Word prayerfully, reverently, one finds, with Abraham Lincoln, that the Bible is the best gift God has ever given to man. All the good from the Savior of the world is communicated to us through this book.

PRAYER: *Lord, make us to be such persons for whom You have such regard. Through Jesus our Savior. Amen.*

AND NOW, A BENEDICTION BY ISAIAH

Isa. 66:10 *Rejoice with Jerusalem, and be glad for her.*

Not mentioned in the books of Job, Hosea, Jonah, Nahum, Habakkuk and Haggai, Jerusalem is centered in the Book of Isaiah more than anywhere else in the Bible, mainly because the author was a lifetime resident of the Holy City. Still, for all its fame, Jerusalem, as of old, is handled like a hot potato with ouches and cries of pain. It isn't freely accepted as the City of Peace when it has witnessed floods of bloodshed for centuries—B.C. and A.D. Also the unsure locations of Holy Places continue to divide people who accuse one another of fraudulence. Nor do the political fratricides help, with their intifadas, broken treaties, and the unforgettable "eye for an eye." Yet in spite of the risks and dangers, both real and imaginary, the pilgrims and tourists swarm into Jerusalem as Isa. 66:20 describes, "Upon horses, and in chariots, and in litters, and upon mules, and upon dromedaries." Now it's in planes, trains, ships, buses, motor homes, autos, and motorcycles. There is a mystique about the place which you can almost inhale. You feel it underfoot whether it's proven holy ground or not. The wisdom of the ages has trodden there and left its mark. And as with much-used buildings, the sounds of old have embedded themselves in the walls and floors and can, with newer technical devices, be extracted. The very stones cry out. Only those who hear take off their shoes with devout respect. This is the City of God for which Isaiah now has a final word. Two words, in fact—Joy and Comfort. Actually, the very last verse in this book (Isa. 66:24) is so horrendous that when it is used in Jewish worship services, after the last verse is read, the one before it (verse 23) is repeated to make for a positive, peaceful finale. This, as we have noted along the way, is also the way the Old Testament ends—bitter. But, as a little girl explained, "Those were the days before God became a Christian."

JOY—is not alone one of the fruits of the spirit, (Gal. 5:22-23) it is also one of the characteristics of God who here imparts His joy to His beloved city—with a river of prosperity. (Isa. 66:12) Like the Nile River, 4,050 miles of some of the richest soil in the world. The river's prosperity is best seen when flying down to Luxor. There is a wide green swath of luxuriant growth on both sides of the life-giving river. But beyond the well irrigated fields there is the crippling desert stretching into the distances on both sides. This sort of ceaseless flow of life-blood now energizes and vivifies the City of Jerusalem. Also now flowing into the city would be the wealth of the nation's. (Isa. 66:12) To see Isaiah's prophesy of joy come alive in our time, visit Jerusalem over Christmas and/or Easter. When the suppressed emotions of gladness are allowed full expression. To see bumper-to-bumper busloads of visitors from around the world inching the distance of five miles to neighboring Bethlehem for the various worship services, and to hear international choirs singing carols in Manger Square at midnight on Christmas Eve. And to see the crowded Churches in Jerusalem. One cannot help but "rejoice with Jerusalem and be glad for her."

In return Jerusalem provides a motherly *comfort* that is not felt anywhere else on earth. In verse 13 "comfort" is used three times. Nobody can give the feeling of at-homeness, and all is well, as can Mother. To be embraced by her from who we entered this life, and from whom we first drew nourishment, is Comfort in every sense of the word. "Com" "Fortis," the gathering together of strength. What will it be like in the New Jerusalem? Indescribably better.

PRAYER: *O Thou in Whom Joy and Comfort are created, grant us both, now and ever. And thank You for Isaiah, as we move along to other experiences in Your Holy City. Amen.*

IS IT I?

Jer. 2:2-3 *Go, make this proclamation in the hearing of Jerusalem: These are the words of the Lord: I remember in your favor the loyalty of your youth, your love during your bridal days, when you followed me through the wilderness, through a land unsown. Israel was holy to the Lord, the first fruits of his harvest; no one who devoured her went unpunished, disaster overtook them. This is the word of the Lord.*

One hundred years after Isaiah, Jeremiah, while quite young, became Israel's prophet. Brought up in a hamlet near Jerusalem, Jeremiah, like his predecessor, spent most of his life in that capital city. To it he was sent on his first mission. To its population he proclaimed God's favorable comments about them.

Their forebears had endeared themselves to God during the forty years in the wilderness. That was pretty generous of the Lord, for, in fact, those forebears had been so disrespectful of the Lord, and so ungrateful that not one of them over twenty years old was allowed into the Promised Land. Not even Moses! Yet, now the Lord in His generosity chooses to recall only the best of that Israelite history: their times of loyalty; those halcyon "honeymoon" hours, when their followership had merit; when they were the apple of His eye.

Thus far sweetness and light. Then the other shoe falls and for the rest of the Chapter the Lord catalogs the evils in which His people are now enmeshed, and for which punishment awaits them.

The trouble was that they were resting on their laurels. Because their forebears had been foremost, they were convinced that it would count to their present standing in the Lord's favor. As with persons who still live on the assumption that because their parents or relatives are intensely religious, that's going to provide easy access for them into heaven. Meanwhile, eat, drink, be merry...John Wesley got the point: "Let, therefore, none presume on past mercies, as if they were out of danger." And John Bunyan in a dream saw that even from the gates of heaven there is a way to hell. St. Paul, remembering those who thought that a glorious yesterday, a lovely today, gave automatic promise of a perfect tomorrow cautioned, "Let him that thinketh be standeth, take heed lest he fall." Unfortunately, unless we watch our step, the progression can turn out to be yesterday, today, and Gomorrah. It is a lesson writ large in the early history of Jerusalem, and Israel.

PRAYER: *Lord, keep us from falling out on the last lap, for he that endures to the end shall be saved. Amen.*

ANANIAS CLUB

Jer. 7:4 *This catchword of yours is a lie; put no trust in it.*

This Temple Sermon, given by Jeremiah as he stood at the entrance to the Temple, begins with a sandwich. The introduction starts and finishes with the same words: "Mend your ways and your doing." (v. 3,5) In between are the words "the temple of the Lord"—three-peated.

It all looks acceptably straightforward—except to the Lord. He sees a yawning chasm between the words and deeds of those who are entering the Temple for worship. They are saying the right things, but doing wrong. So He calls their bluff. "This catchword of yours is a lie."

The people were so sure of their utterance, that they could not believe that it was anything but on the right track. Wasn't this the Holy Land which the Lord had gifted to His chosen people? Wasn't this the Holy City of Jerusalem in which He had chosen to reside? Wasn't this the Holy Temple in whose holy of holies He had found permanent residence? And, in that Temple weren't worshippers safe? (Jer. 7:10) "No" replies the Lord. Where there is privilege, there is responsibility. And these people had not fulfilled their part of the deal. They were dealing unfairly with one another. Aliens were being oppressed, and orphans and widows. Innocent blood was being shed. Other gods were being worshipped. There was stealing, murder, adultery, perjury—abominations of all kinds. (Jer. 7:6-11) No, insists the Lord, unless you "mend your ways and your doings...I will fling you away out of my sight.. the whole brood." (Jer. 7:3,15)

Nor are we free from the danger of being ensnared by catchwords—minefields of them. "As long as you attend church you are safe." At an Alcoholics Anonymous meeting I heard one man tell how, on Saturday nights he would go on a drinking spree. But Sunday morning he would be in his place at church, "and fool the preacher for another week."

Such temple trickery comes in myriad variations. Or if you are a hefty giver to charities, you can be sure that the celestial moving men will land you safe on Canaan's side. Or God is love, and so is sex. What's the diff? Or if there's safety in numbers, why not serve two or more masters?

How tempting it is, on checking out of church, to go to the code room and pick up some catchwords for use beyond the church doors. But here, the Lord through His prophet, is urging His people everywhere, for all time, to snag those catchwords, cash words, mish-mash words, catch as catch can words, rash words, and commit them to the incinerator. And listen to the Lord as to how to proceed—not to denominational parlance or neighborly freakonomics.

"Be imitators of me," Paul boldly urged, "as I am also of Christ." And what does Christ say to us in such binds, since He was tempted in all points like as we are? "You cannot (yea, we must not) serve two masters." (Matt. 6:24) You may have dual citizenship, but a divided loyalty is not for those who are cherished by God.

PRAYER: *Lord, save us from being two-faced: acting as if we are wholly committed to You, but not really. I surrender ALL. Amen.*

MY GOD

Jer. 10:6 *Where can one be found like thee, O Lord?*

Brilliant Albert Einstein dismissed the idea of God as the product of human weakness. Centuries before, equally historic Jeremiah concluded that nobody could compare with God. But there were also unbelievers like Einstein in Jeremiah's time. More familiar with nature's movements, humans explained the mysteries of life in terms of sea and sky, death of plants in the autumn, and resurrection in the spring. Noting the power of sex, that, too, received God-like respect. Then, to make such super-powers more readily available to answer human petitions, images of them were made of clay, wood, silver, gold. Ancient Babylon was called a "city of gold" (Isa. 14:4) because in one of its fifty-three temples there were golden images of Bel and Ishtar (goddess of sex) and innumerable altars for the worship of Ishtar. And still there is fabulously expensive idolatry reverenced across the world of the present day.

In Jeremiah's time (600s B.C.) there had been an alarming turn away of the Jewish people from God to the bent knee before idols of stick and stone and gold. Displeased, God Himself took action, and through His mouthpiece, Jeremiah, defined His unparalleled position and powers in the universe. Then, lest anyone forgets this full-length portrait of God's abilities, (Jer. 10:12-16) it is repeated at the end of the book. (Jer. 51:15-19) It reminds one of Moses repeating the commandments to his fellow journeymen, as he says goodbye to them on the verge of their crossing Jordan to enter the Promised Land. (Num. 36:13; Deut. 1:3) Here, Jeremiah is refreshing the memory of God's people concerning the incomparable stature of the God they once served and who has chosen them as His own. Such a refresher course is always, in all ways, welcome.

Worth remembering is that "God made the

earth by His *power*." (Jer. 10:12) When we consider the power manifest in all the "osophies" and "ologies," we realize that the finding of such power is owed to countless individuals across the centuries. But when Jeremiah attributes power to God (as above), he means that all the power that ever was coheres in the Maker of the universe.

"The heavens declare the glory of God and the firmament showeth his handiwork. There is no speech or language where his voice is not heard." (Ps. 19:1,3) What "ism" or "wasm" has such all-inclusive potency?

Also, Jeremiah writes that our Creator God has "fixed the world in place by his wisdom...(and) understanding." (10:12) How precious little wisdom and understanding we humans have, and for what a short time. For example, astronomers may have mapped the night sky. Then, surprisingly, here comes another occupant of sky-space. It's new to us, but it's just that its light has been traveling toward us for eons, and has finally reached our macular-degenerated eyes. It is so spectacular out there, and so optically piecemeal down here. Robert Browning had a more expansive suggestion in his poem "Rabbi Be Ezra"—"trust God, see all, nor be afraid!"

Yet, we can see all, not be afraid, but still just get a micro understanding of this earthly life as it flashes by. Our main determinant, therefore, is to trust God for He alone fully understands what life here and hereafter is all about. Our finitude does not allow us to comparably comprehend as He does.

PRAYER: *Gracious Lord, Although we do not need proof of Your divine supremacy, we confess that we have spent time at pagan altars. Forgive us, heavenly Father, Reinforce our attachment to You, now and ever. Amen.*

Free at Last

Jer. 10:17 *Living as you are under siege.*

Jerusalem was surrounded by Babylonian troops who planned to stay and starve the city dwellers, or break their way in and kill or capture the Jerusalemites.

The Babylonians may be remembered for their Tower of Babel, where people babbled in different languages until there was one seething mass of confusion. But when it came to this siege business, the people of Babylonia became masters of the art and showed it in the construction of their own capital city. It could be described as siege-proof. H. H. Halley in his *Pocket Bible Handbook* p. 300, explains "Ancient historians said that its wall was 60 miles around, 15 miles on each side, 300 feet high, 80 feet thick, extending 35 feet below the ground so that enemies could not tunnel under; built of brick one foot square and 3 or 4 inches thick; 1/4 mile of clear space between the city and the wall all the way around; the wall protected by wide and deep moats (canals) filled with water; 250 towers on the wall, guard rooms for soldiers; 100 gates of brass. The city was divided by the River Euphrates into two almost equal parts; both banks guarded by brick walls all the way, with 25 gates connecting streets and ferry boats; one bridge, on stone piers, 1/2 mile long, 30 feet wide, with drawbridges which were removed at night. A tunnel under the river, 15 feet wide, 12 feet high. Excavations of recent years have, to a large extent, verified the seemingly fabulous accounts of ancient historians."

Let our minds circulate around these statistics and we can see how these Babylonians would consider the conquest of Jerusalem as a piece of cake.

Meanwhile, on the inside of the Holy City, the populace was suffering all the paralytic seizures of being besieged by the Superpower of the time.

Describing some of their terrors, Jeremiah recalled a feeling of having the community's tent ropes severed. Young family members who could have helped had escaped through secret exits. Leaders, shepherds of the people, had turned out to be "mere brutes." (10:21) They never consulted the Lord. Then came the fearsome news that the enemy was going to make Jerusalem and sister cities "a haunt of wolves." (10:22) The worst scenario in siege situations, and from early times, at meal times, was cannibalism.

Nor do humans live as under siege only in times of war. When Wall Street sings the blues and one's business is out of business, and the old folks at home are standing in a bread line—fears run rampant. Where to sleep—in the bus station, or the subway? And, on those below zero days—sit on a hot air grate on the sidewalk? Or build a campfire under a bridge?

A siege by any other name is terrifying. A no-win physical ailment, loneliness, job loss, the death of a cherished companion...It comes to everyone. It did for Jesus at Calvary; at the stoning of Stephen, at the beheading of St. Paul. Ah, but the Lord has saved and will again. "Therefore this is the word of the Lord about the King of Assyria. He will not enter this city (Jerusalem)...That night the angel of the Lord went out and struck down 185,000 in the Assyrian camp." (2 Kings 19:32,35)

PRAYER: *Jesus "thou didst suffer to release us; Thou didst free salvation bring. Hail, Thou agonizing Savior,*

Bearer of our sin and shame; By Thy merits we find favor, Life is given thro Thy Name."[1]

THE DIVINE LETTER WRITER

Jer. 11:4 *If you obey me and do all that I tell you, you shall become my people and I will become your God.*

In verses 2-8, God uses the term "this covenant" four times. It is surprising that He uses it even once. Why should He covenant with these people who had let Him down at every turn? Time and again He had reaffirmed their understanding of His ability to do anything for them that they had requested. But in spite of warning these people about their apostasy of serving idols, they had blatantly continued the practice. Wasn't the Lord justified in responding that He would not listen to their cries in the hour of their disaster? (v. 14)

Yet, in spite of all to the contrary, He now gives His rebellious, but still loved, ones another chance—a new covenant in which they can become, in very truth, His people, and He would be their God.

The old order changed. But why? How?

Since the Lord does not see as man does, looking into the distant past and the far future, He saw that the old regimen of stated prayer time, the observance of the main festivals—Pentecost, Passover, Atonement, Tabernacles, Lights, Purim, and burnt offerings for sin, guilt, peace, and all the other ritualistic customs with their Mosaic recipes, besides the additional business of each day—had served their purpose of disciplining a people who had been enslaved for 400 years, and had their

---

[1] John Bakewell

thinking done for them. The time had now come to step up to a more universally acceptable coupling of humans with their Savior. And only our Living Lord could have created such an effective network. This time His law would be written, not on stone, which can be ground to dust and blown away, but on that human centerpiece, that command center of your persona and mine—our throbbing hearts. But how can we know what's written there? Who will interpret those instructions to us? This is unseen writing in an unspoken language. Yet, how, in timely fashion the networking began at Pentecost, with the coming of the Holy Spirit, the Interpreter, who makes all messages plain. Then, to clarify further, there is God's approved Word—Old and New—with its rearview mirror present operating procedures and guides, and a glimpse at where we are headed.

Together with the remembrance that the Lord will never leave us nor forsake us, there is our personal responsibility to be faithful to Him.

So the New covenant (or Testament) was inaugurated by Jesus at the Last Supper, when He said: "This is my blood of the new covenant which is shed for many." (Mark 14:24) The writer to the Hebrews quotes Jeremiah's reference to the New covenant. (8:8-12) And St. Paul expands on it in 2 Cor. 3:5-18. Luke 24:32 tell how the Risen Christ walked and talked with two men on the Road to Emmaus, and how their hearts were strangely warmed. Paul had a similar experience on the Road to Damascus, as John Wesley did more recently in London. It is a more workable formula that the Lord has provided for us in His new covenant. Obeying the instructions He writes on our hearts, and which are interpreted by the Holy Spirit, we become His people, and He our God.

PRAYER: *"Into my heart, come into my heart, Lord Jesus. Come in today, come in to stay." Amen.*

THIS IS THE DAY OF SALVATION

Jer. 18:11 *Go now and tell the people of Judah and the citizens of Jerusalem that these are the words of the Lord: I am framing disaster for you and perfecting my designs against you. Turn back, every one of you, from his evil conduct, mend your ways and your actions.*

Again, Jeremiah is sent to the same people, but with a final warning. Having been directed to the Potters house to learn the art of pottery, Jeremiah now better understands how the Lord moulds His people according to His plan. When, as with the clay, people sometimes foil the Divine Potter's hopes. He balls them up and starts again. That is the current warning that Jeremiah is to deliver.

His hearers, the Prophet knew, would readily understand the Potter's context. Potters were a common sight. Much pottery was used in the home. Especially in Jerusalem. There potters would get their clay from the Potter's Field—which later became a burial ground for the indigent. Pottery, in fact, is the first to turn up, in abundance, at any archaeological excavation. After all, the Potter's wheel was invented in Egypt in 3400 B.C.

At one time or another, just about everyone had watched a Potter give birth to a vessel out of a blob of clay. Then, suddenly, against the will and skill of the creator's hands, something went awry. Squashing the clay back into its original squishy nothingness, the Potter built a new creation.

The people of Jerusalem and Judah had resisted God's expectations for them. As Isaiah had pointed out (45:9ff) it is none of the clay's business to question the Potter, or to criticize Him. But these people of Jerusalem, who had come from dust and would return to the dust—these clay things of God, were behaving as if they were the Creators of the Universe. They had become like the one whom God questioned in the Book of Job (38): "Who made you General Manager of the Universe?" They were the same sort of people whom Jesus wept over. He, too, wanted to make them vessels fit for the Master's use but they "would not."

"Almost persuaded now to believe, almost persuaded Christ to receive. Seems now some soil to say, 'Go, spirit, go thy way, some more convenient day on thee I'll call.'"

Almost persuaded, harvest is past. Almost persuaded, doom comes at last. Almost cannot avail, almost is but to fail. Sad, sad, the bitter wail, almost, but lost.

PRAYER: *Just as I am, Lord, I come, I come to Thee. Amen.*

FROM SIN TO THE SON

Jer. 23:14 *Among the prophets of Jerusalem I see a thing most horrible: adulterers and hypocrites. They encourage evildoers, so that no one turns back from sin; to me all her inhabitants are like those of Sodom and Gomorrah.*

It was inevitable. Encouraged to do evil by (oh, horrors!) the prophets, and stubbornly defying God, the people of Jerusalem descended to the lowest depths of depravity. In the words of the Lord Himself, they had become like the people of Sodom and Gomorrah, those twin, sin cities.

Historians remind us that no incident in history ever made such an impression upon the Jewish people. It is mentioned in the books of Deuteronomy, Amos, Isaiah, Jeremiah, Zephaniah, Lamentations, Ezekiel, Matthew, Luke, Romans, 2 Peter and Revelation. William Barclay adds that "the glare of Sodom and Gomorrah is flung down the whole length of scripture history."

Those two cities were flourishing at the end of the twentieth century, B.C. The area had everything going for it. When Abraham and his nephew, Lot, were dividing up the land flowing with milk and honey, Lot was given first choice. What an enviable position to be in. He must have felt like a monkey on a banana plantation—he didn't know where to begin. With so much lush acreage to choose from, what did Lot select but the area containing Sodom and Gomorrah. It was an acreage fit for a King. In fact, Sodom and Gomorrah were known as royal cities. They were rich in soil, vegetation, livestock, and something for which we still scramble—oil.

Slowly the people succumbed to evil. God said that He wouldn't destroy the place if even fifty righteous people were found there. By the time the counting was done only forty were found. All right, God relented, He would settle for forty. By then the number had dropped to thirty, then twenty, then ten. (Gen. 18:20-33) All sorts of carnalities were practiced, not the least of which were homosexuality and sodomy—taking its name from Sodom.

When God looked at Jerusalem of Jeremiah's

time He recognized the goings-on. He had seen it all, ages before, in Sodom and Gomorrah. He was ready to do to His chosen city what He had done in the twin, sin cities—let punishment rain down upon them.

Two New Yorkers were in the Big Apple at Broadway and 42nd Street. Surveying the scores of pornographic movie houses, massage parlors, total-nudity shows, rambling hookers and such, one man said, "Tell me, do you think Sodom and Gomorrah were like this?" "No," said the other, "it wasn't as expensive." Indeed, the price keeps escalating and the wages of sin is death.

PRAYER: *Save us from false prophets, Lord. Wolves in sheep's clothing are a menace to our souls. We cling to You, good Shepherd. Amen.*

BE NOT AFRAID

Jer. 26:7-9 *The priests, the prophets, and all the people heard Jeremiah say this in the Lord's house and, when he came to the end of what the Lord had commanded him to say to them, priests, prophets and people seized him and threatened him with death.*

No matter where we turn in the Book of Jeremiah, we hear an echo of this text. Certainly one comes across the outline of this doleful sermon in Jer. 7:1-15; 11:1-17; 17:19-27; 34:8-22. And no wonder that the Book of Lamentations, which follows the Book of Jeremiah is attributed to Jeremiah. He always seemed to be regrettably mournful about something, so that, since then, any prolonged complaint has been termed a jeremiad. One can also understand why Rembrandt, the master artist, portraying Jeremiah on canvas, used his father as a model. The elderly Rembrandt, white-bearded, sits disconsolately resting his face on his hand, looking as if the whole world has caved in on him.

For this reason many otherwise able persons back-pedal when it comes to the ministry of preaching. Moses made all kinds of fancy excuses. He almost sounded like a speeding motorist trying to convince a state trooper that he was safely within the law. Jeremiah tried that too. When God called him to the ministry, Jerry was only twelve years old. "Ah! Lord God" he protested, "I do not know how to speak; I am only a child." But the Lord said, "Do not call yourself a child; for you shall go to whatever people I send you and say whatever I tell you to say. Fear none of them, for I am with you and will keep you safe." (Jer. 1:6-8)

This is not to say that the Lord calls His chosen ones to be doom-sayers, spoil-sports, fear-mongers, praying "give us this day our daily dread—to spread." Nor does His call to service mean flowery beds of ease, a twenty-minute sermon once in a while to the accompaniment of a contemporary jazz ensemble to make the congregation happy enough to shell out, gracefully. Oh, there must be joy—but joy in obeying the word of the Lord. As it was said of Jesus, "for the joy that was set before Him He endured the cross, despising the shame."

There's always a cross in serving Him. That's what appeared in Jeremiah's sermons, and the hearers were dismayed, and, instead of repenting of their wrongdoing, they wanted to put the preacher with this hell-fire preaching to death.

One vegetarian, shown his veggies under a microscope, saw little creatures on the leaves, and smashed the microscope. That's one way of getting rid of what doesn't fit our desired agenda. Death to the truth-sayer. So the timid preachers head for the tall grass and their self-tenured parishes.

Not the Jeremiahs, though criticized as they continue to be. As Pope John II explained: "The Gospel is certainly demanding...At the same time, however, He (Christ) reveals that His demands never exceed man's abilities. If man accepts these demands with an attitude of faith, he will also find in the grace that God never fails to give him the necessary strength to meet those demands." (*Crossing the Threshold of Hope*, pp. 222-223)

Indeed, this guarantee rests on Jesus' final Beatitude (be happy attitude) in Matt. 5:122: "Rejoice and be exceeding glad, for great shall be your reward in heaven, for so persecuted they the prophets which were before you." We're in good company.

PRAYER: *For Your undergirding assurance we give You hearty thanks, O Lord. Ratchet up our unbelief. Amen.*

A FAITH THAT'S FIT

Jer. 27:4-5 *These are the words of the Lord of Hosts the God of Israel: Say to your masters: I made the earth with my great strength and with outstretched arm, I made man and beast on the face of the earth and I give it to whom I see fit.*

And whom did the Lord deem fit—but the unfittest of all!

At the time the world ruler was Nebuchadnezzar. King of Babylon. An atheist—one who had ruined the Holy Land and taken God's people into captivity—was the one upon whom the Lord looked with favor. Unbelievable. But the Lord had His reasons.

It seemed to all the nations that had been suppressed by Nebuchadnezzar that now was their window of opportunity to break out of their bondage. Intelligence reports had it that Babylon was in a vulnerable position both inside and out. So an undercover summit meeting was planned in Jerusalem. But God had other ideas. Instead of backing these hotheaded allies that opposed the supreme conqueror, God threw in His lot with the enemy. Startling! Worse, He warned everyone else to do the same, Jeremiah included. Other prophets ordered the people to disobey God's directive.

Why it is at times that God makes such seemingly satanic requests, like when He ordered Abraham to sacrifice his son, as if the son was a ram or a goat?

Well, for one thing, because God sees not as man sees.

Look again at Jer. 1:4-5 where, even before Jeremiah was born, God could see the prophetic tendencies in the embryo as it moved through the maternal passageways toward Jeremiah's birthday. Nobody else has such insight. Such divine amplitude in itself needs no further witness of God's superlative knowledge. God can see the end from the beginning. He was not infatuated with Nebuchadnezzar. He knew the man inside out. But God also knew the evil doings of His own people and their inability to extricate from sin. "Oh, what a tangled web we weave when first we practice to deceive." Nebuchadnezzar, though unfit to be a servant of the Lord was in some other ways, which only the Lord could discern, just the Kingpin the Lord needed to achieve His purpose of straightening out the crooked nation of Israel.

Also, God's timing differs from man's. In July 1997, astronomers at Hawaii's Keck Observatory and the Hubble Space Telescope discovered an infant galaxy 13 billion light years from earth. It's been in existence for ages, but we are only now seeing it and learning about it. The lesson here is that only when we are ready and able (with the right telescope) will God's works be revealed to us. ("Give it to whom I see fit.") "A thousand years in Thy sight are but as yesterday when it is past, and as a watch in the night."

Our problem at this point is unbelief: How do we know that this is the word of the Lord? Even in Jeremiah's time there were false prophets that the Lord warned His people about. (Jer. 27:9) It took the Israelites a long time to concede and say in their language of the day, "You know what? God, through Jeremiah, was right on the money. Why did we ever disbelieve?" William Carey, the great Baptist missionary to India, had tested his signature exhortation before recommending it to others: "Expect great things from God. Attempt great thing for God."

PRAYER: *With Your "great strength and outstretched arm," nothing is too knotty for You, Lord. You are the only One who can take the imp out of the impossible. Amen.*

OPEN THE GATES OF THE TEMPLE

Jer. 29:4-7 These are the words of the Lord of Hosts the God of Israel: To all the exiles whom I have carried from Jerusalem to Babylon...Build...plant...marry (that)...you may increase there and not dwindle away.

The Lord knew His people better than they knew themselves. And He still does. He knew that His exiled national family was demoralized. Leaving behind in the Holy Land all that was precious to them, what was there left to live for? How could they sing the Lord's joyful song in a strange land? So they began to dwindle physically, mentally, spiritually. That is when the Lord sent them a buck up message through Jeremiah. Otherwise, if these Israelites should unravel, what would their new neighbors think of them and their God? Were God's people panty waists? Couldn't they make a go of life in the thriving City of Babylon? What kind of faith did these wobbly, wimpy Israelites possess? God could see and hear what was being bandied around in the social circles of Babylon, and knew that His chosen people were made of sterner stuff. So He tells them, in effect: "The Lord is on thy side. Bear patiently the cross of grief or pain. Leave to thy God to order and provide. In every change He faithful will remain. Be still, my soul, thy best, thy heavenly Friend, through thorny ways leads to a joyful end."

For one thing, the exiles were to believe that God was not like some household item they had forgotten and left behind in Jerusalem. No, He was not imprisoned, in the Temple's holy of holies. He was alive and well, and right with them. By which He infers that the world is His parish, and ours, and it is our duty, with His help, to so live in whatever circumstances we are placed, as to be a powerful influence for good in the lives of people around us. There's no reason to dwindle; every reason to prosper.

That's a timely, heartening word for changing

times which come to all of us in varying forms, every day. Instead of languishing because times are not as they once were, to seek the Lord in the unfamiliar, and follow His guidance to new and higher peaks of performance; to see His challenges emerge not only from the immoveable mountains, but also from the swiftly tossing rapids—is to be the kind of adventurer who is near to the heart of a God in whose image we were made.

Nor is the Lord confined to the boundaries of this world parish. He reaches beyond it, through the millennia to the extremities of space, and back to our habitable globe and to us individuals. In what capable hands we are. He is omnipotently free to be omnipresent and not shackled to Jerusalem, this planet, universe, us. He is here and everywhere adored.

What a liberating faith this provides for those denominations, churches, countries, races that claim that He belongs to them alone. That church across town couldn't possibly have Him as a member. But He persists in being my heavenly Father, and theirs, and ours, and yours.

PRAYER: *Under no circumstances would You have Your loved ones dwindle, Lord. Expand our faith. Amen.*

OUT OF THE DEPTHS

Jer. 32:2 *At that time the forces of the Babylonian King were besieging Jerusalem, and the prophet Jeremiah was imprisoned in the court of the guard house attached to the palace.*

An imprisoned prophet—how come? Jeremiah claimed that the Lord had told him about the conquest of Jerusalem by the Babylonians. That was interpreted as sowing a defeatist attitude among the people of Israel, and stiffening the resolve of the enemy. Considered treason, Jeremiah was jailed. It was more of a detention center, a state prison, but where food was assured and a certain amount of freedom. But when Jeremiah purchased some land in his hometown and attempted to leave Jerusalem to go to inspect his property, he was re-arrested. The authorities believed that the prophet was in cahoots with the enemy and was fleeing (with valuable intelligence) to join their ranks, as others of his countrymen had already done. For this serious offense, Jeremiah was put in a maximum security prison.

Actually, it was a cistern or bottle-shaped dungeon cut out of limestone rock. Once in such a pit, with no way out except outside help, prisoners were left to die hideously.

Fortunately a palace servant had pity on the prophet. Along with helpers, ropes, and rags (to cushion the ropes), the servant engineered the lifting of Jeremiah out of his squeeze-bottle. Still a jail-bird, however, the prophet was sent back to the much-less-constricted guardhouse.

In the Book of Lamentations, which Jeremiah wrote, he mourns: "they flung me alive into a pit and cast stones on me...I cried out...from the depths of the pit." (3:53,55) How often Jeremiah was in the pits, literally, emotionally, mentally. Yet, each time he was uplifted by unknown, unseen allies. God has myriad ways in which He sends help. F. W. Robertson of Brighton (U.K.) said: "If I had not met a certain person, I should not have changed my profession." Instead of becoming a well-known preacher, Robertson would have served as a foot soldier in India. How did the change come? One night Robertson's dog barked and upset a sensitive girl whose mother complained to Robertson. That mother, in time, introduced Robertson to a person who changed his life and profession.

Then, too, God spoke directly and helpfully to Jeremiah. As the hymn goes: "This is my Father's world, and to my listening ears, all nature sings and round me rings the music of the sphere...in the rustling grass, I hear Him pass. He speaks to me everywhere.

PRAYER: *Lord, rescue us from our deep blue moods and abysmal ignorance, now and ever. Amen.*

THE ONLY COMPLETE CURER

Jer. 33:6 *I will heal and cure.*

The sun must have shone brighter through the bars of Jeremiah's prison when he heard the Lord say: "If you call to me I will answer you, and tell you great and mysterious things which you do not understand." (Jer. 33:3) But that lightening word was not for Jeremiah alone. Jerusalem and the whole country could throw their headpieces in the air for joy. This word, straight from heaven, was for everyone. And there was more to it than met the ear. For the Lord added: "I will heal and cure...and will let my people see an age of peace and security." (33:6-7)

The real sunshiner is still ahead for anybody at anytime in the two words "cure" and "understand." Healing is often skin deep. With soap and water and the formation of a scab, one is convinced that all is well. Then comes the day when a rash appears and ointments and flesh-colored Band-Aids don't help. The irritant is underneath...In like manner the Lord spots troublemakers that we can't identify—cancerous thoughts which affect our deeds. Ably, subtly, He informs us that He will reveal to us great and mysterious things that we do not understand because they are somewhere underneath and undetectable even by lasers and micro-cameras—terroristic plans or a feeling of insecurity that ripples through our nervous system.

The Lord had seen the havoc such underlying, untaken-care-of wrongs had done to His chosen people. Now He would more than heal them. He would cure them from the depths of their core values and out.

On our own we don't seem to be able to locate the canker within, much less to cauterize it or quadruple bypass it, or have a transplant. We deceive ourselves about the seriousness of our terminal spiritual ailments.

Eugene Peterson explains how this underlying rot is overlooked, even in the church, or should we say *especially* in the church since it is inexcusable there.

"Parish glamorization is ecclesiastical pornography—taking photographs (skillfully airbrushed) or drawing pictures of congregations that are without spot or wrinkle, the shapes that a few parishes have for a few short years. These provocatively posed pictures are devoid of personal relationships. The pictures excite a lust for domination for gratification, for uninvolved and impersonal spirituality...a tall-steeple church with a cheesecake congregation...I am still vulnerable to seduction."[1]

---

[1] E. H. Peterson, *Under the Unpredictable Plant,* p. 22

Further, on the same topic, Peterson adds that we mistake "religious cancer for spiritual growth."[1] Then, quoting Erwin Chargall: "Man is only strong when he is conscious of his own weakness. Otherwise the eagles of heaven will eat his liver, as Prometheus found out. No eagles of heaven any more. No Prometheus: now we get cancer instead—the prime disease of advanced civilizations."[2]

Knowing these imperiling undercurrents, the Lord cleans, cures and heals. What a Savior.

PRAYER: *Dear Lord and Father of mankind, from the shadows You keep watch above Your own. We strive to be worthy of Your saving grace. Amen.*

NEW—THROUGH AND THROUGH

Jer. 33:10-11 *These are the words of the Lord: You say of this place, 'It lies in ruins, without people or animals throughout the towns of Judah and the streets of Jerusalem. It is all a waste, inhabited by neither man nor beast.' Yet in this place will be heard once more the sounds of joy and gladness, the voices shouting, 'Praise the Lord of Hosts, for the Lord is good; his love endures forever,' as they offer praise and thanksgiving in the house of the Lord. For I shall restore the fortunes of the land as once they were. This is the word of the Lord.*

From beginning to end, misfortunes and fortunes, all are under God's watchful care. Nothing escapes His attention. We have His word on it. Jeremiah, while still in the guardhouse, had a releasing experience when his All-knowing God gave him a soul-satisfying description of what was,

---

[1]*Ibid* p. 138
[2]*Ibid* p. 138

and what was to come.

"This place" (meaning Jerusalem and adjoining towns) at present was in shambles. Most of the 20 Kings, since the scintillating days of David, were rotters. So-called prophets had gone off their rockers, setting a poor example, misguiding people through wide gates and broad ways that led to destruction—because of the carnalities they practiced.

Such ruination could have blotted out the area forever. As happened with Sodom and Gomorrah. Just an ink-blotched memory.

But "this Place" was too precious to the Lord. Besides, He had had many restoration experiences, beginning with the new world He presented to Noah after the Flood. The remaking of Jerusalem and its environs would be nothing new. He would be happy to reconstruct that which was so near to His heart. It would be patterned after what it had been at its finest, no less. Best of all, "This Place" would ring with the joy of religion which had been missing for too many lamentable centuries. There would be joy of the kind known at weddings. But that full-throated delight would be directed at the Lord for His goodness and never-failing love. Songs of praise will be sung, as are to be found in Ps. 106, 107, 118, 136. And this uninhibited and unlimited praise and thanks would be expressed in the house of the Lord. At last the people would come back home to their heavenly Father. What a blessed reunion—which is the kind of reclamation that is possible for sinners in any age.

There will be the joy of forgiveness. And God also gives the joy of courage, which, in Hebrew, denotes "firmness in the knees." Also, God gives the joy of healing, which means, "I will cause new skin to grow."

PRAYER: *Lord, in "this place" where we now live, grant us the joy of Thy salvation, now and forever. Amen.*

A ROSE BETWEEN TWO THORNS

Jer. 34:1 *The word which came to Jeremiah from the Lord when King Nebuchadnezzar of Babylon and his whole army, along with all his vassal Kingdoms and nations, were attacking Jerusalem and all her towns.*

The Babylonian war machine was poised to flatten "Jerusalem and all her towns." Nebuchadnezzar was taking no chances. No doubt he had heard how, a hundred years before, Sennacherib had fully expected to come "like a wolf on the fold," and make short work of "Jerusalem and all her towns." But, alas, overnight, that mighty army was slain. At dawn, 185,000 warriors lay dead.

Nebuchadnezzar made sure that he would not suffer such a fate. He would throw at the enemy everything in his arsenal. And that was daunting, since everyone knew that Nebuchadnezzar had dominated the Middle East for forty-three years.

Imagine how the citizens of Jerusalem must have shuddered with fear. Yet in the middle of all that tension and apprehension came the word of the Lord. He had not abandoned His people. He was still on hand, still concerned about the welfare and future of His beloved. Things would have to get worse before getting better, but the best was yet to be. He would see to that!

How God consistently creates calm in the center of cyclonic times. How, in barbed wire days, He sees to it that His people can rest assured and sing merrily between the barbs on the wire.

The world reserves its longest ticker tape and cheers for those who can make a go of it—in the midst of adversity. But it is the Lord who makes it possible. He did for Paul and Silas. (Acts 16:16-26) Subjected to brutalities and indignities, these men were lynched, stripped of their clothes, beaten, hurled into a dungeon, with their feet fastened in stocks. Yet at midnight, a time when the sharp spines of torment run through men's skulls like rapiers, Paul and Silas prayed and sang praises to God. Perilously placed amid death-dealing circumstances, those two men sang cheerily between the barbs on the wire.

In Jerusalem there is barbed wire surrounding the Garden in which the Easter tomb is located. One Sunday morning, children from the Jerusalem Blind School filed into the Garden for worship. Their opening hymn, which they sang with gusto, was, "O Worship the King all glorious above, O *gratefully* sing His power and His love."

From Jeremiah to the present, in Jerusalem there have been Hallelujah choruses heard from between the barbs in barbaric hours. God's word gives hope and joy, yesterday, today, and forever.

PRAYER: *Lord, we hear You telling us to go and do likewise. By Thy grace we will. Amen.*

"WILT THOU BE MADE WHOLE?"

Jer. 35:13 *These are the words of the Lord of Hosts the God of Israel: Go and say to the Judeans and the citizens of Jerusalem: "Will you never accept correction and obey my word?" Says the Lord.*

Babylonian army units were harassing the homeland of Israel.

The Rechabites, a small Hebrew community,

slipped into Jerusalem for safety's sake. They were descendants of the Children of Israel who had exited Egypt with Moses. But whereas the rest of those who entered the Promised Land became landowners, settling into homes in towns and cities, the Rechabites continued the nomadic, tent existence of their forebears. But it was their faithfulness to the God of their forefathers that really mattered, and which, here, God uses as a contrast with the faithlessness of His supposed followers in Jerusalem. Despite repeated opportunities to correct their evil conduct, turn from serving other gods to obeying the living God, these stubborn Jerusalemites simply refused to amend their ways.

Why, as God asks, will some people never accept correction and obey the word of the Lord? Because for one thing, they claim the right to be wrong. Then complication sets in when they explain, that which was supposed to be wrong eventually turned out to be absolutely right and what was supposed to be right, in time was proven wrong. The danger, however, is that—free to choose the better, there is an innate tendency to choose the worse, the easy. Then a minimum has a funny way of becoming a maximum. Then the question becomes: How far into wrong does one go before reaching the point of no return? How long does one play the part of Mr. Hyde before ceasing to be the kindly Dr. Jekyll altogether?

In a doctoral dissertation on the nature of ultimate realities, a student was sure that the riddle of the universe could be solved by the recognition of God. Yet the student argued, if he accepted the reality of God, he could no longer do as he pleased. And that was unthinkable. God must be shut out.

To be sure, God grants humans the right to be wrong. He's not afraid of that. But He also grants the right to be right, so that persons may walk with Him in the paths of rightness for His name's sake.

Abraham Lincoln outlined it in his Second Inaugural address: "With malice toward none, with charity for all; with firmness in the right, as God gives us to see the right."

That's what God was asking of His people back then—as He still does.

PRAYER: *We stand corrected, Father. And we trust and obey, for there's no other way. Through Christ. Amen.*

HIS WORD IN OUR WORLD

Jer. 36:10 *Then Baruch (the scribe) read Jeremiah's words (from God) in the house of the Lord out of the book in the hearing of all the people.*

The congregation in the Temple heard the Word of the Lord, but if they responded in any way it is not reported. Yet here are other reports about this Bible reading. Some officials were stirred up enough by the reading to go "down to the palace" (36:12) and repeat all that they had just heard. Unsatisfied, Baruch was sent for and requested to read again what he had uttered in the Temple. That made the hearers tremble. (36:16) It didn't sound good. They knew enough about temperaments in high places. They foresaw an explosion waiting to happen, especially when they turned to each other with the same words: "We must report this to the King." (36:17) Then came the impending threat that Baruch and Jeremiah better head for the tall grass for having written this document. Their lives were in danger.

The scene changes to the royal winter quarters, with his majesty trying to keep warm near the fireplace. Having heard about the questionable scripture reading, the King called for the allegedly objectionable manuscript. As the scroll was read, the King, showing his disgust, cut each column, amid cries to desist, and flung them into the fire. (36:23) Intending to do the same to Jeremiah and his secretary, the King with temper now hotter than the brazier, sent for the prophet. "But the Lord had hidden them." (36:26) Hidden His own, but exposed the one who scorned the sacred Word.

Burning the Bible, literally or in any other way, brings disaster. It did for this sacrilegious King, who went on to commit murder, incest rape, theft, as do those who distance themselves from God's Holy Word.

Look, in contrast, at another King, Josiah. Coming to the throne at the age of eight, with an obnoxious family legacy of a father and grandfather who were idolatrous and merciless, Josiah is honored in Hebrew history as being second only to David. "Before him there was no King like him...nor did any like him arise after him." (2 Kings 23:25) He read the scriptures publicly at church, and lived by their tenets. Destroying anything idolatrous left by his predecessors, he organized a Passover feast to celebrate the commitment of his country to the Lord. Nothing like this had been done for 400 years to show, unashamedly, how devoted the nation was to God. (2 Kings 23:22)

And that can happen in our time. Sadly, quite the opposite is raising its ugly form, indicating our drift from the living Word.

In this morning's paper it told about Comedy Central's animated series about Jesus Christ living in modern day New York, "a half hour animated show about JC wanting to escape his father's enormous shadow and to live in NYC as a regular guy." Or even if we tried what Jeremiah did in the Temple, we would disturb a beehive. A U.S. District Judge recently ruled that the National Day of Prayer authorized by federal statute in 1952, "is an unconstitutional endorsement of religion."

The signs of our times increasingly point to the imperative need for reinvigorated Bible study. That's where the Laws for and guidance toward righteous living abide—now and ever.

PRAYER: *Again many thanks for Your Word, Divine Author. Help us to incarnate it daily as never before. Amen.*

UP THE DOWN STAIRCASE

Jer. 43:2 *(A group) had the effrontery to say to Jeremiah "You are lying; the Lord our God has not sent you to forbid us to go and make our home in Egypt."*

Approaching the terminus of Jeremiah's life, the rearview mirror reflects much lamentable information from the Lord concerning the people of Israel. Lamentable, often, was Jeremiah's own psyche, which makes it understandable why it is assumed that this prophet also wrote the Book of Lamentations. His dour experiences continue until the end as recorded in our text for today. He had just informed his people that though the Babylonians were planning the invasion of Jerusalem and the entire country, the Israelites were not to flee to Egypt for refuge.

Usually heeded, this time Jeremiah was given

the brush-off. Worse, and for the first time in his prophetic career, he was called a downright liar. Worse yet, Jeremiah was insolently accused of having been manipulated by his coworker and secretary, Baruch.

The leader of the opposition, having reduced Jeremiah to gibbering unimportance, took (forcibly?) him and his scribe in stubborn disobedience to God's will—and moved to Egypt to live under Pharaoh's protection—not God's.

Yet, knowing Jeremiah's fortitude and faith, it is conceivable that he even requested to go to Egypt. Confident that God would never forsake him; knowing the optimism of uncertainty and the certainty of optimism, in Egypt he could still be in a position to mentor his bewildered countrymen in their physical and spiritual incertitude. He could hereby set the format for the faithful in future centuries.

Insightful Jesus, recognizing this, relayed the message through His own generation: "rejoice and be exceeding glad for great shall be your reward in heaven; for so persecuted they the prophets which were before you." (Matt. 5:12)

To be in such elite company emboldens the battered. As it did for the Christ Himself. He articulated this Beatitude out of personal experience. God did not send His prophets into some of the worst kinds of messes just as a trial run before sending His son. Jesus suffered all the worsts that the prophets had endured, and then some. Jeremiah was not the last truth-sayer to be called a liar. Jesus, the Truth, had His face slapped for suspected insubordination. (Matt. 26:67) His whole life has been called a lie. His virgin birth has been scoffed at for millennia. His walking on the Galilean Lake has been joked about in beer halls for ages. His resurrection and appearances thereafter; His going in and out of closed doors. His raising of the dead on several occasions. His ascension...it goes on and on. Then there was His assassination which not all the prophets suffered. Then, for the Son of God there was that ultimate humiliation: "My God, why have You forsaken me?" Yet He bore our sins in His own body on the tree, willingly, grateful to have been chosen to lead the way to glory—giving us a foretaste of what it will be like in that house not made with hands, eternal in the heavens. And thank you, Jeremiah, for preparing the highway for our God, and for us.

PRAYER: *Gracious Lord, work in and through us even at the worst of times, that we, too, may join the favored few. Amen.*

SINGING IN THE REIGN OF TERROR

Lam. 1:7 In the days of Jerusalem's misery and restlessness she called to mind all the treasures which were hers from days of old, when her people fell into the power of adversaries and she had no one to help her. The adversaries looked on, laughing at her downfall.

In what is known as Jeremiahs' Grotto, located beneath the hill of Golgotha where Jesus died, Jeremiah cried. With inconsolable grief he recorded the dire condition of Jerusalem, following her mincemeat experience in Babylon's meat-grinding machine. The city was pulverized—Temple, walls, homes, the infrastructure—you name it, all were a junk pile. And if the Exiles were sitting down by the waters of Babylon and weeping, so, too, were Jeremiah and the few scattered survivors doing in the once-fabled City of Jerusalem.

Had Jerusalem been an inconsequential cowtown out on the prairie, its loss could have been written off and forgotten. But how could anyone forget its historic magnificence? It had drawn people from all over the world for trade, as a tourist attraction, as a magnet for pilgrims attending sacred feasts, as the Super-center for worship. Then, to witness the stark contrast between past and present was agonizing, gut-wrenching. (1:20) Tears came in Niagara proportions, especially as one was overwhelmed with a shroud of helplessness and hopelessness. To add insult to injury, those who had caused the ruination just threw back their heads and guffawed at the hapless downtrodden. How the mighty are fallen! And humiliated. Could any curse be worse?

Jerusalem in tatters is not that unusual. Such decimating experiences come sooner or later to all humans. There is crying and sighing and dying. "The mass of men lead lives of quiet desperation." The question then becomes: What happens next? Are we on our own? Is God sitting in His heaven doing nothing? On the contrary. He is more interested in the outcome than we are. But He waits to see how willing we are to learn from past errors, and to make mid-course corrections, however sand-papery to our souls that may be. It's never a hopeless situation for Him. He knows how to work all things together for good to those who cooperate with Him. On the underside He weaves the knots and blots to look surprisingly beautiful—from the top. He wants us to have the last laugh—with Him.

PRAYER: *In life's long silences and blackouts, we feel about us the movement of thy security forces, Lord, and we are undismayed. Thank You. Amen.*

CLEANSE ME

Lam. 1:8 *Jerusalem had sinned greatly, and so she was treated like a filthy rag.*

Indeed, this Book of Lamentations looks more like a laundry list of dirty thoughts, mucky words, and smelly deeds. Nor is the unpleasantness Cloroxed out by making the book into five poems. Yet there are at least two reasons why we dare not leapfrog over Lamentations and move on to Ezekiel. According to how we learn from the past, we will either 1. repeat the errors of history or 2. redeem them. And who would want to repeat Jerusalem's recent fouled past?

It had been a big bustling beautiful queen of a city. Now having been besieged, robbed, ravished the solitary queen was widowed, friendless, put to forced labor, left to weep the night through without a single comforter.

Where once pilgrim's flocked to the Holy City for the great festivals, making the several city gates crowded thoroughfares, now a ghostly quiet had settled upon the area. You could almost taste the bitterness in the air. And the handful of survivors knew well why the situation was in dire straits; the countless misdeeds of the people. All signs of majesty had vanished. Princelings were like disturbed deer on the run with no game parks to call their own. Then the cruelest blow fell as Gentiles, mind you, rank outsiders, were seen entering the sanctuary, something inconceivable, unallowable by God in the good old days. How much more discredited could God's personal residence on earth become? Yet the twin question here is: Why did this era become so vitally important in Jewish archives, so that it has been given a place beside Judaism's proudest accomplishment—the Exodus under Moses' leadership? The very inclusion of Lamentation's in the Bible points not to a moody broody, offensive five chapters, but to a phoenix-like uprising from the ashes of an inglorious episode.

And that resurrecting surge is detected in the people's courage to submit to self-examination. "The Lord was in the right, it was I who (wantonly) rebelled against His commands." (Lam. 1:18,20) Still, God, ever the dispenser of Goodness and Severity, did not desist from punishing the evildoers (chapter 2).

Making confession and receiving due punishment for wrongdoing was not the living end for God's loved ones. He is always more concerned about them than they are about themselves. As Jeremiah, the author of Lamentations, found: "The Lord, I say, is all that I have (3:24)...therefore I will wait patiently: the Lord's true love is surely not spent." (3:21-22)

Then, in the waiting, prayerful, expectant interlude there comes the confirming belief that "the Lord will not cast off His servants forever. He may punish cruelly, yet He will have compassion in the fullness of His love; He does not willingly afflict or punish any mortal man." (Lam. 3:31-33)

Putting the first three chapters in capsule form, Jeremiah exhorts us to "examine our ways and put them to the test and turn back to the Lord." (3:40) What's so lamentable about that? We are redeemed. That's all-sufficient.

PRAYER: *Lord God of Hosts be with us always, for nobody can bring us from rags to riches and redemption as You can. We thank You. Amen.*

TASTE AND SEE

Lam. 2:13 *How can I cheer you? Whose plight is like yours, daughter of Jerusalem? To what can I compare you for your comfort, virgin daughter of Zion? For your wound gapes as wide as the ocean—who can heal you?*

The national situation remains under a cloud, especially Zion, city of our God. Strongholds are in smithereens. Palaces in pieces. Mourning is multiplied. The sanctuary and altar are now the property of pagans. The law is no more. (2:9) The elders are in the depths of dejection, draped in sackcloth, with sprinkled dust on their heads, like decaying roadside posts.

Surveying the baleful scene, the prophet knows his people well enough to know that their basic needs at the moment are how to keep their sunny side up and how to pack up their troubles in the old kit bag and smile...

Through the ages, whenever people have learned of the invincible power of God, they have been laughingly confident. In Rome's Coliseum, when Christians faced the wild beasts and flashing blades, they were laughingly confident. Their bodies might be mutilated, but their spirits were buoyant. As Bernard Clausen noted: "We have enough of that pitiable human breed that sees difficulty in every opportunity. We could stand a few more heroes...who will see opportunity in every difficulty."

The prophet foresaw that likelihood, and how the Lord, if given half a chance, would show the downcast people of Jerusalem how to smile at all their foes.

Also there was evident need among God's banged-up people for comfort. Nothing was going right for them. The troubled waters ran deep within their lives. Their foundations were shaken. And in order to keep from caving in, and to stabilize their rockiness at ground zero, their vulnerable state cried out for deep strength, which, as Isaiah (30:15) had found, could come only with quietness and confidence, adding: "they that wait upon the Lord shall renew their strength. (Isa. 40:31)

Last, prophetic analysis found that there was a need among Zion's zonked-out populace for healing. The stricken wayfarer beside the Jericho road had nothing on these people. A 911 call to Dr. Diet, Dr. Quiet, Dr. Merryman, and any other attending physicians, would have been in order. Yet, the prescriptions for healing had long since been made widely available. By the psalmist, for one: "Bless the Lord, O my soul, and all that is within me, bless his holy name. Bless the Lord, O my soul, and forget not all his benefits: Who forgiveth all thine iniquities; who healeth all Thy diseases. (Ps. 103:1-3) Then there was Isaiah's prescription: Messiah "was pierced for our transgressions, crushed for our iniquities; the chastisement he bore restored us to health and by his wounds we are healed." (53:5)

PRAYER: *Lord, You have not left us without instruction as to how we may be cheerful, comforted, healed. We go now to the medicine cabinet and take the dosage. Amen.*

FINALLY SONSHINE

Lam. 4:11, 12 *The Lord glutted his rage and poured forth his anger; he kindled a fire in Zion, and it consumed her foundations. This no one believed.*

How often, and from how many authors have we heard this lament? Speaking on behalf of the Lord, Jeremiah issued the warning that this would happen if the people didn't turn from their evil ways. (Jer. 26:2-8) Angry at such impunity, Jeremiah was threatened with death. (Jer. 26:8) Even the Psalmist proclaimed that nothing bad could ever happen to Jerusalem, because "God is in her midst; she will not be overthrown...the Lord of Hosts is with us; the God of Jacob is our fortress." (Ps. 46:5-7) Isaiah made a similar prophecy regarding the invincibility of the Holy City, which is verified in 2 Kings 19:31-34. The stalwart warrior Sennacherib, learning of Zion's strength, backed away to keep from endangering his reputation as an unstoppable conqueror. Even the tiny Jebusites, early settlers in Jerusalem, were so sure of the natural fortifications that they made light of the great David's intended assault upon them. (2 Sam. 5:6-8) It was as if oncoming generations of Hebrews couldn't, in their wildest imagination, see their sacred capital city ever lying in splinters.

Still, everything that couldn't and shouldn't happen to God's dwelling place—did. Why? Why? Why?

Well, if twenty percent of humans think, and twenty percent think that they think, and the rest would rather die than think—the ultimate destruction of Jerusalem got a lot of people to put on their thinking caps and ask, for one thing: Why did this happen? That is what the Lord had been eager to learn. Why did they continue in their ungodly ways while persuading themselves that in no way, certainly not in the shattering of their famed city, would the Lord lay upon them painful penalties. Then came the wake-up call and demand for a self-examination: "Lord, is it I?" That's always a cleanser. "Lord, revive Thy Church, beginning with me."

Introspection can cause the realization that "it is a terrifying thing to fall into the hands of the living God." (Heb. 10:1) "For we know who it is that said, 'Justice is mine: I will repay'; and again, 'the Lord will judge his people.'" (Heb. 10:30)

That is, until we fall into His everlastingly endearing arms. Then to our astonishment we find that this God who so loved the world loves us exceeding abundantly above His need to punish us.

Sometimes we cannot believe that God so loves. For 2,000 years the Jews could not call their once capital city their own. They were on the leashes of several nations, feeling the tug of authority from afar.

In 1954, visitors to Jerusalem had to carry their luggage across No-Man's Land with guns trained on them from both sides. On June 7, 1967, when Israeli Paratroopers recaptured Jerusalem they went to the Western (Wailing) wall and prayed and wept with gratitude. Moshe Dayan, then Minister of Defense, said, "We earnestly stretch out our hands to our Arab brethren in peace, but we have returned to Jerusalem never to part from her again."

PRAYER: *Almighty God, You have taught us through the experience of others. Inspire us to learn and behave. Through Jesus our Savior. Amen.*

THE SOURCE OF PURITY

Ezek. 4:14 *O Lord God, I have never been made unclean, never in my life.*

In an acted prophecy, Ezekiel envisions the Lord instructing him to ready God's people (especially in Jerusalem) for the coming siege of the city and for their removal to far-away Babylon as exiles.

So helpful is the Lord (as always), that in a detailed list of instructions He guides His people in preparing for what their daily routine will be when they are surrounded by enemy garrisons, and finally severed from any assistance from local supporters.

At one place in the process, the intake of the besieged would be reduced from bread and water to a starvation diet. Even the few stray grains of "wheat and barley, beans, and lentils, millet and spelt" (4:9) were to be ground together and baked over a fire fueled by human dung. (4:12)

That's when the prophet Ezekiel exploded with disgust. No, he objected, that would cause him to be unclean, something he had never been and was unwilling to be, even in desperate siege conditions.

Graciously the Lord conceded. "So He allowed me to use cow dung instead of human dung to bake my bread," (v. 15) which immediately takes us to the case of Peter on the rooftop of Simon the tanners house at Joppa. (Acts 10:9-16)

There Peter has a vision of a sheet let down from heaven. In the sheet are creatures of every kind—beasts, reptiles, birds. A voice ordered Peter to "Kill and eat." (v. 13) But Peter, a good Jew like Ezekiel, responded, "I have never eaten anything profane or unclean." (v. 14) Both men were remembering the Mosaic requirements for purification—in four instances: 1. Circumcision of a male child; 2. Contact with a corpse; 3. Certain diseases, such as leprosy; and 4. In sacrifices and in eating, only certain types of birds and animals could be used. As for animals, only those that chewed the cud and whose hooves were cloven were considered clean. But seeing even unclean animals in the sheet, Peter protested. Still, the voice from above persisted: "It is not for you to call profane what God counts clean." (v. 15)

Therefore the question is: Why did the Lord change His mind and give Ezekiel the benefit of the doubt, but held Peter's feet to the fire? With so many grades of impurity it is always a problem to decide which to refuse and which to use. It is not that God is unable to make up His mind and needs help from us humans—because in His objective wisdom He sees what is best for us in similar situations but for dissimilar reasons. For Ezekiel it was no big deal to change from human to cow dung. For Peter the lesson was a transitional one of historic proportions. The Lord was teaching Peter a lesson which was soon to be pressed into application, namely the inclusion of Cornelius, the Roman centurion; a non-Jew and therefore an outcaste, as a new convert into the Christian community—the beginning of Christianity; open-door policy to the rest of human kind. The New covenant was jump-started and was on the move. Which is why the Lord's help must be sincerely sought, up front. He will guide with certainty both in old and new circumstances. He is the same (not us) yesterday, today and forever.

PRAYER: *If purity of heart is a prerequisite for seeing Thee, O Lord, that's what we desire more than all. Amen.*

DEM BONES

Ezek. 4:16 *He then said, "O man, I am cutting short their daily bread in Jerusalem; people will weigh out anxiously the bread they eat, and measure with dismay the water they drink."*

Transported along with 8,000 exiles, Ezekiel had found lodging in Babylon. It was along an irrigation canal connected with the River Euphrates. Here Ezekiel, the fourth of the Great Prophets, preached the same message that Jeremiah was spreading in Jerusalem—that sin brings punishment. A visionary, though laughed at by his fellow exiles, Ezekiel's visions justified his prophetic power when in time they were clothed with reality.

And here was one vision that he had of what would happen in his dearly loved, but now faraway Jerusalem. Because they had sorely displeased the Lord, Jerusalemites would be besieged by enemy troops. Under siege, God's people would have to resort to food rationing, a symbol of "belt tightening" in all areas of living. One sees it in the terms which Ezekiel uses: "cutting short," "weigh out," "anxiously," "measure with dismay." Fellow exiles, living beside a freshwater canal, could only vaguely envision how their brother Hebrews in Jerusalem would be bordering on perpetual thirst—and hunger.

Yet, the underlying warning for both the exiles and the besieged (and for all of us since then) is that "man does not live by bread alone, but man lives by every utterance of the mouth of the Lord." (Deut. 8:3; Matt. 4:1-4) For "bread" is not confined to a baked loaf, or even to food in general, but to material possessions. "What does it profit a man if he gains the whole world, and loses his soul?" (Matt. 16:26) That, in fact, was why both besieged and exiles were in such straits: things of this world had played a dominant role in their lives. And God's Word, which repeatedly had brought them through troubled waters and set their feet upon a rock had been exchanged for a mess of pottage, or some unprofitable prophet's potted message. No wonder that all such end up in Ezekiel's valley of dry bones! (Ezek. 37) And, no wonder that Ezekiel was put to death by his fellow exiles for preaching the Word. It is still happening. "For so persecuted they the prophets which were before you." (Matt. 5:12) Yet, in following Ezekiel's example we are "Blessed," made happy. (Matt. 5:11)

PRAYER: *Lord, we hear Your word, and proclaim it—that our dry bones may come alive. Amen.*

THE "I" IN IDOL

Ezek. 8:17 *He said to me, "Man, do you see that? Is it because they think these abominations a trifle, that the Jews have filled the country with violence?"*

If Ezekiel had his squeaky-clean senses offended by being ordered to cook his food over human excretion, he hadn't heard or seen anything filthy yet.

Realizing that His prophet was an innocent babe in the woods who had not understood why God had punished His own chosen people, the Lord arranged for Ezekiel to be taken in a vision to Jerusalem. There Ezekiel could see for himself the evil doings that had displeased the living God.

Arriving at the entrance of the Holy City, Ezekiel saw the image of Astarte, goddess of Lust. The farther the prophet went the worse the vileness became. On a wall in a dark chamber were carved idols of vermin, with Jewish elders worshipping the beastliness. Having persuaded themselves that God had abandoned them, the Jews felt free to worship anything they pleased.

The next shocker for Ezekiel was at the gateway to the temple, where women were bowing before a fertility god. He had died, but was rescued by his sister Ishtar, a fertility goddess. They married and brought dead vegetation to life in the spring. In an inner sanctum there were men with their backs turned to the holy place while they worshipped the rising sun.

Was it possible that Ezekiel, with his telescopic spiritual vision was looking down the centuries, and into ours?

O, let us not think only of the River Ganges, where any morning thousands of people worship the rising sun. Think also of those Sunday mornings when motor cars are zealously washed, waxed, pampered, but never turned in the direction of a church worship service. Or there is that other household god, the big $ with two strikes against it—$, which nevertheless influences most decisions everywhere.

Then there are the addictions that get the full allegiance of too many in our human fellowship—sex, gambling, alcohol, private planes, palatial estates. Why, the very address of a regal residence once brought Hollywood tourists to their knees: "Pickfair," owned by movie stars Mary Pickford and Douglas Fairbanks. There's no end to the listing of household gods first recorded in Gen. 31:19, where Rachel stole her father Laban's homemade and in-home cherished gods. And although 400 years later such idolatry was forbidden in the Second Commandment (Exod. 20:4-5; Deut. 5:8-9), such deities have become household names and fixtures. The gardens with expansive acreage superintended by famed caretakers; Olympic-sized and equipped swimming pools; those costly walls adorned with masterpieces of art; libraries with first editions of authors of repute. Not alone among the wealthy are such worship centers (shrines) to be found. On all levels of society, an adulation for things like unto piety is to be found.

Ezekiel was not called "the Prophet of the long view" for nothing. He has spotlighted us, but also turns the light on God—who is the one who deserves our full allegiance.

PRAYER: *Thank You, Lord, for cornering us. We've been caught red-handed with our secret idolatries. With Your help we return to worship You in spirit and in truth. Amen.*

FINDING FAVOR IN HIS SIGHT

Ezek. 9:11 *The man clothed in linen...brought back word, saying, "I have done as thou didst command me."*

In a vivid vision Ezekiel is given a full-length account of what is going to happen to vile Jerusalem. Evildoings had long since permeated the very heart of the city: the Temple.

The true and living God was no longer worshipped there. An acknowledged den of vice (also mentioned as such by Jesus centuries later), the Temple housed foreign gods, idols, animals, insects, and other paraphernalia that were being bowed to and exalted in chaotic worship. Beginning with the priests and the upper levels of society, reaching to the commoners—all lacked the divine standards by which decent living is ordered. Bedlam prevailed, spreading throughout the capital city and beyond.

The Eternal Judge saw no way to correct the sprawling decadence but to wipe the slate clean by exterminating the pagan falsifiers.

In such desperate and terrifying conditions, somehow the other part of God's nature is forgotten, namely, His love. For here, having given the command for the slaughter of those who caused and continued to practice corruption, God now sends a person in a distinctive white (in contrast to the blackness of sin) linen garment. This servant of the Lord was instructed to look for blameless people, those who were opposed to what the wicked were indulging in, and put a mark on their foreheads.

It is reminiscent of what happened at the first Passover. If the Israelites wanted the angel of death to pass over them, they were to mark their doorposts with a slash of lamb's blood. (Exod. 12:7,13)

But, in Ezekiel's vision how was this white linen–clothed person to know who in Jerusalem was good or bad? He would need to be certain in his own judgmental balancing act as to which was which.

On sight can you size up a person who is good? There can be all kinds of diverting deceptions that convey wrong impressions. How do we see ourselves as others see us, and see others as they see themselves? It calls for perception, understanding, experience, God-inspired affection.

Seriously committed to his task, this seeker of persons who bore the shining image of the Master in their face, moved determinedly through the community noting just who was worthy to be saved and preserved as a fertile remnant full of future promise.

Too often God's negatives, as in His stringent methods of ridding the world of ungodliness, are held against Him. "What are You doing to us, Lord?" is the bitter, insulting complaint. "Why us, why now, why the overkill?"

What is so often overlooked is His final and Positive move—designed to rescue us from danger we are not even aware of. There's a positivity to incorporate in our lives: to become one of the Lord's white linen–clad seekers of those who are on the Lord's side, able to report at the last judgment, "I have done as Thou didst command me." "Enter thou into the joy of Thy Lord."

PRAYER: *Speak and make me listen. Thou Guardian of my soul. Amen.*

ABIDE WITH HIM

Ezek. 11:16 *For a while I became their sanctuary.*

Coming to the close of his visionary visit to Jerusalem, and just before being transported back to Babylon, Ezekiel is informed by God of future plans for His exiled people.

We recall that the Prophet, in his vision, saw firsthand the evils perpetrated by the Jews, for which the Lord had allowed them to be conquered and carted off to Babylon as exiles. But now a new day was dawning for the exiles and Ezekiel was being made aware of it—from the days of tragedy to the coming age of triumph.

Yes, the exiles had come to their senses. Admitting their infidelities, they repented. Far from their Temple (in Jerusalem), they became reacquainted with God. Slowly they learned to do without all the Temple trappings which they once believed were vitally essential for worship.

The Word of the Lord was beginning to energize these removed people. God could see down the future vistas how the growth factor was multiplying because several prophets were planting the same message with their differing talents. And the message was, that no matter where we are, we can have all the help and comfort and healing that the Temple could ever afford—for God is not shut away in some distant holy of holies, but is with us wherever we are. It had to come gradually. We humans, by and large, are slow learners, with a truth-intake that has a handbrake on.

For forty years in the wilderness, the Tabernacle indicated the physical presence of God. Each time Moses ordered a move to the next camp, the tented Tabernacle was folded, carried to the new rest area and set up again. Eventually, in the land of promise, the tent became inadequate and was replaced by Solomon's ooooh-aaaah Temple in Jerusalem. It was a world treasure. Yet though this building and two others stood at that spot for more than 1,000 years, the living end came in A.D. 70 when the Romans did their destructive job. None but the Muslim Mosque of Omar has stood on that site in the last 2,000 years.

Which is far from saying that worship is no more. The Lord works in ways past our understanding. Perhaps He has always had this best-of-all method hidden until its time had come—

namely that He Himself would be our sanctuary, anywhere, anytime. Nor was He going to keep us in the dark as to how it came about. As Ezekiel was shown at firsthand what deviltries by the Jews had caused their punishment, so we have been afforded a step-by-step history of how we have arrived at this state of having a personalized sanctuary—24/7/365.

Jesus, centuries later explained: "The time is coming, indeed it is already here, when true worshippers will worship the Father in spirit and in truth. These are the worshippers the Father wants. God is a spirit, and those who worship him must worship him in spirit and in truth." The woman answered, "I know that Messiah (that is, Christ) is coming. When he comes he will make everything clear to us." Jesus said to her, "I am he, I who am speaking to you." (John 4:23-26) Revelation 21:22 gives the last word on this subject: "I saw no temple in the city, for its temple was the Sovereign Lord God and the Lamb." The Lamb of God is Christ. He is all the sanctuary we need.

PRAYER: *Gather us into Your sanctuary, Yourself, Lord. Now and forever. Amen.*

TO SUIT THE CASE

Ezek. 12:4 *Bring out your belongings, packed as if for exile.*

In His rebellious peoples' future, God saw the inevitability of punishment. For obstinately not seeing or hearing what He would have them do, they would be conquered and led away in captivity to a foreign land.

God's mercy, however, holds sway over His judgment. He never puts burdens upon us that we are unable to bear. For example, we have seen a Himalayan woman trying to heft a piano on her back. Rather, God provides ways in which the job can be humanely managed. As in our text.

The prophet Ezekiel is instructed by God to enact a parable: give the prospective exilers an idea of how to prepare for such a total break with the past. Unprepared, the community could find itself under back-breaking conditions. This way, the people watching Ezekiel and not knowing what he was up to, would ask questions, and in his answers they would see and hear what they should do under emergency conditions.

First, what to pack as if for exile? Bare necessities. Persons who climb Everest, sail solo around the world, land on the moon, and other such exilic experiences, know what Ezekiel meant when "you can't take it with you" determines your every move; you must think in terms of core essentials. Especially when one is aware of the daily obituaries and the fact that there is also packing to be done for that crossover to the afterlife. What to take? That, no doubt, was what God wanted His people to face. For wasn't it their turning away from Him that had caused their downfall? If they wanted to be with Him forever, they better start packing into their beliefs and behavior those vitals which are well-pleasing to the Lord.

There were His commandments carefully numbered so that they would be easily remembered at the fingertips of both hands. Or, more compactly, as Jesus reduced its size from Ten to two: Love God, Love your neighbor. That packs all the passport we need for getting us through the pearly gates.

For refreshment and sustenance on any journey, there's the Bread of Life. We should never leave home without Him who said, "The bread that God gives comes down from heaven and brings life to the world." "Sir," they said to him, "give us this bread now and always." Jesus said to them, "I am the bread of life. Whoever comes to me will never be hungry, and whoever believes in me will never be thirsty." (John 6:33-35) That means more than the wafer and the fruit of the vine at Holy communion. Yet the energy supplied by the Bread and Water of Life is not automatic as St. Augustine defined it: "Without God we cannot; without us, God will not." To ingest His principles into our system will be done as often as mealtimes, at least, with as much chewing on His teachings as it takes to have them enter the mainstream of our being, to produce health and strength through eternity. Happy packing!

PRAYER: *Thank You for the Parable on packing, Father. Just in time to make an eternity's difference. Amen.*

GOD'S WHISTLEBLOWERS

Ezek. 13:1-2 *The word of the Lord came to me: Son of man. Prophesy against the prophets of Israel.*

Being a Prophet was no easy task. He was not a weather forecaster, a reader of tea leaves, or one who gazed into a crystal ball for life's answer. He was called of God to this exacting ministry. Amid life's temptations he had to work at being God's man, consistently. Also he had to know God's people pastorally. Which meant living among them, becoming familiar with their joys and sorrows, their ambitions and their low ebb moods. Then it was his business to know the voice of the

Lord and interpret His instructions so that the people would grasp the meaning. In like manner the prophet interceded on behalf of the people, and did so appealingly that God would often change His plans and adapt those suggested by the prophet.

Having the world as his parish, Ezekiel thought he had adequate support from "the prophets of Israel." But God had a different perspective. He could see those prophets were on their best behavior when in Ezekiel's presence, and just the opposite when they were not. As God saw it, these falsifiers prophesied "out of their own minds" (v. 2); they foolishly followed "their own spirit." (v. 3) They were "like foxes among ruins." (v. 4) There are still people like those foxes who feel most at home among the ruination caused by others. The foxy persons always sound so distinctive and above the fray. It is easy for them to castigate the fallen. They hip-hop, having a fun time at the expense of those who are enduring miseries. Their sole desire is heard in their plea: "Give us this day our daily DREAD to spread. "The "foxes" in some historic remains are nothing but bandicoots, snakes, vermin. That was more the kind these prophets were.

It was probably as it is today when you are starting a business. You are advised to buy up as many politicians as possible. In Ezekiel's time it was false prophets. Under a popular brand label ("prophets"), they were already household names. As such they were accepted, employed, trusted, revered as God's associates and messengers. That's what made them treacherous. They were wolves (foxes) in sheep's clothing. They were not innocent lambs, nor were they shepherds. They were two-faced, fork-tongued. They said: "Says the Lord," when He had not spoken to them. (v. 7) They prophesied "out of their own minds." (v. 2)

Another example of prophetic shoddiness was a whitewashed wall. Instead of building, for example, a barrier that could withstand foreign troops in a time of war, or constructing individual and communal character which could overcome Satan as Jesus did during His wilderness temptations, these false prophets covered their skimpy efforts with window dressing or eye-catching whitewash—another proof of their paltry ministry, which was a mumbling fib.

Jesus excoriated the scribes and Pharisees with this same whitewash metaphor. (Matt. 23:23-33) In their own pernicious way the scribes and Pharisees had been false prophets. They paid tithes of mint and dill, but neglected the weightier demands of the Law. They cleansed the outside of the cup, but the inside was full of greed and self-indulgence. They were like tombs covered with whitewash, but full of corruption.

"Snakes, vipers' brood! How can you escape being condemned to hell?" Even authentic prophets were not that venomous. But Jesus saw extreme hazards in false prophets.

PRAYER: *O Thou who art the Truth speak in and through us. Apart from You we are subject to falsity. Amen.*

ON MAKING HIS THREE

Ezek. 14:14 *Even if those three men were living there, Noah, Daniel and Job, they would save none but themselves by their righteousness.*

On God's behalf, Ezekiel now tries to give as sordid a picture as possible of the utter depravity of Jerusalem and the country of which it was once the capital—a glittering crown jewel.

This sinfully dark picture is seen at its worst in a contrast with the brightest and best of the sons of the morning—the three most upright men who ever lived, men of God's own choosing—Noah, Daniel, and Job. They are mentioned four times in six verses.

God had been known to relent about destroying many another sin-city because of the redeeming character of a single shining soul among them. But in the case of Jerusalem and its environs, things were so debauched that even for these Three Exemplars complete destruction would not be stayed. Also the evildoers could not escape punishment. God had them cornered—in all four corners: sword (war), famine, wild beasts, pestilence. Those who survived war would suffer from an ensuing famine, when the stronger, more crafty wild beasts would overpower the emaciated humans. Any lone human survivor would be at the mercy of myriad pests—fevers, roaches, locusts, and other bugaboos. All doors to escape were tightly shut.

Yet, look again at the Three Wise Men. How did they maintain their goodness and faith in the Lord? How may we?

It was not that they escaped suffering for wrongdoing. In fact, they suffered much more than most people do. And it was a suffering that was undeserved. They went like lambs to the slaughter, while holding fast a steady faith in God.

At 500 years of age, Noah was instructed by God to build an Ark. That project took Noah 100 years to finish, while critics laughed him to scorn. A ship? And where was the water? It would come to him? Oh, Yeah! Still Noah persisted, and became the Second Father of humankind inasmuch as the first lot, sired by Adam, were all washed away by the Flood. Though closeted with wild animals for months, Noah was untouched. Being the bond between Adam's progeny and his own, Noah is now the symbol of unity among humans. For Noah's sake God laid down his bow (that weapon of attack), and gave the world a beautiful rainbow (sometimes double!)—as a sign of peace.

Then there was Daniel, caged with lions that had been subjected to famine conditions that they might get their share of well-nourished Daniel's body. Yet those Kings of the forest became puppified in the presence of a praying Daniel. They may have snarled, just to show that they could. Mostly they sniffed around their tantalizingly delicious human meal, and slunk off into their appointed corners to hear their tummies grumble.

We know, too well, Job's losses—family, health, wealth, and the urging of his wife to curse God and die. But Job hung on, declaring boldly, and quite contrary to his soul mate: "Though He (God) slay me, Yet will I trust Him." And Job joined Noah and Daniel in Faith's Hall of Fame.

It's possible for us too.

PRAYER: *Thank You, Lord, for showing us how to rise above the sinning crowd, and become like one of the Three. Amen.*

TOO BAD TO BE TRUE

Ezek. 14:21 *The Lord God says: How much less hope is there for Jerusalem when I inflict on her these four terrible punishments of mine, sword, famine, wild beasts, and pestilence, to destroy both people and cattle!*

The Unholy City had reached the ultimate depth of degradation. "How much less hope" could one have for the once wholly, lovely city? And just in case the distant exiles in Babylon should receive this word, and find it incredibly hard to believe the wretched picture is word-painted in all its vile guile and bile by the Lord God Himself.

Jerusalem would have been deserving of any one of the punishments that were about to descend on her. But not according to the Lord of heaven who sees not as man sees. We look on the outward appearance. He, looking in to the hearts of those people, saw that just one of these scourges would be a mere knuckle rap. They deserved the whole nine yards!

So, He would send the "Sword." That signified a rampaging horde of conquerors bent on mass destruction. They would spare no one in the once holy city—men, women, children, the aged, the infirm, all would be slaughtered. Nor would the respected and sacred be spared. It would be a slash-and-burn invasion.

Next, whoever survived were gripped by a famine. Why not? Who was left to cultivate the fields, to harvest, to sell the produce? Where were the caretakers of the livestock, the milkmen, the butchers? Lacking local food supplies and suppliers, where to turn for bodily nourishment?

As if the worsening situation were not alarming enough, wild beasts attracted by the dead bodies of humans and farm and domestic animals, would be emboldened to invade towns and villages. Faminedebilitated humans would be unable to combat the beasts, and the predators and carnivores would take over.

Last, but not least, would come pestilence—flies, mosquitoes, locusts, boils, fevers, epidemics.

Even Sodom and Gomorrah were given a chance to be saved. For the sake of a small handful of righteous persons the devastation would have been put on hold. But not here, in Jerusalem. Not even if Noah had been living there, and Daniel, and Job. What a holy trinity they were. Yet their high standing in the Lord's estimation was not enough to stem the tide about to be unleashed on Jerusalem, the hopeless city.

PRAYER: *Lord, have mercy on us sinners. For Christ's sake. Amen.*

GRAFTED TO THE CHRISTLY VINE

Ezek. 15:6 *The Lord God says: As the wood of the vine among all kinds of wood from the forest is useful only for burning, even so I treat the inhabitants of Jerusalem.*

Since the Lord deals with the ageless as we mortals cannot, here He chooses the vine as a teaching tool. Certain that the grape vine was known widely by humans, the Lord likens it to the disappointingly unfruitful city of Jerusalem.

At first, however, that choice city was regarded as a promising vineyard. The potential was abundant. Fertility was plainly evident. The eternal Gardener lovingly cultivated it, removing obstacles, keeping a constant eye on it as if from a central watchtower. So confident was the divine Caretaker that there would be a harvest like none other, that He made preparations, as a viticulturist would do by hewing out wine vats, to receive and use and widely distribute the overflowing outcome of righteousness. People could taste and see that the Lord and His chosen people were good. (Isa. 5:1-2) Yet, fasten your seat belt, for "all it yielded was a crop of wild grapes." (Isa. 5:2)

The Lord was heartsick. "What more could have been done...than I did?" He grieves. "Now listen," He continues, "while I tell you what I am about to do..." (Isa. 5:4-5)

But they wouldn't listen. Hence the final disposal of the vineyard (Jerusalem), by burning.

The everlasting truth of such consequences following such promise was so powerful that Jesus used it 600 years later. "I am the vine; you are the branches, anyone who does not abide in me is thrown away like a withered branch. The withered branches are gathered up, thrown on the fire, and burned." (John 15:5-6)

At the entrance of the Temple one would see an engraving of a grapevine, a reminder of what the spies brought from the Promised Land. The Lord of the harvest promises returns of good measure, pressed down, shaken together and running over. But He won't put it in our mouths. There's hard work to do, and loads to lift. Failing to do our part we become brands flung to the burning. That's His eternal word.

PRAYER: *Pluck us from the burning, Lord, and grant us the fruits of the Spirit. Amen.*

THE LIFE-SAVING POTENTIAL OF POISON

Ezek. 16:60 *I will remember.*

This text, uttered by the Lord, must have struck terror in the hearts of those to whom it was addressed. Hadn't God remembered enough about Jerusalem's deplorable past? Ezekiel, chapter 16, for the most part, is one of the most sickening sections of the entire Bible. It is a series of shockingly decadent activities which made even Sodom and Gomorrah look like Sunday School sweeties. And, unbelievably these satanic immoralities were perpetrated by God's favorite people, in His choice city of Jerusalem. They had sunk to the depths of depravity. On top of all that, here was God, thundering our text: "I will remember." What could He mean but the complete annihilation of all these rotters?

Indeed, the wrongdoers had received justly deserved punishment which had lasted almost a century. Exiled in a faraway land, many of the newly born were never to see their homeland, or their once acclaimed holy city, or their now destroyed second-to-none Temple.

Slowly the banquet of consequences was digested—and survived. With perseverance the prophets among them performed their ministry of teaching, worship, healing, while the Lord, never giving up on His loved ones, planned to do His part. "I will remember," He intoned. But it was not to be a recalling of the worst but of the best memories of Israel's pristine covenant with God. Granted a new covenant by a merciful Lord, the reformed people must do their part. "I will remember," (v. 60) is to be balanced with "You will remember." (v. 63) That meant a creative transfiguration of the past to solve present problems—like learning about God. That's where most of our problems begin. Either we lack an understanding of our Savior or we, too, soon forget Him, as Christmas and Easter attendees. It is not easy to comprehend God when we are told that He is everywhere, that He knows everything, that He has always lived and will forever live. Under such pressure it is easier to forget Him. How does one get a handle on such super naturals?

Fortunately, for Christians, there is a direct route to learning about God: the life of Jesus Christ who affirmed: "I and the Father are One. He that has seen Me has seen the Father."

Though we latter-day sinners have not seen Jesus, He encouraged us with His blissful comment: "blessed are those who have not seen (me) but yet have believed."

Some people cannot accept that except as a placebo. Yet they will believe that there is a wind blowing, when nobody can see wind. The breeze announces its arrival by tossing your hair, waving branches, forcing you to lean into it. Wind is known by its effects. And so does the Holy Spirit. On the day of Pentecost "there came from the sky what sounded like a strong, driving wind...They were all filled with the Holy Spirit." (Acts 2:2,4) But Peter said, "These people are not drunk, as you suppose...No, this is what the prophet Joel spoke of: says God, "I will pour out my spirit on all mankind, and you sons and daughters shall prophesy; your young men shall see visions, and your old men shall dream dreams." (Acts 2:14-17) Indeed, they turned the world right side up. That's rememberable.

PRAYER: *Father, our prayer is: "More about Jesus let me learn, More of His holy will discern; Spirit of God my teacher be, Showing the things of Christ to me."*[1] *Amen.*

---

[1] E. E. Hewill

All My Nature Refine

Ezek. 22:19 *Therefore, these are the words of the Lord God: Because you are all alloyed, I shall gather you into Jerusalem.*

The full picture is framed in verses 17-22. Wanting His chosen people to be precious as silver, shining, distinctive in their many finely chiseled lifestyles, universally acceptable, treasured, the Lord finds, instead, that His people have become nothing of the kind. They are a messy mix "debased with copper, tin, iron, and lead." (v. 8) They have lost their uniqueness and all the shining possibilities that go with such distinction. And, where the Lord would have put such persons into a crucible, as it were, fiery furnace experiences in order to purge the dross and to release valued virtues, He is ready to use Jerusalem as a melting pot in which to consume the people who are nothing but dross, and no silver lining.

God is always on the lookout for the merest traces of silver, of burnished bravery, of gleaming goodness, a reflection of His presence in our faith and works. Finding that, he does His utmost (through searing trials, perhaps) to enhance and to bring that treasure to the surface—for multiple uses. Jesus showed how it was done. Said He to His disciples, "You are the men who stood by me in my trials." That was magnanimous of Him. Actually, they had been pretty lousy supporters. Peter denied Him, Judas betrayed Him, then they all forsook Him and fled. Yet He honored that vein of silvery aspiration for the best which He detected in them, and He dug that out, draining the dross with what radiant results worldwide.

According to Ezekiel's report, however the

opposite happened to too many of his fellow Israelites. They had allowed too many impurities into their lives. Which sullied beyond recognition and detection any good that may once have been present. What is to be done with a useless outfit like that? The crucible—not to release the good, there wasn't any—but to consume, to vaporize the scrap.

We are seeing this kind of conclusion repeatedly, in a wide variety of forms. And, because it is in the Old Testament we deceive ourselves by believing it can't happen in these New Testament times. My soul, have a care. Strive for that joy without alloy which comes in partnership with the Savior.

PRAYER: *"Let the beauty of Jesus be seen in me, all His wondrous compassion and purity." Amen.*

THE LORD'S LAST CALL

Ezek. 23:2-4 *There were two women...they played the harlot in Egypt...As for their names, Oholah is Samaria, and Oholibah is Jerusalem.*

Oh-Oh! Trouble ahead.

Both Samaria and Jerusalem had reached the depths of filth and vulgarity. Their citizens had kicked off the traces, jumped over the fence and indulged in harlotry with people of any nation that came down the pike. God had tried several times in various ways to bring these people, whom He had loved, to their senses. But they just slid further into the slime. What would shake them awake? Certainly not a diatribe regarding their foul relations with Egyptians, Assyrians, Babylonians. That only diplomats would understand.

So He put it down where the masses, who

know about the messes of life, would understand. And He put it in the most dire language. The sins of these two sisters (cities) are dragged out into the sunlight for all to witness. Unfaithfulness was practiced in as many forms as human ingenuity could conjure up. There was adultery, the defilement of God's sanctuary, the desecration of the Sabbath, drunken orgies. Even the sacrifice of children—selling them for personal gain and/or lust. All these ungodly activities were summed up in the lives of prostitution of the two OH sisters.

Even *Encyclopedia Britannica* felt the need to turn to the *Shorter Oxford English Dictionary* for a definition of female prostitution as "the offering of the body to indiscriminate lewdness for hire."

God's people had allowed themselves to be influenced by countries around them that observed fertility rites. That is, they saw nature dying in the autumn, then believed that in the spring the fertility goddess made herself available for the bringing of new life. Religious prostitution was practiced in the Temples of Ishtar, Aphrodite, Astarte, fertility goddesses. The Aphrodite Temple in Corinth had 1,000 prostitutes. A man would go to one of these sex-for-hire women. The money he paid her would go toward the upkeep of the Temple. Both the man and the paid woman were led to believe that they were fulfilling their religious duty. And because it was lucrative, the priests encouraged it—to such an extent that the priests were considered the country's financial experts! Such were some of the moral pitfalls that engulfed God's people. And still do. Since the caprice of the passions has been considered as a necessary evil, prostitution has been tolerated, and limits and laws have been shifted and twisted to suit changing lifestyles, community pressures, or modified religious doctrines. Brothels at Southwark, near London Bridge, were licensed by the bishops of Winchester and then sanctioned by Parliament.

The Oh-Oh sisters are still among us: those who are kept by men of independent means, those who live in apartments and carry on their independent trade from there, those who use this as a sideline to their regular low-paying jobs. This kind of immorality is found from local to international. God still warns us from Jerusalem.

PRAYER: *We sing with dear Fanny Crosby: "Redeemed—how I love to proclaim it! Redeemed by the blood of the Lamb; Redeemed thro' His infinite mercy, His child, and forever, I am." Amen.*

PRIDE'S LAST RIDE

Ezek. 26:1-2 *The word of the Lord came to me: "Son of man, because Tyre said concerning Jerusalem, aha, the gate of the peoples is broken, it has swung open to me; I shall be replenished, now that she is laid waste."*

Tyre and Jerusalem were once alike in name and fame. Jerusalem is familiar, coming to its zenith during the David-Solomon era.

Tyre is different, unfamiliar, older, and as easily forgotten as a blown-out automobile tire spelled the European way. But Tyre, a Phoenician city-state was the Mistress of the Mediterranean Sea. It was the most powerful maritime city of its day, the people, though Semitic, had cultivated a very un-Semitic love of the sea. Some sixty miles from Nazareth, and in the area of today's Lebanese capital of Beirut (the Paris of the East), Tyre arose on the mainland, with its own port. Later, needing more space, both on land and sea, it developed the nearest rocky island with its own harbor, joining them to the mainland with a cause-way, thus giving Tyre two cities and two ports, just right to accommodate the trade routes coming and going from east and west.

Known as seafarers, the Tyrians (Phoenicians) had city-states all around the Mediterranean, and on the east and west coasts of Africa.

Blessed with a well-watered plain stretching to the foot of the Lebanon Mountains, and to the mouth of the River Leontes, Tyre was a fertile producer of grains and fruits. According to the fifteenth century B.C. Armana Tablets, Tyre specialized in glassware, dyes, gold, silver, copper, along with numerous artisans—who not only beautified Solomon's Temple in Jerusalem, but built ships so that the two nations made joint merchandising voyages to Arabia (Opher, for gold), East Africa (for ivory and animals) and India (for spices and silk).

But all this was 400 years before Ezekiel's time. At the time of Ezekiel's writing foreign invaders had plundered both Tyre and Jerusalem, and left Jerusalem, especially, flattened out.

That's when Tyre showed its ugly side (in today's text)—uncovering the evils it had been harboring against its closest competitor; remembering how Jerusalem had knocked them off the winners platform, and basked in the glitter which Tyrians felt should have been theirs. And when Jerusalem was out for the count, Tyre arose to avenge all the friction it was supposed to have suffered at Jerusalem's hands.

The way Tyre reacted with glee, "Aha" was unpardonable, arrogant, a return to jungle beastliness. And God would not tolerate it, not just because Jerusalem was His beloved city, but because here is a universal lesson to be learned, namely, that Pride is the chief of the seven deadly sins, and must be put down. Pride holds the reins of Envy, Anger, Dejection, Avarice, Lust, Anxiety.

Five hundred years after our text, Jesus visited Tyre (Mark 7:24ff) and in His own way, rejoined it to Jerusalem through peace and healing: Pride flees when Christ comes.

PRAYER: *Heavenly Father: Hold us in check. Take the reins from our prideful hands. Put us in the hands of the Caring, Sharing, Daring Christ. In His Name. Amen.*

A Caring Ministry

Ezek. 34:8 *My shepherds have not asked after the sheep but have cared only for themselves.*

Living in a land like New Zealand, where sheep outnumber humans, Palestine, likewise, in Ezekiel's era, was sheep-oriented. And not, as today, mainly in the meat industry. For the early fathers of the faith—Moses, David, Jeremiah, Ezekiel and a host of others needed the woolly animals, by the millions for blood sacrifices.

On the night Jesus was born, the shepherds who watched their flocks by night were specialists in sheep-breeding. How to have unblemished lambs and keep them in pristine condition until they were required at the Temple altar five miles from Bethlehem. It was a profession passed on for generations.

Naturally, the sheep herding entered into daily

conversation as buzz words still do. And, of course, the preachers lost no time in utilizing the fleecy flocks and their keepers in Sabbath and other preachments—throughout the Bible. Yet, lest people thought, as in the best-loved psalm (the 23rd) in the world that all shepherds were like the Good Shepherd, the Lord, through Ezekiel, here describes the ins and ughs of pastoring. In fact the Lord is disappointed with the shepherds of Israel—all those in overseeing, care giving positions—national rulers, priests, community leaders. Expected to at least serve God's people as devotedly as shepherds did for their flocks, these leaders were instead "caring only for themselves." They fattened themselves off the sheep's milk, meat, and wool—that is, the people's work output and profits, and publicized woolly prosperity. But leaders did not feed the sheep, that is, the people's personal well-being, such as encouraging the weary, having an adequate health care system, searching for stragglers and persons in many kinds of lostness. (34:3-6) It all made what today would be called a fractured infrastructure. And the Lord could still be castigating, not Ezekiel's transgressors, but those who are shamefully neglecting their care-giving ministries in the twenty-first century.

In the world's richest country, hundreds of thousands of homeless souls spend nights under bridges, on park benches and sidewalks, and in abandoned subways. Amid the finest health care system, millions still go to a painful and early grave.

Addictionologists cannot keep up with the growing number of addictions and addicts.

At the same time there are those who could be

care-giving but who loll on their state-of-the-art yachts, or have permanent reservations on round-the-world cruises, or permanent seats at casinos that forever bloat the casino owners' bank accounts while the pusher of buttons goes home with empty pockets.

Though the Lord has promised to level the playing field (34:11-16), there will be consequences to suffer by those who refuse to play by His rules.

PRAYER: *"Savior, like a shepherd lead us, much we need thy tender care. We are Thine, do thou befriend us, be the guardian of our way; Keep Thy flock, from sin defend us, Seek us when we go astray."*[1] *That we may learn from Thee to dare to care and share. Amen.*

ON BEING SINGLED OUT

Ezek. 34:17 *As for you, my flock, these are the words of the Lord God: I will judge between one sheep and another.*

Having given the shepherds a few welts with their own crooks, the Lord does not let the sheep (His chosen people) off their hooks. He won't allow them to shift all the blame for their own faults on to the shepherds. Individuals can be as beastly and rambunctious (or more so) as shepherds and animals of field and forest. Consider the bull-headedness of some people, even on Church committees. Or those with elephantine memories, and those who eat like a horse. Or the long-horned type of person who will not let you forget his physical and mental superiority. Or the tiny unemployed woman who wins the lottery and is worth a mint; how peacocky she becomes overnight. Oh, the wretchedness of humanity outdoes

---

[1] Dorothy A. Thrupp

the savagery of the forest. The wildest of animals cannot think up or devise with an evil purpose all those things that are reported in the daily news that people have done to their neighbors. And God sees it even if we don't, and here He draws attention to it. Nor was it affixed to Ezekiel's time. It's probably worse now, with less excuse. How easy it is for the office worker to step out of his air-conditioned office into his air-conditioned car and irritably honk aside a sweaty day laborer in his rattletrap. That, essentially, is what happened when King David stole another man's wife. As the prophet Nathan subtly brought it to the King's attention (2 Sam. 12:7) of how a rich man wanted to entertain a guest. Instead of taking a sheep from his own flock for the banquet, he took a poor man's (Uriah) lamb (Bathsheba). How heartlessly manipulative we can be with other people's lives and property. It is this sort of frequently repeated unfairness among us sheepish humans that God is addressing here. And not often enough. For if on this every day, work-a-day level we could live more respectably and amiably, we would breed better flock masters (national and community leaders). It is from our own cribs and preschools that they must ultimately arise. Then, at best, we shall need little leading, for the Lord has promised to set over us One Shepherd (Jesus) v. 23, who will bring peace and an absence of fear. (v. 25) What other kind of leader is worth following? We've watched the irreligious kind haven't we? They and their hangers-on have been convinced that these leaders, with all the qualifications and university degrees therewith, were born to lead. But, proceeding on fragile unproven, slick techniques, they have skidded into inextricable tangles. Whereas, following Jesus' leadership is the best credentialed way. (John 10:25) Not only did He affirm that "the Father and I are one," (John 10:30) but also that Jesus could claim "I am the good shepherd," (John 10:11) and more defining "I am the door of the sheepfold...anyone who comes into the fold through me will be safe." (John 10:7,9) Ahh! Safe at last—and forever.

PRAYER: *Impartial Judge of the universe, make us ever mindful that we have to make a personal accounting at thy judgment throne. Help us each step in the countdown to that day. Amen.*

FLOCK TO HIM

Ezek. 36:38 *As Jerusalem is filled with sheep offered as holy gifts at times of festivals, so will their ruined cities be filled with flocks of people. Then they will know that I am the Lord.*

In spite of the wickedness of His people, and His avowed intention to destroy them, God cannot bring Himself to obliterate His people. Greater love has no one than this! Instead, He foresees a new day for Israel. The spirit of the Shepherd's psalm (23) pervades the situation. But it is approached from another angle.

At festival time, God's people, by now dispersed in many lands, would flock to Jerusalem, there to observe the required rites and ceremonies at the Temple. One of the rites, being to sacrifice sheep as a sin or thank-you offering to the Lord. And, unable to sacrifice just any sheep, unblemished animals were available at suitable locations. These purebreds were raised in special flocks by Temple-appointed shepherds—such as those in Bethlehem who were chosen by God to receive the initial good news for the coming of the spotless Lamb of God to take away the sins of the world. (Matt. 2:8-19) They would understand better than anyone the significance of such purity and sacrifice. They could identify more closely, even than the priests, with every phrase in Ps. 23.

Through Ezekiel, God was prophesying that this was the sort of person who would populate Jerusalem in that new post-exilic day. God's newly minted people would no longer look upon Him as vengeful (the impression of God that outsiders had also received), but as a loving, caring Shepherd of "flocks of people." Their wants would be satisfied, their situation Edenic (Ezek. 36:35), their souls restored after suffering grinding grief and lamentation. Passing through the valley of the shadow, or dry bones (Ezek. 37:1-14)—they would fear no evil because they would be energized by the Lord's presence, by His rod, His staff, His goodness, His mercy. Their final assurance would be to dwell in the Lord's House (imagine that!) forever and ever. Amen.

That coming glory, Ezekiel portrayed for his fellow exiles, would be far superior to the perks they were enjoying in Babylon, the greatest city of its time. Not imprisoned, the exiles were free to make a life of their own in the green pastures and beside still waters of the river along whose banks they resided. Yet, in the future Jerusalem, God's people would be at home, under the care of the good Shepherd, giving Him the best sacrifice of all—not sheep—but a broken and contrite heart. Furthermore, that's the enviable homeland in which people of faith are always welcome.

PRAYER: *"Savior, like a shepherd lead us, much we need Thy tender care; In thy pleasant pastures feed us, for our use thy folds prepare."*[1] Amen.

---

[1] Dorothy Thrupp

ARISE, YE SAINTS

Ezek. 37:3 *Can these bones live again?*

God posed this question in order to evoke an answer in which all humans are, and ever have been, vitally interested, since it is common knowledge that all but the bones are decomposed five years after death. Why So? Is it because these bones can live again? Certainly Ezekiel didn't have the foggiest idea, so he handed the question back to the Lord, saying helplessly, "Only thou knowest that, Lord God." (v. 4) Let's leave it there for a moment and consider how this scene has been cleverly put together in words, music, costumes, lights, dance, and has placed Ezekiel on many a Broadway stage with appearances around the world. It has made Ezekiel the best known prophet on the great white way of stage and screen. Unfortunately chapter 37 remains, for many, an entertainment feature. In fact, if it's not burlesque the public wants none of it. It's too macabre, however otherwise important it may be, as here it is.

These particular bones were either of those persons slain in a battle near Jerusalem or of those who perished long before this war. With all of them death was the terminal factor and the dry bones the terminal condition. And there's that returning echo with its haunting question: "Can these bones live again?" Suddenly the scene changes as if in answer to the question. Somebody, following an unmentioned, unseen DNA blueprint makes a rustling sound (verse 7), whereupon the bones connected with their original partners. Sinews, flesh, skin added bulk and a finishing touch. Wind blew life into the motionless forms, and what do you know, there "rose to their feet a mighty host." (v. 10) Then to certify the reality of this resurrection and its implication for God's people everywhere, the Lord announces the great good news: "I will open your graves and bring you up from them." "I will put my spirit in you and you shall live." (v. 12,14) And an earlier Easter was celebrated. How better could the Lord inform us in Old Testament and New B.C. and A.D. that death is not the last horrendous word. And yes, it is something to dance about, since it reveals more than we were shown before our entrance into this world. Where Ezekiel, looking ahead, asks, "Can these bones live again?" The paleoanthropologist, looking backward asks, "Can these bones have lived seven million years ago?" Did they live in the trees or walk upright on the ground? Did they roam the woodlands of Africa, the plains of Asia, the mountains of Europe? Did they have opposable big toes? Could they have lived in both worlds at the same time? All valuable questions and findings impacting our knowledge of past and present. Yet the ultra concern for hominids (humans) has always been—is there a life beyond the fossil stage? The final word is with the Spirit of the Lord (v. 14): "I will put my spirit into you and you shall live." What a jolly enlivening way to end our brief encounter with Ezekiel—to know that there is a resurrection ahead for God's seemingly skeletal chosen people.

PRAYER: *"He speaks and listening to His voice, New life the dead receive; the mournful, broken hearts rejoice, the humble poor believe."*[1] *Hear our sung prayer, Lord. Amen.*

---

[1] Charles Wesley

BRIDGED TO HIM

Dan. 1:3-4 *The King ordered to take certain of the Israelite exiles...and fit (them) for service in the royal court.*

Two epochs in Jewish history have been unforgettable lessons for people globally. The first was the Exodus from Egypt, about 1400 B.C., the second was the Exile (from Palestine) in Babylon about 606 B.C. There was Ex-ing in both, whether it was leaving home and homeland, or moving from childhood to adulthood, single to married life, parentage, a change of employment, nationality, advancing age, bodily changes, and in the locality around us. Ex-ing never ceases for anyone, though its silent unobtrusive movement causes us to lose track of its nonstop all-pervading and altering actions. And therein lies its peril. Amid the fluctuating conditions of Ex-ing, we are prone to adapt, without thinking, the faith of our Fathers' holy faith to the not so holy society in which we find ourselves at the moment. This was the insidious temptation that caught many of the exiled Jews off guard. But not Daniel and his three companions.

All the specially selected, smart young exiles were promised top jobs in their new land of bondage—if they learned the language, literature, customs, of the locals. Also attractive were the meals, which would come, yum, yum, from the King's Kitchen.

Most of the Jews in this regal program took the bait, and were hooked. Not so the Faithful Four. It was not that they didn't care for the taste of Babylonian food even from the palace. It simply wasn't Kosher, the God-directed way in which Jews were to prepare their meals.

So the Faithful Four kept a tight hold on their traditional values and customs, and made it to the top echelons of that foreign exilic society.

Even at the end of his long life in Babylon, Daniel was riveted to the faith of his fathers. Trapped by Babylonians who were jealous of this foreigner's high office in their government, Daniel was about to be dropped into a den of lions. But Daniel, who "had had windows made in his roof chamber looking toward Jerusalem, and there he knelt down three times a day and offered prayers and praises to his God as his custom had always been." (Dan. 6:10)

Daniel continued to practice the custom that he had learned early in life, namely, that when a Jew was far from the Holy Land, at prayer time he was to turn in the direction of Jerusalem. Even Mohammed instructed his Muslim followers to turn to Jerusalem at their five prayer periods every day. But when Mohammed had a falling-out with the Jews, he ordered his people to turn at prayer time, not to Jerusalem but to Mecca. Daniel was never deflected from his one-way devotion to the Holy Land, Holy City, Holy Temple, and almighty God. Ex-ing never turned him from God.

PRAYER: *Dear Lord and Father of mankind, we are grateful for Your promise never to leave us. Likewise whatever the Exodus and exiling situations may be, we are Yours now and forever. Amen.*

No Fooling

Dan. 5:2 *Under the influence of the wine, Belshazzar gave orders for the vessels of gold and silver which his father Nebuchadnezzar had taken from the temple at Jerusalem to be fetched, so that he and his nobles, along with his concubines and courtesans might drink from them.*

The sacred vessels, carefully fashioned by artisans over a period of hundreds of years and strictly used and preserved in the Jerusalem Temple, numbered 5,400 pieces. (Ezra 1:9-11) But King Belshazzar was of a mind to show his drinking companions how really great he was. He would take these treasured vessels and use them for any obscene purpose he desired. By such high-handedness, all would see that Belshazzar was no one's underling, not even God's. Did his concubines and dancing girls want to have fun with the sacred vessels—let them feel free to go ahead and do what they wished. But it wasn't long before Belshazzar was cut down to size, slain that night by a new conqueror of Babylon. Belshazzar's impudence and act of sacrilege were not tolerated by God.

Most people do not realize the sanctity of these vessels that came into existence during the Exodus from Egypt. Thirty of that forty-year journey were spent in the lush oasis area of Kadesh Barnea, in the Sinai desert. During their 400-year enslavement in Egypt, the Hebrews had learned much about crafting, from jewelry to larger pieces. Upon their departure from Egypt, the Hebrews had been given much gold and silver by their grateful Egyptian friends and overseers. Remember how these Hebrews put together a golden calf in no time, in the desert? Later, under God's direction, a Tabernacle was erected, a Tent wherein God was said to dwell. This portable worship center, which went ahead of the people, was a Holy of Holies, even in the Promised Land, where it was finally rested in Jerusalem by David and became a part of Solomon's Temple.

So that by the time Belshazzar got his impious hands on those spotlessly purified vessels—dishes, spoons, bowls, cups, candlesticks, snuff dishes or censers, lavers, they were hundreds of years old. To make them more precious, Henry Soltau (1805-1875), born in Plymouth, England, and a graduate of Cambridge University, gave up his law practice to delve into a study of those Holy Vessels. All down the line he found meaningful symbols that pointed to the life and death and resurrection of our Savior, Jesus Christ. As John explains (1:2-4): "He (Jesus) was with God at the beginning, and through him all things came to be; without him no created thing came into being."

Belshazzar was not the last one to diabolically (proceeding from the devil) insult the holy. The Holy Bible, the holy sacraments, and all other specified holiness, are still spat upon (as Jesus was), joked about (holey), trampled on, vilified...But, as Jesus brought it to a head: "If anyone speaks against the Holy Spirit, for him there will be no forgiveness, within this age or in the age to come." (Matt. 12:32)

PRAYER: *Holy Father, keep our tongues from speaking guile, at all times. Amen.*

WINE, WOMEN, AND WRONG

Dan. 5:2 *Under the influence of the wine, Belshazzar gave orders for the vessels of gold and silver which his father Nebuchadnezzar had taken from the Temple at Jerusalem to be fetched, so that he and his nobles, along with his concubines and courtesans might drink from them.*

To his banquet Belshazzar had invited a thousand of his top-ranking executives along with enough female company to keep the place in a tizzy of excitement. Wine flowed almost as abundantly as the River Euphrates did through the city, and it was that wine that addled the King's brain. Egged on by his equally besotted companions, Belshazzar sent for the sacred vessels, those vessels that had been filched from the Temple at Jerusalem, when his father conquered that city.

You have to credit Nebuchadnezzar with a certain decency. For, although he was the conqueror of Jerusalem and the plunderer of its Temple, at least he took the sacred vessels from that Temple and stored them out of harm's way. But not Belshazzar. He was bent on showing his drinking party-goers how really great he was. He would take the treasured vessels and use them for any obscene purpose he desired. By such highhandedness all would see that Belshazzar was no one's underling, not even God's. He would show God a thing or two. Did his concubines and dancing girls want to have fun with the sacred vessels—some 5,400 pieces, which had been carefully fashioned over a period of hundreds of years, toss them around, stamp on them, wear them as headpieces? Belshazzar's authoritative word was final.

But was it? Just when all of that riotous festivity was at its noisiest and basest, suddenly there was another word, and another, and another. Not the words of Belshazzar this time, but the words of God's warning, written by a ghostly hand on the wall. Immediately the banquet came to a screeching halt. The Bible says that when Belshazzar saw those words on the wall, his mind was filled with dismay and he turned pale, he became limp in every limb and his knees knocked together. (Dan. 5:6)

> The Moving Finger writes; and have writ
> Moves on: nor all thy pity or wit
> Shall have it back to cancel half a line
> Nor all thy tears wash out a word of it.[1]

That very night the end came, by the sword of the Persian conqueror Cyrus. Since the River Euphrates ran under the city wall, Cyrus had his engineers divert the river into a new channel, and, guided by two deserters from Babylon, Cyrus marched on the dry riverbed into the city. Finding the place unguarded with King Belshazzar and his commanders having an intoxicatingly hilarious banquet, Cyrus captured Babylon and slew Belshazzar. The wages of sin is this kind of an end.

PRAYER: *Lord, save us from weak resignation to the evils we deplore. Grant us a firm jaw, determined to be Thine alone. Amen.*

ON SHUTTING LIONS' MOUTHS

Dan. 6:10 *When Daniel learned that this decree had been issued, he went into his house. It had in the roof-chamber windows open toward Jerusalem; and there he knelt down three times a day and offered prayers and praises to his God as was his custom.*

Before returning to his own country of Persia, Cyrus appointed a man named Darius to rule over Babylon, and a new era began.

One of the first reforms enacted by King Darius was to allow the exiled Jews to return to their homeland if they so desired. Few went. After seventy years of exile they had forgotten Palestine. To those Jews born in Babylon, their homeland of Palestine was the foreign country. For Daniel, too,

---

[1] Edward Fitzgerald, *Omar Khayyam*

Babylon had become home. And because he stayed, and was of increasing help to the new administration, he was envied by native-born Babylonians over whom he had leapfrogged to a high position in the government. This was a challenge to those who coveted Daniel's power and prestige. So the jealous ones joined forces and planned a crafty maneuver.

When Daniel was out of town, the sneaky operators went to Darius and urged him to sign a decree that said that in a period of thirty days no one should present a petition to any god or man other than King Darius. (6:7) Anyone breaking this law would be thrown into a den of lions.

Lions? Why not the fiery furnace? Well, because these new rulers, the Persians, were fire-worshippers. Their god was Ahura Mazda, the god of light. Consequently, death in the fiery furnace was unlawful and was replaced with a den of lions. The Persians were noted hunters, and always had an ample supply of big cats from India and Africa to consume human lawbreakers.

When Daniel came home and heard of the decree enacted by the King, the first thing he did was to pray, as he had been in the habit of doing every day, three times a day—facing Jerusalem. Jews had been taught that if they were outside the Holy Land, they were to turn in its direction for prayer. Inside the Holy Land, they should turn toward Jerusalem for prayer. In Jerusalem they should turn toward the Temple, or go to the Temple for prayer.

That's all that Daniel's enemies needed to see—him on his knees, making supplication to his God. (6:11) To them, that was a violation of the King's decree, and they reported it to his majesty.

Darius realized that he and his friend Daniel had been tricked by these scoundrels. But there was nothing to do but go through with the prescribed punishment.

In the apocryphal book *Daniel, Bel and the Snake*, we learn that Daniel was in the lion's den for six days. There were seven lions in the den, and every day two men and two sheep were fed to the animals. But before Daniel was thrown in, the lions were given nothing to eat. Yet they did not touch Daniel—as someone remarked, because Daniel was two-thirds grit and one-third granite. Actually, the Lord was his Deliverer. And He promises to be ours, from every den of iniquity.

PRAYER: *Inspire us, Lord, to overpower Satan who prowls around like a roaring lion, seeking whom he may devour. In Your name. Amen.*

DIVINE INSTRUCTION

Dan. 9:2 *I, Daniel, was reading the scriptures.*

Just because this is the only mention of Daniel deep in his Bible, it does not mean that this is the only time that he referred to the good book. As any part of a circle gives us a good idea of its total circumference, this brief notation regarding Daniel's immersion in God's word shows us from where Daniel was drawing much of his spiritual nourishment and guidance. And as an exile in a foreign land he needed such help to withstand the pressures of being a stranger in a strange land. In his native Jerusalem, spiritual sustenance had been readily available. One could go to the Temple services. At other times one could attend schools or classes where teachers would expound on the sacred texts and answer questions. Then, again, for centuries, the only way that Jewish people could restore their broken relationships with God was by bringing sacrifices to the Temple. But now, in far-away Babylon, none of this was possible. This, for some Jews, became an excuse for not cultivating their spiritual lives. But not for Daniel and his companions. From the beginning of their captivity they were determined to maintain their spiritual vitality (which in fact, was on what the rest of their lives depended) by studying the scriptures. At the time the Biblia—the Bible, comprised the first five books of our Bible, plus Isaiah and Jeremiah (who lived just ninety years before Daniel), Job, Obadiah, Micah, and a collection of Psalms. That makes eleven as compared with the thirty-nine books in our Old Testament, for a total of sixty-six books in our complete Bible.

Daniel and the faithful few had been careful to take the sacred books with them from Jerusalem. Then in Babylon, during their seventy years of captivity, the faithful ones copied these books for each other's use. "These books became for them the place of encounter with the living God Himself. And as they listened and read...they found themselves listening to the same living voice as their prophets and priests had so often claimed to hear and bring them and it comforted and challenged them with no less power and relevance than it had in the lives of their forefathers and mothers in the faith. In this way they were allowed to discover what today is always a new and wonderful mystery—that God has tied up real and loving religion so closely with the Bible."[1]

---

[1] Ronald Wallace, *The Message of Daniel*, p. 149

Indeed, that is how it worked out for Daniel.

Many people are proud of having read the entire Bible through several times, as if this marathon achievement is, in itself, a passport to heaven. But not for Daniel. The more he and God communicated through the Word, the more Daniel got into gear. For the next thing he records is, "I turned to the Lord God in earnest prayer and supplication with fasting and sackcloth and ashes." (v. 3) He was in high gear now confessing the sins of his people (v. 8), and his own misdeeds. (v. 20) Then there dawns upon him an enlightened understanding (v. 22)—with the coming end to the Exile and the restoration of Jerusalem. His word is Life; let's live it.

PRAYER: *Lord, help us to "dare to be a Daniel"—fueled by Your enriching Word. Amen.*

THE BOOKS OF DANIEL

Dan. 9:2 *I, Daniel, was reading the scriptures and reflecting on the seventy years which, according to the Word of the Lord to the prophet Jeremiah, were to pass while Jerusalem lay in ruins.*

From the beginning of their captivity, Daniel and his companions were determined to maintain their spiritual vitality by taking nourishment from God's Word—the Bible (the Biblia), since there was no Temple in Babylon. At the time the Bible consisted of the first five books of our Bible.

Not only did his study of the Bible help Daniel to stand firm in difficult times, but it also provided him with a reliable timetable for the events of his own day. Studying the Book of Jeremiah, Daniel came upon Jeremiah's prophecy (Jer. 25:11-12; 29:10) regarding the seventy years which were to pass while Jerusalem lay in ruins.

If Daniel was doing his arithmetic correctly, he would have figured that 490 years had passed between the occupation of Palestine by the children of Israel and the time they were taken in captivity to Babylon.

Just as God had ordered humans to rest one day in seven (and we are never at our best without it), so He ordered one year in seven to be a year in which the land, unworked, unplowed, unseeded, could replenish its resources. But Israel would not obey the Lord, working the land to death for 490 years. Which meant that seventy sabbatical years had been skipped. Accordingly, the Lord packed off His disobedient people to Babylon for seventy years, while the land enjoyed its sabbaticals to the full. (Lev. 26:33-35)

Learning from his Bible that by now the Promised Land must have renewed itself and was ready for the return of its former occupants, Daniel thought the land might be ready for them, but were they ready for it? They were still sinful, greedy, disobedient. If they returned, things would be just as bad as when they left.

So in chapter 9, verse 3, Daniel says, "I turned to the Lord God in earnest prayer." Then follows one of the most moving prayers to be found anywhere. No wonder that before Daniel could say "Amen," his prayer was answered.

PRAYER: *Thank You, Lord, for Your Word and for prayer. With them we are equipped to whip the enemy. Amen.*

THE INNER BRACES OF PRAYER

Dan. 9:7 *Lord, the right is on your side; the shame, now as ever, belongs to us, the people of Judah and the citizens of Jerusalem, and to all the Israelites near and far in every land to which you have banished them for their disloyal behavior toward you.*

It is no surprise to find Daniel in prayer. That's where one finds him consistently. When he is almost executed, Daniel prays with faith, earnestness, perseverance, purpose. In fact it was his prayer life that had him thrown to the lions. Yet whereas on other occasions Daniel is *seen* in prayer, now he is *heard* praying. Further, this prayer shows how steeped Daniel was in the scriptures, subtly weaving in quotations from Ex. (20:6); Deut. (7:21; 10:17); Jer. (7:10); Ps. (44:16; 130:4); 2 Chron. (36:15-16); Ezra (9:6-7,15); Neh. (9:10,17,32-34).

This prayer speaks of the great Rightness and the right Greatness of God. That has contemporary significance. We've lost sight of His rightness and greatness. Believing that if we keep Him in His exaltedly righteous position, He can't be of much help to us lowly humans, we get Him off His pedestal by addressing Him as "You." Sometimes our tone of voice is no different from "Hey, You, God, look—I'm hurting, and You better do something about it. And I mean right now." We want to cut Him down to our size, to be a kind Uncle Willie who will babysit for us, take the dog for a walk, find a handsome marine for Suzie.

Daniel shows that because God is greatly right and rightly great, our acknowledgment of His exaltation engenders within us the assurance that He is in charge of the universe, and we have nothing to fear.

Daniel's prayer also speaks of God's mercy. (9:9) That word "mercy" comes from the Hebrew word for "womb." It denotes a maternal compassion—the Mother love of God, which is given repeatedly.

Daniel's prayer also includes his homeland, his home city, and his fellow Israelites wherever they may be scattered. And there we find the cross in Daniel's prayer. The vertical line drawn between himself and his exalted God is crossed by the horizontal line of concern for others like himself. Every valued prayer ought to have such a cross at its heart: an agonizing before God on behalf of sinful needy souls everywhere.

But Daniel doesn't just plead for the sins of others to be forgiven. It is always easier to confess the faults of others. Rather, in 9:20, Daniel says, "Thus I was praying, confessing my own sin and my people Israel's sin."

PRAYER: *With a cross-purpose in our prayers, O Lord, we would dare to be a Daniel. Amen.*

UP THE DOWN STAIRCASE

Dan. 9:16 *Lord, by all your saving deeds we beg that your wrath and anger may depart from Jerusalem, your own city, your holy hill; on account of our sins and our father's crimes, Jerusalem, and your people have become a byword among all our neighbors.*

Noting the condition of Jerusalem as it once was, compared to its present pitifully unenviable situation, Daniel appeals to the Saviorhood of God. Now nothing but God's saving grace will suffice to rescue and reinstate the Holy City and its worship center. And first, the crushing pressure and denouncement imposed by God's wrath must, please Lord, be removed. For look at the avoiding eyes and the ducking out of sight of the Jerusalemites when mocked by people of neighboring states—the Ammonites, Edomites, Moabites. It was a reflection of contempt upon God Himself. What a comedown from the time when the psalmist proclaimed what was universally accepted, namely that "Great is the Lord and most worthy of praise in the city of our God. His holy mountain is fair and lofty, the joy of the whole earth. The mountain of Zion, the far recesses of the north, is the city of the great King. God in her palaces is revealed as a tower of strength. (Ps. 48:1-3) And now this degradation and humiliation. "Lord...we beg."

Having begged for the removal of God's anger, Daniel begs for the forgiveness of the sins of the people—both present and past. The sins of the fathers never disappear when the fathers do. The weedy element seems to reproduce itself more quickly and consistently than the good, and calls for stern measures to be stopped. Again, only the goodness and severity of God are equal to the challenge.

How to get back on top after having bottomed out is a perennial human problem, in all facets of daily life. The Prodigal Son showed, in Daniel style, which way to begin. "I will arise, and go to my father," my Savior. Then the confession: "I have sinned..." Finally "make me." The procedure worked for Daniel, and for the later prodigal, and will work for us latter-day prodigals. How can we be sure? Because His Word is sure. "How may a young man [or anyone] lead a clean life? By holding to Your words. (Ps. 119:9)

PRAYER: *As we press on the upward way, new elevations we are gaining every day. Lord, thanks to Your Saviorhood. Amen.*

On Living Again—and Again

Dan. 12:2 *An angel says to Daniel: "Many of those who sleep in the dust of the earth will wake, some to everlasting life..."*

Here is one more conduit in the Old Testament that feeds into the New: resurrection. How excitingly conclusive. No other subject is more important. As Michael Green writes: "Central though it is, the resurrection is a subject that is curiously avoided by many who call themselves Christians. Lord Ismay records that when he was Chairman of the BBC, only one of the 6,000 sermons preached on the air had shed any light on this subject." (*The Day Death Died*, p. 13)

To be sure, other Christians will discount this mention of the resurrection because it was given by an angel. If there are no angels what do we do about the angels that are mentioned from Genesis to Revelation? In the Old Testament they appear twenty-three times. In the life of Christ they appear thirteen times—from the announcement of His birth to the announcement of His resurrection. The Master, Himself, spoke of angels on twelve different occasions. In the Book of Acts they appear seven times, and in Paul's Epistles and the Book of Revelation—another eight times—for a total of sixty-three times covering a 4,000-year period. Even beyond Bible times the recognition of angels has persisted. Charles Wesley, the great hymn writer, voiced the belief of many when he said: "Angels where'er we go: Attend our steps where'er betide. With watchful care their charge attend, And evil turn aside."

Not only does the Book of Daniel tell of angelic messengers that assist us in life, but also

Daniel asks the question which all of us ask, sooner or later—how is it going to end? And where others may leave us dangling, Daniel provides an answer in our text for today.

That is as far as Daniel is able to take us. The rest comes to us from the Lord Jesus Christ whom Daniel foreshadowed. For whereas Daniel's being lifted out of the lion's den has been looked upon as an earlier type of resurrection, he went down into the grave as it were and came up alive—Jesus actually went to the grave and then cheated it on the third day to arise to life everlasting. Thereby He served notice that we can go and do likewise.

Like Daniel in Babylon, Jesus was a stranger. At His birth there was no room for Him in the Inn. "He came unto His own, and His own received Him not." He had nowhere to lay His head. Later He was flogged and derided, killed, buried in another's tomb. He was called the Stranger of Galilee.

The whole drama of riding into Jerusalem on a donkey was not only an unfolding of God's plan for Jesus' life, but also by it our Lord deliberately made a Messianic claim—since the Prophet Zechariah (9:9) had prophesied: "Rejoice, daughter of Zion, shout aloud daughter of Jerusalem, for see, your King is coming to you...humble and mounted on an ass."

As strangers, since this earth is not our home, we have the blessed assurance that if we live out our lives according to God's purpose for us, he will give His angels charge over us, to keep us in all our ways, now and evermore.

PRAYER: *Thank You, Lord, for binding the Two Testaments with the most dependable fastener of all—the resurrection. Amen.*

The Ever-Living Word

Joel 2:28 *And it shall come to pass afterward, that I will pour out my spirit on all flesh.*

After Daniel, the Bible books continue with Hosea, Joel, Amos, Obadiah, etc., and since the six books—Hosea, Job, Jonah, Nahum, Habbakuk, Haggai—don't mention Jerusalem, we move next to the wise counsel of Joel, whose hometown was Jerusalem, and who was well-informed on the writings of other prophets.

Today's text is important for Christians. It stands out of Joel's little book of three chapters, since it was quoted by Peter on the Day of Pentecost, the day on which the Christian Church was born.

The question here is: How did Peter make the connection between what he was going through at the moment and Joel's prophecy that had been made hundreds of years before? And if the devil can cite scripture for his purpose (as he did during the temptation of Jesus in the wilderness) why can't we, God's people?

Knowing the assaults of the devil better than we do, God has put the Bible ("the sword of the Spirit, which is the Word of God") into our hands. It has all the answers we need to rebuff the devil, with the aid that the Holy Spirit gives us.

So how can we learn the procedure from Peter? On the day of Pentecost, when the Spirit came upon the faithful, they spoke in tongues and were understood, without translators, by persons from many lands who were in Jerusalem for the celebration of Pentecost.

As usual, the unbelievers made fun of this mishmash of languages, claiming that it was caused not by the Holy Spirit, but by spirits in alcoholic beverage.

At that moment, Peter, newly convinced of the reality of the Holy Spirit after his denial of and forgiveness by Jesus, recalled how critical Joel was of drunks. (Joel 1:5) No, Peter affirmed as he launched into the first Christian sermon, this Pentecostal joy was not drunkenness, but what Joel had gone on to call the pouring out of God's Spirit on all flesh. (2:28) The result of that sermon was that 3,000 persons were converted. (Acts 2:41) How did Peter make that timely connection? For one thing, Peter had companioned with Jesus for three years. Today the tour guides of Jerusalem take you to the Mount of Olives to a cave that Jesus used as a sort of classroom—retreat center. That's plausible. It is close to the Garden of Gethsemane, where Jesus often went for seasons of prayer. In the cool cave the Master and His 12 Men would no doubt have their Bible studies, getting an understanding of vital passages and how to use them credibly and winningly in everyday circumstances; unlearning earlier mistaken meanings; filling in knowledge gaps; grafting in new findings. Nor was such learning only a cave experience on their long walks up and down the country, they were in a walking-talking-teaching-learning mode. Even in His Post-Easter days Jesus continued this on-the-march teaching method.

Just as validly as Joel had perceived every good reason for prophesying the outpouring of God's Spirit in some fuzzy future, so rightly did Peter perceive every good reason for accepting Joel's prophecy as being fitting for that particular happening on Pentecost. The prophets (projectors) are in the Bible. The receptors are us. "With us in mind, God had made a better plan, that only with us should they reach perfection." (Heb. 11:40)

PRAYER: *Grant us, Gracious Lord, to be keen receptors of Your Word, and how and when to credibly and winningly connect it to our everyday living. Amen.*

JOEL'S FIRST NOEL

Joel 2:32 *Then everyone who invokes the Lord's name will be saved; on Mt. Zion and in Jerusalem there will be a remnant as the Lord has promised, survivors whom the Lord calls.*

Joel's first word "Then" refers to what the Lord has just spoken through him. They are words (2:28:31) of such prophetic import that Jesus used them in His "little apocalypse" in Mark 13:24. And Mark, whose gospel is believed to depend heavily on Peter's memoirs, shows why he included this Joel reference—Peter himself was impressed by Jesus' use of it, and used it himself in his first sermon on the first Pentecost, the birthday of the Christian Church. (Acts 2:17-21)

"Then," adds Joel, following the fulfillment of that prophesy, everyone who calls on the name of the Lord will be saved. And again the connection is made with Jesus. For, as Matthew records it, an angel told Joseph in a dream what was happening to his wife Mary. "She will bear a son, and you will give him the name Jesus, for he will save his people from their sins." (Matt. 1:21) And with another "then," Saint Paul appropriates Joel's affirmation: "Everyone who calls on the name of the Lord will be saved." (Rom. 10:13)

Continuing to lay emphasis on the "call," Joel now turns from people calling upon the Lord, to the Lord calling people. With this difference, not "everyone" is called, only a remnant, a dedicated few. "Many are called, but few are chosen." For the Master's minority He has the highest regard. Finger-ring collectors sometimes display what they proudly call a Regard ring. The word "Regard" is spelled out in precious stones with which the ring is set. R is the ruby. E, the emerald. G, the garnet. A, the amethyst. R, another ruby, and D, a diamond. It's precious. And that is the kind of regard that the Lord has for the remnant of the righteous—the redeemed and redeeming minority. The masses who are determined to go their own ways, keep going over the brink and into the drink. Only the remnant survives, as they did in Jerusalem—the small dedicated, God-connected souls; the church from every race and nation. They become the leavening influence in each succeeding generation—until that time comes when every knee shall bow, and every tongue confesses that Jesus Christ is Lord.

PRAYER: *We respond to Thy call, O Lord, committing ourselves to service in Thy select and selected fellowship. Amen.*

A WONDERFUL SAVIOR IS JESUS

Joel 2:32 *Everyone who invokes the Lord by name shall be saved.*

There was a time earlier in American history when it was easy to become a citizen. Requirements were at a minimum.

That, at first sight, appears to be the name of the game in our text.

"Everyone." There's a wide-open door or no door at all. "Everyone" is inclusive. Unconditional. Every nation, color, sex, creed. Even unbelievers. You would think that applicants were lined up around the block, overnight. What sort of belief system is this? "Who invokes the Lord by name?" Many people use the name of the Lord as an angry swear word. Does that disqualify them? Doesn't sound like it. "Everyone" still enfolds them.

"Shall be saved." There's another open-ended promise. The worst, the lowest, the sinner on his deathbed, a thief on a cross. The furthest removed from the Lord—no negatives apply. "Come on in," the welcome proclaims. "Come one, come all."

So attractive is the invitation that the publishers of the New Testament felt justified in connecting to Jesus this verse from Joel. In particular, Saint Paul did: "Everyone who calls on the name of the Lord will be saved." (Rom. 10:13) But, as we do, Paul went on to question the rationale of the verse. "But how could they call on him without having faith in him. And how could they have faith without having heard of him? And how could they hear without someone to spread the news? And how could anyone spread the news without being sent?" (Rom. 10:14-15)

To sharpen his point, Paul calls in two heavyweights. First, Moses quoting God: "I will use a nation that is no nation...and a foolish nation" to stir and arouse His languid people. Second, Isaiah: "I was found by those who were not looking for me; I revealed myself to those who never asked about me." (Rom. 10:19-20)

Despite the vagaries of logic, and contrary to conventional wisdom, we here see the Lord taking fumbling nations that are a menace to themselves and the global family and using them for His honor and their glory; taking accidental happenings and turning them into happy memories for all concerned.

Paul then brings it to a head: "It is by grace you are saved through faith; it is not your own doing. It is God's gift, not a reward for work done." (Eph. 2:8-9)

At His word the impossibles slink away into obscurity. Though Mt. Zion, the site of the Temple, was obliterated. "When the Lord gives the word there shall yet be survivors on Mt. Zion." And in devastated Jerusalem His enlivening word remakes a Remnant. (Joel 2:32) Then, as we have since learned, in every community—mega or shrimpy—it is always the Remnant, the virile central command, a handful of people, who keep things ticking. Which is to say that the Lord still looks to us, not to save Him as much as to save ourselves from lounging on flowery beds of ease and letting Him do everything.

PRAYER: *We call on You, Jesus, for, as the angel promised, You will save us from our sins. (Matt. 1:21) Amen.*

JUDGMENT AHEAD

Joel 3:1 *When I reverse the fortunes of Judah and Jerusalem...*

When His people were back in His good graces, God's plan was to deal severely with their overlords. Those who had been merciless toward the Hebrews would now get their turn under the scourge. Though for a time God used other nations to teach His people a lesson He could not let those nations off the hook for their irrational overkill treatment of those they had conquered.

Coming together eagerly, as if for war against a common enemy, those nations would see blood (the blood of God's people) on their hands. Then would come the accusations.

First, that these nations had scattered God's people. As in scattering ashes, it was done sparsely and irregularly—therefore deliberately. Taken into captivity, God's people were intentionally separated, not only to intensify their isolation from their homeland but also from home folks, kindred spirits with whom they might team up and become a menace. Enforce estrangement in their ranks, keep them off balance and so render them dehumanized and powerless. That meddling with his loved ones, God determined, was unacceptable.

A second accusation was that these nations that had conquered the Holy Land and Holy City, finding few if any landowners (who had been deported and scattered) took immediate possession of whatever they could lay their hands on. That didn't set well with the Lord of heaven. It was His property, to which He had guided His chosen people. It was in that city and Temple that He would make His earthly dwelling. How dare these interlopers usurp what was not rightly theirs.

The third crime of the nations brought to judgment is condensed into two incidents in verse 3:
i. Boys were sold into any kind of slavery the owners had in mind. The money gained from such an exchange went to pay prostitutes. Boys of that time must have often heard not the threat, "I'll take you

behind the woodshed," but "if you don't behave I'll sell you."

ii. Girls were bartered for the price of a drink which is guzzled in no time. Obviously children, particularly those of a low grade nation, were of little value.

Looking in these mirrors we see the likeness of our own present-day inhumanities. We have our own methods of scattering humans, often under cover of some charitable label: saving souls, emigration to a better life, adopting children from other lands, employing foreigners for service labor and/or prostitution.

How nations and religions have moved into each others' territories and built their empires there—business empires like gambling, which is another way of dehumanizing people, has tainted all peoples throughout history. These days gaming machines are calibrated by state-of-the-art security devices to give the "house" the advantage over the players. Since there is cheating and stealing by both players and employees, catwalks in the ceiling allow the surveillance crew to look straight down through one-way glass. In the United States there are at least 174 gaming enterprises plus 400 Native American gaming establishments.

The Lord was not easy on the offending nations in Joel's day, and He is the same Lord—yesterday, today, and forever!

PRAYER: *Lord of all time and eternity, preserve us within the confines of Your jurisdiction, that we may pass Your tests at the time of Judgment. Amen.*

WHY BE HOLY?

Joel 3:17 *Thus you will know that I am the Lord your God, dwelling in Zion, my holy mountain; Jerusalem will be holy, and foreigners will never again set foot in it.*

How would Joel and the faithful few know that the Lord was their God and not a god of another kind? How does anyone come to know the one true God? Other gods may have their own propagandists. The present Lord makes His own case, leaving His hearers and observers and analysts to make their studied judgments.

The Lord addresses the enemies of His people—that He has seen the way they have mistreated the Israelites, and now He is going to reverse the fortunes of His beloved, making the deeds of the enemy recoil upon their own heads. (3:7) Then, summoning His own people to arms, granting them a fruitful land, and causing the enemy to shudder with apprehension, He gives, in such a critical mass, undeniable proof of His Godliness. Thus they came to an understanding of and belief in the God of the first Commandment, beside whom there are no other gods of any consequence.

Then comes the double use of the word "holy." In one library I found this word listed under every letter in the alphabet—all the way from Holy Alliance and Bible and City to Holy Year of Jubilee and Holy Mt. Zion. Part of the problem with holiness is this long association with taboo. That is, anything holy was to be stayed away from. No, St. Paul disagrees. To be holy is to be pure, free of sin, healed of the wounds caused by moral wrongdoing. "I appeal to you therefore brethren," Paul urges, "to present your bodies as a living sacrifice, holy and acceptable to God." (Rom. 12:1) And, because God had purified Zion and Jerusalem, He henceforth desired such an undefiled city to be peopled by those who were cleansed of their sins. In fact, that is what the people were required to do when they were called to arms. They went through the kind of purification ritual, and sanctification as they would in preparing themselves for worship in the Temple. Such were acceptable to the Lord. The spiritually unclean were aliens, "foreigners." They lacked the passwords and passport and therefore were not allowed where the Lord's own were welcome. As in the parable of the Ten Bridesmaids: those who were prepared went in to the banquet hall. To the unprepared, the "foreigners," the groom said, "Depart from me, I never knew you."

PRAYER: *We claim You as our God, O Lord. Accept us into the holy joy of Your Salvation. Amen.*

A CALL FROM CENTRAL INTELLIGENCE

Amos 1:2 *He (Amos) said, the Lord roars from Zion and thunders from Jerusalem; the shepherds' pastures are dried up and the choicest farmland is parched.*

Though mentioned third in the list of the Twelve Minor Prophets, Amos is credited with being first off the starting block in the golden age of prophesy. And not without good reason. Called a herdsmen, he was more akin to the royal rancher in 2 Kings 3:4. He supplied royalty with sheep, goats, cattle. The sycamore trees that he raised produced a poor grade of fruit, used mostly as fodder for his animals. A man of means and well educated, Amos lived just twelve miles south of Jerusalem, a city which he no doubt frequented—for trade and educational opportunities. A man of God, he was aware of the spiritual plight of his countrymen up and down the land. In fact, God was burdened for His people, and laid that burden on the heart of Amos.

Without hesitation, this burden-bearer made God's message known to the country for the inexactly known period of two weeks—to two years. Then he wrote it all down. Later, this second verse, in poetic form, was used for public worship in the Temple.

With so many farm animals under his care, Amos must often have heard the bone-chilling roar of lions on the prowl. To such an equivalent of a forest-wide nuclear blast, everyone paid attention. Add thunder to that, and the attention of the universe is riveted. In like manner, Amos contended, God wanted His peoples' attention. And He wanted it all, or not at all.

As for the parched farmland, some versions say, "and the top of Carmel withers." Mt. Carmel, overlooking the Mediterranean Sea, has always been known for its lush woodlands. But here is the first reason for listening to the Lord: "Look at the Withering Heights. They symbolize the state of the country. You think all is well with you. You convince yourselves that you are as flourishing as you ever were. The reality is that there is dry rot in your souls." They were playing at being better than they were. Self-deceived, they were unfocused, unable to tell right from wrong.

Only God knows how such staggering wrong-headedness deserves His thunderous roaring to bring us to our senses. Here sweet-talk and niceties only add to the problem.

PRAYER: *Alarm us awake, O Lord, lest we lapse into a spiritual stupor. Amen.*

FROM THE STRONG COMES SWEETNESS

Amos 1:2 *The Lord roars from Zion.*

This is the very first line that Amos writes in

his brief book, outside of which his name is not heard. And the roaring was actually not from Jerusalem, but from twelve miles south in the area of Tekoa, which extended some twenty miles east, 4,000 feet down to the Dead Sea. Much of the Tekoan landscape was wild, where, indeed, lions roared. As a cattleman (what more could lions ask for?), Amos was familiar with the all-encompassing voice of the King of the forest and transferred that form of expression to the Lord—for several reasons!

You notice for one thing, even in a zoo, that when a lion roars all else is silent and listening. Not that a lion waits for silence before speaking. In the quiet of an African jungle night he roars, causing the lesser creatures—the monkeys, jackals, hyenas, zebras, deer—to hush. And when Amos realized that everybody was concerned and talking about an earthquake, which did in fact occur as a mighty shocker taking 30,000 lives, he knew that only the loud exhortation of the Lord would get the attention of His people. "Be still and know that I am God." "In quietness and in confidence shall be your strength." (Isa. 3:15)

We humans, at our best, like nature, mirror the image of God. Our defects remind us that we are only His image.

That is the attitude which Amos is taking in this first line in his book.

Also, the lion's full-throated announcement has an enveloping effect. No one is left out, far or near. The big cat's message is: "All creatures that on earth do dwell—listen up; I've a story to tell to the nations."

> The Lord is the need of the world,
> and for Him it cries.
> Though it babble of gold and fame,
> it lies, it lies.
> Though it would not have us know,
> Its secret it cannot keep.
> The Lord is the need of the world.
> And it tells it, awake or asleep.

Not alone does the Lord's invitation come from His beloved Jerusalem, seeking our silent attention to His universal message—but there's also an urgency to it. As the wisdom writer urged: "Whatsoever your hand finds to do, do it with all your might." (Eccles. 9:10) With no less wisdom another writes that "being everlastingly on the job beats carrying a rabbit's foot."

Moreover, there's a ferocity in the divine "roar." On the surface there was a false calmness. But as Amos drilled below the surface, he reported: "These are the words of the Lord: For crime after crime of Israel I will grant them no reprieve." (Amos 2:6) What were these crimes? Slave trading and raiding villages for more slaves. The poor were ground into the dust, father and son resort to the same girl (2:7), the profaning of God's name, "and in the house of the Lord they drink liquor." (2:8) And that was only the beginning. The Lord's roar and ferocity were necessary. How accurate Amos was in putting his opening thoughts in a jungle setting with silence, attention, ferocity, inclusiveness. For "the fear of the Lord is the beginning of wisdom, and to depart from evil is understanding." (Ps. 11:10)

PRAYER: *We hear You Lord, and respond to Your love call. Amen.*

BREATHE ZION'S ENLIVENING ATMOSPHERE

Amos 6:1 *Shame on you who live at ease in Zion.*

Having severely criticized the "cows" (the women, in 4:1-2), Amos now lays it on the bulls, the leaders of society. He focuses on all the expensive, licentious aspects of their social lives. He sees them lolling on beds inlaid with ivory, sprawling on couches, feasting on fatted calves. (6:4) They drink wine by the bowlful and anoint themselves with the richest of oils. (6:6) "Therefore," he concludes, "you shall lead the column of exiles; that will be the end of sprawling and revelry." (6:7)

Some interpreters feel that here Amos is speaking like a countrified hick who has a natural dislike for citified slouches on couches, and that God does not necessarily feel the same way about it. Yet there is a decadence that goes with opulence, which must be addressed. And Amos deserves our gratitude for doing so.

At the moment, for example, there is a leading golfer who is pocketing $110 million a year. He has been so highly praised and paid, that in a better mood he confessed the personal conviction that he was entitled to do whatever he pleased. Often far from home he engaged in extra-marital relations. Indulging, even minimally, has become a major freefall for him morally. In turn, the shake-up in his morale has affected his professional acumen, causing his drop in international rankings.

Amos' message here is by no means provincial, applying only to those of his time who lived within the meridians of lassitude and loungitude. Amos' message is international. His global outlook is evident in the number of cities and areas he names, near and far.

Jesus encapsulated this issue in Luke 12:48: "Where someone has been given much, much will be expected of him; and the more he has had entrusted to him the more will be demanded of him."

If we don't measure up to the requirement, and rest back on what we believe are entitlements owed to us, we will be deserving of all the negatives that will most surely engulf us.

Not that the Lord is heartless. But to take Him for all He's got is shameful and brings its own built-in punishings.

And how much He has given us? Never, of course, what our greediness hungers after, but more than what we deserve. "We love Him *because* He first loved us." How wonderfully He brought us to birth, without one creative twitch from us. How He inducted others to take over and guide us to grown wisdom, stature, and in favor with God and man. How He then brought to our opening minds the saving knowledge of Jesus Christ, who lived, suffered, died for us, that we might go on with Him to that " house not made with hands, eternal in the heavens." How much more generous could He have been? In the face of such super gift-giving, dare we drag our feet like Lazy bones— "loafing in the sun. How you 'spec to get your day's work done? You'll never earn a dime that way." Instead of sitting down to sing it, let us "Rise up, O men of God! Have done with lesser things, give heart and mind and soul and strength to serve the King of Kings."[1]

PRAYER: *Forgive us, heavenly Father, for our indolence. It never fails to get us bogged down in muck. Raise us, cleanse us. Now and ever. Amen.*

SELF REFLECTIONS?

Obad. 11 *On that day when you stood aloof, while strangers carried off his wealth, while foreigners passed through the gates and shared out Jerusalem by lot, you were at one with them.*

In this shortest of Old Testament books, nothing is known of the author, although there are eleven Obadiahs in this earlier Testament. Nevertheless, he comes right to the point, which is that here God is taking aim at Edom, a once distantly related to Israel nation, east of the Dead Sea. Since David's time, 500 years before this, the Edomites had been building a case against Israel. Then when the Babylonians under Nebuchadnezzar besieged and destroyed Jerusalem (it took them a month), the Edomites saw their chance for revenge.

But God was watching. Though He was punishing His own people at the hands of the Babylonian invaders, He was not turning a blind eye to the criminal intervention of the Edomites into Israel's invasion, for this Edom would receive in kind. "You will be treated as you have treated others." (v. 15)

Of what were they guilty? Verses 10-14 list ten charges.

1. Violence done to a brother. It would have been inexcusable enough lifting a hand against a fellow human, even though he was an enemy. To purposely

---

[1] William P. Merrill

trample a kinsman was to arouse God's wrath.
2. Aloofness, when a helping hand was desperately needed. There lies the glaring sin of knowing what is right, and not doing it. Instead,
3. the Edomites behaved as if they were part of the Babylonian contingent that stormed Jerusalem carrying off its wealth, which included thousands of gold treasured vessels from the Temple, and brazenly sharing out the Holy city among themselves.
4. Then noting the tightening noose that strangled the Israelites, the Edomites gloated. So pronounced was this nefarious clucking, that it is given double exposure in verses 12 and 13.
5. Nor was that dastardly enough—the Edomites broke out in a public display of jubilation at the downfall of their neighbors.
6. Then there was swaggering over the way the Israelites had been squashed.
7. With such a vile attitude that put them at odds with God, the Edomites took the liberty of impertinently entering the city gate, when it was none of their business. To help would have been acceptable; to
8. loot, no. That was jackal behavior.
9. When King Zedekiah of Jerusalem, and fellow fugitives could have made a getaway, the Edomites, knowing the local escape routes better than the Babylonians, trapped the King and company.
10. Then, with ultimate shamelessness, the Royal booty was delivered to the enemy—no doubt in exchange for a regal reward.

Little wonder that God was riled. As His Son said: "He who is not with me is against me, and he who does not gather with me scatters." (Luke 11:23) So in time, both the Babylonians and Edomites were scattered to destruction. Let him who thinks he stands, take heed...

PRAYER: *Thou God seest us. Keep us from gloating and boasting and looting. Help us to love our neighbors as ourselves. Through Christ. Amen.*

FULLY ANSWERED QUESTIONS

Mic. 1:5 *All this for Jacob's crime and Israel's sin. What is the crime of Jacob? Is it not Samaria? What is the sin of Judah? Is it not Jerusalem?*

What high-octane preaching was flowing across the land. Micah and Isaiah in the south, Amos and Hosea in the north. And it sounds as if these men shared their findings; the moral state of the nation, and the remedy. Micah though now not as well known as his contemporaries, was in that time the best known. His defining of the national spiritual slump was helpfully accurate. When you know the target, you have the best chance of achieving your objective. As the big-game hunters of Africa affirmed: "It's not how hard you hit 'em, but where."

In the north, Micah ascertained that Samaria was the breeding ground for crime. Calf-worship, to which the Israelites had been exposed for 400 years in Egypt, and which burst out in the golden calf incident in the Sinai, was given extended devotion after the Hebrews settled down in the Promised Land. And Samaria was the hotbed. Also there was Baal worship, a fertility cult, some of which was imported, but much of which was native to Canaan. The result was that many Hebrews didn't know which God to worship.

In the south, Micah, who knew Jerusalem

well, saw that this city was the source of sin. Wealthy landowners oppressed the poor, officers of the law were cannibalistic, nor could religious leaders be trusted. Addressing these three groups, in chapter 6:8, Micah says they should do justly, love mercy, and walk numbly with God.

To deal with this crime and sin, Micah writes, God was going to do "all this." 1. God would leave His dwelling place. (1:3) In 5:2 it is more explicit: "from you, Bethlehem in Ephrath, will come a King for me over Israel." That was God's son. 2. God would dissolve mountains like wax (1:4), and 3. He will tear open the valleys (1:4); that, too, is a reference to Christ's coming—when mountains will be leveled and the valleys exalted. (Luke 3:5)

"All this," through the sacrifice of God's Son, washes away crime and sin and sets the spiritually imprisoned free. And not only in Samaria and Jerusalem, for Micah's prophecy has eternal and universal application. That was and is God's desire—to send a major note through a minor prophet.

PRAYER: *What a wondrous long-distance operator You are, Lord. Your word is as clear and helpful to us as it was back then. Many thanks. Amen.*

RECLAIMING RUINS

Mic. 3:12 *Therefore, because of you Zion will become a plowed field, Jerusalem as heap of ruins, and the temple mount rough moorland.*

The previous meditation gives the gist of the charges brought against the Hebrews, and what would be done about them in God's good time.

Now Micah lists the detailed sins (3:2, 3, 9-11) and spells out the short-term consequences thereof. (3:12)

Leaders of the country were thought of as shepherds: they led and cared for persons in their jurisdiction. At least, that was the hope. Actually, however, the shyster shepherds, instead of tending their "flocks," tenderized and consumed them. Knowing that the poor would always be around, the ruling class exploited them. Nor has the situation changed. The picture of an impoverished Bangladeshi child can start a hefty cash flow into many an exploiter's coffers. Using low-income neighborhoods for political gain can make czars out of Party Bosses. And this shell game was no different in Micah's day than it is now.

The Law, too, has always been manipulateable. In the name of justice, many a court decision has been and still is made according to the lawyer's personal code of ethics, and/or because of the bottom line—money.

Or thinking that a fair deal will be found among religious leaders, people turn from administration, politics, law, only to find that religion has its share of shady dealers. False preachers and prophets have kept their genre going from Bible times to the present. As of old, there are the shepherds of religion who, to use Ralph Sockman's apt phrase, "temper the winds to the shorn lambs in fur coats."

So Micah lashed out at these perversions of rectitude. And if Micah's prophetic forthrightness was still making an impression a century later (Jer. 20:17-19), it had an effect on his own emperor, King Hezekiah. Left a morally questionable legacy by his father Ahaz, Hezekiah did some cleaning up in the Kingdom and Temple, enough to merit a word of distinction in the history book. Second Kings 18:6-7 records that Hezekiah "remained loyal to the Lord and did not fail in his allegiance to him, and he kept the commandments which the Lord had given Moses. The Lord was with him and he prospered in all that he undertook."

"Stand up, stand up for Jesus, ye soldiers of the cross." You can never tell where God will direct the ripples of righteousness.

PRAYER: *Lord, make us mighty in prayer and Micah in speaking out on Your behalf. The rest we leave in Your creative hands. Amen.*

CAPSULED CHURCHMANSHIP

Mic. 4:2 *"Let us go up to the mountain of the Lord, to the house of Jacob's God, that he may teach us his ways and we may walk in his paths." For instruction issues from Zion, the word of the Lord from Jerusalem.*

Long ago Bible scholars agreed that Micah could hardly have been the author of this second half of his book. Yet the sublimity of the above text remains, casting Jerusalem in the role of the world's capital, a magnet for the world's populace, drawing people from all climes—for at least seven good reasons: 1. To "go up." The words echo through the parable of the Prodigal Son and beyond. "I will arise and go." It is a movement back to where a person belongs, to the Rock from where he was hewn; to a reinstatement with the Father; to a new beginning. 2. "To the mountain of the Lord—a flashback to Moses on the mountain of the Lord, Mt. Sinai. There Moses received the Word of God which was to serve as a blueprint for establishing God's kingdom on earth. But here, in Jerusalem, God's own city, not just as Moses could ascend to the heights of holiness, anyone was welcome, from anywhere in the world. 3. "To the house of Jacob's God," the place of worship. How deep calls to deep despite the myriad reasons conjured up for deploring worship. Our hearts are denied basic security until we find security in the Lord—through worship in prayer, reading the scriptures, having them explained and applied to daily life, and joyously singing the faith. 4. "That He may teach us His ways," which are not our ways. That unlearning of wrong ways and retraining in the divinely accepted modes can be as difficult as moving out of the sandlots to the big leagues and world Olympics. 5. "We may walk in His paths." Continuing the previous point, it is not as cushy as it sounds to walk where Jesus walked—on the Via Dolorosa, among other tortured trails. Discipline is required and dedication and discipleship. "Heaven is not reached at a single bound..." 6. "Instruction issues from Zion, that is, through the ministrations of trained teachers of the word. Bogus instructors, sowing the seeds of untruth, can cause irreversible damage in human lives. 7. "The word of the Lord from Jerusalem." The King of Kings has the last word from His epicentral capital, Jerusalem. Hear ye!

Every time I fly out of the Holy Land, I thank the Lord that He has not confined Himself and His teaching to that beautiful little country, I thank Him for making the place whereon we stand—holy ground. There we can go to Him and achieve all that Micah envisioned happening in good old Jerusalem.

PRAYER: *Working with You, Lord, we would bring in the Kingdom through our church, and this community, both now and ever. Amen.*

A WHOLE AND HOLY PEACE

Mic. 4:3 *They shall beat their swords into mattocks (plowshares) and their spears into pruning knives.*

Micah's better-known contemporary, Isaiah, records every word of the above text in his second chapter, verse 4. But the prophet Joel expresses the opposite idea in his chapter 3, verse 10. Who is right? That is what the world still can't figure out. Should we transform our weaponry into farm equipment and study war no more, or should we transfer the time, money, and raw material designated for the peaceful pursuits of farming and gardening over to the beefing up of our military arsenals?

It's an age-old dilemma. And here even the Bible is of two minds. And the world still is. One reason is, as Jerome Davis explained, "Wars are becoming more frequent as civilization advances." After an exhaustive study done at Harvard of the number of wars, their duration, the participants, casualties, and the proportion of combatants to the total population, it concluded that the intensity of war has steadily increased: Twelfth century, 18; Thirteenth, 24; Fourteenth, 60; Fifteenth, 100; Sixteenth, 180; Seventeenth, 500; Eighteenth, 70; Nineteenth, 120; and the Twentieth, 3,080...The monetary cost (of war) has steadily increased. In Caesar's time it took only about $0.75 to kill one man, but by the Napoleonic era $3,000 was needed. Some years later when the American Civil War occurred this amount had risen to $5,000. In World War I the cost rose perpendicularly to $21,000 per man killed, and in World War II it was $50,000. The direct cost to the United States of World War I is estimated to have been at least $22 billion, which roughly equals all the money appropriated by the American Congress from its foundation to the start of the war. The United States spent roughly $400 billion in World War II.

According to William Eckhardt, research director for the Lentz Peace Research Laboratory in St. Louis, one of the most horrendous aspects of war is that all wars have one thing in common, namely the majority of people killed; ninety-one percent are civilians, not soldiers.

In the little town of Bethlehem they tell you that every Christmas Eve the bells in the carillon tower are rung—and the message of "Peace on earth, good will among all people" is transmitted across the world.

The promise that peace is possible is still held out to us. How to grasp it and make it a reality?

Micah forges ahead, when no one else does. He affirms that One will come out of Bethlehem. (5:2) And He did in the Person of Jesus Christ. "Whose roots are far back in the past." (5:2) And His were. "He was with God at the beginning." (John 1:2) "He shall appear and be their shepherd." (Mic. 5:4) He did lay down his life for the sheep." (John 10:11) "And he shall be a man of peace." (Mic. 5:5) He was. "Peace is my parting gift to you, my own peace, such as the world cannot give. (John 14:27)

As the Bishop of Jerusalem has repeated in his Christmas Eve message at the Church of the Nativity in Bethlehem: "Here not only was the Prince of Peace born, but the principles of peace." This is where Micah directs us to the source of peace, "that He may teach us His ways and we may walk in His paths." (Mic. 4:2) The "ace" in peace is to come first to Him. Learn from Him the basics, lest we walk off the map to world peace.

PRAYER: *Prince of Peace, as only You can, help us to be incarnators of Your peace in our time. Amen.*

WAR BEGONE

Mic. 4:3 *Neither shall they learn war any more.*

With this line Micah puts the finishing touch on his peace proposal. It was as affixed in stone as the Commandments were at Sinai—"For the Lord of Hosts Himself has spoken." (4:4) Yet the malingering question is how to stop and unlearn what we have about war? For across the world the learning about armed conflict continues unabated, beginning with our highchair and playpen days. There's the flailing of arms and the spitting out of baby food that is disliked. The playpen prison bars are rattled with resentment—with tit-for-tats involving school-time bullies and sex rivals.

More organized and focused on militarism are such Preparatory Schools as the Virginia Military Institute, The Citadel, and schools attached to the five armed forces that are joined at the top by the Pentagon in the nation's capital. The education and research that readies students for war proceeds through special colleges; the ROTC; the Service Academies for Army, Navy, Air Force, Marines and Coast Guard; plus the War Colleges for each service. The U.S. Army command and General Staff College is the graduate school for U.S. Armed forces. As a government reporter said:

"We will do everything necessary to maintain our arsenal."

To be sure, there are also persons who are working for "a world without nuclear weapons," "a bold initiative consistent with America's moral heritage." On the other hand, as always, there are the Caesars, Hitlers, Mussolinis and terrorists. Are we then to keep building hexagons to house the makers of smarter war games and toss aside the word of the Lord as impractical?

Coming closer to the issue, the framers of the Constitution of UNESCO wrote into the preamble, "Since wars begin in the minds of men, it is in the minds of men that the defences of peace must be constructed." And Prof. Paul E. Johnson adds, "The inner motivations of the Soul are the original battleground of war. It is likewise the ground of peace."

From the battlefront, a serviceman wrote home to his wife asking her to please stop nagging him so that he could fight this war in peace. That hit the bull's-eye. The making of peace takes all the effort and sacrifice a war calls for—without the armed conflict. Why is the city of Jerusalem called "the City of Peace" when it has had more turmoil than any other city in history? And it is not just because the city's name Salem, Shalom, Salaam means peace. Yet the people there and everywhere else have failed the Lord repeatedly. But He has held out the possibility of peace on earth, not as a carrot on a stick but as an achievable reality on earth. In the name of Jesus every knee shall bow. (Phil. 2:10) In Him all things hold together. (Col. 1:17) Moreover, He taught us to pray that His kingdom might come on earth. That is repeated at the close of the Bible, that there will be not only a new heaven, but also a new earth. (Rev. 21:1) Peace on earth has been foreordained, in spite of man's warring madness. All provision has been made. His promise shall be fulfilled. (Mic. 4:8) "Why are you now filled with alarm?" (Mic. 4:9) The future is His and ours.

PRAYER: *O Lord, "Let peace begin with me; let this be the moment now, With every step I take, let this be my solemn vow, to take each moment and live each moment in peace eternally. Let there be peace on earth and let it begin with me."*[1]

LISTEN UP

Mic. 6:1-2 *Up, state your case...Hear the Lord's case.*

The setting for this debate between God and a wayward nation of Israel is a courtroom. It could just as readily be between the Lord and an individual, anywhere. How necessary are such face-to-face, no-holds-barred encounters. The Lord encourages it, not to talk us down but to get clearer understanding on both sides.

In this case He is at a loss to know why His chosen people are meandering around in a no-man's land. One can almost hear a sob. He asks in despair, "O my people, what have I done to you?" (v. 3) He thought He had done rightly by them releasing them from Egyptian slavery, providing top quality leaders both in Sinai and the Land of Promise. What more could they have wanted?

Acknowledging their alleged ingratitude, the people answer in effect: "All right, Lord, what do You want us to do to make You happy? You like

---

[1] Sy Miller and Jill Jackson

blood sacrifices—how many thousand animals would satisfy You? How about oil? Say the amount that was spilled in Alaska and the Gulf of Mexico combined? Or would You prefer us to lay our children on the sacrificial altar?" Without pointing to their contemptuous insults and the sacrilege, God, through His prophet Micah, gives a simple, straightforward, three-pointed reply, which, since then, has guided myriads of misguided persons into the paths of righteousness. (v. 8)

First, "do justice." In America today people are found to lie 200 times a day; in our courts it's no longer "May the best man win," but "May the best lie win"; and a criminal defense lawyer in New York City reports that "there's a rampant amount of perfidy in civil litigation." Both sides commit perfidy, and if "a major impediment to a free society is a dishonest judicial system,"[1] then God is still speaking to us, for justice is truth in action. It is impossible for us to do wrong and feel that's the way it ought to be. Unfortunately, too many people still wish to be shipped "somewhere east of Suez where the best is like the worst, where there are no Ten Commandments, and a man can raise a thirst" (Kipling). As long as humans use the judicial system to satisfy their biases, the more we need to heed the divine injunction: Do justice, with integrity.

Second, love kindness, mercy. Shakespeare's lawyer, Portia, in her famed speech, noted that mercy is twice blest, it blesses the one that gives it and the one that takes it. And one is most like God when mercy seasons justice. And where did

---

[1] Laura Schlessinger, *The Ten Commandments,* pp. 272-274

Shakespeare find that truth but in the Bible. There the mercy of God is mentioned more often in the Old Testament than any other topic—which is why Jesus used it in His fifth Beatitude: "blessed are the merciful..."

Three, walk humbly with your God. Jesus showed His wisdom again by including humility in His Beatitudes. "Blessed are the meek (not the weak) for they shall inherit the earth." That is how Tennyson felt, that "true humility—the highest virtue, mother of them all." Paul goes into further detail in Phil. 2:6-11 about Christ "who being in the form of God counted it not a prize to be on an equality with God, but emptied himself, taking the form of a servant...he humbled himself" It is living within this divine trinity that we find favor with God and man.

PRAYER: *How can we thank You enough, Lord, for Your threefold prescription for a good life here and hereafter? Amen.*

LIVING GOD—LIVE IN US

Zeph. 1:4 *I shall stretch my hand over Judah, over all who live in Jerusalem. I shall wipe out from that place the last remnant of Baal, every memory of the heathen priests.*

The autumn celebration in the Temple was a time of happy thanksgivings for a bountiful harvest. But Zephaniah, the last of the nine Minor Prophets before the Babylonian exile, chose to throw a monkey-wrench into an otherwise joyful occasion. Starting where God started at the Creation, and in God's own words, the Prophet warned of the coming de-creation of the world. In the reverse order in which they were made, every living creature, beginning with humans, would be swept clean off the earth. (v. 2-3)

Neither would the Holy Land nor the Holy City be spared. That's when the jubilation in the Temple must have come to a screeching stop. "He's talking about us," they likely whispered. "Let's listen." And what they heard was: 1. Worshippers of the pagan fertility god Baal (and most of the listeners were of this persuasion) would be wiped out. Why? Because this deity was their lord and god, and thereby they were disobeying the first commandment, "Thou shalt have no other gods..." (Exod. 20:3) 2. Heathen priests would be swept not under the rug, but out of existence for they, too, were breaking God's primary command. On the rooftops, the priests worshipped the astral deities in the starry sky. (v. 5) Therefore the priests and their congregation, though worshipping in the Lord's house, were disconnected from the Living God. The huge hoax was more akin to the present-day celebration of Xmas. The "X," instead of standing for Christ and the celebration of His birth, crosses Him out. The season has become whatever one wants to make it: Happy Holidays, White Christmas, Santa's Workshop, Rudolph the Red-Nosed Reindeer, partying, gift-giving, making the cash register play "What a Friend We Have in Jesus." And in spite of annual attempts to put Christ back in Christmas, the charade continues on its giddily worsening way. We are not hot for the Lord, neither do we give Him the cold shoulder. We are lukewarm, so He promises to spew us out. How's that for a spitting image of the Church? Where is Zephaniah when we need him? For nobody else seems to be sounding a prophetic clarion call to be up in arms as soldiers of the cross. Yet the prophets pronouncement of doom on such chicanery still applies.

PRAYER: *Save us, Lord, lest we perish. Amen.*

The Might of Light

Zeph. 1:12 *At that time I will search Jerusalem by lantern-light and punish all who are ruined by complacency like wine left on its lees, who say to themselves "the Lord will do nothing, neither good nor bad."*

The Lord really didn't have to search for anything. He knows such personal particulars as the number of hairs on our head (or the lack of hairs), and He knows our inner makeup physically, mentally, spiritually. No grounded sparrow escapes His attention. Besides, as the Light of the world He needs no lantern nor a helicoptered searchlight. Yet He speaks here of searching Jerusalem in lantern-light terms that would be understood by His human listeners, for this was the way their own law-and-order officers nightly combed the streets and back-alleys for miscreants. The Holy City harbored its share of unholy humans. With His revealing presence the Lord penetrated the nooks and crannies where the actual sources of Israel's corruption resided. These were the unseen termite-like people who had chewed away society's moral fiber. Revival had to begin with their removal by a pest-control treatment.

And what did the Lord find was at the root of the rot? Just what He expected—complacency. He also found that the people took no blame for being the way they were. Rather, they blamed God. He was setting the bad example, they claimed. They were only being like Him who sat in his heaven and did nothing.

How tempting it is to retreat to our sleepy hollows, and slouch in comfy hammock-swung ease, leaving the active forces of evil to wreak any kind of havoc they wish. No stubborn response by us to sin's dominance. No firm "Here I stand, I can do no other. So help me, God." From us—only avoidance; only a transference of blame. "If God doesn't take a hand in fighting terrorist of attacks on the soul, what do you expect me to do?" So His swift reprisal descends upon us who call ourselves His followers. Oh, that He might stab our spirits broad awake, by taking some pointed pain, some killing sin, and to our dead hearts running them in.

Light can be a life-saver. To escape a storm, a mountain climber spent the night in a cave. When dawn's light shone into the cave, the climber leaped away in alarm. The light had revealed a den of rattlesnakes.

If it were not for Christ, the Light of the world, the fangs of evil would find us. Welcome His searching, saving, enlightening lantern.

PRAYER: *Shine on us, Lord. Shine in us and through us—that others, too, may pay homage at Thy pierced feet. Amen.*

JOY WITHOUT ALLOY

Zeph. 3:14 *Zion, cry out for joy; raise the shout of triumph, Israel; be glad, rejoice with all your heart, daughter of Jerusalem!*

After all the gloom and doom and ka-boom that this prophet has thrown around like hand grenades, you would have thought that the universe had disappeared. "That's the end, there ain't no mo'." Then, surprise! All heaven breaks loose with Hallelujah Choruses. The joy bells ring out from the hilltop of Zion—spreading to all God's chosen people (Israel)—and on to the Temple and beyond (Jerusalem). The decibels mount. All available descriptive words pertaining to joy are strummed. For the Lords' ultimate desire is not to punish and destroy. Those have their places in his plan. His foremost purpose is to love, forgive, provide for a fresh start that leads to Eden, at last. "I will bring you home." (3:20)

That is a cause for super celebration. At Olympic games you see medalists "cry out for joy." Toughest of the tough, these athletes weep uncontrollably at the relief of putting behind them the grinding work, the failures, heartaches—and suddenly after all the cyclonic training sessions, stepping out into the calm of a rainbow-hued dawn once believed impossible. Usually pictured with mouths wide open such athletes gulp in the God-given golden moment. It's a win-win situation—for the individual, the team families, towns, nation, and the commercial enterprises attached thereto. This crying, these tears, are not hot and bitter. Their salt tastes tremendous. With tears like this, who cares what they cost?

Such is the message of the Eternal for His people. The pratfalls will come. The frustrations and disappointments, the faded hopes and off-course humiliations, and all the weaknesses that flesh is heir to—these are a part of the turf and must be faced. Always we can count on the Lord's help, if we will accept and use it. But even when He has to deal roughly with us, it is for our salvation, whether we acknowledge it as such or not. He wants to strain out all that is harmful to us, retaining only that which will put us on that central pedestal in laurelled triumph. If that doesn't make one cry out for joy, nothing else will. Taste those tears—that's ambrosia.

PRAYER: *Thank You, Father, for leading us back to Eden, and a paradise regained. That's our goal, from this day forward. Amen.*

BACK TO A BRIGHT FUTURE

Zech. 1:17 *Proclaim once more: These are the words of the Lord of Hosts; My cities will again brim with prosperity; once again the Lord will comfort Zion, once again he will make Jerusalem the city of His choice.*

Three times are the words "once more" repeated in this passage. And, in the Bible, such a three-part always indicates a hinge of history on which the future is determined.

One determinant is the proclamation of God's word. Always a "once more" is in order, especially since we are constantly barraged by the words of others. It was difficult enough in the prophet's time to withstand the onslaught of words in a marketplace, in parades, national observances, community high-jinks, intergenerational reunions. Those, if allowed to be one's only exposure to words, could be habit forming. But what kind of habits? Were they to be judged alone by fellow humans like ourselves? Surely that would be as perilous as trying, in the present day, to put together a personal philosophy of life from the myriad media commercials with which one is assaulted relentlessly. Always there is a deathless need to proclaim and to hear "once more" (which is never too often) "the words of the Lord of Hosts." These are determinative. Without them the future is a predetermined wreck. With Him cities brim with prosperity that finds favor in His sight.

Another is the Lord's conferring of comfort. Not everyone can be a comforter. Oh, they think they can be. It doesn't come naturally. Job's comforters proved that. Nor do courses and in-service training guarantee desired results. But "there's something about that Name." To know that underneath us are His everlasting arms—ah! In the very thought one feels the warmth and strength of His comfort.

Finally there is the remaking of Jerusalem. When one thinks of the City of Peace and the rivers of blood that have run down its streets again and again, and again, for centuries, its reclamation and reconstruction appear impossible. Certainly by humans. They've tried often enough. Only the Lord can do it. And if He can do that—and He will since nothing is impossible for Him—think of the limitless possibilities that open up for remolding squishy lives, and mending fractured relationships, healing interracial, interdenominational, international wounds. We try to be a part of the answer, of course. But ours is a partial answer, because we're only on this earth part time. The Creator has been giving earth's occupants His concerned attention from earth's inception. Father knows best. The Prince of Peace, with His principles of Peace, are provably dependable, particularly when involved in what is "His choice."

PRAYER: *Once more we extol You, our God, for Your incisive guidance, both now and ever. Amen.*

OUR ALL-EMBRACING GOD

Zech. 2:5 *"I myself shall be a wall of fire all round it (Jerusalem)," says the Lord, "and a glorious presence within it."*

In the days of the Prophets, cities that were worthy of defending were heavily guarded. A wall around the city was always the first line of defense. Around Babylon, for example, the wall was fifteen miles long each way. From the wall to the city there was a quarter-mile of space. Should an enemy breach the wall, they could be picked off more easily while they raced across the quarter mile clearance—which also could be spiked and booby-trapped. Babylon's wall was 380' high, 85' thick, 35' below ground, with 250 guard rooms on top. There were also 100 gates of brass. The city of Nineveh had five daunting walls and three deepwater moats. All of which caused concern in Jerusalem when returnees from the Babylonian exile began to rebuild the Temple and not the walls. Unprotected, they felt that they were begging for trouble.

Actually, however, the Lord had a double concern for His people. Knowing that they had been imprisoned for seventy years, He wanted them to feel unconfined, unwalled, limitless in every sense of the word. They could come home in unlimited numbers from every corner of the Dispersion. Here their talents could be given free rein. And God would pour on them blessings in good measure, shaken together and running over.

"Yes," the people responded in their own way, "we don't want to be fenced in any longer. But, without a wall around the city, are we not inviting invasion?" But the Lord had taken care of that too.

He Himself would be not just a wall. That could be penetrated. Rather, He would be a wall of fire. Even today a forest fire can overwhelm state-of-the-art firefighting. In the Serengeti they still keep the King of the beasts and his subjects at bay by keeping a huge bonfire going all night. Fire, one of the four basic elements, is still a power to be reckoned with. It worked in favor of the Israelites for forty years in the Sinai, and God would see that it worked again for Jerusalem.

Nor would the Lord be only an outer protection. He would be an inner one as well. Taking up His abode in the Holy of Holies of the Temple, again, He would know what local protection was needed and provide it—in individuals, in homes, in businesses, in politics.

PRAYER: *Protector Supreme: You know who to safeguard and why and how. Our apprehensions flee. Our hearts are at rest in Thee. Amen.*

THE WRECK OF THE SATANIC

Zech. 3:2 *The angel said to Satan, "The Lord silence you, Satan! May the Lord, who has chosen Jerusalem, silence you! Is not this man a brand snatched from the fire?"*

This is one of the twenty-three times that an angel is mentioned in the Old Testament. And angels didn't vanish when B.C. became A.D. In the life of Christ angels appear thirteen times. Twelve times they are spoken of by Jesus, seven times by Luke in his Book of Acts, and eight times in Paul's letters and the Book of Revelation, for a total of sixty-three times in a book that was put together over a period of more than 2,000 years.

This vital, abiding messenger of God expressed the paramount need for Satan to be silenced, because what the evil one says is with a forked tongue. It splits the truth as it spits venom at God. Though the Lord chose Jerusalem for His cherished own, Satan vented his spite on God's choice, therefore on God Himself, as he had done in the Garden of Eden—turning Adam and Eve, God's own, away from Him. That is why Satan deserves to be silenced, His tongue is too active. He has chronic palpitation of the tongue as he consistently contradicts the Creator.

In his accusation, Satan is not just wordy. That word "accuse" means "to tear the flesh off and eat it." That's savagery, cannibalism. But that's the nature of this beast.

By worlds-apart contrast, the Lord is a Savior. The brand snatched from the fire is finely descriptive of His Saviorhood. He not only saved Joshua, the high priest from exile, but Jerusalem was also rescued from annihilation. Understandably John Wesley, the founder of Methodism, applied this phrase to his own experience as a six-year-old. His home was afire and neighbors, climbing on each others' shoulders, reached an upstairs window to pluck the little brand from the burning. Later, the Lord snatched Wesley from a hot situation and made him the revivalist of Europe in the eighteenth century.

That has been largely the Lord's mission through the ages—pulling Lot out of the fire and brimstone that rained on Sodom and Gomorrah; walking in the furnace with Shadrach, Meshach and Abednego; sustaining Polycarp being burned at the stake; making holocaust victims more than conquerors over the Nazi ovens. And still He does it. "When through fiery trials thy pathway shall lie, My grace, all sufficient, shall be thy supply." That becomes the final silencing of Satan. He cannot accomplish his main objective—to destroy the good, to annihilate God. There's always the divine silencer and Savior, who, with His legions of angels has the last word and deed.

PRAYER: *Heavenly Father, as You claimed the penitent thief for paradise, so redeem us in the nick of time. Amen.*

THE KING IS COMING

Zech. 9:9 *Daughter of Zion, rejoice with all your heart; shout in triumph, daughter of Jerusalem! See your King is coming to you, his cause won, his victory gained, humble and mounted on a donkey, on a colt, the foal of a donkey.*

Christians admit that this is a cherished verse. All four gospel writers made the connection between it and Jesus' triumphal entry into Jerusalem. The Church gives it top priority every Palm Sunday. And all of the Christianizing of this verse has come about because, initially, Jesus saw Himself as the fulfiller of this prophecy and daringly followed Zechariah's script. And the crowds of His day, used to processions of Kings and pilgrims, entered into the occasion, adding their enthusiastic shouts as only Jerusalemites knew how to do. The usualness of the crowd's response vanished quickly when they realized who, exactly, they were cheering for, and within the week they yelled for Him to be crucified.

Is that what Zechariah had in mind? Who knows? As a prophet he did his job as a pipe through which Omnipotence made His pronouncement. That ended Zechariah's involvement. His was not to ask how or why. Weather forecasters only explain barometric conditions. They do not make the rain or turn on the faucets. That's when the Creator of the universe takes over. Is this why it's called "an act of God?" Indeed. In the case of today's text, God put the words in the prophet's mind and voice and pen. He knew what He was about and how His Son would enact the entire drama.

Early on, Jesus began preparing Himself for this event. In His home synagogue in Nazareth, invited to read the scripture to the congregation, Jesus turned to Isaiah's description of Messiah as the Suffering Servant—a picture into which Jesus fit perfectly. Then, knowing that the phrase "Your King is coming" was referring to the Messiah, and certain that though He was to die, His cause had won, His victory gained, He entered the city on a donkey—as majestic figures did. When a King rode in on a horse, it signaled his warlike intentions. Peace was never more form-fitted as the Messiah than when He mounted a donkey on that first Palm Sunday. His position, the procession, the praise, the paradox of triumph and humility, couldn't have been anything but an act of God. That's how mysteriously He works.

PRAYER: *Father of our Lord Jesus Christ, what wonders You perform. How masterfully Your script is written, Your enactors chosen and coached, and the whole drama pulled off to perfection. We beg to be included in Your plans. Amen.*

ARMS AND THE MAN

Zech. 9:10 *He will banish the chariot from Ephraim, the warhorse from Jerusalem; the warrior's bow will be banished, and he will proclaim peace to the nations. His rule will extend from sea to sea, from the River to the ends of the earth.*

Having established the identity of Messiah, the bringer of Peace, His very first peaceful procedures turn to the disarming of the military establishment. What would be truthful about crying "Peace, Peace" while still procuring and brandishing the weapons of warfare? The real ace in peace would be a national laying down of arms, displaying a confidence in moral rectitude, no longer wrestling with flesh and blood but with principalities, powers. That puts the armaments on the inside. It is then the Spirit is girded with the whole armor of God.

So the first line of defense, the chariot, is the first to be banished, no longer brandished. Solomon had perfected the chariot as a fearsome war machine. Horses, chariots, charioteers were posted in strategic positions up and down the land—the best known being at Megiddo, in the north—a pass through which all invaders of the country had to enter. And for centuries, Solomon's descendants kept up the chariot tradition.

Swifter than a weighty chariot was the warhorse. It could carry its cavalryman into action in a flash. Its bulk would knock foot soldiers right and left out of its way, trampling and kicking them to death. So this beast, trained to be destructive, and stabled in Jerusalem, also had to be turned out to pasture. That took care of demobilizing in both north and south.

There was the warriors bow that had to go—since it was the longest range missile of all. Bows could send their arrows a tremendous distance. At shorter distances fiery darts were shot with slack bows so that the speed would not extinguish the flame.

Devoid of armaments, not only in Palestine would peace prevail but also on all the earth. And only that Man on a donkey has the power to bring about such a paradise regained—and keep it that way.

PRAYER: *Lord, take from our souls the strain and stress, and let our ordered lives confess the beauty of Thy peace. Amen.*

THE SECRET OF SUCCESS

Zech. 12:5 *Then the families of Judah will say in their hearts, "The inhabitants of Jerusalem find their strength in the Lord of Hosts, their God."*

Because of poor baton passing, succeeding generations do not seem to get the message that if the Lord is for us, who can be against us? The lesson is here reemphasized.

Judah, the northern Kingdom of Israel, had made an unholy alliance with the nations of the world—or worldly nations. They moved against Jerusalem, bent on its overthrow. But Jerusalem refused to roll over. And it was quite beyond the understanding of the obviously superior power.

Then Judah had its eyes opened. They got the message, namely, that victory did not lie in brute force, but in the Lord of Hosts—where Jerusalem found its strength.

Certain now that there was no further use in hammering on Jerusalem's gates, Judah became a turncoat and joined Jerusalem's cause.

Moreover, when Judah disengaged from its untrustworthy alliance, it threw the rest of the alliance into confusion and a mass withdrawal from the conflict.

How the Lord networks increasing blessings in favor of His loved ones—above what they ask or think. And the blessings ripple out to completely turnaround the stance of enemies. And what better victory is there than to make an enemy into a friend? Political appeasement policies never accomplish that. On the surface there is an armistice, a laying down of arms. But let's be honest, beneath the appearance of peace isn't there a seething hatred for the victors—a vendetta which looks for the earliest opportunity to revive the conflict? Rivalries are never solved until there is a change of heart. That is where God works best.

At the heart of things. "Man looks on the outward appearance, but the Lord looks at the heart." (1 Sam. 16:7) That's where the vital connections are made, as they are in our physical bodies.

Ultimately, weapons of mass destruction or instruction do not bring strength and win-wins, although they are always touted as being able to. The dodged reality is that only those who "find their strength in the Lord of Hosts, their God," win.

PRAYER: *Savior of the world, lest we forget. Keep this lesson before us, constantly. With gratitude we pray. Amen.*

HE LEADETH ME, O BLESSED THOUGHT

Zech. 12:8 *On that day the Lord will shield the inhabitants of Jerusalem; on that day the weakest of them will be like David, and the line of David godlike, like the angel of the Lord going before them.*

"On that day," used twice for emphasis in succeeding lines of the text, is a day chosen by the Creator and known only to Him, to which all of His created beings move. And as at the primal creation, chaos gave way to order; so the present chaotic situation that looks as if it will have the final word will in the end, again, become the fertilizer from which comes the beauty of eternal orderliness.

However, on the way to "that day," the chaos that engulfs God's chosen city will be deflected by the Lord's protective shield. No description is given as to what kind of safety device(s) would be used, denoting the need of the people to put their trust in the Lord. "Vengeance is mine, I will repay," says the divine Guardian.

With such reassurance, the morale of Jerusalem's inhabitants would no longer resemble those Israelite "warriors" who were terrified of Goliath's rawboned challenge. Rather, the most timid of them would be infused with a David-like winning spirit. "The Lord will deliver you into my hands." That's the "rage" in courage.

More than being like David the shepherd boy, these God-protected people would have a bloodline that would culminate in one who was godlike—a prophecy that the New Testament writers saw fulfilled in Jesus Christ, the "Son of David." It is one of twelve references to Messiah in the Book of Zechariah.

Finally, there is the angelic figure in whom is the explanation of all that has gone before. What more protective shield would God's people need than was given to the angel by the divine commander? The heavenly messenger would carry out the Commander's every order. The angel would infuse the weakest, most scared folk with lionheartedness, and check on their genealogy so that it flowed in the direction of godlikeness. Also, like the good shepherd, the angel would lead—into the paths of righteousness, through the valley of the shadow, seeing that goodness and mercy bring up the rear, that none stray or are stolen—that all may dwell in the house of the Lord forever. From "that day" on.

PRAYER: *We cannot slip out of Your arms, Lord. Tighten Your grip on us, now and ever. Amen.*

WHOLE HOLINESS

Zech. 14:21 *Every pot in Jerusalem and Judah will be holy to the Lord of Hosts, and all who come to sacrifice will use them for boiling the flesh of the sacrifice.*

When that time comes, no longer will any trader be seen in the house of the Lord of Hosts.

In today's text is found not only Zechariah's final statement regarding Jerusalem, but also the last time that the Holy City is mentioned in the Old Testament. Crossing this historic divide in history, the Eternal City moves from B.C. to A.D. But not without an "Eden at Last" touch.

Ancients, the world over, are known for their pottery. There was an abundance of it. Archaeological digs turn up pottery, if nothing else. Potters were everywhere to replace the clay things of society. And now for Jeremiah to use the words "every pot" means "everything, everywhere would be holy to the Lord." That is paradise regained when the seemingly impossible will be realized, namely that no trader will desecrate the Lord's Temple by trafficking in it.

Knowing Zechariah's word on this matter, and observing the return of this parasitical problem in His own time, Jesus cleansed the Temple at both the beginning and end of His ministry. Since then the great Reformers have felt duty bound to follow Jesus' example. For despite Zechariah's prophecy, the defamation of the Lord's house makes a comeback in every age.

Nevertheless, "When that time comes," the Lord's appointed time, the prophecy will be fully realized. Meanwhile, everyone in Zechariahs' succession will strive to drive out the spirit of buying and selling and money lending from the house of worship, making it a house of prayer for all nations. That will hasten the kingdom's coming on earth, as it is in heaven, when not just the pots will be holy—but when every knee shall bow and every tongue confess that Jesus Christ is Lord.

Watch that trader, he can so quickly infect God's people with a spirit of secularism and rot their guts. Yet, "The Lord is in His holy temple..." He will drive out the demons.

PRAYER: *Make us to be house cleaners in Thy church, O God. Now and ever. Amen.*

A TREASURED ENDING—OR BEGINNING

Mal. 3:1 *Look, I am sending my messenger.*

Malachi is bringing the Old Testament to a close in the way it was designed to be.

It didn't look like a preconceived, well-ordered script at first. It was interesting to learn how our religious forefathers described in understandable terms how our habitable world was put together. Then, as artists do, there was a rubbing out of errors and a starting again, as in Noah's flood. With the introduction of Abraham, Moses, and the Exodus, we could detect a hazy outline of mission moving toward a desired objective. David and Solomon, Ruth and Esther—Prophets, both major and minor, always a war somewhere—gave indication that all of humanity was involved in formulating a way of life that had been meant for the Garden of Eden, but foiled.

To those who were insightful, the blurry outline of the Master Artist became apparent. The more those who lived through these times and the more they recorded the happenings and experiences, and the more these annals were carefully brought into one binding, the more they were heard to sing in unison of One who alone could save humanity from its own inherent faults. Beginning with the Book of Genesis and ending with Malachi, thirty-four out of the thirty-nine books of the Old Testament, in 93 passages, tell of the coming of God's Messenger.

It is unfortunate that many commentators have fumbled all over the landscape in their endeavor to identify this Messenger. Some have stated in their scholarly superiority that it is impossible to make an honest identification. Others were too easily tripped up by the Hebrew meaning of the name Malachi, which is, "my messenger." So their conclusion is that Malachi is this Messenger of the ages that God is about to send.

Others have thought God, Himself, to be the Messenger, or some angelic being, or another prophet, or a priestly figure, or Ezra, or someone now on the scene, like John the Baptist. All these commentators are like the two men on the road to Emmaus on that first Easter evening. They never did recognize Jesus, until after He disappeared.

No, all of scripture, and in particular here in Malachi, God has no one else who is wholly fitted to save the world but Jesus. How right on cue is Malachi. He here uses the words "Suddenly," and that the Messenger "is here, here already." How right he was, for all you have to do is to turn the page, and there He is in Matt. 1:21: "You shall call His name Jesus, for He shall save His people from their sins." Right on the button!

And if the writers of the Old Testament, coming from different backgrounds and different countries, and separated, sometime, by thousands of years, could unknowingly yet under the artistic guidance and skill of the Creator put together the Figure of Jesus Christ, that, in itself, is an impressive miracle worthy of total acceptance. Add to that the Life of Christ, and His sacrifice for us of all the ages, His nearness to us in Spirit, and His promise to be with us forever. It is well with my soul.

PRAYER: *Heavenly Father: You saw our need and gave us all we needed—Jesus. Amen.*

BORN TO SET US FREE

Matt. 2:1 *Jesus was born in Bethlehem in Judaea during the reign of Herod. After his birth astrologers from the east arrived in Jerusalem.*

Local Bethlehemite traditions and universally approved historians have factualized the birth of Jesus. Most births are documented and remembered, as noted on most tombstones, by date and location. But, see how, with Jesus, His arrival is immediately buttressed by facts. Astrologers, always respected for their knowledge and wisdom, aroused the interest of the capital city's intelligentsia. That brain trust, in turn, alerted the palace. What the heavens were retelling the Wise Men unnerved the King and "the whole of Jerusalem." (v. 3) Now everyone was in the act, not just Jesus' parents, and the shepherds who kept watch over their flocks by night, or the angels who informed them of what had just occurred in a manger. Heaven and earth were full of the tidings. It was an unforgettable event. Yet, strangely, not a single reference is made to it for the rest of Jesus' life.

If anyone else had had such an auspicious beginning it would have been capitalized on, as with the Dionne Quintuplets. They were heralded the world over for nothing but being part of an unusually large multiple birthing. In Jesus' case, He was the fulfillment of prophecies of His coming, which are found in almost every book of the Old Testament. Yet though He was factualized at birth, marginalized in life, and scandalized in death—"it was our afflictions he was bearing, our pain he endured, while we thought of him as smitten by God, struck down by disease and misery. But he was pierced for our transgressions, crushed for our iniquities; the chastisement he bore restored us to health, and by his wounds we are healed." (Isa. 53:4-5)

"Bethlehem" means "house of bread." There, too, was the well which David longed to drink from. (2 Sam. 23:14) In Christ both are available—the bread and water of life. That, too, is a fact. Come, eat, drink, and live.

PRAYER: *Fill our cup, Lord. Feed us till we want no more. Amen.*

BLESSINGS IN UNEXPECTED PLACES

Matt. 4:5 *The devil then took Him to the Holy City and set Him on the parapet of the temple.*

This is the second of the three temptations which Jesus wrestled with in the wilderness called "the most sacred of all stories." It is reported by Matthew and Luke.

The original manuscripts do not use the word "tempted" with the meaning we give it today. It was more a time of "testing" for Jesus. Could He pass the stress tests to prove His Messiahship? Another correction is that here the devil is personified. Martin Luther should have known better than to throw this ink bottle at what he claimed was the devil. He had more likely made a glaring mistake on his manuscript, and in a fit of irritation, blamed the ink—as a golfer might crack his club over his knee in disgust at missing an easy shot. Besides, Jesus and Luther both knew that there's a good Dr. Jekyll and an evil Mr. Hyde within all of us, and they battle it out daily, as in this scripture. We know the experience, and here Jesus shows how we can be the victor as He was. The first test had to do with bodily hunger. (v. 3) Could Jesus withstand the agony of a 40-day fast without crumbling spiritually? Esau caved in after one day of hunting in the woods. He gave up his valued birthright for a bowl of soup.

The second test took Jesus from a local, personal situation to a public one. And where were the most people to be found but in the capital city of Jerusalem. From His visits to Jerusalem it is evident that Jesus was impressed by the person who mounted the pinnacle (parapet) of the Temple each morning at sunrise to call the city to prayer. What a precarious perch that was, and how exposed to public view. To jump from that 450-foot perch into the Kedron Valley—without committing suicide would surely be proof positive of Jesus' Messiahship. Didn't Psalm 91 promise that angels would snatch Him up before He reached the rocks below? Nothing to it. The third test moved from local to city to the world. He could claim the world as His oyster, impearled!

Looking back one sees that the second test gathered into itself the experiences of the other two. It was Central. In a city you can also starve. In a city like Jerusalem, the nations of the world were represented, certainly among the pilgrims, on festive occasions. Then to jump from the Temple's pinnacle in full view of a multitude of international pilgrims, without being hurt would get the message of His invincible Messiahship out to the uttermost parts in a flash. What a priceless opportunity to become the World's Ruler, at the drop of a...Tested at all points, as we are—physically, mentally, spiritually—Jesus shows us in this triangular experience how it is possible to reach extremities in body, mind, spirit, without crashing. His weapon of choice in each case was the sword of the Spirit, which is the Word of God. Being conversant with the scripture, Jesus struck down each devilish proposal with Deut. 8:3; 6:16; 6:13. The inner impulse, even if it had horns and a tail, feeling the point of each counter thrust, vanished. Greater things than these can we do, the Lord promised, with His help. Our inclination toward evil, when looked at not as an inducement to do wrong but as a challenge to be more than conquerors for the right, can be a blessing—hidden in full view.

PRAYER: *Divine Pathfinder, for Your pioneering the way to success through stress, we bow before You in grateful adoration. Amen.*

LORD OF ALL

Matt. 4:25 *Large crowds followed him, from Galilee, and the Decapolis, from Jerusalem and Judaea, and from Transjordan.*

When Jesus said "Come unto me," they came from north, south, east and, in time, across the sea from the west. They came to Him because He first went to them. That was His approach in fishing for humans. Neither fish nor humans will come to you, unless there is a lure (or allure). And He is the attraction: "If I be lifted up, I will draw all persons unto me." All these strategies entered into His conclusive commission to go into all the world and make disciples of all nations, knowing that thereby, in time, every knee will bow and every tongue will confess that Jesus Christ is Lord.

There is "much in little" in this seemingly bland text. Note the "large" crowds. Nothing exceeds like success. Word-of-mouth being the main form of mass communication at the time, and the most effective form of communication in every age, indicates that Jesus' ministry had spread like a forest fire touching households up and down the land—from northern Galilee to southern Jerusalem. That expanse goes beyond mere numbers to encompass cultural differences. Galileans, with their strange guttural brogue were looked down upon and laughed at by the self-appointed elite of Jerusalem. There was the contrast between the more agrarian and fisher folk. Then there were the Greek-speaking people of the ten cities of the Decapolis area of Palestine. Entranced by the Stranger of Galilee, these foreigners took His teachings back to their homeland to make Him no stranger to Greece. As for persons from beyond the Jordan, Arabs moving west from desert lands, with another kind of complexion, clothing, speech, religion—they made the melting pot even more universal—in short, making the two-line text the shape of things to come: every knee, every tongue. Here we have in microcosm a Christ of the Cosmos.

PRAYER: *Lord of all being, in Your Kingdom, no person is left behind. We are Yours, and You are ours. Amen and Amen.*

WHERE ACTIONS NEED TO SPEAK LOUDER

Matt. 5:35 *Nor by the earth, for it is his footstool, nor by Jerusalem, for it is the city of the great King.*

"I swear on a stack of Bibles," or "On my God" are oaths whose early equivalents are found in these lines from Jesus' sermon on the mount. In verses 34-36 there are four such emphatic statements usually made for the purpose of canonizing one's intention. But Jesus believed that such passionate preludes were not only unnecessary, but also were, in fact, a cover-up for insincerity. As one may say, "to be very honest with you," only to camouflage a basic dishonesty.

Demolishing the popular expressions one by one, the Lord sermonized that, first, swearing "by heaven" was blaspheming. Divinity's throne is Central Command for the Universe, not to be used as a convenient expression which is supposed to put the stamp of unquestioned acceptance upon a questionable deal. Nor, second, is swearing "by the earth" permissible. It is God's footstool. That piece of furniture provides as much necessary support as a throne does. In throne rooms the presence of the footstool is a given, therefore it, too, is not for common, loose use. Jerusalem, being no throne room, one might have thought, would be well respected enough to swear by and make it stick. Yet, third, Jesus makes even this a no-no, because "it is the city of the great King." Jerusalem is no ordinary city, as its long God-guided history has already shown. It's God's chosen, a holy city, and must not be denigrated by paltry usage.

Alright then, can't I at least swear by my own head? That is, I will take full responsibility for the consequences of this oath. "Not so," responds Jesus for a fourth time, "since you cannot turn one hair of it white or black." It belongs to the Creator.

Instead of resorting to unlicensed aids, Jesus' final word is: just speak the truth, live rightly. That needs no enhancement. In fact, any added word could open a can of worms—"Not everyone who says 'Lord, Lord' shall enter the Kingdom of heaven, but he who does the will of my Father who is in heaven."

PRAYER: *Help us, Lord, to show what we believe—in deed and in truth. Muffle us when we are prone to speak words that are not proven by what we are. Amen.*

HOLD THE GARNISH

Matt. 15:1 *Then Jesus was approached by a group of Pharisees and scribes from Jerusalem, with the question...*

Though this question triggered a discussion about one of the cherished traditions of Judaism, and although it led to further teaching of crowds of people and of the disciples by Jesus, it was Jerusalem's influence that configured the occasion.

Those who approached Jesus, at the time in Galilee, were from the religious elite establishment of the capital city. That they had taken time off from their duties to make the better part of a week's roundtrip journey from Jerusalem speaks of the critical nature of their assignment. This was no ordinary question. It went to the heart of a centuries-old belief that affected the well-being of persons throughout the Hebrew faith. And, if it were being given a spin, as it was reported that Jesus and His followers were doing, the religious hierarchy in Jerusalem demanded to know why. To allow the blasphemy to continue could only lead to widespread corruption.

Nobody in Galilee, or for that matter, anywhere else, was raising objections about this seemingly petty proposal of washing or not washing hands before eating. But to the lawmakers and monitors at the nation's hub it was crucial. That characterized them. It exposed their devotion to outward forms unmatched by inward graces, words unbacked by deeds, wolves in sheep's clothing, whited sepulchers. And Jesus called them on the carpet for it, here calling revered Isaiah to His defense: "Because this people worship me with empty words and pay me lip-service while their hearts are far from me, and their religion is but a human precept, learned by rote, therefore I shall shock this people yet again adding shock to shock: the wisdom of their wise men will vanish and the discernment of the discerning will be lost." (Isa. 29:13-14, condensed in Matt. 15:8-9)

The more Jesus collided with these Uncle Shams, the more He portrayed them as hypocrites (15:7), and the more determined were they to get Him out of the way. Therein lies the true unveiled meaning of clean and unclean—and its consequences.

PRAYER: *Drop the scales from our eyes, dear Lord, that we may behold the truth as it is in Thee. Amen.*

EVEN BEYOND FOREVER

Matt. 16:21 *From that time Jesus began to make it clear to his disciples that he had to go to Jerusalem and endure great suffering at the hands of the elders, chief priests, and scribes, to be put to death, and to be raised again on the third day.*

In the first of seven statements made in this first of three predictions of Jesus' passion, we find our Lord concentrating His remaining time and effort on His passiontide and its undertow. Tides, though powerful movers and shakers, are not generally understood, and can be a life-endangerment. Some disciples, familiar with the sea, would better understand tides than their buddies who didn't know port from starboard. Likewise, the turbulence of Jesus' passion, He judged, needed explaining.

So He began to make it clear, knowing that because of the disciples' unbelief and denial of the reality of His Messiahship—they saw through a glass darkly and through a materialism murkily—"he had to go to Jerusalem."

Why such compunction? Obviously He could see that in at least ninety-three sections of the Old Testament there was a transparently recognizable formation of a Messiah Figure. Identifying with that Figure, Jesus' shared this incarnation with His townsfolk in a Nazareth synagogue. Quoting Isa. 61:1-2, He added, "Today...in your hearing this text has come true." (Luke 4:21) He had to take the tide at its flood. Hence the compulsion to go to Jerusalem—city of destiny.

Disregarding the fact that He had offended the Pharisees (from Jerusalem), thereby making that city a veritable minefield for Him. Jesus nevertheless chose to endure great suffering. That has drawn and bound humans to Him. His endurance is endearing.

Suffering came "at the hands of" not only those who recently approached Him in Galilee. Now the chief priests, who probably were the instigators of the Matt. 15:1ff incident, came out of the closet with fury.

The whole hunting hierarchy was bent on tracking down their quarry, that He might be "put to death."

Yet, what a joyfully unexpected finish there is to a perilous prediction: "to be raised again." Death is not the last word—for Him or us.

PRAYER: *Easter Master, thank You for making hope spring eternal. Amen.*

GETTING TO KNOW HIM

Matt. 21:10 *When he entered Jerusalem the whole city went wild with excitement. 'Who is this?' people asked.*

One must be fair; there was already excitement before Jesus entered the city. After all, the people, from far and near, were celebrating their most enduring and joyful religious festival, Passover. They recalled how it began—with their release from the land of bondage, and its ongoing promise of being protected by a divine Savior.

And, yes, Jesus' entry has been rightly called Triumphal, not alone because it added voltage to the prevailing arousal of emotions, but also because He was fulfilling, the script outlined by the prophet Zechariah (9:9) 500 years before. Seeing the well-known prophecy coming to life before them, the populace was shaken to the core.

Then, naturally, came the question, not *what* is causing this intense expectancy but *who*?

Locals would have known the answer. As we've noted, the people of the land had been following Jesus in multitudes. They had heard His teaching and preaching; had witnessed His healing miracles. It was more likely the foreigners, those of the dispersion who inflated the city's population from a few thousand to two and a half million at festival time. They wanted to know for whom the hosannas were being shouted.

What answer did they get? That He had been typified in one-word cameos such as the Good Shepherd or Physician or the stone which the builders rejected, or the bread of life, the light of the world, the truth, the vine, the door—to mention a few. So many descriptions of Jesus—hundreds of them can be confusing—that one may never come to know precisely who He is. Knowing this, Jesus personalized the question. "Who do you say I am?" (Matt. 16:15) It is only when we know Him intimately that we can give the correct answer as Peter did. "You are the Messiah, the Son of the living God." (Matt. 16:16)

PRAYER: *Come into our hearts, Lord Jesus, Without Thee, none of our answers come out right. Amen.*

THIS IS MY FATHER'S HOUSE...NE'ER FORGET

Matt. 21:13 *My house shall be called a house of prayer, but you are making it a bandits' cave!*

Verses 12 and 13 in this chapter will forever stand guard over the Hebrew-Christian place of worship, in all nations. And the verses don't wait for some noted Reformer to put the scriptural word into deed. Rather, they continually press their demand upon every worshipper to help keep the place of worship spiritually clean.

The air quality will be judged by prayer quality. Are worshippers in sync with the Lord's prayer? Do they acknowledge the heavenly Father and hallow His name? Are they bringing His Kingdom on earth by doing His will? Accepting daily sustenance at God's hands, do suppliants ask divine forgiveness, as they in turn forgive? Believing that outer defilements vanish when the evil within is vanquished, do God's people look to Him to create within them clean hearts? What fanner bees are to the hive, prayer can be in our lives. Fanner bees congregate on one side of the hive and fan their wings desperately. This draws in the fresh air, and expels the bad.

Without such prayer quality, on the authority of Isaiah (56:7) with a side reference to Jeremiah (7:11), Jesus warns that the resulting condition will resemble a bandit's cave. With that refuge from justice Jesus was well acquainted, which occasioned his parable of the Good Samaritan. On the seventeen-mile highway from Jerusalem to Jericho, travelers descended from 3,000 feet to 850 feet below sea level. In summer laboring upward, foot-weary journeymen needed the coolish comfort of caves. And the highway robbers exploited those rest stops—attacking from the deep recesses of the hideout.

Such a situation prevailed in the Jerusalem Temple. Sellers of items for Temple sacrifices plundered the purses of buyers, within the comfort zone of worship. Cavernous banditry! Counteracting, Jesus welcomed needy folks, the blind and crippled, and He healed them there (verse 4). That cleared the air for prayer.

PRAYER: *God of all the nations, help us to keep Thy Temple/Church unspotted from the world. Amen.*

THE WONDERS OF HIS LOVE

Matt. 21:15 *When the chief priests and scribes saw the wonderful things he did, and heard the boys in the temple shouting, "Hosanna to the Son of David!" they were indignant.*

Had these of the priestly class seen the even more wonderful things Jesus had done, they would have been overwrought with bewilderment. As it was, the few brief clips they did see made them vehemently vitriolic.

For one thing, they saw Him cleanse the Jerusalem temple—a big job in a short time. Annas the high priest had vested interests in the commercial trafficking within the temple precincts. Lesser priests, though not in favor of such a desecration of the sacred, dared not interfere. But when Jesus vigorously evacuated the evil doers, some Rabbis must have, under their breaths, expressed gratitude for Jesus' intervention.

Restoring the temple area to its God-appointed use, Jesus then welcomed the blind. They didn't seek out the priests. The blind, as they still do in oriental lands, lingered around places of worship—near the money boxes. There they hoped to be recipients of at least the small change. But in Jesus they recognized (and/or heard) One who gave more than money. He gave life to the deceased. He gave sight to the blind. He gave the deaf their hearing. He gave the lame leg power. And the authorities witnessed it.

Then, seeing how the disabled were being saved from an astonishing assortment of maladies, some youngsters got in the action. "Save us," "Now" they hollered. Children have always wanted everything pronto. And if they are not obliged immediately, they shout louder, as these did.

If that didn't get Jesus' attention, the chief priests and scribes took heed. Why not? The list of "wonderful things" Jesus did was getting longer by the minute. It was reflecting badly on the religious leaders. They were the ones who were supposed to be doing "wonderful things." And they were not.

They were highly insulted at the impudence of Jesus. By what authority was He doing these things, they demanded to know. Emotions broiled, and the way to Jesus' cross was marked "One Way."

A servant is not greater than his Lord. Yet, glory be, the servant is duly rewarded by the Lord with an overflowing cup of joy. It is still happening—from Jerusalem to Java, Jiddah and Jubbulpore.

PRAYER: *Wonder-working Lord, work wonders through us, that others, seeing our good works may glorify our Father who is in heaven. Amen.*

THE AUTHOR IN OUR AUTHORITY

Matt. 21:23 *So they answered, "We do not know," and Jesus said: "Then I will not tell you either by what authority I act."*

It was not that Jesus was dodging the question about the source of His authority to perform these "wonderful things." (Matt. 21:15) It was that He saw through the questioners' masked sincerity to their real intention—namely, to ensnare Jesus in a legal trap. In foiling what could have been fatal, Jesus countered with a question about John the Baptist's baptism. Consulting one another as to what would be the winning answer, and concluding that they were hoist on their own petard, the questioners conceded defeat. So Jesus, according to the agreement, never did explain to whom, or to what authority, He turned for His workaday instructions. Yet that was far too important a matter to be callously flicked off His sleeve.

To eyes that sincerely wanted an answer, it was clearly visible in the Master's life and teaching.

Was, then, His authority the fellowship of believers (the Church)? To be sure, Jesus thought highly of the church, saying, "On this rock I will build my church, and the powers of death shall never conquer it." (Matt. 16:18) Later, Paul wrote: "Christ loved the church and gave himself up for it." (Eph. 5:25) Yet Jesus also declared: "There is something greater than the temple here." (Matt. 12:6)

Then was that greater authority the Bible. In the wilderness of temptation and indeed throughout His ministry, He used to great advantage the sword of the Spirit which is the word of God. Yet here again He pointed to a higher authority than scripture, repeatedly emphasizing: "You have heard it said, but I say unto you." (Matt. 5)

Noting how Jesus stands out over the church, and the scripture, we must conclude that it is the Spirit of God working in Him that is His, and our supreme authority for all matters in day-to-day living. We must turn to that Spirit for instructions. Sometimes the Spirit will speak to us through the church, or through the scripture, or through the Law or through friends...We cannot choose the channel through which He guides. Our main job is to stay close to Him who promised: "Lo, I am with you always." And maneuver us through the days of our years He will. We can count on that.

PRAYER: *Guide us, O thou Great Jehovah, pilgrims in this barren land. Through Jesus Christ our Lord. Amen.*

THE RIGHT OF WAY

Matt. 21:32 *For when John came to show you the right way to live, you did not believe him but the tax-collectors and prostitutes did; and even when you had seen that, you did not change your minds and believe him.*

Too long have we thought of Jesus' cleansing of the Temple as being complete when the money-changers and other such defilers were chased out at the end of a whip. But that was only an outer cleansing, like dust and cobwebs. Now came the more difficult inner cleansing, that probing for hidden destroyers, the spiritual termites that can eat away the very foundations of one's life. And there, in the Temple, among the religions leaders who were considered the pillars and undergirding of the Lord's house, there Jesus uncovered a rotting situation.

For one thing, the Temple elite, who should have been setting a shining example of righteousness—were not. They had been eaten away by a decaying faith. So putrid had they become, that even those who were considered social pariahs—the tax-collectors and prostitutes—were more acceptable in God's sight. The last came in first, and the first last.

But hold it! Don't Jesus' words "and even when you had seen that" indicate that the first were still granted the time to redress their wrongs and finish first? Losing that opportunity to overtake their spiritually sluggish competitors, the spiritual "leaders" proved to posterity their true worthlessness in the work of the Lord and His Temple/Church.

How deftly Jesus brought to life His current parable of the Two Sons. (Matt. 21:28-31) But the chief priests and elders didn't even make that connection with themselves. So accustomed had they become to believing that they were the Lord's special operational forces, that the pride of it blinded them to the fact that they represented the son who said to the Father, "I will do the job," but didn't lift a finger. And, never of a mind to say "I will not" to the Father, these persons couldn't conceive of such a negative response being applauded. But Jesus cornered them into applauding, and then turned the knife in the wound by telling them exactly who they were cheering—tax-collectors and harlots.

How right was Sir Walter Scott: "O what a tangled web we weave, when first we practice to deceive." The cobwebs are the outer sign of the need for more intensive cleaning.

PRAYER: *Lord, heal me at the heart that my mind, too, may be wholly clean. Amen.*

LET'S GET GROWING

Matt. 21:33 *There was a landowner who planted a vineyard: he put a wall round it, hewed out a wine-press, and built a watchtower; then he let it out to vine-growers and went abroad.*

What more could a landowner, in Jerusalem, or anywhere else have done for prospective renters? He surveyed the available properties, made his choice, went through the legalities of purchasing, hiring workman, bringing seeds and gardening equipment, and saw the first sproutings of a vineyard. Aware that he had an appointment abroad, the owner installed a winepress to enable the property to profit from the sale of both fruit and juice. Then, to ensure the security of the whole operation, a watchtower for surveillance was built on the grounds, and the entire acreage surrounded by a substantial wall. Indeed, here was a landowner who was not only a caretaker but also a caregiver. All he wanted in return was "the produce due to him." (Matt. 21:34)

And that is all our loving heavenly Father asks of us His renters on earth. Instead, as with the renters in the above parable, we harry those servants of the Lord who come to collect His dues. We thrash and stone and kill them. Even when the Son of Earth's Creator and Owner comes, we still give Him a rough time. Yes, we Christians. Yes, even so-called Christian bishops and elders and theologians and all those who belong in what has aptly been termed a Christless Churchianity. We want to get Christ out of the way because He comes to collect the fruits of the spirit and all we have to offer Him is the forbidden fruit on which we have already gorged. The love, peace, joy and all the rest of the fruits He was expecting were too difficult to produce. They called for careful nurturing and pruning and protection from thieves in the night, and we were not committed enough to the Master's cause to do His will. So instead of re-applying our energy with diligence, it was easier to slay the Savior. Oh that we may take heed and belong to "a nation that yields the proper fruit." (Matt. 21:43)

PRAYER: *Lord of the harvest, we would be worthy laborers in Thy Kingdom. Now and forever. Amen.*

THE REWARDED REMNANT

Matt. 22:14 *Many are invited, but few are chosen.*

In the same way as when many are cold, but few are frozen, the difference lies in the inner bodily conditions. Some persons are more acclimated to the cold and can endure, without harm, arctic temperatures. Other persons having partaken of intoxicants or drugs are susceptible to hypothermia at higher temperatures.

In war times, when a country needs militia, there is a general call-up for conscription, a draft. All men (and perhaps women) of a certain age must report at local centers. Yet, after each person is examined, not all are drafted. In fact in some places, our text for today becomes literally a reality. Only the chosen few are deemed fit for service, the kind of service that is foreseen by the Commander in Chief.

The idea is seen originally in Isa. 10:22: "Israel, your people may be many as the sand of the sea, but only a remnant will return."

The "critical mass" then is not so much the invitation. Where God is concerned, the invitation to come to Him has always been wide open, as wide as the arms of Calvary's cross. It's a "come all" welcome, with no exclusions. Even persons loafing the byways. No, the universal dateline which causes the great divide between the many and the few, the great unwashed and those finally accepted and selected—is at the point of personal responsibility. Do we want to be just part of the crowd, or part of the inner beltway where the action is? And if it's the latter, the remnant, what does it take to get there? Is it not that those who get the final nod of approval are those who have diligently prepared for the position and are already living and working as if they had arrived at their hearts desire? Those are the wise ones, with lamps trimmed and burning brightly; with an extra supply of fuel, ready to enter the banqueting hall the moment the doors open. Or, uniformed, trained, and "At your command, Sir."

Persons who have first chosen for themselves

to be the Master's Own are those who are most pickable by Him. He takes it from there, honing them into the kind of servicemen and women He needs in His Holy City and throughout the world.

PRAYER: *King of our lives, grant that we may be Thy choice coworkers, both now and ever. Amen.*

TRYING TO FOOL JESUS

Matt. 22:18 *Jesus was aware of their malicious intention and said, "You hypocrites! Why are you trying to catch me out?"*

Well versed in the ways of men, Jesus could discern from the tone of His accusers' voices, from telltale facial expressions, from fidgety hands, from an almost imperceptible wink, that they were setting Him up, positioning Him for a pratfall. He could almost hear the mocking laughter and hoots that would follow. So He made the pre-emptive bluff call: "You hypocrites!"

How right He was. The opening remarks of these crafty Jerusalemites sounded to Jesus too saccharin to be sincere. (v. 16-17) Then came their questions, loaded with explosives—should or shouldn't they pay federal taxes? Either way, they had stealthily calculated, Jesus would trip the trap for Himself. A "Yes" would have enraged the populace. Who, in any age, has wanted to pay taxes? "No, they shouldn't," would have brought government regulators screaming for Jesus' imprisonment.

Deftly the master turned a potential insurgent's bombshell into an unforgettable teaching tool. "Pay to Caesar what belongs to Caesar," Jesus calmly advised, agreeably, since the coins used to pay taxes were stamped with Caesar's image and literally belonged to him. That defused an explosive issue among Jews.

Foiled and wanting to slink away with egg on their faces, the accusers were, in a trice, put on the defensive. The ball was in their court. Why were they trying to catch Him out, Jesus wanted to know.

Now there's a cricketing term, and quite understandable in this New English Bible version of our text. Why did the accuser want to get rid of Jesus while at the same time making out as if they were all on the same team? Jesus asked the two-faced bounders! Then He bowled them over with a fast ball (stumps and all). Pay "to God what belongs to God." (v. 21) That took out the center of their wicket, since this was exactly what these religious leaders were not doing.

They were giving what belonged to God to the emperor. It was easier. All that Caesar asked for was a pinch of incense thrown on an altar fire, once a year, while the worshipper said, "Caesar is Lord." And the tax money that should have gone to Caesar, people wanted to keep for themselves.

The Lord always nabs offenders, whether they are going or coming. No wonder they are "taken aback," and leave Him alone. (v. 22)

PRAYER: *Lord, You know the tricks of our trade. Straighten us out. We thank You. Amen.*

ON BEING BIBLE BASED

Matt. 22:29 *Jesus answered: "How far you are from the truth! You know neither the scriptures nor the power of God..."*

That was a tough call—that one about a woman successively marrying seven brothers. (Matt.

22:23-28) Whose wife will she be in the resurrection? The question still comes up in cases of multiple marriages, even when no brothers are involved. Whose wife will belong to whom in eternity? Those who have had satisfyingly lengthy marriages can't think of heaven without the partner they had on earth. Others, for diverse, or divorce reasons, favor a change in the afterlife. Who on earth has the authoritative answer? Well, some of those tricky, sticky religious elders thought they would see how bright Jesus was by confronting Him with this conundrum.

As at other times, Jesus showed not that He had all the answers but that anyone could have God's word on the subject from out of the scriptures (which these questioners did not know). Therefore, first, they were far from the truth.

First, when one throws aside a Standard Reference book to what or to whom does one turn for standards? For truth? If each person has a different Standard Reference book, imagine what babbling chaos would result. It would be a rebuilding of the Tower of Babel in Babel—on and on. Doing what is right in one's own eyes or in the eyes of some pundit, one is still far from the truth. How come? Because God's word is truth. That word became flesh and dwelt among us full of grace and truth. And our distance from the truth is in direct proportion to our distance from (or nearness to) Christ, the truth incarnate.

Second, without the Scripture (the Word of God), one is disconnected from the power of God. Plugged in to the scripture by daily meditation and Sabbath observance, we feel the power of the Holy Spirit surging through the circuitry of our body, mind, and spirit. His word becomes a lamp to our feet, a light to our path. Without that light, which is dependent on power, we can lose our way, stumbling into danger and premature death. And this, Jesus indicated, was the plight of His questioner. Scripturally illiterate, they were strangers to truth and power—the two ingredients necessary for solving the "marriage in heaven," and other such puzzles.

PRAYER: *Help us to search the Scriptures, Lord, that in them we may find eternal life and truth and power. Amen.*

WHEN TWO BECOME FLESH

Matt. 22:36 *"Teacher, which is the greatest commandment in the law?"*

These Pharisees and Sadducees just wouldn't admit that the likes of Jesus had bettered them. Yet their hatred toward Him drove them on to try again. This time with the Law as bait. The Law was central. It was Mosaic. It was controversial— just the kind of dynamite that, with the slightest friction, could cause the demolition of Jerusalem's religious enclaves, and earn Jesus time on a cross. So the incendiary question: Which is the greatest of the Ten Commandments?

The First?—to which the Second and Third are linked? Who or what is more important than God? Or, how about "Remember the Sabbath Day," which, as one British Prime Minister believed, is "the greatest Worker's Protection Legislation in human history"? Or there's the transitional Fifth Commandment, which heads the second tablet and is written in stone. Then, from Six to Nine there are the prohibitions against humans murdering, committing adultery, stealing, bearing false witness. Or last, the finger-pointing at the individual who covets. A prickly list, indeed!

Shouldn't the laws regarding God be considered the greatest? Isn't that precisely why they are atop the Decalogue? And if this was the answer Jesus' questioners were hoping for, did it mean that He thought less of the other Commandments? And, if that's the way He rated the Commandments, wouldn't everyone else give diminishing attention to those demands at the bottom of the list?

Jesus' agile mind, computing the possible permutations and combinations of this tenfold puzzle and always wanting people to incarnate what they first fully understood—simplified the Ten Words from Sinai without tampering with "the Law and the prophets." (Matt. 5:17) Masterfully, and for the first time in history, Jesus compressed the Ten Commandments into Two.

First, a portion of the Shema (Deut. 6:5), with its ten directives on how to remember to love God. "That is the greatest, the first Commandment," (Matt. 22:38) Jesus said. Then, lest anyone thought that's where their obligations ended, the Lord added second, "Love your neighbor as yourself. Everything in the law and the prophets hang on these Two commandments." (Matt. 22:39) Neat! Through the Two, all Ten are magnified, certified, glorified.

PRAYER: *O Voice from Sinai, who spoke through Your Son Jesus in Two Words, help us to enflesh those Words in our daily living, now and ever. Amen.*

THE GODFORSAKEN CHURCH

Matt. 23:38 Look! There is your temple, forsaken by God and laid waste.

Who could have figured, even with a Global Positioning System (GPS), that Jerusalemites would ever find themselves in such a Godforsaken position? Their city was at the crossroads of the world. Their temple was second to none. Their potential was such that it could have maxed out the rest of the best of mankind. Had they followed divine instructions, the future was assuredly putty in their palms. But they blew it, as Samson did. He, too, did not even realize that the Lord had forsaken him. Is there anything more lamentable?

But there were justifiable reasons for it. You can understand one man's sex drive. (Judg. 17:20) But the Jerusalem populace? And in at least fourteen God-forsaking ways?

People had followed the self-defeating example of their religious leaders—the Scribes and Pharisees, who, for one thing, interpreted the Mosaic Law (the Ten Commandments) to suit themselves: "Say one thing and do another." (Matt. 23:3) Two, they were not about to get their shoulders under a fellow human's load. (v. 4) Three, all they did was with one eye on the publicist's camera, as it were. (v. 5) Four, they misjudged where true authority resided. (v. 8-10) Five, they proudly preened themselves. (v. 12) Six, blindly following inept leaders, people were spreading the germ of waywardness, making others twice as fit for hell as they were themselves. (v. 15) Seven, there was more desire for material wealth than for the spiritual. (v. 16-21) Eight, there was a blaspheming of God. (v. 22) Nine, there was a majoring in minors. Values were reversed. The picayune was given precedence over the pre-eminent. (v. 23-24) Ten, externals to be seen of men were valued more than internals which mean more to God. (v. 25-26) Eleven, there was an outward appearance of aliveness which was really a hoax. Inwardly, the resemblance was to that of a tomb. (v. 27-28) Twelve, an abolition of the best of the past (v. 32) such persons were doomed. (v. 33) Last, there was a spurning of the Christ. (v. 37) What need was there of further witnesses? Why shouldn't the Lord turn away from the Jerusalem Temple? (v. 38) A Church that has no more influence than to produce such a bag of wormy members—must be "condemned to hell." (v. 33) Thus says the Lord!

PRAYER: *Heavenly Father, the present-day Church is too frighteningly similar to the one You forsook. Send help, Father, lest we perish. Amen.*

HIS WORD FOR OUR CHURCH

Matt. 24:1-2 *Jesus left the temple and was walking away when his disciples came and pointed to the temple buildings. He answered, "Yes, look at it all. Truly I tell you: not one stone will be left upon another; they will all be thrown down."*

These men were among the last few to gaze on this Temple. Seven years after its completion, the whole thirty-five acre Temple area would be no more. It was the third and last Temple on the hallowed spot where Abraham, some 2,500 years earlier, was ordered to sacrifice his son Isaac. This Temple, erected by King Herod, equaled the grandiloquence of Solomon's famed first Temple. It was in Herod's Temple that Jesus, at the age of 12, was found in serious discussion with the doctors of the law. It was here, as we have been seeing, that the Lord did much of His end-of-ministry teaching. Which is why He could prophesy with such authority and finality—the demolition of this historic structure. Keen observer and analyst of the moral and social scene, He was well qualified to make pinpoint prophesies: this one being fulfilled by the Romans in A.D. 70.

Jesus knew His Jerusalem. Yet He considered the entire country as His parish. Covering the length and breadth of Palestine on foot gave Him the opportunity to interconnect with all sorts of people along the way. These people were not specially selected by an advance team. Questioners and answerers were not tutored in what they should say or the manner in which they should conduct themselves. They were honest-to-goodness, face-to-face, heart-to-heart confrontations. No wonder that the singles and the masses heard Him gladly. Nor did they forget Him. To be sure, the Jerusalem crowds cried for His blood. But the seed of the Word had been so widely and wisely sown across the land, that whatever the apostles did or did not ultimately do, the informed masses nurtured the Word—which flourished quickly—and the Kingdom was on its way. It was this "Early Church" to which we still refer as the gold standard for Christian Churchmanship. And the joyous thought is that the recipe has been given and, if followed, will yield similar results.

The Church constantly needs to be looked at. All of it. Not just the structure or the finances, the programs, the worship services. All of it—that mountainous problems might be brought low, and the rough relationships made plain. Otherwise history will repeat itself. Not one stone will be left upon another.

PRAYER: *Father we now know that it is not enough to point to the Church. We must take a hard, long look at it and with Your help make the corrections. Amen.*

THE BIRTH OF THE BEST

Matt. 24:8 *All these things are the first birth pangs of the new age.*

It is well to remember, as these daily devotions proceed, that everything that is said and done in these pages has been in the Jerusalem area where humans are still living out their days. These are no fairytales, no harry potters but that of which life on earth is made.

As with "all these things," (v. 8) which include false messiahs (v. 4,5, 23-26), persecution of the faithful (v. 9), a turning away from the faith (v. 10,12), the spread of lawlessness (v. 12), and desecration of the holy (v. 15).

Atop the Mount of Olives in what is now believed to have been a cave, Jesus had a private chat with His disciples. (v. 3) They questioned Him regarding His Coming Again. Outside the Epistles, this is the only place where Jesus' Second Advent is mentioned. It appears four times in this chapter 24. (v. 3,27,37,39) What signs, the disciples are anxious to know, will precede Jesus' second arrival on earth? So Jesus lists "all these things."

Yet He makes clear that "all these things" and a lot worse, do not mean the end of the world. Only God knows that zero hour. Rather, a convergence of the worst things one can imagine should not alarm us. (v. 6) For there is an excruciating pain called "birth pangs," which, astonishingly, does not signal an end-all, but a new creation, such as none other. Bud-like, spring-like, the unfolding potential defies the imagination. The Forthcomer is capable of quantum leaps and exponential growth. Jesus chose His words definitively, promising enormous gain in pain; inexplicable joy in sorrow.

So not to worry. Not to fear. The best is still ahead, though it is designed to follow the screaming agony of labor pains. They do not have the crushing terminal word. His word supersedes that, and it is one of triumphant bliss. Shouldn't we have expected it to be that way? With that assurance the Master's men went out and turned the world right side up.

PRAYER: *Through peril, toil, and pain, Lord, may Thy message of hope sustain us. Both now and ever. Amen.*

PRUDENTIAL LIVING

Matt. 25:8 *The foolish said to the prudent, "Our lamps are going out; give us some of your oil."*

In this parable, the number five plays a dominant role. How better to remember the important than by putting it on the five fingers of one hand?

There are five wise and five foolish bridesmaids, distinguished by the five who were in the right, from the five who were left out.

Then "lamps" are mentioned five times. And "oil" too, either named or referred to. And Jesus starts the story with this preface: "When the day comes, the Kingdom of Heaven will be like this." (Matt. 25:1) Like what? A blissful, nuptial-like union is anticipated. But because of the dark time on earth, and the subsequent shadowy valley of life that must be traversed, a guiding light is needed, a light that has a dependable, long-lasting source of power: in this instance, oil. That olive oil, be it remembered, was not just for lamps but also for healing (as when the Good Samaritan poured oil into the wounds of the stricken wayfarer), and for cooking.

It then becomes a question of not *what* is such a

source of light and healing and bodily sustenance, but *whom*? Nobody but Christ qualifies. He is the light of the world, the soothing Savior, the bread of life. So the choice is up to us. Will we choose the right way or be left out "when the day (of final reckoning) comes"? Nor should we wait to make the choice at midnight. The penitent thief on Calvary's cross just slipped in under the radar, but only because of Jesus' timely intervention. The Master stressed the timeliness of the Now. "Now is the acceptable time. This is the day of salvation." This way we have a longer time with our divine Companion, in Spirit, making it easier to recognize Him when He does appear again in the New Jerusalem. In this way there will be no surprises, no deathbed confessions, which a fatal accident will puff out in a sec. One can fully enjoy the final union with the Lord Jesus Christ, now and forever. No known wedding will generate the ultimate bliss that can be expected on that Day.

PRAYER: *Thine is the Kingdom and the power, and the glory, O God. Today we make our commitment to Him, who alone can guarantee our entrance into the Kingdom. In His name we pray. Amen.*

Only Trust Him

Matt. 26:2 *"You know that in two days' time it will be Passover, when the Son of Man will be handed over to be crucified."*

After a lengthy period of teaching, all of which pointed to end-times, Jesus concluded by saying to His disciples: "You Know." They should have known a lot by then but in this case there were at least two unforgettables He knew they knew. One was the fast-approaching Passover Festival day after tomorrow. The Passover had been instituted by God at the time of Israel's exodus from the land of bondage. And because of its application to life's many imprisoning circumstances and the freedom there from, that it had become the most mentioned incident in the Bible and in Hebrew history—for 1,400 years. Second, Jesus knew that His disciples were aware of His impending death. On three different occasions He had predicted His passing. (Matt. 16:21-28; Matt. 17:22-23; Matt. 20:17-19) Here we see certified certitude on the part of the Master and His men.

By way of contrast, verse 3 of Matt. 26 opens with "Meanwhile." Against the backdrop of calm confidence in Christ, there is a clammy Caiaphas with his scheming politicos, all of Jerusalem's religious aristocracy. He thought he knew how to dodge the bullet. At a time when there had been twenty-eight high priests in thirty years, Caiaphas held that office for eighteen years. Kowtowing to the Roman occupational authorities in Palestine, Caiaphas had polished his political pandering to perfection. But such perfidious politicians are never right. Caiaphas wasn't.

Also in contrast to Jesus and His men, Caiaphas and his clique were not certain about two issues. One was how to get rid of Jesus. It was discussed at such length, but it died of old age. Their vaunted punditocracy fell on its own sword. And Jesus may have lived on if Judas had not offered to be a foil for the Caiaphas connection. "Still as of old, men by themselves are priced. For thirty pieces Judas sold himself, not Christ." Second, the schemers decided that Jesus' death "must not be during the festival (Passover). (v. 5) But it was. They were all wrong. Jesus was all right. It's always safer to take our cues from Christ. Look to Him, the Author and finisher of our faith.

PRAYER: *Heavenly Father, help us to keep our eyes on the Bethlehem star, that it may bring us to the Savior. Otherwise we lose our way. Amen.*

JESUS, I COME

Matt. 26:22 *Greatly distressed at this they asked him one by one, "Surely you do not mean me, Lord?"*

At a Passover meal, an air of remembrance and thanksgiving normally prevailed. In this setting, Jesus' last meal with His disciples, you could have cut the tension with a knife. It had been caused by the Lord's blood pressure raising accusation: "Truly I tell you: one of you will betray me." (Matt. 26:21) Only one? Yes, but which? That was the arrowhead that stuck in each man's gizzard. Could he be the one? It was an individualized question that received an individualized response.

In earlier times the answer could or would have been evaded. The Second commandment affirmed: "I, the Lord your God, am a jealous God, punishing the children for the sins of the parents to the third and fourth generation of those who reject me." (Exod. 20:5; Deut. 5:9) Any blame could have been laid at the door of a great-great-granddaddy. Eight hundred years later Jeremiah reports (31:29) that the same idea was going the rounds in another form: "Parents have eaten sour grapes and the children's teeth are set on edge." Six hundred years later, Jesus' disciples revealed that the idea, though revoked, (Jer. 31:30) was still in operation. (John 9:20) And it could have been invoked at the Last Supper. Yet our Lord kept the revocation alive. That is, blame could not, should not be shifted to another's shoulders; it must be borne personally.

To be sure, Jesus believed implicitly in the Law (the Ten Laws from Sinai). He came not to destroy the Law but to fulfill it. There are many gene traits that run in the family for generations. "Like father like son." Yet, Jesus recognized the danger of an individual absolving himself from sin because he was merely suffering the consequences of his parent's wrongdoing. Understandably, then, the exoneration of oneself is passed on to the devil, or to any other handy scapegoat. And the actual perpetrator of the crime flies free to do more dirty deeds.

By the time of the Last Supper, Jesus' lesson had been well learned. "Surely you do not mean ME, Lord." "Not my brother nor my sister but it's me, O Lord. Standing in the need of prayer." Studdert Kennedy was right on when he wrote that at the Last Judgment we shall be asked only one question: "Well, what did You make of it?"

PRAYER: *Save us, Lord, from "passing the buck." Grant us the grit to admit. Amen.*

FROM HERE TO FRATERNITY

Matt. 26:29 *I tell you, never again shall I drink from this fruit of the vine until that day when I drink it new with you in the Kingdom of my Father.*

We are noticing in these devotionals how many "helps" for life's journey have been spoken by God through His choice souls—in Jerusalem. And here is another signpost to glory, tersely described by the only begotten Son of the Father.

He, the Christ, makes five points as He approaches the closing of the Passover meal. One, "never again" denotes not only the end of the Lord's own life but also the passing of the old covenant. At the first Passover in Egypt, the Hebrews who were to exit the land were instructed to mark their doorposts with the blood of a lamb. That was God's promise (covenant) that the angel of death would pass over the blood-marked homes. Now, Jesus teaches, that old covenant would be superseded by the blood (His own) of the Lamb of God which takes away the sins of the world. Two, "When I drink it" refers to fellowship or communion with the Lord. As He explains further in Rev. 3:20: "Here I stand knocking at the door, if anyone hears my voice and opens the door, I will come in and he and I will eat together." A relaxed close relationship is indicated. Three, "new" in contrast to the old or initial covenant. But more than that, with Christ all things become new. He grants us safe arrival in the Promised Land, not in a compromised one. Nor is its capital the Holy City of Jerusalem but the Eternal City in the New Jerusalem. (Rev. 21:2) Four, "with you" is the personal "you" that we saw in the previous devotional, but it is also in the sense of "you all"—the worldwide fellowship of believers in Christ—the Church. Five, "in the kingdom of my Father." There are all kinds of Kingdoms, and, lest we choose the Kingdom we prefer, the Lord clearly defines what kinds of persons we must be if we want to enjoy His tightly knit companionship in the Kingdom of God, His heavenly Father.

So all the distress at the Last Supper; all the uncertainty and conscience-searching and sorrow were not to be the last word. Jesus keeps the best for the last—from the first miracle (changing water into wine) to the end of His time on earth. That's the joy of our hope, that momentum from in front that we can draw on, now and ever.

PRAYER: *Thank You, Father, for the five-finger posts that point us to the Prince of Peace. Amen.*

OUR GO AHEAD SAVIOR

Matt. 26:32 *But after I am raised, I shall go ahead of you into Galilee.*

Why did Jesus have to leave Jerusalem? Or, if it was a danger zone, why not go to Nazareth? There's no place like home. Or to Bethany, His headquarters for His southern ministry? Or—? Yet, as the shepherd of a scattered flock, (Matt. 26:31) He knew exactly where He wanted His followers to go—and why.

Galilee, sixty miles north of Jerusalem, had been the area of most of His ministerial action along with these same persons. Ten out of thirty-three of His miracles of healing had been performed in Galilee. There, in a natural amphitheater, He had preached His sermon on the mount. His varied forms of teaching had been received by thousands of listeners who had been drawn there from all points of the compass.

And Galilee, Jesus foresaw, would continue to be a venue for Christian activity. As, indeed, it became in A.D. 70 when Jerusalem and its Temple were destroyed by the Romans, and the Jews were expelled.

Further still, with celestial vision, Jesus saw that the final conflict would play out nowhere but in that same Galilean area—at Armageddon.

Then, in case the faithful should feel lost and leaderless in the melee, Jesus said trust Me. "There are many dwelling places in my Father's house...I am going to prepare a place for you...that where I am you may be also." (John 14:1-3) In the spirit of Galilee, which means "circle," Jesus completes His encircling plan for His faithful followers.

And they, are they to follow as mere sheep? No, since Galilee has another immemorial lesson for us. The Lake takes in water from the snows of Mount Hermon and from Springs. Then the Lake gives that water to the River Jordan to be delivered to the Dead Sea. The Lake of Galilee gets and gives and lives. The Dead Sea gets and keeps—and dies. To give is to live. To deny is to die. Persons who live with the Savior are reassured that He will go ahead of us now and forever. His resurrection power guarantees it.

PRAYER: *For Your leadership through time and eternity, we praise You, O Lord. Amen.*

STAY WITH HIM AND PRAY WITH HIM

Matt. 26:36 *Jesus then came with his disciples to a place called Gethsemane.*

Outside the Garden of Eden, Gethsemane is the best-known garden in history.

At the time of our Lord, citizens of Jerusalem were not allowed to have gardens in the city. Gardens called for manure and such fertilizers that did not belong in a holy city. However, people could own and operate gardens on the Mount of Olives adjacent to Jerusalem, on the east. There, Mary, mother of John Mark, owned this Garden of Gethsemane and Mark was keeper and perhaps the operator of the olive oil press (which oil gave its name to Gethsemane). As friends of Mary, Jesus and His disciples were given access to the Garden's solitude—which lent itself to prayer and meditation. Where else, then, would Jesus think of going when His heart was ready to break with grief (v. 37)—but to the beautiful Garden of prayer?

Three times he prayed, much the same agonized prayer, and each ending with "not my will but Yours (heavenly Father)." (v. 39,42,44)

Another triple occurrence was Jesus' earnest plea for Peter, Jame,s and John to stay awake (v. 39,40,41) with Him as He prayed.

Then the scene shifted from pray to betray—with Judas' kiss.

The Church of All Nations is built over the huge rock on which it is believed Jesus knelt to pray in Gethsemane. Symbolic thorns are much in evidence as a reminder of the heart-tearing and emotion-ripping experience that the Lord endured there. That is what prayer and self-sacrifice involve. Prayer is not an invitation to put one's mind in neutral and nod off. That is when we ought to be most awake, beseeching the Lord, wrestling with the angel as Jacob did; crying, "I will not let you go until you bless me." Little wonder that it is recorded that as Jesus prayed in Gethsemane His sweat came as drops of blood. (Luke 22:44) The effort was intense and tightly focused, calling for wide-awakeness. "Awake thou that sleepest"—especially at prayer time. That's the soul's high hour. And our Gethsemane can be anywhere.

PRAYER: *Lord, teach us to pray as You did, valiantly, in the Garden. Amen.*

HIS CENTRAL CALM

Matt. 26:51 *At that moment one of those with Jesus reached for his sword and drew it, and struck the high priest's servant, cutting off his ear.*

What was so important about this incident that moved all four gospel writers to include it in their narratives? You can see how Matthew draws heavily on Mark's account. They are starkly the same, devoid of details. Luke and John mention specifics that the other doesn't name. Yet, together, instead of opening themselves to criticism about being too diverse—all four writers make a full-dimensioned and meaningful picture.

First, the "one" with Jesus had a name. He was not just a "bystander." (Mark 14:47) It was Peter. (John 18:10) Second, Peter "reached for his sword." Yet he was not the only armed disciple. They all had swords. (Luke 22:49) Third, Peter "struck the high priest's servant." Here again was no nameless ninny. He was Malchus, endowed with high priestly power to act on behalf of his chief who couldn't be present. Issuing orders, Malchus became the center of apostolic attention. And Peter, the apostolic leader, responded with his well-known impetuosity cutting off—according to Luke 22:50, and John 18:10—Malchus' *right* ear. Why the right ear? Was it a random stroke? Or, as surgeons are very careful in amputating the offending limb and not the good one, had Peter seen Malchus cupping his right ear that he might hear better? Or, instead of beheading the offensive Malchus, did Peter mercifully decide to lop off a disposable body part? Whatever motivated Peter, Jesus saw it differently. To the Master, the human body was the Creator's design to be treated with respect. And Luke, the Physician, alone records that Jesus lost no time in healing the severed ear, one of five instances where Jesus healed by a touch. And not only that ear, but there was also a healing of other relationships—divided by a sword or anger or opinions or religious viewpoints were all brought together by our cohering Christ. "Stop," He commanded. "No more of that." (Luke 22:51) We are one in Him and by Him. He states the bottom line.

PRAYER: *End all our cuts and bruises, Lord, with Your touching ministry. Amen.*

ARMED WITH HIS WORD

Matt. 26:55 *Jesus spoke to the crowd: "Do you take me for a bandit, that you have come armed with swords and cudgels to arrest me? Day after day I sat teaching in the temple, and you did not lay hands on me."*

At the end of the day the Gethsemane narrative centers around the word "bandit." There was the "crowd" from whose overwhelming numbers no bandit could escape. They had come "armed," expecting a fight with a terroristic bandit whom they meant to "arrest" by "laying hands on" Him.

It was a well-chosen word—"bandit." For it has been confidently asserted that the Temple authorities in Jerusalem were in cahoots with the bandits of the Jericho Road. Didn't the priest and the Levite turn a deaf ear and a blind eye to the stricken wayfarer in Jesus' parable of the Good Samaritan? We've had our home-grown theories about those Temple authorities failing to lend a helping hand because they were hurrying to a lecture hall to expound on brotherly love and peace, or that they saw that the victim had been robbed already!

"Day after day" as Jesus taught in the temple, He could conceivably have learned from "classified sources" of such collusion, namely, that the priests overlooked unlawful practices on the well-traveled Jericho Road in return for a percentage of the loot.

In Gethsemane, then, Jesus said that He was not this kind of a person—either a highway bandit or a clerical collared one. And that implication was enough to put the mark of execution upon Jesus. Reading between the lines, Jesus disciples could see the obvious—that Jesus was doomed. There and then they forsook their Leader and fled. (Matt. 26:56)

Since a servant is not greater than his Lord, we may expect to be looked upon as bandits too. Indeed, in the present day, it is widely believed that the world's greatest enemy is Christianity, namely the followers of Jesus Christ. Bandits! Should we take to our heels and flee for the tall grass? Or, as Jesus did, can we disprove the charge by 1. by teaching the Word of God, 2. day after day—and not just on the Sabbath and at midweek services, 3. in the temple (a "church that is in the home"; in the Temple of the Lord which is our own body; or the center, where, as is our custom, we worship regularly). Can we do this openly, fearlessly, and with such passion as to be innocently un-arrestable? He did. We can.

PRAYER: *Heavenly Father, give us the fortitude to stand up for Jesus, now and ever. Amen.*

WOUNDED FOR ME

Matt. 27:42 *Let him come down now from the cross, and then we shall believe him.*

Jerusalem at this Passover time was abuzz with multitudes of people, but Jesus, who often ministered to such multitudes, was now alone. His disciples had distanced themselves from Him. The frenzied crowd, shark-like and smelling blood, circled Him for the kill. The Roman soldiers who knew that Jesus was at their mercy had their Abu Graib sport with Him in the barrack rooms. Passersby hissed and dissed Him. Even the bandits crucified on either side of Him were emboldened to act superior to Him, voicing their contempt for Him. Then the chief priests and elders, with acidic sarcasm, defied Jesus to come down from the cross at their instant command. Only then, they said (feebly smothering their fiendish glee) they would become, mind you, believers of His!

Lonely and pained though He was, Jesus could see through their lying teeth that these hypocrites had absolutely no intention of believing in Him.

But He could have come down from the cross. Angels could have attended to that as they could have lifted Him up had He jumped from the precipitous pinnacle of the Temple.

Yet He stayed on the cross, for one thing, because He felt destined to fulfill the prophecy concerning His death. (Zech. 13:7) How could He, at this critical moment, be untrue to the trust that His heavenly Father had put in Him?

Second, because He wanted to experience being tempted in all points (plus) like we are. He might teach and preach and heal and prove His humanity. But as the Son of God that he claimed to be, and was believed by many to be, could He in the face of subhuman humiliation die well?

And because, for the joy that was set before Him, He endured the cross, despising the shame. He has won the admiration of the ages and their obeisance. Who now wouldn't want the arm-in-arm confidence of walking with the Savior through the valley of the shadow of death? No, Lord, don't come down from the cross. Let me come up on my cross beside You. "I shall fear no evil, for Thou art with me."

PRAYER: *In the cross of Christ I glory, Towering o'er the wrecks of time. Amen.*

DEATH, BEGONE

Matt. 27:53 *And coming out of their graves after his resurrection entered the Holy City, where many saw them.*

It is at this point that myriads of people have parted company with Christ and Christianity: the resurrection of humans from the dead.

People can find pretty plausible reasons for just about anything startlingly different in the gospels—even the virgin birth. But the resurrection, oh come on, not even Houdini could pull that one off.

But Jesus was never in doubt at this point. So confident was He that death did not have the final word, that He proved it by bringing to life again—Jairus' daughter, the son of the widow of Nain, and Lazarus. "Death cannot keep his prey, Jesus, my Savior. He tore the bars away, Jesus, my Lord." (Robert Lowry) After that He unhesitatingly proclaimed: "Because I live, you too shall live." (John 14:19) And this promise we see being fulfilled in our text for today—an open-ended promise, till He comes again.

After being so sure of an afterlife, it was then Jesus' turn to real-ize it in His own life. Was He just talking off the cuff, or was it the gospel truth?

Easter morning dotted the I's and crossed the T's on the bewildering mystery of the resurrection from the dead. Jesus started the disentombment movement, which quickly grew in number—with all persons heading for the Holy City, which the

Psalmist called "God's resting place." (Ps. 132:4)

Could this not be a preview of what Jesus knew was going to happen when He said, "I go to prepare a place for you"? (John 14:3) On resurrection day the dead in Christ shall rise, heading for the New Jerusalem. There the Master will have lodging for us in the many mansions or dwelling places prepared by God the Father. (John 14:2)

If all of this cocksureness is troubling; if now we have many more misgivings than we had at first; how do you get out of a grave after several years? Which way do you then turn? Is this bunkum? Isn't dying the nevermore for life? "NO," replied Jesus to doubting Thomas, "I am the way," just follow Him. "I am the truth," believe Him. "I am the life." And because He lives, we too shall live—forever.

PRAYER: *Lead on, O King eternal, we follow not with fear. Amen.*

THE LORD'S NEED OF US

Matt. 27:55 *A number of women were also present, watching from a distance; they had followed Jesus from Galilee and looked after him.*

How does one look after Jesus? We can surmise how His parents looked after Him—from the time of His conception—to Bethlehem—to Egypt—to Galilee. We can also reasonably assume that these female watchers at Calvary who had accompanied Jesus on His journey to Jerusalem, took care of Him by preparing food, cleaning clothes at wells and streams along the way, and by finding lodgings.

But now, having done all they could to look after Jesus, and now caught in circumstances beyond their control, these women looked on from a distance. What could they do for Him now? What can we do for Him—distanced as we are, not just in feet and inches, but in centuries? Can He still use our services, or are we excused?

Since Jesus said, "Lo, I am with you always," that dispenses with linear measurements and the centuries. He is right here, always, and all ways. Now what do we do?

Bless His heart, He foresaw our predicament and kindly offered suggestions: "Inasmuch as you have done it for the least of these my brethren, you have done it for me." That's where we can begin to look after Jesus: by being practically concerned about the last, the least, the lost, the unlisted.

Elsewhere Jesus told His congregation: "Whosoever doeth the will of my heavenly Father, the same is my brother, and sister, and mother." Think of it—we can have that family feeling with Jesus. We can know His preferences, His dislikes; what makes Him sad and what makes Him glad. With such intimacy, we can be among the qualifiers who do that which is well-pleasing in His sight.

Then God's will is repeated in The Lord's Prayer: "Thy Kingdom come, Thy will be done." It is the pivotal phrase on which the prayer goes around and gets around. God's will is for the kingdom to come on earth as perfectly as it is in heaven. And it did come to earth in Jesus. To serve the Christ, then, is to do the Father's will. Can we be counted on as Christ's caretakers?

PRAYER: *We would cease to be watchers from a distance, Lord, and closely attend You. Amen.*

A Tomb Full of Joy

Matt. 28:8 *They hurried away from the tomb in awe and great joy, and ran to bring the news to the disciples.*

Who hurries, nay *runs* away from a tomb except perhaps when passing a graveyard on a moonlight night with an owl silhouetted against the moon and giving his haunting, bloodcurdling "Whoooo"? But the two Marys did on the first Easter dawn. Why did they flee—especially when the angel at the tomb steadied their nerves with the assurance that they had "Nothing to fear"? (28:5) Yet they bolted. Why? The circumstances, of course.

For one thing, there was a "violent earthquake." (28:2) Then an angel rolled away the stone from the mouth of the tomb. And even if the two women were emotionally controlled thus far, seeing the guardsmen at the grave shake with fear and fall to the ground as if dead, (28:4) the ladies got the chills and took to their heels.

Or could that swift departure have been caused not by fear, but by joy? After all, the women had been invited to see for themselves that the gravesite was unoccupied. Then on the strength of that revelation, the angelic deliveryman passed on a message which the women in turn were to pass on—to the disciples. The message was that the resurrected Christ would be seen soon by His followers. Delivering such mail is always an assignment of great joy.

Or is it? Doesn't our increasing emphasis on Easter bunnies and finery and food prove our willingness to dodge the seriousness of the resurrection of Jesus? The subject is annually and violently earth-shaking. The urge is to flee in fear. Yet it is the fear that flees when: 1. The full realization dawns upon us that Jesus is alive. That full awareness comes slowly, like the dawn. One preacher reports that saying "Christ is alive" shook him awake to a new meaning. Growing more excited as he repeated "Christ is alive!" He said to himself, "Christ is as alive as I am, as these people are walking down the street." Then determined to share the gripping news, he started the tradition of singing an Easter hymn every Sunday morning of the year in his church services. That, in turn, made the church alive and fearless; 2. In knowing that Christ promises to be with us, and that we shall see Him as He is, also sends the phantom of fear skedaddling; and 3. When fear sees the bearer of such good tidings speeding away with joy, fear knows he's already beaten, and takes off in the opposite direction.

We hurry away from Easter not because it scares us, but because we can't wait to get the irrepressibly good news to a waiting world—and start a lifelong Easter celebration. Joy to the world. The Lord has risen, and is HERE NOW.

PRAYER: *Living Savior, no longer would we flee and fear, but tarry and tell. Amen.*

THE FORERUNNER'S BATON

Mark 1:5 *And everyone flocked to [John the Baptist] from the countryside of Judaea and the city of Jerusalem and they were baptized by him in the River Jordan, confessing their sins.*

Mark, the writer of the gospel from which Matthew and Luke copied copiously, introduces his good news bulletin not with Jesus, as the other two do, but with our Lord's cousin, John.

At the moment Jesus was in the north country, far from and unacquainted with the Holy City—where His life was to end. And what turned His attention south was John's ministry there. But for this, Jesus may have conducted His entire preaching-teaching-healing-leadership training career as the Stranger of Galilee.

John redirected that perspective.

And what was the attraction? John's magnetic mass evangelism, "Everyone flocked." The flock came not only from the countryside to hear this countrified preaching, but also the citified flocked too. The simple and the sophisticated mingled freely as they sought to appease their hunger for redemption, readily confessing their wrongs in order to live aright. Then came the dip in the Jordan—that outward symbol of an inward cleansing.

So powerful had been the report of the Baptizer's redemptive ministry, and so far and wide had the word been heard that Jesus, Himself, became one of those who flocked with the Judeans and Jerusalemites, to the Jordan. (Mark 1:9)

Nor was the flocking without significance. Mark had seen the sheep do it in the countryside, and the humans do it in the city, as had John the Baptist. Now Mark perceives what John is aiming to do and brings it to our attention, namely, that there was One, the good Shepherd, who could draw all persons unto Him. And John would try and be a humble forerunner of that Movement.

Redemption needed a Redeemer, and John discerned who that was. That takes sharply defined insightfulness. "After me comes one mightier than I am...he will baptize you with the Holy Spirit." (Mark 1:7-8)

No wonder that the Baptist is called the first prophet of Israel after a four hundred year hiatus. He looked beyond—past the public acclamation of his own ministry, which, in itself, has caused many a would-be prophet to look no further. John also looked beyond Jesus' as—yet parochial ministry—to the saving of humankind by the Lord Jesus Christ.

PRAYER: *Heavenly Father: How You synchronize the minutest details of daily life. Without this country preacher we may have looked elsewhere for the world's Savior. Amen.*

WHAT'S A CHURCH FOR?

Mark 11:16 *And he would not allow anyone to carry goods through the temple court.*

What a strange little verse to interject into the narrative. And what barefaced audacity it discloses. Here was a wandering, unordained religious reformer coming to the capital city for the first time (at least according to Mark), entering the famed thirty-acre Temple area and immediately ordering people around as if he owned the place. Little surprise that the Temple authorities were outraged. Who gave this self-inflated newcomer the pomposity to impose his will on everyone present, commanding that their profit-making activities be brought to a screeching halt? The official response, understandably, was: "Kill him."

Not so the crowd that "was spellbound by his teaching." (Mark 11:18) And what could He possibly have taught that would make His seemingly unorthodox, unauthorized behavior spellbinding?

Well, for one thing, His unequivocal stand on the unshakeable foundation of Holy Scripture.

That galvanized His listeners and confounded His critics. Revered Isaiah couldn't have been a better reference where he said: "my house will be called a house of prayer for all nations," (Isa. 56:7) for all people, mind you. But in the Jerusalem Temple, with its profiling courts, where the uninitiated dare not go on pain of death—all people were not welcome.

Referring to another prophetic heavyweight, Jesus called the Temple desecraters a den of thieves. (Jer. 7:11) And those who had suffered at the hands of such crooks were firmly in Jesus' corner as He called the prophet's to witness the present thievery.

Elsewhere, Jesus had seen how people had been ripped-off by a roped-off religion. Now in Jerusalem, at city center, He found the template for that exclusiveness in the Temple, and He lashed out at it.

The goings-on in the Temple belied its magnificence. And it was resplendent. Herod had spared no expenses in its construction. Gold and white marble were lavished upon it, causing rabbis to exclaim years after its destruction that "whoever has not seen the Temple of Herod has never seen a beautiful building in his life." Yet, the atmosphere had become spiritually toxic. As the first renowned act of His public ministry, Jesus de-toxified the Temple.

For those who confess to follow the cleanser of the Temple, that ministry remains in every age. Spiritually toxic conditions are ever prevalent. We breathe them in. We walk through moral messes. The Lord's house—whether in the temple of the soul or in the church or in the marketplace—

needs waste managers. Here am I, Lord, count on me. And you?

PRAYER: *We hear Your cry for supporters, Lord, and we know the consequences. Here we come. Amen.*

TAKE THAT!

Mark 12:9 *He will...give the vineyard to others.*

Unable to trip Jesus with a trick question, the doctors of the law were incensed.

Now it was Jesus' turn to take the initiative. A quick thinker, familiar with God's Word, and able at a moment's notice to apply a divine lesson where it fitted. Jesus did not hesitate to use Isa. 5:1-7, with additions from His own insight and foresight. He recalled the Isaiah passage (that should have been familiar to His judicial Jewish questioners), which we now know as the Parable of the Wicked Husbandmen (renters).

In parabolic terms, it was about God's prodigal generosity to the chosen (Jewish) people. He had given them a land flowing with milk, honey, money. They were buttressed with perks and additives that they could never have thought of, much less provided for themselves. But God did. Yet in spite of His cornucopias providence, the Jewish people scorned Him.

He sent courteous messages through His prophets. Still nothing penetrated their rigid self centeredness. As a last resort, He sent His only begotten son, confident that if the Son couldn't bring the rebel renters to their senses, nobody could.

In telling this part of the parable, Jesus was talking personally, having become aware of His own death, and with the consent of this very audience. And the closure of God's relationship with the Jewish people would come, declared Jesus, with God transferring His favor to others.

That wasn't long in coming. In A.D. 70 the Romans took over the Holy Land. More wars have been fought there than anywhere else on earth. Jerusalem has been captured twenty-six times in its history. Christians occupied the land in the third century. The Persians had it during the seventh century. Arabs and Ottoman Turks had their turns at it from A.D. 1517—until 1917 when General Allenby marched in and placed the country under British Mandate, which ended in 1948 when the United Nations partitioned Jerusalem between Israel and Jordan.

Why does God permit the giveaway of His people despite His insistent promise that He will never forsake them? Could it be that the answers appears to be more in our court? We hold God to His promise that His last word for us will be LOVE. At the same time, with the liberty He has bestowed upon us and with increasing pride in our scientific breakthroughs we cannot resist overriding God's word to give our own last word. Yet the heavenly Father patiently loves us back to His awaiting embrace.

PRAYER: *How grateful we are, merciful Lord, that at the end of the day Your tough love overpowers our squishy faith. Amen.*

A TALE OF TWO CITIES

Mark 12:15 *He saw through their duplicity.*

Where our text for today has been interpreted as "knowing their hypocrisy," or "Jesus knew well that they were acting a part" or "he saw how crafty their question was," the one word "duplicity," which the New English Bible inserts, gathers all the other descriptions into its crosshairs and draws a bead on bull's-eye central.

For numerous reasons Jesus' accusers had adopted a no-holds-barred policy toward Him. In their front line was duplicity, that consistently successful, 5,000-year-old secret service operative.

A number of Pharisees and men of Herod's party (Mark 12:13), who were as different as chalk and cheese, came together for espionage purposes. This unusual alliance was undoubtedly to give Jesus the impression that even such bipartisan, across-the-aisle chumminess denoted respect for Him, especially when with forked tongues they sweet-talked to Him: "Master, you are an honest man, we know, and truckle to no one, whoever he may be; you teach in all honesty the way of life that God requires." (Mark 12:14)

That was as lovely a confession as Peter ever made, (Matt. 16:16) and which Jesus had treasured. But with these men, Jesus recognized the King Cobras in them—the serpentine eyes, the poison glands, the ready-to-strike–poise. He "saw through their duplicity." Familiar with the true ring of honesty, integrity, sincerity (without wax), Jesus' keen perception heard the unfamiliar off-beats of a forged attempt to sound authentic. His clear-eyed vision of what His opponents were up to "left them completely taken aback." (Mark 12:17)

But do you notice how these satanic men duplicated (there's that *duplicity* again) the three temptations with which Jesus was afflicted in the wilderness? (Matt. 4:1-10) 1. "Master, you are an honest man." Even if He turned stones into bread they would have believed Him. 2. Since Jesus didn't yield weakly (truckle) to anyone it was evident that He would not hesitate to jump from the Temple parapet—450 feet into the valley below (without a hang glider?), knowing that angels would swoop in and bear Him up. 3. And teaching the way of life that God required, it would be no problem for Jesus to briefly bend a knee to the devil in order to become the Owner of the whole world. All of which is to say that this duplicity, and the temptations that it fostered, were for Jesus a case of "been there, done that." Indeed, as the old hymn assures us, "Each victory will help you some other (victory) to win."

The secret, not the secret service, is to turn our eyes upon Jesus and learn from Him the immovable standards for honesty, unyielding strength and godliness. For all cohere in Him. As St. Paul helpfully adds: "We speak of these gifts of God in words taught us not by our human wisdom but by the Spirit." (1 Cor. 2:13)

PRAYER: *"Dear Master, in whose life I see*
All that I long and fail to be,
Let Thy clear light for ever shine,
To shame and guide this life of mine.
Though what I dream and what I do
In my poor days are always two,
Help me, oppressed by things undone
O Thou, whose dreams and deeds were one."[1]

THE EVER-LIVING WORD

Mark 12:24 *Jesus said to them, "How far you are from the truth! You know neither the scriptures nor the power of God."*

Still Tuesday of the first Holy Week and Jesus

---

[1] Dr. John Hunter

was up to His lips in controversy. In the Capital City the capitalists were on His neck. So were the politicos and the religionists. The Festival atmosphere provided the ideal emotional temperature. And the time for attack had struck. And it all conjoined painfully on this one day. Whew! But prepared in soul for His demise, Jesus took on the attackers.

This textual issue concerned the resurrection from the dead, which the questioners disbelieved. Their intent was to corner Jesus into confessing that, after all, they were in the right.

Not so, was the Lord's comeback. "How far you are"—not only from the rightness of the resurrection doctrine but also from the scriptures (which make crystal clear that hope of eternal life); finally and regretfully, you are far from knowing and being a choice recipient of the power of God.

The implication is apparent. The Sadducees, and all of us who stray from the Word of God, wander afar into error and are not even aware of our lostness. Compass-less, we falter into dark, endangering life-situations from which God could rescue us if we remembered and believed in the extent of His power.

On this subject and on another occasion, Jesus went further and deeper: "The Father who has sent me has borne witness on my behalf. His voice you have never heard, his form you have never seen; His word has found no home in you, because you do not believe the One whom He sent. You study the scriptures diligently, supposing that in having them you have eternal life; their testimony points to me, yet you refuse to come to me to receive that life." (John 5:37-40)

Therein lies the root cause of anyone's prodigal wandering into the far country, refusing Christ as Savior. God's Word gives the stamp of approval to Jesus' Saviorhood; in and through the Lord Jesus Christ we have eternal life; in Him is the power of God made manifest. All that is good coheres in Christ. He is the world's standard of reference. Without His "mission control" of our lives, we are off course and at loose ends in interplanetary space, headed for nowhere. But with the Master in charge, the "nowhere" becomes "now here." He is our very present help and hope, now and forever. Amen.

PRAYER: *Lord, help us to tear up the misleading maps that land us in trouble. Lead us in the paths of righteousness for Thy Name's sake. Amen.*

ONCE UPON A SCRIBE

Mark 12:34 *When Jesus saw how thoughtfully he answered, he said to him, "You are not far from the Kingdom of God."*

"How far is not far?" asked the fellow who came in second in an Olympic sprint. To miss by a split-second, a helping hand, is to drown. This was the word of intense caution that Jesus was conveying to a legal expert. The man knew his law books and logic. And he had discovered after much diligent searching just the Right Man (Jesus) to further his knowledge. He received a satisfying answer as to which was the leading commandment. Nor was that as easy as it sounds. It was believed that Moses had received 6,143 principles on Mt. Sinai. David reduced those to eleven in Psalm 15.

Isaiah squeezed the eleven into six, (Isa. 33:15) and Micah did better, cutting the six in half. (Mic. 6:8) Habakkuk found one phrase that included all the above. (Heb. 2:4)

But all was not well that ended well with the Law professor. Jesus had a different take on the matter. "You are not far," but you are not quite there. And much depends on what you do about it.

It was apparent that the lawyer was not interested in doing his homework and heartwork. His life-changing knowledge was not being ingested and digested. Worse yet, he failed to recognize Jesus as the Savior of the world.

How many times Jesus had dealt with people like this. To the woman taken in adultery He gave a straight forward command: "Go, and sin nor more." Did she obey? Or did she remain "not far" from her Kingdom's goal? Then there were the thieves who hung on either side of Him at Calvary. Both were "not far" from their Savior. Yet only one made it to paradise. What made the difference?

St. Paul had a similar experience, revealing the continuance of this human problem. King Agrippa said to Paul, "With a *little more* of your persuasion you will make a Christian of me." (Acts 26:28)

One night a preacher was expounding this topic. Three persons slipped into a back pew—two men and a woman. After a while they began to titter and dig each other in the ribs, whispering, "He's trying to scare us. There will be other times when we can make our decision."

After the service the pastor locked up the church. As he made his way home across the railroad tracks, here came a man running along the track, waving a lantern. He said there had been an accident up the line. Sure enough and it involved the three at the back of the church. One man was dead, so was the woman. The other man was crawling around on his hands and knees moaning, "Oh, my God." After the service, they had had some drinks, and had been hit by a passing train.

"Almost persuaded, now to believer; almost persuaded Christ to receive. Seems now some soul to say, 'Go Spirit, go Thy way, some more convenient day on Thee I'll call.'

"Almost persuaded, harvest is past! Almost persuaded, doom comes at last! Almost cannot avail; Almost is but to fail! Sad, sad, the bitter wail, Almost but lost."[1]

But the penitent thief, committing his all to his Savior, received an instant reply: "Truly I tell you today you will be with me in Paradise." (Luke 23:43)

PRAYER: *Take my life now and let it be consecrated, Lord, to Thee. Amen.*

I SURRENDER ALL

Mark 12:41 *He watched the people dropping their money into the chest.*

Always on duty for the Kingdom, Jesus deposited Himself in view of the Temple treasury. It consisted of a line of trumpet-shaped containers into which contributors put their offerings for the Temple's various needs.

No doubt the Lord was remembering His recent encounter with the fellow who was not far

---

[1] P. P. Bliss

from the Kingdom, not yet fully committed to finding newness of life in Christ. But the thought connection is clearer in Luke (20:45-47) where He had been talking about widows being shafted by wealthy donors who sought the limelight wherever they went. Now Jesus sees an enactment of what He may previously have heard rumored. What He now sees at the Temple treasury was a living example of what He ached to tell the lawyer but decided that the better part of discretion was to let the man discover it himself. As when Dr. George Washington Carver asked God, "What's in this peanut?" God replied, "You have brains, go find out." And he did—to the enrichment of the world.

Calling together His disciples for a teaching moment, Jesus said, referring to a widow's total commitment in her financial contribution, "This is the truth." (v. 41) He was certain that this was the way all people should give, whether money, time, talent, or life itself.

In today's churches at offering time the playing field has been leveled. The once noisy collection plate that drew attention to the giver's benefactions is now silenced in an envelope placed in a velvet-covered plate, or into a deep, soft bag. But Jesus heard the jingle of coins designed to turn heads and elicit comments of oohs and aahs. That, as Jesus saw it, was the main intent of the swankoboasts.

Then came the easy-to-identify penniless widow. What, if anything, did she have to trumpet? But Jesus' keen sight and hearing couldn't miss the two thin wee mites which were all that she possessed. How did He know that, unless He knew her personally; knowing her as one who was wholly given to God in body, mind, spirit. Unsurprisingly, He hastened to enthrone her in faith's Hall of Fame: "The others who have given had more than enough, but she, with less than enough, has given all that she had to live on." (v. 44)

Peter must have heard that first edition of what just happened. Mark, who wrote his gospel even before Matthew wrote his, retrieved this episode from his mentor Peter's memoirs. And Luke, who at this time was not a disciple, later copied (with a briefer treatment) from Mark.

How the good, though seemingly insignificant and hardly seen, emerges to bless and encourage the human race until the end of time.

The two mites couldn't have purchased a sparrow. But the commitment behind that meager legal tender fling open heaven's gates to welcome the widow in. It still works that way.

PRAYER: *Ever-watchful Master. Not a mite would we withhold. All we are, is Thine. Amen.*

THE HANDS OF HIS TIME

Mark 13 *As Jesus was leaving the temple...*

This thirteenth chapter, called "The Little Apocalypse," because it echoes the fire and brimstone sections of the Book of Revelation, is also one of the five major discourses, or teaching episodes, in the life of Christ. While it touches on a variety of subjects, there are four areas that appear to be of special concern to Jesus, for He comes back to each three or four times for added emphasis.

The first, and it was the first off His tongue in this Olivet discourse, was "Be on your guard." (13:5,9,23,33)

After three years of assuring His followers that underneath them were His everlasting arms; that faith was the victory; that there was nothing to fear, this wake-up call to sentry-duty, must have shaken His inner circle of four men. The Lord must have sensed that He had some sleepyheads among His followers. Didn't the faithful few prove Him to be correct later, in Gethsemane? Who among us doesn't? And why does our divine Leader, make our number one priority a wide-open-eyed-and-eared alertness?

Because, second, we are too easily misled. (v. 5,6,22) Shysters come in all shapes and sizes. Their drumbeats get us to stamping to their rhythm, and, unless we are attuned to Jesus' marching band of believers, we follow that "other drummer." To where? To what? So, as these four emphases interact with one another, the being on-guard is a crucial moment of fine-tuning; tuning out the misleading media madness and chat-room gossip and tuning in the proven helpfulness of the Holy Spirit, who intervenes behind the scenes.

Third, there is "the end," which echoes through verses 7, 10, 13, 29. The first "end" refers to the demolishing of the magnificent Temple in Jerusalem in A.D. 70. That came to pass. And just as surely will the "living end," before the Lord comes again. For that, too, we must watch. About that, too, we dare not be misled. Nobody knows the calendar date of that end. Only the Father does. And He is looking forward to gathering us to Himself.

Fourth, "the chosen." (v. 20,22,27) Such persons, not knowing that they are His chosen have nevertheless learned from His Word that we love

Him because He first loved us. Continuing in a love relationship with the Savior of the world, such persons qualify as His chosen. Being on guard, not misled, preparing themselves for the Master's coming again—they are assured of an open-arms welcome by Him.

What the Lord said to the quartette of disciples, He says to everyone: "Keep awake." (13:37)

PRAYER: *O Thou who never slumbers nor sleeps, (Ps. 121:4) teach us how to "keep awake," even at slumber time. Amen.*

UNITE THE UNTIED

Mark 14:15 *Make the preparations for us there.*

In verse 12 the disciples talk as if they were preparing a Passover meal for Jesus. It doesn't sound as if they were thinking of themselves as being included. Perhaps Jesus wanted a last supper. They would provide it.

But Jesus quickly corrects their distorted view of the situation. It was not to be a solo meal, but a communal one—a holy communion. It was not them at the dining table. It was "us." Him, yes, but also His chosen 12. They might not think that they are included, but He does. (Mark 9:40; John 20:17; Rev. 3:20) In Revelation He goes beyond the twelve and makes it a wide-open invitation to "anyone."

This makes of secondary importance all the seemingly important details which must be observed in pulling together a Passover meal. For what use is food and drink and elaborate ritual and robes if He's not there? In fact, what is any meal without a strong sense of the presence of the Unseen Guest? It's just grub. But invoking His blessing before taking the first mouthful; to express thanks for His gifts of sustenance; to express awareness of the need to feed unfortunates; to dedicate our refreshed energies to His service is to sup with Him, and He with us.

Moreover, how intuitively Jesus saw the value, not only of the relations between Himself and the twelve, but also between the twelve themselves. He had forewarned them that they wouldn't always have Him around. What, then, if under His followership that had not become a fellowship? Divided they would have been ineffective and snuffed out. United they bore a prodigious witness to the ages.

It is no surprise that the apostolic band, bonding with Christ and with each other at the Passover meal, used that same Upper Room in which to come together and prepare for the coming of the Holy Spirit at Pentecost.

Indeed, this had been pre-visioned by the prophet when he wrote in Psalm 133—"How good and how pleasant it is when brothers dwell in unity! It is like the precious oil upon the head...It is like the dew of Hermon, which falls on the mountains of Zion! For there the Lord has commanded the blessing, life for evermore." The blessing is long-abiding.

PRAYER: *You count on us, Lord, and we are nothings without You. Together, as You have always wanted it, we can bring Your Kingdom on earth, as it is in heaven. Amen.*

Do You Know Him?

Mark 14:71 *I do not know this man you are talking about.*

Sad to report, too many church members

could say that and not be accused of denying Jesus. They occasionally hear His name, but the Savior they have never really known.

But Peter? Who could have known Jesus better? The four gospels make no bones about who was the Lord's forefront follower: Peter. And, at Gethsemane, when Peter struck a blow for Christ by cutting off an ear of the high-priest's servant—does that look like one who didn't know who Jesus was?

And weeks later in his first sermon (after Pentecost) Peter said, "Men of Israel, hear me: I am speaking of Jesus of Nazareth, singled out by God and made known to you through miracles, portents, and signs, which God worked among you through him, as you well know..." (Acts 3:22) And Peter well knew too. Then what should one know about the Master to be wholly His? With all his discipleship qualifications, what did Peter lack?

First, the record shows that as long as Jesus was near, Peter was his Master's man. But separated, as on the Sea of Galilee, Peter sank. Yet after denying Jesus three times, which is recorded by all four gospels, and is retold by Peter through Mark, Peter made an honest confession. He stepped into the shadowed courtyard and wept bitterly—tears of repentance. That was his first step to a clearer understanding of Jesus.

Second, as Peter told the would-be converts at Pentecost: "be baptized in the name of Jesus." (Acts 3:38) That symbolic ritual of cleansing, which cries for serious and meaningful reinstatement in our time, gives a lasting reminder of one's immaculate soul-cleansing. As with the physical rules of hygiene, which set standards for outer purity, baptism is the high-water mark for being unsoiled in Spirit.

Even with repentance and baptism, Peter, himself, was still "not far from the Kingdom." As yet he did not have what it took to be the Lord's own. He could still operate in a denial mode. It was not until he received the gift of the Holy Spirit that the final piece was in place. Then, and then alone, did Peter grow in spiritual stature. Now he could be strong and unafraid and unequivocal. Jesus was no longer with Peter in body. But He was with Peter, forevermore in Spirit, as He is for us. (See Mark 1:7-8)

PRAYER: *Spirit of God, descend upon my heart. Teach me to feel that Thou art always near. Amen.*

A MOCKUMENTARY OF JESUS

Mark 15:20 *When they had finished their mockery they stripped off the purple robe and dressed him in his own clothes.*

It all started with the Wise Men at the time of the first Christmas. That had been recalled by the religious hierarchy. In Jerusalem they inquired: "Where is he that is born King of the Jews?" They reported to Pilate that Jesus had claimed to be a King. (Luke 23:2) That seems to have touched a nerve that gave Pilate pain. He was proud of his position as an emperor-appointed governor. Now here came a wandering preacher who claimed a status equal to the mighty Roman emperor Caesar.

That weighed too heavily on Pilate's vanity. Jesus must be cut down to size—the more diminishing the better. And Jesus detected the governor's testy tone choosing thereafter to remain silent.

But Pilate's Roman cohorts did not remain silent. Taking their cue from their governor (and perhaps instructions from him), the soldiers filled out in deeds what they had heard in their superior's words.

First, the soldiers took Jesus "inside the governor's residence." (Mark 15:16) Then the whole brigade was marched in. Was this a full-fledged humiliation of "the King of the Jews," staged privately for the one who was most outraged by this "King"?

It even looks as if the soldiers had dress rehearsals for the occasion. For, second, they dressed Jesus in purple, the color of royalty (easily procured in the residence of one who yearned to be a royal and in secret wore such purple vestments just for the feel of ultimacy).

Third, of course, would be a crown. And if uneasy lies the head that wears a crown, why not make this fellow's crown of plaited thorns? Fourth, what King is not saluted? So the soldiers, all professional saluters, snapped to attention, but with scathing hilarity hailed or heiled Him "King of the Jews."

Fifth, to prove their loathing contempt of this King thing, each soldier, as in running the gauntlet, hit Jesus over the head with a stick and spat on Him.

Sixth, there was kneeling by the whole assembly before Jesus. Ironically they paid homage to the King of Kings.

Seventh, as our text for today puts it, when the charade was over, the purple gown was returned to the Resident-in-chief, and Jesus was re-clothed in His own garments.

Note that at Calvary, the soldiers did an about

face. They had forgotten the purple robe. Now they coveted His robe and cast lots for it. (Luke 23-34)

His is always the last word. He claims us at the end. He takes the mocking and mugging, the spitting and spouting. In every age the Master has suffered tortures of body, mind, Spirit. He has taken the worst that a corrupt world could throw at Him. And yet, in the end, knees bend, heads bow, hearts turn from stone into gifts for Him. For there is no other whereby we can be saved—except the Lord Jesus Christ, King of King, Lord of Lords, the Mighty God, the everlasting Father, the Prince of Peace.

PRAYER: *Heal my wounded, broken spirit, Lord. Save me by Thy grace. Amen.*

WHEN THE CASUAL BECOMES CAUSAL

Mark 15:21 *A man called Simon, from Cyrene, the father of Alexander and Rufus, was passing by on his way in from the country, and they pressed him into service to carry his cross.*

The significance of Simon was not that he might have been a black man or that his sons were known in the Christian community, but because he was, at the moment, a nameless passerby on his way into Jerusalem for some unnamed purpose. In an instant his path crossed that of Jesus, with electrifying consequences. Hauled out of his private preoccupations into the public glare of history's stage, Simon was thrust under the burden which Jesus was no longer able to shoulder.

There was reason for Jesus to stumble on His three-quarter-mile journey to the place of the skull. Of the fourteen stations of the cross, five are from various traditions; but nine are from the gospels, and this is one of the nine.

Jesus' first tumble was just before He started an uphill climb, and at that point He caught sight of His pain-wracked mother. No wonder His limbs went limp and He needed a helping shoulder to heft His cross. What did He see in Mother's eyes that took the starch out of Him? Was it the remembrance that she had once shared with Him of Simeon predicting that a sword would pierce her soul? (Luke 2:35) Was this the sword, which would soon literally pierce His own side? Since Mary kept such treasured memories in her heart (Luke 2:19), was she now recalling the gift of myrrh which symbolized sorrow and death? Was this a gift, or was she going to lose Him again as she often had, but this time forever? Not losing sight of her Son, Mary kept pace with the procession, for she is mentioned next beside His cross at Calvary. (John 19:25)

Meanwhile, Mary must have been grateful for the timely aid of Simon. Later, Simon, stripped of his anonymity, was given respectful recognition for his sacrificial service. Whether more than his two named sons had life-changing experiences because of this incident, we can only surmise. But through the ages countless numbers of persons have been inspired by Simon to go and do likewise—as with the monument that greets one at the entrance to Boy's Town in Omaha, Nebraska—"He ain't heavy, Father, he's my brother."

W. Graham Scroggie notes in a comment on Simon, that "there are no accidents in the programme of Providence. At some time or another Christ will cross your path, and give you your supreme opportunity. What you do in that hour will tell eternally."[1]

Any passing moment can be "that hour" urged the hymn writer. "Give every flying minute, something to keep in store." We do not have to go looking for historic moments in which to impress our legacy in the ages. It hardly ever happens that way. Rather, golden opportunities lie on the surface of everyday happenings. Blessed are those who have eyes to see. Often, however, as with Simon, Providence pressures us into action. Then, to be willing accomplices of His, whatever the sweaty consequences, is to be stamped with His image.

Anywhere can be CROSS country. But cross-bearers are scarce. The penitent thief saw and seized the moment—and arrived in paradise that very day. Other passersby hurled insults at Jesus. (Mark 15:29) Simon, the passerby, hurled himself into the service of Christ. Simon says, "Come, follow me to Christ." Let's go and make the unreturning minute rememberable.

PRAYER: *Lord, grant that we may see the potential in all that we encounter daily. Press our shoulder to the task that must be done for Jesus' sake. Amen.*

HOW TO SAVE A WORLD

Mark 16:8c *Afterwards Jesus himself sent out by them, from east to west, the sacred and imperishable message of eternal salvation.*

Before Christ was born, indicators pointed toward Him as the coming Savior of the world. (John 3:16) But in His lifetime He saved some

---
[1] W. G. Scroggie, *The Gospel of Mark*, p. 270

people in a wee section of the Middle East.

That didn't mean the world had heard the last of Jesus. That was just getting His foot in the door. For in today's verse His forever plan is disclosed. And that plan will reach fulfillment only when every knee shall bow, and every tongue confess that Jesus Christ is Lord. (Rom. 14:11)

Lest the plan be lost in a single exposure, the recorders three-peat it in Mark 16:15,20; Matt. 27:16-20; Luke 24:49 (plus Acts 1:4,9).

First, the plan is stamped with Christ's imprimatur: "Jesus himself." It is not to be attributed to the apostles or Paul or any of the New Testament authors. The Author and Finisher here is the Master Himself, since "full authority in heaven and on earth had been committed to Him." (Matt. 27:18) This was His Magna Carta. He had earned the right to blueprint it, and see it through to completion. This is a Savior's ministry.

Second, He "sent out by them." He could have done it all Himself, since "He was with God at the beginning, and through him all things came to be; without him no created thing came into being." (John 1:2-3) Rather, Jesus preferred to work with and through those whose world this is. Instead of being onlookers, they would learn more and be more committed as participants. Each worker would bring his own talents, and all would be richer for the sharing.

Third, there was the territory to be covered. "East to west" appears in Mark 16:8b as "the whole creation" and in Mark 16:8c as "far and wide." So it's no less than the fact that the world is our parish. How grateful we ought to be that His plan didn't cover only that almost unnoticeable strip of land along the eastern Mediterranean coast. That is why I, for one, offer a prayer of thanks every time the plane goes aloft from Tel Aviv—that the Lord Jesus is not confined to what is called the Holy Land. He is Lord of all.

Fourth, the marrow of this mission is the message, Jesus quoted scripture which foretold that persons who repented of their sins, in His name, would be forgiven. (Luke 24:47) Here is salvation which is sacred and not to be taken lightly. It is also an imperishable cleansing; it has no expiration date.

Nor is this the last word. Jesus didn't just send these fellows out with a pat on the back, wishing them good luck. Mark's gospel doesn't end at 16:8a with the word "afraid." Instead at 16:20 where Jesus fulfills His own promise "Lo, I am with you always." He continued to work with His missioners (in Spirit), "confirming their words by the miracles that followed."

His continuing help in every age and in every clime is of an eternal quality. Count on it.

PRAYER: *Thank You, Lord, for Mark's gospel from Peter's memoirs. These closing verses take away fear and instill us with faith and fortitude. Amen.*

THE LOOK OF REVELATION

Luke 2:38 *Coming up at that very moment [Anna] gave thanks to God; and she talked about [Jesus] to all who were looking for the liberation of Jerusalem.*

What else we know about this prophetess appears in the previous two verses. She was a childless, long-widowed octogenarian who prayed and fasted in the Jerusalem Temple from which she was never detached. Though this was the temple which Jesus called a den of thieves, Anna's templed life was exemplary, which is why she shared these few rare moments in the exclusive company of the Holy Family and Simeon.

But how did Anna know that this child was the promised Savior of the world?

For one thing, Temple talk and teaching must often have turned to the subject of the coming Messiah. Indeed, that hot topic had been around for centuries. Yet there had been no sign of Him. How then, could Anna suddenly recognize this baby as the ONE?

To be sure, the arrival of the Wise Men, and their inquiries about a newborn King, stirred up a cauldron of trouble in the capital city. And the Temple, being a mission control center, would get such news first.

Still, the Wise Men were looking for one destined to be an earthly ruler of the caliber of their Babylonian Monarchs. Hence their gifts—fit for a King. Did the bubble burst when the child was found in a lowly cattle shed instead of in a palace? Is this why the Wise Men didn't have the nerve to go back to Herod and give their report as he had requested? Were they embarrassed to have Herod see the egg on their faces?

There were mixed signals filling the air. Even the chief priests and scribes, though right on target in telling King Herod that the coming One would be born in Bethlehem (Matt. 2:5-6), didn't know just *when* in Bethlehem, or just *where*.

Yet Anna recognized the Infant the moment she saw Him. Even His parents were astonished to hear what she and Simeon said about His affinity with divinity.

Let's get to the point: What was Anna's secret? Four powerful factors came together to form a detecting device within her: the holy spirit, worship, prayer, fasting. As physically, there are detection devices that reveal the unseen, (such as landmine detectors, high-tech devices that secretly track anything that moves: "your car or your kid, or your kid in your car," and X-rays that reveal the sex of an unborn child), so is it in the area of the Spirit.

Worship sensitizes souls that can become calloused by the world's materialism (eating, drinking, sex, money). *Prayer* goes deeper, higher, wider reaching out to talk to and with God who is a Spirit. *Fasting*, by disciplining the human body, tunes out desires that crave immediate satisfaction, allowing for an openness and entryway for the incoming *Spirit* divine. Thus equipped persons see what others with eyes see not.

PRAYER: *Drop the scales from our eyes, Lord, that we may know You, and serve You, now and forever. Amen.*

TO FIND AND BE FOUND

Luke 2:40 *Why did you search for me? he asked. Did you not know that I was bound to be in my Father's house?*

The first recorded word that Jesus spoke, at least according to Luke, is the word "Why?" And it was close to one of the last words which Jesus uttered on the cross: "Why have You forsaken me?" "Why," in itself, is a searching word.

When Jesus asked His parents: "Why did you search for me?" it involved the question, "Where did you search for me?" Did they look for Him in the relative's home in Jerusalem, where He obviously got

His meals and lodging during the three days He had been missing? Had the parents inquired at their usual pit stops along the highway?

The question "why" also included the question "*When* did you search for me?" After three days? That doesn't sound like very caring parents. Nowadays the cops would be called much sooner. Search squads, neighbors, friends would all be on Amber alert. But three days! Shame, shame. Is that all the boy meant to his parents?

And Jesus "why" presupposed *how* the search was conducted. Was it a diligent concerned look in every corner? Was no stone left unturned? Did they ask, seek, knock, and keep on knocking, as years later, Jesus advised searchers to do? Get the "why" answered in full, and you can tell just who in the account is lost.

In the mountains of New Hampshire a little girl strayed away from her picnicking family. The message went out across the area: "Mary Moore is lost." Hundreds of volunteers combed the woods for hours. Then they found Mary. Put in touch with her father by two-way radio the first thing Mary asked was, "Daddy, where have *you* been?" She was not lost, her Dad was!

In many ways that was true of Jesus' parents. Others with spiritual insight recognized the Messiah in Jesus while His parents had not yet come to a knowledge of that truth. You see it in the way the boy Jesus gently takes the emphasis off Mary's words "your father" and puts it on His own acknowledgment of "my Father." In the same way, years later, the morally undiscerning couldn't grasp Jesus description of the Beyond: "In my Father's house are many mansions..."

Once the disciples said to the Master, "Everyone is searching for You." (Matt. 1:37) Indeed, they still are. "The Lord is the need of the world, and for Him it cries. Though it babble of gold and fame, it lies, it lies. Though it would not have us know its secret it cannot keep. The Lord is the need of the world, and it tells it awake or asleep."

The search for Jesus is still on. Much depends on why we search. Is it to get loaves and fishes? And where do we search for Him, and when, and how?

Let's go to our heavenly Father's house and find out.

PRAYER: *Good Shepherd, all we like sheep have gone astray, and are counted as lost. We look to Thee, from whence comes our help. Amen.*

THE SHUN IN TEMPTATION

Luke 4:9 *The devil took him to Jerusalem and set him on the parapet of the temple. "If you are the son of God," he said, "throw yourself down from here."*

The devil told Him to do it. And, as always, with princely perks. To go to Jerusalem, in itself, was a privilege beyond Jesus' chief joy, especially since God had chosen that city—where His name should be. (2 Chron. 6:6) Then, to be set (even in imagination) on the parapet of the temple was a high honor. There a select priest would take his stance just before sunrise. As the first rays of sunlight appeared, the priest's horn summoned worshippers to make their morning sacrifice.

Continuing his appeal to human pride, the mealy-mouthed manipulator went for the jugular. After all, Jesus was not just a son of God, but *the* Son, wasn't He? Or wasn't He? That would twang

Jesus' divine aspirations into a flustered state of agreeing with His adversary.

Finally, there was the ultra stroking of Jesus' pride: just a mere jump of 450 feet into the valley. No harm would be done. That was scripturally assured. (Ps. 91:11-12)

Jesus was tempted in all ways like as we are, the good Book avers. But this temptation with all its layers of lies and studied deceptions is surely more than any human encounters. Yet here again, the Lord pioneers a way that we can follow, if we watch closely and learn from Him.

In love with Jerusalem, Jesus still viewed it objectively enough to be able to weep over its weaknesses. That steadying stance kept Him from falling head over heels at the mere mention of the place.

The lofty and central position of the temple parapet was after all a routine, daily, physical location. How much better it could be to awaken the hearts of humans to sacrifice their time and talents for the betterment of the world. And as for jumping from that parapet why not rather "Rise up, O men of God. Have done with lesser things?" Why not throw oneself upon the mercy of God? Throw ourselves into His arms? Throw our best efforts into Kingdom-building? Fall, if any falling is to be done—at God's feet.

Throughout, Jesus sensed the negativity of the devil's devious devices, outscripturing His oppressor who quoted scripture only for his own satanic purposes.

Physical attraction, lofty personal attainment, sensationalism to gain wide public recognition, make a powerful undertow that can sweep the misguided soul into the depths of defeat.

How much we need our Eternal Lifeguard.

PRAYER: *Lead us not into temptation, but deliver us, O Great Deliverer. Amen.*

NO OTHER GOD

Luke 19:44 *You did not recognize the time of God's visitation.*

When you go up the Jericho Road, as Jesus did here there comes a point on the Mount of Olives when suddenly a panorama of Jerusalem breaks upon your sight. It is more impressive and heartlifting than Mount Everest at dawn. It is a cheering sight. But for Jesus it was a tearing sight. He hadn't wept so much since He stood at Lazarus' grave. Because this time Jesus wept for His favorite city and its inhabitants. And why?

It had to do with the matter of recognition, recognizing God's presence.

Before Jesus came to earth, God was known vaguely; a Voice from a mountaintop, a Voice in the night, deep-speaking to the deep thoughts of prophets and such.

Then came the Incarnation—the Word was made flesh, and dwelt among us. As the gospels chronicle it from Jesus' "birth, through His life and ministry, was" the time of God's visitation to His people in human, easily understandable form.

Yet, though a few persons recognized God in Christ, reconciling the world to Himself, the masses didn't, certainly not the masses in Jerusalem. And that's what brought the tears to Jesus' eyes. He had hoped for something better from the capital city's citizens. From the time when the Wise Men broke the news to Jerusalem of His coming and His encounter with the doctors of the law in the Temple, along with all the time He gave to nurturing Salem in the metropolis, and trying to spread His protecting cross-destined arms to protect His "brood"—you would think that here would have been a wider recognition of God's presence in a "Holy City." But, having eyes, they did not, would not see. They "did not recognize." They were like Philip who said to Jesus, "Lord, show us the Father; we ask no more." Jesus answered, "Have I been all this time with you, Philip, and still you do not know me? Anyone who has seen me has seen the Father." (John 14:8-9)

No wonder that Jesus felt His mission was complete when Peter recognized exactly who Jesus was when he said: "You are the Messiah, the Son of the living God." (Matt. 16:16) As a result, Peter was made the bedrock of Christ's Church and handed the Keys of the Kingdom of Heaven. (Matt. 16:18-19)

It is the recognition of Christ as Lord of all, or Lord not at all that makes for an unconquerable church. It provides us with the Master's Keys. His hand is on the openings and closings of life on earth, as it is in heaven.

PRAYER: *Weep not for us, Lord Jesus. Now and ever You are all the God we need. Amen.*

STANDING ON THE PROMISES

Luke 21:19 *By standing firm you will win yourselves life.*

In the last verse of this twenty-first chapter, Luke tells us how busy Jesus was in His closing days on earth. Early each morning Jesus made His way to the Jerusalem Temple, where people flocked to hear Him teach.

Those teaching sessions continued all day. Each night the Master would head down to Kedron Valley and then trudge up the Mount of Olives (possibly to the Garden of Gethsemane, His favorite prayer haven).

But right in the middle of all this teaching and exhausting ministry, (in our text for today) Jesus urges His listeners to stand firm. Luke skillfully puts this verse at the dead center of the chapter, making it serve as the axis on which the meaning of chapter 21 revolves.

The reason for standing firm is outlined in the first half of this chapter. It had to do with the destruction of Jerusalem by the Romans in A.D. 70. But not that historic event alone. God's people would also experience a wide assortment of experiences that would rock the foundations of human life—wars, earthquakes, famines, plagues, persecution, betrayals by loved ones, helplessness, confusion, and who knows what else. Ah, yes, there would be a crying need for Christians to set an example, and stand firm.

At this point one can almost hear the echo of Moses' challenge to Joshua, as the new young leader was about to enter the Promised Land: "Be strong." (Deut. 31:6) To win ourselves life in any land of Promise, there must be a standing firm, strongly.

But where are the helps and helpers for us who come from dust, and return to it? Talk about Promises? There is the promise that the Son of Man will come in a cloud with power and great glory. (Luke 21:27) That's all the help we need. But more is available. There is the promise that our liberation is near (Luke 21:28), free from sin.

Freed from the bonds of earth.

And there's prayer. The invitation is to pray "at all times for strength to pass safely through all that is coming and to stand in the presence of the Son of Man." (Luke 21:36)

There! If that doesn't put firmness in our knees and our resolve, nothing else can. "You will win."

PRAYER: *Lord, we also take heart from Your servant who said: "God himself accompanies you; he will not let you down or forsake you." (Deut. 31:6) Amen.*

A VERY PRESENT HELP

Luke 22:4 *And he (Judas) went to the chief priests and temple guards to discuss ways of betraying Jesus to them.*

The account of how Jesus was finally corralled by the religious authorities begins and ends with the public, Jesus' "security force." The priests' problem was how to keep Jesus' adoring public out of the way long enough to whisk Jesus into the custody of His enemies." Timing was crucial. The Passover, with its expected inflow of multitudes of pilgrims, was approaching, adding fuel to fiery emotions.

Enter Satan. He always seems to have the best sense of timing when death and destruction are required. He knows when and how to ignite an inflammable situation.

Verse 3 says that "Satan entered into Judas." But Satan also entered into the chief priests and scribes, and then brought the two scheming sides together: Judas to penetrate the security surrounding Jesus, and for the chief priests to finish the nasty disposal of the carpenter from Nazareth.

So the ball was in Judas' court. And he had qualified for this round. He was called "Iscariot" because he was once a member of a certain activist zealot group that was swift with the dagger when it came to stabbing Roman troops who occupied Palestine.

Next, Judas was "one of the Twelve." (v. 3) Jesus had chosen this man, having seen potential powers for good in Judas' persona, which made this always last-mentioned disciple special. Having traveled up and down the land with the Master for three years, and being of that stealthy type he had informed himself of Jesus intimate relationships and whereabouts—as one had to do as a Zealot. And apparently Judas had never lost his touch where that was concerned. Jesus noted it when He said "one of you is a devil." Jesus was not unacquainted with Satan. He had wrestled with that evil spirit in the wilderness for forty days, and every time He cast such spirits out of His patients. Now Satan was manipulating Judas and his priestly accomplices in their discussion of "ways of betraying Jesus."

How many ways are there to betray Jesus? Greed? Under cover of a privileged position? Treachery? Oh, myriad ways. Unable to serve two masters, Judas had transferred his allegiance from Christ to the prince of darkness, and all of Satan's artifices were at Judas' beck and call—as they are for anyone who exchanges Christ for chaos.

If Judas had only let in the fellowship of believers. Instead, he shut them out and himself became the most pathetic shut-out in history—when he could have had a close and everlasting companionship with the Savior, through His followers.

All one body, we. Onward Christian soldiers.

PRAYER: *Lord, help us to remember the strength there still is in Your tactical units of believers. Amen.*

How Come Union?

Luke 22:24 *Then a dispute began as to which of them should be considered the greatest.*

Holy Communion is the high point in Christian worship. It was for Jesus. That is why He longed to celebrate it with His disciples. (22:15) His desire was intensified not only because this would be their last worship service together, but also because the lessons of the service would be invaluable in their everyday personal lives.

In fact, the fracturing process took the communion place throughout the communionizing process. Even while the elements of bread and wine were partaken of, at least three cracks appeared in that seemingly solid togetherness.

For one thing, Jesus was aware if nobody else was, of the presence of His betrayer. And He knew which one of the twelve it was. The Lord could see and feel the devilment in Judas. Having discussed the dastardly deed with others of his kind, Judas' conclusions were ripe and bursting for action.

Next, the entire fellowship crumbled when each disciple thought that he might be the betrayer Jesus had in mind. Each of the eleven searched his own soul for any such motives, and, finding none, turned to look at his fellows with narrowed eyes of suspicion. Could it be this one or this? What sort of a hornet's nest had this become?

Then, with frazzled emotion and teeth on edge, a rancorous dispute broke out about who among them was the greatest. It probably spewed out, rather late, because of the seating arrangement. Used to being seated to the right and left of the host according to their importance, and here at the Last Supper sitting where they could find a seat, some attendees were riled. Pride was sore and the accusations flew.

What an unholy mess! And at Holy Communion!

Jesus was sensitive to such stormy conditions and must have known that their breakout was near. Hence His emphasis on service, and giving way to the brethren.

"This cup," He intoned, "is the new covenant, my blood which is shed for you…This bread is my body which is broken for you…I am among you like a servant."

That otherness, that givingness, that suffering servanthood, must be at the heart of everyday living. To be sure, it is not designed to prevent the intervention of malicious thoughts and practices. Those, as we say, go with the turf of life. They are to be expected as a part of the crossing and clashing of human emotions in the daily efforts to co-exist. The mass of men lead lives of quiet desperation.

Our Lord foresaw this, not only for the Supper in the Upper Room, but for all human endeavors. And servanthood, He determined, was the key to harmony. His entire life and teachings exemplified this truth encapsuled in the Eucharist. Take, eat, drink, digest this lesson of putting Jesus first, others next, then yourself and, as we've found from Sunday School days, it does spell JOY.

PRAYER: *Lord, give us this daily bread and drink that we may be sustained in the living of these days. Amen.*

See Here

Luke 22:64 *They blindfolded him, and kept asking him, "If you are a prophet, tell us who hit you?"*

It is usually believed that here the Temple police, into whose keeping Jesus was entrusted, were insulting Jesus; having fun with Him; treating Him as if He were a child. His blindfolding was as if He had to pin the tail on the donkey. But is it not also probable that, unsure of Jesus' prophetic ability, these fellows wanted to find out for themselves? That is the way one of the thugs at Calvary saw it: "If you are the Messiah, save yourself and us." Prove your power to us!

This is the way many unbelievers and believers view Jesus. Since Jesus promised "Ask anything in my name and it shall be done," we take Him at His word. "Give us this," we plead. And when it is not forthcoming, doubts arise. People turn away from Him and seek others for answers. Well, isn't this what we would do with a medical doctor? He has a long, expensive schooling in the science of medicine. But if he doesn't bring our loved one through a critical ailment, we become critical—and look for second, third, fourth opinions. "God and the doctor all men adore, when sickness comes, but not before. When health returns (or doesn't) alike requited, God is forgotten and the doctor slighted."

Wherein lies the problem? Can He or can't He? For the human there are limitations. For the divine there is a paradox. At times when people believe that the Lord will heal, for example, He doesn't. As in the case of Lazarus' death. Lazarus' sister gently chided Jesus: "If you had been here my brother would not have died." But Jesus, though learning of the death of

His good friend, took three days to respond to the distress call—for His own very good reasons. On the other hand, when people felt that Jesus couldn't or wouldn't help He did help. As with the centurion's servant. Distance, which seemed an impediment to the centurion, was overcome in a jiffy by Jesus.

Which is to say that He knows best which is the right combination of circumstances in which to act—or to desist. Leave it in His capable hands, beginning each request with, "If it is Your will, Lord." His own such prayer at the most crucial time of His life was, "Not my will, but Thine be done."

He knows the strokes of insult from the hem-of-the-garment touch of faith, and He responded in his own time and way. With Him, and for our utmost good, all things are worked out for the salvation of the world. You can't fool Him. The temple guards were the ones who really were blindfolded and fooling themselves. Jesus was fully aware of what was happening. He always is. Take Him on faith, and be safe and saved.

PRAYER: *Take off our blinders, Lord. Help Thou our unbelief.*

THE DIFFERENCE FAITH MAKES

Luke 22:71 *At that they said, "What further evidence do we need? We have heard this ourselves from his own lips."*

These people were in an enviable position and didn't know it. There is likely no Christian believer in history who has not said: "If only I could hear Jesus speak, I would need no further evidence. I would never again doubt Him."

For others, just to have seen Jesus would have sealed the deal of their discipleship.

Still others long to have seen Him perform a

miracle. After that, they pledge, no more questions would be asked and every controversial word or deed of Jesus would be chalked up in His favor.

Then there are the combatants who vow that if they had been at Calvary, they would never have allowed Jesus to be crucified; they would have fought it with tooth and the nails lying there ready for use.

Well, that's what we all nobly blather, in our moments of playing to the gallery.

But when faced with similar opportunities to help Him and believe in Him, how our ballooning aspirations deflate, and we become no better than those who still disbelieved Him, though seeing and hearing Him; still looking for more loaves and fish to save money on a free lunch—while unmindful of the miracle they had just seen but been blind to. Understandably, knowing what was in man, Jesus said: "Blessed are those who have not seen (or heard, or tasted or touched) and yet have believed."

It is not, then, the actual, physical contact with Him that is as all important as we think it is. Likewise, distance, time, place, circumstances, age, nationality, don't mean a scrap. Faith, face it, is the victory. That's the invisible means of support, the spiritual factor, that is the Great divide—the Fault for the faithless. "The just shall live by faith."

In Saint Paul's epicentral thirteenth chapter and thirteenth verse in First Corinthians, three virtues take their stand on eternity's podium. Though Love is in first place here, elsewhere in his letters Paul gave equal recognition to the other two. Faith has its day of triumph when it can be said: "The greatest of these is Faith."

PRAYER: *O Invisible, we view Thee. O Intangible, we find Thee—with us, always. Amen.*

Know the Rest of the Story

Luke 23:5 *His teaching is causing unrest among the people.*

How much rest is associated with Jesus. There is the physical rest He promises: "Come unto me all ye that labor and are heavy laden, I will give you rest." And He ensures rest for the soul. Accordingly, the hymn writer confidently asserts, "O Rest in the Lord." On into eternity Jesus prepares for us His mansions of rest, where we reach the heights of Ever-rest. Yet the chief priests and scribes of Jerusalem portrayed Jesus as quite the opposite kind of person: one who was causing unrest and in at least five different ways.

First, Jesus was charged with subverting the nation. The nation, mind you. He, from wee Nazareth in the boondocks, was a national figure, Public Enemy Number One!

Second, Jesus was on a blacklist of anti-tax activists. At any time when a pocketbook is raided, most especially the State treasury, watch out for the brickbats, in word and deed.

Third, there was Jesus' claim, His accusers claimed, to be "Messiah, a King." Hearing that, Pilate, the presiding official, asked Jesus point blank, "Are you the King of the Jews?" (23:3)

Fourth, all the above were said to have stirred up a boiling cauldron of unrest, not only in Judea, but

Fifth, throughout the land. (23:2-5)

From the sound of the accusations, the entire nation seemed to be on the point of imploding. Jesus, a man of rest, indeed! Who said that?

Well, too many still insist that Jesus and His teachings continue to cause unrest among the people of the world. Some are certain that the world has become gray with His breath; that the global village would be better off without Him as an inhabitant. Let each person be his own God. Turn to some of the less demanding tenets in other world religions. Two thousand years with Christ is surely enough. It's time to clear Him out, out, out. And many sectors of society have already swept Him out of their doors.

Yet there He stands, knocking and He is not about to go away. "Behold, I stand at the door and knock and knock and knock..." Because He knows that the world is not through with Him, it's through without Him.

Unrest among the people occurs when they reject the Christ and bring their ears to His enlivening, enduring word. Our hearts are unrested until we seek the rest which only He can give, and none can wrench from us. And it's not that "hurry up and relax" kind of rest. To rest in the Lord is to have the Rest which passes all understanding and misunderstanding.

PRAYER: *Father, we would let go and let God in Christ take charge. Amen.*

HIGH COMMUNION FIND

Luke 23:12 *That same day Herod and Pilate became friends; till then there had been a feud between them.*

Right in the middle of recording Jesus' court trial, Luke feels obliged to include seventeen words that had nothing to do with Jesus or His trial.

Why?

It was no secret that the powerful Roman Prefect, Pilate, of Jerusalem, and Herod, the provincial Jewish ruler of Galilee, up north, had no time for each other. Pilate could hardly be expected to retain his anger upon hearing that Herod had exceeded his limits of power in having John the Baptist beheaded. And, of course, any foreign official, as Pilate was, would be despised by Herod, an indigenous Jew.

How long the ugly situation had lasted suddenly made no difference. For when Pilate turned Jesus over to Herod (who happened to be in Jerusalem), it was just what the doctor ordered for Herod. He was pleased as punch. Once believing that Jesus was John the Baptist come back from the grave, Herod had often wished he could meet Jesus and see Him, perform some death-to-life miracle. And here was Herod's chance! Thank you, Pilate.

And then when Herod sent Jesus back to Pilate, showing Pilate that he, Herod, was hereby acknowledging Pilate's superior power and canceling out any misdemeanor Pilate held against him, Pilate was made to feel good. Thank you, Herod. Let's shake hands.

With Jesus, the bridge-builder between them, how could these two former enemies keep from becoming friends?

This was, this is, Jesus' mission. "In Christ there is no east or west, In Him no south or north. But one great fellowship of love. Throughout the whole wide earth."

But since Herod and Pilate both had a part in Christ's crucifixion, both of those murderers faced a bridge to nowhere. Herod died in exile. Pilate committed suicide.

You see this again on the cross, with Jesus between two thieves. At least one thief crossed the bridge to Jesus—and paradise. The other thief went—who knows where.

In each case the individual was given a last chance to redeem himself, with the help of the Redeemer. Yet, as with the people of Jerusalem whom Jesus wanted to take under His wings, most spurned the opportunity. Only the penitent thief and those like him, took the tide at its flood and were swept into glory.

Herod and Pilate became friends—strange bedfellows, endangered species. They preferred to feud with the Friend of all—the foe, the friendless.

PRAYER: *Divine Companion, it is through You that we would make friends worth having. Amen.*

RING THE DECIBELS FOR HIM

Luke 23:23 *But they persisted with their demand, shouting that Jesus should be crucified. Their shouts prevailed.*

The Holy Bible, though associated with silent meditation and prayer, resounds throughout with shouts. Recent generation, with their boisterous demonstrations have done no less shouting than their forefathers. And the results have been the same—depending on the reason for the uproar, as brought out by our text for today.

Herod and Pilate, as judges, found nothing for which Jesus should be punished. But the hostile Jerusalem crowds inflamed by the chief Priests, thought otherwise. And, convinced that they were not getting their message through the thick skull of Pilate, shouted the word "Crucify" as if to shoot the word into Pilates' brain.

Pilate, already threatened by a demotion was reeling with emotional wounds and visibly vulnerable. A good shout from a demanding mob might bring Pilate's walls tumbling down. And it did, and they did. "Their shouts prevailed."

Is this the winning way to get what you want?

Moses wouldn't have thought so. On their way down Mt. Sinai, Joshua told Moses that it sounded as if the children of Israel were at war. Had all hell broke loose? But Moses was more discerning. No, Moses, responded, it was neither the jubilation of victory in war nor the wailing of defeat. Upon getting closer the two men saw that it was indeed all hell let loose. The Israelites were having a wild time enjoying their newly fashioned god, a golden calf. (Exod. 32:18ff)

But their shouts didn't prevail. The Mosaic anger was aroused, the calf was smashed, pounded to dust, mixed with water—which the revelers were forced to drink. And none of them were allowed to enter the Land of Promise.

So it was with those who gleefully and maliciously shouted for Jesus' execution. They enjoyed their dance of death, but their evil intent died with them. And Jesus lives on.

Then, which shouts are worth the lung-bursting, throat straining effort? Certainly not those which erupt from the rumbling depths of hate. That kind spews out fire and brimstone—elements of the nether regions.

On the other hand, listen to the Psalmist as he remembers joining a throng and leading the procession to the house of God, "with glad shouts and songs of thanksgiving." (Ps. 4:4) They couldn't control their joy. They found so much for which to be grateful—as they longed and thirsted for the living God. They didn't care who heard their loud hosanna. They were happy and comfortable in the Lord, and couldn't wait to get into God's house to sing their Old Testament equivalent of "The Church's one foundation is Jesus Christ our Lord. He is the new creation by water and the Word." That's the shout that prevails, both now and ever.

PRAYER: *To Thee, and for Thee, we sing aloud our faith, O God. In the name of Jesus. Amen.*

THE FUTURE IS NOW

Luke 23:31 *For if these things are done when the wood is green what will happen when it is dry?*

Jesus' seven last words were spoken while He hung on the cross. But the last words which He spoke while still on His feet are the eighteen that make up our text for today.

The words from the cross were addressed to the Heavenly Father, the Penitent Thief, Mother Mary, and John. The words from ground level were to the crowd on the via dolorosa, addressed directly to the weeping women ("Daughters of Jerusalem," v. 28), in their terms ("wombs, breasts" v. 29), and in a proverb which they, especially, would grasp on the run.

Women, among their household chores, were familiar with the daily routine of gathering firewood for cooking. They knew the difference between dry wood (and the drier, the better), and green wood that wouldn't ignite.

Then, as Jesus often did in His teachings, He used the state of the wood to explain why He had just told the crying women not to weep for Him but for themselves. After all, for the joy that was set before Him, He was going to endure the cross despising the shame. But for those who lived on—worse things were ahead. The situation would become so unbearable that people would desperately call upon the mountains to fall on them and end their misery; they would beseech the hills to protect them. (v. 30) And that's not all.

Our Lord found that, as a teaching tool, turning things upside down drew the listener's attention quicker. And here He employs such a technique: "For if," He states finally, the innocent Son of God can be crucified amid peaceful conditions, what is going to happen when the conditions are politically brittle, and there is carelessness with fiery language? A firestorm can sweep the land.

What to do? What is the Master saying in this His final word?

Is it not that we should centralize the Prince of Peace in our personal lives and in our institutional lives, that the green growth might be seen in our relationship with God and with humankind? He wants it that way. He came to show us how and why His Kingdom can come on earth as it is in heaven. And the more we strive to actualize that kingdom, here, the less fear will there be for walking later over minefields, and having a world in flames.

The Life Assurer is with us. Why crucify Him in favor of some thief?

PRAYER: *Savior of the world, straighten out our crooked thinking, that with Thee we may enter the straight gate, and walk the narrow way which leads to life eternal. Amen.*

FROM NOTHING RIGHT TO NOTHING WRONG

Luke 23:41 *In our case it is plain justice; we are paying the price for our misdeeds. But this man has done nothing wrong.*

The reporter of the above text must have been within hearing distance of the three crosses at Calvary, for he (or she) heard each man speak from his cross. And the neon-lit three areas which call for closer attention: "justice," "misdeeds," and "nothing wrong." These were the words of the Penitent thief in an open-air public confessional.

Most people in this fellows position would have pleaded "not guilty." Or, if guilty, it would be made out as a case of the law being at fault; glaring injustice. On the contrary, he comes out with the unbelievably honest approval of "plain justice" being practiced; the law was doing to the two offenders exactly what was happening. And rightly. Then there is the mention of "misdeeds" on the part of both thieves. At least this fellow realized (a little too late) that there is a difference between good deeds and misdeeds. While he was breaking the law he found reasonable excuses, or excusable reasons for doing what he wanted. But now (suddenly?) he saw the difference. Was it because, for the first time, he saw the moral compass for goodness in that Figure on the Central Cross? Or is this where that ancient legend kicks in? It tells of the time when Mary and Joseph were taking the baby Jesus to Egypt. Stopped by bandits, the Holy Family was saved from harm by the young son of the robber chieftain. The boy was captivated by the Holy Child, asking the Baby to have mercy on him.

Then, says the legend, that time came on Calvary. The youth, now a full-fledged robber recognized the Christ in His ageless purity and, at last, became aware of his own life soiled with misdeeds.

Finally, this confessing thief saw "nothing wrong" in Jesus the Righteous. How did he know that? Was it because of what he had heard persons around the cross witnessing to what the Master had done for them? Or was it because the reforming lawbreaker had been transformed in an instant? This by one of the Words from the cross which Jesus uttered? Whatever it was, Jesus recognized in this man one who had taken the necessary steps to conversion.

History remembers this fellow in the brotherhood of the crucified as the malefactor who confessed his sin. And "if we confess our sin, He (Jesus) is faithful and just to forgive us our sins, and to cleanse us from all righteousness," which is what Jesus did immediately, adding, as was His nature, "good measure, pressed down, shaken together, and running over" saying to the fellow who had exteriorized his rottenness, "Today shalt thou be with Me in paradise." That is where one walks in the palace garden with the King!

PRAYER: *Our Lord and Savior, it's never too late for us to be saved. And it's never too soon. We surrender all to You. Now. Amen.*

GOOD GRIEF

Luke 23:56 *Then they ("the women who had accompanied Jesus from Galilee," v. 55) went home and prepared spices and perfumes; and on the Sabbath they rested in obedience to the commandment.*

What an astronomical distance there was between these women and the way they reacted to Jesus' death, and "the crowd who had assembled for the spectacle"—"when they saw what had happened, went home beating their breasts." (Luke 23:48)

For the crowd it was like witnessing a tragedy that would appear in the headline of the evening newspaper. "Hear all about it!" A "spectacle" with which they had no personal connection. But it was stunning enough for them to beat their breasts in bereavement; moving enough for them to memorialize the event for years to come. Today, such events are followed by wreaths, bouquets, cards, love letters, piled up at the site, with annual pilgrimages to the place.

With those who knew Jesus best, one notes no public outpouring of grief. It was as one of the early church fathers wrote that when a non-Christian died, his friends fussed and paraded their torn to piecesness. But when a Christian died, his friends escorted his body, as if he were making a journey from one place to another, near.

Sure, the Galilean women were heartbroken. On the way to Calvary they must have been among the "many women who mourned and lamented over him (Jesus)." (Luke 23:27) Yet those who knew Jesus best were quietly and confidently comforted. Had He not told them on the Mount: "Blessed (happy) are they that mourn, for they shall be comforted"? To be sure, that "mourning" was over their sins. But if He could give comfort then, He could give comfort now. And He did—so that they went to their lodgings in full control of their emotions.

Then, knowing the therapy of work, they prepared for the embalming of Jesus' body. And, instead of forgetting Sabbath observance for their own good reasons, they "rested," "in obedience," "to the commandment," and in obedience to the influence of Jesus' calming Spirit. Hadn't He promised "Lo, I am with you always"?

Those who felt, as St. Paul stated later, that they were determined not to know anything except Jesus Christ and Him crucified, those people found solace in the home, at work, with rest, and worship on the Sabbath. In quietness and in confidence was their strength.

PRAYER: *We thank You, Lord, for teaching us, through the women from Galilee, the four steps to assuaging grief. Amen.*

ON SAVING APOSTLES!

Luke 24:7 *The Son of Man must be given into the power of sinful men and be crucified, and must rise again on the third day.*

(Note: In and around Jerusalem is where Luke finds all of Jesus' resurrection appearances taking place.)

The women of Galilee are still in control not just of their own emotions, but of the whole resurrection experience. The women were center forward, where the eleven apostles, at the moment, were bungling unbelievers.

When the two angelic guardians of Jesus' tomb reminded the women how Jesus had predicted His crucifixion and resurrection, the women remembered how the apostles, on those two former occasions (Luke 9:22, 44) couldn't make sense of what Jesus was saying. And it happened here again. Though these women kept dinning into the apostle's heads what had just occurred at the empty tomb—the apostles sloughed it off as insane blather.

To many persons it still seems incomprehensible that the Son of God must be handed over to sinful men. That concept has scared multitudes away from the Christian faith.

Worse yet is that sinful men have the overwhelming power to subdue the King of Kings and Lord of Lords. With that kind of Leader, what chance do the rest of us have? Should we look for a heftier Savior?

But just when we cannot understand the logic of this prediction, although it is mentioned in similar terms on three different occasions, there comes another *must*. That is the ace. It trumps all the previous appearances of supremacy—"[He] *must* rise again on the third day." He *must* have the last word. His hidden power rises to assert itself, just when there seems to be no hope, and just at the right time: His own good time.

Of this the women were the first to be convinced. The men fell apart. As a group they were pathetic. Judas betrayed. Peter denied. Thomas doubted. They all forsook Jesus and fled from Him. How much more could they have shown their backbonelessness?

To be sure, the men finally were shaken awake by Jesus' reappearance and His eating food before their startled eyes. Yet, had it not been for the women and their faith and their hammering today's text into the minds of the men, those eleven followers may have zeroed out.

Jesus and the women had learned of the power of God from Mary's Magnificat. To her God had shown "the might of His arm." (Luke 1:51) That "might," they knew, would overcome any other "power."

Thank you, ladies, you saved the day.

PRAYER: *And thank You, Lord Jesus for empowering those women to get their fellow disciples back on track. For Thine is the Kingdom and the Power (dynamic, dynamite, dynamighty), and the Glory, forever. Amen.*

STAND BY ME

Luke 24:36 *As they were talking about all this, there he was standing among them.*

After their late night arrival in Jerusalem, Cleopas and a companion couldn't wait to recount to the eleven and the rest of the company assembled (v. 33) in the Upper Room, behind locked doors, the details of the Emmaus encounter with the risen Christ.

But was this phenomenon the same Jesus that the believers had known in the flesh? And what reason had anyone to believe that there was any connection between the Two?

Most in the present assembly had heard Jesus predict that the prophet's writings would find fulfillment in Him. (Luke 18:31) That had been reiterated to the Emmaus travelers that very night (Luke 24:27)—and was to be three-peated before the whole throng moments later. (Luke 24:44) Indeed, as we now look through the writings of Moses, the prophets, the Psalms, and the rest of the Old Testament, we see how much on target Jesus was. There are ninety-three passages in almost every book of the Old Testament that verify Jesus' triple claim. As Henry Halley notes: "by the time we come to the end of the Old Testament, the entire story of Christ has been pre-written, and pre-figured, in language and picture, which, taken as a whole, cannot possibly refer to any other person in history." (H.H. Halley, *Pocket Bible Handbook*, p. 346)

Then, to put the final stamp of validity on His resurrection, "THERE HE WAS standing among them"—having come through locked doors.

Still, those once-believers went retro into unbelief. See the description of their many-sided state of shock: startled, terrified, thought they were seeing a ghost, perturbed, doubting, incredulous, astounded, too good to be true. (v. 36-41)

Breaking the spell by showing His nail-pierced hands and feet, Jesus concluded serenely, "So you see that scripture foretells the sufferings of the Messiah and his rising from the dead on the third day." (v. 46)

Now everything fell into its proper place and made sense, Jesus was the Messiah, the Word made flesh, who lived and died and rose again. It is understandable, then, that Luke had nothing more to write in his gospel. He quickly concludes that the assembly was full of joy, spending "all their time in the temple praising God." (v. 52)

That's what our faith is essentially about, believing in Jesus our crucified and Easter Savior. The whole Bible proclaims it. There is no other name given under heaven whereby we can be saved.

THERE HE WAS when the disciples needed Him most. HERE HE IS for us, in fulfillment of His sacred covenant "Lo, I am with you always." That brings abounding joy. That drives us willingly to the place of worship—wherever that may be—the church, home, school, office. Which means that in every waking moment we worship through all we do, praising God's holy name.

PRAYER: *Ever-living Lord, You are always THERE for us. We are joyful and grateful, now and forever. Amen.*

Upset to Set Up

John 2:15 *He made a whip of cords and drove them out of the temple, sheep, cattle, and all. He upset the tables of the money-changers, scattering their coins.*

In the gospel of John, this is Jesus' first public appearance in the Capital City. And, as some would say, it was a picture of a bull in a china shop. Jesus is blazing with anger at the unabashed merchandising in the Lord's house. Wouldn't this be the reaction of anyone who witnessed the desecration of a prized possession? Here a den (animal-like) of thieves was ransacking the dwelling of the Divine.

Either making a whip, or taking one from a cattle drover, Jesus used it, as the drovers did to drive the for-sale animals out of the sacred area. No doubt the cattle and sheepherders went after their galloping beef and mutton.

Then the rampaging Redeemer turned on the money changers. They presented slight resistance. In an instance their tables, with stacks of coins carefully sorted in their denominations, were tipped over. And there went the coins, every which way—some into the gutter, some toward persons who could put a foot on them and pocket them when no one was looking. What confusion! What an arousal of fiery feelings! Was it at all necessary? Wasn't there a more loving, pleasant, Savior-like way to rid the Temple of claptrap?

Very simply, this typifies the life of Christ. He was not an army tank crashing His way through society, sending mice and men spinning off into destruction. The bruised reed He did not break nor the smoking flax quench. He turned the other cheek, went the second mile to the cross to save the world from sin.

But yes, His was also an upsetting ministry. "I came not to bring peace, but a sword," He stated fearlessly. Whipping animals out of the Temple and overturning the tables of the moneychangers was no onetime deal for Jesus. He was highly sensitive to the presence of human corruption—dealing with it quickly and surgically. He left clean wounds to heal, not infections to worsen.

And Jesus had the best teachers for this type of Kingdom-building. Moses, the prophets, the Psalmists were pioneers in driving out demons and overturning upside down values. God motivated them in the eternal cleansing movement. After all, said Job: "It is God who moves mountains before they know it, overturning them in his wrath." (9:5) Jesus' mother was also of this mind. Her Magnificat shows it. (Luke 1:49-53) E. Stanley Jones called it "the most revolutionary document in the world," especially when she declares that God "scatters the proud in the plans of their hearts." St. Paul, coming later, but imbued with the same no-nonsense, forward thrust wrote to the Corinthians: "I will not have you become partners with demons. You cannot drink the cup of the Lord and the cup of demons. You cannot partake of the Lord's table and the table of demons." (1 Cor. 9:20-21) There are, in every generation, demons to be driven out, their tables overturned, and their sinful profits scattered.

Who will do it? Here am I, send me.

PRAYER: *Loving Lord, steadfast standard bearer, we rally to Your cause, cost what it may. Amen.*

THE CHURCH ETERNAL

John 2:21 *But the temple he was speaking of was his body.*

Upon cleansing the Temple, Jesus was challenged by irate witnesses to justify His impertinent action. So attention was turned from cattle and coins to the titanic temple's already forty-six years in the building, with eighteen more years until completion.

The Lord had not emptied one of the Temple courts of its offensiveness for nothing. He was on His way to a deeper message. He foresaw that the Temple was doomed to destruction, no matter how squeaky clean it was kept, physically. The more lasting house of worship He was to declare, was within His body—and ours. Then, though the templed body dies, as His did, and as ours will—there will be an arising, as at Easter, for the Risen Lord and His loved ones.

But how is the human body the dwelling place of the Most High? Where is the worship center and who leads worship? When? How? And does this make unnecessary what we do in the local church?

St. Paul, one of his Lord's fine-tuned interpreters and amplifiers, was amazed that Christians didn't know the answers to the above questions. "Surely you know," he said hopefully, "that you are God's temple, where the Spirit of God dwells. Anyone who destroys God's temple will himself be destroyed by God, because the Temple of God is holy; and you are that temple." (1 Cor. 3:16-17) Or, again, "do you not know that your body is a temple of the indwelling Holy Spirit, and the Spirit is God's gift to you? You do not belong to yourselves; You were bought at a price. Then honor God in your body." (1 Cor. 6:19-20)

Returning to this subject in a Letter to the

Ephesians, Paul helpfully adds, "You are built on the foundation of the apostles and prophets, with Christ Jesus himself as the cornerstone. In him the whole building is bonded together and grows into a holy temple in the Lord. (2:20-21)

Here we are, then, templed bodies with the best blest cornerstone and foundation, and Master Pastor—the Holy Spirit. And we're not grounded, immovably, in a few acres. We're temples on the move, as the Tabernacle was in the Sinai. We can take the church to work, to play, in the home, into exile, to person (for our faith) to the ghetto—wherever the Spirit guides. That's the way He prefers it.

Oh, the local church will always be needed. As Jesus insisted, He came not to destroy but to fulfill. The church is the repository of the history of our faith. It brings us together in a growing fellowship. With its organization it can multiply our individual endeavors for God's glory—worldwide.

Nor should we forget what we've just seen Jesus doing—cleansing the Temple. Consistently that must continue in His church and in our templed bodies—through confession of sin, repentance, scripture, prayer, praise, and Holy Communion.

PRAYER: *With Christ in us, heavenly Father, the gates of hell shall never prevail against the Church. Amen.*

ON REMOVING THE RUST FROM TRUST

John 2:23-24 *While he was in Jerusalem for Passover many put their trust in him when they saw signs that he performed. But Jesus for his part would not trust himself to them. He knew them all.*

Though unrecorded, Jesus' impressive works won

a host of believers in Him. With such success everyone is usually well pleased. And Jesus should have been. Didn't He invite such followership? Weren't ALL welcome? Wasn't His promise that "in no wise" would anybody be cast out?

One hears the door shut with the word "But." Yes, Jesus the open-armed welcomer hasn't changed. The problem is with persons who have disregarded His conditions for discipleship. Ineligible, they can expect the shut-out response, "depart from me, I never knew you." In fact, He knows them better than they know themselves. They may be kidding themselves about their eligibility to belong in His company, but they are not hoodwinking Him. Without research assistants, think-tanks, scanners, screeners, polls, or psychoanalysis, Jesus knows us all, and knows all in us. As with the celebrity status, He was "too shrewd, a reader of human nature to be unduly impressed by it." (A.M. Hunter)

Those who ate of the multiplied loaves and fishes and who, thereafter, followed Jesus as their Free-Lunch-Distributor, learned their lesson in sharp order. He would have none of that "milk faith" as Luther called it.

What, then, is Jesus looking for in us? What is He hoping to find before He puts His trust in "us"? "Not everyone that saith to me, Lord, Lord, shall enter the Kingdom of heaven, but he that doeth the will of my Father in heaven."

And what is His will for those He cherishes? Certainly part of His will is for prospective, in-earnest disciples to deny self, take up their cross daily, and walk in His footsteps.

That's too authoritarian, too confining, too

dictatorial for too many church members today. Sadly, church membership and Christian discipleship parted company when they ought to be united. Church membership today is not unlike the Jerusalemites in the above text, Christ is turned to and called upon, only when He can burnish human pride, hand out the mild and honeyed words, and see that the Sermon on the Mount brings in the right amount.

No wonder that He withholds His trust and the church is no longer His Bride. She's too fickle; too infatuated with things that titillate her fancy for the moment.

The Lord, for His part, will not trust Himself to us who wish to call ourselves His own—until He hears from us the kind of firm-jawed loyalty He heard from King David's lips: "I will not offer the Lord God that which cost me nothing." (2 Sam. 24:24) It's not calling for a grim grind of a Christian life. But He wants that binding oath—for better or worse; in sickness and in health; to love and to cherish, with heart, soul, mind and strength, now and forever.

PRAYER: *Trust us, Lord, we pray, for we henceforth are wholly Yours, sincerely. Amen.*

GROWN BY HIM AND FOR HIM

John 3:3 *Jesus answered, "In very truth I tell you, no one can see the Kingdom of God unless he has been born again."*

In this section (John 3:1-21), before Jesus exits Jerusalem, He encounters Nicodemus, by night, and leads him to the light.

It is significant that this lesson on being born, born again, and yet again, sees first light in the cradle of Judaism. Then, like the Good News which it is, it spread from Jerusalem—through the New Testament and to the uttermost parts...

But, at first, Nicodemus, well established in the top bracket of the religious hierarchy, was too encumbered with the baggage of religiosity to understand any of it but natural, physical birth. Being born again in any other terms was incomprehensible. Impossible.

With truth on His side (mentioned four times), Jesus brushed aside the "impossibles" of Nicodemus, explaining that there was also a spiritual birth. In general terms, this birth has some of the features of the physical birth. We are fed on the milk of the Word. We grow in wisdom and stature, and in favor with God and man. We now relish the meat of the Word. We are ready to put on the whole armor of God; "For our struggle is not against human foes, but against cosmic powers, against the authorities and potentates of this dark age, against the super human forces of evil in the heavenly realms." (Eph. 6:11-12)

Born again, we are new (altogether) in Christ Jesus.

Nicodemus' truth-intake couldn't accommodate. He had to grow into it. And knowing that, Jesus gave the man a glimpse of still another birth into life eternal, which is mentioned twice, in John 3:15 and the famous 16.

This third birth can be more bewildering than the first two together. How can a body, cremated or buried or mutilated, come alive again? Well, Jesus showed how it was possible—wounds and all. Then St. Paul took it from there—to explain, as his Lord did in physical, understandable word pictures. What the birthing from death to eternal life entails. "But, you may ask, how are the dead raised? In what kind of body?" "What you sow is not the body that shall be, but a bare grain, of wheat perhaps, or something else; and God gives it the body of his choice, each seed its own particular body...so it is with the resurrection of the dead: what is sown as a perishable thing is raised imperishable...sown a physical body, it is raised a spiritual body...flesh and blood can never possess the Kingdom of God, the perishable cannot possess the imperishable...we shall be changed in a flash...then the saying of scripture will come true...Death is swallowed up; victory is won. (1 Cor. 15:35-57)

Speaking further of those who have been born again, Paul adds that they are citizens of heaven, "and from heaven we expect our deliverer to come, the Lord Jesus Christ. He will transfigure our humble bodies, and give them a form like that of his own glorious body, by that power which enables him to make all things subject to himself." (Phil. 3:20-21)

PRAYER: *Creator God: We now know the Destiny that shapes us. It is You, gracious Lord. Father us through all the birthings of our existence. Now and forever. Amen.*

THE YOU IN TRUTH

John 3:21 *Those who live by the truth come to the light so that it may be clearly seen that God is in all they do.*

Jesus is still speaking to Nicodemus. It must have been a long night but an enriching one. For tradition has it that Nicodemus became a believer in Christ. How could it have been otherwise? Nicodemus was searching earnestly for the truth and found it in Jesus who is the Truth.

Since Nicodemus had sought Jesus during the hours of darkness, it was inevitable Jesus should use darkness and "light" to educate this mature student in the faith.

You would think, Jesus explained, that people would prefer light to darkness. Most of life is lived during daylight. We even change our clocks to enjoy added daylight time. Those are the hours for seeing the work that requires doing. To be sure, with artificial lighting much work is now carried on around the clock. Yet that aspect of it didn't concern Jesus at the moment. The moral and spiritual qualities of light and dark better defined what He wanted to communicate to Nicodemus.

Jesus found people prefer darkness. Why? Because their deeds are evil. "Wrongdoers hate the light and avoid it, for fear their misdeeds should be exposed." (John 3:20)

So! People prefer to cling to their misdeeds. God, cleanse me—but not yet, not completely. Let me enjoy my shady deals. Allow me to be financially well fixed while I find comfort in the shadow of a doubt.

Shadows appear when some object gets in the way of light. Trouble in the soul begins when something gets in between Christ, the Light of the World, and us. Shades of darkness appear, inviting areas in which to secrets away the cherished questionables of daily life. They afford too much fun and frolic to give up.

Adam and Eve let the forbidden fruit black out the radiance of God's presence. Immediately, they saw a need to cover up, to hide, to lie, to quibble. Lurking in the shadows they couldn't quite see where they were going or what they were thinking or doing.

An uncertainly, a fear of being found out, doubts about their creator, where to find fig leaves. The contrast with having lived in the light, instead of being in a cooling comforting shade—was increasingly terrifying, deeply disrupting.

But one doesn't have to live that way. We have the option, Jesus insists on keeping the way unobstructed between His brilliant Sonshine and ourselves. It is not that we shall never err. His light shows up the truth of a situation which indicates that we are in the wrong. But, through repentance and obeying His corrective instructions, we are extricated from quicksand and our feet set again on solid ground. Freed from the need to uncover our covert ways, determined to lie in the revealing, healing light of divine truth, we and others will see clearly (no longer darkly) that God is in all that we do.

Light has come into the world and, with the help of Him who is that Light, we shall make our preference, not lite, but L I G H T.

PRAYER: *Dear Lord, thank You for seeing that Your priceless lesson for Nicodemus finally reached us. "Light of the world illumine this darkened earth of Thine, till everything that's human, is filled with the divine." Amen.*

THE WILL TO BE WELL

John 5:6 *Jesus saw him lying there, and knowing that he had been ill a long time he asked him, "Do you want to get well?"*

Following a pastoral visit to Samaria and Cana, Jesus found reason to return to Jerusalem. It was Festival time and the Sabbath.

Since the Sabbath was made for man to do good, Jesus was drawn to the pool of Bethesda where the sick were known to be prevalent. Walking among them, making inquiries, the Master came upon a worst-case scenario—a cripple who had made that healing center his dwelling place for a longer time than Jesus had lived, thirty-eight years.

Able to size up persons and situations in a jiffy, as we have noted, Jesus asked the cripple what to many seems an impertinent, insulting, hurtful question: "Do you want to get well?" After lying around there helplessly, who wouldn't want to get out of there in a hurry?

But Jesus did not retract his probing question. Why? Dr. Arthur gossip, assuming that the cripple had tried to get into the healing waters—unsuccessfully, every day, for thirty-eight years—figured that the man had made some 14,000 attempts to get well. But who is to know? He might have tried twice every day. Or given up after the first year or so. In which case it would have been the better part of valor to accept his inescapable physical condition. After all, if only the first person to step into the bubbling water was healed, this cripple had a lot of competition. And since misery loves company, the Bethesda fellowship could be quite binding and difficult to think of leaving. Nobody was dying of hunger, so food was being brought in. To maintain relatively hygienic conditions, clothes must have been cleaned, floors swept, "rest room" facilities provided. And one didn't have to work to pay for it all.

Today in some large cities, thousands of people live this way underground, like moles, and they love it. Many, of course, are on the run from family, friends, jobs, justice. But they love where they are. They are among their own kind.

But there was something more about the cripple which Jesus learned and/or suspected. "A little later Jesus found him in the temple and said to him, 'Now that you are well, give up your sinful ways, or something worse may happen to you.'" (John 5:14)

In spite of the cripple's sinful ways and his highlighting his thirty-eight years, which, to good Jews, would put him on a par with the Israelites wandering in the wilderness for forty years, Jesus looked beyond the man's foibles, and healed him—on the Sabbath. Jesus did that at the expense of His own life. "This made the Jews all the more determined to kill [Jesus], because not only was he breaking the Sabbath but, by calling God his own Father, he was claiming equality with God." (John 5:18)

Do we want to get well—physically mentally, matrimonially, financially, spiritually? Take the Divine Healer at His word: "Stand up. Well."

PRAYER: *Love divine, all loves excelling, we are grateful that You never give up on us, we will stand up, stand up for Jesus. We shall stand on His promises and no longer lounge on the premises. Amen.*

OUR TIRELESS PROTECTOR

John 5:17 *He defended himself by saying, "My Father continues to work, and I must work too."*

How to observe the Sabbath was the cause of much controversy in Jesus' time, as it still is in ours.

For having healed the Bethesda cripple on the Sabbath, Jesus was accused of working, therefore desecrating the holy day.

Refusing to be cornered, the Lord went on the offensive with the reminder that the heavenly Father never ceases working. Why shouldn't Jesus follow that best Exemplar?

Right away that confused His accusers, God working on the Sabbath? Didn't He, Himself, forbid such labor, since He, Himself, had rested on the seventh day of creation?

Yet the Rabbis and wise men would support Jesus' position. Since all of life keeps going, Sabbath or not, God cannot sleep. He must be constantly aware of the proper functioning of the universe. He rested after His work of creating the world, without slackening on His responsibility to keep His creation in running order. That, Jesus persisted, was all the permission He needed to do what He did at Bethesda and what He proposed to continue doing on any Sabbath day that called for His services.

Lest we forget, Jesus came not to destroy the Fourth Commandment, but to fulfill it. The extremists and nit-pickers were the destroyers. They made a career out of defining, re-defining, re-designing "work" to ludicrous lengths. There were literally thousands of ifs, ands, and buts that made their way of keeping the Sabbath workless, worthless.

As God pronounced that demandment on Sinai, and as Jesus properly understood and practiced it, it has become, as former British Prime Minister Harold Macmillan phrased it: "The greatest piece of workers' protection legislation in history."

And how did Jesus keep His Sabbath, and mean for us to keep ours?

One unbroken habit was that Jesus attended public worship on the Sabbath—either to teach/preach and/or to pray, listen, chant, respond in a fellowship of believers. Nor did He exist on this once-a-week ingestion of the Bread of

Life. "Give us this day our daily bread," He prayed and received and partook of, in solitary places and with associates. His was a life in which He was always about His Father's business.

But not just holding His Father's hand. With Jesus' other hand He reached out to all persons who were in need—on the Sabbath or any other day. He was the connecting power line between the Source of all Power and the weak human recipient in need of regenerating.

Paradoxically, these days, we must work hard to set aside a time for rest on the Sabbath. Otherwise the tsunami of "must dos" will storm any quietude out of existence. And the last state will be worse than the first "Seven devilish."

PRAYER: *Lord of the Sabbath, who showed us how to keep the day holy, make us examples of Your right observance. Amen.*

THE LORD'S BEST KEPT SECRET

John 5:24 *In very truth I tell you, whoever heeds what I say and puts his trust in Him who sent me has eternal life; he does not come to judgment, but has already passed from death to life.*

In these swift moving times when milliseconds are worth their weight in platinum, briefer is better. But no more succinct than our text. *Multum in parvo*—much in little. A world of meaning in a nutshell. All we could ever ask for, for the taking. And all in four forthright statements. That's the way Jesus thought and spoke—to be understood even on the run.

"In very truth" is always Jesus' warning that He is about to express a fact of life that deserves acute attention. Listen up, He urges: First, "heed what I say." Why did the Lord have any doubt about being taken seriously? There were those who proclaimed Him as a Teacher come from God. The common people heard Him gladly. Multitudes followed Him and hung on every word He uttered. The Palm Sunday acclamation which He received from the populace was usually reserved for the triumphal entry of a conquering King.

Yet Jesus was insightful enough to know that truth has its vilifiers, those who can't or won't understand it. Or if they do understand, they attack it for its innate revelation of their own sins. Such unheeding persons were found not only among the masses who heard Jesus' teachings and witnessed His miracles, they were to be counted even among His apostles.

So it was not a preacher pleading with His listeners to shake off their slumbers and turn up their hearing aids. It was Jesus' challenge to take Him at His word, and make that word incarnate in their everyday activities.

Second, trust the Father who sent His son. That is why much depends on the first point. For the person who trusts the Word of the Lord Jesus Christ, and believes in Him, naturally feels likewise about the divine Sender, the Heavenly Father, the God who so loved the world that He gave His only begotten Son to redeem the world.

If the accomplishment of One and Two find favor in the sight of the Lord, then the reward is forthcoming. And the best part is that there is no waiting period. Often we are left yearning for our wages in the afterlife. Do we have to hope along with sick hearts because that hope is deferred until Judgment Day? Then suppose the judgment goes against us? All our heeding and trusting would have been in vain.

Not on your life, the Lord affirms. "In very truth" when One and Two have passed the expectations of our loving Lord, there is no Judgment Day in our future. The reward is presented to us in the here and now. Life in the Lord is what eternal life is all about, not in some distant era or in some other universe, but where we are at this moment. We have already been translated "from death to life."

That, in very truth, in His word. Read it again at the top of this page, and enjoy that new Life—Now.

PRAYER: *Dear Lord, many thanks for this precious verse. We shall keep it in the locket of our hearts—and live by it. Amen.*

HIS SHUT-OUT WORD

John 5:38 *His word has found no home in you, because you do not believe the one whom he sent.*

The fallout from the Bethesda healing (John 5:1-9) was still raining down on Jesus. He was being charged for breaking the Sabbath, but also for "claiming equality with God." (John 5:18)

Jesus now takes verses 19-47 of chapter 5 to explain His position as Son of the heavenly Father.

In today's text Jesus informs His accusers that God's Word has found no dwelling place in their lives. But their knowledge of God's Word was the one certainty, they were convinced, no one would dare to question. The Jews, especially these religious leaders who were breathing heated, hate-filled breaths down Jesus' neck, were people of the Word.

It was in their minds and on their tongues throughout each day. On what grounds, then, did Jesus, who was brought up in that same Jewish tradition, have the nerve to tell His fellow Jews that for all their knowledge of God's Word they were not standing on its promises? They were merely sitting on the premises?

These accusers of His, Jesus responded, showed that they didn't believe in the Word of God, since they didn't believe in Jesus, the One whom God had sent to redeem the world, the One whose coming the Old Testament points to, throughout.

And the proof of their unbelief in Jesus was evident, not only by the discriminatory way they used God's Word, but also by the way they became deaf to that Word, because they refused to hear the voice of the Father in heaven. They couldn't recognize the Word as belonging to God.

Had the accusers known the Father, they would have known the Son; would have known others in the family of God. Having claimed to be part of that family, there would have been a familial, comfortable understanding of each other, ease of movement, with all doors open, no secrets hidden would be the order of the day.

Instead, in this situation, Jesus found that God's Word was homeless. It needed a welcome, but was met with a "no admittance" sign. It needed room in which to be read, marked, learned, inwardly digested. But there was no place for the Unseen guest at every meal, the Silent Listener to every conversation. Where was the place and time for private meditation and family prayers? Nowhere. Where was the cleanliness (body, mind, spirit) that is next to Godliness? Look again.

No room in the homey inn was reenacted in Jesus' adulthood.

Is that the unwelcome sign that is still being hung out for Him? Lord, is it I?

PRAYER: *Lord Jesus we do believe that You are the Son God sent to us. Hereby we are assured that His Word has found a permanent home in us. Amen.*

THE FELLOWSHIP OF THE UNASHAMED

John 7:13 *No one talked freely about him, however, for fear of the Jews.*

After a tour of the Galilee area, Jesus returned to Jerusalem much against His will.

Though no one openly talked about Jesus, His name was on the lips of nearly everybody attending the feast of Tabernacles. He was the talk of the town, that is, in whispers, behind closed doors, in unfrequented alleyways. The dread attached to Jesus' name not only from the vastly differing opinions which people had of Him, but also because the Jewish religious professionals, astonished at His blatant breaking of commandments and jealously guarded traditions, were looking for the right moment to trap, torture, and put Him to death. To be even overheard mentioning the name of "Jesus" would result in serious repercussions for the speaker.

In our text for today "the Jews" get the blame for the great hush that prevailed over the city concerning the person Jesus Christ. Yet all through the ages, "the Jews" have been replaced by unnumbered cases for zipping people's lips when it comes to expressing themselves about the Stranger of Galilee.

You can understand it when unbelievers shut Him out of their minds and lives and conversations. At best He is a matter of jest for them. As when Jesus was sculptured full size, in chocolate, and called "Our Sweet Lord."

What is more worrisome is when believers, given an opening to proclaim Christ as Savior, go mealy-mouthed and dither to a stuttering halt.

Especially is this noticeable in this era, when being politically correct must take precedence over all else.

In our racially complex society, Christians are scared numb and dumb at the thought of fear of the Hindus, Muslims, Buddhists, Transcendentalists, et al.

A missionary lectured at a University. In the question period, one student asked, "You spoke all about Christianity. What about Islam, Hinduism?"

"Why?" asked the missionary. "Are you Muslim?" "No," replied the student. "Are you Buddhist?" "No." "Then, what are you?" "I guess I'm a kind of a Christian," replied the student. "That's interesting," said the missionary. "I've worked for forty years among Muslims. Never once have I heard a Muslim say, 'I guess I'm a kind of a Muslim,' or a Hindu saying, 'I guess I'm a kind of a Hindu.' Son, your problem is with Jesus Christ. Get to know Him first and all these other things will be added unto you."

That was Jerusalem's problem. As Jesus found—"they would not."

Who does not want to talk uninhibitedly about the love of one's life? Who is going to stop you?

Jesus loves me, this I know. Do I love Him

enough to speak really freely about Him—anywhere, anytime?

PRAYER: *My Jesus, I love Thee....Take my life and let it be ever, only, all for thee. Hear it—all ye—from the housetops. Amen.*

GRAND CANYONS

John 7:43 *Thus he was the cause of a division among the people.*

The Festival of Tabernacles had reached the peak of its meaningfulness on the last day of its observance. The crowds were never larger than they were at this time. The faithful never more devout. And Jesus took that tide at its flood, perhaps while the ceremony of pouring water from the Pool of Siloam on the altar took place.

Raising His voice, Jesus declared that it was in Him that living water (not just Siloam water) found its source.

That pressed the red button that bestirred the listeners to take varying views of Jesus. "Thus he was the cause of a division."

But can the Savior, who with outstretched arms invites all people to come to Him, be just the opposite? Is He really the One who came, as He asserted, not to bring peace, but a Sword? Is He the great cleaver causing a divisive Christianity? Does this account for the infighting within each denomination, each local church, each doctrine, each line of the multiple versions of the Bible? Is this why Christianity is said to be the cause of war and never its cure? Where is there any unanimity to be found in the Christ who is prior to all, and in whom all things cohere?

In general that's the picture which the adversaries of Christianity would have the world accept. And once that notion is bought into, no part of Christendom is viewed as holy. It becomes a target full of the buckshot of skepticism.

Yet this is because the apartheid, for which Jesus is blamed, is wrongly interpreted. It all depends on where the emphasis is put, as with the expression "a gray day." Said one way, it is depressing. Said, rather, that it is "a grade A," is encouraging, uplifting.

Indeed, Jesus came not to bring peace but a sword. The sword, however, was not a weapon of annihilation which He wielded. The only such frightful use of a sword, in Jesus' presence, was done when Peter cut off of a human ear—which Jesus instantly healed (His last miracle). The Master had a more incisive, refined purposes for His two-edged sword. More helpfully it would accomplish what King Solomon suggested for discovering the truth in the case of the two women who claimed the same baby as their own. Solomon commanded a sword to be brought (1 Kings 3:24) and for the child to be divided and given to each woman. The sword was never used, but it definitely brought the truth to light.

The only cleavages Jesus had in mind were the lines drawn in the sand, beyond which one dare not go. No more fuzziness between good and evil. "This is the way," and none other.

PRAYER: *Uniting Savior, keep us ever aware of the divides we dare not cross, and the divisions we must obliterate. Amen.*

UNLOOSE HIM

John 7:45 *The temple police went back to the chief priests and Pharisees, who asked them, "Why have you not brought him?"*

For the heavy lifting in security matters, the Roman occupation forces in Palestine were in charge. They also patrolled the sensitive Temple area in Jerusalem. Adjacent to the Temple precincts there was a Roman garrison quartered in what was called the Tower of Antonia (named in honor of the Roman Emperor Mark Anthony). During the big Jewish Festivals, when hundreds of thousands of pilgrims swarmed into the Capital City, emotional outbursts could ignite an explosive situation, and often did—when the military alone had the weaponry and expertise to maintain order.

In local matters of security, Jewish religious leaders were allowed, by their Roman overlords, to have their own policing system. These were known as the Temple police (in today's text). John mentions them five times in his gospel.

Concerned about Jesus' quickly growing popularity among the townsfolk, religious leaders gave orders for Jesus to be arrested. (John 7:32) But the police returned empty-handed, trying their bumbling best to explain why. They had never heard anyone speak so winsomely as this Jesus. They came under His spell, and were strangely unable to treat Him as a lawbreaker.

In John 18:3, Temple police figure in the eventual arrest of Jesus, at His place of prayer in Gethsemane. This time, to ensure the arrest, a military escort was sent to embolden the wavering police.

In John 18:22, a Temple policeman, showing off in front of his employer, the high priest, smacked Jesus' face for being cheeky to the boss man.

In John 19:6, when Pilate presented Jesus as one who was faultless, the chief priests and their

Temple police led the cry against Jesus: "Crucify, Crucify."

"Temple police" still operate inside the Church and outside. Often alerted by the clergy, these spotters lay heavy hands on any movement that would make Jesus overly popular, and lead to a congregation known as "Jesus people." But confronting Jesus personally, such Church vigilantes are impressed by Him, and confused in their own attitude toward Him.

Egged on by persons for whom Church means going through the motions, and to whom Jesus is a recurring annoyance to their conscience, the policing brethren finally put a silencer on this Jesus business, and have little hesitancy in calling for an up-to-the-minute crucifixion. "Were you there when they crucified my Lord?"—and the church goes merrily on its way as a secular institution? A Christless Churchianity.

PRAYER: *Heavenly Father, we want to report that we have brought Jesus to church, and to the uttermost parts. Amen.*

TOUGH LOVE

John 8:11 *Go; do not sin again.*

This was Jesus' sternly compassionate dismissal of the woman caught in the act of adultery—a highly controversial episode, which for centuries has been swatted around, now rejected, now accepted.

Although it looks as if it would have fitted in after Luke 21-38, because it and John 8:2 refer to the same occasion, it now appears at the end of John's gospel in a special section called John 8:1-11, with several explanations and disclaimers.

Apparently the chief Executive Officers (or Officious?) going over the original Manuscripts and styles and vocabularies, decided that this might be a true story, but that it did not belong in the Canon (our authorized Bible). The main reason, it finally comes out, is because Jesus seemed too easy on this sinner. It was seen as a lowering of moral standards. Safer to leave it out.

Actually, it tells more about the shaky beliefs of those who made such ominous decisions. Questioning Jesus, indeed! They were no better than the Scribes and Pharisees who started this firestorm (John 8:3).

Nor has there been any need to try and get Jesus off the hook, as some gallant scholars have felt obliged to do. Our Lord knew exactly what His opponents were up to. As we learn earlier in this gospel, Jesus "had no need of evidence from others about anyone, for he himself could tell what was in people." (John 2:25)

The religious officials were hell-bent on killing Jesus. They felt that He had backed them into a corner often enough. He had to go. And this was another such attempt: set a carefully prepared trap, with a woman allegedly caught in the act of adultery, placed in the exposed center of a crowd in the temple, with Jesus giving a verdict on the case which would be against the law! Perfect crime. Spring the trap.

But these plotters never did realize who they were trying to kid. The situation is clearly portrayed in a picture in the National Art Gallery in London. Jesus stands before His inquisitor. But you can tell at a glance who is in charge: the Christ.

In the Jerusalem scenario, once again Jesus turned the tables on the real deviates, allowing mercy to season justice for the adulteress. Obvious defeat and the stabs of conscience took care of those who knew better but did worse. They slunk away noiselessly.

And there stood the woman, alone, with her Rescuer. What would be His final word? First, because the supposed charge had fizzled out, Jesus let it go at that: "Neither do I condemn you." (8:11) This is where the critics have rushed in to condemn Jesus. But for Him it didn't stop there. Second, "go," He added. She was free—no longer under anybody's coercion; no longer under threat of being stoned to death. Yet Jesus never let her off scot-free. Three, could have been more painful, and for a longer time than stoning: "do not sin again." That's putting on the restraints—if one reads what Jesus said about adultery in His Sermon on the Mount. (Matt. 5:27-30) "If your right eye causes your downfall, tear it out and fling it away; it is better for you to lose one part of your body than for the whole of it to go to hell." There's nothing lax about that. And the rest of the Bible backs Him up. (Ezek. 18:4; Rom. 6:23; 1 Cor. 6:9; Gal. 5:19-21)

PRAYER: *Lord, Your lesson is for all of us. Take away our bent to sinning. We want to "go" with You all the way. Amen.*

RIGHT SIGHT BY HIS LIGHT

John 8:12 *Once again Jesus addressed the people: "I am the light of the world. No follower of mine shall walk in darkness; he shall have the light of life."*

Unable to make a dent in the steely attitude of

the religious hierarchy, Jesus returned to the populace that was always anxious to give Him a hearing.

Always a contextual speaker, Jesus spoke out of the midst of the customary Illumination ceremony in Jerusalem. Bouncing His claim off the breathtaking sight of the illumined Temple, He proclaimed that He was not just like this local lighting system but the light of the world, no less. Then, as always, He didn't leave the message on distant horizons, but instantly made it personal in the here and now. And notice the two assuring and reassuring promises that include the word "shall." No shilly-shallying. Not one of His followers shall walk in darkness. Each *shall* have the light of life.

What does it mean when someone says: "He/she is the light of my life?" Doesn't it mean, for one thing, that this person is a shining example worth copying? And when we lose such a person, there is an outage of power in our lives. The lights go out. Even the brightest day has a pall over it. We can't think quite as clearly. Work is abnormally burdensome, for the spark of enthusiasm is absent. All of which makes for a wake-up call to be more dependent on the One who assured His followers that they would never be at the mercy of power outages. As controller of all power and authority, God-in-Christ is the only One who can finger the switch that turns the Universe on or off. Already he has taken care of past and present. That we know, even if at times we cannot believe it. But when, by faith, we get a solid grip on the reality and reliability of Christ's ever-lastingness, the future will be no more hazardous than the past or present, but a head-lighted highway to the Gloryland.

As Jesus had quadruple meanings to much that He taught (a timesaver in a brief three-year ministry), the setting of this address near the Temple Treasury that was within the Court of the Women, had ricochets off money and women.

How much we humans have always needed the light of understanding where money is concerned. We love the "filthy lucre," making it the root of all evil. Lives are destroyed by it; so are families and nations. But Jesus shows the healthy way to be wealthy.

And then there was His emancipation of women. Theirs was a gloomy existence. It was Jesus who tore that veil to shreds and started the ladies on their long and widened way to world leadership.

St. Paul knew this "light of life." It enabled him to report: "I am toiling strenuously with all the energy and power of Christ at work in me." (Col. 1:29)

PRAYER: *Light of the world, illumine this darkened earth of Thine until everything that's human be filled with the divine. Amen.*

THE HE(ART) OF SOUL-WINNING

John 8:30 *As he said this, many put their faith in him.*

For those of us who seek souls for Christ, this is intriguing. What to say that will bring disciples to the Master? Of course, we know that what He was—the main magnet. Yet here the report is that Jesus' words captured the allegiance of "many" listeners.

And that was astounding, when we remember that Jesus, on those occasions, was confronted by a rebellious, unbelieving, insulting, life-threatening mob. Still He won "many," though not all, to His side. How?

For one thing, He said: "You will die in your sins unless you believe that I am what I am." (8:24) That would shake-awake their slumbering consciences. As it did for the Penitent Thief, who swiftly recognized his last chance to be saved—and grabbed it. A life-buoy! The other thief waited for yet another chance or brazenly swept it aside—once for all. And that was the division among those people who heard Jesus' wake-up-call and who still do.

He also said: "What I heard from Him (the heavenly Father) I report to the world." (8:26) Later He was to say (8:28): "I tell you what I have seen in my Father's presence." How much more authentic and authoritative could Jesus' words have been when He had *seen* and *heard* them from Father God Himself? Nor did Jesus want to keep that good News to Himself. He wanted the whole world to benefit from it. They were not going to hear any better news anywhere else, from anyone else.

And He said: "He who sent me is present with me, and has not left me on my own." (8:29) Certainly here is one message from God that was passed along to the world in Jesus' own "Lo, I am with you always. I will never leave you nor forsake you." The divine detachment from humankind was itself abandoned by Jesus. Instead, He portrayed a Father God who was perennially putting His everlasting arms about His children of earth.

Jesus also asserted: "I always do what is pleasing to Him (the heavenly Father)." (8:29) How much this depends on the preceding. How could Jesus have known what was pleasing to the Father, unless they were close and communicative? This, at least, is how we learn to please each other on the local level. With intimacy, frequency of give and take over the years, comes a comfortable and mutual fluency in understanding, aided by the Holy spirit.

Little wonder that many put their faith in Jesus. He was in close touch with heaven and earth. You can't miss being on His side. Let's tell others about Him, that they may join us at His side, now and forever.

PRAYER: *To whom else shall we go, Lord Jesus; You have all that we will ever need. Amen.*

O COME, ALL YE FAITHFUL

John 10:22 *It was winter.*

Hanukkah. Lights. Festivities. Jerusalem was in its original Christmas mode. And Jesus was there, perhaps celebrating His own birthday in the Capital City and/or in nearby Bethlehem.

This gospel writer, John, a Jerusalem Jew, knew well that his hometown, in "winter" could be bitterly cold. With an elevation of some 3,000 feet, it is often snow-covered at Christmas. The specific mention of Solomon's Portico (in the Temple, v. 23) suggests that those who were "gathered round him" were sheltering from a snowfall. And what better way to get warm than by starting a heated discussion. "How long are you going to keep us in suspense? Tell us plainly: Are you the Messiah?"

The Festival of Lights apparently did little to enlighten the minds of these questioners who huddled around Jesus. Others may have been singing the equivalent of "O come, O Come, Emmanuel," but not these cynical, songless Semites. They had a voice, though a harsh one, for Jesus.

Not only was the Temple lighted up, so too were private homes, in remembrance of how Judas Maccabeus and his brothers reclaimed the land from that hideous despoiler of it, Antiochus Epiphanes, but it was also a time for rejoicing. Although it had been at least 200 years since the country and its capital, had been ransacked and desecrated—then ritually cleansed and reconsecrated—the populace was in high spirits, except for those like the scowlers by whom Jesus was hemmed in. They were not about to be distracted by any of the season's festivities.

It was not that Jesus refused to answer their question as to whether He was the Messiah. "I have told you," (v. 25) He replied. In fact He had stated His case straight-forwardly on several occasions. But that was not the answer they wanted. They grimly clung to their homespun version and would accept no other. They were to become that section of humanity over whom Jesus wept with disappointment. He offered them His saving grace, but they refused His Saviorhood.

Is this an earlier blueprint of what Christmas has now become? We know its central meaning. The prophets have repeatedly heralded the Messiah's coming to earth; that He would reclaim the world which had slipped yet again after being cleansed by Noah's Flood. Then Jesus came, fulfilling all the Old Testament prophesies about His coming. What more could He do to prove His Messiahship?

Yet the Christmas lights, which should remind

us of the Light of the Word, are considered as more holiday adornments (and good for the economy). And the music, which should be joyous acclamation for our Redeeming Lord, has melted down into jangled bells.

Let us shrug off the chilly, wintry approach to Christ the King, and warm up to Him.

PRAYER: *Lord, Be born in us today, that newness of life might be ours, from now on. Your kind of life. Amen.*

TO BE CONTINUED—NATURALLY

John 12:2 *They gave a supper in [Jesus'] honor at which Martha served, and Lazarus was among the guests with Jesus.*

Actually a suburb of Jerusalem, Bethany is still less than two miles east of the Mount of Olives. But it was the capital of Jesus' closing ministry.

John, the beloved disciple, here writes a chapter and a half, some seventy-seven verses about another beloved companion of Jesus—Lazarus. Well known is the account of Jesus bringing the deceased Lazarus to life. That stirred the wrath of the religious hierarchy to kill both Jesus and Lazarus. Jesus, for performing the miracle, so that all the world seemed to become His followers (12:19); Lazarus, for being Exhibit A of Jesus' supernatural power. Seeing is believing. Moreover, shortly after, during the Passover Parade (Palm Sunday), the crowds were usually large, excited, vociferous. They had all heard about Jesus and, like all rubberneckers, shoved their way into positions where they could see Him—on a donkey.

Not so well-treated, because one's attention is too quickly diverted by Mary's anointing of Jesus' feet (v. 3), is the supper in a lower room. Friends, knowing Jesus' intention to attend the Passover Festival in Jerusalem, honored Him en route, at Bethany. One can only guess at the number of dinner guests. No matter. The best-knowns were there. Lazarus, who had just spent four days dead, in a tomb and Jesus who restored him to life. There's not another setting like this in all of history.

What a time (and so little of it) that was for filling in the information gaps. As Lazarus was dying, he wouldn't have known how it all ended. But there could have been persons at the dinner table who tended Lazarus in his last moments, preparing for the funeral, conducting the burial;, setting up the information network by which the Great Healer was alerted. And then there would be the recounting of all that occurred when Lazarus's grave clothes were removed. What now? Could he walk? What were his first words? What, if anything, did he crave to eat, to drink? Did he recall anything of his four-day stint (or "stink" as his sister Martha called it [11:39]), in a cave-grave? (11:38) And then there would be Jesus' comments! What dinner conversation. Nothing ever like it.

And yet, Jesus never leaves us floundering. All this has a meaning, a message for *us* too. What happened to Lazarus is but a preview of what will happen to us. Oh, let us not take it literally, with dinner guests and that setting. But the essence of it is that in God's own time and place, we, too, shall have new life breathed into us, beyond the grave. All the missing pieces, which we believe we are going to miss during a long period of sickness and burial, are all being saved, "that nothing may be lost." Our Conserving Creator sees to that. Somewhere its being recorded to be replayed in His appointed time. And then we shall recognize it as our personal version of a Bethany Supper—with our Savior. What we have feared will be a lonely bewildering walk through the valley of the shadow of death, really turns out to be a perfectly natural, understandable transference from earth to glory—under the Savior's watchful direction.

PRAYER: *Forgive us, Lord, for anticipating evil when we enter death's door. With our hand securely in Yours, we enter triumphantly. Amen.*

A STIR AT EASTER

John 12:16 *At the time his disciples did not understand this, but after Jesus had been glorified, they remembered that this had been written about him and that this had happened to him.*

The Triumphal entry of Jesus into Jerusalem, prophesied in Zech. 9:9, is recorded by all four gospel writers. Yet it was only John the beloved disciple who grasped the full significance of the occasion—that it was not a donkey ride, a publicity stunt to impress hundreds of thousands of pilgrims thronging the holy city for the most important of the Feasts—Passover. Nor was the ride symbolic of the entry of a war hero, but of a peace bringer. And though welcomed and hailed by the jubilant multitude, Jesus' unusual behavior was a puzzle to His own followers. They didn't remember the prophetic word uttered several hundred years earlier about such an event in their future, neither did they make the connection between that scripture and what they were now witnessing. Hence puzzlement. Recognition dawned, the lights came on when "what had been written about him" was connected with what "had happened to him (Jesus)." But who or what brought these two power lines together to generate a huge new surge of energy to the disciples, and through them to the entire world? John gives the answer in one word: "glorified." Analyzed, the glorification of our Lord is made up of two experiences—His resurrection and Ascension.

In a way, it is sad to think that Jesus' three years of living with the Twelve, and teaching them daily, didn't produce the enlightenment and missionary zeal that enraptured the apostles only after Jesus resurrection. Easter was the turning point, granted. But why not before? In fact, prior to Easter, none of the Twelve could be counted on, in spite of their three years in divinity school. Peter talked persuasively as if he would never forsake his Master though everyone else might. But it was Peter who turned out to be the master denier of his Master. Philip was censured for not really knowing who Jesus was even after years of fellowshipping with Him. Or doubting Thomas. Or Judas, the arch betrayer. Then, at the last, they *all* forsook Him and took to their heels.

That's a disillusioning commentary on the ineffectiveness of Jesus' ministry. But it happens. It happened, as we have seen, to Jesus favorite Old Testament pastoral prophet, Isaiah. All his superlative teaching was, as we now say, "Thrown under the bus," and at the end Isaiah was sawn in half. And still pastor's experience the law of diminishing returns operating in their ministries. A servant is not greater than his Lord!

Knowing all this, our merciful Lord provided the eventual turntable on which expected tragedy became and becomes a triumphant finale: His glorification, that is, His Resurrection and Ascension. That unbreakably joined to what had gone before, turned on the lights to make what was seen darkly through a glass now fully seen and understood. The secret is out, the whole story completed. Our Lord is victor over life and death. "Thanks be to God who giveth us the victory through our Lord Jesus Christ." (1 Cor. 15:57)

"After his resurrection his disciples recalled what he had said, and they believed the scripture and the words that Jesus had spoken." (John 2:22)

PRAYER: *Father, we sing our prayer with Charles Wesley: "His Kingdom cannot fail, He rules o'er earth and heaven; the Keys of death and hell are to our Jesus given: Lift up your heart, lift up your voice! Rejoice, again I say, rejoice."* Amen.

THE COST OF DISCIPLESHIP

John 12:21 *[Some Greeks, Gentiles] approached Philip, who was from Bethsaida in Galilee, and said to him, 'Sir, we should like to see Jesus.'"*

Of what use was it to record this Greek request and leave it at that, so that even seasoned commentators skip over it with the laconic comment: "We don't know if they ever saw Jesus."

Its just that this gospel writer wrote cryptically. If we take the time (as he probably hoped we would) and join the dots, the picture appears.

Non-Jewish Greeks were not an uncommon sight at the Jerusalem Festivals. In fact they weren't an uncommon sight anywhere. Known as world travelers, with minds eager for increased knowledge, tongues eager to share their findings, hands anxious to realize their ideals, they couldn't help but hear about the Man of the Hour. And they were not going home without seeing Him in person.

How else but through their information internet did they find disciple Philip (a Greek name) from Bethsaida, a Greek-speaking area on the Northeast shore of Galilee? Sensing his need for help, Philip turned to fellow disciple Andrew, also a Greek name also from Bethsaida. Both had served with John the Baptist as disciples and Andrew had joined Jesus as the first of His disciples. No two men were better fitted for the task of interpreting the Greek's messages to Jesus, and the Lord's messages in Aramaic to the Greeks.

But what did the Greeks say? Or had they just come to see Jesus, to gawk at Him, to see the color of His eyes, His physique, His sandals? Hardly. "Jesus replied," (v. 23) suggests that He was asked a question; by whom could it have been voiced but by the Greeks? By their very presence, these serious-minded gentiles, moving across many lands, were offering their missionary services to Jesus. Wasn't this an answer to His prayers for those "other sheep, not of this fold"? These Greek missioners could open up the way for the later Apostolic thrust "unto the uttermost parts of the earth." Whether the Greeks verbally asked questions or not, the sensitive Savior got the message and replied: "The hour has come for the Son of Man to be glorified." (v. 23) The hour of destiny had struck. The Good News was on its way around the globe.

It would not come without a stiff price, though, Jesus wanted His Greek missioners-in-the-making to know. Such a ministry includes dying (in many of its forms). But the final outcome (and it is a matter of outgrowth, as with the planting of a grain of wheat) is that "it bears a rich harvest." (v. 24) Additives are that the dying definitely includes dying to self, and the harvest abundant comes when such laborers in the mission field (which can be anywhere, since the world is His parish) "will be honored by the Father," (v. 26)—God.

If these Greeks came to "see Jesus," they got an eye-full and an ear-full, and an agenda-full. As with the Three Wise Men before them, they went home by another way—a straight and narrow way, with a new, Eternal Life Supporter accompanying them.

For anyone going this way, the directions are not Greek. They are easily understood.

PRAYER: *Lord Jesus, to see You is to be drawn into Your everlasting arms, in total commitment to Your Kingdom's coming. Amen.*

On Being Saved

John 12:42 *For all that, even among those in authority many beloved in him, but...*

Centuries before, Isaiah had recognized the difficulty, almost an impossibility, of believing in the Lord. Yet here the gospel writer gives Jesus high marks for attracting believers from the ranks of the sternest of critics. And just when we think Jesus has nothing more to worry about, John flags us to a standstill with that wretched little stop sign "but." So there's trouble ahead. The "believers in our retinue had left home with only half a passport. And you can't get to heaven like that. The public confession of their faith was missing. "They valued human reputation rather than the honor which comes from God." (v. 43) And here we've been persuaded that faith in the Lord was the full and only permission slip needed. We have preferred to hear man's congratulatory "well done, good and faithful" to God's.

Why has this moral equation hardly ever changed? And in spite of the lopsided rewards? The Lord offers far more than man. Yet man's magnetism outdraws God's. Why?

Immediacy is always more appealing, and more sharply portrayed in Jesus' parable of the big dinner party for which many invitations were sent out. But when dinner time arrived, so did the excuses. The apologies came first, profusely. When examined, each case was decided in favor of immediacy. Yes, the dinner would be a privilege to attend; the food would be scrumptious; fellow-guests compatible; a lovely evening would be enjoyed by all, but—. One invitee begged off because he had to inspect property he had just purchased. That was nearer and dearer than a steak dinner. Another excuse-maker was hindered from dining by his compulsion to break in new oxen. After all, much farm labor depended on capable beasts of burden. Still, another spin-meister dodged his dinner obligation because of his sudden marriage. Shades of Hollywood. No wonder the dinner Host was "furious." He had been stood up by an anonymous bit of property, a bull, and an impromptu wedding. That was a lot of bull. Yet their importance lay in their being near at hand. The dinner was distant. Immediacy and proximity made a weighty duo.

And there is publicity. The authorities who believed in Jesus but failed to confess Him openly, were restrained by the "bad press" it would give them. "The honor which comes from God" was too fuzzy and distant. "Human reputation," was immediate, near, with promising publicity. It was too good to miss. Take the tide at its flood!

How history keeps up its repetitive chorus.

We've heard it from Sinai to Sin City. The Israelites declared their undying belief in God. But—when Moses seemed to tarry too long on the Mount, that tricky trinity—immediacy, proximity, publicity did their alluring dance around that nearer, dearer, glitter, the Golden Calf. A lot of bull, indeed.

What the Lord still wishes to see is believers proving their commitment to Him—in word and deed, everywhere. Then the passport is complete and valid. "Enter into the joy of Your Lord."

PRAYER: *To be wholly Thine, is not easy, Lord, but it is possible. Save us from praying as Augustine did: "Lord, make me pure, but not yet." Guide us safely all the way. Amen.*

HIS NIGHT LIGHT

John 13:30 *It was night.*

This is one of those *Multum in Parvo* (much in little) signature sentences which mark John's gospel.

At first it looks superfluous. So it was night, so what? Night has darkened the world with monotonous regularity since the Creation. What more can be said about it? Leave it to the Beloved Disciple. From prelude to postlude he never lets his readers forget the Light of the world and the contrasting blackout. "That life was the light of mankind. The light shines in the darkness, and the darkness has never mastered it." (1:4-5) Then at the end (20:1): "Early on the first day of the week, while it was still dark, Mary of Magdala came to the tomb. She saw"....the Light beyond. (v. 16)

John knew the Genesis value of light, where, at Creation's beginning, God said, "Let there be light...and he separated light from darkness. He called the light day, and the darkness night." (Gen. 1:3-5) But John also knew the Jesus value of light, that, since God's word is a lamp to our feet and a light to our path, (Ps. 119:105) and since that word became flesh and made His home among us, (John 1:14) Jesus rightfully called Himself the Light of the World (John 8:12) and that no follower of His shall walk in darkness. And why not? First, people walk in darkness when their deeds are evil. "Wrongdoers hate the light and avoid it, for fear their misdeeds should be exposed." (John 3:19-20) In contrast, "Those who live by the truth come to the light so that it may be clearly seen that God is in all they do." (John 3:21) Second, no follower of Jesus walks in darkness, because "if he walks after nightfall he stumbles," whereas "Anyone can walk in the daytime without stumbling, because he has this world's light (The Light of the World) to see by." (John 11:10)

Jesus was not that unseeing and unknowing that He would not have experienced missteps and tumbles during the daytime hours of bustling pedestrian traffic. It was those who trafficked in evil businesses that He focused upon here. And Judas was in those crosshairs. "Night" described in a bombshell his stealthy, stumbling moral depravity. And to make the night utterly moonless, starless, pitch black, was the fact that he had less excuse for such a deplorable demise.

Judas, despite his obvious character deficiencies (as we all have), was singled out by the Lord as one who had the potential for good. Yet entrusted as Treasurer of the Apostolic group, Judas failed to be accountable. "He was a thief. (John

12:6) Accorded special privileges by Jesus at the Last Supper, Judas was again a disappointment. Realizing he was a misfit among Christ's close companions, Judas turned out the Light of his life and went out into a life of darkness, despair, self destruction. Where upon Jesus upped the inner lighting by turning on five lights. For in the next two verses, (13:31-32) He uses that electrifying and illuminating word "glorified" five times. The brief Dark Age of conspiratorial intrigue was over, Judas was alone with the night. The Eleven were with the Light and in the right. On which side are we?

PRAYER: *Lord, save us from stumbling out into the dark night of the soul. Draw us nearer to Thy sacred heart. Amen.*

SHOW ME THE WAY TO GO HOME

John 13:33 *Where I am going you cannot come.*

Up until this time Jesus' disciples knew His daily schedule. We know now that He was with them for three years. But, at the time, they didn't know it. For them it was a life commitment. They had given up their jobs, homes, loved ones, to serve His cause, however long He needed them. But His announcement in today's text brought them to a shuddering halt. Judas had just left without a word. Now here was Jesus, moving in the same direction. What was going on? They had reached a crossroad, a place of separation for which they were unprepared, confused, feeling suddenly abandoned. Not only were the Master's men not told where He was headed, but also, for the first time, they were prohibited from accompanying Him. "You cannot come." But fiery Peter, never afraid to talk back to close Friend Jesus, asked: "Lord, where are You going?" (v. 36) The answer was no help. "I am going where you cannot follow Me now." Then, seeing the enlarging question marks on every face, Jesus added: "but one day you will," which didn't make the puzzle simpler. This "not now" and "but one day" was too blurry for the big Fisherman. "Lord," he persisted, "Why cannot I follow you NOW?" (v. 37)

With Lazarus's return from the grave, and Judas's abrupt departure, and now Jesus' goodbye echoing through the chambers of their consciousness, the faithful Eleven were put on alert. As their spokesman Peter voiced it for them, how did they as a group, and more important as individuals, fit into this state of flux, volatility? Even if they had to disband they could always go back to the single or family lifestyles they had known before their response to Christ's invitation to join Him. They were not initially, personally, group-thinkers. Nobody is. We come into this world and leave it as individuals, unless one is joined at the hip with another. And, thrown back on oneself, the ultimate uncertainty about going away and where and how has to do with our final withdrawal from our earthly bodies—which is what Jesus was here tenderly trying to make known to His men. It's a delicate subject which requires gentle handling. And Jesus, whose frail hands were broken by nails showed us how it is done. First, He goes ahead to prepare a place for us. (14:2) That's comforting. The horrific nightmares about Intensive Care Units, last rites, weeping family members, the funeral hearse, and being lowered into a muddy hole or pigeon-holed in a mausoleum, or cremated—are all over-shadowed by the heavenly home ahead, with a personal welcome by the Savior. (14:3) Second, until that happens, we are not even left floundering. The Holy Spirit, the Third Person in the Trinity, will be assigned to taking care of us (14:16) until "the roll is called up yonder." Third, we are not left Christless. "I shall come again and take you to myself" (14:23) He promises. "I," no substitutes. "Shall" is determinative. Even if we are uncertain about it, He isn't. "Come," in any tone, is soft and caring and inviting. "Take" my hand, precious Lord, and here He does. "You" is unconditional—whomever you are. There is always a personal touch to His word. "To Myself," it's One on one. He delivers us safely to our soul's final destination. "So that where I am you may be also." Neat. Cool. Must be heaven—not the other place.

PRAYER: *Lord, how deftly You guide us through misty mysteries to abiding joy. How ashamed of ourselves we are forever doubting Your divine directing. Have mercy upon us, now and always. Amen.*

START AT THE HEART

John 15:25 *"They hated me without reason."*

Jesus was steeped in the Psalms, and here is another example of it. (Ps. 35:19, 69:5) Our text comes out of those two. And having recorded it in his gospel, and been impressed by their accuracy and repetition through the ages, John refers to the latter Psalm in his Book of Revelation. (3:5, 13:8, 16:1, 17:8)

Rebels without a cause is the way our Lord described those persons who could never see anything good or godly about Him. In fact, it was precisely that He had done nothing evil that they detested.

Later, Pilate cross-examined Jesus and could not for the life of him find any fault in the Stranger of Galilee. (Luke 23:14, John 18:38) Yet no extinguishers could dampen down the searing scorn of the hate-mongers. Why is this still rampant?

Anti-Christs will never admit that their animosity toward Jesus is to be found in His three-liner in John 15:22: "If I had not come and spoken to them, they would not be guilty of sin: but now they have no excuse for their sin." As with vegetarians who will take no life, are shown tiny lives on a vegetable under a microscope. They smash the microscope. Unwilling to own up to their aberrant behavior, such persons ride roughshod through and over the rules of decency and Christlikeness, causing widespread chaos—as happened at the Master's crucifixion.

And lest any think that such venom emptied itself on Calvary, let us remember Jesus words of caution: "I have told you all this to guard you against the breakdown of your faith...indeed , the time is coming when anyone who kills you will suppose that he is serving God." (John 16:1-2)

Oh the rebels claim to have a cause, a very good reason(s) for feeling the way they do about Christ. Just look at His Church, they point, it's in pitiful condition with entertainment-oriented worship, pedophilia, licentious leaders, money-laundering, a New Testament to what—a spin master's effort to bring publicity and money into the fold? A thousand-fold?

Or consider the impotence of Christianity. When has it ever boosted society, say, as the stock market can do on a daily basis? When has it held a nation together, say, as a Roman Emperor did, or a

Napoleon? For all Christianity's bluster and convoluted theology, how much better is the global village? Wars never cease, famines continue, the marketplace, upon close analysis, increasingly resembles a den of thieves. Where is the renewing transforming effect that Christianity is touted to have? The hatred for the central figure in all this ineptitude, far from ceasing, is steadily increasing.

In an art gallery, a visitor was audibly vitriolic in his criticism about a masterpiece. One of the gallery attendants said: "Sir, the problem is not in that masterpiece, but in the eye of the beholder." Again, how right Jesus was and is. Personal sin erodes all of life. A heart attune to the Lord's will brings a life of content, and intent to make a better world.

PRAYER: *Heavenly Father, help us to brighten the world by first brightening the corner where we are. In Jesus' name. Amen.*

FROM GRIEF TO BLISSFUL BELIEF

John 16:20 *You will weep and mourn, but the world will be glad, but though you will be plunged in grief, your grief will be turned to joy.*

Christians do not care to be known as weepy, griefy, mourners. Their Hebrew-Christian tradition has built into them a promise that they are born to be cheerful, not tearful. Yet how quite the opposite the reality proves to be. It's the Christless ones who are envied. Its Christ's followers who have a constrained, mild-mannered, third-rate, artificial, improvised "cheer."

To be sure, Jesus starts today's text by giving His followers ample warning of their inescapable times of sadness. At the same time, He adds, the "world" of unbelievers will be glad. But what the "world" does not know, the Lord does. The "world" can only see the beginning from the end. The Lord sees that, too, but He also sees the end from the beginning. He sees the final triumph and perfected joy awaiting only the faithful.

Knowing from time immemorial that we would ask the doubt-filled questions we now ask about a joyful end, the Lord also pre-buttressed our discipleship by giving us the eight Beatitudes, each starting with the word "blessed" or "happy." And the primacy of the placement of these happy attitudes was no accident. For if the Sermon on the Mount (in which the Beatitudes are included) is considered the essence of Jesus' teaching, and if the Beatitudes are the essence of the Sermon on the Mount, then it is obvious that the Beatitudes are the essence of the essence of Jesus' teaching. And they are all joy or bliss, because happiness is really chancy, a happenstance.

In earlier times the island of Cyprus was known as the Blessed Isle, or the Isle of Bliss. Cyprians were a world unto themselves. They did not live off imports as less fortunate countries did. That island's residents had all that humans could ask for anywhere the kind of non-parasitical ecstasy promised in the Beatitudes. Yearning for life, liberty, and the pursuit of happiness, but spurning Jesus' Beatitudinal offering, most people wander off elsewhere in pursuit of happiness. Some try "smiley faces" either drawn on paper, or on their own faces. Others turn to alcohol and drugs. Physical fitness freaks are sure that exercise is the answer. Hearing "Las Vegas calling," that siren song is eagerly turned to. In 2007, Pepsi put out their first new slogan in four years: "More Happy." "One of the nice things about the word 'happy'," Pepsi effervesces, "is it's really multidimensional." To promote this slogan Pepsi put thirty-five new can designs on the market. Surely this would put the United States in first place as the world's happiest nation. In fact, an international study on happiness has shown Denmark as first (with the second-highest suicide rate in Europe?); Switzerland, second; Austria, third; Iceland, fourth; United States, twenty-third; Germany, thirty-fifth; Britain, forty-first; France, sixty-second; Japan, ninetieth. The least happy people on planet earth are found to be in Burundi, Zimbabwe, and Congo.

To go forward there is no other way than back to Jesus. The hippie happpies mislead by dodging any mention of sadness. From them the promise is miles of smiles all the way. Not so. Says the Christ, "in very truth I tell you, you will weep and mourn, but...your grief will be turned to joy," bliss, forever.

PRAYER: *Now we know, Lord, why You have taught us the gain of pain. The progression is toward bliss, now and ever. Amen.*

THE UNVEILING OF TRUTH

John 16:25 *Till now I have been using figures of speech; a time is coming when I shall no longer use figures, but tell you of the Father in plain words.*

One wonders why Jesus used hard-to-understand figures of speech over one hundred different kinds. Mark 4:34 reminds us that Jesus "never spoke to them except in parables: but privately to his disciples he explained everything." Why didn't He always speak in plain words? For the moment He did, at the end of this chapter 16,

He was instantly and clearly understood. As the disciples promptly told Him: "Now you are speaking plainly, not in figures of speech! We are certain now that You know everything, and do not need to be asked; because of this we believe that You have come from God." (v. 29-30) Why didn't Jesus speak plainly from the beginning to all of us? Wouldn't we have understood Him quicker and deeper?

Knowing "everything," Jesus had His reasons for "using figures of speech." First, there was the time element. He was under pressure. There was no time for lengthy, juvenile explanations. He had to speak with "pregnant brevity." As when George Washington Carver asked God to tell him all there was in a peanut, Carver declared that the Lord replied: "I gave you brains, go find out."

The intensity of the situation is magnified in John's gospel. Actually, John deals with only three weeks out of Jesus' three-year ministry (which in itself was short enough). Further, John takes almost half of his gospel to tell about the week before Jesus' crucifixion. The time squeeze caused Jesus to encapsulate His teachings as compactly as possible.

Second, figures of speech have more than quickly caught (and, as often, quickly forgotten) meanings. They call for time (of which we have more than Jesus did) and mental effort. We much better remember what we have striven to unravel by our own sweaty exertion.

Third, in Jesus' figures of speech—parables, similes, symbolism, proverbs, metaphors—had in them seed thoughts, embryos capable of producing bigger and more far-reaching thoughts in their own appointed time. To disinterested unbelievers some of these figures of speech (which contained profound spiritual truths) fell as it were on stony ground or among thorns or simply trodden under the feet of men. As they still are. On the other hand, believers who are anxious to mine the depths of truth, are rewarded with lessons of gem-like quality; or nurturing seed thoughts the faithful find, as the Psalmist did, that these fertile teachings become like trees planted beside water channels, yielding their fruit in season, with foliage that never fades. (Ps. 1:3)

The apostles learned that in due season, when they first heard Jesus' figures of speech, they didn't mean much. But the stories, and the uniqueness of their wording were not difficult to store in the memory or to retrieve when needed. For instance, what John records in 12:16, the other three gospel writers echo it in one form or another: "At the time his disciples did not understand this but after Jesus had been glorified they remembered that this had been written about Him, and that it had happened to Him."

Aware of Jesus' unusual way of presenting His teachings is no reason for us to turn a blind eye and deaf ear to them. Prayerfully plumbing the depths promises rich finding. The ages have proved it.

PRAYER: *What treasure troves await our patient penetration of Your word, O Lord. Thank You for showing where and how to drill with a will. Amen.*

ONE WITH THE FATHER

John 17:8 *I have taught them (the men whom in you gave me out of the world [v. 6]) what I learned from you, and they have received it: they know with certainly that I came from you, and they have believed that you sent me.*

In the Upper Room, or on the way to Gethsemane, Jesus offered what has been traditionally called the High Priestly prayer. And since the High Priest alone could enter the Temple's most sacred area, in this seventeenth chapter, we enter the Holy of Holies in the New Testament. "This great chapter in which John Knox cast his anchor, contained the longest recorded and only prolonged prayer of Christ." (Joachim Jeremias, *The Prayers of Jesus,* p. 106)

True to His customary orderliness, Jesus has three sections in His exemplary prayer: 1. The Son and the Father (v. 1-5); 2. The son and the disciples (v. 6-19) and 3. The Son and the world. (v. 20-26)

Starting the first section (v. 1) with the word "Father," Jesus showed how He was practicing what He had preached when asked to teach the Twelve how to pray. "When you pray," He replied, "say, Our father..." And so this, His own prayer, followed the entire pattern that He had outlined for the apostles. That is why we still use the Paternoster just as He gave it.

Coming to the Second section of the High Priestly prayer, which includes today's text, that word "taught" catches the eye. Oh, how He taught. It was central in the Leadership training portion of His ministry. To be sure, Jesus was concerned about the welfare of all souls, as the third section of this prayer unequivocally states, yet, first He saw the need to give basic training to the specially chosen and commissioned group of His missioners. Matthew's gospel magnifies this point in 5:1-2: "When He saw the crowds He went up a mountain. There He sat down, and when His disciples had gathered round Him, He began to address them." The "crowds," for all their magnitude and public relations value, though not undervalued, received Jesus' attention *after* He addressed the disciples. In fact, Matthew uses the word "disciples" sixty-five times, focusing on the small revitalized group of the Master's Men, rather than on "crowds" or "people."

And what did Jesus teach but what He had learned from His heavenly Father. And not just bits and pieces. The Father, too, had done the prior teaching thoroughly—all that He wanted His people on earth to know through the Son— so that Jesus was able to report to His Men: "I have disclosed to you *everything* that I heard from my Father." (John 15:15) And as rightfully as we can discern, *all* that God wanted us to know for righteous living on earth is now readily available.

Next, records John, the disciples "received" Jesus' teaching. The teaching was not a one-way bridge to nowhere. It had takers, receivers; the bridge made contact. Now here could be questions and answer, two-way mental and spiritual interchange and infra structuring. And the central point of the knowledge which had been given and received had to do with Jesus and His heavenly Father being One. Jesus was not just a philosophical or mystical incarnation or reincarnation, thought up for the justification of a certain religion's beliefs. Here was "certainty," a trusted-and-tried foundation upon which was built, once and for all time, for all people, a "faith that would not shrink, though pressed by every foe, that would not tremble on the brink of any earthly woe." "This," said Jesus (v. 3)—"This is eternal life; to know you, the only true God, and Jesus Christ whom you have sent." So eternal life can begin right now.

PRAYER: *Thank You, Lord, for putting in one sentence what we thought we would never understand. Amen.*

ON KNOWING JESUS

John 18:2 *The place was known to Judas.*

"The place" was the Garden of Gethsemane, on the Mount of Olives. It was owned by Mary, the Mother of John Mark. Mark was the Garden Keeper and conceivably the caretaker of the oil press within the Garden precincts. Jerusalem landowners were prohibited from having gardens in the city because of crowded living conditions, and also because no fertilizers, like manure, were allowed in the Holy City. Mary had apparently made the Garden available to Jesus and the Twelve as a quiet spot for teaching sessions and prayer. And Judas knew all of this, and the times when the gates would be open for them and when closed. Judas also knew the schedule of prayer times. And he knew who would be there, even if nobody else was. The Place, the Prayer, and the Person were well known to Judas, but this last time, for purposes which would become known to the world as devilish.

Of course, there have been people of great distinction who have seen Judas in an entirely different light. They have made him to look faultless, and shifted the blame to Jesus. The fact remains that although the Master specially chose Judas for all his potential good, and though the Lord tried until the end to save Judas from his own weaknesses (even as Jesus wanted to save Jerusalemites), but Judas (and Jerusalem) resisted Him. And we see how that worked out in today's text.

First, Judas knew the Place that Jesus loved. A Teacher on the move, Jesus lost no time in sharing His message "where crossed the crowded ways of life." Yet, throughout His ministry, you see Him taking withdrawal time—to get His Spiritual battery recharged. It can't be empowered by a constant diffusion of power. And in the hectic Jerusalem area, especially at the important Festival season when He was usually there, the private quietude of Mary's olive garden was balm for His soul.

And Judas knew the time when the garden could be used for prayer and not for oil pressing. That would separate Jesus from His ever-loving listeners who might intervene on His behalf on seeing Him being arrested.

Second, Judas knew that Prayer was the purpose for Jesus' hike to the Mount of Olives. Prayer meant calmness. Prayer turned thoughts away from physical surroundings. Prayer called for an inward look at one's soul, and an uplook for help from the Father above—just the ideal setting for an ambush, especially in a privately owned piece of property.

Third, there was the Person. Though Judas resented some of his fellow apostles who treated him as a thief who, as treasure, dipped into their collective purse, Judas was out for no one but the Head Man, Jesus. Nor did Judas want Jesus to pray for him. The Person, the Prayer, the Place didn't mean what they once did to Judas. Nothing ever does when one drifts from the Savior. The place of prayer becomes a den of thieves. Prayer itself loses its potency and its allure, and is dropped by the wayside, and left as litter. The Person of Christ is handed over to accusers, to be jeered at, spat upon, banished from the halls of learning, and law, and international relationship. The thirty pieces of silver, symbolizing money in general, means nothing to anybody anymore. And, with the kiss of death, the Judas's of every age are left hanging!

But Jesus, though crucified, Lives. And so can those who believe in Him.

PRAYER: *Thou, O Christ art all I want. More than all in Thee I find. Amen.*

THE LORD'S TURN (LUKE 22:61)

John 18:27 *A cock crowed.*

This rooster fulfilled the prophesy made by Jesus, namely, that Peter, who boastfully offered to lay down his life for the Lord, would instead betray the Lord, not once, but thrice, before the cock crowed. (John 13:37-38) So literally has this been taken, that today at the site of the high priest's home, there is a church—with a rooster on top—called the Church of the Cock Crowing.

Others have tried to explain that it was not a barnyard bird but a trumpet blast. The Roman garrison in Jerusalem divided their night watch into four segments of three hours each, from 6 P.M. to 6 A.M. At the end of the third watch, at 3 A.M., a trumpeter sounded the time for the changing of the guard, which was called the "cockcrow."

It has also been argued that Jesus would hardly have known that Peter's betrayal would coincide exactly with a rooster or trumpeter, since roosters are not always on time, nor can anyone tell them when to do their strut on the dunghill.

It is more likely that Jesus and His disciples had an in-house understanding of one's conscience being awakened by old poultryman Chanticleer. The fact is that a troubled conscience can be aroused by association with almost anything. As Emerson found: "The prosperous and beautiful to me seem not to wear the yoke of conscience masterful, which galls me everywhere." Even while fleeing to distant Tarshish, Jonah's conscience became his deadliest foe. Everything on board ship, and in the whale's belly reminded him of his disobedience to God's will. Even after Peter made amends for his betrayal, legends have it that critics never let Peter forget his moral failure. At his approach they would "cocka-doodle-do," or laughingly chide, "Here comes the chicken hearted brave man."

Peter is always mentioned first on the apostolic list. Judas, last. Yet both of them flunked their final exams. And, who doesn't? Always there is life beyond the finals and much depends on how that postlude is handled. Judas, though confessing his sin, found that "a burdened conscience never needs a hangman; he hung himself." (Matt. 27:5) Peter, on the other hand, hearing the rooster and at the same moment exchanging a brief glance with Jesus (and reading therein Jesus' "I told you so, but I forgive you") went outside and poured out his confession to the full, in bitter tears. (Luke 22:61) Cleansed and given a second chance, Peter regained his moral footing and his position of leadership among his brethren.

What a glorious example Peter set for all of

us—until the end of time. We don't have to be cowed by a barnyard bird, cooped up with the chickens, though the temptation to do so remains. "I am beyond redemption, where is the nearest noose?" Not so, says Jesus' reassuring look. "Lo, I am with you, always, even into the end of the world." If the Big Fisherman, the impetuous apostle, the Peterooster who said his Paternoster, the faithless sinker in Galilean waters could finally give his name to the greatest church in Christendom, St. Peter's, there's still a chance for the least and lowliest of us to be saved. Look to the Lord.

PRAYER: *Thank You, Lord, for providing us with this real-life enactment of how to rise from rags to riches in glory. Amen.*

HEART AND HAND JOINTS

John 18:20 *The Jews themselves stayed outside the headquarters to avoid defilement, so that they could eat the Passover meal.*

Pilate, the Roman governor, had his military headquarters in Caesarea ("little Rome") on the Mediterranean coast. But when Pilate went to Jerusalem on business, he headquartered in the Herodian palace. This was where Jesus was sent by the high priest for further interrogation. So why did Jesus' Jewish accusers fear defilement if they entered Pilate's domain?

First, because it was the beginning of the Passover festival when the main emphasis, for eight days, was on cleanliness. For 1,400 years the Jews had been annually celebrating their freedom from bondage under Pharaoh, when, because of their quick exit from Egypt, they baked their unleavened bread in the searing heat of the Sinai desert. Without leaven, the bread was flat. It is fermenting leaven, therefore, that has been banned from the Passover festival and, entering a non-Jewish household, the Hebrews would have been in danger of fermentable uncleanness. In their own homes, prior to Passover, the man of the house diligently searched the premises for any semblance of Hometz (leaven), praying that if any bit of leaven had been accidentally, mistakenly missed, that it should be completely erased. Such was the thoroughness of the cleansing. (Exod. 12:15-20)

Because of their personal need to be wholly unblemished, plus the ever-present fear of being defiled by contact with anybody or anything Gentile, these Jewish accusers of Jesus forced even such a superior authority as Pilate to conduct business with them *outside* his residence.

At the same time, however, these outwardly scrupulously spotless accusers showed their shockingly transparent hypocrisy. With clean hands they were unashamed to wear their impure hearts on their sleeves. Even pagan Pilate was baffled by the disconnect between their strict religious observances and their devilish deeds. Especially astonishing to Pilate was the Jews' avowal that they had "no King but Caesar." (John 19:15) Even if Pilate didn't know it, Jesus could see how they had flip-flopped from a short while ago when they said to Him: "God is our father, and God alone." (John 8:4) On that occasion Jesus correctly foresaw what was now taking place. Said He: "If God were your father, you would love me...Your father is the devil and you choose to carry out your father's desires." (John 8:42,44)

If this had been the only time that those who profess the Hebrew-Christian faith had defaulted, it would have been sad and bad enough. Two thousand years later we are still seeing this unpardonable disconnect between clean hands and impure hearts: whitewash over a tomb full of decay. Must Jesus bear the cross alone, again? When will the clean hands and pure hearts be conjoined? The profession and confession? When will the more difficult inward rightness catch up with the relatively quick and easy outward side-show, and convert it? Lord, heal me at the heart, and let the world come on; wash me and I shall be whiter than snow, from the inside out.

PRAYER: *Heavenly Father, we would do more than avoid defilement and remain negative. We would be wholly Thine. Now and ever. Amen.*

THE HOLY ARMOR OF GOD

John 19:23 *When the soldiers had crucified Jesus they took his clothes and, leaving aside the tunic, divided them into four parts, one for each soldier. The tunic was seamless, woven in one piece throughout.*

The clothes of the crucified One were given to the militia who had been assigned to this unsavory job—as part payment. It was ho-hum compensation for the soldiers, depending on their personal needs. But think of what Christies and Sotheby's auction houses would ask for such articles today. Millions.

As with most troopers who serve overseas, these Roman guards may have taken these clothing items home as souvenirs. "Look," they would have said to family and friends. "These sandals belonged to one who was called 'King of the Jews.'

Imagine, a Jew's shoes!" Or so it could have played it making for the possibility, in some future time, for some Roman who had become a Christian, to realize, "You know what? When my grandfather was on active duty in Palestine, this tunic (or belt, or robe, or headpiece) belonged to Jesus, our Savior!" The further possibility is that these items are lying somewhere, waiting to be discovered—even as Mary Leakey found *Australopithecus boisei*, the two-million-year-old "Nutcracker Man," in Kenya.

The seamless tunic, we understand, was made by Mary for her son Jesus. Mary not only copied Hannah's song (1 Sam. 2:1-10) in her own song, the Magnificat (Luke 1:46-55), but Mary followed Hannah's example in making a seamless tunic: Hannah, for son Samuel, and Mary for her Messiah. Significantly, such a seamless garment was worn by the High Priest, who went by the name Ponitfex—the bridge builder. He was the connector between God and His people, as was Jesus, the Savior.

St. Paul included these same five items in what he called "the whole armor of God." (Eph. 6:13) Jesus' sandals, for Paul were "let the shoes on your feet be the gospel of peace, to give you firm footing." (Eph. 6:15) The tunic becomes Paul's breastplate of integrity nearest the heart. Kept in place by the belt of truth. (Eph. 6:14) The outer robe, in Paul's armor is "the great shield of faith." (Eph. 6:16) The shield, over the breastplate, provided double protection, as did the woolen robe over the linen tunic. Jesus' headpiece becomes Paul's helmet of salvation. (Eph. 6:17) Paul, however, adds one piece of armor, that doesn't appear in Jesus' list, and that is the sword of the Spirit, which is the word of God. (Eph. 6:17) On second thought,

Jesus Himself is the word made flesh, if not a sword. The poet picks this up:
> I saw the conquerors riding by
> with cruel lips and faces wan:
> Musing on Kingdoms sacked and burned
> There rode the Mongol Genghis Khan;
> Then came Alexander the Great, Caesar, Napoleon
> then all they perished from the earth,
> As fleeting shadows from a glass,
> And, conquering down the centuries,
> Came Christ the swordless on an ass.

PRAYER: *Even stripped of clothing, O Christ, You are more than conqueror. Empower us likewise. Amen.*

THE CENTERPIECE OF OUR FAITH

John 19:41 *Near the place where he had been crucified there was a garden, and in the garden a new tomb...*

"Near the place where he had been crucified," today has become two places—The Church of the Holy Sepulcher and The Garden Tomb. While most authorities stand by the authenticity of the church's location, the garden is more clearly aligned with our text for today. If only the garden could be at the church site, everyone would be happy. As it is, sadly, both sides not only resent each others' presence, but each, within its own ranks, does a slow boil.

For example, the lines are drawn in the Church of the Holy Sepulcher as to which of the six religious communities can do what and where and when and how. Intent on exerting their rights, several groups on multiple occasions have engaged in fisticuffs leading to bloodshed. The un-Christian behavior among the six Christian denominations housed in the church is probably no better than that of the Romans and Jews in Jesus' day.

Furthermore, at the sacred spots, in the Church, it is difficult to visualize where Jesus' cross stood, or where the malefactors hung on either side of Him, or where is Jesus tomb? There are altars, candles, electric lights, a silver disc here, a black marble disc there—this for the Franciscans, that for the Greek Orthodox, or Armenians, Syrians, Copts, or Abyssinian.

Then there is the Garden Tomb and "Gordon's Calvary." In 1882, General Charles Gordon of the British Army saw what appeared to be a skull-shaped hill. Further inspection revealed two caves for eyes, the rounded skull above, and a mouth-like opening below. Close by was found a rock-hewn tomb. In between Calvary and the Tomb, a lovely Garden flourishes with trees and flowers. Here Christians from all over the world come and are at liberty to have services of any kind they wish—in their own languages—in that Green Cathedral.

There we have it, as it was in the Master's time—three positions: a thief on each side, and the Lord of Life in the center. Now there is Calvary and the Tomb—with a Garden full of life in the middle.

At the Creation there was a Garden. (Gen. 2:15) In the end time there will be a garden. (Rev. 22:2) Why are humans made to be so intimately associated with Gardens? For one thing, because of the eternal quality of trees. They were in existence 300 million years ago. Second, although a tree may look exactly as it did a year ago in the spring, it is altogether new. The old leaves fell off last autumn and during the hibernation season of winter, new birth took place throughout roots and trunk. Third, renewed, replenished trees provide several kinds of therapies. (Rev. 22:2) They give shade and sustenance for man and birds and beasts. No wonder the Garden of Eden was a small-scale model of the kind of world God desired for those who were made in His image. And how wonderfully God brought all these factors together—eternal life, new birth, healing of the nations—in Jesus Christ, in the "Garden" of our text, on Easter morning! Hallelujah!

PRAYER: *Thank You, Father, for fulfilling these promises in Jesus. In Him, with Him, we can enjoy them, and a lot more. Amen.*

FIRST CLASS

John 20:4 *They ran together, but the other disciple ran faster than Peter and reached the tomb first.*

On that first Easter morning, these close friends of Jesus were not doing their daily jogging. But run they did to and from the cemetery. And the author of this gospel should know he was one of them. And he was proud of coming in ahead of the confirmed leader of the apostles—Peter.

The reason for this agitated sprinting was that, alarmingly, Jesus' tomb lacked His deceased body. Body-snatchers—that was it. There was much of it at the time. Yet a careful examination and putting the circumstantial evidence together, joining the dots, recalling scripture pertaining to this scenario, (John 20:9) they saw and believed" (v. 8) that it was nothing short of a Resurrection.

Nor was such a confirmation a disconnected, isolated one. Subsequently the Risen Christ was seen, and conversed with by hundreds of people on several different occasions until the time for His Ascension.

But there again, John was the first to see and know Jesus' resurrection as a life-transforming fact. From then on he couldn't wait to spread his eyewitness account. Putting his fishing days on the Sea of Galilee behind him, this "Son of thunder," this disciple whom Jesus loved, this youngest of the apostles who sat next to Jesus at the Last Supper and to whom Jesus entrusted the care of His mother Mary, gave the rest of his long life (dying when he was about one hundred years of age) to at least three New Life ministries: looking after Mary; Preaching the gospel of a Risen Savior; and writing this gospel of John, the three Epistles of John, and the Book of Revelation. Run, run, run.

John's first and immediate responsibility was Jesus' mother, John's aunt. Though in agony on His cross, Jesus sensed the utter isolation of His widowed mother. Unsure that His siblings would care for her, and having seen how John affectionately treated his own mother Salome, and knowing that John was more financially able than any of the other apostles, Jesus committed His beloved mother to John's care. And the fact that from Calvary, "and from the moment the disciple (John) took her (Mary) into his home," (John 19:27) indicates that Mary didn't really have much of a home of her own. In his Jerusalem home John saw that Mary was amply cared for. At death, she was buried in the Kedron Valley. Only then did John feel free to leave home to preach and heal and administer to the growing number of churches abroad. He partnered with Peter in much of this ministry, after Pentecost.

Because of his bold utterances concerning the Risen Savior, John was imprisoned by the Roman authorities. Instead of executing him, they sent him into exile on the cordoned-off island of Patmus. There, realizing that he was about the only eyewitness of Jesus' ministry left at the end of the first century—he documented past and future happenings.

So, this man, the first in history to be made altogether new by the Easter message, brings our Bible to a close with a reassuring benediction. All is well.

PRAYER: *"Lord, what beauties in John's face did shine reflected ever from Your face divine."*[1] *Do it for us too. Amen.*

OH SAY CAN YOU SEE?

John 20:18 *Mary of Magdala went to tell the disciples, "I have seen the Lord!"*

Peter and John saw an empty tomb. Magdalene knew why. She had seen the occupant. Another first, even getting ahead of sprinter John.

To be sure, John believed in a living Savior even though he did not see Him. But he could have actually seen Jesus because he had been in exactly the same place where Mary was for her sighting, and he was there before she was. But John gave up on any further inquiry and "went home again." (John 20:10) That was the end of his early morning jog.

But not Mary. Although she had done her own running prior to the men, she returned to the tomb to seek until she found the One for whom she was looking. And it wasn't easy—there and back home as it had been for the two disciples.

---

[1] John Wesley

Mary arrived in the early morning darkness, where even a lantern would have been little help in an unfamiliar and heavily guarded private burial garden. The first pleasant surprise, which soon turned into shocking bewilderment, was to find the tomb's stone blockage removed from the entrance. Immediately Mary bolted for help.

After Peter and John came and left, Mary was back—seeking. Through her tears she saw two angels in the empty tomb. To them she expressed her concern that several persons ("they" v. 13) had made off with Jesus' body. Where did they go? Then a man behind Mary, whom she took for the Gardener (who else could it have been?), asked her why she was weeping. Answering, she changed her grievance from "they" to "you" and then to "I" (v. 15)—so confused was she. Yet, nothing deterred her. She pressed on with her search. And it paid off. It always does. That's the promise. "Seek (and keep on seeking), knock (and keep on knocking), and you will find, it will be opened." For the "Gardener" turned out to be none other than the Risen Lord Himself. Seeing Mary's honest efforts in seeking for a solution, Jesus put Himself in a simply findable position. You find that He's in the habit of doing that. God helps those who help themselves. He will not suffer us to be tempted, taunted, more than we are able to bear. He provides exits in more ways than this world dreams of. Behind the scenes He intervenes. A sign in the Garden Tomb, today, says: "Don't look for Jesus, here. He is risen." He is abroad in all the world, helping every Magdalene and John and

Peter as He did on that first Easter. And thus shall it continue to be.

Moreover, when Mary turned away from the grief and death and cemetery scene—she saw the Light of the World. Her darkness turned to dawn. Her tears to cheers. It turned into an even greater day than when Jesus cast seven demons out of her. (Luke 8:2) Oh to have been chosen as Mary was, to proclaim for the first time in history to all the world, "I have seen the (Risen) Lord!" She earned it. We, too, can learn and earn. He's right behind us to help.

PRAYER: *Lord, every day can be Easter when we discover You in a gardener, a guard, a grandmother, a recent graduate...Give us eyes that see beyond the dark and dawn. Amen.*

HIS BREATHING BUSINESS

John 20:22 *Then he breathed on them, saying, "Receive the Holy Spirit!"*

Since this granting of the Holy Spirit occurred prior to Pentecost (Acts 2:1-4), it has off-handedly been referred to as a "Johannine Pentecost"—a private Pentecost recorded only by John. Yet it is not to be taken lightly. In fact, it is a critically important turning point in the life of our Lord.

Heretofore Jesus, the Messiah for whom the ages had been yearning, had come in human form, tempted in all ways like we are. Born in a borrowed cattle shed, buried in another's tomb, Jesus taught and fought to establish His heavenly Father's Kingdom on earth as it is in heaven.

His death terminated the "Man" of the God-Man. And the first showing of His return to divinity was when He entered through locked doors (no

Houdini hoax) and stood among His disciples. (John 20:19) Then, to verify where He had come from (His humanity), "he showed them his hands and his side." (20:20) This was also possibly to arouse awareness about the fakery that has long been associated with dead men walking. As Alex Boese found: "Some celebrities never die. They just go into hiding. It's not clear why some celebrity deaths inspire death-hoax rumors while others don't, but once a rumor takes hold, it can have amazing staying power. And no celebrity clings more stubbornly to life after death than Elvis Presley. The official story is that he died on August 16, 1977. The unofficial story is that the corpse in his coffin was a wax dummy, and nobody was buried in the meditation garden at Graceland. People keep seeing him all over the place: pumping gas in the Australian outback; eating cheeseburgers in St. Paul, Minnesota; or ordering double lattes in Pensacola, Florida." (*Hippo Eats Dwarf*, pp. 261-262)

Jesus' nail-pierced hands and spear-pierced side were seen for the first time by His disciples, except for John who was present at the crucifixion.

Now, having reverted from humanity back to divinity, Jesus wasted no time in sending His close associates on their great commission unto the uttermost parts. "As the Father sent me, so I send you." (v. 21)

But how could they go without empowerment? No more than Adam could before life was breathed into him. (Gen. 2:7) So Jesus—who "was with God at the beginning, and through (whom) all things came to be; without him no created thing came into being" (John 1:2-3)—did once again what He had done with Adam, "he breathed on them, saying, 'Receive the Holy Spirit!'"

How was this done? Breathing into the nostrils of each person present? Following the Adamic procedure? Or was it in one big whoosh on the whole group? Or was it a mouth-to-mouth resuscitation? Whatever it was, they were instantly readied for their mission outreach.

Far from being an anticlimax, when the day of Pentecost did come there was a thunderous sound as of a driving wind. It filled the whole house. Tongues of fire came to rest on the head of each person present. They were filled with the Holy Spirit, and began to speak in other tongues. That day 3,000 believers were added to their number. How could they have believed without the fireworks? And day by day the Lord added new converts. (Acts 2:1-4,41,47) And the apostles all ready were off to a flying start. How blessedly foresighted of Jesus. His plans and timings never fail.

PRAYER: *"Breathe on me, breath of God. Fill me with life anew that I may love what Thou dost love, And do what Thou wouldst do."*[1] *Amen.*

AN OPEN SECRET

John 20:29 *Happy are they who find faith without seeing me.*

In closing His association with Jerusalem (at least according to the author of this gospel), Jesus gives us a final beatitude. What a joyous note on which to sing "Amen." No wonder that John followed his Lord's example and under the spirit's di-

---

[1]Edwin Hatch

rection brought the entire Bible to a close with a glad hosanna. The Lord knows our inner cry for happiness.

But hold everything. How can one ever rejoice without seeing the giver of every good and perfect gift? Is faith only for the sightless? Emily Dickinson weighs in with her comment that "Faith is a fine invention for gentlemen who see; but microscopes are prudent in an emergency!" Seeing is believing.

Or isn't it? For there are those who claim that they can't believe what they are seeing. Others believe only what they can taste or hear or smell or touch. Now where do we go from here?

This is a cryptic saying of Jesus. He didn't have time to give a detailed explanation. Besides, His hearers by now, knew how to decipher what the uninitiated would think of as psychobabble. The disciples, knowing the code, put it in plain words in their later writings.

One discovers such a faith by learning how it has worked for others. This is how Jesus learned it. In His home and synagogue He had heard of such a working faith in the life of Job. Jesus did no writing, but His sibling James did, shedding light on our text for today. "We count those happy who stood firm. You have heard how Job stood firm, and you have seen how the Lord treated him in the end, for the Lord is merciful and compassionate." (James. 5:11)

And how did Job show his firm stand but by stolidly confirming, "I know that my vindicator (Redeemer) lives." And how did Job find such a faith, without ever having seen his Redeemer?

First, Job had to be sure of the source of wisdom. "Where, then, does wisdom come from? Where is the source of understanding? No creature on earth can set eyes on it. (Job 28:20-21) God alone understands the way to it, He alone knows its source (20:23)...it was then he saw wisdom and took stock of it, he considered it and fathomed its very depths. And he said to mankind: 'The fear of the Lord is wisdom, and to turn from evil, that is understanding.'"(28:27-28) To fear (love) such a God, sight unseen, would be understandably wise.

To companion with such a God and thereby grow in knowledge of Him, even as a pen-pal at first, there is the study of His Word—as given to those who have known Him more intimately. And there is that companiable talking with Him, as in prayer, and in the silences listening with the inner ear to His responses.

Job, with his undeserved sufferings and his firm faith in his Redeemer, is an Old Testament preview of the Christ of Calvary. Learning the basics from Job, we find fulfillment in Jesus our Savior, here and hereafter. There lies His promised bliss in this beatitudinal benediction. What better to keep us blessedly upbeat until we see Him full face in glory?

PRAYER: *Thank You, Lord, for this parting Word. And thank doubting Thomas for evoking it. We join Your troopers with our shield of faith. Amen.*

THEY ALSO SERVE

Acts 1:4 *He (Jesus) directed them not to leave Jerusalem: "You must wait," He said.*

After Jesus' sobbing dismissal of Jerusalem as a city reputed for murdering prophets and stoning messengers sent to her, a city that had rejected His proffered help, a city whose temple had been forsaken by God—you would think that the Master would have urged His followers to flee from this wicked city. It smelled like Sodom and Gomorrah. "Run for your lives." You would have expected His last words to be before ascending to heaven. "And don't look back!"

Still, in spite of all He raged at about the city, He had an innate affection for the dear old place, as most people have always done. We echo our Amens to the Psalmist's tender expression: "If I forget you, Jerusalem, may my right hand wither away; let my tongue cleave to the roof of my mouth if I do not remember you, if I do not set Jerusalem above my chief joy." (Ps. 137:5-6)

Remembering Jesus' disappointment with Jerusalem's behavior, the disciples were, indeed, planning to distance themselves from the city. That is why Jesus didn't just direct them, but as some versions word it, "Jesus commanded them not to leave Jerusalem." It was to be redeemed yet again, for God's purposes.

First Jesus pressed upon His men, they "must wait." That is always risky. There are people who like nothing better. For such it's a time for kicking off your shoes, finding the nearest sofa and becoming a couch potato. Without disrespect, their theme song is "Leaning on the everlasting arms," because in three stanzas they ask you to "lean" twenty-five times. That was a lot more leaning than the Lord expected of His waiters. That could have brought on a National Procrastination Week.

What the disciples had learned from Jesus about waiting involved what has come to be known as the Law of Alternation. We see it in operation at least ten times in the gospels. Jesus would draw apart, or wait, when He knew that something was ahead that would require His total output. So the tarrying was a time of renewal, charging His batteries through prayer, meditation, scripture. And the Jesus fellowship did just that. They readied themselves to be qualified recipients of the promised gift (v. 4)—the Holy Spirit.

That is empowerment plus. That can be dangerous, unless there are positive outlets for super power, which now, on reflection, makes the waiting essential. For the Law of Alternation's passivity is now complemented by activity: "You will bear witness for me in Jerusalem." (v. 8)

If Jesus had deemed His ministry in Jerusalem a failure, His followers would need ultra lionheartedness to stand up for Jesus in that city of spiritual sterility.

And if that were not difficult enough they were to branch out to witness for the Savior "throughout all Judea and Samaria"—where there was only one Good Samaritan we've ever heard about! And the embracing arms of the Good News opens even wider to include "even in the farthest corners of the earth."

When the Lord commands and we obediently respond, see what happens. On the Day of Pentecost when the newly energized Christians were accused of being drunk, empowered Peter addressed "all who live in Jerusalem," (2:14) and the gospel was on its way to the farthest corners of the earth. Within thirty years it reached India and China. That's what creative waiting can accomplish.

PRAYER: *Leash us, Lord, until we hear Your full instructions for what comes next. Amen.*

FROM WHENCE OUR SIGNALS COME

Acts 1:26 *They drew lots, and the lot fell to Matthias; so he was elected to be an apostle with the other eleven.*

At the time (as in the previous meditation), the disciples couldn't be blamed for not fully realizing the weighty importance of Jesus' command for them to "WAIT." He could even have pronounced it "WEIGH IT." The pause was heavy with meaning—which showed up the moment Jesus ascended to heaven. (1:9) He was gone, now what should they do—scatter to Galilee as they had after the resurrection?

"Two men robed in white" (1:10) broke their upward gaze and daze, asking, "why stand there...?" (1:11) The waiting period was over, a new era had begun. This, actually, is the moment at which B.C. broke away from A.D. For the first time the followers of Jesus were receiving guidance from Him through His helpers. Their last instruction was from Him, now it is per kind favor of the Holy Spirit.

But the disciples' difficulties in bridging the transition to a new age was only beginning. How much they had needed that waiting period without knowing it. Thank God Jesus knew. For His chosen leader of the group, Peter, repentant and replenished, had done his homework in waiting. Peter notes the gap in the group left by Judas and urges immediate plugging of the hole in the dike.

Now, how to do this? The last time Jesus did it. So they followed the path that the Master had trod; looking for "one of those who bore us company all the while the Lord Jesus was going about among us, from his baptism by John until the day when he was taken up from us." (1:21-22) Hesitant about making new decisions and choices, they fell back upon the trusted and tried followers whom Jesus had stamped with His imprimatur.

Of all the scores of the faithful, two were singled out—Justus and Matthias, about whom nothing more is known. Then came a communal prayer asking the Lord Jesus to declare which one He had chosen. (1:264) But instead of waiting for His new age answer, they reverted to the old traditional Jewish way of determining God's will: They drew lots. (1:25) That is, they cast lots, dice, called Urim and Thummim. The way these cubes fell revealed God's will for each particular case. So it was decided to choose Matthias. Is this why we never hear of him again? This might be the world's way of beguiling itself into believing that they are doing God's will. But it is not His way, now. Those early Elders were forgiven, for they knew not what they were doing. During their waiting period this was one factor that was not factored in.

No wonder the very next line after Matthias' selection is: "The day of Pentecost had come." (2:1) It couldn't come soon enough to show the faithful who was to be their new guardian and guide Interpreter of God's will, from now until Jesus comes again—the Holy Spirit.

But for those who will not accept the gift of the Holy Spirit, the lots or lotteries still prevail—pre-pentecost. "Lord, if you let me win the jackpot, I promise to give most of it to the church and charity." Or "I'll do whatever you want me to do, Lord, if You heal this dear soul." Always a bargaining chip. Rather, with the dawn of the new dispensation there came the fulfillment of Jesus' promise that "when the Spirit of truth comes, he will guide you into all the truth. (John 16:13) He will guide sometime through friends or strangers or the church or the Scriptures...Our main job is to stay close to Him, for "the Holy Spirit is given by God to those obedient to Him." (Acts 5:32)

PRAYER: *"Spirit of life, in this new dawn...Touch thou our dust with spirit hand and make us souls that understand. Amen."*[1]

PURPOSE DRIVEN SCRIPTURE

Acts 2:14 *But Peter stood up with the eleven, and in a loud voice addressed the crowd: "Fellow Jews, and all who live in Jerusalem, listen and take note of what I say."*

The new twelve apostles (renewed in number and in Spiritual power) stand together (having been separated) in public for the first time in the new era.

Prime apostle Peter has to speak loudly since his congregation (as he is going to preach) is made up of people "from every nation under heaven." (2:5) It is significant for the present day, that the long list of ethnic groups in the crowd, begins with Jews and ends with Arabs! (2:5-11) Which also, incidentally, reveals the universality of the Christian Gospel.

Peter asked his listeners to "take note," and someone did, for here we have the first Christian sermon, and the first of twenty-four to twenty-eight speeches (not all by Peter) in the Book of Acts.

What Peter said was in response to the public's criticism of those persons who were involved in the Pentecostal experience. Normally Galileans

---

[1] Earl Marlatt

were known for their difficult-to-understand accent. Peter had been confronted with this problem. "You must be [a Galilean]; your accent gives you away!" (Matt. 26:73) But at Pentecost, when the Galileans went about witnessing to their new faith they were easily understood—even by foreigners! But critics made light of it, accusing the Galileans of suffering from an alcoholic binge. That's what triggered Peter's tongue.

Addressing his "Fellow Jews," (2:14) Peter built his remarks around three scripture references by two Jerusalem-based prophets. That immediately created an old boy's fellowship, and Peter had their rapt attention.

Peter then quotes Joel 2:28-32 and Acts 2:17-21. What a perfectly admirable choice of scripture—which perfectly fitted the situation. How did Peter do it—plain fisherman that he was? Of course, during the past three years he had seen how Jesus did it, and with such issues as Peter was now handling. Further, we see indications of how well Peter had been instructed in his hometown synagogue in the scriptures. Now at Pentecost, the Big Fisherman has his mind, heart, and tongue joined for action by his new help-mate—the Holy Spirit. No wonder that Peter became the mind behind Mark's gospel—from which Matthew and Luke copied.

The second scripture that Peter used to strengthen the point of his sermon was Psalm 16:8-11. It is possible that Peter, seeing Arabs in his congregation, recalled how this Psalmist was being pressured by Arabs to participate in their pagan rites. The psalmist then calls upon God for protection. Reassured, the psalmist is filled with glowing joy. In every line one reads of his unshakeableness, his gladness and rejoicing—exactly the traits that were evident in the high spirits of those who couldn't contain their pure delight at Pentecost.

In a further word on Ps. 16, Peter shows (Acts 2:27) how the Psalmist (David) had fore knowledge that one of his descendants would be the resurrected Messiah (Christ: the Greek form of the Hebrew word for Messiah). See Ps. 132:11.

The third scripture that Peter quoted was Ps. 110:1 (the most quoted Psalm in the New Testament), where Jesus is entitled to be called "Lord." Then in a masterful conclusion, Peter brings together the authority of "Lord" and the Messiahship of "Christ." "Let all Israel then accept as certain that God has made this same Jesus, whom you crucified both Lord and Messiah." (2:36) What a finale, with what results. "They were cut to the heart." (2:37)

PRAYER: *Thank You, Lord, for redeeming Peter. You could foresee what an upstanding preacher he could become. Raise up his descendants to go and do likewise. Amen.*

I SURRENDER ALL

Acts 3:2 *Now a man who had been a cripple from birth used to be carried there and laid every day by the temple gate called Beautiful to beg from people as they went in.*

This incident almost duplicates Jesus' healing of the cripple at the pool of Bethesda. (John 5) It is likely that Peter and John were present on the former occasion, and now branching out on their own, followed their Master's procedure.

Though not mentioned here, the setting must

have been the same, with "great number of sick people, blind, lame, and paralyzed" (John 5:3) asking for alms. For begging could be lucrative, or the families and friends of these infirm persons would hardly have carried them every day for years to the temple gate, seen to their sanitary needs and feeding, and carried them home at night. Some families might even have depended on the income of beggars, as they still do. But whereas the fellow Bethesda's sheep gate was more intent on being healed, this fellow at the Beautiful gate had his eye on the coins that conscience-tender worshippers might throw in his lap. Also this fellow, more intent on money, failed to realize two differences. One, he didn't believe that Peter and John had no money. They looked well-dressed enough! Yet during their ministry with Jesus, they had become accustomed to going without money. Treasurer Judas had taken care of their finances, disbursing money where and when necessary. And now, after Pentecost, "all the believers agreed to hold everything in common." (Acts 3:6)

After sitting in one place for decades with feet and ankles failing bone-density tests, to be suddenly told to "get up" must have sounded cruelly impossible; and then to "walk"! Lord, have mercy. But Peter gave the cripple a hoist, and up he came, with bone-density's immediate return. Then, as if he had never known years of frustrating disability, the dear brother "entered" the temple with [Peter and John] leaping and praising God as he went." (Acts 3:18)

How much we miss by keeping our eyes on moneybags. But attention, in our time, as in most other times, is fixed on the bottom line—legal tender. And we can never get enough—the billionaires prove that. Unable to break away from that fixation, we miss many splendored things. Like health—forgetting that health is wealth. As with this cripple, the constant cry for greenbacks restricts us to remain at the entrance way to the place of worship. If we have the money, we figure, Saint Peter will welcome us through the Pearly Gates, for a good tip. Not to worry. So all the life-sustaining resources of worship go by the board.

Or see how much more the cripple would have denied himself by remaining a money-hungry fixture at the gate, however Beautiful that was. For accompanying Peter and John, the man came to Solomon's Portico. (3:11) That was now hallowed ground. The last time the Portico was mentioned, (John 10:23) the Lord Jesus was teaching there! And what other unsearchable riches of Christ accrued to the cripple, we shall never know. They may have been inestimable.

Two officials at the Vatican are reported to have had this exchange: "No longer need our church say with Peter, silver and gold have we none." "I know," said the other, "But neither can we say, 'get up and walk.'" Choose this day which you prefer. There's a Christ of a difference between them.

PRAYER: *Lord, take what life I have; it's all Yours. Amen.*

THE PRIZE IN SURPRISE

Acts 3:12 *Peter saw them coming and met them with these words: "Men of Israel, why be surprised at this?"*

Surely Peter was not that naive. Why shouldn't the crowd in the temple be surprised—especially if they had regularly entered through the gate called Beautiful? The lame man now healed and leaping around like an antelope, was well known, easily recognizable. No doubt he had been the recipient of a few donations from many in the crowd. And why shouldn't they be surprised—if not shocked? Had this whirling dervish been "lame" under false pretenses? And if so, here they came, swarming toward him to get their money back!

Even if that had been the scenario, Peter rapidly transposed the thinking of the crowd from money to the Master, especially since few if any persons had heard Peter's quiet, personal confession: "I have no silver or gold; but what I have I give you." Then the invitation: "In the name of Jesus Christ of Nazareth, get up and walk." (Acts 3:6)

The crowd could see that the lame man was now different, but they didn't know how or why. Still, because the healed man clung to Peter and John, the crowd surmised that the apostles had some connection with this newness of life. No, said Peter in his disclaimer: "The name of Jesus, by awakening faith, has given strength to this man whom you see and know and this faith has made him completely well, as you can all see." (3:16) Then, in case some in the crowd had never heard of Jesus, and if to others He was already a dim memory, Peter launched into his second inaugural address since Pentecost. Briefly, it was that Jesus had come in fulfillment of prophecy, and that they, the crowd, should listen to everything the Lord says through His prophets.

God had done all He could for His people (Peter's "fellow Jews" and "friends." (2:14, 3:17) Now Peter lays it on the line as to what the listeners should do.

First was repentance. Even before Jesus broached that subject, John the Baptist, the first

Prophet, after a 400-year silence, had made it his initial thrust: "Repent, for the kingdom of heaven is upon you." (Matt. 3:2)

One shows no courtesy or respect in sticking out grimy hands for an Emperor to shake, any more than it makes sense to come to God with unclean hands and an impure heart. To be sure, His love is all-embracing, but are we willing to grab His unsearchable riches with messy fingers? Repentance is the first step to Godliness—when we renounce our evil ways, and seek the Lord's further ownership of our lives. He completes our cleansing by wiping out our sins. (3:19)

Second, declares Peter, we are granted "a time of recovery" (3:19)—or as another version clarifies it "that your sins may be blotted out, that so there may come seasons of refreshing from the presence of the Lord." Refreshingly recovered from damages inflicted by a sinful society upon the soul, we learn to live as the Lord desires. Under the guidance of His Holy Spirit we listen to everything the Master says, and incarnate it in our daily lives. That is what life on earth is for: becoming what the Lord made us to be and just in time for His coming again to receive us to Himself, now and forever. No surprise. He fulfills what He promises—for Peter, for us, for ALL.

PRAYER: *It doesn't surprise us, Lord, that You work all things together for our good. That is Your nature. Praises be. Amen.*

I SERVE A RISEN SAVIOR

Acts 4:2 *Annoyed because they were proclaiming the resurrection from the dead.*

Religious officialdom had its news reporters everywhere in Jesus' time. No cell phone batteries dying on them, no speedy access computers jammed or scammed by hackers, hot news reached central command promptly. And here the temple authorities closed in, with robes flying, having heard that Peter and John were preaching about a resurrected Savior.

Some scholars are convinced that the alarmists were afraid of a political uprising, which they were sure would be suppressed harshly by Rome's occupying troops.

Yet whatever the subsequent interpretation of the situation may be, the fact remains that the core irritant was the proclamation of the resurrection of the crucified Christ. And it still is.

Every year at the approach of Easter, if not at other times, the spin meisters come out of hiding and trot out their familiar theories about why Jesus couldn't possibly have risen from the tomb. Scripture texts are given new and novel twists and the whole subject is pretzeled out of shape. Better to stick with the spring theme, the bunnies, the ham, colored eggs, chocolates, new clothes, and vacations. Much safer this way; everyone's happier, less stressed, and the economy gets its second-best boost of the year—next to Christmas.

It could be that all this flim-flam has inched its way in, in order to push Christ out. Who needs to be constantly reminded of His death and resurrection? What earthly use does it have for our workaday lives whether we believe in a living Savior? Nobody lives, or has lived, for 2,000 years. Come on, get with it.

When the very first pronouncement was made regarding Jesus' resurrection, all that the unbelievers and cynics had to do to stop the eyewitness accounts in their tracks was simply to exhume Jesus' body and allow a public examination of it. But that was never done. Rather, the proof that Jesus was alive multiplied rapidly and became impossible to confute. Years later, Paul, confronting a lingering disbelief in the resurrection, found from personal experience on the Damascus road that "the truth is" Christ was raised to life—the first fruits of the harvest of the dead." (1 Cor. 15:20)

And Jesus rose for a purpose—several purposes: First, that being One with the Father, He is back at His position of Chief controller of the Universe. (John 1:2) How reassuring. "God saw all that he had made, and it was very good." (Genesis 1:31) He knows better than anyone else how to keep all things in very good condition—or to make midcourse corrections, working all things together for our good. Also, from personal experience, Jesus knows what life on earth is all about; that it is just the first fruit of our existence, there is more beyond. Therefore, second, He showed how we will break out of this cocooned physical existence and move on to the next phase that has been prepared for us. "Since it was a man who brought death into the world, a man also brought resurrection of the dead. As in Adam all die, so in Christ all will be brought to life." (1 Cor. 15:21-22)

One can only pity those who continue to be annoyed about and resist the resurrection. It is the bedrock of life. It's in our past, present, and future. "If it is for this life only that Christ has given us hope, we of all people are most to be pitied." (1 Cor. 15:19) But the truth is, Christ "lives, and grants me daily breath; He lives, and I shall conquer death; He lives, my mansion to prepare; He lives, to bring me safely there." (Samuel Medley)

PRAYER: *Lord, help us to bring others to a knowledge of Your uprising, that this fore knowledge of glory may not be annoying but enjoying. Amen.*

UP THE DOWN STAIRCASE

Acts 4:4 *But many of those who had heard the message became believers, bringing the number of men to about five thousand.*

Readers who stop at verses 1, 2, 3, and don't turn the page are left with the impression that here goes the promising, exciting new faith down the tubes. Before that, Pentecost had burst upon the scene in a fireworks display that had everyone looking up at the wondrous speaking in tongues, the sparkling preaching, the rapid multiplication of new church members, the potential for winning the world for Christ. Then, just as quickly as the colored stars and crackling sounds fall to earth, the Pentecostal period appeared to have had its day in the spotlight. The resurrection theme was pounced upon and silenced, and its chief proclaimers—Peter and John—were imprisoned. So much for another attempt to get the Jesus movement off the ground! Then, ready to return to our old ways of eating, drinking, making merry, we hear James Russell Lowell singing: "Though the cause of evil prosper, yet 'tis truth alone is strong; Though her portion be the scaffold, And upon the throne be wrong; Yet that scaffold sways the future, And behind the dim unknown, Standeth God within the shadow keeping watch above his own."

When all seemed lost, there was net gain. Behind the scenes He intervenes. "Many of those who had heard the message became believers."

What a blue-ribbon harvest of converts!

And that was only the beginning of the continuing good news of salvation. The day after their overnight in jail, Peter and John were summoned to appear before the religious establishment. It was a picture of overkill—all these rulers and elders and priests frowning down on two "uneducated laymen." (v. 13) As it turned out, the swaggering authorities were caught between Peter the rock and a hard place and "had nothing to say."(v. 14) It was Peter, "filled with the Holy Spirit," (v. 8) who did most of the saying, ending with another apt quote from scripture. (Ps. 118:22)

What a beautiful choice of Psalms: It "is a unique liturgy of national thanksgiving which celebrated God's repeated deliverance of Israel across the centuries."[1] The procession of worshipers, led by the choir, entered through the Temple Gates on New Year's Day.

Peter had much for which to be thankful...the surging interest in a living Savior, another deliverance of His people from the confinements of manmade laws to the fresh air of Christ's liberating teachings; a New Era for humans. Then Peter turned the screws on the officials, many of whom, just a few weeks before, had taken part in the unjust trial and crucifixion of Jesus. Adapting Psalm 118 for this particular moment, Peter boldly stated, "This Jesus is the stone, rejected by you the builders, which has become the corner-stone." (Acts 4:11) That is, Jesus, once considered useless enough to throw on the trash heap, has become the One on Whom all else depends. Putting it in

---

[1]Elmer Leslie, the Psalms, p. 112

his own words, Peter concludes with a cornerstone comment: "There is no salvation through anyone else; in all the world no other name has been granted to mankind by which we can be saved (other than the name of Jesus)."(Acts 4:12) In his Lyman Beecher lectures at Yale in 1966, Bishop Lesslie Newbigen concluded: "To claim finality for Jesus Christ is not to assert that the majority of men will someday be Christians, or to assert that all others will be damned. It is to claim that commitment to Him is the way in which men can become truly aligned to the ultimate end for which all things were made."[1]

PRAYER: *When we feel weakest, Lord, You make us feel stronger than ever. Many thanks. Amen.*

DRAW ME NEARER

Acts 4:13 ...*took note that they (Peter and John) had been companions of Jesus.*

Though the officials had been informed at least three times that the apostles association with Jesus, it had failed to penetrate their gray matter. But suddenly it did. The shadows recoiled as the light of understanding dawned.

Who or what turned on the light? Had someone seen a reflection of the stranger of Galilee in these two men from Galilee? How else does one see a shining example except when actions speak louder than words? And those who had seen and heard Jesus began to note the similarities between Him and these two witnesses of His.

Yes someone would recall this healing of the man by the Beautiful Gate, for which Peter and

---

[1] L. Newbigen, *The Finality of Christ*, p. 115

John were being given the credit, was a striking parallel to Jesus' healing of the cripple by the pool of Bethesda. Where else, how else could these single fishermen have learned the healing art?

As for Peter's sermons—crisp, scriptural, close-fitting the condition of the moment—were they sudden inspirations, were they out of the blue? Hardly, because by now it was known far and wide that Peter had been Jesus' right-hand man, the skipper of a twelve-oared boat, and John was "the disciple whom Jesus loved." With such a tight affinity, these two would be present at most if not all of Jesus' teaching sessions. On the Mount of Olives, today, one is taken to a cave where tradition claims Jesus often took His committed hours of in-depth study and questions and answers regarding God's word and its bearing upon the daily rigors of everyday living. This was the theory part of discipleship. Then came the practice—"where cross the crowded ways of life, Where sound the cries of race and clan. Above the noise of selfish strife. [They] heard thy voice, O Son of Man!"[1]

Just in the area of our Lord's miracles there was an assortment of at least thirty-five that were recorded—either in all four gospels, narrated only in three gospels or two gospels or only in one gospel. The feeding of the 5,000 caught the interest of Matthew, Mark, Luke and John. And we are called always to remember that Mark, though not an apostle, wrote, as the interpreter of Peter, "accurately all that [Peter] remembered of the things done and said by Christ."[2]

---

[1] Frank Mason North
[2] Ronald Brownrigg, *The Twelve Apostles*, p. 58

Which is to conclude that Peter didn't miss much of what Jesus said and did. Knowing that, the other gospel writers—at least Matthew and Luke—faithfully copied Mark's gospel, which is now considered the first one to have been written.

Once Peter accepted Jesus' invitation to be a fellow-worker, sponge-like he soaked up his Master's masterful example. He bore that shining image of the Master in his face. And, in his own way, John did too. It came as it still comes, from a flowing together of lives. One sees it in husbands and wives who have lived together, through sunshine and shadow for decades. They talk like each other, can finish each others' sentences, tackle jobs with equal verve, are one heart in two bodies. If officialdom in the Jerusalem temple had been unable to recognize the Christ in Peter and John, there would have been something terribly out of whack in their craniums.

PRAYER: *"Jesus, confirm my heart's desire, to work and speak and think for Thee, still let me guard the holy fire, and still stir up thy gift in me." Amen. (Charles Wesley)*

TELL IT OUT

Acts 4:18 *They then called them in and ordered them to refrain from all public speaking and teaching in the name of Jesus.*

In our newfangled terms, the above would be called mandatory micro management. In the previous verse (17), the committee had decided to "caution" the two apostles "never again to speak to anyone in this name" (Jesus). But when the committee's action was spelled out to the accused, it became more than cautionary; it was mandatory.

If this did not sound so familiar, we would hop over it. But, these days everywhere we turn, every word of v. 18 echoes and re-echoes "remember me," and "don't you forget it." Actually, Peter and John were better off than we are. This order was for them alone; as yet it hadn't embraced Christendom. Now it has.

The present sensitivity toward ethnicity and political correctness and a pluralistic society, has not so subtly demanded the elimination of the "scandal of particularity." Level the playing field is the order of the day. Secularize society. Remove any semblance of religion, especially Christianity, which it is claimed has been too elitist, too power-hungry, too divisive. Accordingly, the public appearance of the Christian faith has been shamed and mocked into the shadows. Breathing this strange atmosphere all week, church members are forgetting how to think and talk any other way, even in church on Sunday. Jesus' name, outlawed all week, sounds strangely familiar in a sanctuary during worship. The Stranger of Galilee is back where He started from. To mention His name anywhere, increasingly is bringing in a feeling of unease in a Christian fellowship. The quizzical looks and whispers (if that speaker leaves the room) betoken "Is he too evangelical?" "Is she a fundamentalist?" "Does he have Alzheimer's?"

Two other changes are noticeable: that prayers said in and out of church rarely include any reference to Jesus. It's as if the Christian community is directly and slavishly obeying the 2,000-year-old mandate voiced in the temple in Jerusalem. Even the Lords' Prayer is omitted and other prayers, if any, are generalized.

Peter, let it be remembered was not about to kowtow to the ordinance: "Is it right in the eyes of God for us to obey you rather than him? Judge for yourselves. We cannot possibly give up speaking about what we have seen and heard." (4:19-20) That kind of rejoinder brings up the second noticeable change in our time. Where is it heard or even echoed? Who is there, not yet intimidated, who boldly asserts, "It is impossible for us to refrain from all public speaking and teaching in the name of Jesus"? That kind of courage, may we ruefully confess, has been crucified and cremated, while we march in lockstep, under orders from men rather than from God.

To be sure Peter did not get away with his outspokenness. Later documents record that Peter and John received "forty lashes less one"—thirteen on each shoulder from the back, and thirteen on the chest from the front. Yet they returned to the temple to preach Christ. It doesn't look as if there is any alternative for those who persist in proclaiming the Savior. A cross awaits. The servant is not greater than his Lord. But a crown also awaits the conquests.

PRAYER: *Heavenly Father, we sing and pray with Isaac Watts: "Sure I must fight, if I would reign; Increase my courage, Lord; I'll bear the toil, endure the pain, Supported by thy word." Amen.*

PROCEED WITH HIS PROCEDURE

Acts 4:24 *When they (the Christian fellowship) heard it (the mandate placed upon the apostles by the court), they raised their voices with one accord and called upon God.*

The Christians were not about to "shut up" about Jesus. Then how should they proceed? Today's protestors plunge straight into demonstrations, catcalls, spitfire responses, erupting into physical violence and loss of life, with no holds barred.

Not those of the early church. They set a gold standard for the way to approach such a radioactive subject. They, first of all, called upon God for guidance.

Uncaring, unchristian folk call such a first step imbecilic. "What can an unseen, unknown God do that we can't?" they ask. And off they go helter-skeltering down the wrong road. These Christians, on the other hand, knew God, knew how, getting an overview of humanity, He could see ends from beginnings and which moves were the wisest. They also know how God makes His will known to earthlings, "by the Holy Spirit." (v. 25) They were convinced of God's sovereignty, "Maker of heaven and earth and sea and everything in them." (v. 25) With such a dependable and easily accessible divine guide, it was second nature for them to turn to Him first. Nor was the Christian call a cry for "gimme." They talked to God as a Best Friend. They talked scripture. And surely Peter was behind that, although he is not mentioned in the text. We have heard Peter, on several recent occasions, quoting scripture that fitted perfectly into the jigsaw puzzle of the moment. As here, once again, from Psalm 2:1,2 (Acts 4:25,26).

The first line describes the condition in which the Christians find themselves: a state of commotion. There was bewilderment on the part of the temple authorities (v. 16), and a court-ordered clamp down on the speech and activities of the Christians. Pandemonium indeed. The rest of the

Psalm is omitted, possibly because the Christian brethren knew how well the whole piece was a duplicate of their own situation. As in the Psalm, the pagan kings were in revolt against Judah's God, so in Jerusalem were the officials against the Lord Jesus. In the Psalm (2:7) God says to the King, "thou art my Son, in whom I am well pleased." (Mark 1:11) In the Psalm (2:8), God says, "I will give you the nations for thy inheritance." For this reason Jesus refused to submit to Satan's temptation to fall down and do him homage, in return for which Jesus would be given "all the kingdoms of the world in their glory." (Matt. 4:8) The long established fact was that the gift of all the nations of the world was already in God's will and testament for Jesus.

Then, having turned first to God and His Word, First Church, Jerusalem, returned to their burning problem of the hour: How should they witness for the Lord after being muffled by the law? They did not give God instructions, as is too often done. They were open to His guidance, whatever that might be. All they asked for was enablement to do His will. And the moment the prayer ended there was a strong sensation of Pentecost revisited. (4:31) "And all were filled with the Holy Spirit and spoke God's word with boldness." (v. 31) God did it up right, as usual, for "every day they went steadily on with their teaching in the temple and in private houses, telling the good news of Jesus the Messiah. (Acts 5:42) So "the word of God spread more and more widely; the number of disciples in Jerusalem was increasing rapidly, and very many of the priests adhered to the faith." (Acts 6:7) And certainly the last verse of Psalm 2 hit the hot button: "Happy are all who find refuge in Him." IN Jesus!

PRAYER: *Thank You for that final Beatitude, Lord. In all of our goings, however painful, the finale is joy. Amen.*

CONSECRATED, LORD, TO THEE

Acts 4:36-37 *For instance...Barnabas...sold an estate which he owned; he brought the money and laid it at the apostles' feet.*

Growing rapidly in number, believers in the risen Christ were soon tormented and penalized into poverty by Jewish officialdom. Undismayed, the new converts rallied around the less fortunate in a communal ministry of sharing. As with the feeding of the five thousand, the Lord saw to it that all had enough and some to spare.

Enter Barnabas with his donation. But why is Barnabas singled out by name out of all the unnamed priests and thousands of commoners who had turned to the Lord? Was Barnabas a standout among men, one whose exemplary sacrifice would kindle the flame of total commitment in others? That's how it looked to author Luke, at least especially when he heard of the contrasting episode of Ananias and Sapphira, and how "Great awe fell on the whole Church and on all who heard of this." (5:11) Without the total giving of Barnabas the subsequent lie to God (5:4) would have been shameful enough. But someone had to set the standard—planting the flag, proclaiming, "Here I stand, I can do no other so help me God." Barnabas had heard of how Jesus did it (set His face toward Jerusalem, knowing He would be crucified there), and a servant is not greater than his Lord.

Nor was this an isolated virtuous act on the part of Barnabas. For the next he appears is in Acts 9:27. Paul had just been converted on the Damascus road, but when his former associates heard that he had switched his allegiance from Judaism to Christ, "They hatched a plot against his life." (9:23) Escaping to Jerusalem hoping to find refuge among Christians, Paul found instead that the Christians were equally distrustful of him. Suddenly he had become as a wounded moose fatally surrounded by wolves. Enter Barnabas once again, risking his life and credibility to rescue Paul from those who would savage him, "and introduced him to the apostles." (9:27) Without the timely intervention of Barnabas, we may never have heard any more about Paul!

Becoming increasingly indispensable, Barnabas was sent to pastor a new church at Antioch. Since some of the members were from the island of Cyprus, as Barnabas was, he was the ideal choice. And Luke adds to Barnabas' credentials— "He was a good man, full of the Holy spirit and of faith. And large numbers were won over to the Lord." (11:24)

Needing an associate pastor to help with his potential mega-church, Barnabas made another bull's-eye decision. He went to Tarsus, Paul's hometown, and invited Paul to be equally yoked in serving the parish at Antioch. And "for a whole year the two of them lived in fellowship with the Church there." (11:26) With such top-flight leadership, the Antioch church was bursting with enthusiasm to get the Good News out to the world. And naturally, their co-pastors were delegated for the task. Antioch became the headquarters for the three missionary journeys that started Christianity on its mission through Europe.

Dividing, after a disagreement, these two coworkers continued their ministries in separate fields; Paul the publicized one and Barnabas the silent innovator. Barnabas is not mentioned again except briefly by Paul in 1 Cor. 9:6; Gal. 2:1, 9,13; Col. 4:10. Local legend at Salamis, Cyprus, Barnabas' homeland, has it that Barnabas, "on a later mission here was stoned to death and that Mark (his cousin) buried him outside the city, placing on his breast a copy of St. Matthew."[1]

How else could Barnabas have been the pioneer of a world-embracing Christianity? Years before, Jesus' word had been laid on the heart of Barnabas.

PRAYER: *"O Lord God almighty, who didst endure thy holy Apostle Barnabas with singular gifts of the Holy ghost: Leave us not, we beseech thee, destitute of thy manifold gifts, nor yet of grace to use them always to thy honour and glory; through Jesus Christ our Lord. Amen."* The Anglican Book of Common Prayer, *collect for June 11.*

ALL OR NOT AT ALL

Acts 5:9 *Why did the two of you conspire...?*

Barnabas had set an Olympic pace in his financial donation. With it he bounded from anonymity to apostleship, as his fellow Christians watched—admiringly, envyingly. Not the least of them were these Two well-to-dos, Ananias and his beautiful wife, Sapphira.

Learning what Barnabas had laid at the Apostles' feet, this couple seems to have persuaded themselves that they could comfortably match the amount that

---

[1]*National Geographic* Dec. 1956, p. 734

Barnabas donated—and still have enough left over for themselves. What they had calculatingly planned, however, was that they would be placed on a par with Barnabas, without really deserving to be. Peter picked up the echoes of his Master's voice in the Temple. On that occasion Jesus "saw rich people dropping their gifts into the chest of the temple treasure." Then came "a poor widow putting in two tiny coins. 'I tell you this,' He said, 'this poor widow has given more than enough, but she, with less than enough, has given all she had to live on.'" (Luke 21:1-2) What Peter was seeing in the donation of Ananias was even more than a replay of the Temple incident. The rich givers Jesus cited merely walked away haughtily, in their self-glorification. Here Peter identifies with Ananias. He sees in Ananias the trembling, hesitant conscience-stricken person he, himself, was when he had betrayed Jesus, and the Lord gave him that long I-told-you-so look. (Luke 22:61) And Peter "went outside and wept bitterly." (Luke 22:62) Oh, what a painful flashback. As Peter looked into the eyes of Ananias he could see a reflection of himself. Jesus had just said, "I am going where you cannot follow me now." (John 4:36) But Peter was determined not to be left behind; determined to be his Master's right-hand man, saying, "Lord, I will lay down my life for you." (John 4:37) Not much later, instead of making the utmost donation, Peter kept back part of the price. Multiply that by three steps as Peter distanced himself from the Christ. Then the cock crowed the wake-up call for Peter's conscience (John 18:27), and he turned to lock eyes with Jesus. That did it, Peter burst into confessional and redemptive tears.

But Ananias did not. Peter's understanding look

did nothing to soften Ananias' tough conspiratorial stance. So convinced was he of the rightness of his cause, he was willing to lay down his life for it. Whereupon "he dropped dead." (Acts 5:5)

Someone was watching the clock, for "about three hours passed" (Acts 5:7) and here came wifey Sapphira the sapphire, with money written all over her, "unaware of what had happened." (5:7) Their family plan was so foolproof that Sapphira had apostles' accolades about topping Barnabas' contribution. Then she figured he would return home with a wink of approval, and a "we dood it" sigh of relief. A con man's dream.

But when Peter started asking probing questions, Sapphira knew that everything had gone awry, especially when Peter asked the heart-stabbing question: "Why did the two of you conspire to put the spirit of the Lord to the test?" That was a fatal blow. She joined her husband in a grave condition. (5:10)

The word "conspiracy" can be divided into two words. It is the *piracy* that is done by the *cons*. "Great awe fell on the whole church and on all who heard of this." (5:10)

He that has ears to hear, let him hear, for its still happening in and out of the church.

PRAYER: *Lord, You can see through us. "Can a human being defraud God? Yet you defraud me. You ask, 'how have we defrauded you?' Why, over tithes and contributions" (Mal. 3:9)—and a lot more. Forgive us, redeem us, that we may be all Yours, now and ever. Amen.*

What Prison?

Acts 5:23 *"We found the jail securely locked at every point, with the warders at their posts by the doors, but on opening them we found no one inside."*

In other places lawbreakers may have been treated more casually. Not in the capital city of Jerusalem—where people came from all over the world for festivals of one kind or another. Under the strict supervision of Roman occupying forces, the building of Jerusalem jails left nothing to chance. And who should be locked up in one of these maximum security persons, yet again, but Peter, John, and perhaps others of the apostles. On the principle that they were obeying God rather than men, the apostles had stubbornly refused to obey the city's religious officials. But when the special temple police went to get Peter and company for the further questioning, they found the jail as tightly secured as ever, but with no one inside. The prison that wasn't! That's God's promise to His people in any of life's confinements: freedom.

We're not talking about escapees from jail. They have their day with the warden and the Judge. But see what Jesus has done, can do, for those who follow His guidance. After all, He is the One who went in and out of locked doors. "Death cannot keep his prey, Jesus my Savior! He tore the bars away, Jesus my Lord!" (Robert Lowry)

See how He has unshackled persons who have been bound by illness. As in Acts 5:16: "The people from the towns around Jerusalem flocked in, bringing those who were ill or harassed by unclean spirits, and all were cured." Or even if there has been no physical cure, the spirit has been set free, made triumphant. As Saint Paul found: "No wonder we do not lose heart! Though our outward humanity is in decay. Yet day by day we are inwardly renewed. Our troubles are slight and short-lived and their outcome is an eternal glory, which far outweighs them, provided our eyes are fixed not on the things that are seen but on the things that are unseen; for what is seen is transient, what is unseen is eternal (1 Cor. 4:16-17)

Oh how He releases—from cramping, crunching circumstances. A study of hundreds of slum boys in Baltimore held out little hope for their future. They all looked like penitentiary prospects. Twenty years later a careful survey revealed that just five boys had criminal records. The rest, all productive citizens, credited a teacher for their turnaround. The teacher, now in a nursing home, simply responded that she loved those boys. Love (and God is love) was the key out of unloveliness.

Oh how He releases—from boredom, bereavement, aging, addictions, broken homes, illiteracy, joblessness, loneliness, trench warfare. Imprisonment comes in myriad forms. But there's always the One who holds the master key. Paul, too, learned that at Philippi. He and Silas were beaten and "flung into prison," an inner prison. Their feet were secured in the stocks and they were kept "under close guard." They were maxed out. And it was midnight! Talk about a lockdown. But here came the divine doorkeeper. Hearing the missionaries singing and praying and lifting the spirits of the other inmates, thereby freeing themselves from bondage, the Holy intervener entered into the freeing process: "The doors burst open and all the prisoners found their fetters unfastened." Even the jailer was converted that night, along with members of his family, rejoicing "with his whole household in his new found faith in God." (Acts 16:23-34)

Another prison that wasn't. It can be yours and mine. Ask the Savior to help you, comfort, strengthen and keep you. He is willing to aid you. He will carry you through.

PRAYER: *"He breaks the power of canceled sin, He sets the prisoner free; His blood can make the foulest clean; His blood availed for me."*[1] *Thank You, Lord. Amen.*

THE DNA OF OUR FAITH

Acts 5:31, 32 *God exalted him at his right hand as leader and savior, to grant Israel repentance and forgiveness of sins. And we are witnesses to all this, as is the Holy Spirit who is given by God to those obedient to him.*

Increasingly one learns why Jesus drew Peter out of a handful of simple Galileans to the leadership of His apostolic team. Jesus had far-ranging vision. From the beginning of their relationship He must have seen Peter as we are now privileged to see him in these first post-Pentecostal days: Christ's man, throughout. The mind that was in Christ had become Peters.

As a hardy fisherman, Peter had seen many a seaman pale and wail and fail in a gale. Whereas Peter had learned how to prevail in a gale. Then he saw, repeatedly, how Jesus did it in everyday living, and how, for the joy that was set before Him, He endured...

Now we see Peter living out that faith in deed, as he has refused to be silenced, even with imprisonments, and now in a condensation of his recent sermons.

---

[1] Charles Wesley

Finding that the law enforcers were not really listening to him but to their own pet peeves, Peter tries once more, putting it in a nutshell: the DNA of our faith.

Back to Jesus, who was the center of contention in the minds of the religious hierarchy, Peter makes four points.

First, that after His death, Jesus was exalted. Peter wouldn't let these accusing priests forget that they put down Jesus—with beating, spit, curses, insults, crucifixion. But God had exalted Jesus; raised Him to the heights. Oh not to empty ether; not rest on some passing cloud nine; but

Second, to a definite signatory position—God's right hand. At all top-scale functions, the guest of honor has traditionally been seated at the host's right hand. That, fittingly, was where Jesus had always belonged—until He submitted to the Father's will to come and show the world how it could be saved—and by life. But, well pleased with His Son's total sacrifice, God returned Jesus to His exalted place of divine prominence, and

Third, as Leader. Not everyone knows how to lead, even when they are given such titles as president, chief executive officer, commander-in-chief, grand master..."He leadeth me" indicates that he has pioneered the way ahead. He knows the paths of righteousness and the valleys with their deceptive shadows. He knows the human need for green pastures and still water, and the restoration of one's spirit. He sees that the stragglers are protected in the rear by those two security men—goodness and mercy. He shepherds.

Fourth, Jesus was exalted to saviorhood. "You shall give Him the name Jesus, for He will save His people from their sins." (Matt. 1:21) He did just that, and was rewarded accordingly.

The other four points Peter makes in our text have to do with us humans. To be worthy of such a Lord, we first need to Repent. That calls for a renunciation of sin and a turning to the Holy Spirit for guidance in living a life well-pleasing to God. Second, to receive forgiveness for our sins, so that we will not be burdened by them ever again. Third, since we are pipes through which omnipotence sounds, we are expected to be witnesses for the living Christ, enabled in that task by the Holy Spirit. Finally there is our continuing from childhood on, lest we miss the Kingdom's goal. Herein lies all the Good News that's fit for abundant living.

PRAYER: *Thank You, Lord, for chiseling Peter into a rock of a man. Under Your watchful care he has given us the vital signs of our faith. Amen.*

WHEN ACTIONS SPEAK LOUDEST

Acts 5:33 *But a member of the council rose to his feet, a Pharisee called Gamaliel, a teacher of the law held in high regard by all the people.*

From here to verse 39 is the only mention there is of this distinguished man. A grandson of the famed Hillel who is still remembered with iconic respect by scholars, Gamaliel was also a teacher of that student whom the centuries have embraced as Saint Paul. Little wonder that when Gamaliel spoke, people hushed, listened, agreed. When he rose to his feet, watch out—there was about to be thunder and lightning.

Of all the dignitaries and celebrities who took history's stage in the time of Christ, not one was without stain. Their hoisted scars and gripes are on full display. But not Gamaliel. He was squeaky clean. A thoroughbred, pure-blooded Pharisee, he was the most respected lawyer of his time. And now was the moment for him to make a conclusive statement about the most aggravating situation that was rocking Jerusalem.

For some time Jesus Christ had everyone's attention—with His teaching, His miracles, His botched trial, and crucifixion, and resurrection. Nor did that end the chaotic situation. Jesus' followers were multiplying daily and the apostolic leaders were becoming defiant of the law. They had been reprimanded, beaten, imprisoned, but that only caused them to rejoice "that they had been found worthy to suffer humiliation for the sake of the name (Jesus)." (v. 41)

Such behavior had to be capped. And who should do it but the presiding elder of the Council, Gamaliel. So he rose to the occasion and did two good things. One, he saved Peter and John and whoever else was involved, from being put to death (v. 33) as the rest of the Council had desired; and, two, he distinguished between the Jesus' movement being manmade or God-made. If the first, it would collapse; if the second, "you will never be able to stamp it out." (v. 39) How right he was. It's still impacting all of humanity.

The sad disclosure here, which leads to Gamaliel's anticlimax is the disconnect between his noble words and his deeds. He failed to practice what he preached, most especially in regard to Jesus.

Where was this esteemed lawyer during that first Holy Week—a Passion Week for Jesus? Everyone knew what was happening in the city, and no one knew better than the ecclesiastical politicos of whom Gamaliel was the leader. It was as if he had taken the advice which he had just dished out concerning Peter and John: "My advice to you is this: Keep clear of these men; let them alone." (v. 38) That is exactly the position Gamaliel had taken with Jesus; he distanced himself at a time when Jesus most needed a helping hand.

Or in a more tolerant mood, we might even allow that Gamaliel was another closet Christian, like one of his associates—Nicodemus. He also seems to have been of the same stripe as King Agrippa: "With a little more of your persuasion, you will make a Christian of me." (Acts 26:28) But both Gamaliel and Agrippa kept a tight rein on their final decision. All in all, Gamaliel is best described by dear, lowly Timothy: "While preserving the outward form of religion they are a standing denial of its power...always wanting to be taught but incapable of attaining to a knowledge of the truth." (2 Tim. 3:5,7) Gamaliel's own words were self-fulfilling where he said: "You risk finding yourselves at war with God." (v. 39) Paul showed the way of deliverance for all such strategized minds: a personal experience with the Risen Savior, Jesus Christ, the Lord.

PRAYER: *Lord, save us from having everything—but You. To whom else shall we go. You are the giver of life, here and hereafter. Amen.*

DIVIDE AND CONQUER

Acts 6:2,4 *It would not be fitting for us to neglect the word of God in order to assist in the distribution...then we can devote ourselves to prayer and to the ministry of the word.*

With a rapidly growing congregation in the

early church, it was to be expected that new and varied problems would show up. And here was one: a discriminatingly unequal distribution of aid to widows. Jewish widows, it was claimed, were getting more than their share, whereas Greek-speaking Jewish widows were getting the short end of the wishbone.

The twelve apostles couldn't take on any more responsibility, they felt, without becoming ineffective in their ministry. One hears their plea in our text for today.

At first it sounds like a wail from a pity party. In fact it sounds elitist, aloof, lofty. It reminds me of a Sunday morning after the church services. One of the church staff members was laughing. When asked why, he replied: "When I was greeting people at the door, I asked a gentleman if he was a minister. 'Oh, no,' he replied, 'I'm a bishop.'" The dear brother was elevated, no longer in the lowlands of picayune pastoralia. Now he was in the upper stratosphere of power, prestige. Now he was in a position to push pastors around like pawns on a checkerboard.

That, at first, is the impression the apostles give. They couldn't stoop to the doing of menial tasks. They could best serve only by being holed up in a monastic ivory tower to pray, meditate, study the scriptures.

Actually, their intent is inadequately expressed in verse 2. What they were really and wisely doing was harking back to Moses' shining example. (Exod. 18:14-36)

Moses had found himself swamped with responsibility, and his father-in-law, Jethro, promptly spotted the problem and rectified it.

Of course, pride was involved. Moses couldn't think of relinquishing any of his responsibilities for fear the whole Exodus project would fall apart. He had been a general in the Egyptian army, with great success. What could now prevent him from being general manager of mankind? But Jethro was up front with Moses. "This is not the best way to do it." (Exod. 18:17) "You will only wear yourself out and wear out the people who are here. The task is too heavy for you; you cannot do it alone." (Exod. 18:18). Then he suggested a sharing out of duties among carefully chosen credentialed persons. And it worked. As it did in the early Church. The particular problem was solved (we never hear of it again), without the Seven selected men neglecting their prayers and studies.

Stephen, one of the Seven, in his defense before the Council (Acts, Chapter 7), showed an encyclopedic knowledge of the scriptures. It is widely believed that if Stephen had been given a chance, he had the potential of being more effective than Saint Paul. Certainly there would have been no Paul without Stephen. It was Stephen's steadfast faith amid the fatal hail of stones that turned the direction of Paul's life from grime to glory, from crime to Christ.

Philip was another of the Seven who both assisted in the distribution to the widows and kept up with his evangelistic missions. He converted an Ethiopian, hereby introducing Christianity into a heathen land. He had a Godly home, where Paul felt at home. And Philip set such a good example, that his four daughters became preachers.

The Twelve and the Seven, dividing their labors, after prayer and the guidance of the Holy

Spirit, expanded the scope of the Kingdom's horizons, so that "The Word of God spread more and more widely: the number of disciples in Jerusalem was increasing rapidly, and very many of the priests adhered to the faith." (6:7)

PRAYER: *Master, show us when to divide, and how to unite. We seem to have our signals crossed. Amen.*

COME AWAY

Acts 7:2-3 *The God of glory appeared to Abraham...while he was in Mesopotamia, before he had settled in Harran and said: "Leave your country and your kinsfolk, and come away to a land that I will show you."*

In the Old Testament one sees, along the way, fingers pointing to a New Testament. At least forty-seven passages from the Psalms and the Prophets testify in detail to the coming of Christ the Messiah. While in the New Testament we are often, as in today's text, pointed back to the Old Testament from whence we have come. For much as we would like to think of the New Testament as a bouquet of fresh flowers, and leave it at that, we cannot. For the New Testament is not a vase of cut flowers. Rather, this fragrant garden is rooted and grounded in the rich, deep soil of the Old Testament—denoting continued growth. Cut it anywhere and it bleeds.

As the action in Acts proceeds in Jerusalem, the High Priest, hearing accusations that Stephen had blasphemed the Temple and the Law of Moses, asked the accused if this was so. (v. 1)

Instead of a direct answer, Stephen chose to approach the question through a brief history lesson. Planning to take a long jump over 2,000 years, Stephen took a long running start up to the take-off line—all the way back to Abraham. (Genesis

12:1) There (our text), God ordered Abraham to do three things: 1. Leave Ur of the Chaldees where he was born, brought up and married, before settling in Harran—500 miles up the River Euphrates at the top of the Fertile Crescent. 2. Leave kinsfolk, all the relatives. 3. Come away to a new land. Three bewildernesses!

One would have been painful enough. Why leave Ur, a flourishing city? Today Ur is about 120 miles north of Basra on the River Euphrates, close to where it joins the Tigris River in Iraq. In the 1920s archaeologists from the University of Pennsylvania and from the British Museum in London unearthed Ur. The leader of the expedition, Sir Charles Leonard Woolley, wrote: "We must radically alter our view of the Hebrew patriarch (Abraham) when we see that his earlier years were passed in such sophisticated surroundings. He was the citizen of a great city and inherited the traditions of an old and highly organized civilization. The houses themselves reveal comfort and even luxury (2000 B.C.). We found copies of the hymns which were used in the services of the temples and together with them mathematical tables..."[1]

Why leave all this glory behind? Yet, because of unsettling conditions, Abraham's father, Terah, moved the family upriver to Harran—a place much like Ur.

As for leaving kinsfolk behind, that, too, must have been a wrench. And Abraham never forgot it. For when he was very old (he died at 175), he said to his most trusted servant, "I want you to swear by the Lord, the God of heaven and earth,

---

[1] Keller Werner, *The Bible as History*, p. 40

that you will not take a wife for my son (Isaac, who was born when his father, Abraham, was 100 years old) from the women of the Canaanites among whom I am living. You must go to my own country and to my own kindred to find a wife for my son Isaac." (Gen. 24:3-4) "And the servant...arose and went to Mesopotamia." (Gen. 24:10) For Abraham, who had found the love of his life, Sarah, at Ur—no woman was worthy of his son, except one of his relatives still residing in Ur. The old gentleman had kept in touch with his kinsfolk in the old country.

Then there was the strange land of Canaan, another 600 miles south of Harran, to which God had called Abraham. But honest Abe went, unhesitatingly. No wonder he is mentioned seventy-two times in the New Testament, more than any other Old Testament person except Moses.

Sooner or later there comes to everyone a three-pronged Abrahamic assignment. Will we be full of detaining, diverting questions? Or will we respond instantly, in faith? The bottom line is that this is what Stephen was urging his listeners to do. But they would not. It was easier to stone Stephen. How is it with us?

PRAYER: *Lord, grant us wisdom, grant us courage, for the facing of this hour. Amen.*

FAITH, IN SPITE OF

Acts 7:4-5 *God led him (Abraham) to migrate to this land (the Holy Land) where you now live. He gave him no foothold in it, nothing to call his own.*

In this long speech, Stephen never wandered. All along the way he made connections with Jesus assuming the knowledge and conscience of his hearers would detect it. So he reports the arrival of Abraham in the land to which God had called him—the place in particular, where this court case is being held: Jerusalem. But what an anti-climax Stephen describes it to be. After the heartbreak of leaving his homeland, dwelling for some years in the intermediary city of Harran, slogging for 1,000 miles along the old caravan routes—only to find in this new God-selected situation, that, in Stephen's words, Abraham had no foothold, nothing to call his own, a promise of descendants without any children of his own, and that the descendants would be slaves in a foreign land and oppressed for 400 years! So much for a personal call from God! Can't you just see Abraham writing to his loved ones in dear old Ur: "Arrived in the Holy Land—and all I have to show for it is this lousy imprinted T-shirt: "There's no place like Home Sweet Hamas."

In Acts 7:39, reporting the Exodus under Moses leadership, Stephen says that the rebellious Israelites "wished themselves back in Egypt." But never once is there any such backward yearning by Abraham. How did he do it, with all the negatives spread across life's roadways? What kept him soldiering on? And there in Jerusalem, and up and down the land?

For an answer we turn to Hebrews, Chapter 11, which lists seventeen names, "and the prophets," (v. 32) in Faith's Hall of Fame.

Abraham gets three verses (8-10). In verses 8 and 9, his faith gets top credit. 1. By faith he obeyed the call to leave his home. 2. By faith he set out, without knowing where he was to go. 3.

By faith he settled as an alien in the land. With all the distractions and disappointments en route, Abraham's faith was unwavering. That denotes a clear knowledge of and an experiential walk and talk with a trustable God. 4. Then there was that exciting promise that Abraham's seed would be multiplied into a great nation. The only trouble was that with an aging wife, and he in his seventies, he had no seed, no son. Yet these were the very gales into which he maneuvered his sail, and was driven in the direction he desired to go. "He was looking forward." (Heb. 11:10)

Nor was this movement merely forward—no matter where it led. Abraham had pinpointed his goal: a city. (Heb. 11:10) He had had enough impermanency as a tent-dweller, with flocks that were always looking for fresh pastures. Abraham had grown up in the helpful and comforting infrastructure of city life. He had accepted the nomadism required of him. But for a final terminus he preferred a city. But not just any city. He had been around enough, here and abroad, and had seen cities, yes, but felt not all were habitable; their foundations didn't have much future left in them. Abraham desired a fixed abode in "a city with firm foundations." (Heb. 11:10) And that underpinning was determined by architects and builders, all of whom were prone to human error. Early in life, according to Jewish and eastern legends, Abraham saw the difference between the idols that his father made of wood and stone—and the Creator of the sun, moon, stars. So he early turned to the architect and builder of the universe: God. And this God of glory is the One Abraham looked to, all his life, for a final resting place. Abraham had faith in the God who had called him: "My Friend."

PRAYER: *Lord Jesus, we know that Stephen was looking beyond Abraham to You, Who said: "I go to prepare a place for you." Thank You, Lord. We, too, have our hearts set on that goal. Amen.*

GIVE OF YOUR BEST TO THE MASTER

Acts 7:22 *So Moses was trained in all the wisdom of the Egyptians, a powerful speaker, and a man of action.*

Stephen is still standing in a court of justice in Jerusalem. But with the strongest muscle in the human body, the tongue (and you thought it was the big toe), Stephen has taken us on a trip to the East, to Ur in Iraq; north to Harran in Turkey; and now his tripping tongue takes us on a trip south to Egypt.

The "So," with which our text begins refers to the previous verse (21), which informs us that when the infant Moses was lifted out of the River Nile in his basket made of reeds, "Pharaoh's daughter adopted him and brought him up as her own son." She, the Princess Bithiah is credited with giving the three-month-old child his name Moses," not only because it meant "taken out of the water," but also because her father was Thutmose I, her husband was Thutmose II, and she was the stepmother of Thutmose III. Later, the Princess, herself, reigned as a Pharaoh for twenty years (1504-1483 B.C.). There was no question, then, that her adopted son, Moses, should be brought up with the finest that Egyptian royalty could offer. Graduating from the University of Memphis, Moses went on to be a General in the Egyptian army, winning an important campaign in Ethiopia. Research has revealed that Pharaoh gave Moses jurisdiction over the mining operations in Sinai. That is where most of Egypt's wealth came from: gold, silver, precious stones, iron, copper. In January, 1978, the Chase Manhattan Bank turned over to the Smithsonian Institution its famous collection of currencies. In the display was 3,500-year-old Egyptian gold ring money. The rings were made about 1500 B.C., which would put them in Moses' era in Egypt.

That was the lap of luxury for which Moses was destined, if he wanted it. Yet, as Professor Halford Luccock of Yale once noted: "Moses comes vividly to mind when one looks at the gold-covered mummy case of the young prince Tutan Khamen in the National Museum at Cairo. The feeling comes, 'There, but for the grace of God, lies Moses.' For that is what Moses would have been had he not struck a tangent to his earlier career—a mummy. According to the tradition in Exodus, Moses was a ward of Pharaoh and would have rated the honor of a tomb in a pyramid. There his body would have rested for 4,000 years and then, one morning, he would have blazed forth in the world's newspapers under some such headline as this: 'Gold Mummy Discovered by Howard Carter,' But Moses did not want to be a mummy."[1]

Instead, Moses, never forgetting his faith-based origins in Judaism, and the lasting influence of his natural parents Amram and Jochebed, moved away from Pharaoh's pagan palace. Without wasting the non-Jewish ways in which he was acculturated (accepting it as God's will for his life), he used the best of it to God's glory. With stupen-

---

[1] H. E. Luccock, *The Acts of the Apostles,* p. 124

dous results. Starting as an unknown castaway, Moses has become the preeminent figure in the Old Testament and the most quoted in the New. Above all, here was one, as Stephen was trying to get his hearers to understand, who was an outline of the coming Savior. At least thirteen similarities have been found between Moses and Jesus—from their infancy perils, to feeding multitudes, to delivering people out of bondage, to their reappearance after death. Still, as Stephen pressed home his point, "Our forefathers would not accept [Moses] leadership but thrust him aside," (7:39) so Christ was thrust aside. And still is.

PRAYER: *We are no better than our forefathers in the faith, Lord. Forgive us for obeying our worst genes as we strive to walk where Jesus walked—in all the wisdom of our heavenly Father. Amen.*

CLOSER DRAWN TO HIM

Acts 7:31 *Moses was amazed at the sight, and as he approached to look more closely, the voice of the Lord came to him.*

Here Stephen recalls the first meeting between Moses and God, as told fully by Moses himself, author of the first five books of the Bible. The location was a burning bush on Mt. Sinai. And Stephen gets the gist of the occasion, namely, when the Lord saw Moses approaching, the Lord came to him. That's always been the Lord's approach: "Come unto me...and I will give you."

It isn't always, however, that the Lord waits for us to move first. After all, the truth of the matter remains that we love Him because He first loved us. But see what Moses gained by taking the time to "look more closely" at this intriguing sight—

most unusual. He could have hee-hawed as others have done, claiming that such "burning bushes" have been seen in many lands—a certain plant which self-ignites when the temperature goes up. Or as others have done, blame it on colored lighting, as one sees with electric logs in a fireplace. But when a voice out of the bush called his name, Moses found himself responding, "Here I am." (Exod. 3:4)

What, then, did Moses learn, inasmuch as we know nothing, to this point, about whether he was religious. Oh the genes were there, and the potential, and the germination was taking place. But now a springtime in the soul had arrived, and birth pangs, and a cocoon cracking open—and a new life a-burning. The first instruction the divine voice gave from the bush was, "The place where you are standing is holy ground."(Exod. 3:5) That brought Moses up short. He had become so familiar with this territory, both as a superintendent of mining operations and then as a shepherd for his father-in-law. It was the same in the area of Sinai, but with a new Owner—God. "I am the God of your father, the God of Abraham, Isaac and Jacob." (v. 6) God explains that He has seen the misery of the Hebrews in Egypt. And Moses' heart and mind, jumping to attention, get the picture. The fire in the bush must be God, for fire is fearsome. That is why today, in the Chapel of the Burning Bush at St. Catherine's Monastery on Mt. Sinai, as you enter you see a large red fire extinguisher!

Yet the bush that Moses encountered needed no extinguisher. That was not a consuming fire.

The illuminating Lord was not a consuming tyrant. He had watched His chosen people suffer long enough in Egypt, and He was preparing to rescue them from the grip of the Oppressor. For fire is also a life-giver: essential for the cooking of food and keeping one from freezing to death.

And what was the Lord of Light, the Fire from heaven aiming at—but to tell Moses: "Come I shall send you...and you are to bring my people Israel out of Egypt." (Exod. 3:10) A burning need had found its hot button. Only the Lord knows how to make such connections.

What are we readying ourselves to be connected with? Are we more typical of the persons in Stephen's audience? The voice of the Lord Jesus had come to them. They had heard Him many times in the Temple in Jerusalem. They had heard about His teachings and healings and miracles. They had seen His power working through His apostles even after His ascension to heaven. His offers to help those Jerusalemites couldn't have been any more attention-getting than a burning bush was to Moses. But, whereas Moses moved closer to God, these in his courtroom, Stephen sadly says, moved away from Jesus. They were stubborn, he concluded, heathen at heart, deaf to the truth, resisting the Holy Spirit. (7:51) And for that, they stoned Stephen to death too. Come to the Lord, embraceable you.

PRAYER: *"Draw me nearer, nearer, blessed Lord, To the cross where thou hast died: Draw me nearer, nearer, nearer blessed Lord, To thy precious, bleeding side."*[1] Amen.

---

[1] Fanny Crosby

AFTER HIS PATTERN (V. 44)

Acts 7:44 *Our forefathers had the Tent of the Testimony in the Desert.*

This "Tent" has also been called the Tent of Witness, The Church, the Congregation, The Tabernacle of the testimony. It was a portable sanctuary. What other form could it have taken for Israelites on the move for forty years? In fact, it was taken into the Promised Land and used there for some 400 years before Solomon built the Temple, the first permanent worship center in Israel's history.

Dubiously helpful interpreters warn against thinking of this "Church in the Wilderness" in terms of a Church as we know it today. But, why not? If it walks like a duck, quacks like a duck, swims like a duck, what is it? For the Israelites in the desert had all the characteristics of what we call a Church. Their pastor was Moses, who "received the living utterances of God to pass on (to the people)." (Acts 7:38) Their assistant pastor was Aaron, Moses' brother. The choir director was sister Miriam. (Exod. 15:20-21) Then there were the usual parish squabbles: banging heads and ideas about the pastors, doctrines, committees, food (quails and manna), water; yearning for the fleshpots of Egypt; pressure for alternate forms of worship; and freedom to choose your own gods. (7:39-40) Looks more and more like your Church and mine doesn't it?

Well, it was, consider that yearning for the fleshpots of Egypt, that hungering, burning desire for the things that appeal to the flesh; the easy way, the broad, wide way that always leads to destruction. In spite of all the warning signs, humans have always reached out expectant arms to embrace the thou-shalt-nots. We are not the first—God anticipated this, after having seen Lot's wife looking back and turning into a pillar of salt (Gen. 19:26), God warned Moses at the very beginning of the Exodus that "the people may change their minds...and turn back to Egypt." (Exod. 13:17) Which they did. And with good reason (the reason is always the best when we want something right here, right now). A papyrus letter from Moses' time, regarding the area inhabited by the Israelites, describes how the Egyptian environment pampered human senses. The fields were rich with fresh vegetables, the pools with fish, the lagoons with birds, the orchards with fruits for wine. Meat was plentiful, and nobody cried: "God help me." Can we wonder why the Israelites felt cheated in the Sinai desert? Their past had its gratifying memories. As it still does for Church members. A new convert said to evangelist Dwight L. Moody: "If I continue in the faith, my friends will leave me." How to get along without those long-term friendships? Or without those free-wheeling (but now questionable) sprees?

To compensate for giving up a sensual past, the Israelites asked their assistant pastor: "Make us gods to go before us." (v 40) In the Tent of the Testimony was the Ark of the Covenant—with its mercy seat, on which God sat. But now the people wanted gods who would get off their mercy seats and go ahead and pioneer and come up with new ideas, new ways to worship that would not be so exacting; a kind Uncle Willie who does whatever he's asked to do. And what did their combined efforts come up with? A golden calf! Eye-catching. A god small enough to be slapped around and not bulldozed by.

There stands, for the ages, the gold standard of a Church, in the wilderness. Let us take the measurements and make the applications to the Church of the present day. How are we doing?

PRAYER: *"Dear Lord and Father of Mankind, Forgive our foolish ways; reclothe us in our rightful mind. In purer lives thy service find, In deeper reverence, praise."*[1] *Amen.*

Turn Evil to Live

Acts 7:58 *The witnesses laid their coats at the feet of a young man named Saul.*

Saint Paul was a rotten specimen of humanity—at first sight. And since first impressions incline to be lasting, some people never did accept Paul, and he was beheaded. He is still cut out of the New Testament by those who accept Jesus and His apostles and no one else.

In a way you can't fault the anti-Pualites, for Paul is introduced to the world in three verses totaling six lines in the Book of Acts. Our text for today is the first verse. The second is 8:1—"Saul was among those who approved of [Stephen's] execution." The third verse is 8:3 "Saul, meanwhile (during Stephen's burial and period of mourning), was harrying the church; he entered house after house, seizing men and women and sending them to prison." A chapter later, when, in the interim, Paul had become the likes of a forest fire raging wildly and widely out of control. "Still breathing murderous threats against the Lord's disciples, went to the high priest and applied for letters to the synagogues at Damascus authorizing him to arrest any followers of the new way

---
[1] J. G. Whittier

whom he found, men or women, and bring them to Jerusalem." (9:1-2) Then armed with all the legal paraphernalia that he thought he needed to cause maximum damage to the Christian cause, Paul set out on his 200-mile journey to Damascus, no doubt taking a sufficient number of hitmen to help him with the dirty work.

Here is the full-length portrait of a religiously motivated terrorist—the worst kind, as was learned painfully on 9/11 at the World Trade Center, the Pentagon, and in Shanksville, PA. Surely this was the devil incarnate at work. Surely Paul would now scrawl FINIS across Christendom.

At this point in history, one can only imagine that there was silence in heaven as the cloud of witnesses watched anxiously.

To demonize Paul even more—was his body. A second century work entitled *The Acts of Paul and Thecla* describe Paul as "a sturdy little balding, bowlegged man, with meeting eyebrows and a somewhat hooked nose"—which could have induced a sense of inferiority. Then he writes in 2 Cor. 12:7, "I was given a thorn in my flesh, a messenger of Satan sent to buffet me; that was to save me from being unduly elated." This "thorn" has been described as a red-hot bar stuck in his head. Others have theorized that the "thorn" was epilepsy or eye trouble or an aggravation in the digestive tract or headaches or malaria. Whatever it was, it plagued him, and made him appreciate Dr. Luke even more on the missionary journeys.

Tormented in mind and heart by the Christians, wracked by physical deficiency in his body, Paul had the makings of a nuclear device ready to detonate.

Enter the Lord Jesus Christ. As He promised He would. As he always has. He saw that Paul, dastardly though he was, had something Paul wrote to Timothy his "true-born son in the faith." (1 Tim 1:2) "Christ Jesus came into the world to save sinners; and among them I stand first. But I was mercifully dealt with for this very purpose, that Jesus Christ might find in me the first occasion for displaying his inexhaustible patience, and that I might be typical of all who were in future to have faith in him and gain eternal life. To the King eternal, immortal, invisible, the only God, be honor and glory forever and ever! Amen." (1 Tim. 1:15-17)

PRAYER: *Thank You Lord, for brother Paul. Do for us what You did for him. Amen.*

THE CONVERT AND THE REVERT

Acts 8:14 *When the apostles in Jerusalem heard that Samaria had accepted the Word of God, they sent off Peter and John.*

What the mother Church heard was that Philip's evangelism had netted the best known person in Samaria—Simon, the magician. Of Simon it was said, "Everybody, high and low, listened intently to him. 'This man,' they said, 'is that power of God which is called "The Great Power."'" (v. 10) Simon was considered a Messiah. He led a movement that competed with the fast-growing Christian faith. History records that during the reign of Claudius, Simon went to Rome where the Senate honored him "with a statue erected upon the Tiber between the two bridges, with the Latin inscription, 'To Simon the Holy God.'" Yet at home in Samaria, when Simon heard Philip preach, "was captivated when he saw the powerful signs and miracles that were taking place." (v. 13) Simon felt dwarfed beside Philip, became a believer, was baptized, and "was constantly in Philip's company." (v. 13) A homerun for Philip.

But when the news reached mission central in Jerusalem something didn't sound quite right, and Peter and John were dispatched to find out. When something is too good to be true, it is. And it was.

As Simon watched the apostles laying their hands on people who then received the Holy Spirit, he was transfixed. Just the laying on of hands could so energize people; it caught Simon's full attention. "I'll buy that," his money-hungry mind responded. If he could add this act to his bag of magical tricks…He already felt immersed up to his armpits in gold. Gold had swallowed him whole. Which naturally led to Simon offering Peter money, with the request: "Give me too the same power, so that anyone I lay my hands on will receive the Holy Spirit." (v. 19) That is when Peter told this devil incarnate to go to hell. (v. 20)

And Simon did. Peter's X-ray vision saw, as he had with Ananias and Sapphira, that Simon's heart was not right with God. It was right with gold. (v. 21) As someone has written: "Still, as of old, men by themselves are priced. For thirty pieces Judas sold himself, not Christ." And so did Simon. But, whereas Judas disposed of himself, Simon became the most vehement opponent of Peter in debates in several cities. "Simony," a term that is still used for the purchase of spiritual gifts, still rings with the sound of money. Simon is also credited with being the founder of Gnosticism, "One of the most persistent and pernicious heresies with which the church has ever had to cope."¹ Even a hundred years later there were heretics called "Simonians," and their sexual libertinism was influential for centuries. Sex for all, and all for sex. Dante, too, picked up on Simon's villainy and introduced him into the Faust series, where he sells his soul to the devil. At the end, we hear, Simon boasted that he would fly. But, without a safety net, and never lowering his wheels, well—!

It was for this reason that Jesus locked horns with the Simons of His time. "You have heard it said," He repeated with monotonous persistence. "But I say unto you." He tried to get the wily Simons to see the truth. Yet with Pilate, they asked muddle-headedly, "What is truth?"—and their house of cards was left to them desolate. In the Master's Spirit that is all Peter and John were trying to do here. They and evangelist Philip learned lessons which are still valuable—if we would learn. Master Central—that's where our directives must come from, for our lasting good.

PRAYER: *Such are the treacherous minefields, Lord. Guide us step by prayerful step. Amen.*

ON BEING A RECYCLED DISCIPLE

Acts 9:26 *On reaching Jerusalem [Saul] tried to join the disciples, but they were all afraid of him because they did not believe that he really was a disciple.*

As yet, Paul had not changed his name. But he was a changed person, B.C. to A.D. (Before conversion to After Damascus) It was now three years since he had become a follower of Jesus. Instead of taking Christian's from Damascus in chains to Jerusalem, as was his intention, he fellowshipped

---

[1]John Phillips, *Exploring Acts*, p. 151

with the brethren in that northern city. So well was he accepted by them, that when it was learned there was a scheme to assassinate him, these new friends smuggled him to safety.

Coming by way of Petra, Paul headed for home in Jerusalem. If he expected an open-arms acceptance as he had enjoyed in Damascus, he was mightily mistaken. He was held at arm's length by the Mother Church in Jerusalem.

Bible students have railed against the apostles and all Jerusalem Christians for their shameful non-acceptance of Paul. Outwardly they couldn't tell the difference: same man, same appearance, same name. He had been known in the city for his severe measures against the Christians. That's all they knew of him. Perhaps anecdotal reports had filtered down concerning Paul's vision of Christ, and other assorted stories. But remembering Paul's vehemence, his secret-agent ability to get his man, his ties to officialdom in the city that would provide him with military assistance, Christians shrank at the very mention of Paul's name. They had not seen anything of an inward change. He was the same old, same old.

Besides, the case of Simon the Magician was still fresh in the minds of the apostles and others. Simon, too, claimed that he was a new person in Christ—until it came to the first test, and he flunked. Paul could be another Simon.

Just then Barnabas took his courage in both hands, and faith in his heart, and reached out to Paul—introducing him around to those who had been considered enemies to be destroyed by Paul. And Paul responded, speaking "out boldly and openly in the name of the Lord, talking and debating with the Greek speaking Jews." (9:29) And that did it. They planned to murder Paul, but, as in the north, the Jerusalem brethren smuggled him to safety.

With two attempts on his life, Paul realized that he was in double danger, as a double agent. If he decided to die for Christ, as he had seen Stephen do, he would have to do more than merely say he was a Christian. With that in mind, he made a beeline for his birthplace, Tarsus, where, for nine years, he realigned his life under the guidance of the Holy Spirit.

Looking back, it was good, then, that the Christians in Jerusalem viewed Paul with suspicion: "They might not believe that he really was a disciple." They drew a line in the sand, which preserved the integrity of the early church, and moved Paul to conduct a self-examination for which he was a better person.

Jesus drew lines in the dust, twice. (John 8:6,8) It was symbolic of the way He believed. The dividing line was not rubbed out because, as today, it is considered ghettoizing, politically incorrect, intolerant. No, He insisted, there are the sheep and the goats, light and darkness, good and evil, Satan and the Savior. It is not that questionable disciples (church members) don't have a chance, and must be ostracized. "Go," said Jesus to the woman caught committing adultery. (John 8:3) "You are free." But, as with all of us, there's still work to be done: "Go, do not sin again." There's restitution and reconstruction and having the mind of Christ. And then we are His, forever.

PRAYER: *When others draw a circle and shut us out, Lord, encircle us with Your TLC, that we may become true disciples. Amen.*

The Church Triumphant

Acts 9:31 *Meanwhile the church, throughout Judaea, Galilee, and Samaria, was left in peace to build up its strength, and to live in the fear of the Lord. Encouraged by the Holy Spirit, it grew in numbers.*

It is not quite a coincidence that when Paul left Jerusalem, perhaps never to return, there was peace in the land. It almost sounds as if Paul had been the troublemaker. When he disappeared, so did the turmoil.

See it this way: We do not hear about Paul until the stoning of Stephen. But before that the apostles had been heckled, beaten, imprisoned by the religious hierarchy of Jerusalem. The threat to the Christians reverberated like firecrackers across the country. But when Paul turned his back on Jerusalem and returned to his birthplace of Tarsus, though the priests retained their positions in Jerusalem there was peace in the land! Circumstantial evidence points to Paul as the instigator of the anti-Christian mob-rule in Jerusalem. Everyone breathed a sigh of relief to hear of Paul's permanent departure. Good riddance, the priests simmered down, and the Christians relaxed their taut nerves. Of course, peace, Shalom, mean different things when used as a noun, a verb, an adjective. In the context of today's text it means "rest." Paul and his cohorts had savaged the church for at least a year. When Stephen was executed "that day was the beginning of a time of violent persecution for the church in Jerusalem, and all except the apostles were scattered over the country districts of Judaca and Samaria." (Acts 8:1) Tune out now for a well-earned rest. Yet "rest," as in music, is for the purpose of giving the following music a boost. And that's what it did for the church. For the next word of importance in the text is "build."

Building entails the drawing of plans—which must be discussed, amended, redone. Building materials are to be assembled, and helping hands enlisted, with training provided. Actual construction whether it be faith or study and worship programs or buildings to house a growing community of believers—all need constant superintending.

Then the church needed to build up its depleted strength. Knowing that a chain is only as strong as its weakest link, and that a bridge will hold up only as long as its weakest connectors do, care is taken throughout the organizational complex. After a recent earthquake in Istanbul, Turkey, many building contractors were sued. They had purposely skimped on the quality of building materials—which caused unnecessary and unusually high casualties. Strength also needs maintenance. A body builder cannot expect calls for regular workouts, year in and year out, and not particularly to be a Mr. or Miss America, but to keep the physical anatomy in working order, until death us do part.

Living in the fear of the Lord does not mean fleeing from Him in fright. Rather, it is "a wholesome dread of displeasing Him, a fear which banishes the terror that shrinks from His presence." In this sense "the fear of the Lord is the beginning of wisdom."

The Holy Spirit, or Comforter (*com fortis*), encourages one to be brave. "Be strong, We are not here to play, to dream, to drift: We have hard work to do and loads to lift, Shun not the struggle: face it—'tis God's gift. Be strong. Be strong!"[1]

---

[1] Mabbie Babcock

No wonder the early church had continuing growth, with no expiration date. Here is the blueprint for the church of the present day too.

PRAYER: *Thy church, O Lord, once an infant, grew to world stature. Help us to keep it fit for the living of these days. Amen.*

STICK TO THE FACTS

Acts 11:4 *Peter began by laying before them the facts as they had happened.*

"When Peter came up to Jerusalem," (11:2) he was ecstatic about his recent experiences. They had concerned a new but amiable relationship, for the first time, with non-Jews. Immediately protesters attacked Peter. They strongly objected to his unseemly, un-Jewish behavior. With nothing to be ashamed about, Peter laid the facts on the table for all to see and question.

It started at Joppa, now a suburb of the great Israeli city of Tel Aviv. While at prayer, Peter had a vision of something coming down from heaven "like a great sheet of sail cloth. (11:5) On the rooftop of a beach house Peter had seen the sailboats on the Mediterranean Sea and began to put the pieces together. Sailcloth, catching the wind of the Spirit, could take him anywhere. But here the sailcloth was "slung by the four corners"—the four corners of the earth? Then Peter's commentary continues that the sailcloth was "lowered from heaven till it reached me." (v. 5) Here was a message from heaven, a special personal delivery for no one but Peter, which made him attentive to every detail in the proceedings. For in the sailcloth he saw animals, birds, reptiles—all edible. But when a heavenly voice invited him to eat, Peter, a

Kosher-true Jew, drew back. And this happened three times—always in the Bible an indication of prime importance. The episode ended with the Lord having the last word: "It is not for you to call profane, what God counts clean." (11:9) The Spirit had blown Peter's sails into a new understanding of Gentiles: they, too, were God's people.

Going directly from Joppa to Caesarea, to the home of the Gentile Roman centurion Cornelius, Peter right away put his new revelation to work, and the whole Cornelius household became Christians. (11:14) Nor was it Peter's doing, as Cornelius credited him. It was Jesus, and Peter was quick to acknowledge his Master's Keynote assistance: "I recalled what the Lord had said." (11:16)

It is difficult to be blown off course as long as we recall what the Lord had said. To whom else shall we go? He has the words of eternal life.

Peter fitted his action to the words of Jesus, instead of rearranging Jesus' words to make Peter's actions acceptable. This latter is the spin mode of our time: Do what you want and find somebody or some murky new Da Vince code to make one's mistaken notions look respectable. *The Smithsonian* (June 2008) has a fun article on the last page called "Moses at the bat. In the Big Inning." It is cleverly done. The author combed through eleven books in the Old Testament, finding a line here and there and rearranging them to give the impression of a baseball game. There were giants in those days as well.

For instance: And Abner said to Joab, "Let the young men....arise and play before us." (2 Sam. 2:14) Behold, Rebekah came forth with her pitcher (Gen. 24:45) the children of Israel...said, "Who shall go up for us first? (Judg. 20:18) And Moses...smote (Exod. 7:20) and...[it] became foul...(Exod. 7:21) and Miriam was shut out (Num. 12:15)...and Moses lifted up his hand and smote...with his rod...(Num. 20:11) a long blast (Joshua 6:5) [outside] the camp (Judg. 7:17) [for] an 'omer (Exod. 16:36)...and the men of Israel and of Judah arose, and shouted...." (1 Sam. 17:52) In like manner, there are people who make the scriptures jump through hoops for the enjoyment of the crowd in their ting-a-ling circuses.

PRAYER: *Heavenly Father, we would rather remember the words of Jesus, and make our actions fit His message exactly. Amen.*

PETER AT HEAVEN'S GATE

Acts 12:9 *Peter followed him out, with no idea that the angel's intervention was real.*

It was now going on fourteen years since Jesus' resurrection. To know that they served a living Savior who was ever-present through the comforting Holy Spirit, Christians enjoyed their faith.

Then disturbing times returned, started by King Herod. Distracting disagreements within the Church, and Herod's iron fist pounding them from the outside, caused the Christians, among other losses, to have a misty memory of the Lord's resurrection and ascension. Then came this incident of Peter being imprisoned once again. The other time (Acts 5:17-19), Peter and John were in the lockup for brief periods before an angel conducted their quickie release. But in this second experience behind bars, there emerges a distinct outline of another resurrection, Peter's.

This time every precaution was taken to prevent Peter's escape. His death was imminent and the similarities with Jesus' end-time are striking. In jail (like a Calvary), Peter was chained to a military guard on each side, with arms stretched out as if he was being crucified between two thieves. All exits were blocked by sixteen soldiers, and with three sets of iron bars for triple backup security that Jerusalem jail was not just a Golgotha, but a tomb as well. And as in Jesus' garden tomb, there was an angel. John Philips helpfully adds: "Throughout the scripture, angels sent to men seem in a hurry to discharge their duties and vanish...They never linger long, nor do they unduly fraternize with men...Perhaps, too, they wish to avoid the embarrassment of man's tendency to worship them." (Rev. 22:8-9) "Quick!" the angel ordered Peter, "Get up...do up your belt and put on your sandals....Now wrap your cloak around you and follow me." (12:7-8) Readied for action, Peter left his sleepy guards behind.

The first person the resurrected Christ saw was Mary Magdalene. The first person the rescued-from-death Peter saw was Rhoda. Then, as Jesus rejoined the apostolic band, so did Peter. Author Luke is obviously paralleling these two resurrections. The difference, though, is that Peter was confused about the reality of the experience. Was it a vivid dream or was it for real? It didn't take long for his awakened soul to believe that this walk-out of prison was closer to full inner sensory perception than the prison itself (where, as media commercials conclude "certain restrictions apply"). In this out-of-the-body experience, Peter's spirit looked beyond the present veil of tears—to the reality beyond—a reuniting with loved ones. After listening to a Beethoven symphony, one man exclaimed, "If reality is like that, I have no cause to be anxious or afraid." That was the enheartening word the early church needed to hear as a thunderclap warned of an approaching storm of persecution. Death was certain, if not by violence then by that expiration date stamped on every human being. But Christ arose, so did Peter, and so shall we. No cause to be anxious or afraid. Because He lives, we, too, shall LIVE. Nothing is more real. Nothing more important worth remembering.

PRAYER: *Thank You, Lord, for the certainty with which we can live now and forever because You live. Amen.*

THE TEMPLED HOME

Acts 12:12 *Once he realized this, he made for the house of Mary, the mother of John Mark, where a large company was at prayer.*

Working on all cylinders, Peter could think of no other place he would feel more at home than at the house of Christ's followers: the house of Mary. A wealthy Jerusalem widow whose life was made new by Jesus' ministry, Mary opened her spacious home for use by this ministry. All the major events of this fellowship, this church, took place at Mary's—The Last Supper, Jesus' resurrected appearance through closed doors, Jesus and doubting Thomas, Pentecost, this visit by Peter, and other unrecorded events.

Nothing is known of Mary's husband, but if their son John Mark is any indication of the top value of his parents, they were at the head of the class. To be sure, in such a home with people like

Jesus, the apostles, Mary the mother of Jesus, Barnabas and friend Paul, and many other believers—coming and going and praying and worshiping and fellowshipping—how could one miss being deeply influenced for good? And John Mark was. We understand that his mother also owned the Garden of Gethsemane on the Mount of Olives (since no gardening, which meant fertilizing with manure, was allowed in the city), and that Mark was the Garden's caretaker. On that terrible night when Mark ran to the Garden to warn Jesus that the police were after Him, he was too late. Someone grabbed Mark's tunic, and he ran away in his undergarment. He alone gives this pen sketch of himself in his Gospel of Mark, written with the help of Peter's memoirs, Peter calls him "my son." (1 Peter 5:13)

How understandable, then, that Mary, this Lady with a Lamp, would have the first Christian Church in her home. Her lamp had been lighted by Jesus, the Light of the World, and, in turn, through a shining example, she passed that light on to uncounted numbers of people; and possibly started the house church movement—there being no church edifices at the time. Saint Paul gave all time publicity to this close-binding oneness in Christ when he sent greetings "to the church that meets at their house." (Rom. 16:5) The practice had spread far and fast.

When the early Methodists felt unwelcome in their former churches, they worshipped in homes. Historians take pains to tell us that those were the days when Methodism was at its strongest. Wherever uncongenial conditions have prevailed, worship in homes has proved to be the cornerstone of the commonwealth. In communist-dominated areas, the so-called "underground church," in homes, has kept the Christian faith alive and alight. Whatever the beleaguered circumstances, such cocoons of Christian contentment and containment soldier on. Herein lies the eternal quality of the Church of Christ. "On this rock I will build my church, and the powers of death shall never conquer it." (Matt. 16:18) The church in the home is the line of defense that has never been breached. But it needs defenders, equipped with the whole armor of God. Those who pray and study God's word daily, have grace at meals, help the needy. Be a merry Mary.

PRAYER: *The head of our table is for You, O Lord, Be here and everywhere adored. Amen.*

NOT TO WORRY

Acts 12:18 *When morning came, there was consternation among the soldiers: what could have become of Peter?*

When morning comes these days, street lights and night lights turn off automatically. Early on, the normal routine was, "Put out your candles, the sun is up." With minimum illumination during hours of darkness, people were expected to be bedded down—as was the case in Peter's prison. Peter, however, had flown the coop. For when the guards had yawned and stretched themselves awake, and found empty chairs where Peter should have been, there was pandemonium. One can only imagine the astonishment of the two soldiers to whom Peter had been shackled. "Where...? Did you feel or hear anything? How...? Maybe the other guards took him for questioning. Perhaps he had to go to the restroom." The more they searched in vain the more nervous the whole prison complex became. All knew the law in such a situation: it was that if a prisoner escaped, the guards would suffer the punishment that the prisoner was doomed to have. For Peter, it was to have been execution. My Lord, what a morning!

And what a reversal of roles. Peter, harmless, innocent at the mercy of a tyrant King, who, for political expediency, had randomly chosen to do away with the head man of a growingly joyful Christian community.

Then there were all the King's horses and all the King's men treating Peter as Public Enemy Number One—impounding him like a gangster, with all the state-of-the-art policing aids they could find. It was over-the-top. Peter, for his part, was putty in the dictatorial hands of monsters. They could do nothing wrong; he could do nothing right. What he did, first, was to believe that his friends were praying for him. Praying? What would that accomplish? Second, when an angel appeared in Peter's jail cell—an angel? Aw, come on. When the angel gave instructions, he did his part and followed the instructions. Third, when God saw the church at work on its knees, and saw Peter do his part, God did His. "He tore the bars away, Jesus, my Lord." There wasn't a thing human ingenuity could muster up to stymie God's plan. And by the time dawn came, Peter was well on his way to a beautiful isle of somewhere. He didn't need dawn's early light. The Light of the world did that. "God is light, in Him is no darkness *at all*." (1 John 1:6) Jesus also said, "I am the door, by Me if any man enter in, he shall be saved and *go in and out* and find pasture." (John 10:9) How Peter shows us the Lord's intervention and guidance even, and especially, in life's imprisoning experiences. The Lord's way always looks naive, impossible. But when the invisibles work on the impossibles, they allow us improbables to win.

In a famous painting, one sees Satan and Faust playing chess. Faust, gambling for his soul, loses. A chess champion, studying the picture, suddenly shouted, "It's a lie! The King and the Knight can move!" Indeed, they can, with the help of the King of Kings.

PRAYER: *Our Father, You are always in the shadows, keeping watch above Your own. Praises be. Amen.*

WHEN GOD CALLS

Acts 12:28 *Barnabas and Saul, their task fulfilled, returned from Jerusalem, taking John Mark with them.*

Paul and Barnabas had not been in Jerusalem for the specific purpose of giving the mother Church moral support during Peter's imprisonment, although it sounds as if they were. With the prediction of a severe famine that would hit the Jerusalem area, the Church at Antioch had taken a collection for the mother church, and it had been delivered by Barnabas and Paul, the co-pastors at Antioch.

On their return to Antioch, these two men were assigned as missionaries. Why? What Galvanic movements had led to this historic turn of events that concluded by Paul being given the title "The Great Apostle to the Gentiles"? For one thing, it was this experience of helping the church in Jerusalem. Usually those at the home base send out aid in all directions. But here these two pastors see, firsthand, that if at headquarters they lack necessities, what must the destitution be like in the back country?

Also, this being Paul's first return to Jerusalem in a dozen years, he had become reacquainted with the apostles and others. They, too, could size up his growth in spiritual stature, and let him in on more firsthand information about Jesus and His teachings, especially His final commission: "Full authority in heaven and on earth has been committed to me. Go therefore to all nations and make them my disciples: baptize them in the name of the Father and the Son and the Holy Spirit, and teach them to observe all that I have commanded you. I will be with you always, to the end of time." (Matt. 28:18-20)

If he had not heard it before, this would be Paul's call to arms in the service of his Savior. Here, historians find, is the source of a more profound influence than an exploding sun. As Yale professor Kenneth Latourette explains, "It is clear that at the very beginning of Christianity there must have occurred a vast release of energy, unequaled in the history of the race. Without it the future course of the faith is inexplicable. The burst of energy was ascribed by the early disciples to the founder of their faith. Something happened to the men associated with Jesus. In his contact with them, in his crucifixion and in their assurance of his resurrection and of the continued living presence with his disciples of his Spirit, is to be found the major cause of the success of Christianity."[1]

Paul's entrance to the mission field was, firsts, opened up by his participation in that outreach ef-

---

[1] K. S Latourette. *A History of the Expansion of Christianity,* Vol. 1, pp. 167-168

fort to restore the mother church in a time of sore need; second, by Jesus' magna carta concerning the worldwide spread of His faith; third, by having a dependable ground crew for Paul, the "sky pilot." Nobody was more fitted for the task, none more unanimously called and set apart to do the work to which [the Lord had] called them." (Acts 13:2) As on an aircraft carrier, the planes can go farther and faster and higher than the mother ship, they are always dependent on the carrier for their life-support, so were these missionaries dependent on the old folks at home.

PRAYER: *"We heed, O Lord, Thy summons, And answer: Here are we! Send us upon Thine errand, Let us Thy servant be. Our strength is dust and ashes, Our years a passing hour; But Thou canst use our weakness to magnify Thy power."*[1] *Amen.*

THE BEAUTY OF THE CANYON

Acts 15:6 *The apostles and elders met to look into this matter.*

"This matter" was that the "Gentiles must be...told to keep the law of Moses." (v. 5) It had been voiced in Jerusalem by "some of the Pharisaic party who had become believers (in Christ, which had made them into stricter Jews!). (v. 5)

It was inevitable. It usually is when humans bump heads over volatile issues. It is no different in the Church, though hotheaded lovers of the Lord have less excuse for their near fisticuff behavior. Here even the apostles were at it. "In Adam's fall we sinned all." And it takes time to purge the hell out of us—the apostolic way.

---

[1] John Haynes Holmes

This contentious subject had been boiling on the front burner ever since Christians had started converting non-Jews.

As a Jew, Jesus lived Jewishly. To be sure, He broke with tradition quite often when he declared, "You have heard it said, but I say unto you," when He healed on the Sabbath day; when He excused His disciples after they walked through a wheatfield on the Sabbath, eating as they went. These, and other violations of the Mosaic Law finally put Jesus on a cross.

Yet the twelve apostles remained steadfast Jews, despite their new faith in Jesus, until they fully realized that Jesus did not come to destroy the Law but to fulfill it. Judaism was too cribbed, cabined and confined to be a worldwide faith.

The cracks appeared with Peter's vision on the housetop at Joppa. (10:9-16) The lesson from heaven was: "It is not for you to call profane what God counts clean." (10:15) Peter knew that he should not have been in the home of a tanner who dealt with leather, something denoting the taking of a life. As a Jew, Peter felt guilty. But God wised him up. The tanner was just as precious to the heavenly Father as anyone else. So the divide between Christians and Jews began to widen. It became a grand canyon when Paul and Barnabas returned from their first missionary journey to report huge successes for Christianity in Gentile lands.

Upon hearing this report, the strict Jews in Jerusalem who had turned Christian, were not happy. You can see it in the contrast between the joyful welcome the missionaries received in Phonenicia and Samaria, and the ho-hum reception they were given in Jerusalem. (15:3-4) The Traditionalists were waiting to explode, and did, "with no small dissension and dispute." (15:2,7) Hence the history—asking Jerusalem Council, at which Peter spoke first. He needed to. He had been part of the problem.

Just as when Peter denied Jesus, he wanted to be on Jesus' side and against him, so he had been twofaced about this Gentile issue. Peter fraternized with the Gentiles when no one was watching (except Paul, see Gal. 2:11-14). But under the scrutiny of the strict Jews, Peter kept his distance from the Gentiles. He was for or against the Gentiles, depending on the company he was in. But, straightened out once again, Peter came out boldly for the Gentiles at the Jerusalem council. As did Paul and Barnabas. Compromises were made and all were comfortable with the results. So Christianity, while retaining the Old Testament route by which it had come, moved out of the crib in which he was born and began its growth into a worldwide faith.

PRAYER: *O Thou, in Whom we are all one, we are grateful to be people of The Book. Amen.*

A MNASONIC BOOM

Acts 21:16 *Some of the disciples from Caesarea came along with us, to direct us to a Cypriot named Mnason (Nay-suhn), a Christian from the early days, with whom we were to spend the night.*

Going ashore at Caesarea, after his third and last missionary journey, Paul and traveling companions headed for Jerusalem, a distance of sixty-five miles. Joining the group was Mnason, who invited Paul and companions to spend the night at his home on the way.

Mnason was respected for having been one of those, beyond the Twelve, Jesus had handpicked. Sensing trouble ahead in Jerusalem for Paul, friends felt that Mnason was just the heavyweight Paul needed beside him for this potentially troubling visit to the Capital City.

Persons such as Mnason, who could give eyewitness accounts of Jesus, were becoming rare. It was now a quarter century since Jesus' ascension. Originals who had known Him personally were dying or scattering far and wide, or having memory loss concerning the Savior. Originals who still had their faculties were becoming valued antiques. Their very presence exuded authority, integrity, dependability. For them just to say, "I know....I've seen....I've heard" would bring immediate compliance. They were invaluable bridges between past and present. They could tell of that which had been tried and failed, and that which had possibilities and had never been given a chance.

To live as if the present is all there is for history, is self-destructive. There is a past, and is not to be flippantly ditched because of age or its curios and queers. If the past is prologue, it has something worth hearing.

What if Dr. Leakey, after finding a human skeleton in the Olduvai Gorge in East Africa, had cast it aside as just another old fossil? Surely it had nothing to teach a modernist. That was then, this is now. Yet, Leakey believed that our conservationist Creator does not allow human events to ebb and flow and to become forgotten forever. There is no indication that the Creator is callously wasteful. Somewhere, sometime there is a finding again and a learning from.

So Paul was directed to Mnason, a Christian from the early days.

In Bali there is a legend that "Once upon a time the people of a remote mountain village used to sacrifice and eat old men. A day came when there was not a single old man left and the traditions were lost. They wanted to build a great house for the meetings of the assembly, but when they came to look at the tree trunks that had been cut for that purpose no one could tell the top from the bottom: If the timber were placed the wrong way up, it would set off a series of disasters. A young man said that if they promised never to eat the old men any more, he would be able to find a solution. They promised. He brought his grandfather, whom he had hidden, and the old man taught the community to tell top from bottom."[1]

The Elderlies have their place in every society and generation. Take them along, as Paul did. Lodge with them, as he did. They have treasures beyond comprehension, to share. Otherwise they are mindlessly chucked in human junkyards as expendable, to the tragic loss of society.

Let's start a society for the Preservation of Mnasons. A Mnasonic society!

PRAYER: *Lord, we pray along with Your servant, Robert Browning. Our times are in Your Hand, Who saith, "A whole I planned, Youth shows but half; trust Me, see all, nor be afraid!" Amen.*

AT GOD'S DISPOSAL

Acts 21:23 *Our proposal is this...*

Man proposes. And how. Back in Jerusalem, Paul was "welcomed...gladly" (21:17) by church members.

---

[1] Attributed to Henri Noumen & Walter Gaggney

It was different when he met with the elders. Paul must have sniffed something in the wind when he greeted the elders without any indication of their being glad to see him after his growingly successful missionary journeys abroad. Instead, they couldn't wait to inform Paul that he was up to his neck in trouble. It was rumored they wanted him to know that he was teaching Jews everywhere that they should reject the highly esteemed Mosaic Law. But they offered, as if to get him off the hook, a strange suggestion. If Paul went through the whole Temple ritual with four men, then the Elders assured him, "everyone will know that there is nothing in the reports they have heard about you, but that you are yourself a practicing Jew and observe the law." (v. 24)

Since this supposedly helpful suggestion actually led to the beginning of the end of Paul's ministry and life, it is worth taking a closer look at it, in slow motion.

It is evident that the Jerusalem Elders never really were enthused about Paul. Either it was that they could never forget his cruel past, or that after his conversion he had been so enormously successful in a way that each of them envied and would have been proud to include in their personal biographies. In their "proposal" you can almost see the Synod throwing Paul to the wolves, and dusting off their hands as if to say "good riddance." And as it turned out, they never had anything more to do with him. He was cut loose to fend for himself.

The picture of the church, at this point, is not bright. It shows, if anything, that Satan is never on vacation. He uses the passing of time to make ancient truth uncouth. Which is a siren, awakening the

Lord's people to the need to stay close to Him; ask for His detailed guidance; follow His instructions through the Holy Spirit's promptings.

As with his Lord, Paul came unto his own people in Jerusalem and his own received him not. They deceived him. Yet if Paul ever realized that he had been blindsided by his father superiors, he lovingly, forgivingly, never said a mumbling word about it in his letters. He made no accusation. Even called himself the chief of sinners.

The elders, Paul, Peter, were all in the same boat—blundering, self-possessed. Knowing what was right and doing it not, therefore sinning. But all were finally straightened out, and, under God, the church was cleansed and strengthened. Still, such tripwires that they fell over are still strung by the Evil One across our daily walkways. Angels have fallen over them. Judases are still in the making. Jesus was not being melodramatic when He soberly cautioned: "What I say unto you, I say unto all, 'watch.'" Watch out. In this fast-moving age, when a fighter pilot firing a cannon can fly swifter than the bullets and shoot himself out of the sky—it is wiser to set our watch by the Lord. "My soul, be on thy guard; Ten thousand foes arise; The hosts of sin are pressing hard to draw thee from the skies."[1]

PRAYER: *Lord, we will "Watch, and fight, and pray; The battle n'er give o'er; Renew it boldly every day, and help divine implore."*[1]

OUR UNFAILING FRIEND

Acts 21:30 *The whole city was in turmoil, and people came running from all directions.*

---

[1]George Heath

Well it happened, as the elders surely knew it would. They were old hands at gauging the eruptive tendencies of the Jerusalem populace, especially at a Festival time. While pilgrims came mainly to worship, they came from vastly dissimilar backgrounds. Customs were at variance. They spoke different languages, ate different foods, had currencies that were divergent in value, dressed and socialized in their own way. They were a volatile lot and could quickly get out of hand. As here. Some incendiary word had ignited their emotions, and people came running, as they always have, to see what's going on.

The "turmoil" soon became "an uproar," (v. 31) then a bubbling, confusing "hubbub," (v. 34) and finally "the violence of the mob...yelling, 'Kill him'!" (v. 35-36) A Vesuvian eruption indeed.

Explosive causal factors were: 1. Persons who could never forgive Paul for becoming a Christian, when he had been a solid, dependable bulwark against them. He could always be counted on to demonize this upstart "cult." But not anymore. Now he was more aggressively for them, than at his worst when he had been against them. And his onetime supporters rallied to stop him. 2. "The Jews from the province of Asia...stirred up all the crowd." (v. 27) Their anger was still smoldering over the way Paul had urged Jews back in their home country, to turn their backs on the Mosaic Law and the Jerusalem Temple (the place of the presence of God on earth!). 3. Those who wickedly started the untrue report that Paul had taken a Gentile into a prohibited part of the Temple and thereby profaned the holy place. (v. 28) 4. As in any such emotionally charged situation, there were the rowdies ready to stir the troubled brew. Those who can't live without sensory titillation. If they can't find it, they induce it.

In the midst of such violence one hears Kipling's, "If you can keep your head when all about you are losing theirs, and blaming it on you." And Paul did. At the center of the cyclone, he kept cool. Though cursed, smitten, shoved around, hoisted by Roman soldiers to be carried to the safe custody of their barracks, Paul showed the unbreakable resilience of which he was made. Onlookers, who were still not sure of the validity of Paul's conversion, must have kept an eagle eye out for any cracks in his composure, any cave-ins of conviction, any readiness to confess that it was all a stunt that he had pulled on the Christian community, and was thus now ready to be freed back to the ruthless crowd to which he had formerly belonged.

Satan must have stormed Paul's ramparts, knowing that he was never more vulnerable—as Jesus had been in the wilderness for forty hungering and thirsting days and nights. Who was going to win—Paul or the maddening crowd? What was holding him steady in such Tsunami conditions? A few minutes later the secret was out. The battle had been won on the Damascus road. There the Celestial Christ said to Paul: "I am Jesus." (22:8) That's all the assurance anyone needs to stay firm.

PRAYER: *Dear Lord: Who was with Daniel's friends in the fiery furnace and with Paul at the center of the storm, be with us now and forever. Amen.*

BORN AGAIN

Acts 22:6 *What happened to me on my journey was this:*
Since these meditations are about happenings

in Jerusalem, we were unable to fully explain the most important segment of Saint Paul's life—because it took place in Damascus.

But now in Jerusalem, with a mob after his blood, Paul addresses the bloodthirsty multitude. Even their raucous calling for his execution simmered into silence as he began to tell of his conversion at Damascus—which grants us the opportunity to review Paul's twice born experience, the centerpiece of the three times it appears in the Book of Acts. (9:1-19; 22:3-16; 26:12-18)

Many believers, since then, have been convinced that conversion to Christ should happen Paul's way or not at all. It should be sudden, dramatic, with a vision of Jesus, asking Him questions, being answered by Him, with accompanying miracles. Yet if Jesus said: "Blessed are they who have not seen (or heard) but still have believed," then the indication is that there are other ways to come to a personal acceptance of Him as Lord. For even with Paul, it was not quite the way many think it was. It was not so much an isolated, emotional, ecstatic turnaround as it was a process, slowly gaining momentum and culminating in a event. Some of the factors that flowed together to create a new man in Christ were 1. The unfulfillment of Pharisaic Judaism left Paul restless. Later in his letter to the Romans, he explained his former predicament. (Rom. 7:7-23) "To sum up," he concluded, "left to myself I serve God's law with my mind, but with my unspiritual nature I serve the law of sin." (7:25) "Wretched creature that I am, who is there to rescue me from this state of death?" (7:24) "Who but God?" he found. "Thanks be to him through Jesus Christ our Lord!" (7:25) 2. As he persecuted Christians, Paul learned that they had something valuable that he lacked. As did the troubled John Wesley learn from the Moravians during a stormy Atlantic crossing. Certainly Stephen's bold witness for Christ made an impression on Paul which he could not shake off. It was probably one of the pricks of conscience that brought him to his knees on the Damascus road. 3. Then, as a Jew, Paul believed in the coming of Messiah. All that he needed to be shown was that Jesus and Messiah were One. That was revealed to him at Damascus. That is why the best known psychologist, Carl Jung, believed that "Saint Paul had already been a Christian for a long time, only unconsciously (subconsciously?); hence, his fanatical resistance to the Christian's because fanaticism is only found in individuals who are compensating for secret doubts. The incident...on the way to Damascus marks the moment when the unconscious complex of Christianity broke through into consciousness."[1]

The Master still breaks through human restraints to lay claim on those persons who are open-doored, open-hearted toward Him. Others may not see that readiness in us. But the Lord sees and makes His move, in His own time and place and approach.

PRAYER: *"Consecrate me now to Thy service, Lord. By the power of grace divine; Let my soul look up with a steadfast hope, And my will be lost in Thine."*[2] *Amen.*

POSSIBILITIES BEYOND CLOSED DOORS

Acts 22:22 *Up to this point the crowd had given him a hearing; but now they began to shout, "down with the*

---

[1] C. G. Jung, *Contributions to Analytical Psychology*, p. 257
[2] Fanny Crosby

scoundrel! He is not fit to be alive!"

"This point" was when Paul uttered the word "Gentiles." That one word brought Paul's otherwise acceptable speech to a grinding, howling halt. That one word was not just a stop sign for Paul's oration, it was more like an irritating red rag to a bull. It enraged the mob into a blinding fury. From listening civilly, the crowd suddenly turned bloodthirsty: Paul must be gored to death!

Humans haven't changed at this point. For each of us there are words that instantly numb the best in us, and inflame our worst selves. And one such word is "Jesus."

He was at the bottom of Paul's problem. Jesus had said, "Other sheep I have that are not of this fold." Today, some interpreters have taken that to mean that the Lord is servicing other planets on which members of His flock reside. Be that as it may, Jesus also had in mind those who were not of the chosen Jewish race. This the Jews couldn't or wouldn't accept. But Paul did, and that to the Jews, was heresy—especially when the Gentiles were absolved from becoming Jewish converts before they became Christians. That absolution had been mandated by the Jerusalem Council. (Acts 15:6-34) But Paul got the searing blame. People, in effect, were crucifying Jesus afresh, through Paul.

Jesus' name is still the point beyond which one proceeds at his own risk. His name has stopped prayers in public schools, colleges, in social gatherings and public places. Jesus must now move over and give equal time and space for Atheists, the Dalai Lama, Scientologists, Muslim, Hindus, Zoroastrians—from A-Z.

In the United States of America, still statistically 77% Christian, the name of Jesus causes more disputation than all the wrangling and filibustering in the world of politics. Jesus' life teachings, miracles, healings are studied with the subtle intention of invalidating the lot. There is more of a tendency to side with Einstein in his belief that the Bible is "pretty childish." That takes care of Jesus too!

Another dead-ended word is "Church." From the time King Herod "launched an attack on certain members of the Church," (Acts 12:1) the attacks have never ceased, either from the outside or within the body of believers. Each group, sad to relate, thinks it is the only one fit to take the name "Church." Others can be chapels, assemblies, fellowships, worship centers, et al., but never "Church." That enthroned word belongs to only one blest people: Themselves.

Then there's that word that is a cut-off point for numberless folk, "Christian." Just who has the right definition of a Christian? Part of the confusion stems from the unnumbered versions of the Bible that have appeared during the last century. Seeing a goldmine in the Bible industry, unauthorized versions, as expected, have been the most popular because they say what people with an uncertified morality want to hear. Hence the return of the Tower of Babel.

The way ahead was shown by Jesus, Paul, and others who have followed their example: by fearlessly walking the way of the cross and witnessing for the ever-living Savior. There is no easy way.

PRAYER: *Heavenly Father, You know the obstructions we face daily. Guide us through or around them—for the advancement of Your cause. Amen.*

Rubbing Out the Rubbish

Acts: 22:27 *The Commandant came to Paul and asked, "Tell me, are you a Roman citizen?"*

Paul replied with a simple "Yes." Nothing more was needed. Everyone across the world knew the coveted meaning of Roman Citizenship. As Cicero said: "How often has this exclamation, 'I am a Roman Citizen' brought aid and safety even among barbarians in the remotest parts of the earth?" For the Roman Empire was in full control of the land that stretched from Britain, across Europe, the Middle East and to the Gates of India. Even beyond the Empire's boundaries, nations watched their p's and q's and lived in awe of Rome for 1,000 years.

Paul was proud to be a Jew, we find at least five places where he expressed that honor. He dated all things with Jewish dates. He kept Jewish laws. He was a man of one book, the Old Testament. He was a Pharisee—one of "The Separated Ones." But he was also privileged to be a citizen of the mighty Roman Empire.

That acquisition had come to Paul through inheritance. It had come either through his father or grandfather. 1. By purchase. Any person of wealth (and the Roman government needed the money) could purchase the rights—a. you could not be bound or b. scourged or c. crucified, you were protected by the weighty, fearsome power of Rome. 2. Conferment upon persons who had given distinguished service to Rome. 3. A whole town or area could be favored with citizenship, for having endeared themselves to some Roman Emperor. And, at least five Emperors had visited or been interested in Tarsus (Paul's birth place), from 175

B.C. to 31 B.C. for Tarsus was well known for trade, manufacture, and its university (where they had more scholars than anywhere else in the world).

Beyond his classic Jewish education, and his prized Roman Citizenship, Paul was a man of means. Part of his wealth was inherited and some from his business of tent-making. That's lucrative! When one remembers that travelers had nothing but their tents for shelter, and pilgrims to the Jerusalem feasts swelled the regular population of 25,000 to several million—tents were in heavy demand. Besides, Paul's travels—and lengthy court trials and appearance before the Emperor in Rome and private lodging for years in Rome—all came at a price. Even some government officials, knowing Paul's financial stature, tried schemes and persuasions to get his assets.

Yet Paul was to write: "All such assets I have written off because of Christ. More than that, I count everything sheer loss, far outweighed by the gain of knowing Christ Jesus my Lord, for whose sake I did in fact forfeit everything. I count it so much rubbish, for the sake of gaining Christ and finding myself in union with him...My one desire is to know Christ and the power of his resurrection." (Phil. 3:7-10) Then, returning to the subject of citizenship, Paul tells the Ephesians and us, "You are no longer aliens in a foreign land, but fellow-citizens with God's people, members of God's household. You are built on the foundation of the apostles and prophets with Christ Jesus himself as the cornerstone." (Eph. 2:19-10)

It all comes down to the glorious fact that none of the honorific titles and medals that the earth bestows upon us can grant more ever ready and everlasting joy than being a citizen of the kingdom of God which rests on Christ, the cornerstone.

PRAYER: *Thank You, Lord, for the bottom line. We rest on that. Amen.*

GOD'S SECRET SERVICE OPERATIVES

Acts: 23:16 *The son of Paul's sister, however, learned of the plot and, going to the barracks, obtained entry, and reported it to Paul.*

Enter Paul's nephew, unnamed, unknown. And after helping his uncle, he silently withdraws to the anonymity from which he had emerged. He is never again heard from, except here in verses 20 and 21, recorded by Luke some twenty years after Paul's martyrdom in Rome. But Paul could have been martyred here in Jerusalem, if it hadn't been for his nephew's timely intervention.

At the time, Paul was in the most unaided, defenseless, vulnerable position of his life. As the disciples of Jesus all forsook Him and fled, so did Paul's onetime compatriots. There he sat alone in the Roman barracks awaiting further interrogation. And then, out of the blue, here came this nephew with the worst possible news a man in Paul's position would want to hear—that his end was near; that forty villains had a foolproof conspiracy worked out for Paul's assassination tomorrow.

Wise to such shadowy deals from his preconversion days, Paul knew what to do next. Since nobody was believing anything he said, Paul sent his nephew to the Roman Commander to hear a firsthand account of the grisly plot. And that did it. Though the commander didn't know the nephew from Adam, the young man's report must have been in sync with what the commander's own undercover agents had heard. For straightaway the commander gave orders for a military escort to conduct Paul safely out of the city. There would be foot soldiers, cavalry, and lancers numbering ten times the number of conspirators. The whole garrison was to slip out of Jerusalem just when the city gates would close behind them for the night and lock the assassins into a frustratingly ineffective bind.

What large doors on little hinges turn. That nephew had no idea that his seemingly meager effort had been multiplied as were the five loaves and two fishes of that other young man whose tiny resources fed 5,000 people—with leftovers, yet! Therein lies the power of the One who intervenes behind the scenes.

It should bring abject fear to those who are not on His side. They can't do anything more than hefty, helpless, Goliath could.

And it should give an ease and confidence to those who are on the Lord's side. His agents and angels are ever on the job of protecting them. Like our own loved ones, now in heaven, who were Nephew-type persons when they were on earth. What better agents and angels could the Lord assign than such combat veterans? "Surely goodness and mercy shall follow me all the days of my life." Oh to be one of them, now and evermore.

Professor Halford Luccock of Yale hoped that since we have an International Order of this, that, and the other, why not a World Order of Nephews of Paul?

Actually, the Lord provided such—before

Paul, and since. He couldn't wait for us foot draggers. In every valley of the shadow He has provided kindred spirits to accompany us. In all imprisoning circumstances the phenomenal nephews come out of nowhere to help until the setting of the sun. Noble needed nephews we didn't even know we had, appear at the Lord's command and in His own good time. Then they vanish like the Spirit-appointed life-savers they were sent to us to be—that we might strive to go and do likewise. Oh to be one of those chosen few nephews.

PRAYER: *Oh, Great Intervener, count us among Your "nephews." And thank You for those "nephews," who, under Your guidance, work all things together for our good. Amen.*

A SERMON ON THE MOUNTS

Acts 23:24 *And provide mounts for Paul so that he may be conducted under safe escort to Felix the governor.*

Having ordered a powerful military garrison to accompany Paul on the sixty-five-mile journey to Caesarea, the Roman commander saw to Paul's comfort and safety. Instead of making Paul walk the distance like a criminal, Paul was to be mounted and set among the cavalrymen as a tighter safety measure. The way *The New King James Version* puts our text for today provokes a new approach to Paul's situation: "mounts to set Paul on." Without being facetious, one may well ask what Paul's sermon on the mounts would have been. For he surely wouldn't have been speechless on that entire two-day journey. Always at ease in an international setting, able to speak to the Roman militia in their language (though they didn't know his), and always interested in Rome—that fascinating hub of the

Empire, Paul would have a lot to chit-chat about. And this, as we look back, prepared Paul for that similar association with the military he was to have on that long, perilous sea voyage to Rome. (Acts 27-28:11)

But on the way to Caesarea, clop-clopping along on horseback, unaware, at the moment, that he was leaving his beloved hometown of Jerusalem for the last time, what were really the mounts, the lifter-uppers, that Paul was relying on to bring him safely to his destination—whatever that was to be ultimately?

Three years before Paul had written to the Corinthians, boosting their sagging spirits. "Such are the promises that have been made to us, dear friends." (2 Cor. 7:1) And what were those promises that Paul was now resting back on? God said: "In the hour of my favor I answered you; on the day of deliverance I came to your aid." (2 Cor. 6:2) That's a quote from Isa. 49:8. A little further, God continues His promises: "I will live and move about among them; I will be their God, and they shall be my people...I will be a father to you, and you shall be my sons and daughters." (2 Cor. 6:16,18) These lines Paul had gathered from Lev. 26:12; Jer. 32:38; Ezek. 37:27; Isa. 52:11; Ezek. 20:34,41; 2 Sam. 7:14. And all these were verified by and incarnated in Christ Jesus. In fact, as Herbert Lockyer found, "It has been computed that there are 30,000 Bible promises. No indication is given as to how this colossal number is reached. Altogether there are 31,173 verses making up the Bible; 23,214 verses comprising the Old Testament, and 7,959—the New Testament. Doubtless this total of verses gave rise to the 30,000—every verse being a promise."[1]

Talking about mounts—the Lord has amply provided for our journey through life. In His Word there are assurances and helps on which we can rest our souls and bodies. Listen to Jesus' promises, which can be twinned with 2 Corinthians 6 and 7: "Seek first the Kingdom of God and His righteousness, and all these things shall be added unto you." (Matt. 6:33)

"Come unto me, and I will give you rest." (Matt. 11:28)

"Whosoever shall do the will of my Father which is in heaven, the same is my brother, and sister, and mother." (Matt. 12:50)

"If you have faith as a grain of mustard seed, you shall say to this mountain, remove hence to yonder place, and it shall remove: and nothing shall be impossible unto you." (Matt. 17:20)

"Fear not, little flock for it is your Father's good pleasure to give you the Kingdom." (Luke 12:32)

What a sermon. What a life. What a Lord.

PRAYER: *Lord, lift me up and let me stand, By faith, on heaven's table land, a higher place than I have found; Lord, plant my feet on higher ground. Amen.*

ROCK OF AGES

Romans 9:33 *Here I lay in Zion a stumbling stone and a rock to trip them up; but he who has faith in him will not be put to shame.*

Explaining the difference between Jews and Gentiles, Saint Paul takes the liberty of combing two verses from Isaiah (8:14 and 28:6). This quote tells of how One will come to Zion (another name for Jerusalem, and used more than 100 times in

---

[1]Herbert Lockyer, *All The Promises of the Bible*, p. 10

the Old Testament) and confound the Jews by His faith-based life, since they strove to attain righteousness by their own efforts and not by relying on God's mercy. And Jesus in fulfilling Isaiah's prophesy, turned out to the "stumbling stone" by His insistence on faith instead of works.

To stigmatize Jesus as One who causes upsets, is, in itself, a slap in the faith. How can the Savior of the world, the One who first loved us, who chose the way of the cross, since that was the only way humanity could be redeemed; how could He possibly be the cause of anyone's downfall? Doesn't He, instead, stand rock-like on life's highway to prevent us from going over the cliff? Indeed. Yet, His prohibitions and inhibitions are irksome to rebellious souls who want their own way.

As with the Rich Young Ruler (Luke 18:18-27) who asked Jesus what had to be done in order to be assured of eternal life. Was it the commandments? If so, the Ruler answered, "I have kept all these (all ten, a remarkable achievement!) since I was a boy." (v. 21) "No," countered Jesus, "sell everything you have and give to the poor...then come and follow me." (v. 22) That is, live by faith. However, "When he heard this his heart sank, for he was a very rich man." (v. 23) He stumbled over the faith issue, and went away dragging his sagging emotions sorrowfully.

Likewise with the woman caught committing adultery. (John 8:3-11) The Pharisees knew that the Law required that such adulterers should be stoned. But when Jesus said, "Let whichever of you is free from sin throw the first stone at her." (v. 7) The Pharisees stumbled over that stone. Not one of them was guiltless, as every last one slunk away. All of the accusers had fallen on their faces, morally. Trying to pick up the stone of accusation to hurl at the woman, the conscience-stricken hypocrites tripped over the stone. They were hoist on their own petard. And as Shakespeare put it: injured by their own cleverness. Elsewhere Jesus was all for hanging a millstone around the necks of such pitiful specimens of humanity. People like this had caused Jesus to weep over His beloved Zion. Taking exception to His precepts, they hurt themselves and others. By ordering their lives according to His teaching; by taking the stone which others had rejected and making Him the cornerstone of their lives (Matt. 21:42), they could have become well-pleasing in the Lord's sight, building "more stately mansions, O my soul, as the swift seasons rule! Leave thy low-vaulted past. Let each new temple, nobler than the last, Shut thee from heaven with a dome more vast till thou at length art free. Leaving thine outgrown shell by life's unresting sea."[1]

Today those stones are shipped all over the world to be foundations and cornerstones for Masonic Lodges.

PRAYER: *Heavenly Father, Grant that Christ, the Living Stone, may be our foundation and cornerstone, that we may be spiritually rock-solid both now and ever. Amen.*

CENTRAL COMMAND

Romans 15:19 *I have completed the preaching of the gospel of Christ from Jerusalem as far round as Illyricum*

We now move on from the Book of Acts,

---

[1] O. W. Holmes, *The Chambered Nautilus*

which, in many ways, is the most indispensable book in the Bible. It is the only bridge we have joining Christ and Christianity, Jesus and Paul, the good news of Jesus and how that news spread into all the world. We have been hearing about Saint Paul via the pen of Luke, the physician. Now for the first time, we hear from Paul, himself, through this letter to the Christians in Rome. It was written in Corinth, three years before Paul went to Rome—not as a missionary as he had hoped, but as a prisoner.

Here he introduces himself to the Roman Church, one which he had not founded, in a city he had longed to visit but never had. As usual, no matter where Paul went, or what the occasion, his dear old hometown of Jerusalem was always on his heart and mind.

A woman went into a store and asked for a compass. The salesperson said, "We have compasses for drawing circles, but none for going places." Paul had both. Encompassed by the desire to fulfill Jesus' Great Commission, Paul went abroad to as many places as time and energy would allow. He evangelized an area of 1,500 square miles in less than sixteen years. Five thousand five hundred and eighty miles were on roads with fellow travelers—pilgrims, millions of them, going to the great annual Feasts in Jerusalem. And there were runaways, traders, teachers, students, tourists. Rome took pride in its highways and waterways, keeping them safe from robbers and pirates. And because horses and carriages cost more, people like Paul walked. Since they could do only fifteen to twenty miles a day, they went by ship—doing an average of 100 miles a day. Paul did 6,770 miles by sea, making his total distance of travel 12,350 miles.

Nor were travel and geography Paul's main interests, although the Book of Acts has been called the Travel section of the Bible. Rather, it was Paul's other compass that was the one he lived by. As in today's text, he puts the first point down in Jerusalem, then with the other point he circles "as far round as Illyricum" (Yugoslavia, or whatever it is called at the moment). Further, it was not the physically structured city that Paul centralized. It was what Jerusalem's Temple symbolized: the place where God lived on earth, and what He expected of His children of earth: worship and connecting it with word and deed in daily life. (Rom. 15:16,18) For God knew that humans are prone to center their lives on money or self or sex or their professions...But, as Jesus magnified, none could miss it—that unless we seek first the kingdom of God and His righteousness, nothing else will work out right. "All things betray thee, who betrayest Me."[1] Paul proved that. In his unconverted state his main point of reference had been to crush Christianity. And nothing worked out for him.

To be sure, some have argued that as a Christian, things seemed to go even worse for Paul. Yet, Jesus, Paul, and many of the saints in glory, lost their lives, but found eternal life. That is more to be desired than what happened to Judas the betrayer. If Paul had made Illyricum his epicentral focus, in starting at the perimeter he would have gone around in circles. Making God in Christ the reference point for all we do, keeps

---

[1] Francis Thompson, *The Hound of Heaven*

us within the circle of His care. He determines our positioning so that we don't lose our bearings.

PRAYER: *Be our mission Controller, Lord, and we can scan the universe in safety. Amen.*

GIFTED GIVING

Romans 15:25 *I am on my way to Jerusalem, on an errand to God's people there.*

Headed for Jerusalem, Paul took with him the money he had asked for and received from churches on his far ranging and final preaching mission. It could have been a sizable collection, the kind that roadway thieves and pirates covet. It would call for other persons, trustworthy, to unobtrusively take different routes and modes of transportation to get this treasury safely to the treasuries of the Mother Church in Jerusalem. Mother needed it, and deserved it.

Jerusalem had suffered a severe famine. Then, after Pentecost, when the Christians were persecuted—losing jobs, homes, income—they resorted to a common purse, all for one and one for all. (Acts 4:32) When Greek-speaking widows complained of discrimination (Acts 6:1), and the Jerusalem Conference imposed a nervous strain on the Church, Paul felt that they needed help. And they deserved it. As Paul states here, the Mother Church "shared their spiritual treasures," (v. 27) with the new churches, so that those who have been helped "have a clear duty to contribute to their material needs." (v. 27) So here comes Paul with a bundle of financial goodwill.

Still, Paul was apprehensive. The Mother Church might be poor, but she still had her pride.

To think of all these little towns and villages sustaining the stately capital—city regals—was too big a pill to swallow. And the blame was dumped on Paul.

Sure enough, just as Agabus had warned (Acts 21:11), Paul arrived in Jerusalem and into a hornet's nest.

But still writing this letter to the Romans, three years before the hornets (both friend and foe) got him, Paul hopefully added, "so when I have finished this business and seen the proceeds safely delivered to them, I shall set out for Spain and visit you (Rome) on the way." (v. 28) Then Paul makes three points with the Roman Christians: 1. Be my allies. (v. 30) He needed help in the ongoing struggles of life, and life in a new world religion. He knew that Christ's teaching would not sit well with everybody. The schools of philosophy would be up in arms. Scientists would trot out their objections, other religions that had dominated the field for centuries were already battering the Person and principles of Christ. And as an ambassador for Christ, Paul was getting hammered on the front line. He needed Christian brethren to interlock their resources with his—to gain the victory. 2. "Pray for me." (v. 30) In retrospect we see where, in spite of all the prayers that were said for Paul, his difficulties never ceased. They still never do. Before World War II, two million people in Britain prayed that war might be averted. But war came with millions of casualties and colossal financial cost. Why? The disconnect seems to come between our short-range requests and God's long-range beneficial answers. God, in His wisdom, determines how long it will take our prayers to have maximum effectiveness. Father (in heaven) knows best. No sincere prayer is ever wasted. It's just that our sense of timing (subject to human limitations) is not as accurate as His; not as millennium time-tested as His. Always His promissory note is cashable: "Ask and you shall receive." And Paul did receive, and we shall, too, in good measure. 3. "The God of peace be with you all." (v. 33) Accept Him. Live with Him. Serve Him. For He is the One who shows us how to be faithful allies of His and of each other. He shows us the dynamism of prayer of fellowshipping with Him in Spirit and in truth. And all our errands to and for God's people will be blessed.

PRAYER: *God of peace, in alliance with You. We learn how to work with others, in prayer, for the good of Your people everywhere. Amen.*

A BUDGET BLUEPRINT

1 Cor. 16:3 *Carry your gift to Jerusalem.*

It would be two years before Paul would make his final delivery of a super donation to the Mother Church in Jerusalem. Meanwhile, wherever he was, his pen was active. Here, to the Church at Corinth, he has just written three memorable chapters. Who can forget the 13th? That love Chapter deserves framing in gold. Or the 14th? Or the 15th, a heartening funeral sermon, which has been used as such for centuries?

Following that trajectory, Paul was headed for heaven, you would suppose. But the very first words of this 16th chapter show that though high-minded, he is never unaware of his earthly duties: "Now about the collection in and of God's people." (v. 1)

As Paul visited established churches and

founded new ones, he established a formula for all those who wanted to contribute to the fund for the suffering Jerusalem Church.

Giving to charity was a long-held custom. Clubs and fellowships did it. Pagans donated for some god or temple. An emperor's birthday seemed a right day for such an offering. Paul, however, adapted the Jewish practice to Christianity. The offering was to be taken on the first day of the week (the day on which Christ rose from the dead), when Holy Communion was served, and when hearts were moved at the remembrance of Jesus' question: "What do ye more than others?" (Matt. 5:47) In such a setting, one was predisposed to share, to serve, in good measure; to sacrifice. So successful was this formula that it has remained the standard procedure in most churches.

The next and last step was the delivery of the donation. That, too, called for cautionary care, since at that point treasurers and/or deliverymen have been known to abscond with the funds. Or the money is used for a sudden local emergency, and cozily justified therewith. Or wrongly addressed, the collection terminates in some cause that is far from needy, and the recipients play whoopee with it. There are too many slips between the rubber and the road, and Paul took no chances. Knowing also that contributors give more freely when they are confident that their sacrificial giving has been handled with armored-car security.

So Paul insisted that the persons who were to make the delivery to Jerusalem must be: 1. Selected by the congregation. (v. 3) The fellowship would know who was rock-solidly dependable. 2. Authorized and instructed by Paul. (v. 3) He would give them directions and addresses to the officials of the Mother Church in Jerusalem. An experienced journeyman, Paul would share valuable tips with these carriers of their congregation's gift to Jerusalem. The caravanserais (Inns) for overnight stops, called for extra vigilance. Food stops, lodging, church helpers at various towns—all these "in house" hints would calm the nerves of those who were first-timers. Especially in the cosmopolitan city of Jerusalem, where people from all over the world were constantly streaming in and out. Slick operators would quickly spot babes from the outback—from whom could be made a fast buck or the whole collection!

These couriers were entrusted with the baton on the last lap to the finish line. Working under Coach Paul's guidance, they and the rest of their congregational team at home could all be gold medalists for God. And thus shall it ever be.

PRAYER: *Show us, Lord, how to make our money an integral part of our worship. That will help to sacramentalize our lives. Amen.*

THE BEDROCK OF FAITH

Gal. 1:18 *Three years later I did go up to Jerusalem to get to know Cephas, and I stayed two weeks with him.*

After a three-year retreat by himself near Damascus, Paul made a beeline for Jerusalem, and Peter's home. These three years have been compared with the three years Jesus gave to teaching His twelve disciples. As a sidebar, this is why three years have become the standard amount of time for a theological seminary education.

But Paul, on his own, though under the tutelage of the Holy Spirit, felt the need for background knowledge of Jesus Christ whom he was determined to serve for the rest of his life. And who could supply any more authentic knowledge than Peter, the Big Fisherman?

When I served a College Campus Church, after one of my early sermons, a history Professor asked me from where I got this quote and the date. I told him what I had in my footnotes. "Yes," he replied, "but what are your primary sources?" That is what we see Paul hungering for as he visits Peter.

Paul was sharp enough to have learned during those days when he was persecuting the Christians in Jerusalem—just who was their acknowledged leader. Everyone pointed to Peter. Jesus had pointed to him, saying, "I tell you, you are Peter, and on this rock I will build my Church...I will give you the keys of the Kingdom of heaven." (Matt. 16:18-19) Peter's fellow apostles soon saw that he was a natural leader, and unanimously allowed him to be their spokesman. Yes, Peter failed His Lord in a time of crisis. But under Jesus' patient encouragement, Peter snapped back to attention and, recommissioned, led the infant church to maturity. Even the church at Rome noted Peter's spiritual superiority and named him their first bishop. Much later, the largest Christian church in the world was named for him—St. Peter's Basilica.

Yes, indeed, this was the primary source Paul was looking for. And to spend fifteen days with such a mentor! One can only imagine the number of questions Paul had been jotting down for three years. He would want details and definitions. And there would be some heated arguments—as there were later (Gal. 2:1), good-naturedly. It must have been a joy for Peter to recall those years with his beloved Jesus. And, who is to know, it could have been Paul who put the idea into Peter's head to have the Life and Teachings of Jesus written down and preserved for posterity! For indeed, as Eusebius (A.D. 270-340) reported Papias (A.D. 70-140), bishop of Hierapolis, saying in a document which has since been lost: "This also the elder said: 'Mark, having become the interpreter of Peter, wrote down accurately all that he remembered of the things done and said by Christ, but not, however, in order. For neither did [Mark] hear the Lord speak, nor did he follow Him, but afterwards, as I have said, he followed Peter,'" who called Mark "my son." (1 Peter 5:13) Now, though placed second in the New Testament, Mark was the first gospel to be written. Nor is it a secret that Matthew, Luke, and John took much from Mark's gospel—thanks, again, to Peter. Or Paul?

Whoever gets the credit, the Spirit of truth worked all these persons and their talents together for our good.

In this era, when we are urged to go contemporary, what about the basics? Do we know Him whose life made the gospels?

PRAYER: *Heavenly Father, "My hope is built on nothing less than Jesus' blood and righteousness; I dare not trust the sweetest frame, But wholly lean on Jesus' name.*[1] *Amen.*

OUR RACE AT HIS PACE

Gal. 2:1-2 *Fourteen years later, I went up again to Jerusalem with Barnabas, and we took Titus with us...to make sure that the race I had run and was running should not be in vain.*

Fourteen years after his visit to Peter (in the previous Meditation), but just four years after

---

[1] Edward Mote

his most recent visit to Galatia...Paul wrote this letter.

In Galatia (now central Turkey), Paul was well received. His meetings were standing room only. At one point he and Barnabas were acclaimed as gods (Acts 14:11). But, throughout history, whenever there has been a certain scent in the air, predators got wind of it and came buzzarding in. These spoilers, seeing the crowds, "were filled with jealous resentment, and contradicted what Paul had said with violent abuse." (Acts 13:45) That not being enough, "a campaign of persecution was started against Paul and Barnabas, and they were expelled from the district." (Acts 13:51) In the next town "the populace was divided...A move was made by Gentiles and Jews together, with the evangelist, won over the crowds...stoned Paul, and dragged him out of the city, thinking him dead." (Acts 14:19) No wonder Paul became unsure that he was on the right track. So up he went to Jerusalem to check with the standard bearers—the leaders in the mother Church.

Paul and Barnabas made a full report of what they had done, and hearing it, "those of repute" (Gal. 2:2) gave it their stamp of approval, accepted Paul and Barnabas as partners "and shook hands on it." (Gal. 2:9)

So what was all the fuss about?

Actually, this was one of the epochal events in Christendom. Up until this point, any non-Jew who converted to Christ, first had to be a Jew. He had to be circumcised, and obey the Mosaic Law. But now that was no longer necessary, since one is not saved by these outer, physical demandments, but by the Grace of God and one's personal faith in Him.

Granted. But how does this play out in the present-day, day by day, in downtown Peoria?

1. Do we know what we believe and whom we believe? Paul said, unashamedly, "I know whom I have trusted, and am confident of His power to keep safe what He has put into my charge until the great day. Hold to the outline of sound teaching which you heard from me, living by the faith and love which are ours in Christ Jesus." (2 Tim. 1:12,13)
2. When we are firm in the faith we are better able to tell the "sham Christians, intruders who had sneaked in to spy on the liberty we enjoy in the fellowship of Christ Jesus. (Gal. 2:4)
3. And how firm are we in the faith—only as far as when we are offered a billion-dollar contract or celebrity status? Pressures of myriad kinds can destabilize our faith. The devil sees to that. Falsities abound, attempting to shape Christianity in the form of some "school of thought," and not the faith once and for all declared to the saints.

Watch it, Peoria, there is much to gain in Christ Jesus, the same yesterday, today, and forever. Hold fast that which is the best.

PRAYER: *Gracious Lord, forgive our coming-in to the sweet talkers. Thy words are our direction finders. We would be attentive to them. Amen.*

GOD'S ALL-SUFFICIENT WORD

Gal. 4:24-26 *This is an allegory; the two women stand for two covenants. The one covenant comes from Mt. Sinai; that is Hagar, and her children are born into slavery. Sinai is a mountain in Arabia and represents the Jerusalem of today, for she and her children are born in slavery. But the heavenly Jerusalem is the free woman (Sarah); she is our mother.*

As this new faith of Christianity caught on in all kinds of societies from which Judaism exempted itself, Christians began asking questions about their faith. What made it so different from Judaism. And, was it valid?

At the time nobody was better fitted to give answers than Paul. Jesus had taught by precept and example, but that was still years away from being preserved in written form. Paul, however, was God's man of the hour. The Apostles had long since been publicly branded as "uneducated laymen." (Acts 4:13) Paul was a scholar, writer, preacher, missionary, seasoned traveler. He had experienced weariness with pharisaic Judaism, even before he was converted to Christianity. By now he was well informed of the divide between the faiths, and here gives a reasonable explanation. Wisely he starts with Abraham, a landmark person in the Old Testament. Who has not heard of Father Abraham and his wife, Sarah, who were too old to have children at ages 100 and 90? Impatient, Sarah gave her slave girl to Abraham, planning to make that baby her own. But jealousy problems arose, until Sarah had her own son, Isaac. Hagar, the slave, and her son symbolized Mt. Sinai from where the Law was given—the law that was so enslaving—with its never-ending rules and regulations about keeping the Sabbath, how Kosher foods should be prepared, what customs to be observed, and on and on. In all the hair-splitting that took place at every turn and twist, strict adherents of the faith hardly had time for anything else. It became an enslavement, an earthly walled-in Jerusalem.

On the other hand, there was Sarah and her

son of promise, who were free. They symbolized the freedom that is to be found in Christ. Hagar's son had come from a brief sexual act. Sarah, barren, unable to bear children, nevertheless by God's grace, in accordance with His promise, has a son. Even as "God so loved the world that He gave His only son (Jesus), that everyone who has faith in Him may not perish but have eternal life" (John 3:16)—in the new Jerusalem, a place not made with hands, eternal in the heavens.

There is the dividing canyon between Law and Love.

Law has its place and time, but as a way of life it has been weighed and found wanting. It clips our wings and keeps us earth bound, earthy. Hagar's son was not born out of love. He was a product of the dictates of impatience and of momentary, fleshly impulses: the laws of the physical body. To be sure, Isaac was begotten by the same birth process, but by a different motivation—that of love.

The two covenants, never before defined, now clearly delineated by Paul, stand apart in their true colors. Choose you this day which you will serve. We cannot serve two masters. Some try and get muddled, and muddle others.

After Paul's refreshing allegory, Christians could with sharper focus see the kind of Christian life that Jesus taught but never had the time to detail for wider usage. Now we know and, Paul-like, can still do our part in clarifying the word for changing times, the Lord being our helper.

PRAYER: *We urge, with Charles Wesley: "Come, let us use the grace divine, And all, with one accord, In a perpetual covenant join ourselves to Christ the Lord." Amen.*

The Crown Awaits the Conquest

Hebrews 12:22 *You have come to Mount Zion, the city of the living God, the heavenly Jerusalem.*

It sounds as if Saint Paul has more to say on the subject he was treating in yesterday's meditation on Gal. 4:24. But, according to modern scholarship, that is impossible—even though Paul was considered the author of Hebrews, from the fifth to the nineteenth century. The King James Version of the Bible (1611) included this Letter as "the Epistle of Paul the apostle to the Hebrews."

Now, at least eleven persons are suggested as possible author of this Letter to Hebrews. On the short list are three names: Paul, Barnabas, and Apollos. But now that Paul has been dropped; and since Barnabas had qualifications equal to those of the famed Alexandrian preacher Apollos; and since Barnabas and Paul worked together in the Church of Antioch for a year; and since Barnabas and Paul did the first missionary journey and together in Galatia; and since Barnabas picked up some of Paul's teaching, such as today's text; and Paul's repeated use of track and field phrases (see Heb. 12:1-2), Barnabas makes a strong finish as author of Hebrews. There exists, in fact, a letter of Barnabas to the Hebrews. And, though Barnabas has been scratched off even the short list, because he never put his name to the Letter, it ought to be remembered that he was a self-effacing person who did his best and didn't care who got the credit. Perhaps Barnabas also noted how Paul overdid it, at times, in making sure people knew that he, too, was an Apostle and on a par with the Twelve.

Still, see how the author of Hebrews picks up Paul's fresh description of the new covenant as the heavenly Jerusalem—and the joy of being citizens thereof. Why such rapture? Because:

1. The Christian is greeted by "myriads of angels (12:22) with their heavenly chorale. Didn't Jesus say that "There will be greater joy in heaven over one sinner who repents than over ninety nine righteous people who do not need repentance"? (Luke 15:7) The angels know how to pull out the stops at a nod from their Conductor. (See also Rev. 5:11.)
2. The Christian is welcomed (this is getting exciting) by all those whose names are on the register of the King of Kings. He chooses the best and "only those shall enter whose names are inscribed in the Lamb's book of life." (Rev. 21:27) How will we contain our ecstasy when being embraced by history's finest?
3. Then the Christian will come face-to-face with "God the judge of all." (12:23) But why be afraid, even of the Judge? He, too, is there to lift our spirit with His "well done, good and faithful servant, enter into the joy of your Lord."
4. Assuming that the "good men made perfect" (12:23) will also be on the register in No. 2 above—
5. The Christian is given the best at the last. "Jesus the mediator of a new covenant." (12:24) To be in His everlasting arms at last will be worth all the tribulation that earthly life splashed and smashed in our faces.

So it was worth being born and reborn. Praise the Lord.

PRAYER: *"Lord, give me such a faith as this; and then, whate'er nay come, I'll taste e'en now, the hallowed bliss of an eternal home."*[1] Amen.

---

[1] William H. Bathurst

Kingdom Gifts

Rev. 3:12 *I shall write on them the name of my God, and the name of the city of my God, that new Jerusalem.*

Coming to the end of the Bible, and a 4,000-year relationship with Jerusalem, we never seem to be any closer to the Holy City than in today's text. It is written into one of the Letters written to the Seven Churches of Revelation: the Church at Philadelphia.

The letter was not alone to those ancient Philadelphians. As the good Book says, "He that hath ears to hear, let him hear what the spirit says to the churches." That includes us.

Besides, since that ancient city of Philadelphia gave its name to our own city of Philadelphia in Pennsylvania, and since our Philadelphia was the proprietary capital of the province until 1776, and since it was the capital of the colonies during most of the Revolutionary period, and since it was the capital of the United States from 1790 to 1800, and since at the beginning of the nineteenth century Philadelphia became the cultural capital of the country, we have more reason than most countries to feel an affinity with those to whom the Apostle John was writing. Then, too, and strangely, see how our country seems to fit so neatly into the city which we have been focusing on throughout these meditations.

JERUSALEM

Moreover in certain Bibles all the words of Jesus are in red type. And here we find, from Rev. 2:1-3:22, all seven churches are quoted in red letters, the largest number of Jesus' own words outside the gospels.

And what is He saying? "Those who are victorious I shall make pillars in the temple of my God." (3:12) That's a promise and a prize, for pillars are critically important. Architects, engineers, and skilled laborers will agree to that. For pillars take unusual stress from the roof, walls, storms, earthquakes. Columns require deep and solid foundations. There must be a central spine of iron or steel within the pillar. Only the Lord's chosen persons can measure up to what is required of those who can support His church. Can they remain firm and faithful through the local Church's stormy periods—and not just the altar calls, but the altercations? Do they have backbones of steel?

Another reward for the faithful is that "they will remain there forever." (3:12) This probably refers to the frequent earthquakes which terrorized the people of that area—and still do. When the Romans occupied the country, they finally stopped building their imposing Romanesque structures, knowing that they would soon be toppled by seismic activity. The faithful, however, would not suffer such uncertainties, especially in their character. They would be steadfast, immovable.

Also, the faithful will be stamped with the name of God in Christ. That is a sign of belonging to Him—the sheep of His fold. As the officials noted with Peter and John "that they had been companions of Jesus." (Acts 4:13) That mark is a special imprint.

Then, too, as our text highlights, the faithful will be imprinted with the name of the eternal city, authorizing them as citizens thereof. And we're at home, at last.

PRAYER: *Father, with Your servant Paul we say,*

"Thanks be to God for His gifts beyond words!" (2 Cor. 9:15) Amen.

THE GREATER CITY OF GOD

Rev. 11:26 *(The outer court of the temple) has been given over to the Gentiles, and for forty-two months they will trample the Holy City underfoot.*

We have been watching the author of Revelation swinging his spotlight on Seven Beatitudes helpfully located at strategic places throughout the book; the Seven Churches; the Four Horsemen, until the beam locks on to Chapter 11—the most difficult and important chapter in Revelation. The measuring of the Temple is called for, but with the exclusion of the outer Court of the Gentiles. Then the spotlight seems to redden and shudder and reveal the beginning of the end of Jerusalem.

For all the city's greatness and centrality; for all the special attention given it by God; for all the promises and prophesies that it would last forever—here is the first indication that it won't.

In fact, the dissolution of the city began to show slowly, unbelievingly over a thousand previous years, Solomon's, around which the city's fame was built, lasted for 400 years, but was demolished by the Babylonians in 586 B.C. Rebuilt under Zerubbabel's supervision, that Temple lasted 500 years, only to be trampled underfoot (as our text reports) for three and a half years, around 168 B.C. At the next Temple, built on the same site as the others by Herod the Great, took 85 years, to complete. Six years later it was sacked by the Romans in A.D. 70. After that, for 500 years, Jews visited Jerusalem at the risk of their lives. In A.D. 1267, a respected Jewish leader wrote: "What shall I say of this land...the more holy the place the greater the desolation. Jerusalem is the most desolate of all."

Today, the only connection which Jews have with the city of their forebears is a wall from the Second Temple. Called the "Western" or "Wailing Wall," it is the most revered place in Judaism.

Right there seems to be the lesson which the Jews and all the rest of us have still not learned, namely, that cities, Temple, walls, material things are not deserving of our devotional affection. Only God is.

At the wall, these days, myriads of people, Jews or not, are soulfully impressed by the history and publicity of the wall and, its imposing esplanade. The thing to do, they believe, is to fondle those massive stone blocks, kiss them, pray at them. Then stick into a crevice between the stones a roll of paper with a pre-written prayer on it—all in the hope that our unseen God sees our very earnest attempts to get His attention for our particular cause.

Jesus' corrective word was "Blessed are those who have not seen and yet have believed." It's not the city or temple or wall or to her reconstruction that will bring a new day, but faith in the Lord who alone can instill within us the joy we crave, now and forever. Besides, how can we have a New Jerusalem without the death of the Old Jerusalem, any more than we can have eternal life without dying to this earthly life? He that has ears to hear, let him hear what the Spirit says to the churches.

PRAYER: *We would not forget Jerusalem, Lord, but we set our affection on the New Jerusalem, and prepare ourselves for citizenship therein. Amen.*

Toward the Brighter Day

Rev. 14:1 *Then I looked, and on mount Zion stood the Lamb.*

What a fulfilling sight. One couldn't ask for anything more. Here's Jesus, the Lamb of God, who takes away the sins of the world, standing atop the Mount of Zion (Jerusalem), the heavenly Father's specially chosen dwelling place—for Himself and His loved ones. And since it is the New Jerusalem: it's heaven!

How different from the recurring refrain in the Book of Revelation—buzzing as from a beehive overcrowded with stingers. One hears some of the awfullest reports of mass killings and blood running in rivulets down the streets. Our feelings are not spared. These are atrocities that are going to happen, and we need to know the facts and make what preparations we can to be overcomers. For the battles can be won, not just forever to be endured lingeringly. So, look up, there on the Mount stands the Captain of our salvation, granting us an exciting glimpse of His "V" for victory sign and sound. With Him are 144,000 persons full of rich meaning. 12 x 12 = 144. That denotes the 12 tribes of Israel and the 12 apostles tying together the saved of the Old and New Testaments. Besides, 12 by 12 makes a perfect square, as these four-square persons are right on all sides. The "thousand" signifies their abundance. That's encouraging since we often get that sinking feeling, seeing all the evil multiplying across the globe, that there are no four-square people left on earth. But these 144,000 actually numberless persons are on the Lord's side. You can read their owner's name on their foreheads. (v. 1)

More encouraging, these brethren were singing a new song. (v. 3) The words and the tune come out of and fit into the newness of a redeemed life. No words or musical intonations recall the old unredeemed days. Didn't Jesus promise to make ALL things new? Not only is the Spirit of the person transformed, the mortal body takes on the form that most pleases the Creator. So the singers chant their way to glory in their entirely purified personalities.

Is all this really possible? Doesn't it finally come down on the side of being vacuously visionary? How does one maintain a perfected condition? Granted that on earth it is virtually impossible—with gross temptations battering at all five senses at the same time. One unguarded sensory perception and those evil adversaries enter in.

But the ransomed of the Lord maintain a consistency of vigilance by following the Lamb of God (Jesus) wherever He goes. (v. 4) Bound to Him, He becomes their "Automatic Pilot." Protecting and/or correcting them on their journey, now and forever.

If, daily, many are joining that heavenly chorale, why can't we? The invitation remains open: "Come, ye blessed of my Father, enter the Kingdom prepared for you from the foundation of the world."

PRAYER: *Thank You, heavenly Father for pointing to our ultimate goal, and for showing us how to get there through Jesus Christ our Lord. Amen.*

THE HOME OF GOD'S ELECT

Rev. 21:2 *I saw the Holy City, new Jerusalem, coming down out of heaven from God.*

Throughout the centuries Jerusalem has been destroyed repeatedly by invaders and reconstructed by new occupants. Yet, whatever state of newness it may be in, it will not be taken UP for a final makeover. Rather, since the Ruler of the universe said, "I am making all things new," (Rev. 1:5) the new Jerusalem is scheduled to come DOWN—and not from some space-centered reconditioning Lab but "out of heaven from God, made ready like a bride adorned for her husband." (v. 2)

If there is ever a definition of "readiness," it is a bride ready for her wedding. Time and money are poured out by family members, friends, wedding professionals, priests, florists, clothiers, jewelers, caterers...Every detail is meticulously micromanaged. That is as close as John could get to describing the perfection for a whole new Holy City. But, where a bride fusses over items that are like grass "which is there today and tomorrow is thrown on the stove" (Matt. 6:30) in the new city of Jerusalem, God attends to everlastings. And the very first item is that "God has his dwelling with mankind." (v. 3)

No surprise, then, that all in the new city is as God wants it. That will be His dwelling. And that's heavenly. Of course, God's Son came to live on earth, to be like us, that we might learn to be like Him. Then He ascended "to prepare a place for you. And if I go and prepare a place for you, I shall come again and take you to myself, so that where I am you may be also." (John 4:2-3) Now, John is telling us, the new Jerusalem is the fulfillment of the Lord's promise: life with Him in the eternal city.

Yes, but what makes this new dwelling so different from any other? 1. "He will wipe away every tear from their eyes." (v. 4) Why? Weren't tears supposed to be good for us—clearing the eyes, challenging us to rise above our failures, separations, frustrations? Sure, the Lord turned them to our benefit. But they were not supposed to be those hot channels running down our cheeks. Sin in the Garden opened those optical faucets, and they have been flowing ever since. Thank the Lord that this saltwater supply is destined for total elimination. 2. "There shall be an end to death." (v. 4) Not just the dearth of the death, but its complete annihilation. What it has done to us the Lord will now do to it. Which is also a double whammy for tears, mourning, crying, pain (v. 4), which are all linked to death. On reflection, all of them also operate quite apart from death. Throughout the days of our years, mourning, for one, hasn't waited until a loved one's graveside to show its sad face. We bemoan the loss of a home, a job, a town landmark. Crying can break out at any time, even staining the pillow during lonely night hours. And pain! How we want to respond, "Tell me about it." Any part of the universe within our bodies can cry out in pain, as the mind can, and the soul does. But, rejoice, these crushers are not to last forever, as they sometimes promise to. They too, have an expiration date. And the Lord's people, on the contrary will have the mark of death removed from them. Also, since thirst is an indicator of a thirst-aid somewhere, and hunger pinches the tummy telling of the existence of food, so our longing for a new Jerusalem is answered here. It is ready for the taking.

PRAYER: *We've had a deep down certainty, Father, that there must be a perfected dwelling somewhere. And there is! Keep us faithful enough to be inheritors of that Kingdom. Amen.*

THE LAND OF BEGINNING AGAIN

Rev. 21:10 *So in the spirit he (an angel) carried me away to a great and lofty mountain, and showed me Jerusalem, the Holy City, coming down out of heaven from God.*

This is the last mention of Jerusalem in the Bible. Much like the previous text (Rev. 21:2), which dealt with the wipeout of life's worst features, this text leads into the only description we have of our new and everlasting home. This, my friends, is the heaven we often talk about and try to visualize.

Although John had a glimpse of it in our last meditation, now he is taken to an elevation from which he can get the best possible view, as from Tiger Hill one can get the only unforgettable sight of Mt. Everest at sunrise.

But why was Jerusalem, even a new Jerusalem, chosen as heaven? Why not New York or New England, or New Delhi? After all, Jerusalem is the most hated city in the world. Yes, but it's also the most cherished by the three major faiths: Judaism, Christianity, Islam, and mainly because it is the place of the presence of God on earth. Even today, people want to be buried in Jerusalem, since it is the closest to heaven. And God alone has His reasons for choosing a new Jerusalem as the eternal abiding place for His people.

To describe the Holy City for us—John was chosen. Surely there could have been a better choice. Look at John: a Galilean fisherman. He was not a writer, not artistic, not prep-schooled or college-trained, not a Rabbi—yet he is called on to describe the most important happening of all time. That, it seems, is how God works in mysterious ways His wonders to perform. Were twenty-first-century persons asked to do this job, he/she wouldn't get beyond one word: "Awesome!" John at least gives it a try, with all the awesomes at his command (as of 2,000 years ago). He uses light, color, gemstone, space (all three dimensions), beauty, and everything that would give us a faint idea of the magnitude and ultra magnificence of the Holy City. And when he's done, the result still seems to be a patchy attempt by an unprofessional, to portray on a giant canvas, or perfected universe. On this side of eternity, a person can't do any better.

All of which is trying, struggling, to convey, to the best of one's human knowledge, that there's only ONE in charge, and has been from the beginning, "the Alpha and the Omega." (Rev. 21:6) He knows best. In His own words (which are very few and far between in the Bible), He said, "these words are trustworthy and true." (Rev. 21:5)

Many have tried their utmost to frame a picture of heaven. "O Beulah Land," "On Jordan's Stormy Banks," "Sunrise." But Bernard of Cluny's hymn has rung heaven's bells around the world since the twelfth century: "Jerusalem the golden, with milk and honey blest! Beneath thy contemplation sink heart and voice oppressed: I know not, oh, I know not, What joys await us there; What radiancy of glory, What light beyond compare. O sweet and blessed country. The home of God's elect! O sweet and blessed country that eager hearts expect! Jesus, in mercy bring us to that dear land of rest; Who art, with God the Father, and Spirit, ever blest. Amen."

PRAYER: *Come, Lord Jesus, and take us Home. Amen and Amen.*

THE SOUL'S SUNSHINE

Rev. 21:23 *The city did not need the sun.*

In the aftershock of learning that the New Jerusalem will have all the most beautiful creations this earth has ever known (Rev. 21:10-21), we are casually informed that the fabulous Temple will be missing. (v. 22) Nor is that the only unexpected deletion. For although the very first act of the Creator was: "Let there be light," (Gen. 1:3), in the new Jerusalem that Light is turned off. Never again sunlight. And since the moon is but a reflector of the sun, forget about moonlight. That old order of day and night will be scrapped, suddenly making the change feel more like Alaska and the northern lands that bask in the midnight sun. Yet even that kind of illumination will disappear. An entirely different radiance will take over: "The glory of God illumines it, and its lamp is the light of the world: he that followeth me will not walk in darkness, but shall have the light of life," (John 8:2) "the Lamb of God," "who takes away the sin of the world." (John 1:29)

Indeed, centuries before Isaiah had given hints of this eventual sunless-enlightenment: "The Lord shall be unto thee an everlasting light." (Isa. 60:19-20) The Psalmist added: "In Thy light shall we see light." (Ps. 36:10) That is, in the authentic, unmanufactured light that emanates from our divine Lord, we will not see foggily as in a smudged mirror—as we now view tears, death, sorrow, crying, mourning, pain (Rev. 21:4). These, in our present world, have black, thunderous sheet-lightning clouds forever attached to them. They are times of depression, and often of submission to the worst in us. But in the fullness of light which the Lord turns on, those former heartaches and breaks shall be no more. Appearing in the Light of the Holy Comforter, what once was scary is transformed into that which is cheery.

To prove the attractiveness of the newly lighted Jerusalem "Kings of the earth (will) bring their glory and honor into it." (Rev. 21:24) Drawn like moths to a flame, these Kings complete what was partially unveiled in a Bethlehem stable on the first Christmas day. There only Three Kings, led by the light of a star found their way to the Baby feet of Him who was destined to be the Light of the World. That was the Alpha part of the story, when the Kings laid their gifts before Him.

In the Omega (finale), the 3 Kings rightfully expand to "the Kings of the earth," bringing to the New Jerusalem (now including Bethlehem) more than tokens of gold, frankincense and myrrh. Now ultimates will be offered Him: "glory and honor."

Didn't you always feel in your innermost being that this was going to be the way the good Lord would bring this incomplete old world to a glorious and honorable end? It's already in place. We have no need for the sun when we have God's Son.

PRAYER: *"Sun of my soul! Savior dear, It is not night if Thou be near; O may no earth-born cloud arise To hide Thee from Thy servant's eyes."*[1] Amen.

HIS NOURISHING WORD

Rev. 22:10 *Do not seal up the words of the prophecy that are in this book.*

This last contributor to the Bible, in his concluding pages, John concentrates on essentials. With his futuristic gift he anticipates what he

---

[1] John Keble

knows has happened before and will happen again—namely that "this book," the word of God, will be sealed and set aside as if it never existed.

How "on the money" he is and was.

Follow Derek Wilson in the newest biography of Martin Luther, *Out of the Storm*:

"Translating the Bible became the biggest affair of his life. He had finished his New Testament in 1522 but he was forever revising it and bringing out fresh editions. The Old Testament occupied him, on and off, for another 12 years. It was a tumultuous relation-ship. At times the translator found himself swept along by the power of the narrative. At others he wrestled for days to unlock the true sense of a single phrase. He was by turns elated and depressed by the results of his labors." (p. 299) "At last in the summer of 1534, the work, including the Apocrypha, was finished." (p. 301) "It was rapturously received by the German evangelical community. But did the novelty quickly wear off? Did familiarity breed contempt? Luther seemed to think so. Six years later he mournfully told his dinner table companions: 'This German Bible (this is not praise for myself but the work praises itself) is so good and precious that it's better than all other versions, Greek and Latin, and one can find more in it than in all commentaries, for we are removing impediments and difficulties so that other people may read it without hindrance. I'm only concerned that there won't be much reading in the Bible, for people are very tired of it and nobody clamors for it anymore.'" (p. 302).

How right was the Revelatory prophet, John,

for biblical lassitude and loungitude demarcate our present position in twenty-first-century history. As Charles Colson asserts: In "today's biblically illiterate Church" there is "rampant doctrinal ignorance among American Christians."[1]

Yet, Dr. Paul Brand, world renowned surgeon and missionary to India, is more positive. His prescription is that when we study the Bible in context, we absorb protein, which makes us grow. Just about everyone occasionally suffers a loss of appetite for Bible study. "These are times for discipline for force feeding." "One day your appetite will be stimulated. Words will leap out again and taste good. One day the spiritual saliva will flow again as God's word becomes relevant to your felt need, and you realize you have passed though a transient period of anorexia."[2]

PRAYER: *"Break thou the bread of life, Dear Lord, to me, As thou didst break the loaves Beside the sea; Beyond the sacred page I seek thee, Lord, My spirit pants for Thee, O living Word."*[3]

THY PERFECT LIGHT

Rev. 22:16 *I, Jesus...am...the bright star of dawn.*

Jesus' last words to us in the Bible are found in Rev. 22:20: "I am coming soon." The second last "I am" ends on a beginning note: "Dawn." That was the paradoxical way in which the Lord moved through His earthly existence. Having said "It is finished" and when everybody took Him at His word, he reappeared on Easter morning. And he has been active ever since.

---

[1] *Christianity Today*, April 2009, p. 72
[2] Dr. Paul Brand, *God's Forever Feast,* p. 32
[3] Mary Lathbury

Having described Himself as the Vine, the good Shepherd, the Way, the Truth, Life, the Light of the world, the Bread and Water of Life, Jesus now gives a final definition of Himself—with Starpower.

Acquainted with his great predecessor David's 19th Psalm, Jesus, too, must have reveled in the fact that "The heavens declare the glory of God, and heaven's vault makes known His handiwork." Especially since He "was with God at the beginning, and through Him all things came to be without Him, no created thing came into being. In Him was life and that life was the light of mankind. The light shines in the darkness, and the darkness has never mastered it." (John 1:2-5) Presumably, then, Jesus would know what astronomers have since discovered, namely, that stars come in different colors, sizes, density, temperature, amount of light emission. As an average star, the sun may be a million times larger than earth, but there are stars a million times larger than the sun.

Then why, among all the varied and spectacular constellations in space, did Jesus choose to identify with the morning star?

Granted that it is beautiful and bright, and chases away the night. But, as often he does, Saint Paul comes to the rescue. In his stirring defensive speech before King Agrippa, Paul affirmed: "I have had God's help to this very day, and here I stand bearing witness to the great and to the lowly. I assert nothing beyond what was foretold by the prophets and by Moses: that the Messiah would suffer and that, as the first to rise from the dead, *he would announce the dawn*." (Acts 26:22-23)

As Easter morning was, and is, the dawn of a new realization that death has been vanquished, so, in the new Jerusalem, Jesus, the undiminishable Light of the World, will turn our yawns into dawns. His Starpower may shine, for instance, on the fact that immense possibilities reside in wee mangers, in out-of-the-way places. And to track down the riches therein we will have access not to "a wisdom belonging to this present age...already in decline...(but) to God's hidden wisdom, his secret purpose framed from the very beginning to bring us to our destined glory." (1 Cor. 2:6-7) Good dawning to you.

PRAYER: *"Light of the world, illumine This darkened earth of thine, Till everything that's human Be filled with the divine; Till every tongue and nation, From seas dominion free, Rise in the new creation Which springs from love and Thee."[1] Amen.*

NO TINKERING WITH THE WORD

Rev. 22:19 *If anyone takes away from the words in this book of prophecy, God will take away from him his share in the tree of life and in the Holy City which are described in this book.*

In early days professional copyists (scribes) made copies of books by hand. In the present day even top publishing houses make mistakes, though manuscripts are machine-corrected all along the printer's pathway—even in the Bibles. For this reason ancient authors added this warning about changing words and meanings, even unintentionally. Yet no book has suffered more

---

[1] John Monsell

in this way than the Book of Revelation, almost making it into a joke book, and the least read book in the Bible. One elite commentator, by suggesting that Revelation "contains problems of interpretation about the solution of which there can be no real certainty"—plays into the hands of biblical pranksters. Distinguished Martin Luther (shame on him) felt that Revelation, with all its complexities, had no place in his Bible, so he tore it out.

That is the danger our text for today is warning about. By heeding the warning we can have our share in the tree of life. What share? Isn't this the nasty tree that got Adam and Eve and all of us into trouble? Isn't it time that withered old yarn was laid to rest? No, the tree in our text is not that one in Eden with a snake wrapped around it—signifying death. This tree, at the other end of the Bible, is Ezekiel's tree of life. (Ezek. 47:12) And see how full of life it is. Extra ordinarily productive it has many different kinds of fruit, all life-sustaining, with leaves for medicinal purposes. (Rev. 22:2) It resembles the fruits of the Spirit: love, joy, peace, patience, kindness, goodness, fidelity, gentleness, self control. (Gal. 5:22-23) Each month of the year this tree of life produces a different fruit, symbolizing the provision of sustenance for people of all ages since from the cradle to the grave we do have vastly differing needs. Nor are these fruits just for a certain type of people, in one area of the world. After all, "this is my Father's World." No one is left behind. The leaves of this tree are for the healing of everyone on earth. Best of all, there's no skull and cross bones sign on this promise, forbidding its use, as in Eden. The invitation is to all to come, see, taste, enjoy, LIVE. Neither do we want to give up our share of the kind of Holy City portrayed in full length. (Rev. 21:9-27) The lighting of that city will be like none other. No need for sun or moon or man's brightest illuminating devices.

"The glory of God illumines it (Rev. 21:23) through Christ "the Light of the world." Then there are twelve gates to the city. As in the case of the fruit providing for each stage of life. So here, the gates swing open for the entrance into the presence of the Lord of persons of all ages and all nations at all times. Since there will be no night there! (Rev. 21:25) Won't that be something? But when the author of Revelation describes the gates of the New Jerusalem each being made of one pearl, there's nothing more spectacular left to say. Nobody should want to miss out on the best that is yet to be.

PRAYER: *Maker of all things bright and beautiful, guide our footsteps, that we might reach the immensities of glory You have in store for us. Amen.*

NOTES

NOTES

NOTES

NOTES

NOTES

NOTES

NOTES

www.ingramcontent.com/pod-product-compliance
Lightning Source LLC
Chambersburg PA
CBHW050246170426
43202CB00011B/1576